St █████ HINS
BARN

ati

te

Nicholas Moussis

Guide to
European policies

11th revised edition
2005

European Study Service

ISBN 2-930119-40-3

© European Study Service
Avenue Paola 43 - B-1330 RIXENSART
TEL.: (+32 2) 652 02 84 - FAX: (+32 2) 653 01 80
RCN: 51147 - TVA: BE-659 309 394

SUMMARY

CONTENTS

FOREWORD

The Flemish master Pieter Bruegel the elder has well illustrated the lack of interest of people for a historic event that takes place under their very eyes. In a painting of 1564, entitled "Christ bearing the cross", he has depicted the Messiah as a small figure sinking down under the cross on his way up the Golgotha. No one of the crowd of Roman soldiers and ordinary people around Him pays any attention to His Martyrdom. They are all looking at a couple of peasants struggling with three soldiers in the forefront of the picture. This everyday brawl is the centre of attention of the crowd and not the event that has changed the course of history. One can hardly blame these people who, at the time of the Crucifixion, were going about their business and were attracted by a boisterous albeit banal happening. As demonstrated by Brueguel, they had not the hindsight that we now have about the importance of the event that they were witnessing.

In the same sense, one should not blame the majority of contemporary Europeans for their lack of interest for European integration. They have no notion that they are witnessing an experience that will most probably change again the history of mankind. This history is marked by wars and all sorts of bloody fights between ethnic, religious and other groups, fights for power, for land, for ideals (real or supposed) or just for the survival of a nation or a group attacked by other nations or groups. The extraordinary event that takes place under our eyes is the fifty year old experience of peaceful and voluntary unification of different and formerly conflicting nations. The European experience is unique by virtue of its objective of establishing the basis for an increasingly closer union between formerly hostile nations. It is also unique because of its institutions, which have no equal in other international organisations. Lastly, it is unique on account of its achievements: never in human history have different nations cooperated so closely with one another, implemented so many common policies or, in such a short space of time, harmonised ways of life and economic situations which differed so greatly at the outset.

Yet this unique experiment is hardly exciting. It is hidden behind tedious negotiations by complicated institutions using a peculiar jargon incomprehensible to ordinary citizens. Curiously enough it is not the lack but the abundance of information that clouds the European horizon. Information about the work of European institutions is abundant and freely available to citizens for the asking, particularly in electronic form. The problem is that the great majority of citizens do not and never will go asking for information about an experiment that they consider as extremely complex and distant from their everyday problems and interests. On their part, many European mass media report on a daily basis new European policies, laws, programmes and internal and external disputes. Yet, these media accounts are for most citizens like the leaves of a tree, which hide the forest that is stretching out behind. Leaves, like the daily news are ephemeral and unexciting, not worthy of particular attention. On the other hand, the dense forest of European institutions, policies and laws, which produces the political and economic oxygen necessary for the blossoming of small and medium European nations, is obscure and terrifying, if one has not a map showing the way through it.

The Guide to European Policies attempts to provide the reader with an overall view and the perspective necessary for understanding the complex organisation, which is the European Community/Union (EC/EU). The emphasis of the book is placed on the common policies developed by the EC/EU. Indeed, **an approach to multinational integration** is advanced, based on the setting up and development of common policies by the participating states. This approach is based on the empirical evidence of the European Union, but may also be applied *mutatis mutandis* to other multinational integration schemes elsewhere in the world.

This book aspires to being a textbook for **any student of European integration**, whether academic student of the European integration process, lawyer interested in Community law, which is ceaselessly growing and modified, economist wishing to acquire the latest information on European economic policies, historian wanting to understand the recent history of the continent or businessman seeking to understand the mechanisms of the large market in which he operates. In fact, European integration cannot be properly approached with the particular methods and tools of political science, international relations, economics or law. *The Guide de European Policies* follows, therefore, an interdisciplinary, pragmatic approach, which is somewhat distinct from the precise lines of the established disciplines. European policies, as all public policies, have both positive and negative aspects and can therefore be approached either in a positive or a negative way according to the viewpoint of the writer. The empirical or pragmatic approach followed here endeavours to present European policies as they are, with a minimum of value judgments as to their performance.

To help the reader find easily the details of any policy or measure he or she is interested in and/or deduce in an unprejudiced way whether a certain policy is good or bad or whether it has achieved the objectives assigned to it, facts and references are presented in a precise, almost scholastic, manner. All statements about past, present and future developments of common policies as well as all references to European law are based on the official texts of Community acts, published in the **Official Journal of the European Union (OJ)** or in Commission publications, such as the monthly **Bulletin of the European Union** and the annual **General Report** on the Activities of the European Union. In addition to their documentary purpose, the references to the OJ are also meant to help researchers find the official texts of their particular interest, as published in the collections of the OJ or in the electronic database EUR-Lex in the Europa server of the Commission.

PART I: Treaties, law and institutions

Chapter 1.   *Introduction to European integration*
Chapter 2.   *The European Treaties*
Chapter 3.   *European law and finances*
Chapter 4.   *The European institutions*

In this part of the book we review, in an introductory chapter, the various theories that have endeavoured to **explain the phenomenon of European integration**. We ascertain that all these theories have shed some light on various aspects of the integration process, but they have all missed the fundamental aspect of this process: the building and management of common policies. We, therefore, propose a theoretical synthesis based on the common policies of the European Union, which are, indeed, the main subject of this book. The theoretical propositions advanced in section 1.1.2 are empirically verified in the rest of the book. In the second section of the introductory chapter we briefly recall how, after the Second World War, an ever-increasing number of European States have decided to set aside their differences and engage themselves in **the process of European integration**.

The main objective of the second chapter is to emphasise the **role of the treaties and their reforms in setting new common policies** and ever-higher goals for pre-existing ones. It shows how the success of the common policies based on the Treaty on the European Coal and Steel Community (ECSC), signed in Paris in April 1951, led to the signing in March 1957, in Rome, of the Treaties on the European Atomic Energy Community (EAEC or Euratom) and of the most important European Economic Community (EEC), extending integration in all economic sectors. We will note that in order to attain their expanding goals, the Member States decided, in Maastricht in 1992, to supplement the amended Treaty establishing the European Community (TEC) as well as the Treaties on the ECSC and EAEC with the new Treaty on the European Union (TEU), which set the objective of political integration. We will see that five years later, the Treaty of Maastricht was replaced by the Treaty of Amsterdam, in order to accommodate the objectives of the new policies on home and judicial affairs and on foreign affairs. We will finally realize that the **Treaty of Nice**, actually in force, seeks the smooth functioning of EU institutions after the accession of ten more Member States, but that a Constitutional Treaty, signed but not ratified as yet, aims at the further evolution of the Union.

In chapter three a metaphorical image is used to explain how **the European Union covers under its roof** the main edifice of the European construction, which is the European Community, and the new wings of the common foreign and security policy and of justice and home affairs. The original **decision-making process** of the Community is clarified, a process that leads to the formation of an equally **original legal system**, based on the treaties and taking the form of regulations, directives and decisions. A particular attention is paid to the **unique financing system** of the European Community based on its own resources inscribed in the Community budget, managed by the Commission.

The final chapter of this part examines the structure and the functions of the main actors of European integration, the **European institutions and consultative organs**, in the order that they appear in the decision-making process: the European Council, the European Commission, the Economic and Social Committee, the Committee of the Regions, the European Parliament, the Council of Ministers, the Court of Auditors and the Court of Justice. The interaction of these institutions and organs is essential for the development of **the common policies that are analysed in this book**.

Chapter 1

INTRODUCTION TO EUROPEAN INTEGRATION

In 1945, just after the Second World War, Winston Churchill described Europe as "a rubble heap, a charnel house, a breeding ground for pestilence and hate". A year later, on 19 September 1946, in his famous Zurich speech, he proposed as a remedy "to recreate the European Family ... and to provide it with a structure under which it can dwell in peace, in safety and in freedom ... a kind of United States of Europe". Half a century later, realising and exceeding Churchill's vision, the western part of the "European Family" had become an island of peace and prosperity in a world ravaged by hatreds, conflicts, civil wars and misery. The successful formula that European nations had invented to overcome their depression was the integration of the formerly antagonistic nation-states into a union of peacefully interacting and competing nations. The multinational integration formula involves the gradual creation of imperceptible albeit innumerable links between the nations taking part in the process. Those links consist of common laws and common policies, which govern the Member States' economic activities and influence the day-to-day lives and occupations of their citizens.

1.1. The theoretical framework

Many theories, stemming mainly from the theoretical frameworks of political science or international relations, have been developed during the second half of the twentieth century about international and, more especially, European integration. Each has focused on a particular aspect of the phenomenon, while neglecting most of the other aspects. Each, therefore, has had its own merits in shedding scientific light on some parts of a very complicated phenomenon, but none has succeeded in explaining the whole, in structuring scientific observations on all its parts and in predicting its future development. After pointing out the main points of prevalent theories, we attempt in section 1.1.2. to present an explanation of the phenomenon of multinational integration based on the evolutionary development of common policies.

1.1.1. A synopsis of prominent integration theories

As early as the 1920s, **federalists** like Coudenhove-Kalergi perceived that European nations, which had just devastated each other in a nonsensical civil war, were a natural entity that could become a significant global force, if only they could succeed in having a federal constitution[1]. After the second catastrophic war for supremacy of one European nation over the others, Altiero Spinelli expressed the view that the national states had lost their *raison d'être*, since they could no longer guarantee the political and economic safety of their citizens and should give way to a federation, called by him "the European Union"[2]. Federalists, thus, put the cart (the ultimate state of European integration) before the horse (the creation of solidarity among former bitter enemies). They had a bright vision, but had not found the means to reach it.

Functionalists like Mitrany[3] rightly pointed out that international organisations are not an end in themselves, but rather the means of addressing the priorities dictated by human needs and have, therefore, to be flexible and modify their tasks (functions) according to the needs of the moment. In their over-optimism, however, for the creation of a cobweb of really international (worldwide), task-oriented organisations, they overlooked and even mistrusted the peacekeeping and welfare functions of a regional organisation like the European Economic Community.

Closer to the European reality, the **transactionalist** theory of Karl Deutsch defines international integration as the attainment, within a territory, of a "sense of community" and of institutions and practices strong enough to assure dependable expectations of "peaceful change" among its population[4]. The assertion that the sense of community among states would depend on establishment of a network of mutual transactions[5] is borne out by the experience of the European Communities. However, this experience proves that first comes the formal institutional framework and on it are built the informal transactions and hence the community spirit, necessary for an effective multinational integration.

Relatively close to the Jean Monnet method of "common action which is the core of the European Community"[6], is the **neofunctionalist** theory, developed mainly by Ernst Haas[7]. Both Monnet and neofunctionalist theo-

---

[1] COUDENHOVE-KALERGI Richard N., *Pan-Europe*, Knopf, New York, 1926.

[2] SPINELLI Altiero, "The Growth of the European Movement since the Second World War", in M. Hodges (ed.), *European Integration*, Penguin, Harmondsworth, 1972.

[3] MITRANY David, *A Working Peace System*, Quadrangle Books, Chicago, 1966.

[4] DEUTSCH Karl W., *Nationalism and Social Communication*, 2nd edition, MIT Press, Cambridge, MA, 1966.

[5] DEUTSCH Karl W., *The Analysis of International Relations*, Prentice Hall, Englewood Cliffs NJ, 1968.

[6] Monnet Jean. "A Ferment of Change", *Journal of Common Market Studies*, n. 1, 1962, p. 203-211.

[7] HAAS Ernst B. The Uniting of Europe: Political, Social and Economic Forces 1950-1957, 2nd edn. Stanford: Stanford University Press, 1968.

rists rejected federalist idealism and brought down Mitrany's functionalism from its international high spheres to the concrete level of several neighbouring states. The Monnet inspired famous declaration of Robert Schuman of 9 May 1950 was quite explicit on the road to be followed by European integration: "Europe ... will be built through concrete achievements which first create a *de facto* **solidarity**". Integration was viewed as a process where the constructive functions of the main actors, the common institutions, would induce positive reactions of the political and economic elites, influence the behaviour of other societal groups and bring together the citizens of the different nations. Neofunctionalist logic was built on the "spillover" effect. This meant that economic integration would gradually build solidarity among the participating nations and would in turn create the need for further supranational institutionalisation. Leon Lindberg (1963)[1] defined the "spillover effect" as: "a situation in which a given action, related to a specific goal, creates a situation in which the original goal can be assured only by taking further actions, which in turn create a further condition and a need for more action and so forth".

Many other neofunctionalist assumptions have been proved correct by European experience, notably that: action by interest groups would not be motivated by idealistic pursuit of the common good, but would be self-regarding and goal driven; perceptions by these groups of shifts in the loci of authority and power would increasingly direct their activity towards the developing supranational arena; the supranational scheme of government at the regional level would be the appropriate regional counterpart to the national state, which would no longer feel capable of achieving welfare aims within its own narrow borders. In economic terms, the creation of a customs union would generate pressures for the establishment of a common market and monetary union. The close economic integration brought about would require supranational regulatory capacity. Thus, political integration would follow economic integration[2].

Some neofunctionalist assertions, namely the withering away of the power-based states system, prompted a strong **intergovernmentalist** alternative to neofunctionalism, despite the strong European evidence in its favour. The Treaties of Maastricht and Amsterdam have, indeed, disproved Stanley Hoffmann's prediction that states would not compromise their sovereignty by moving their integration from the areas of "low politics" (read economics) to the sphere of "high politics", i.e. foreign and security policy[3]. **Liberal intergovernmentalist** analysis provided by Andrew Moravcsik (1993)[4] has failed to explain how national interests, voiced by national

---

[1] LINDBERG Leon, The political Dynamics of European Economic Integration, Stanford CA, Stanford University Press.

[2] BALASSA Bela, *The Theory of Economic Integration*, Allen and Unwin, London, 1962.

[3] HOFFMANN Stanley, "The European Process at Atlantic Crosspurposes", *Journal of Common Market Studies*, No 3, 1964.

[4] MORAVCSIK Andrew, "Preferences and Power in the European Community: A Liberal Intergovernmentalist Approach, Journal of Common Market Studies, No 31 (4).

governments in international negotiations, can merge and allow European integration to prosper.

Although the neofunctionalist theory has come closer to the European integration process, particularly thanks to its emphasis on the spillover effect, some critics rightly point out certain deficiencies in neofunctionalist reasoning. By highlighting the **multi-level governance** (European, national, regional, etc) of the EC/EU and the interaction of political actors across those levels, Gary Marks *et al.* (1996)[1] have shown the theoretical trap of imagining either the withering away of the state or its stubborn resilience. **Neoinstitutionalists**, like March and Olsen (1984)[2], have demonstrated the importance of institutions (not just formally established supranational organs, but also informal interactions) in providing contexts where actors can conduct a great number of positive sum bargains.

Although the neofunctionalist theory has come closer to the European integration process, particularly thanks to its emphasis on the spillover effect, it, like the other integration theories has overlooked the main element of this process, which is the gradual formulation, development and multiplication of common policies. In the next section an empirical approach is advanced taking into consideration this important element.

1.1.2.   An empirical approach based on the development of common policies

The multinational integration process may de defined as the voluntary establishment by treaty, concluded between independent states, of common institutions and the gradual development by them of common policies pursuing common goals and serving common interests. Being "voluntary", a multinational integration process is clearly distinguished from any form of coercive governance or coalition of nations or states. A "multinational" integration process between several nations should be distinguished from a Mitranian "international integration", involving all or most nations of the world. It should also be distinguished from "regional integration", a concept frequently used to denote the integration of various states of a region of the world, but which should, in fact, be reserved to the integration of various regions of a state, a process that is going on in most countries of the world. Multinational integration may go on inside one state containing different nationalities, but, in this case, its institutions are based on a constitution rather than on a treaty between independent states.

The "gradual development" of common policies implies that multinational integration is a constantly evolving process without a clearly defined end. Since the process is voluntary, it ensues that independent states may

[1] MARKS G., SCHARPF F., SCHMITTER P.C. and STREECK W., Governance in the European Union, London, Sage.

[2] MARCH J.G. and OLSEN J.P., "The New Institutionalism: Organizational Factors in Political Life", American Political Science Review, No 78.

join it at any point, following the procedures and criteria laid down by the group, or leave it, if they consider that the common policies developed or envisaged by the group, according to the majority definition of the common interest, do not coincide any more with their national interests.

The primary goal of multinational integration is the **achievement of peace and security** among the member states as well as between them and the rest of the world. But, unlike a military alliance where this goal is pursued by various pledges of political and military nature, a multinational integration scheme is built gradually **by means of a large number of common policies**, cementing common interests and creating a real solidarity among the member states. In the words of Jean Monnet, the intellectual father of European integration, "union between individuals or communities is not natural; it can only be the result of an intellectual process... having as a starting point the observation of the need for change. Its driving force must be **common interests** between individuals or communities".

Characteristically, the Treaty on European Union (TEU) [see section 2.4.] declares in its preamble that the goals of the High Contracting Parties are: "... ending of the division of the European continent", "... [deepening] the solidarity between their peoples while respecting their history, their culture and their traditions...", "... [implementing] policies ensuring that advances in economic integration are accompanied by parallel progress in other fields"..., [thus continuing] "the process of creating an ever closer union among the peoples of Europe". In its Article 2, the TEU sets a number of objectives, such as the promotion of economic and social progress and the assertion of European identity in the international scene, but does not mention the obvious - i.e., the maintenance of peace among the Member States - as an objective of the Union. In fact, the TEU relies on the implementation of common policies for the consolidation of peace among the participants.

More explicitly, the Treaty establishing the European Community (TEC) clearly declares in its Article 2 that "the Community shall have as its task, by establishing a common market and an economic and monetary union and by implementing **common policies or activities** referred to in Articles 3 and 4, to promote throughout the Community a harmonious, balanced and sustainable development of economic activities...". Articles 3 and 4 of the TEC serve, in fact, as legal bases for common policies in a great number of sectors or for common measures in some other fields (the distinction between common policies and common measures being quantitative rather than qualitative).

Common policies foster both **political and economic integration** of the participating states. Although multinational integration depends on political decisions, it greatly affects the economies of the member states. Increasingly, through the stages of customs union, common market and economic and monetary union [see part II], it opens up the participating economies to multinational trade and competition. Obviously, the economies of the member states are greatly influenced by common economic and other policies. As these economies are gradually opened up to multinational trade and competition, **all economic parameters change**: trade increases enormously within the large internal market, both supply and demand conditions are modified drastically, state intervention is seriously curbed and new dynamics are set in motion, notably concerning trade and investment opportunities, mergers and acquisitions. The creation and/or extension of multinational companies and the cross investments between them and national companies tend to bind the economies more closely together. The common policies build, in fact, a new concept and context of political economy, which affects the actions of political leaders and the activities of businessmen of the member states.

Indeed, by bringing about tougher conditions of competition than the ones existing inside the previously protected economies, multinational integration brings about **radical changes in business habits** and creates new business opportunities. Unsurprisingly, business associations, constituting powerful interest groups, try to influence the integration process in their favour. They intervene by way of demands, suggestions or criticisms addressed to the principal actors - the common institutions and the governments of the Member States - at various stages of the decision-making process concerning particular policies or the advancement of the integration process itself, which they usually support [see section 9.4.].

In the case of the EC/EU it is clear that the political elite were and still are influenced by an **open-minded and dynamic economic elite**. In fact, more than by considerations of security or balance of power at world level, over-emphasised by political scientists, the historic decisions of the Member States were motivated by economic factors: revitalising the two most important economic sectors in the post-war period, coal and steel; creating a large market in order to give a new dynamism to their economies stifled by protectionism; completing the single market to further facilitate trade and investment within a large market; strengthening the single market with a single currency to further facilitate internal transactions and allow European businesses to better face global competition. These decisions and the ensuing common policies were supported, if not provoked, by influential economic groups in the Member States.

Economic pressures alone cannot start the integration process by themselves, however. The necessary condition for setting the multinational integration process in motion is that the political, economic and other elite of neighbouring countries are earnestly seeking to **serve the interests of their nations**, rather than their own interests or those of a particular class or societal category. Under this condition - which implies democratic regimes - economic and political leaders would sooner or later agree among themselves that trade liberalisation would better serve the supreme national goals of peace and prosperity than existing protectionist economic policies [see sections 5.1. and 6.1.]. They would then have an option: either to pursue mutual trade liberalisation through intergovernmental cooperation or through multinational integration.

Intergovernmental cooperation is a conventional shelter of national interests, entrenched in the solid and familiar bulwark of national sovereignties defended by national governments. It does not need strong central institutions or a great deal of common legislation. The agreement that it governs depends more on the goodwill of the participating governments than on common legislation enacted and enforced by supranational bodies. In contrast, **multinational integration** is a dynamic venture of promoting national interests, depending on many unpredictable internal and external parameters and moved forward perpetually by the ever-changing requirements of the partners and by the extra energy provided by the combination of their forces. While safeguarding the interests of big and small countries alike, it requires common institutions and leads progressively to the establishment of a great number of common policies, to the harmonisation of legislations and to the common management of significant parts of national sovereignties. Small and big countries participating in the process have the same rights and obligations. They pledge themselves to pursue common goals, which go much beyond trade liberalisation. In addition to this goal, the nations participating in an integration process wish to liberalise also the movements of persons and capital and to facilitate the establishment and provision of services by companies from the partner countries.

The second course of action, the **fundamental decision to establish a multinational integration process**, outlined in a treaty, would be the catalyst, which would precipitate a sequence of secondary decisions formulating various common policies. If the implementation of these initial common policies gave satisfactory but not optimal economic results, it would reveal the necessity for more common policies and would thus have a multiplicative effect on the process. There is no predictable end to this process, as it depends on all sorts of internal and external factors. Depending on the stimuli exerted on the actors by those factors, the process may temporarily be slowed down or speeded up, but its general trend is progressive. An abrupt end to the multinational integration process is theoretically possible, but becomes increasingly improbable as the process itself continuously strengthens and multiplies the economic, political and cultural links between the participating nations.

The dilemma of choice between intergovernmental cooperation and multinational integration may present itself again, after the launching of the integration process, for those fields (namely political) that had been left out of the initially economic integration process. In this instance, however, if the member states chose the first course, the common policies existing in the economic fields would keep generating common needs, thus exerting multiple pressures on the participating governments to take up, for the policies initially reserved to their cooperation, the practices successfully tried in the economic area. This has happened in the case of the EC/EU concerning justice and home affairs (JHA) policy and may happen progressively concerning the common foreign and security policy (CFSP) [see chapter 8].

Multinational integration is based on common policies, which develop and multiply thanks to the Community decision-making procedure that characterizes it. **A common policy**, as far as multinational integration is concerned, is defined as a set of decisions, measures, rules and codes of conduct adopted by the common institutions set up by a group of states [see section 4.1.] and implemented by the common institutions and the member states. Multinational integration is, in fact, a basic common policy decision, juxtaposed to isolationism or intergovernmental cooperation. Integration is, indeed, the fundamental course of action (the trunk), decided voluntarily, in common, in a treaty or other multinational agreement, from which all secondary horizontal or sectoral policies depend or emanate (as the branches of a tree). As the integration process develops in stages, the passage from one stage to the next - from customs union to common market, then to economic and monetary union and finally to political union - is also based on a fundamental common policy decision inscribed in a treaty [see part II].

Common policies develop when, where and to the extent that the governments, representing the parties to a treaty, believe that the individual interests of their states are better served by them than by national policies. Decisions on fundamental common policies, affecting national sovereignties, are taken by the participating governments and are outlined in treaties, signed by those governments and ratified after agreement of the parliaments of the Member States [see chapter 2]. Decisions on secondary common policies, including guidelines and legal acts based on a treaty, are normally taken by the **common institutions** set up by the treaty [see section 4.1.], according to procedures and following the legal forms agreed in the treaty [see sections 3.3. and 4.3.]. To create a sentiment of mutual confidence, the formulation of a common policy by the common institutions must clearly indicate the **common need** that it addresses, the **common goal** that it pursues and the **common interest** that it serves [see section 3.2.].

It is normal that some common policies better satisfy the national interests of some participants than those of others. It is abnormal and impracticable that all common policies better satisfy the interests of some members of the group to the detriment of the rest. Indeed, no party to a multinational integration scheme should feel that its national interests are being permanently and systematically damaged by the common policies proposed; but, on the other hand, no party to such a scheme may systematically obstruct the common policies proposed by claiming that they do not fully satisfy its national interests. Hence, all parties to a multinational integration scheme must be prepared to give ground in one field, expecting to gain ground in another field. The hundreds of decisions taken every year by the EC/EU institutions demonstrate the fact that its Member States play the game according to this rule. The few exceptions confirm the rule.

In EC/EU usage, "common policies" are the ones that take the place of the essential elements of national policies (agriculture, fisheries, foreign trade). The policies that support and supplement national policies are called "**Community policies**". But, in fact, the distinction, between the two categories is not at all clear-cut. Indeed, all common policies, whether called thus by the Treaties or by Community practice, are in a process of development. They start as mere objectives set specifically or in more general terms by the Treaties or the institutions and are gradually built up by common or "Community" legal acts. In this book, the terms "common policy" and "Community policy" are used alternatively, as the latter is taken to mean "the common policy of the Community" in a certain field.

This book brings enough empirical evidence to test the hypotheses advanced above. Chapter 4 examines the structure, the functions and the role of the main actors of European integration, which are the common institutions. The second part of the book examines the fundamental common policies, which correspond to the **stages of the European integration process**. These basic policies are framed by secondary decisions presented in the relevant chapters of the Part II and they are supported by horizontal and sectoral policies analysed in the rest of the book. Part III focuses on policies that are of particular concern to the citizens of the Union and touches upon the role of political parties and the media in the multinational integration process. Part IV examines the **common horizontal policies** - such as social, competition or environment protection - which affect the overall conditions of the economies and societies of the Member States. Part V analyses the **common sectoral policies**, which concern certain sectors of the economies of the Member States, namely industry, energy, transports and agriculture. Part VI, presents the **common external policies**, which steer the relations of the Member States with third countries. In the final chapter, conclusions are drawn on the effectiveness of the European integration process and on its possible future development.

1.2. Birth and growth of the Community

In his declaration of 9 May 1950, Robert Schuman proposed the creation of a **common market in two important economic sectors** which had until then been used for military purposes, namely the coal and steel sectors: it would be a matter of integrating Germany economically and politically into a European Coal and Steel Community with France and other willing countries. He advocated some transfer of sovereignty to an independent High Authority, which would exercise the powers previously held by the States in those sectors and the decisions of which would bind those States. That was to say that the cooperation of the Member States in those sectors should be much closer than that obtained with a traditional intergovernmental cooperation. The choice of coal and steel was not fortuitous. In the early 1950s those sectors were the basis of a country's industrial and military power. In addition to the economic benefits to be gained, the pooling of French and German resources in coal and steel was to mark Franco-German reconciliation.

Beyond the Coal and Steel Community, Robert Schuman envisaged the creation of a common market for all products, on a scale comparable to that of the United States, in which the conditions would be fulfilled for rapid and regular economic expansion through economies of scale, better division of labour and the improved use of new production techniques. It is true that, beyond economic integration through the merging of the essential economic interests of the European countries, Schuman looked forward to political integration through the creation in stages of a "**European Federation**". But this was to be achieved in an advanced stage of European integration, after the creation of conditions of mutual trust through concrete achievements based on common policies.

Although the appeal from the French Minister for Foreign Affairs was addressed to all European countries, only five - Germany, Italy, Belgium, the Netherlands and Luxembourg - gave a favourable reply. Therefore, only six States signed the Treaty establishing the **European Coal and Steel Community (ECSC)** in Paris on 18 April 1951 [see section 2.1.]. The "little Europe of Six" began its construction on 23 July 1952, the date of entry into force of the ECSC Treaty. The United Kingdom, on the other hand, favoured the intergovernmental method of liberalising trade through a European free trade area, which would not involve any transfer of national sovereignty. According to the British standpoint, customs duties should be abolished between member countries, but the latter should remain autonomous with regard to commercial policy vis-à-vis third countries. Denmark, Norway, Iceland, Austria, Portugal and Switzerland supported that argument and, therefore, did not sign the ECSC Treaty.

In parallel with the integration of their economies, the six founding States of the ECSC wanted to integrate their armies. They, therefore, signed in Paris, on 27 May 1952, the Treaty instituting the **European Defense Community (EDC)**, which aimed at the creation of a supranational integrated army, placed, however, under the supreme command of NATO, barring unanimous opposition of the Six. The EDC project was rejected, on 30 August 1954, by the French parliament. This project may develop in the framework of the European constitution, after the creation of the conditions, which were lacking fifty years ago [see European perspectives in the conclusions].

The very first years of the functioning of the common market in coal and steel showed, however, that economic integration was possible and worthwhile and that it could be extended to all economic sectors. Already in June 1955, the Ministers for Foreign Affairs of the Six discussed the possibility of creating a common market embracing all products and a separate Community for nuclear energy. Speedy negotiations conducted by the Belgian Minister for Foreign Affairs, Paul- Henri Spaak, were concluded in April 1956 and on 25 March 1957, the Six were able to sign, on Capitol Hill in Rome, the Treaties establishing the two new Communities [see section 2.1.].

The United Kingdom proposed then to the Six the creation of a vast European free trade area between the European Economic Community and the other Member States of the OECD, but the discussion were interrupted during the autumn of 1958 owing to intractable differences of opinion between France and the United Kingdom. The separation between states, which wanted to try the Community method and those, which preferred the intergovernmental cooperation for trade liberalisation took shape in 1959 with the creation of the **European Free Trade Association (EFTA)**, to which the United Kingdom, Norway, Sweden, Denmark, Austria, Portugal, Iceland and Switzerland acceded, with Finland joining at a later date.

Having been impressed, however, by the early successes of the European Community, it was not long before the British Government was rethinking its refusal to play an active role in the work of European unification. It was aware that the United Kingdom could not maintain its political influence in Europe and the world through the intergovernmental association of the EFTA. So in August 1961, the United Kingdom submitted an initial official application to become a full member of the European Community. UK candidature of the EEC was followed by two other EFTA member countries, namely Denmark and Norway, and also by Ireland.

Accession of those countries initially met with the opposition of the President of the French Republic, General de Gaulle, who, being very distrustful of the United Kingdom's intentions, declared, right in the middle of the negotiations in 1963, that he wished to discontinue them. The second British application for accession, in 1967, with which Ireland, Denmark and Norway were yet again associated, was not examined for much time owing to France's misgivings. The issue of the accession of those countries could not be resolved until, following General de Gaulle's resignation in April 1969. After laborious negotiations, the Treaties of Accession were finally signed on 22 January 1972. The **accession of the United Kingdom, Ireland and Denmark** took effect on 1 January 1973, following favourable referenda (Ireland and Denmark) and ratification by the national parliaments. Norway's accession was prevented, however, after 53.49% of the Norwegian population opposed accession to the European Community in a referendum.

Once democracy was restored in Greece, Portugal and Spain, those countries submitted applications for accession to the European Community, in 1975 in Greece's case and in 1977 in the other two cases. **Greece** acceded to the Community on 1 January 1981, and **Spain and Portugal** on 1 January 1986. Those countries thus chose to step in the novel and hence risky experiment of the EEC rather than in the secure but limited refuge of the EFTA.

With the signature of the Single European Act, in June 1987, the Twelve Member States of the EEC decided to complete their internal market on 31 December 1992. One year before that date, in December 1991, they decided in Maastricht to develop within the single market an economic and monetary union, a judicial and home affairs policy and a common foreign and security policy, thus transforming the European Economic Community into a **European Union (EU)**, including a refurbished European Community (EC).

Since the 1st January 1995, the Europe of Twelve became the Europe of Fifteen, with the **accession of Austria, Finland and Sweden**, the people of Norway having again voted against membership of the Union by a majority of 52.8%. The remaining countries of the European Free Trade Area (minus Switzerland), i.e., Norway, Iceland and the Liechtenstein signed with the European Community a Treaty on the **European Economic Area (EEA)**, which came into force on 1 January 1994, creating a large free trade area involving several common policies of the EC/EU [see section 25.1.].

The enlargement of the EC/EU is still in progress. After the fall of the iron curtain in 1989, one after the other the countries of Central and Eastern Europe applied for membership in the EU, thus clearly opting for multinational integration rather than for intergovernmental cooperation inside EFTA. The EU encouraged their application by political and financial means [see section 25.2.]. The Laeken European Council, in December 2001, welcomed the considerable progress made in the accession negotiations with **Poland, Hungary, the Czech Republic, Slovakia, Slovenia, Estonia, Latvia, Lithuania** plus **Cyprus** and **Malta**. After conclusion of the negotiations at the Copenhagen European Council, in December 2002, these ten countries signed the Treaty of Accession in Athens on 16 April 2003[1]. Romania and Bulgaria could accede in 2008. Negotiations could start with Turkey, after this country would satisfy the criteria for Union membership established by the European Council in Copenhagen in 1993.

1.3. The attractiveness of the Community method

The preceding summary of events demonstrates the **extraordinary attractiveness of the multinational integration process**, the Community method, compared to its rival, the intergovernmental cooperation method. The countries, which had originally advocated the latter method, have come, one after the other, to solicit their participation in the integration process. The countries of Western Europe, which still shy away from this process, are nevertheless following many of the policies decided by the countries participating in the process, thanks to the European Economic Area agreement (EEA) [see section 25.1.]. The countries of Central and Eastern Europe, which, after their liberation from the iron curtain, had the option of joining the outer circle of the free trade EFTA/EEA or the inner circle of the EC/EU, have unhesitatingly opted for the latter. The facts speak for themselves. There could be no better demonstration of the validity of the multinational integration (Community) method than the attraction that it exerts to outsider neighbouring countries.

What is even more extraordinary is that the membership has kept growing together with the tasks assumed by the team, which means that the newcomers accede to an ever closer union and undertake to adopt all the

---

[1]   OJ L 236 and OJ C 227E, 23.09.2003.

"acquis communautaire", i.e. all the ever-growing legislation enacted by the institutions set up by the elder members. Earlier accessions happened at the time that the Community had just realised its customs union and was struggling to complete its common market in order to make it a single market. The newcomers could well believe that the integration process would stop at this stage and, in fact, some still wish that it did and feel betrayed that it marches on and on. But, later day accessions happened at times that the Community/Union had declared, in revised Treaties, its intention to proceed to the stages of economic and monetary union and even to political union. Hence, when they signed and ratified these Treaties, they were fully aware that European integration is a process without a specified end, but with the declared objective of bringing the European peoples ever closer together. This means that recent newcomers and applicants are attracted by the economic and political advantages of integration, which, for them, outweigh the disadvantage of ceding parts of their national sovereignties to supranational institutions.

The attraction continues and it seems likely that all the countries in the periphery of the Union will someday ask for accession to it. On its side, the Union does not seem disposed to close its door. The **Constitutional Treaty** declares that the Union shall be open to all European States which respect its values and are committed to promoting them together (Art. I-1). All this is very well, but there is a problem of definition of the concepts **"European States"** and **"respect its values"**. These concepts may be defined either in a narrow or a broad sense. Who will define them? The European institutions (Commission, Parliament, Council) or the peoples of the Union through referendums? And, if these last are asked to give their opinion, who and how will adequately inform them in order to enable them to express themselves on such difficult subjects?

Furthermore, the problem is not so much the continuous enlargement of the Union as that **its actual structures and institutions cannot support its expansion** without their reinforcement. The signing of the Constitutional Treaty was an initial endeavour to strengthen the structures and institutions of the Union. But, it seems that the majority of citizens in some of the twenty-five nations believe that this effort is not sufficient for the further enlargement of the Union, whereas the majorities in other nations believe quite the opposite: that this strengthening should be avoided in order to discourage the progress of the integration process. In other words, some nations would like a stronger Constitutional Treaty, which could, not only allow further enlargements, but also help the Union to stand up in the international arena and differentiate itself from other existing and developing superpowers, particularly concerning the social protection of citizens. On the contrary, other nations would like to see the abolishment of the Treaty on the European Union and the solitary existence of the Treaty on the European Community, restraining further integration and conferral of national sovereignties. To better understand the argumentation of the two sides, we should know what these various Treaties stand for.

General bibliography on the EU

- BAIMBRIDGE Mark, HARROP Jeffery, PHILIPPIDIS George. *Current economic issues in EU integration*. Basingstoke: Palgrave Macmillan, 2004.
- COMPSTON Hugh (ed.). *Handbook of public policy in Europe: Britain, France and Germany*. Basingstoke: Palgrave Macmillan, 2004.
- DOBSON Lynn, FØLLESDAL Andreas. *Political theory and the European Constitution*. London; New York: Routledge, 2004.
- GRABBE Heather. *The constellations of Europe: how enlargement will transform the EU*. London: Centre for European Reform, 2004.
- JOWELL Jeffrey, DAWN Oliver (eds.). *The changing constitution*. Oxford: Oxford University Press, 2004.
- MENON Anand. *Leading from behind: Britain and the European constitutional treaty*. Paris: Groupement d'études et de recherches "Notre Europe", 2004.
- MOUSSIS Nicholas. *Access to European Union: Law, Economics, Policies*, 13th rev. ed. Rixensart: European Study Service, 2004.
    - *Accès à l'Union européenne: droit économie, politiques*. 11e édition révisée. Athènes: Papazissis; Bruxelles: Bruylant; Paris: LGDJ, 2005.
- OBERDORFF Henri. *L'Union européenne*. Paris: Armand Colin, 2004.
- SWENDEN Wifried. "Is the European Union in need of a competence catalogue?: Insights from comparative federalism", *Journal of Common Market Studies*, v. 42, n. 2, June 2004, p. 371-392.

DISCUSSION TOPICS

1. On the basis of the contents of this book, can you assess the importance of common policies for multinational integration?
2. Why did R. Schuman call for a treaty on coal and steel and not for the constitution of a federal state?
3. Does multinational integration imply the disappearance of nation-states?
4. Discuss the evolution of the membership of the European Community/Union.
5. Which in your view are the primary objectives of the nations that take part or are seeking participation in European integration and how do they pursue them?

Chapter 2

EUROPEAN TREATIES

Paris 1951	Rome 1957		Brussels
ECSC Treaty p 20	EAEC Treaty p 20	EEC Treaty p 21	Single Act p 21

Maastricht 1991, p. 22			
ECSC Treaty	EAEC Treaty	EU Treaty	EC Treaty

Amsterdam 1997, p. 23			
ECSC Treaty	EAEC Treaty	EU Treaty	EC Treaty

Nice 2000, p. 24		
EAEC Treaty	EU Treaty	EC Treaty

Rome 2004. p. 24
Constitutional Treaty

We shall not linger over the basic Treaties of the Communities, as we shall examine their objectives and main clauses in the later chapters in connection with the legal base of each common policy. Here, we shall simply review the main objectives of the original Treaties and those of the Treaties which have been adopted to revise some of their provisions and to lay the foundations of more advanced stages of European integration.

2.1. The original Treaties

As we saw above, the first European Treaty, the one establishing the **European Coal and Steel Community (ECSC)**, was signed in Paris on 18 April 1951 and entered into force on 23 July 1952. Its main objective was to eliminate the various barriers to trade and to create a common market in which coal and steel products from the Member States could move freely in order to meet the needs of all Community inhabitants, without discrimination on grounds of nationality. Capital and workers in both sectors should also circulate freely. In order that all this could be achieved, the Treaty laid down certain rules on investment and financial aid, on production and prices, on agreements and concentrations of businesses and on transport and Community institutions, including a High Authority and a special Council (of Ministers), the decisions of which would be binding on all Member States. Ambitious despite its restricted scope, the ECSC Treaty introduced a European Assembly and a European Court of Justice. The avowed intentions of the founders of the ECSC were, indeed, that it should be an experiment, which could gradually be extended to other economic spheres, culminating in a "European Federation". For this reason, the duration of the ECSC Treaty was limited to fifty years. On 23 July 2002, when it expired, the specific rules concerning the coal and steel sectors were integrated in the Community law and their particular resources, programmes and international obligations were taken over by the European Community[1]. The coal and steel sectors, previously covered by the ECSC Treaty, are dealt with respectively in the chapters on energy and industry.

The Treaty establishing the **European Atomic Energy Community (EAEC**, but more commonly known as **Euratom)** was signed in Rome on 25 March 1957 and came into force on 1 January 1958. Its aim was to create a common market for nuclear materials and equipment, establish common nuclear legislation, introduce a common system for supplies of fissile materials and establish a system for supervising the peaceful use of nuclear energy and common standards for nuclear safety and for health and safety protection of the population and workers against ionising radiation. The key elements in this Treaty were, however, the coordination of the research programmes of the Member States and a joint research programme, implemented in a Joint Research Centre, which was to develop technology and stimulate nuclear production in Europe [see sections 18.2.4. and 18.3.]. Although it was very much in the spotlight at the time of its establishment, Euratom has experienced many ups and downs as a result both of disillusionment as regards the economic prospects for nuclear energy and of the ambition of some Member States to develop their own nuclear industry, and not purely for civil purposes. Nevertheless, the EAEC Treaty is still in force. The subjects concerning it are examined mainly in the chapters on research and energy.

Signed at the same time as the Euratom Treaty on the Capitol Hill in Rome on 25 March 1957, the Treaty establishing the **European Economic Community (EEC)** was likewise brought into force on 1 January 1958. Although the EEC and EAEC treaties are sometimes referred to as the "Treaties of Rome", the "Treaty of Rome" is obviously the EEC Treaty. The essential task, which the Treaty of Rome assigned to the Community

---

[1] Decision 2002/234, OJ L 79, 22.03.2002, Decisions 2002/595 and 2002/596, OJ L 194, 23.07.2002 and Decisions 2003/76 and 2003/77, OJ L 29, 05.02.2003.

institutions, was **the creation of a common market** between the Member States. That involved: (a) the achievement of a customs union entailing, on the one hand, the abolition of customs duties, import quotas and other barriers to trade between Member States and, on the other hand, the introduction of a Common Customs Tariff (CCT) vis-à-vis third countries [see chapter 5]; and (b) the implementation, *inter alia* through common policies, of **four fundamental freedoms**: freedom of movement of goods, of course, but also freedom of movement of salaried workers, freedom of establishment and freedom to provide services by independent persons and companies and, finally, freedom of capital movements [see chapter 6].

Although in the preamble to the Treaty the Member States declared that they were determined to lay the foundations of an ever closer union among the peoples of Europe, the Treaty itself constituted the charter for a common market. That fact is worth emphasising, because, in order to understand clearly the difficulties in developing, and the scope of, the various common policies which are analysed in this book, it must be borne in mind that the EEC Treaty was conceived so as to govern only relations between Member States up to the common market stage. However, through its Article 235 (Art. 308 TEC), it gave Member States **the possibility to act in the fields not provided by it** by taking unanimously the appropriate measures to attain one of its objectives. This has allowed the Member States to implement a large number of common or, so called, Community policies without amending the Treaty.

An important amendment to the Treaties establishing the European Communities took place on 1 July 1987 with the coming into force of **the Single European Act**. Supplementing in particular the EEC Treaty, the Single Act committed the Community to adopt measures with the aim of progressively establishing the internal market over a period expiring on 31 December 1992.

2.2. The Treaty of Maastricht

The integrationists in the original six Member States were, already before the completion of the single market, pushing their new partners to step into the next integration stage, that of the economic and monetary union and even to sketch the final stage, that of political union. The defenders of the intergovernmental method were, however, reticent. The compromise solution found in Maastricht, in December 1991, was to split the integration venture in half. Hence, the so-called Treaty of Maastricht, which was signed on 7 February 1992, was in fact made up of two separate but interrelated Treaties: the **Treaty on the European Union (TEU)**; and the **Treaty establishing the European Community (TEC)**. These two Treaties separated the European construction into three pillars or edifices [see section 3.1.], distinguished mainly on the basis of the decision-making process: the main pillar or edifice, which is the European Community and where the common work of the participants is regulated by the TEC and where the Community method prevails; the pillar or edifice of justice and home affairs; and the pillar or edifice of the common foreign and security policy (CFSP). The method of construction of the two new pillars or edifices was based on intergovernmental cooperation, since the TEU required unanimity for decision-making and, hence, any Member State could veto a common action. A so-called "Social Protocol" excluded the United Kingdom from the social protection objectives of the TEC.

Thus, since the putting into effect of the Treaty of Maastricht in 1992, the European Union accompanies and complements the European Community; but since the Treaty on the latter governs a far greater number of activities and in a much more forceful way than the Treaty on the European Union, it is more exact to speak of the **European Community/Union (EC/EU)**, in order to keep in mind that they are two different organisations and legal entities. In true fact, for the time being, only the European Community has a legal personality, whereas the European Union has no legal personality at all and can therefore not sign treaties or other international legal instruments.

2.3. The Treaty of Amsterdam

The Treaty signed on 17 June 1997 at Amsterdam, only six years and a half after the signature of the Treaty of Maastricht, did not bring fundamental changes to the integration process, but it marked some progress in several policies. The most important development was the transfer into the European Community wing, entailing the Community decision-making method, of policies related to the free movement of persons, notably concerning visas, asylum and immigration [see section 8.1.]. In particular, it made the Union's **institutional structure** more efficient by extending the co-decision procedure (Parliament/Council) and qualified majority voting in the Council [see section 4.3.]. Another important objective of the Amsterdam Treaty was to place employment and **social protection** at the heart of the Union [see sections 13.3. and 13.5.3.]. While confirming that the Member States bear primary responsibility for employment, the revised Treaty on the European Community engaged them to act together to find solutions to unemployment. The Labour government of the United Kingdom accepted the social objectives of the Treaty and therefore the social policy agreement, excepting the UK from this common policy, was abolished.

In its European Union wing, the Amsterdam Treaty strengthened the common foreign and security policy by making the European Council (heads of State or government) responsible for defining common strategies to be implemented by the Union and the Member States and by designating a High Representative for the CFSP (the Secretary General of the Council) and a Policy Planning and Early Warning Unit under his responsibility [see section 8.2.].

2.4. The Treaty of Nice

The Treaty that was signed in Nice on 26 February 2001, only three years and a half after the signature of the Treaty of Amsterdam, did not aspire to give a new impulse to the European integration process, but only to prepare the institutions of the European Community/Union to function with the representatives of ten new Member States. This Treaty, which will stay in force until replaced by the Constitutional Treaty, revised the Treaty of Amsterdam concerning mainly four institutional matters: the replacement of unanimity by qualified majority in decision-making procedures, the enhanced cooperation of some Member States[1], the weighting of votes in the Council and the size and the composition of the Commission.

The Treaty of Nice extended the qualified majority voting to new subjects, thereby boosting the role of the European Parliament in the codecision process with the Council. It reinforced and facilitated the enhanced cooperation of some Member States, in cases where an agreement cannot be reached by normal decision-making procedures. The Protocol on the enlargement of the European Union, adopted at Nice, redefined the weighting of the votes of each Member State in the Council and introduced a population element by specifying that decisions taken by qualified majority on the basis of a Commission proposal should gather at least 72% of the total votes of the members, representing at least 62% of the total population of the Union. As regards the composition of the Commission, the same protocol provides that after the enlargement of the Union each Member State will have one Commissioner until such time as the 27th Member State joins the European Union, but thereafter the number of Commissioners will be smaller than the number of Member States.

The coming into force of the Treaty of Nice was initially held back by the negative result of a referendum of the Irish people, held on 11 June 2001, but the problem was resolved by the positive outcome of a second referendum, held on 19 October 2002. The Treaty of Nice, thus, came into force on 1 February 2003. Under the heading of the city in which it was signed, the Treaty of Nice, as the repealed Treaties of Maastricht and Amsterdam, includes in fact two Treaties: the Treaty on the European Union (**TEU**) and the Treaty establishing the European Community (**TEC**). The existence of two separate Treaties for the Community and the Union, their frequent modifications, the new numbering of their articles and the technocratic language of their texts are daunting and hardly likely to mobilise the public opinion in favour of European integration [see sections 10.1. and 10.4.]. A greater transparency was expected to be achieved with the constitutional Treaty, which, at least, would bring the two Treaties into one. **This book follows the numbering of the articles of the TEU and the TEC** adopted in Nice and actually in force, except when referring to past legislation based on previous versions of the Treaties.

---

[1] OJ C 325, 24.12.2002.

2.5. Towards a European Constitution

Convinced of the need for a substantial reformation of the institutional framework of the enlarged Union, the Nice European Council, in December 2000, called a new Intergovernmental Conference (IGC) to propose a new and extensive modification of the Treaties. In order to prepare for the Intergovernmental Conference as broadly and transparently as possible, the Laeken European Council (14-15 December 2001) decided to convene a **Convention on the Future of Europe**, with the former President of the French Republic, Mr Giscard d'Estaing as Chairman. The IGC, which began its works in Rome on October 2003 with the participation of representatives of twenty-five States, took largely on board the proposals of the Convention and the new Treaty was signed in Rome on 29 October 2004 by the heads of State or government of the Twenty-five[1]. But its coming into force is suspended, since it required its ratification by all the twenty-five Member States and some of them have asked their citizens to pronounce themselves on this ratification and the outcome is already negative in two such referendums.

The Constitution **would simplify the European construction**. As of the coming into force of the new Treaty, the existing Treaties on the European Union, the European Community and the European Atomic Energy Community would be repealed, thus eliminating the confusion between the Community and the Union. The Union would have a single legal personality under which it would negotiate, sign and implement all its external commitments, policies and activities, including trade, aid to development, representation in third countries and in international organisations. Both from the interior (its citizens) and from the exterior (its counterparts) the Union would, thus, be seen as a whole construction [see section 3.1.].

Other **important innovations** of this Treaty are the attribution of constitutional weight to the Charter for Fundamental Rights, the solemn acknowledgement of the Union's values and objectives, the definition of the conditions for membership of the Union (including conditions for voluntary withdrawal from the Union) and a clearer presentation of the principles determining the distribution of competences between the Union and its constituent parts. The Constitution jointly vests the Parliament and the Council of Ministers with the legislative and budgetary functions. The co-decision procedure is extended and renamed "ordinary legislative procedure". Hence, the Parliament becomes co-legislator in almost all cases (95% of the legislative areas), with the exception of a dozen areas, where it will only be consulted [see section 4.1.3.]. The "European laws" will replace the actual legal instruments of the Union [see section 3.3.], thus simplifying the legal system of the Union and facilitating its understanding by the citizens. The Constitution establishes a permanent President of the

---

[1]   OJ C 310, 16.12.2004.

European Council, who will take on the work currently assigned to rotating Presidencies [see section 4.1.1.].

The Constitution does not extend the Union's competences considerably. The content of most provisions that govern **the Union's policies** thus remains unchanged, which means that they will continue to develop with the "Community method", which should in the future be called the integration method. The integration method is not extended to the **common foreign and security policy (CFSP)**. Nevertheless, the creation of the post of Union Minister for Foreign Affairs, who would be a member of the Commission responsible for the representation of the Union on the international scene, would merge the present tasks of the High Representative for the Common Foreign and Security Policy with those of the Commissioner for external relations. Although a member of the Commission and as such in charge of the Commission's responsibilities in the field of external relations, this "European Minister of Foreign Affairs" would chair the External Relations Council and coordinate the other aspects of the Union's external action. This function could considerably strengthen the Union's role in world affairs [see section 8.2. and Part VI].

2.6. The treaties as instruments of progress

Few citizens realise that the Nice Treaty, which is in force since the 1st February 2003, is in fact composed of two separate Treaties: the Treaty on the European Union and the Treaty instituting the European Community. Even fewer citizens realise that there is a fundamental difference between the two Treaties. The EC Treaty was based on the tested "Community method" [see section 4.3.], which had instituted and managed the common policies of the common market. The new policies of the EU were to be governed by a method akin to intergovernmental cooperation, in order to persuade eurosceptic nations to advance in the stage of political integration without conceding bits of national sovereignty [see section 1.1.2.]. The experience from the development of the European Community/Union to date indicates, however, that this differentiation is neither inevitable nor eternal.

The frequency and vigour of the amendments of the European treaties show that their authors, i.e. the governments of the Member States, do not consider them as sacred and unalterable, but they use them as perfectible instruments of the multinational integration process. The Treaties and the future Constitution are the base on which decisions are taken that give substance to the common policies at a certain time in a certain internal and international context. Given that the problems of European states change continually under the pressure of internal and external factors, the common policies must develop regularly, in order to face them successfully. This is the reason why the Treaties, which are the primary source of European law and hence the legal basis of common policies, have to be modified frequently. This should also be the case for the future constitutional treaty.

Bibliography on European Treaties

- DIMITRAKOPOULOS G, KREMLIS G (eds.). "A new constitutional settlement for European people", Athens: Editions Ant. N. Sakkoulas; Bruxelles: Bruylant, 2004.

- ERIKSEN E. O., FOSSUM J. E., MENÉNDEZ A. J. (eds.). *Developing a Constitution for Europe*. London; New York: Routledge, 2004.

- EUROPEAN COMMISSION. *A Constitution for Europe: Constitution adopted by the Heads of State and Governament: Presentation to citizen.* Luxembourg: EUR-OP*, 2004.

- GOEBEL Roger. "The European Union in transition: the Treaty of Nice in effect; enlargement in sight; a Constitution in doubt", *Fordham International Law Journal*, v. 27, n. 2, January 2004, p. 455-502.

- KILJUNEN Kimmo. *The European Constitution in the making*. Brussels: Centre for European Policy Studies, 2004.

- MICCÙ Roberto, PERNICE Ingolf (eds.). *The European Constitution in the making*. Baden-Baden: Nomos, 2004.

- MOUSSIS Nicolas. "Réussir la constitution: l'adopter, puis l'adapter à la majorité", *Revue du marché commun et de l'Union européenne*, n. 476, mars 2004, p. 151-152.

- PHILIP Christian, SOLDATOS Panayotis (sous la dir. de). *La Convention sur l'avenir de l'Europe: Essai d'évaluation du projet de traité établissant une Constitution pour l'Europe*. Bruxelles: Bruylant, 2004.

- SCHWARGE Jürgen. "The Convention's draft treaty establishing a Constitution for Europe", *Common Market Law Review*, v. 40, n. 5, October 2003, p. 1037-1045.

- TEMPLE LANG John. "The main issues after the Convention on the Constitutional Treaty for Europe", *Fordham International Law Journal*, v. 27, n. 2, January 2004, p. 544-589.

The publications of the Office for Official Publications of the European Communities (EUR-OP) exist generally in all official languages of the EU.

DISCUSSION TOPICS

1. Which were the principal goals of the Treaties of Rome?
2. Which were the new goals set by the Treaty of Maastricht?
3. Which were the new goals set by the Treaty of Amsterdam?
4. Is the signing and ratification of a treaty necessary for the passage from one integration stage to the next?
5. Discuss the advantages and disadvantages of a constitutional treaty for the European Union.

Chapter 3

EUROPEAN LAW AND FINANCES

3.1. European Community and European Union

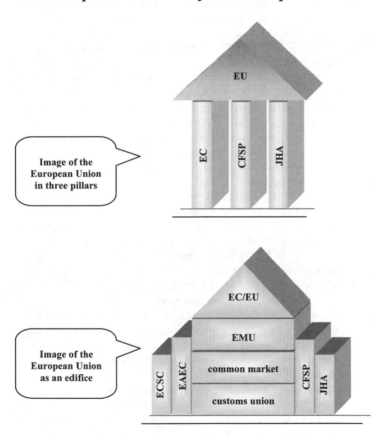

Image of the
European Union
in three pillars

Image of the
European Union
as an edifice

One often hears about **the three "pillars"** of the European Union, the first being the European Community (EC), the second the common foreign and security policy (CFSP) and the third justice and home affairs (JHA). We should say, however, that the image of the EU as three pillars minimises the place of the Community, which is preponderant, since it contains all common policies instituted in the framework of the three original Treaties and all the legislation adopted on their bases since 1952.

The European Union is better visualised **as an on-going construction.** In this image, the European Community constitutes the main edifice, solid and functional, thanks to the existence within it of a great number of common policies, which are at various stages of development. Next to it, the CFSP and especially the JHA are still at the stage of foundations, built following the plans drafted under the Treaty on the European Union. Their edifices need to be patiently built with common legal acts. Moreover, the Treaty of Amsterdam has transferred into the Community edifice many subjects, which were originally under the JHA wing. In this wing, intergovernmental cooperation is presently confined to police and judicial cooperation in criminal matters [see section 8.1.2.]. It would be absurd to represent this cooperation as a pillar of the European construction.

A closer look at the metaphorical image of the European construction shows that **the main edifice, that of the Community**, is divided horizontally by floors. The floor of the common market is built on the foundations of the customs union. Apart from the four fundamental freedoms (free movement of goods, persons, services and capital), the common market floor consists of numerous horizontal and vertical compartments, which contain the common policies that constitute the bulk of this book. The compartments of coal, steel and nuclear energy, built with the Community method provided by the ECSC and Euratom Treaties, are also found on these first floors of the Community edifice.

The floor of **economic and monetary union (EMU)** was built above the floor of the common market and, therefore, inside the Community edifice [see chapter 7]. The Treaty on European Community has drawn the architectural plans and the "memorandum of understanding" that the builders (European institutions and Member States) need to respect in order to succeed in the construction of the EMU. Some of the contractors (Member States), who have advanced faster than others, find themselves already in the "penthouse" of the Community edifice, which shelters the single currency, and have started setting up common policies inside it. The others, including the new Member States will continue to work inside the lower floors, until the time that they are ready and/or willing to join the pioneers in the top floor of the collective edifice.

The "European Community" exists thus and grows under the roof of the "European Union". This is also true for the other two Communities, that of coal and steel and that of atomic energy, which are often mixed with the European Community and indistinctly called "the Community". It is correct to speak about the "**Community**" in respect of everything that happened and that was built up until the 1st November 1993, when the "European Union" came into being. It is even correct to speak about the "Community" for measures taken after that date by following the Community procedure on the basis of the EC Treaty (but also the ECSC and EAEC Treaties). The term "**European Union**" should, however, be used for all measures that concern the new edifices of the construction and, in general, for designating the organisation of European countries, which have decided to create an ever closer union among their peoples, covering relations much broader than the economic relations governed by the original Community.

3.2. The competences of the European Community/Union

When the member states of a multinational integration scheme adopt a fundamental or secondary common policy, they implicitly recognise that it has an added value in relation to their previously independent national policies in a certain field. Certainly, as common policies advance, national policies lose some of their independence in terms of goals and means, since segments of national sovereignty are blended into a new concept of **"shared sovereignty"** that is intended to serve better the various national interests. But, this loss of independence is circumscribed by two means: the continuing influence of the member states in the development of a common policy after its inception, through the common institutions in which they participate [see chapter 4]; and the possibility left to the member states to choose the means that suit them best to attain the common goals of a common policy, by virtue of the principles of subsidiarity and proportionality explained below.

The **principle of subsidiarity** means that the Community must not undertake or regulate what can be managed or regulated more efficiently at national or regional levels. This principle, implying multi-level governance [see section 1.1.1.] must be exercised in a spirit of cooperation between the various levels of power. According to the Treaties (Art. 2 TEU and art. 5 TEC), the Community must act within the limits of the powers conferred upon it by the Treaties and of the objectives assigned to it therein. In areas which do not fall within its exclusive competence, the Community must take action, in accordance with the principle of subsidiarity, only if and in so far as the objectives of the proposed action cannot be sufficiently achieved by the Member States and can therefore, by reason of the scale or effects of the proposed action, be better achieved by the Community. Any action by the Community must not go beyond what is necessary to achieve the objectives of the Treaties. Article 308 of the EC Treaty enables the Council, by unanimity and after consulting the European Parliament, to introduce the provisions needed to attain a common objective, but does not make it possible to create new powers for the Community. An interinstitutional agreement sets out the procedures for implementing the principle of subsidiarity[1].

---

[1] Interinstitutional agreement, OJ C 329, 06.12.1993.

The **principle of proportionality** implies that, if a Community action proves to be necessary to attain the objectives of the Treaty, the Community institutions must further examine whether legislative action is required or whether other sufficiently effective means can be used (financial support, encouragement of cooperation between Member States by a Recommendation, inducement to take action by a Resolution, etc.).

The "**open method of coordination**" applies the principles of subsidiarity and proportionality in many common policies. It involves setting common objectives, translating these objectives into national policy strategies and periodic monitoring on the basis, inter alia, of commonly agreed and defined indicators. In those instances, the scale of European action leaves a wide margin of manoeuvre to the national authorities, but, owing to its intergovernmental nature, it prevents the democratic control of the European Parliament and the judicial control of the Court of Justice over the decision-making process.

The **Constitutional Treaty** does not depart from current practice on the question of transfer of sovereign rights from the Member States to the Union, but it defines in detail the principles which govern this transfer and guarantees that these principles should not be infringed. According to the Constitution, these principles are: the principle of conferral, under which the Union shall act within the limits of the competences conferred upon it by the Member States in the Constitution (Art. I-11); the clear distinction of the Union's competences into areas of exclusive competence, of shared competence and of support of national policies (Art. I-13 to I-17); and the exercise of these competences in accordance with the principles of subsidiarity and proportionality under the control of national parliaments.

3.3. The Community legal system

Common policies, which are the essence of multinational integration, are based on **common legislation**. Inherent in the concept of a common policy [see section 1.1.2.] is its **binding force on the member states**. The latter must give the common institutions the legal means to implement common policies and to enforce their decisions on all the parties concerned and on their citizens. Hence, common policies are shaped by legal acts agreed by the common institutions, implemented by the member states and/or the common institutions and controlled by the common institutions [see chapter 4]. The national laws of the member states are harmonised in a great number of fields in the context of common policies. A special law, based on the treaties and called acquis communautaire, is thus built to bring into being common policies, a law that is superimposed and takes **precedence over national law**, even the constitutional law, of the Member States, whether national legislation predates or postdates Community legislation. In fact, according to the Court of Justice, the Member States have definitively transferred sovereign rights to the Community they created, and they cannot subsequently go back on that transfer through unilateral measures[1], unless they decide to break away from the EC/EU. This is another feature of the multinational integration process, which distinguishes it from intergovernmental cooperation, where decisions may have political consequences, but do not carry a legal binding force on the participating states. A multinational integration process, such as that of the EC/EU, could not function, if each Member State could circumvent its legislation by bringing into play its national - including its constitutional - law.

The legal acts, which substantiate the common policies, may be undertaken by the competent institutions with legal effect only if they are empowered to do so by the European Treaties (principle of attribution of powers). Article 249 of the EC Treaty provides for five forms of legal act, each with a different effect on the Member States' legal systems: some are directly applicable in place of national legislation, while others permit the progressive adjustment of that legislation to Community provisions.

The **regulation** has a general scope, is binding in all its elements and is directly applicable in each Member State. Just like a national law, it gives rise to rights and obligations directly applicable to the citizens of the European Union[2]. Regulations enter into force on a date which they lay down or, where they do not set a date, on the twentieth day following their publication in the Official Journal of the European Union. The regulation substitutes European law for national law and is therefore the most effective legal instrument provided for by the EC Treaty. As "European laws", regulations must be complied with fully by those to whom they are addressed (individuals, Member States, European institutions).

The **directive** binds any Member State to which it is addressed with regard to the result to be achieved, while allowing the national authorities competency as to the form and methods used. It is a sort of Community framework law and lends itself particularly well to the harmonisation of national laws. It defines the objective or objectives to be attained by a common policy and leaves it to the Member States to choose the forms and instruments necessary for complying with it. Since the Member States are only bound by the objectives laid down in directives, they have some discretion, in transposing them into national law, in taking into account of special national circumstances. They must, however, "ensure fulfilment of the obligations arising out of the Treaty or resulting from action taken by the institutions of the Community" (Art. 10 TEC). Although they are generally published in the Official Journal, Directives take effect by virtue of being notified to the Member States to which they are addressed. The latter are obliged to adopt the national measures necessary for implementation of the Directive within time-limits set by it, failing which they are infringing Community legislation.

---

[1] Judgment of 15 July 1964, case 6/64, Costa/ENEL, ECR 1964, p. 1160.

[2] See on this subject, notably, the judgments of the Court of Justice of 14.12.1971, case 43/71, Politi, ECR 1971, p. 1049 and of 7.2.1973, case 39/72, Commission v Italy, ECR 1973, pp. 114-115.

The **decision** is binding on the addressees it indicates, who may be one, several, or even all the Member States or one or more natural or legal persons. This variety of potential addressees is coupled with a variety in the scope of its contents, which may extend from a quasi regulation or a quasi directive to a specific administrative decision. It takes effect on its communication to the addressees rather than on its publication in the Official Journal. In any case, according to the Court of Justice, a decision can produce direct effects creating for the individuals rights that national jurisdictions must safeguard[1].

The above legal acts are normally used, on the basis of the Treaty and following the Community method [see section 4.3.], for harmonising or approximating national legislations and their effects are binding on the Member States, the Community institutions and, in many cases, the citizens of the Member States. This is the case of laws or decisions which must apply uniformly in all Member States. However, the objectives of the common policies are also sought by **non-binding concerted action**, taking the form of coordination of national policies, mechanisms for exchanging information, bodies for cooperation, Community programmes and/or financial support.

Therefore, in addition to the above binding acts, which form the Community law, the Council and the Commission can adopt **Recommendations** suggesting a certain line of conduct or outlining the goals of a common policy and **opinions** assessing a current situation or certain facts in the Community or the Member States. Furthermore, the Council and the European Parliament adopt **Resolutions**, which are also not binding, suggesting a political desire to act in a given area. These instruments enable the Community institutions to suggest guidelines for coordination of national legislations or administrative practices in a non-binding manner, i.e. without any legal obligations for the addressees - Member States and/or citizens.

While Resolutions and opinions are published in the "C" series (communications) of the **Official Journal of the European Union (OJ)**, binding acts and recommendations are published in the "L" series (legislation) of the OJ, in order to stress their political importance. The same is true about the **common positions** and **joint actions** of the common foreign and security policy and of justice and home affairs (Art. 12 31 of TEU) [see sections 8.1. and 8.2.1.]. They are published in the L series of the OJ, although they have not a legal binding force on the Member States, since the Court of Justice of the European Communities does not have jurisdiction on their interpretation and implementation. They embody, however, political commitments for joint behaviour and/or action.

The **Constitutional Treaty** renames and simplifies the legal instruments of the Union. After its coming into force, the institutions would

---

[1] Judgment of 6 October 1970, case 9/70, Grad, ECR 1970, p. 838 and judgment of 12 December 1990, joined cases 100/89 and 101/89, ECR 1990, p. I-4647.

adopt European laws, European framework laws, European regulations, European decisions, recommendations and opinions (Art. I-33). A **European law** would be a legislative act of general application, binding in its entirety and directly applicable in all Member States (as the actual regulation). A **European framework law** would be a legislative act binding, as to the result to be achieved, but will leave to the national authorities the choice of form and methods (as the present directive). The European laws and framework laws would be adopted by the European Parliament and the Council in accordance with the ordinary legislative procedure (Art. I-34) [see section 4.3.]. A **European regulation** would be a non-legislative act of general application for the implementation of legislative acts and would have the binding force and applicability of the main act. A **European decision** will be a non-legislative act, either binding in its entirety or binding only those to whom it is addressed. The European Council would adopt decisions, the Council, the Commission and the European Central Bank would adopt regulations and decisions (Art. I-35). **Recommendations** - usually adopted by the Council and in specific cases by the Commission or the European Central Bank - and **opinions** - usually adopted by the advisory Committees - would have no binding force.

3.4. The Community finances

The conventional international organisations such as the UN or the OECD are financed by contributions from their member countries. In most instances their financial requirements amount to staff and operational expenditure: if they are entrusted with operational tasks, their financing is generally provided on an "à la carte" basis by those member countries which decided on those tasks. It is virtually never a question, in such organisations, of financial transfers or even of financial compensation. The European Community, on the other hand, although it is not a federation in the formal sense, pursues many federating common policies, which call for a transfer of resources from the national to the supranational level.

Some common policies of the European Community/Union are clearly in the interest of the stronger and wealthier Member States. This is the case notably of the internal market, competition and taxation policies, because they open the markets of the weaker and poorer Member States to their products and services. Therefore, some other policies are needed to **balance the benefits of the integration process**, by operating capital transfers in favour of the poorer Member States: e.g. the agricultural, regional and social policies. These transfers of capital are also in the interest of the wealthier Member States, since they allow their poorer partners to buy more of their products and services. This balance of the benefits of the Member States, which distinguishes, *inter alia*, a multinational integration scheme from a free trade area one, is organised by the Community budget.

The implementation of many common policies requires, indeed, not only legal but also some financial means. Certainly, not all common policies need common financing. For example, competition and taxation policies are based almost exclusively on legal measures. But the implementation of most common policies is based on a mixture of legal and financial measures. Common regional, education, aid to development policies, e.g., would be seriously restrained without Community financing of their common programmes. There could be no common agricultural or fisheries policies, in the sense that we know them, without common support of prices and/or incomes [see sections 21.4.2, 21.4.3 and 22.3.]. It is a political value judgment whether there should be more or less common financing of this or that common policy and this judgment is subject to a long debate carried out every year among the budgetary authorities of the Community, politicians from the Member States sitting in the Council and the European Parliament, on the basis of technical reports and proposals provided by the Commission. The result of this multinational political debate is recorded in the **Community budget**.

In the beginning of the European Economic Community, the contribution of the Member States to the Community budget was determined on a scale according to GNP shares or other criteria. Provision had been made in the EEC Treaty for replacing the Member States' initial contributions by **own resources** after establishment of the Common Customs Tariff (CCT) [see section 5.2.1.]. The transfer of customs revenue to the Community budget was a spillover effect [see section 1.1.1.] of the realisation, provided for in the Treaty, of a genuine customs union[1]. In such a union the country of import of goods from a third country is not always the country of final destination of those goods. The revenue from customs duties is therefore often collected in a country other than the country of destination or of consumption. Only the payment of that revenue to the customs union, in this instance to the Community, makes it possible to neutralise that effect. This is, moreover, an important integrating element, which again differentiates a customs union from a free trade area [see the introduction to part II].

However, since the realisation of the customs union in 1968, the importance of customs duties was continually diminishing inasmuch as they were being progressively abolished or reduced under the General Agreement on Tariffs and Trade (GATT) and the various tariff concessions granted to the least developed countries [see section 23.4. and chapter 24]. For that reason it was decided, in 1970, to use a proportion of the **value added tax (VAT)** as an additional source of Community financing. That tax, which has a uniform basis of assessment, takes fairly accurate account of the economic capacity of the citizens of the Member States, as it is levied at the consumption level [see section 14.2.1.]. The "**uniform base**", which was adopted for calculating the proportions of the VAT yield which

---

[1]   Decision 70/243, OJ L 94, 28.04.1970.

countries must pay to the EU, is made up of all taxable supplies of goods and provisions of services in the Union.

Since 2001, the system of the European Communities' own resources is based, since 2001, on the following elements[1]:

- the **maximum ceiling** on own resources is fixed at 1.27 % of gross national income (GNI) of the EC/EU;

- **traditional own resources** - essentially customs and agricultural duties - minus 25% retained by the Member States as collection costs;

- 0.5% of the maximum call-in rate from **VAT resources**, aiming at correcting the regressive aspects of the system for the least prosperous Member States;

- **technical adjustments** aiming at the correction of budgetary imbalances in favour of the United Kingdom and originating in the famous battle cry of Margaret Thatcher of 30 November 1979: "I want my money back".

As far as **Community expenditures** are concerned, we should note that they have increased between the early 1980s and the early 1990s from 1.7 to 2.4% of all public expenditure in the Member States. They still represent, however, little more than one percent of the cumulative Gross Internal Product of the Member States. More than 90% of the receipts of the European Union are redistributed to the Member States and serve to finance the objectives of the various common policies (redistributive function of the Community budget).

The **management of the Community budget** is entrusted to the Commission (Art. 274 TEC) and is exercised according to a Financial Regulation, which sets the principles and ground rules governing the establishment and implementation of the budget and financial control, ensuring more efficient and effective management and control of European taxpayers' money[2]. Article 280 of the EC Treaty stipulates that the Member States must coordinate their action aimed at protecting the financial interests of the Community against fraud and must take the same measures to counter fraud affecting the financial interests of the Community as they take to counter fraud affecting their own financial interests[3].

---

[1] Decision 94/728, OJ L 293, 12.11.1994 and Decision 2000/597, OJ L 253, 07.10.2000.
[2] Regulation 1605/2002, OJ L 248, 16.09.2002 and Regulation 2342/2002, OJ L 357, 31.12.2002.
[3] COM (2000) 358, 28 June 2000.

Bibliography on European law and finances

- BAIMBRIDGE Mark, Whyman Philip (eds.). *Fiscal federalism and European economic integration.* London: Routledge, 2004.
- BIEBER Roland, MAIANI Francesco, KAHIL-WOLFF Bettina. *Précis de droit européen*, Berne: Stämpfli, 2004.
- BORRÁS Susana, GREVE Bent, JACOBSSON Kesrtin (eds.). "The open method of co-ordination in the European Union", *Journal of European Public Policy,* v. 11, n. 2, April 2004, p.181-336.
- CATTOIR Philippe. *Tax-based EU own resources: an assessment,* Luxembourg: EUR-OP*, 2004.
- CRAIG Paul. "Competence: clarity, conferral, containment and consideration", *European Law Review,* v. 29, n. 3, June 2004, p. 323-344.
- EUROPEAN COMMISSION. *Protecting the Communities' financial interests: Fight against fraud: Action Plan for 2004-2005,* Luxembourg: EUR-OP*, 2004.
  - *Building our common future: Policy challenges and budgetary means of enlarged Union, 2007-13.* Luxembourg: EUR-OP*, 2004.
- KERSBERGEN Kees van, VERBEEK Bertjan. "Subsidiarity as a principle of governance in the European Union", *Comparative European Politics*, v. 2, n. 2, August 2004, p. 142-162.
- STONE SWEET Alec. *The judicial construction of Europe.* Oxford: Oxford University Press, 2004.
- TRIDIMAS Takis, NEBBIA Paolisa (eds.). *European Union law for the twenty-first century: rethinking the new legal order.* Oxford; Portland, Or.: Hart, 2004.

DISCUSSION TOPICS

1. Comment the imagery of the European Union in three pillars and as an edifice.
2. Discuss the importance of the principles of subsidiarity and proportionality.
3. Compare the legal system of the Community to that of a national state.
4. Consider the Community finances from the point of view of multinational integration.
5. Discuss the interaction between national and Community administrations in the fight against fraud.

Chapter 4

THE STRUCTURE AND FUNCTIONS OF EUROPEAN INSTITUTIONS

In the first part of this chapter is analysed the structure and the role of the institutions or organs of the European Union. In the second part is examined their interaction which leads to the formation and enforcement of European law. In the third part of the chapter we make some suggestions for a drastic reform of the institutions in view of the enlargement of the EC/EU and its evolution towards a political union.

4.1. The European Institutions

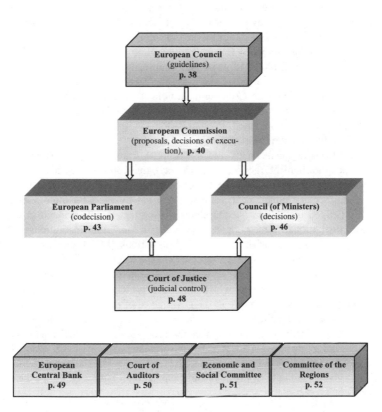

Common policies, which are the essence of the multinational integration process, are the fruit of intensive negotiations among the parties, which participate in this process. In order to be acceptable to all parties (member states), the conception of a common policy must try to satisfy or, at least, not injure the national interests of the parties and, therefore, the governments of all member states must participate in the decision-making process. Their participation, however, may be direct or indirect. Decisions on fundamental common policies, requiring new transfers of national sovereignties to the shared or supranational sovereignty, are taken by the participating governments (in intergovernmental conferences) and are outlined in treaties, signed by those governments and ratified by them after authorisation by the national parliaments [see chapter 2]. Decisions on secondary common policies, i.e. those needed to attain the goals set in the treaty, including policy guidelines and legal acts based on the treaty, are taken by the **common institutions** set up by the treaty, according to procedures and following the legal forms agreed in this treaty [see sections 3.3. and 4.3.]. In contrast to an organisation based on intergovernmental cooperation, where the governments are the main actors, in a multinational integration process the governments of the member states direct the play from the backstage, but they leave the stage to the actors, that is their representatives, appointed by them and/or by their citizens.

The principal actors of European integration are called "**institutions**" by the European Treaties. However, the qualification of an organ as institutional is changing in various revisions of the Treaties following the development of the European Community/Union. According to the EC Treaty (Nice version) the basic institutional structure of the European Union consists of five institutions: the European Parliament, the Council of Ministers, the Commission, the Court of Justice and the Court of Auditors. According to the Constitutional Treaty the institutional framework comprises: the European Parliament, the European Council, the Council of Ministers, the European Commission and the Court of Justice of the European Union. The European Council is therefore recognised by the Constitution as a fully-fledged institution, but the Court of Auditors is not included in the basic institutional framework. It is included in the "other institutions and advisory bodies", as is the European Central Bank (ECB), the Economic and Social Committee and the Committee of the Regions.

For analytical purposes, we consider as principal actors of European integration the five organs which intervene principally in the decision-making process and therefore in the governance of the Community/Union: the European Council, which sets the goals of the common policies; the European Commission, which makes the proposals for the decisions to be taken and is mainly responsible for the implementation of the common policies; the European Parliament and the Council of Ministers, which take the decisions; and the Court of Justice, which controls the legality of these decisions.

4.1.1. The European Council

The European Council is made up of the **Heads of State** (the President of the French Republic and the Presidents of the Republics of Cyprus, Latvia and Lithuania, responsible for foreign and European affairs) **or of Government** (the Prime Ministers of the other Member States) of the EU and the President of the European Commission. Begun on an informal basis as "Summit meetings" in the early 1960s, the European Council is now explicitly provided for in Article 4 of the Treaty on European Union (Nice). This Article provides that the European Council shall meet at least twice a year, under the chairmanship of the Head of State or Government of the Member State which holds the Presidency of the Council. Departing from the letter of the Treaty, the Seville European Council (21-22 June 2002) has agreed that it shall meet in principle four times a year (twice every six months) and that, in exceptional circumstances, it may hold an extraordinary meeting.

The European Council is the architect of European construction. It provides the Union with the necessary impetus for its development; it defines the general political guidelines thereof and resolves the most important problems of the construction. The European Council is above all **a forum for free and informal exchanges of views** between the responsible leaders of the Member States. Its strength is its spontaneity and its informality, which bring about a sort of *"esprit de corps"* on the part of Europe's political leaders. Being a venue where package deals can be struck, and thus being free from the rigidity that sometimes paralyses the proceedings of the Council of Ministers, the European Council often acts as an appeal body for politically and economically important business which is deadlocked at ministerial level.

It should be noted, however, that the Heads of State or Government **do not adopt legal acts formally binding** the Member States [see section 3.3.]. Their deliberations result in the publication of declarations containing guidelines and general directives for future Community action. These declarations have undeniable political value, but no legal binding force. They give the political impetus necessary for common policies, but the latter are constructed with Community provisions adopted subsequently in accordance with the procedures laid down in the Treaties. The situation is quite different in the sphere of the common foreign and security policy where the European Council, in addition to adopting common strategies, can decide upon joint actions or common positions, which bind politically, if not legally, the Member States [see section 8.2.1.].

Apart from considering the European Council as a main institution of the Union, **the Constitution** establishes a permanent President of the European Council, who will take on the work currently assigned to rotating Presidencies. He or she will be elected by qualified majority, for a term of two and a half years, renewable once (Art. I-22). This new institutional arrangement is designed to lend a degree of visibility and stability to the

Presidency of the European Council. The Permanent President will necessarily have the same nationality as one of the members of the European Council, but will not participate in the voting procedure within this institution.

4.1.2. The European Commission

From the very beginning of the Community until 2004, the European Commission, usually referred to simply as **the Commission**, was made up of two nationals from each "big" and one national from each "small" Member State. Hence, the Treaty of Nice - adopted at a time that the European Community/Union numbered fifteen Member States, five of which were considered as big (Germany, France, the UK, Italy and Spain) - stated that "the Commission shall consist of 20 Members, who shall be chosen on the grounds of their general competence and whose independence is beyond doubt" (Article 213 TEC). Anticipating the enlargement of the EC/EU, this Treaty provided, however, that the number of members of the Commission could be altered by the Council, acting unanimously. In fact, in the Act of Accession of the ten new Member States (article 45), it was agreed (not without difficulties) that any State acceding to the Union should be entitled to have one of its nationals as a member of the Commission and that a new Commission composed of one national of each Member State should take up its duties on 1 November 2004, after the European elections of June 2004.

Thus, actually, the Commission is composed of 25 members (Commissioners), who are proposed by the government of each Member State and are appointed, for a period of five years, by the Council, acting by a qualified majority and by common accord with the nominee for President. The members of the Commission may not, during their term of office, engage in any other occupation, whether gainful or not. They must not take instructions from any government and all governments must respect this principle and not seek to influence the members of the Commission in the performance of their tasks (Art. 213 TEC).

The Heads of State or Government, acting by a qualified majority, nominate the President of the Commission and the nomination must be approved by the European Parliament. The President and the other Members of the Commission are subject as a body to a vote of approval by the European Parliament (Art. 214 TEC). The Parliament examines every Commissioner as to his or her programme and ideas and may put forward objections as to his/her suitability for his/her particular responsibilities inside the Commission, but may not reject his/her appointment. Hence, in case of objections expressed by the Parliament for certain members of the Commission, its President has the option of either assigning other responsibilities to the members in question or of risking the rejection of the body by the Parliament.

The **Constitutional Treaty provides** that the current composition of the Commission – one Commissioner per Member State – is maintained until 2014. From then on, the Commission will comprise a number of Commissioners corresponding to two thirds of the number of Member States. The members of the Commission will be chosen according to a system based on equal rotation among the Member States, guaranteeing equal treatment and reflecting the demographic and geographical range of all the Member States (art. I-26). The President of the Commission shall be proposed to the European Parliament by the European Council, acting by a qualified majority. The Parliament may elect the candidate, acting by a majority of its component members. The European Council, acting by a qualified majority, with the agreement of the President of the Commission, shall appoint the Union Minister for Foreign Affairs, who will be a Vicepresident of the Commission (art. I-28). The President, the Union Minister for Foreign Affairs and the other members of the Commission shall be subject as a body to a vote of consent by the European Parliament (art. I-27).

The Commission is the driving force for European integration. Under the Community decision-making process provided for in the European Community Treaty [see section 4.3.], it alone **has the initiative to make proposals** with a view to the taking of Community decisions. No other body and no individual State can replace the Commission in this task. It alone can amend its proposal, with the sole exception of there being unanimity in the Council to do so. The **power of initiative**, which is held by the Commission, is particularly important for the development of the common policies and therefore for the progress of the multinational integration process. All common policies, all Community legislation, all Community programmes have been adopted by the legislative bodies with Commission initiatives in the form of explanatory communications and proposals of legal acts.

In its proposals, the Commission is entrusted with the task of defining the common interest in each policy, legal measure or action that it proposes and the representatives of the Member States can only unanimously substitute it in this role. This means that even if only one state believes that the amendment to the proposal of the Commission, promoted by the majority, is contrary to its interests, the proposal cannot be adopted by the Council with qualified majority voting. The proposal must be amended by the Commission itself, which must find a compromise solution that comes closer to the common interest. Of course, if the Commission considers that the minority is exaggerating or filibustering, it can amend its proposal in the sense wanted by the majority, which may thus adopt it. In most cases, however, in the course of the deliberations and negotiations within the Council, the Commission amends its proposal repeatedly in order to encourage concessions here and there and thus reach agreement.

It should be stressed, however, that the Commission **only proposes legal acts or actions** of the EC/EU. The decisions are taken, usually in tandem, by the European Parliament and the Council with the codecision procedure or, in some cases, by the Council alone, i.e. by the representatives of the Member States. The Commission does not legislate. On the one hand, it proposes legal or administrative measures. On the other hand, it implements the acts and decisions taken by the Member States themselves through their representatives in the Parliament and the Council. The slogan concerning "the laws taken by the technocrats of Brussels" is a myth well cultivated by europhobic media.

The Commission is also the **guardian of the Treaties** and of the "acquis communautaire" (i.e., all the Community's legislation) [see section 3.3.]. One of its main tasks is to ensure fulfilment of the obligations of the Member States and/or proper application by them of the provisions of the Treaties and of secondary legislation (Art 226 TEC). For that purpose it has investigative power, which it exercises at its own initiative or in response to a request from a government or a complaint from an individual. If, following its investigation, the Commission considers that there is **infringement of Community legislation**, it invites the State concerned to submit its comments within a given period. If the State in question does not comply with the provisions or if the explanations that it provides do not convince the Commission, the latter issues a reasoned opinion to which the Member State is obliged to conform within the prescribed time-limit. If the Member State fails to conform to the reasoned opinion, the Commission refers the matter to the Court of Justice, which arbitrates the dispute and, more often than not, sanctions the irregularity as noted by the Commission and requires the recalcitrant Member State to conform to the Community legal order.

The Commission is also the **executive body** of the Community and plays, therefore, an **administrative role**. The Treaties confer upon the Commission extensive powers of execution to ensure the attainment of the objectives set out in them: good functioning of the single market, control of the rules of competition, supply of fissile materials, etc. But the Commission's powers are constantly increased by the powers conferred to it by the Council for the implementation of common policies (Art. 202 TEC)[1]. It is the Commission, which implements the decisions of the legislative bodies (the Council and the Parliament) and manages the Community budget [see section 3.4.] and in particular the various Community Funds[2] [see section 12.3.] and the research and technological development programmes [see section 18.2.2.]. The implementation decisions of the Commission usually take the form of the main decisions (regulation, directive or decision).

Finally, the Commission plays a **representative role** by ensuring the representation of the European Union in third countries and in many international organisations. The role of the Commission is particularly important in the conduct of the common commercial policy and of the aid to de-

---

[1]   Decision 1999/468, OJ L 184, 17.07.1999 and Regulation 1882/2003, OJ L 284, 31.10.2003.
[2]   Regulation 1105/2003, OJ L 158, 27.06.2003.

velopment policy. Acting on behalf of the Community on instructions from the Council, the Commission negotiates tariff agreements, formerly in the context of the General Agreement on Tariffs and Trade (GATT) and now of the World Trade Organisation (WTO) [see section 23.4.], trade and partnership agreements with third countries, association agreements and even, in practice, the agreements on the accession of new member states to the European Union. In order to carry out its representative role, the Commission has its own representations in more than 160 countries with which the EC/EU has diplomatic relations and in international organisations such as the Organisation for Economic Cooperation and Development (OECD), the WTO and the Council of Europe.

The **Constitutional Treaty** confirms all the above tasks of the Commission. It asserts that this institution shall ensure the application of the Constitution, and measures adopted by the institutions pursuant to the Constitution. It shall oversee the application of Union law under the control of the Court of Justice. It shall execute the budget and manage programmes. It shall exercise coordinating, executive and management functions, as laid down in the Constitution. With the exception of the common foreign and security policy (CFSP), and other cases provided for in the Constitution, it shall ensure the Union's external representation (Art I-26).

The exception of the CFSP from the external tasks of the Commission is relative, since the **Union Minister for Foreign Affairs** will have the power of proposal and will, thus, have a strong voice in the development of the Union's common foreign and security policy, which he or she should conduct and carry out as mandated by the Council. The same will apply to the common security and defence policy (Art I-28). Indeed, the role of the Union Minister for Foreign Affairs will be twofold, one part played in the Commission, as its Vice-President, and one in the Foreign Affairs Council, as its President. He or she shall be responsible within the Commission for tasks incumbent on it in external relations and for coordinating other aspects of the Union's external action. Within the Council, he or she shall ensure the consistency of the Union's external action.

4.1.3. The European Parliament

The number of Members of the European Parliament has increased with the successive enlargements of the Community/Union. After the 2004 enlargement, **the number of seats was increased to 732, which were allocated as follows:**

99 to Germany;

78 to each: France, Italy and the United Kingdom;

54 to each: Spain and Poland;

27 to the Netherlands;

24 to each: Belgium, the Czech Republic, Greece, Hungary and Portugal;

19 to Sweden;

18 to Austria;

14 to each: Denmark, Slovakia and Finland;
13 to each: Ireland and Lithuania;
9 to Latvia;
7 to Slovenia;
6 to each: Cyprus, Estonia and Luxembourg; and
5 to Malta.

Thanks to its direct election by the peoples of the Union, the European Parliament is the only real multinational legislative assembly in the world and plays an increasingly important role in the European integration process. In fact, although under the original Treaties the Parliament's role was purely advisory, it has kept growing, by virtue of the increasing political influence it has gradually managed to secure. At present **it exercises four functions**: legislative, political, supervisory and budgetary.

The European Parliament's first task under the Treaties establishing the original Communities, that of **consultation**, whereby Parliament gives its opinion on Commission proposals, was strengthened by the Single Act of 1987 which introduced a procedure of cooperation with the Council in many Community decisions. The **legislative function** of the Parliament was considerably increased with the Treaties of Amsterdam and Nice. Article 192 (TEC) provides, in fact, for the participation of the European Parliament in the process leading up to the adoption of Community acts through exercise of its powers under the procedures laid down in Articles 251 and 252 (co-decision and cooperation) [see section 4.3.]. Furthermore, the Parliament has the right to give or withhold its **assent** as regards the conclusion of certain international agreements, the accession of new Member States and the structural and cohesion funds.

The **political function** of the Parliament is also essential. As it represents 450 million citizens (EU-25) and is the European forum *par excellence*, the Parliament is the virtual contractor for European construction. It often calls upon the other protagonists, the Commission and the Council, to develop or alter existing common policies or to initiate new ones. Indeed, the Treaty gives it the right to request that the Commission submit any appropriate proposals on matters on which it considers a Community act is required (Art. 192 TEC). In case the Commission or the Council fail to act as required for the purpose of implementing the Treaty, the Parliament may initiate proceedings against them before the Court of Justice (Art. 232 TCE) [see section 4.1.5.]. The Commission and the Council have to report to the Parliament for their acts. The European Council itself reports to the European Parliament on each of its meetings and annually on the progress achieved by the Union.

The **monitoring function** of the Parliament is exercised in particular vis-à-vis the Commission. The President and the other members of the Commission are subject as a body to a vote of approval by the European Parliament (Art. 214 TEC). The Commission is answerable to the Parliament alone, so as to obviate its bowing before the will of the national governments or of some of their number. The Commission has to account to the European Parliament, defend its position before parliamentary commissions and in plenary sessions. The Parliament may, at the request of a quarter of its members, set up a temporary Committee of Inquiry to investigate alleged contraventions or maladministration in the implementation of Community law (Art. 193 TEC). In case of a serious maladministration, the Parliament may, moreover, pass a motion of censure against the Commission by a two-thirds majority of its members and thus compel it to resign (Art. 201 TEC), as it has threatened to do in March 1999.

The European Parliament appoints an **Ombudsman** empowered to receive complaints from any citizen of the Union or any natural or legal person residing or having its registered office in a Member State and concerning instances of maladministration in the activities of the Community institutions or bodies, with the exception of the Court of Justice and the Court of First Instance acting in their judicial role[1]. In cases where the Ombudsman establishes that mismanagement has occurred, he refers the matter to the institution concerned, which has three months in which to inform him of its views. The Ombudsman must then forward a report to the European Parliament and the institution concerned and inform the person lodging the complaint of the outcome of such inquiries (Art. 195 TEC).

As regards **budgetary functions**, the Parliament has to give its agreement to any major decision involving expenditure to be borne by the Community budget. It is effectively the Parliament which, at the end of a conciliation procedure with the Council, adopts or rejects the budget proposed by the Commission. Thus, it exercises a democratic control on the own resources of the Community [see section 3.4.]. It monitors also Community expenditure, since it has the power to give a discharge to the Commission for the management of the Community budget (Art. 272 and 276 TEC).

According to the **Constitutional Treaty**, the European Parliament shall be composed of representatives of the Union's citizens, who shall not exceed 750 in number. Representation of citizens shall be degressively proportional, with a minimum threshold of 6 deputies per Member State, in order to make sure that, even in the least populous Member States, all the major shades of political opinion will have a chance of being represented in the European Parliament. It follows that, since the number of EMPs will never exceed the total of 750 and, since the smaller Member States will always be allocated at least 6 EMPs each, the larger Member States will have to hand down a number of their seats to the acceding Member States.

The Constitutional Treaty **enhances significantly the functions** of the European Parliament. As of its coming into force, the Parliament shall, jointly with the Council, exercise legislative and budgetary functions. The Constitution extends the codecision procedure, renamed "ordinary legislative procedure", to a large number of articles. The Parliament therefore be-

---

[1] Decision 94/114, OJ L 54, 25.02.1994, Decision 94/262, OJ L 113, 04.05.1994 and Decision 2002/262, OJ L 92, 09.04.2002.

comes co-legislator in almost all laws and framework laws of the Union, with the exception of a dozen cases, where it will only be consulted. The request for accession of new Member States will be subject to the approval of the European Parliament, which could thus turn down a candidate, even despite the unanimous approval of the governments of the Member States. In future the President of the Commission will be elected (not approved) by the European Parliament by a majority of its members, acting on a proposal from the European Council. This amendment would clearly establish the responsibility of the President of the Commission vis-à-vis the Parliament. In fact, the European Parliament's legislative powers are growing with each amendment of the Treaties. It has to be said, moreover, that the national parliaments rarely exercise their legislative and budgetary powers to the full, subject as they are to the will of the parties which support the governments submitting legislative drafts to them. The European Parliament is not subjected to such constraints.

4.1.4. The Council

The **Council** is composed of a representative of each Member State at ministerial level, authorised to commit the government of that Member State (Art 203 TEC). While it is usually referred to broadly as "the Council" or "the Council of Ministers", it actually consists of nine specialised **configurations** regrouping several related areas, e.g. general affairs and external relations or economic and financial affairs[1]. Each Council configuration is composed of the ministers with responsibility in the matter, but several ministers may participate as full members of the same Council configuration, e.g. the ministers responsible for health and social policy. Although Commission proposals are discussed inside the specialised Council configurations, decisions agreed by all the Member States can be taken without a debate (as "points A" in the agenda) by any Council whatsoever, and this is often the "**General Affairs and External Relations Council**", composed of the Ministers of foreign affairs. This is the principle Council configuration and holds separate meetings (with separate agendas and possibly on different dates) dealing, respectively, with: (a) preparation for and follow-up to the European Council, institutional and administrative questions, horizontal dossiers which affect several of the Union's policies; and (b) the whole of the Union's external action, namely common foreign and security policy, foreign trade, development cooperation and humanitarian aid.

The **Council Presidency** changes every six months to another country in alphabetical order, and it is therefore the Minister of the country holding the Presidency who chairs each Council meeting[2]. The rotation of the Presidency has the advantage of giving each country a chance to prove its

---

[1] Decision 2004/338, OJ L 106, 15.04.2004.
[2] Concerning the order of the exercise of the Presidency see OJ L 1, 01.01.1995.

efficiency in promoting common policies, on the basis of Commission proposals, thus encouraging emulation among the Member States in the advancement of European integration. In order to obviate the problem of differing priorities of twenty-five presidencies in the enlarged Union, its legislative work is henceforth based on a three-annual strategic programme adopted by the European Council.

The Council is assisted by a General Secretariat, consisting of "Eurocrats" of all the nationalities of the Union, separate from their counterparts in the Commission but organised in a similar way. The Council is also assisted by many working parties of national civil servants, which examine the proposals of the Commission and report to the **Permanent Representatives Committee (COREPER)**, which is responsible for preparing the work of the Council and for carrying out the tasks assigned to it by the Council" (Art. 207 TEC). The Coreper sits in two parts: Coreper Part 1, which is composed of the Deputy Permanent Representatives and examines technical questions on the whole, and Coreper Part 2, which is composed of the Ambassadors themselves and deals with political questions on the whole. The European Commission participates in all the meetings of the working parties of national experts, of the Coreper and of the Council to explain its positions and assist the Presidency in reaching agreement on its proposals. After examining an issue Coreper either submits a report to the Council, preparing the ground for its discussions by drawing attention to the political aspects which deserve particular attention, or, if unanimous agreement has been reached between the Permanent Representatives and the Commission representative, Coreper recommends that the Council adopt the prepared text "as **an 'A' item"**, i.e. without discussion. In both cases the Council's work is facilitated thanks to Coreper's intervention.

On the basis of the original Treaties, the Council was the only legislative authority of the Community and this was the main reason for the then existing democratic deficit of the Community [see section 9.5.]. Subsequent amendments of the Treaties have joined, ever more closely, the European Parliament in the decision-making process, thus making the Council one of the two legislative authorities [see section 4.3.] and reducing, consequently, the democratic deficit. Going a step further, the **Constitutional Treaty** specifies that the Council shall, jointly with the European Parliament, exercise legislative and budgetary functions (Art. I-23). Hence, the legislative functions of the Council will come close to those of an Upper House or Senate, representing the governments of the Member States, and sharing these functions with the European Parliament, representing directly the peoples of the Union. However, in addition to its legislative and budgetary functions, the Council ensures coordination of the general economic policies of the Member States [see section 7.3.] and plays an important role in defining and implementing the common foreign and security policy (CFSP) [see section 8.2.1.]. The Constitutional Treaty separates the responsibilities of the Ministers of Foreign Affairs from those of the Ministers of European affairs.

4.1.5. The Court of Justice

In a community of states the common rules adopted by the decision-making bodies might be interpreted and applied differently from country to country, if only national courts controlled them. Therefore, the general task assigned to the Court of Justice and to the Court of First Instance is to ensure that the Community **law is observed in a uniform manner** in the interpretation and application of the Treaty, of the legal acts and of the decisions adopted by the Council and the Parliament or by the Commission (Art. 220 to 245 TEC). The judgments of the Court of Justice, many important ones of which are referred to in the footnotes of this book, consolidate the European law to which are subject the governments, the national courts, the parliaments and the citizens of the Member States. Although European law is a statute law passed by legislative bodies, it is often amended by them in accordance with the case law of the Court of Justice. The Court plays therefore an important role in the European integration process by clarifying ambiguous legal provisions, adopted sometimes under the pressure of reaching agreement between law-makers of different cultures concerned about various national interests.

The Court of Justice consists, in fact, of two bodies, with their seat in Luxembourg: the Court of Justice proper and the Court of First Instance. **The Court of Justice**, often called European Court of Justice (ECJ) consists of one judge per Member State. It sits in chambers or in a Grand Chamber, in accordance with the rules laid down in its Statutes. It is assisted by Advocates-General (Art. 221 TEC). The **Court of First Instance** comprises at least one judge per Member State, which means that it may include judges of the same nationality. The number of Judges is determined by the Statute of the Court of Justice, which may provide for the Court of First Instance to be assisted by Advocates-General (Art. 224 TEC).

The **Court of First Instance (CFI)** is the common law judge for all direct actions, i.e. proceedings against a decision (Article 230 TEC), action for failure to act (Article 232 TEC) and action for damages (Article 235 TEC), with the exception of those the statute reserves for the Court of Justice and those which are attributed to a specialised chamber. The judgments of the CFI can form the subject of appeals, confined to points of law, to the Court of Justice (Art. 225 TEC).

Being the supreme court of the Communities, the **Court of Justice** not only gives a coherent and uniform interpretation of European law, but it ensures that all the Member States and their citizens comply with it. Apart from the tendency of governments to interpret European law in the interest of their nations, it is new law and not always well known. The national judges, who are the judges of first instance of the rules and behaviour relative to European law, may turn to the Court of Justice by means of a **referral for a preliminary ruling** to ask it to adopt a position on the interpretation or evaluation of the validity of the provisions of European acts. Although they are normally optional, referrals for a preliminary ruling are obligatory where judicial remedy under national law is no longer possible, i.e. when the court, which has to apply the Community law, is taking its decisions in the final instance. Through its preliminary rulings, the Court plays the role of a legal council whose opinions are binding on the parties concerned. The referral for a preliminary ruling is appreciated by the national courts and stimulates the cooperation between them and the ECJ.

Disputes falling within the unlimited jurisdiction of the Court are made up in particular of cases relating to non-compliance or to the interpretation of the Community's rules of competition. Hearing an appeal by undertakings (firms, businesses) penalised by the Commission for infringing competition law, the Court gives a ruling on the merits of the Commission's decision and on the appropriateness of the penalty imposed on the undertaking.

According to the **Constitutional Treaty**, the Court of Justice of the European Union shall include the Court of Justice, the General Court and specialised courts. Hence, the term "Court of Justice of the European Union" will officially designate the two levels of jurisdiction taken together. The supreme body is called the "Court of Justice" while the Court of First Instance is renamed "General Court", but their actual composition and tasks are not changed (Art. I-29).

4.2. Other institutions and advisory bodies

As mentioned at the beginning of this chapter, the institutions of the EC/EU are evolving along with the evolution of European integration. Of the institutions and advisory bodies that we consider in this section, only the European Economic and Social Committee was provided for in the original Treaties. New institutions and bodies have been created to cover new needs, notably the Committee of the Regions and the European Central Bank. The Court of Auditors is considered as a main institution by the Treaty of Nice, but not by the Constitutional Treaty.

4.2.1. The European Central Bank

In the framework of the economic and monetary union that it has launched, the Treaty of Maastricht has established a **European system of central banks (ESCB)** and a **European Central Bank (ECB)** [see section 7.2.4.]. The two organs are closely associated. They act within the limits of the powers conferred upon them by the EC Treaty and by the Statute of the ESCB and of the ECB annexed thereto (Art. 8 TEC). The ESCB is composed of the ECB and of the national central banks and is governed by the decision-making bodies of the ECB which are the Governing Council and the Executive Board. (Art 107 TEC). The Governing Council is composed of the Governors of the central banks of all the Member States of the

EC/EU, whereas the President, the Vice-President and the other members of the Executive Board of the ECB are appointed by common accord of the governments of the Member States, which have adopted the euro[1]. Neither the ECB, nor a national central bank, nor any member of their decision-making bodies may seek or take instructions from Community institutions or bodies, from any government of a Member State or from any other body (Art. 108 TEC). The objectives of the ESCB are, primarily, to maintain price stability and, without prejudice to this objective, to support the general economic policies in the Community (Art. 105 TEC). The basic tasks of the ESCB are: to define and implement the monetary policy of the Community, to conduct foreign-exchange operations, to hold and manage the official foreign reserves of the Member States and to promote the smooth operation of payment systems. The ECB, which has legal personality, has the exclusive right to authorise the issue of banknotes within the Community's eurozone (Art. 106 TEC).

The **Constitutional Treaty** gives the European Central Bank the status of an institution, in order to emphasise its independence. It brings together the general provisions on the ECB and the ESCB, without introducing any substantive changes. Accepting the fact that not all the EU Member States need to adopt the euro as their currency, the Constitution declares that the European Central Bank, together with the national central banks of the Member States whose currency is the euro, which constitute the Eurosystem, shall conduct the monetary policy of the Union, while those Member States whose currency is not the euro, and their central banks, shall retain their powers in monetary matters (Art I-30).

4.2.2. The European Court of Auditors

The Court of Auditors consists of one national from each Member State. The Members of the Court of Auditors are chosen from among persons who belong or have belonged in their respective countries to external audit bodies or who are especially qualified for this office. They are appointed for a term of six years by the Council, acting by a qualified majority after consulting the European Parliament. They are completely independent in the performance of their duties (Art. 247 TEC).

The Court of Auditors examines the accounts of all revenue and expenditure of the Community, particularly the annual budget managed by the Commission, and of all bodies set up by the Community. It examines in particular whether all revenue has been received and all expenditure incurred in a lawful and regular manner and must report on any cases of irregularity. The audit must be based on records and, if necessary, performed on the spot in the other institutions of the Community, on the premises of any body which manages revenue or expenditure on behalf of the Community and in the Member States, including on the premises of any natural or

---

[1] Decision 98/345, OJ L 154, 28.05.1998.

legal person in receipt of payments from the budget (Art. 248 TEC). The Court must provide the European Parliament and the Council with a statement of assurance as to the reliability of the accounts and the legality and regularity of the underlying transactions. The annual and the specific reports of the Court of Auditors are acknowledged to be a valuable input to Parliament's debates on the discharge to be given to the Commission for its execution of the budget.

The **Constitutional Treaty** does not modify the structure and the functions of the Court of Auditors. It confirms its status as an independent institution, which shall examine the accounts of all Union revenue and expenditure, and shall ensure good financial management (Articles I-31, III-384 and III-385). The only significant change is that it requires the Court to send its annual report to national parliaments, for information, thus increasing the democratic control of the Union's finances.

4.2.3. The Economic and Social Committee

The ESC is the official body, which enables the Community institutions to evaluate and take into account in the conception of common policies the **interests of the various economic and social groups**. Its 317 members are proposed by the governments of the Member States (Germany, France, Italy and the United Kingdom proposing 24 each; Spain and Poland 21; Belgium, the Czech Republic, Greece, Hungary, Netherlands, Portugal, Austria and Sweden 12 each; Denmark, Ireland, Lithuania, Slovakia and Finland 9 each; Estonia, Latvia and Slovenia 7 each, Cyprus and Luxembourg 6 each and Malta 5) and are appointed for a term of four years by the Council after consulting the Commission. They must provide a wide representation of the various categories of economic and social life (Art. 257-262 TEC) and divide voluntarily into three groups: the Employers' Group (known as "Group I"), which is made up of representatives of industry, banking or financial institutions, transport operators' federations, etc.; the Workers' Group (known as "Group II"), mainly composed of representatives of trade union organisations; and the Various Interests Group (known as "Group III"), which comprises representatives of agriculture, skilled trades, small and medium-sized enterprises, the professions, consumers' associations and organisations representing various interests, such as the families or ecological movements.

The Committee **must be consulted** by the Council or by the Commission in certain areas provided for by the Treaty establishing the European Community. The Committee **may be consulted** by these institutions in all cases where they consider it appropriate. Furthermore, the ESC may issue an **opinion at its own initiative** when it considers such action appropriate (Art. 262 TEC). Whether they are requested by the Commission or the Council or issued at its own initiative, the Committee's Opinions are not binding on the institutions, a shortcoming that weakens their significance. However, the Committee plays the role of a forum in which the interests of the various socio-professional categories, rather than national arguments, are expressed officially and assessed. The opinions of the ESC on the proposals of the Commission reflect the concerns of economic and societal groups and provide valuable indications of the opposing arguments, of the divergences of interests and of the possibilities of reaching agreement at Community level. Furthermore, the ESC associates in the preparation of Community legislation the economic operators who are ultimately the most directly concerned by the practical effects of the common policies on the European economy. For that reason the Commission often adjusts its proposals to take into account the official positions of the interest groups of the Community. In this limited way the Committee influences decisions and makes its contribution to the formulation of common policies, a contribution that could be greater if better exploited.

The **Constitutional Treaty** does not make any fundamental changes to the structure and functions of the Economic and Social Committee, other than lengthening the term of office of its members to five years, so as to coincide with that of the members of the European Parliament. It limits the number of members of the Committee to 350, notwithstanding future enlargements, and specifies that the composition of the Committee will be determined by a European decision adopted unanimously by the Council on a proposal from the Commission (Art. III-389). Before adopting the list of members drawn up in accordance with the proposals made by each Member State, the Council may obtain the opinion of European bodies which are representative of the various economic and social sectors and of civil society to which the Union's activities are of concern (Art. III-390). This would be an improvement to the system of selection of the members of the Committee, but it would certainly be better if the national and European bodies concerned were more involved in the establishment of the list of the members [see section 4.4.].

4.2.4. The Committee of the Regions

The Treaty establishing the European Community officially acknowledges the regional diversity and the role played by regions in the governance of the Community through the Committee of the Regions made up of **representatives of regional and local bodies** (Art. 263-265 TEC). The 317 members of the Committee and an equal number of alternate members (with the same national distribution as the members of the ESC) are proposed by the governments of the Member States and appointed for four years by the Council, acting unanimously.

The Committee of the Regions **must be consulted** by the Council or the Commission on matters relating notably to employment guidelines, legislation on social matters, environment, education, vocational training, culture, public health, European networks and the Structural Funds. It **may be consulted** in all other cases considered appropriate by one of the two institutions, in particular those which concern cross-border cooperation. It can also issue an **own-initiative opinion** when it considers that specific regional interests are at stake (Art. 265 TEC). The Committee of the Regions thus involves regional and local authorities in the decision-making process and expresses their views on all common policies concerning them. Yet again, these views could have a greater impact on these policies than they now have, if a way was found to make the decision-making organs to take them more seriously into consideration [see section 4.4.].

As in the case of the Economic and Social Committee, the **Constitutional Treaty** only lengthens the term of office of the members of the Committee of the Regions to five years, limits their maximum number to 350 and stipulates that the Committee's composition would be determined by the Council acting unanimously on a proposal fro, the Commission (Art. III-386). However, the Constitution does not encourage the Council to obtain the opinion of the regional and local bodies concerned and, therefore, the appointment of the members of the Committee of the Regions will depend, then as now, almost entirely on the proposals of the governments and, consequently, on national rather than on regional political criteria [see section 4.4.].

4.3. The Community's decision-making process

The Treaties establishing the Communities defined the objectives to be attained, laid down the rules to be implemented, set out timetables to be met and established an institutional framework which provides the Community with an original method of decision-making and legislation. The **Community method implies a decision-making process** entailing: (a) a single and supranational source of the right of initiative; (b) usually codecision of the European Parliament with the Council, deciding by qualified majority; and (c) control of the decisions by a supranational judicial authority, the European Court of Justice. The Community method is, indeed, an **original combination** of: **technocratic proposals** emanating from the Commission, worked out with the technical advice of experts from all the Member States; **and legislative acts and** political decisions taken by the Council, representing the governments of the Member States, usually in tandem with the European Parliament, representing the peoples of the Union.

The Community method does not imply legislation by the European Commission. The Community Treaties authorise the Commission to propose legislative acts and to execute the legislative and other decisions taken by the legislative bodies. The rhetoric about the "decisions taken by the technocrats of Brussels" (meaning the Commission) is maliciously erroneous. The fact is that the technocrats propose the Community measures; but it is the political institutions representing the democratically elected governments (the Council of Ministers) and the citizens of the Member States (the European Parliament) that take the decisions. Except in a few areas, such as competition, where the Treaties give it full competence, the Commission may only adopt acts implementing the decisions of the legislative bodies.

As we saw above, **the initiative for the Community's decision-making procedure** lies with the Commission [see section 4.1.2.]. It prepares all proposals for Council Regulations, Directives and Decisions. The Commission's role is political in so far as it chooses and prepares the ground on which the construction of the Community is undertaken, but otherwise its role is technocratic as its proposals are based on technical considerations and/or scientific grounds. Using an "impact assessment method", the Commission analyses the direct and indirect implications of a proposed measure (e.g. concerning businesses, trade, employment, the environment and health). The results of each assessment are made public[1]. Moreover, the Commission is responsible for defining in its proposals the common interest or the interest of the Community. To make sure that its proposal is adopted, the Commission must take into consideration the often-divergent interests of the Member States and endeavour to detect and express the common interest. If it does not succeed in this definition or if it does not itself amend its proposal, taking into consideration the positions of the other Community organs, all the Member States together, in total agreement within the Council, must find a different definition of the common interest inherent in a proposal of a common policy or a common measure (Art. 250 TEC); something that happens very rarely.

When adopted by the Commission, a proposal is submitted to the European Parliament and to the Council for decision and, very often, to the Economic and Social Committee and to the Committee of the Regions for an opinion. **Detailed discussions** begin within the working party of competent national experts, who prepare the Council's decision, the relevant Parliament Committee and the groups of experts of the Economic and Social Committee and of the Committee of the Regions. The interest groups at national and Community levels, alerted in good time of this preparatory work, lobby these various technical and political experts and, if the issue is important, public opinion. The Commission has published general principles and **minimum standards for consultation** of interested parties[2]. They enable all those affected by a proposal to express their opinions and, thus, to participate in the legislative process through Internet portals. A database of information on the different bodies consulted gives an overview of the way civil society consultation is organised at European level[3]. The general public has access to the different stages of the legislative process through the Internet-based EUR-Lex service[4].

The interaction of these actors, representing all the Member States and all the interests concerned tends to confirm or redefine the common inter-

---

[1]   COM (2002) 276, 5 June 2002.
[2]   COM (2002) 277, 5 June 2002.
[3]   http://europa.eu.int/comm/civil_society/coneccs/index_en.htm.
[4]   http://europa.eu.int/eur-lex/en/index.html.

est of the proposal formulated by the Commission. As, more often than not, a common policy cannot fully satisfy all national interests, negotiations have to take place within and between the main actors in order to find the common denominator that best satisfies most national interests. The text ultimately adopted by the Council alone or by the Council and the Parliament (with the co-decision procedure) takes into account all national, professional and other interests voiced at various points of the lengthy preparatory work.

It goes without saying that **the Community interest may not harm an "essential interest"** of a Community State, but the definition of an "essential interest" is inevitably subjective. Each Member State has a natural tendency to exaggerate its own problems and minimise those of the others. In other words, the Community decision-making process risks frequently to come to a deadlock, and it has to be emphasised that it is through the joint mediation efforts of the Commission and the Council Presidency that the deadlock can on most occasions be avoided. On the one hand, the majority has to be persuaded to make the necessary concessions to accommodate the minority and, on the other hand, the Member State upholding an extreme or isolated position has to be persuaded that the general advantages of an agreement are more important than its individual interests. Even though they first and foremost assert the interests of their respective governments, the members of the Council must respect the objectives and needs of the EU as a whole and they usually do so. This is what distinguishes the Council from an intergovernmental conference, where national interests prevail over the common interest [see section 4.1.4.].

The European Parliament is ever more involved in the Community decision-making process under two procedures, co-decision and cooperation with the Council of Ministers. Article 251 (TEC), defines the **co-decision procedure** of the Council with the European Parliament. This procedure was introduced by the EC Treaty at Maastricht and was largely extended by the Amsterdam and Nice amendments of the TEC. It is now applied to practically all important matters covered by this Treaty, including the implementation of the freedoms of the internal market, social policy, environment policy and consumer protection.

In the co-decision procedure, the Council acting by a qualified majority adopts "common positions", which may be accepted, rejected or amended by the Parliament. If the Council does not agree with the amendments proposed by the Parliament, a **conciliation committee**, composed of equal numbers of representatives of the two institutions, must bring together the different points of view. In the rare cases where a compromise solution is not found, the Parliament may reject the proposed act by absolute majority of expressed votes. Thus, the Parliament has the final word in this legislative procedure. Regulations, Directives and Decisions adopted under the Article 251 procedure are signed both by the President of the European Parliament and the President of the Council. The Commission can act as an arbitrator between the two decision-making bodies, by accepting in its amended proposal some of the amendments proposed by the Parliament. The co-decision procedure has worked well so far. Indeed decisions have been taken fairly quickly as a result of a good working relationship between the institutions.

Article 252 (TCE) defines the **cooperation procedure,** where the Parliament is involved in the legislative process by means of its two readings and the proposal of amendments to the Council's common position. In this procedure, the Commission plays an arbitration role, since it may adopt some or many of the amendments of the Parliament in its own amended proposal; but the Council has the final word, since it may unanimously reject the amended proposal of the Commission. However, this procedure is now limited to a few subject matters.

At present, where the treaties do not provide otherwise, the Council takes decisions by a simple majority of its members. This is rarely the case, however, as in the vast majority of instances the treaties provide that decisions are taken either by unanimity or by qualified majority. Unanimity is undemocratic, because the vote of the smallest country weighs as much as that of the largest and any country can block a decision wished by all its other partners. Therefore, the successive amendments of the Treaties have extended qualified majority voting, notably in the areas where there is participation of the Parliament in the decision-making process. **Qualified majority** is calculated on the basis of votes allocated to each Member State under Article 205 (TEC), as modified by the Accession Act of the ten new Member States. According to the latter, the total number of votes in the Council is 321 and is distributed to the twenty-five Ministers in a weighted manner, so that the influence of a Member State in the decision-making process is more or less related to the size of its population. Actually, **the votes of the Council members are weighted as follows**:

- Germany, France, Italy and the United Kingdom 29 each;
- Spain and Poland 27 each;
- Netherlands 13;
- Belgium, the Czech Republic, Greece, Hungary and Portugal 12 each;
- Austria and Sweden 10 each;
- Denmark, Finland, Ireland, Lithuania and Slovakia 7 each;
- Cyprus, Estonia, Latvia, Luxembourg and Slovenia 4 each; and
- Malta 3.

As a rule, decisions taken by qualified majority on the basis of a Commission proposal must gather at least **72% of the total votes of the members, representing at least 62% of the total population** of the Union. The same conditions apply to Article 34 of the EU Treaty, but the 232 votes in favour should, in any case, be cast by at least two-thirds of the members. Whilst the qualified-majority voting system of the Treaty of Nice technically opened the door to enlargement, the weighting of the votes in the Council is no improvement regarding the efficiency and transparency of the decision-making process, a fact which gives cause for serious concern as to how it may operate in a Union of 27 or more Member States.

Responding to this concern, **the Constitutional Treaty**, firstly, generalises qualified majority voting in the normal legislative process. Secondly, it abandons the weighting of the votes in the Council and, thus, simplifies greatly the system of qualified majority, applicable from November 2009. In effect, Article I-25 of the Constitution defines qualified majority as at least **55% of the members** of the Council or the European Council (72%, if the Council is not acting on a proposal of the Commission or of the Union Minister for Foreign Affairs), representing **at least 65% of the population of the Union**.

The constitutional system respects the equality of Member States as each one has one vote counting for the first criterion, whilst their different population sizes are taken into account in meeting the second criterion. Council decision-making would be facilitated as a greater number of combinations of Member States could constitute a qualified majority than under the system prescribed by the Treaty of Nice. In the enlarged Union, this is essential for its ability to act and for the smooth operation of its institutions. Moreover, according to Article I-25, a blocking minority should include at least four Member States, so as to preclude that just three "big" Member States, representing more than 35% of the Union's population, form an alliance to block a decision. Last but not least, the constitutional system, which defines once for all the criteria of qualified majority, would prevent, during subsequent enlargements, long negotiations on the allocation of votes to Member States and the definition of the qualified majority threshold.

So as to prevent one or two Member States from blocking further progress of the Union in certain fields, the Treaty of Nice has reinforced and facilitated **enhanced cooperations**, which aim at safeguarding the values and serving the interests of the Union as a whole by asserting its identity as a coherent force on the international scene (Art. 27a to 28 and 40 to 45 (TEU) and 11 (TEC). **In connection with the EC Treaty**, the veto possibility is removed. Member States which intend to establish enhanced cooperation between themselves must address a request to the Commission, which should submit a proposal to the Council to that effect or inform the Member States concerned of the reasons for not doing so. The assent of the European Parliament is required for an enhanced cooperation in a field coming under the co-decision procedure (Art 11 TEC). **In connection with the common foreign and security policy**, enhanced cooperation is possible for the implementation of a joint action or common position, except in the sphere of the security and defence policy (Art 27b TEU). The Council should act by qualified majority, but the 232 votes in favour of the decision should be cast by at least two-thirds of the members (Art. 23.2 TEU). According to the **Constitutional Treaty**, enhanced cooperation should aim to further the objectives of the Union, protect its interests and reinforce its integration process (Articles I-44 and III-416 to III-423).

4.4. Prospects of European governance

Thanks to the Community method of making and implementing decisions, the often conflicting national interests are passed through the **successive filters of three institutions**, each defending different but complementary interests: the Commission, the common interest; the Council, the interests of the Member States; the Parliament, the interests of the citizens of the Union. Community policies thus rarely - if ever - can promote the interests of some Member States at the expense of those of some others. In the absence of such filters, an intergovernmental cooperation scheme wishing to serve equally all national interests would have to give equal weight to the positions defended by each one of the participating governments and this would lead to a standstill. If it gave policy leadership to a few Member States, namely the bigger ones, intergovernmental cooperation would lead to conflicts of interests and hence to secessionist tendencies.

"**European governance**" - i.e., the rules, processes and behaviour of the actors that affect the way in which powers are exercised at European level - has worked relatively well up to now, since it has made possible all the achievements of the common policies examined in this book. Therefore, the role of the existing institutions should not be radically changed, nor should new institutions be added, because the rules of the functioning of the protagonists of European integration might be altered, with unknown consequences. However, European governance has already reached its limits of efficiency, even after the improvements brought about by the Treaty of Nice and by the Constitutional Treaty. It is doubtful that it could function efficiently in a union of twenty-five - and soon more - Member States, which could in addition have the ambition to deepen their political union. In order to enable the Union to better face internal and external challenges, a future reform of the institutions, brought about by an amendment of the Constitution, should aim at their increased efficiency, legitimacy and rapprochement with the citizens of the Union.

The structure of the **European Commission**, in particular, should be democratised in parallel with the reinforcement of its role, because its technocratic character, useful as it may be, engenders its remoteness from the citizens of the Member States. The Commission is already the executive body of the Community, since it proposes the legislation to the legislative bodies, executes their decisions and controls their implementation by the Member States. It thus plays the role of a "proto-government" of the Union, which has not full democratic legitimacy, since it is not elected directly by the peoples of Europe.

The actual handicap of the Commission is its technocratic character, due to the fact that the Commissioners are not elected but are appointed by the governments of the Member States. If the problem were stated in such simple terms, its solution would also be simple. It would be to entrust the citizens themselves with the election of the members of the Commission at the occasion of European elections. At the same time as they would choose the members of the European Parliament, the voters of each country could elect the Commissioner having the nationality of this country from a short list of candidates prepared by the national parliament. With this system of election in two phases, the national parliaments would play an important role in selecting (by successive votes) two or three personalities capable of assuming European functions, but the Commissioner for each nationality would finally be elected by the citizens of each nation (with the simple majority of the votes cast).

The **president of the Commission** and the **vice-president,** who could also be the Union Minister for Foreign Affairs (according to the constitutional treaty), should be chosen from among these elected personalities by the European Council, acting by qualified majority, and be elected by the European Parliament (as provided for in the Constitutional Treaty). The big difference between the system proposed here and the actual system or the one set forth in the Constitution is that the president and the vice-president of the Commission would first be elected by their respective countrymen and then would be chosen by the majority of the representatives of the peoples of the Union. They would not come out of the sole inspiration of the heads of State or government and would thus have a double democratic legitimacy, national and European. The European Parliament should also have a strong opinion on the suitability of the members of the Commission for the posts assigned to them by the President of this institution. With such a system of democratic designation of the jobs of the Commissioners, the citizens would have an important incentive to elect strong personalities as members of the European executive organ, hoping that their compatriot could qualify for a top job, including that of the president and vice-president of the Commission. Moreover, the citizens would feel that they participate in the governance of the Union, since they would elect directly not only the members of one branch of the legislative authority (the European Parliament), but also the members of the executive authority (the European Commission).

Moreover, the European Parliament should play an important role not only in the investiture of the executive authority of the Union, but also in its monitoring. In addition to the legality of the actions of the Commissioners, the Parliament should permanently control their independence in respect of their country of origin and their efficiency in the implementation of their pre-approved work programme. The political role of the European Parliament would thus resemble that of a national parliament, which controls the government of its country.

Bibliography on the European institutions

- BLUMANN Claude, DUBOUIS Louis. *Droit institutionnel de l'Union européenne*, Paris: Litec, 2004.

- DONNELLY Brendan (et al.). "The democratic accountability of the EU and the role of the European Parliament", *The International Spectator*, v. 39, n. 2, Apri-June 2004, p. 7-60.

- GERVEN Walter Van. "The European Union institutions in the draft Constitution for Europe", *European Review: Interdisciplinary Journal of the Academia Europaea*, v. 12, n. 4, October 2004, p. 465-479.

- HAYWARD Jack, MENON Anand (eds.). *Governing Europe*. Oxford; New York: Oxford University Press, 2003.

- KAUPPI Heikki, WIDGREN Mika. "What determines EU decision making? Needs, power or both", *Economic Policy*, n. 39, July 2004, 221-266.

- MOUSSIS Nicholas. "For a drastic reform of European institutions", *European Law Review*, v. 28, n. 2, April 2003, p. 250-258.

- PERTEK Jacques. *Droit des institutions de l'Union européenne*, Paris: PUF, 2004.

- PETERS Anne. "European democracy after the 2003 Convention", *Common Market Law Review*, v. 41, n. 1, February 2004, p. 37-85.

- PINELLI Cesare. "The powers of the European Parliament in the new Constitutional Treaty", *The International Spectator*, v. 39, n. 3, July-September 2004, p. 83-96.

- SMITH Andy (ed.). *Politics and the European Commission: actors, interdependence, legitimacy*. London: Routledge, in association with European Consortium for Political Research - ECPR, 2004.

DISCUSSION TOPICS

1. Discuss the similarities and dissimilarities between the institutions of the European Union and those of a federal state like Germany or Belgium.

2. Explain the role of the European Commission in the Community decision-making process.

3. Do the functions of the European Parliament differ from those of a national parliament?

4. How does the work of the Council of Ministers differ from that of an intergovernmental conference?

5. Consider the role of the European Court of Justice in the European integration process.

Part II: Integration stages

Chapter 5.   *Customs Union*
Chapter 6.   *Common market*
Chapter 7.   *Economic and Monetary Union*
Chapter 8.   *Towards Political Union*

Although the multinational integration process is continuous, it can be distinguished into **four large stages**: customs union, common market, economic and monetary union, political union. In the isolationist period, usually following a devastating war, like the Second World War, states erect **high protection barriers against foreign trade** and therefore against international competition. These may be customs barriers (tariffs, quotas and measures having equivalent effect), fiscal barriers (higher levels of taxation for goods largely manufactured outside the country), administrative barriers (complicated bureaucratic procedures for imports) or technical barriers (concerning, for example environment or human health protection) serving in one way or another, to discourage or even prohibit imports [see section 6.2.]. This is the zero point in the scale of multinational integration.

Such a protectionist system leads to **great dissatisfaction on the part of consumers**, whose choice is very restricted, and on the part of the most dynamic and/or less protected businessmen, who find their field of activity limited by the barriers. Dissatisfied citizens, as consumers and voters, and progressive businessmen, as influential interest groups, press the political elite to reduce external protection. Under the sine qua non condition that the later were susceptible to such pressures and were sincerely seeking the maximisation of national interests - two prerequisites that exclude authoritarian regimes - they would normally start discussing the possibilities of trade liberalisation with like-minded elite in neighbouring countries [see section 1.1.2.]. If the economic and political elite of several states would agree on the desirability of mutual trade liberalisation, they would still have the option to pursue it either within a framework of bilateral or multilateral intergovernmental cooperation or in the framework of a multinational integration process.

A **free trade area** is based on intergovernmental cooperation. In such an area, member countries abolish import duties and other customs barriers to the free movement of products manufactured in the territory of their partners. However, each country retains its own external tariff and its customs policy vis-à-vis third countries. It also retains entirely its national sovereignty. Trade liberalisation is a common policy of a group of states, but, since without concessions of sovereignty, there can be no spillover from this unique common policy to other policy areas [see section 1.1.1.], a free trade area should be placed at a low level of multinational integration, before the commencement of the evolutionary process.

By contrast, in a **customs union**, which is the first stage of the evolutionary multinational integration process, free movement concerns not only products manufactured in the territory of the partners, but all products, irrespective of origin, situated in the territory of the member countries. Furthermore, the latter lose their customs autonomy and apply a common external customs tariff to third countries. In order to manage the common customs tariff, the members of a customs union must have a common commercial policy. In addition, trade liberalisation has in this case spillover or multiplicative effects on other common policies. There is therefore, already at this stage some concession of segments of national sovereignty to the common institutions that run the customs union [see chapter 5].

If the implementation of these initial common policies linked with the customs union gave satisfactory but not optimal results, it would reveal the necessity for more common policies inside a **common market** and would consequently have a multiplier effect on the process. In fact, if the members would like to turn a customs union into a real internal market, they would need to ensure not only the free movement of goods and services, but also the free movement of production factors, namely labour and capital. In order to obtain these fundamental freedoms of a common market, the member states would need to develop a great number of common policies, calling for further sharing of national sovereignties [see chapter 6].

However, the single market would still not resemble a genuine internal market, if currency fluctuations and the exchange risk could create new barriers to trade, restrict the interpenetration of the financial markets and impede the establishment of businesses in places where the factors of production would be most propitious for their activities. In order to optimise the conditions of trade, investment and production, the member states of a common market would need, therefore, to move forward to the next stage of economic integration, viz. **economic and monetary union (EMU)**. This would imply a single monetary policy, necessary for the management of a single currency, and the convergence of national economic policies, with a view to achieving economic and social cohesion.

Even before that integration stage was wholly completed, the member states of a multinational integration scheme would have developed so many economic and political links between themselves that they would feel the need to step forward into the final integration stage, that of political union, by harmonising their justice and home affairs policies, in order to protect efficiently their area of freedom, security and justice, and their foreign policies, so that the economic giant that they had created through economic integration would have a voice commensurate with its size in the international arena [see section 2.3.and chapter 8].

Chapter 5

CUSTOMS UNION

Diagram of the chapter

Acustoms union is a stage of multinational integration, during which the member states agree, by treaty, to refrain from imposing any customs duties, charges having equivalent effect or quantitative restrictions on each other and to adopt an external common customs tariff in their relations with third countries. The common customs tariff implies, not only a common customs policy, but also a common foreign trade policy [see chapter 23]. Furthermore, the freedom of movement is applicable in a customs union regardless of the origin of goods, thus eliminating customs controls at internal borders.

The founders of the European Economic Community had, from the start the goal not only of setting up a customs union, but also a common market in which goods, services and capital could be traded freely. In economic integration, they foresaw not only a formula offering economic advantages, but also the means to set up the conditions for political union in Europe. In order to achieve this, **a sound foundation** was required. Customs union was, accurately enough, such a foundation; it allowed for unprecedented trade growth in the participating Member States and the construction upon it of the entire European edifice. In fact, all the common policies examined in this book would be unthinkable were they not based on customs union.

5.1. Intra-Community trade

Before the Community treaties came into force, every European country protected its national production with **customs tariffs**, preventing the import of goods at prices lower than those of the national production, and **quantitative restrictions**, preventing the import of certain products in quantities exceeding those which were necessary to satisfy local demand not covered by national production. Thus, a country would import the quantities and qualities not normally supplied by its internal production. As industry was well protected, it saw no need to make large-scale efforts to modernise or reduce production costs. The European consumer, faced with a limited choice and high prices for low quality goods, was the main victim of this **protectionism**. The customs union, limited initially in the coal and steel sectors governed by the ECSC Treaty, but rapidly extended to all products and services, thanks to the EEC Treaty [see section 2.1.], aimed at correcting this situation.

5.1.1. The abolition of customs barriers to trade

According to article 23 of the EC Treaty, the Community is based upon a customs union which covers all trade in goods and which involves the prohibition between Member States of customs duties on imports and exports and of all charges having equivalent effect, and the adoption of a common customs tariff in their relations with third countries. The customs union of the EC **covers "all trade in goods"**. This means that products coming from a third country can move freely within the Community if the import formalities have been complied with and any customs duties or charges having equivalent effect, which are payable, have been levied in the importing Member State (Art. 24 TEC).

Articles 13 and 14 of the Treaty of Rome provided that **customs duties and charges having equivalent effect** to customs duties on imports were to be progressively abolished during the twelve-year transitional period from 1 January 1958 to 31 December 1969. Although the Treaty gave the Member States the option of varying the rate of reduction of customs duties according to product (should a sector have difficulties), the reduction was constant and problem-free. The rate of tariff dismantling was even accelerated by two Council decisions, and completed on 1 July 1968, 18 months ahead of schedule. This demonstrates that tariff dismantling caused no major problems to the industries of the Member States, as any country's objection would have prevented the change of schedule provided by the Treaty. The States, which acceded to the Community later on, had a five-year transitional period to eliminate customs duties in intra-Community

trade. This was also problem-free. Surely, many of the previously protected industries were obliged to renovate or shut down, but many new industries were created or expanded on sound premises.

The accelerated completion of the tariff union meant that, as of 1 July
1968, intra-Community trade had been freed of customs duties and quantitative restrictions on imports and exports. However, **other trade obstacles,**
such as charges having equivalent effect to customs duties and measures
having equivalent effect to quantitative restrictions, were far from gone.
The proper functioning of the tariff union required the elimination of these
obstacles too by the end of the transitional period. Indeed, the Treaty of
Rome expressly noted the necessity of "reducing formalities imposed on
trade as much as possible" (Art 10 EEC). In reality, as soon as tariff disarmament was accomplished, the "formalities war" was stepped up between
Member State administrations anxious to protect national production and at
the same time prevent the decrease of their own functions and powers. Of
course, every form, every stamp required for cross-border trade had a reason: tax collection, statistics, and customs checks aimed at preventing the
import of products not conforming to national regulations, etc. But each
stamp meant time and money to the Community's businesses.

A great number of those **trade barriers were hidden in regulations,**
such as consumer or environment protection standards, which varied from
one State to another [see section 6.1.]. Their restrictive effects were often
more damaging than customs duties and quantitative restrictions. Indeed,
while customs barriers raised the price of imports or quantitatively limited
them, various regulations could completely block the import of a product.
Fortunately, such extreme cases were rather limited. However, as seen in
the chapter on the common market, the elimination of non-customs barriers
to trade proved to be much more difficult and took three times as long as
did the elimination of customs barriers.

Despite the non-completion of the customs union by 1968, **the economic results of the free circulation of goods** achieved by it were indis-
putable. From 1958 to 1972, while trade between the six founding Member
States and the rest of the world had tripled, intra-Community trade had
been multiplied by nine. Such exceptional trade growth was a key factor to
economic development and the raising of the standard of living in all
member countries of the original EEC. The stimulating effect of the wider
market created a feeling of business confidence, which resulted in investment growth. Consumers emerged as the overall winners; supply was
much more diverse and products cheaper than before tariff dismantling.
The welfare objective of European integration was undoubtedly well pursued through the customs union. The task of the common institutions was,
therefore, to eliminate the remaining problems and increase the benefits of
the customs union.

5.1.2. Elimination of internal borders

The good results of the customs union **spurred the completion of the common market**, examined in the next chapter, itself needed for the completion of the customs union. Indeed, the customs union and the common market, which were the goals of the Treaty of Rome, both suffered from the same problems and finally benefited from the same remedies. Heartened by the evident benefits of the customs union, the Community institutions under the leadership of the Commission waged a "war of attrition on formalities", which, thanks to the Single European Act of 1987 [see section 2.1.], reached a successful conclusion on December 31, 1992.

Since January 1, 1993, no customs formalities are required for trade within the Community. Hence, all checks and all formalities in respect of goods moving within the Community have been eliminated[1]. The Community henceforth forms **one single border-free area** for the purposes of the movement of goods under cover of the TIR (international road transport) and ATA (temporary admission of goods) carnets[2]. This saves a great deal of time for economic operators and thus helps cut the cost of transporting goods within the Community. The absence of duties and formalities bolsters intra-EU trade (dispatches and arrivals) which represents around 65% of the total trade of the Fifteen and up to 80% of the total imports or exports of some countries of the Union.

5.1.3. Veterinary and plant health legislation

Veterinary and plant health legislation is important not only for intra-Community trade, but also for the protection of the environment and of human health. It is in the interest of all Member States to strengthen their common legislation in these fields and, at the same time, not to upset intra-Community trade of foodstuffs.

The **plant health arrangements,** which came into force on 1 June 1993, have made it possible to remove all physical obstacles to trade of plants and plant products[3]. These arrangements include the rules applicable to the intra-Community trade of plants and plant products imported from third countries, the standards for the protection of the environment and human health against harmful or undesirable organisms and the protective measures against the introduction into the Community of organisms harmful to plants or plant products and against their spread within the Community[4]. The Community Plant Variety Office supervises the protection of plant varieties in the Community[5].

---

[1] Regulation 2913/92, OJ L 302, 19.10.1992.
[2] Regulation 719/91, OJ L 78, 26.03.1991 repealed by Regulation 2913/92, OJ L 302, 19.10.1992.
[3] Directive 91/683, OJ L 376, 31.12.1991 and Directive 93/19, OJ L 96, 22.04.1993.
[4] Directive 2000/29, OJ L 169, 10.07.2000.
[5] Regulation 2100/94, OJ L 227, 01.09.1994 and Regulation 2506/95, OJ L 258, 25.10.1995.

In the **veterinary field**, the efforts of the Community are mainly geared towards **protecting the health of animals and consequently human health**, while allowing the smooth operation of the internal market. Since January 1, 1992, veterinary checks at intra-Community frontiers have been abolished and are instead carried out at the point of departure[1], while measures were taken to monitor zoonoses and zoonotic agents and thus prevent outbreaks of food-borne infections and intoxications[2]. At the same time, the Community has switched from a system characterised by a policy of systematic preventive vaccination against foot and mouth disease, which could act as an obstacle to the free movement of animals and products, to a policy of non-vaccination and slaughter in the event of an infection source appearing.

Although the elimination of controls at internal frontiers was necessary for the free circulation of animals and animal products in the internal market, it brought about other problems. The epizootic disease of bovine spongiform encephalopathy (BSE - **"mad cow disease"**), which first appeared in the United Kingdom in 1996 and then spread to several other countries, is indicative of the importance of veterinary questions for the customs union. Despite the prohibition of exports of bovine animals over the age of 6 months, of meat and specified meat products from the United Kingdom, the certification of animals and animal products in tandem with increased veterinary checks in the consigning Member State[3], the consumers' concerns spread in all the Member States and the beef market collapsed in the whole Community [see sections 11.2. and 21.4.2.].

Similar problems were created after the detection, in Belgium in June 1999, of **contamination by dioxins** of certain animal products intended for human or animal consumption. The protective measures, taken under the safeguard clause, obliged all Member States to ensure the withdrawal from the market and destruction of any poultry or egg products or food products containing poultry-related products which had come from suspect farms[4]. These cases demonstrate the fact that in a customs union the market problems of a single Member State are **in reality problems of the single market**. Therefore, the measures taken in order to face the problems of a country concern all the members of the Union.

5.1.4. Customs cooperation

The abolition of administrative procedures on crossing the internal frontiers of the Community heightens the **risk of fraud**, if all the Member States do not apply equivalent control measures. Administrative cooperation must encourage a comparative level of checks, thus ensuring the uni-

---

[1] Directive 89/662, OJ L 395, 30.12.1989.
[2] Directive 2003/99, OJ L 325, 12.12.2003.
[3] Directives 96/90 and 96/91, OJ L 13, 16.01.1997.
[4] Decision 1999/449, OJ L 175, 10.07.1999 and Decision 1999/601, OJ L 232, 02.09.1999

form application of Community law at every point of the EU external borders and guaranteeing mutual trust and equal conditions of competition. The efficiency of a customs union depends, indeed, as much on homogeneous rules as on the quality of its operational structures.

Customs officials make up an important **human network** of the EU. Since they collect customs duties, which must be transferred to the Community budget [see section 3.4.], and guard the external frontiers against illicit trading, the customs officers of the Member States **act in fact in the name of the Community** and must apply the Community law. They must be open to cooperation both among themselves and with the Commission in the spirit of Article 10 of the EC Treaty.

Article 29 of the EU Treaty urges the Council to take measures in order to strengthen cooperation between customs authorities and police forces, both directly and through the European Police Office (Europol). In fact, such measures are taken both in the context of the customs union and of justice and home affairs cooperation [see section 8.1.]. Thus, the Council Regulation on the **mutual assistance** between the Member States' administrations and on their collaboration with the Commission aims to step up fraud prevention, ensure the proper application of customs and agricultural regulations, providing *inter alia* for the administration of a computerised "customs information system" (CIS)[1]. The **Naples II Convention** on Mutual Assistance and Cooperation between Customs Administrations aims to crack down on the proliferation of illicit trafficking in breach of national and Community provisions by making customs cooperation faster and more effective[2].

5.2. Trade with non-member countries

Apart from removing obstacles to intra-Community trade, a customs union includes the harmonisation of customs regulations on trade with non-member countries. The efforts aimed at implementing such regulations in the European Union take two solid forms. On the one hand, the Community has established, and manages, a **Common Customs Tariff (CCT)**; on the other hand, Community rules fit into an international context, whose evolution they must follow. Thus, arrangements agreed previously in the context of GATT and, henceforth, of the World Trade Organisation must be transposed into Community law [see section 23.4.].

Customs union requires more than just having a common customs tariff. This tariff must also be applied according to identical rules throughout all Member States. Failure to do this could result in different values attributed to goods for customs purposes or different rules on the release of goods for circulation according to the importing Member State. The

---

[1] Regulation 1468/81, OJ L 144, 02.06.1981 and Regulation 515/97, OJ L 82, 22.03.1997.
[2] OJ C 24, 23.01.1998.

Community Customs Code (CCC), which groups together all the provisions of the Community's customs legislation, aims precisely at removing the risk of different interpretations of EU rules in trade between the Member States and third countries[1] [see section 5.2.2.]. The common customs legislation grouped together in the customs code is an attribute of the customs union.

5.2.1. The Common Customs Tariff

A customs union is characterised by the existence of **a single external tariff** applied by all Member States to imports coming from third countries. Such imports only have to clear customs once and can then move freely within the common customs area. Reaching an agreement among the original Member States on a single external tariff required a complex striking of balances and compromises, given the different national interests, stemming from the different products that each country wished to protect. The common customs tariff adopted by the European institutions in 1968 is, therefore, a major achievement of European integration.

For the member countries, the CCT meant both the loss of **customs revenue**, which, since 1975, has been a resource of the Community budget, and the option of carrying out an independent customs or trade policy [see sections 3.4. and 23.1.]. No member country can unilaterally decide on or negotiate tariff matters; **all changes to the CCT are decided by the Council** following negotiation (if necessary) and proposal by the Commission. All bilateral (between the EU and non-member countries) and multilateral (in the past inside GATT and now inside WTO) negotiations are carried out by the Commission.

As of 1968, **the Member States are not entitled to unilaterally carry out customs policy,** i.e. suspend customs duties or change CCT. Only the Council can waive the normal application of CCT by means of regulations adopting various tariff measures. Such measures, whether required under agreements or introduced unilaterally, involve reductions in customs duties or zero-rating in respect of some or all imports of a given product in the territory of the Community. They take the form of Community tariff quotas, tariff ceilings or total or partial suspension of duties.

The most important tariff concessions were granted by the Community in the context of the **General Agreement on Tariffs and Trade (GATT).** In the course of several international negotiations, namely: the "Dillon Round" (1960-62), the "Kennedy Round" (1964-67) and the "Tokyo Round" (1973-79), substantial reductions of customs duties were made on most industrial products. The "Uruguay Round", which was launched on 20 September 1986 and was concluded on 15 December 1993, has achieved major tariff reductions on the part of the 117 participating countries in the sectors of industry, agriculture and services. It has also imposed

---

[1]   Regulation 2913/92, OJ L 302, 19.10.1992 and Regulation 1427/97, OJ L 196, 24.07.1997.

new rules and disciplines to international trade, rules that the EU has incorporated into Community law [see section 23.4.].

Since 1995, the customs tariff of the European Union takes account of the outcome of the **GATT Uruguay Round of negotiations** [see section 23.2.]. In principle, for each item and sub-item of the tariff nomenclature, both the autonomous rates and the conventional rates resulting from the GATT negotiations are indicated. Several technical annexes to the CCT set out the specific import regimes, such as the import regime for certain agricultural products or the regime for pharmaceutical substances which may benefit from exoneration on duties.

5.2.2. The Community Customs Code

A customs union, without borders, presupposes that the customs relations of the Member States with the rest of the world be regulated in the same way. The common customs legislation is, in fact, applicable to the jurisdictions of all Member States as internal law. For this purpose, the **Community Customs Code (CCC)** groups together and presents all of the provisions of customs legislation governing the Community's trade with third countries in the light of its undertakings within the World Trade Organisation[1] [see section 23.4.]. It aims to guarantee the clarity of Community customs regulations and remove the risk of divergent interpretations or legal vagueness.

The Code contains, first of all, **the basic rules of common customs legislation**: customs territory of the European Union, customs value, goods origin, etc. The definition of the **customs territory** of the Community includes inter alia the coastal Member States' territorial sea, a matter of particular importance to the fishing and offshore activities of Member States. **Value for customs purposes** can sometimes have a greater impact on trade than customs duties. The Community Customs Code specifies the method by which such value is determined, the customs clearance criteria for goods finished or processed out of their country of origin, and the conditions under which goods are temporarily exempt of import duties. The **rules of origin** determine to what extent products coming from third countries may be exempt of duty by determining the degree of processing or transformation they have undergone. These rules are important for the proper application of preference systems and several provisions of the commercial policy of the European Union [see sections 5.2.2., 23.2.1. and 24.5.].

Common customs regulations, uniformly applicable in the Community's trade relations with other countries, involve setting up **various customs procedures** with economic impact. The Community Customs Code harmonised the legislative, regulatory and administrative provisions relative to customs warehouses procedures, free zones procedures, and usual

---

[1]   Regulation 2913/92, OJ L 302, 19.10.1992 and Regulation 955/1999, OJ L 119, 07.05.1999.

forms of handling, which can be undertaken in customs warehouses and free zones[1]. Thus, it includes provisions on: the customs treatment of goods entering the Community's customs territory and on the temporary storage of these goods; goods brought into the customs territory of the Community until such goods have received a destination for customs purposes[2]; returned goods in the customs territory of the Community; and admission to free circulation of goods[3]. **Transit systems** (Community transit, common transit and TIR) are at the heart of the customs union and the common commercial policy, but these systems are subject to fraud. A common transit procedure exists between the EC countries and the EFTA countries[4]. The EU implements the principles of the revised Kyoto Convention on the simplification and harmonisation of customs procedures[5].

The CCC governs also the **export procedures** of Community goods, the deferred payment of customs duties on imports or exports, the refund or remittance of these duties and the post-clearance collection of export duties not imposed on goods entered for a customs procedure. For Community exports, the Commission has adapted the model certificate of origin to the overall frame recommended by the UN[6]. A Community system of relief from customs duties exists[7].

5.3. Appraisal and outlook

The first ten years of the European Economic Community were the years of glory for customs union. The removal of customs duties and quantitative restrictions on imports and exports and the introduction of a common customs tariff, in July 1968, were important achievements of the young Community. They ruled out any "national preference" and gave rise to the "Community preference" for the products of the Member States. They provided formidable stimulus to intra-Community trade and, as expected by the EEC Treaty, were the foundation for the common market and all the common policies examined in this book. This **contributed to the material wellbeing of the Member States' citizens**, through a remarkable increase of better quality goods at lower prices. Tangible manifestations of the customs union are the products from all over the continent, which are available at affordable prices in local stores in all the Member States. The customs union has also greatly facilitated the travel of the citizens from one country of the EC/EU to another.

---

[1] Regulation 2913/92, OJ L 302, 19.10.1992 and Regulation 1427/97, OJ L 196, 24.07.1997.
[2] OJ L 367, 31.12.1988.
[3] Regulation 2913/92, OJ L 302, 19.10.1992 and Regulation 1427/97, OJ L 196, 24.07.1997.
[4] Convention, OJ L 226, 13.08.1987.
[5] Decision 2003/231, OJ L 86, 03.04.2003.
[6] Regulation 2454/93, OJ L 253, 11.10.1993 and Regulation 1662/1999, OJ L 197, 29.07.1999.
[7] Regulation 918/83, OJ L 105, 23.04.1983 and Regulation 355/94, OJ L 46, 18.02.1994.

What the Treaty had not foreseen was the perseverance of the national administrations, which quickly found obstacles other than those of customs to hinder trade between Member States, protect national production in an arbitrary way and, at the same time, defend their own functions and very existence (as in the case of the restructuring of customs administrations brought about by the abolition of customs controls).

As will be explained in the next chapter, the customs union was finally completed, together with the completion of the single market in 1992. The most striking manifestation of the customs union was the disappearance of customs checks at the borders between Member States. The abolition of customs checks at internal borders was achieved thanks to the abolition of customs administrative documents, which burdened intra-Community trade every year, a far-ranging reform of indirect taxation, examined in the chapter on taxation [see section 14.2.2.] and the entry into force of a series of provisions reorganising fiscal, veterinary, phytosanitary, sanitary and safety checks and the collection of statistical data. The most meaningful aspect of this process is the lightening of the administrative burden of companies carrying out intra-Community sales and purchases and, therefore, the encouragement of intra-Community transactions.

In addition to the internal environment of the Union, **the international environment of customs and commerce** has been profoundly modified in the 1990s. The opening up of free international trade to the Central and Eastern European countries as well as those of the former Soviet Union and the entry into force of the new GATT agreements have been powerful catalysts in the globalisation of trade. At the same time, however, there has been a growing globalisation of illicit traffic in all areas, such as drugs, arms, nuclear material and protected animal species. From a customs viewpoint, this requires strengthened cooperation and mutual assistance between the customs administrations of Community countries and those of third countries, notably those of other European countries.

Therefore, the abolition of customs formalities at internal borders must be counterbalanced by the **reinforcement of measures at external frontiers.** Customs checks at the Community's external frontiers have to be strengthened for illegal imports from third countries and customs cooperation must ensure that differences in regulations do not give rise to fraud or problems for consumers. National security problems (crime, drugs, terrorism, firearms traffic) will have to be settled jointly and by a detailed exchange of information between the police and security forces of the Member States in the context of police and judicial cooperation in criminal matters [see section 8.1.2.]. Common policies are necessary regarding citizens of non-member countries circulating freely within the Member States, once they have crossed the borders of one of them [see section 8.1.4.]. It is obvious that the customs union has had and continues having important spillover or multiplicative effects [see section 1.1.1.] on a great number of common policies in other economic and even political fields.

Bibliography on Customs Union

- ARCHER Clive, Norway outside the European Union: Norway and European integration from 1994 to 2004, London: Routledge, 2005.
- BERR Claude, TRÉMEAU Henri, *Le droit douanier: communautaire et national*. Paris: Economica, 2004.
- EGGER Peter. "Market power, multinationality and intra-EU industry exports in the 90s", *Scottish Journal of Political Economy*, v. 51, n. 5, November 2004, p. 626-640.
- EUROPEAN COMMISSION. *Integrated Tariff of the European Communities (TARIC), Introduction*. Luxembourg: EUR-OP*, 2003.
  - *The European Community's Rules of Origin for the Generalised System of Preferences: a Guide for Traders*. Luxembourg: EUR-OP*, 2003.
- KEPPENE Jean-Paul. "La libre circulation des merchandises", *Journal des tribunaux. Droit européen*. v. 12, n. 113, novembre 2004, p. 275-280.
- OLIVER Peter, JARVIS Malcom. *Free movement of goods in the European Community, under articles 28 to 30 of the EC Treaty*. London: Sweet & Maxwell, 2003.
- PERRON Régine (ed.). *The stability of Europe: the Common Market, towards European integration of industrial and financial markets? (1958-1968)*. Paris: Presses de l'Université de Paris-Sorbonne, 2004.
- Ülgen Sinan, Zahariadis Yiannis. The future of Turkish-EU trade relations: deepening vs widening. Brussels: Centre for European Policy Studies, 2004.
- VENABLES Anthony J. "Winners and losers from regional integration agreements", *Economic Journal*, v. 113, n. 490, October 2003, p. 747-761.

* The publications of the Office for Official Publications of the European Communities (EUR-OP*) exist generally in all official languages of the EU.

DISCUSSION TOPICS

1. Which are the main attributes of a customs union?
2. Consider the inferences of the increasing membership of the Community customs union and the decreasing one of the EFTA.
3. What was more important for multinational integration: trade liberalisation among the Member States or the common customs policy towards third countries?
4. The "mad cow disease" (BSE) demonstrated the effects of the customs union on the common agricultural policy and on the consumer protection policy. Outline the interactions between the three policies and the lessons to be drawn from this disastrous experience.
5. Can fraud prevention in a customs union be dealt with national measures or does it require a common policy?

Chapter 6

COMMON MARKET

Diagram of the chapter

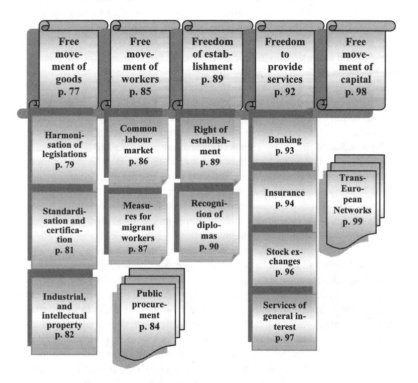

The creation of a single European economic area based on a common market was **the fundamental objective of the Treaty of Rome** [see section 2.1.]. Article 2 of that Treaty set out that objective as follows: "The Community shall have as its task, by establishing a common market and progressively approximating the economic policies of Member States, to promote throughout the Community a harmonious development of economic activities, a continuous and balanced expansion, an increase in stability, an accelerated raising of the standard of living and closer relations between the States belonging to it". It is obvious that the common market was not an end in itself, but a means to achieve economic and political goals.

It is useful to define here the concepts of "common market", "single market" and "internal market" which are used almost synonymously but which have significant nuances of meaning. The **common market** is a stage in the multinational integration process which, in the words of a Court of Justice ruling, aims to remove all the barriers to intra-Community trade with a view to the merger of national markets into a **single market** giving rise to conditions as close as possible to a genuine **internal market**[1]. It is worth noting that the Treaty establishing the European Community ignores the concept of the "single market". It refers generally to the stage of the "common market" and to the end result of it, the "internal market", which according to its Article 14 comprises "an area without internal frontiers in which the free movement of goods, persons, services and capital is ensured in accordance with the provisions of this Treaty". The Community had to clear many obstacles during the common market stage in order to reach the goal of a single market by the end of 1992, a goal set, in 1985, by the then President of the Commission, Jacques Delors.

The establishment of the common market first required the **elimination of all import and export duties** existing between Member States before the foundation of the Community. We saw in the previous chapter how the Member States effectively removed the customs barriers and how immediately after tariff dismantling, they began erecting technical barriers which, in some cases, were even more difficult to overcome than customs ones [see sections 5.1. and 6.1.]. In the first section of this chapter, we shall look at how the Member States decided to complete the common market and what measures they decided to take to eliminate technical obstacles to trade and to open up public procurement.

The creation of a common market resembling an internal market implies not only the liberalisation of trade among the participating member states, it also necessitates the **free movement of production factors**. Hence, in order to speak about a common market, we need to have between the Member States that make it up the existence of **four fundamental freedoms**: freedom of movement of goods, thanks to the elimination of all trade barriers; freedom of movement of workers, thanks to the elimination of all restrictions to their entrance and residence in other Member States; freedom of establishment of persons and companies in the territory of any Member State and of the provision of services by them in the host country; and freedom of capital movements for business or personal purposes. It appears that the **keyword of the common market is freedom**.

6.1. Completion of the internal market

In January 1985, the President of the newly appointed Commission, **Jacques Delors**, presenting to the European Parliament the main guidelines for its action over the following four years promised to put an end to the image of a feudal Europe that offered only barriers, customs, formali-

---

[1]   Judgment of May 5 Gaston Schul, , case 15/81, ECR 1982, p. 1409

ties and red tape. According to Delors, all internal European borders should be eliminated **by the end of 1992**. The Commission had, thus, taken up the challenge to create a genuine common market without internal borders by the end of 1992, but, of course, it could not carry out this formidable task alone. Therefore, in June 1985 the Commission forwarded to the European Council a **"white paper" on completing the internal market**[1]. That programme for the elimination within seven years of all physical, technical and fiscal obstacles was characterised in particular by a more flexible approach to harmonisation methods, the proposal of some 300 legislative texts aimed at removing barriers to trade and a binding timetable to achieve this goal.

The Milan European Council (28-June 1985) welcomed the programme established in the white paper and decided, by a majority of its members, to call an intergovernmental conference with the brief of drawing up a draft Treaty covering, on the one hand, political cooperation and, on the other, the amendments to the EEC Treaty required for the completion of the internal market. The Commission's proposals for a **"single framework"** for the amendment of the EEC Treaty and for political cooperation were endorsed by the European Council at its meeting in Luxembourg on 3 December 1985 and were finalised in the form of a **"Single European Act"** by the Ministers for Foreign Affairs meeting in Intergovernmental Conference on 27 January 1986 [see section 2.1.]. By making significant changes to the Community decision-making process (qualified majority voting in the Council acting in cooperation with the European Parliament) [see section 4.2.], the Single Act not only succeeded in removing the technical barriers to trade, thus creating the Single Market, but has had important spillover effects [see section 1.1.1.] on many common policies, such as transports, taxation and environment protection.

6.2. Free movement of goods

Tariff disarmament completed thanks to the customs union, in July 1968, had eliminated customs barriers to intra-Community trade. But there still remained technical obstacles to trade and the EEC Treaty had not fixed a timetable for their elimination. **Technical barriers to trade result from national regulations** obliging the producers of industrial products and foodstuffs to satisfy certain criteria or to meet certain standards and technical specifications. This legislation is necessary for various reasons: standardising industrial production, guaranteeing the safety of workers, protecting the health of consumers and preventing or reducing environmental pollution, etc. The problem for the common market was not the existence of national regulations, but the differences between them and also the fact that those regulations could be used to protect the national market from products from other Member States which were subject to

---

[1] COM(85)310 final.

products from other Member States which were subject to different standards.

The disparity that existed between countries in terms of technical requirements stemmed from **historical and economic considerations**. A country in which a product was imported rather than manufactured tended to impose stringent requirements on it and checks prior to its being placed on the market, without concerning itself greatly about the economic cost, which that represented. On the other hand a producer country of an industrial product tended to be more tolerant taking into consideration the economic implications of requirements and controls, an excessive stringency of which would penalise its industry. In any case, the various technical regulations could hinder trade even more than customs duties (eliminated thanks to the customs union) [see section 5.1.2.]. Indeed, even a high customs tariff could be paid and a product originating in one country could enter the market of another, if its consumers preferred it. On the other hand, if a product did not comply with the different technical standards, its entry to that country's market was completely blocked.

The result was that the industrialist who wished to export to the other EEC member countries was obliged to bear additional research, development and production costs in order **to comply with all the national standards** which his products had to satisfy. Thus the disparity of the legislation within the Community compelled producers to manufacture different components, increase their production lines, diversify their stocks according to country of destination and have specialised distribution and after-sales services for each country.

All the above **made production on the Community scale more costly** than it should have been and favoured large undertakings (firms, companies) rather than small and medium-sized enterprises (SMEs). Large undertakings, in particular multinationals, had the structure, experience and personnel required to meet the specific requirements of the markets in several countries and could spread the additional costs over long runs in such a way that they represented a negligible fraction of the unit cost of the product. For small companies, however, the additional costs represented a substantial fraction of the production unit cost and could be prohibitive to any exports. The abolition of technical barriers to trade eliminated this disadvantage of SMEs.

The free movement of goods within the Community established by Articles 25 to 28 (TEC) is in actual fact safeguarded by the **infringement procedure** provided in Article 226 of the EC Treaty [see section 4.1.2.]. The Commission invokes those procedures whenever it records an infringement of Community provisions attributable to any authority whatsoever of a Member State (including judicial authorities[1]). It may consider a case as a matter of routine in the light of information provided by Members

---

[1] See Judgment of 30 September 2003, case C-224/01 Gerhard Köbler v Republic of Austria; ECR 2003.

of the European Parliament or published in the press or in the official journal of a Member State. Usually, however, a **complaint** is brought before it
by a company, an association or even another Member State in respect of
draft standards or technical rules of a Member State. Article 30 (TEC) allows some restrictions on imports on grounds of public morality, public
policy or public security, but specifies that they must not constitute disguised restrictions on trade between Member States[1]. According to the
Court of Justice, willing to ensure the survival of a company cannot be a
justification founded on this Article[2].

6.2.1. Harmonisation of legislations

The removal of technical obstacles to trade in **industrial products** is
normally based on Article 94 of the EC Treaty (Art. 100 EEC), which provides for the **approximation of** such **provisions** laid down by law, regulation or administrative action that directly affect the functioning of the
common market. Such alignment is not as easy as it seems at first sight. As
technical regulations relate to production systems and consequently investments already made, and as their harmonisation sometimes entails the
need for industrialists in some Member States to change their production
systems by means of new investment expenditure, the removal of technical
obstacles to trade used to be the subject of interminable discussions. Each
member country tried to persuade its partners that its own technical regulations were the best and should be adopted by the Community.

Until now some 250 **directives on the harmonisation of laws** have
thus been adopted by the Council, a large number of which have on several
occasions been adapted to technical progress. They harmonise the national
regulations in fields as diverse as motor vehicle equipment, foodstuffs and
proprietary medicinal products. Thus, considerable progress has been made
in the motor vehicle sector, in particular as a result of the entry into force
of the EC type-approval for motor vehicles and their trailers[3]. In the foodstuffs sector a body of Community inspectors is responsible for evaluating
and checking the control systems in the Member States[4]. Directives have
been adopted in the particularly sensitive areas of food additives, colour-
ings and sweeteners[5]. The harmonisation work relating to pharmaceutical
products has culminated in the creation of the single market in medicinal
products and in the establishment of a European Agency for the Evaluation
of Medicinal Products[6].

---

[1] See in this context the Judgment of the Court on German beer, case 178/84, ECR 1987, p.
1227.
[2] Judgment of 28 March 1995, case C-324/93, ECR 1995, p. 1-0563.
[3] Directive 92/53, OJ L 225, 10.08.1992.
[4] Directive 93/99, OJ L 290, 24.11.1993.
[5] Directives 94/34, 94/35 and 94/36, OJ L 237, 10.09.1994.
[6] Regulation 2309/93, OJ L 214, 24.08.1993.

The laborious procedures involved in the approximation of laws leads to results, which are **very useful for economic integration**. Indeed, once the standards are the same in all member countries, type approval of a product granted in any member country is recognised by all the others. The manufacturers need only guarantee that all examples of a product will conform to the prototype that has been approved in the directive. Items which do not conform may not be sold anywhere in the common market, including the producer's home market. Conversely, no Member State may apply more stringent national rules to oppose the import or use of products which meet Community requirements. But, the harmonisation of legislations is also very useful for consumers, since it guarantees them the quality and safety of products circulating in the large market.

However, whilst some problems were being resolved through the harmonisation of legislations, the Member States, tempted by protectionism, in particular during the gloomy economic climate of the 1970s, were adopting new legislation and **creating further technical obstacles to trade**. The Community institutions' laborious work to remove those obstacles therefore resembled the endless tasks of the Danaides, punished by Greek gods to fill a bottomless cask. For that reason, the Commission considered a fresh approach to the problem. For that it relied upon the case law of the Court of Justice. In its judgment of 20 February 1979 in the "**Cassis de Dijon**" **case** (concerning the sale in Germany of blackcurrant liqueur produced in France), the Court of Justice gave a very broad definition of the obstacles to free trade which were prohibited under Article 30 et seq. of the EEC Treaty (Art. 28 to 31 TEC)[1]. It stated that any product lawfully manufactured and marketed in a Member State should in principle be admitted to the market of any other Member State.

Even if they are applicable without distinction to domestic and imported products, national regulations may not create obstacles unless they are necessary to satisfy mandatory requirements and are directed towards an objective of general interest which is such as to take precedence over the requirements of the free movement of goods, that is one of the basic rules of the Community. In plain language, a country must not bar the way to competing products from another Member State solely because they are slightly different from domestic products. If it does so, the Commission will take proceedings against it as far as the Court of Justice, where it stands every chance of being condemned on the basis of existing case law. According to another Court judgment, **national provisions must not discriminate** against the traders to whom they apply or have the effect of discriminating between the marketing of national products and that of products from other Member States[2].

In parallel with the application of the "Cassis de Dijon" principle, the Commission secured, in 1983, the adoption by the Council of a **procedure**

---

[1]   Judgment of 20 February 1979, Case 120/78, ECR 1979, p. 649.
[2]   Judgment given on 24 November 1993, Joined Cases C-267/91 and C-268/91, Keck and Mithouard, ECR 1993, p. I-6097.

for the provision of information by the Member States on any new technical standards and regulations that they envisage. This procedure was codified in 1998[1], while a new Directive extended its field of application to information society services[2]. Thanks to the information procedure, the Commission is notified by the competent authorities of any new technical standards or regulations that they envisage and can thus notify the other Member States and request amendments before their entry into force. This is an example of shared sovereignty: the Member States have agreed to lose their independence of action in the field of standardisation, but have gained in exchange the right of surveying the actions of their neighbours [see section 1.1.2.].

6.2.2. Common standardisation and certification policy

As regards the existing rules and standards, at the instigation of the Commission, the Council adopted, in 1985, a **new approach to technical harmonisation and standards**[3]. In cases where full harmonisation of technical standards cannot be applied, because divergences are too great between the essential aims of different national laws, legislative harmonisation is confined to the adoption of the **essential safety requirements** (or other requirements in the general interest) with which products must conform, in order to enjoy free movement throughout the EU. The European standardisation bodies, mentioned below, then prepare technical specifications, which the manufacturers must meet in order to produce and put on the market products which comply with the essential requirements laid down by Community directives adopted by the Council and the European Parliament with the co-decision procedure [see section 4.2.]. No mandatory nature is attributed to these technical specifications, which have the status of voluntary standards. Industrialists are not obliged but have an interest, if they want to market their products in all the common market, to manufacture them in accordance with the Community directives and hence with Community standards. On the other hand, the national authorities are obliged to recognise that products manufactured in conformity with harmonised standards are presumed to conform to the essential requirements laid down in that Directive. Member States must notify the Commission of any measure that they may take for some reason, which may obstruct the free movement of a model or type of product that is lawfully manufactured or marketed in another Member State[4].

The key to the implementation of the new approach to technical harmonisation is the **common standardisation policy**, i.e. the establishment of standards that determine the specifications for industrial production. The

---

[1]   Directive 98/34, OJ L 204, 21.07.1998 and Directive 98/48, OJ L 217, 05.08.1998.
[2]   Commission proposal, OJ C 65, 28.02.1998.
[3]   OJ C 136, 04.06.1985, p. 1-9.
[4]   Decision 3052/95, OJ L 321, 30.12.1995.

standards are adopted by European bodies, which have the task of elaborating technical specifications that meet the essential requirements laid down by the technical harmonisation Directives, while ensuring that those standards are the result of agreement of all parties concerned: producers, users, consumers, administrations, etc. These bodies are: the European Committee for Standardisation (CEN), the European Committee for Electrotechnical Standardisation (CENELEC) and the European Telecommunications Standards Institute (ETSI).

In order to be able to exercise their positive effects, European standards must, however, also be **certified and recognised by the relevant national bodies**. Reciprocal recognition of certificates of conformity with rules and standards is therefore essential to the free movement of goods. Hence, the Council laid down the guiding principles for the European policy on the mutual recognition of tests and certificates[1], provided for the setting up of the European Organisation for Testing and Certification (EOTC) and adopted conformity assessment procedures, intended for use in the technical harmonisation Directives for the marketing of industrial products[2] [see also sections 17.3.6 and 19.2.1.]. The **principle of mutual recognition** enables, especially in sectors which have not been harmonised at Community level, the competent authorities of importing Member States to recognise technical specifications, standards and rules applicable in other Member States and the validity of tests carried out by approved laboratories in other Member States offering adequate guarantees of reliability and efficiency.

A **single "CE" marking** is used in order to facilitate controls on the Community market by inspectors and to clarify the obligations of economic operators in respect of marking under the various Community regulations[3]. The aim of the CE marking is to symbolize the conformity of a product with the levels of protection of collective interests imposed by the total harmonization directives and to indicate that the economic operator has undergone all the evaluation procedures laid down by Community law in respect of his product. Consumers who see the **Community marking CE** on a product have thus an indication (not necessarily the proof) that this has been manufactured in conformity with Community standards.

6.2.3. Protection of intellectual and industrial property

Community-wide protection of **intellectual and industrial property** plays an important role in breaking down barriers to the free movement of goods and services. Adequate and strong protection of **copyright and related rights**, ensuring a fair balance between the interests of right holders and the interests of users, is considered to be one of the keys to added value and competitiveness [see also sections 10.3. and 23.4.].

[1] OJ C 10, 16.01.1990, p. 1-2.
[2] Decision 90/683, OJ L 380, 31.12.1990,.
[3] Decision 93/465, OJ L 220, 30.08.1993.

A Directive **protects on the territory of the Community every trade mark** in respect of goods or services which is the subject of registration or of an application in a Member State for registration as an individual trade mark, a collective mark or a guarantee or certification mark, or which is the subject of a registration or an application for registration in the Benelux Trade Mark Office or of an international registration having effect in a Member State[1]. Member States remain free to fix the provisions of procedure concerning the registration, the revocation and the invalidity of trade marks acquired by registration.

Companies that wish to adapt their activities to the scale of the Community have at their disposal the legal instrument of the **Community trade mark**, enabling their products or services to be distinguished by identical means throughout the entire Community[2]. A Community trade mark may consist of any signs capable of being represented graphically, particularly words, including personal names, designs, letters, numerals, the shape of goods or of their packaging, provided that such signs are capable of distinguishing the goods produced by one firm from those produced by other firms. The Community trade mark provides uniform protection throughout the Community, which can be obtained by means of a single procedure. This protection enables the proprietor to prevent any other person from using the mark for the same products or services or for similar products if there is a danger of confusion. The Community trade mark is granted (registered) for a period of 10 years, which is renewable, by the Office for Harmonisation in the Internal Market (OHIM) based in Alicante. Its protection on all the territory of the Union is reinforced by the existence of quasi-judicial bodies - the Boards of Appeal of the Office for Harmonisation in the Internal Market - whose decisions may be challenged before the Court of Justice.

As regards industrial property, a Directive seeks to guarantee effective legal protection for **industrial designs** (in machinery, tools, electronic equipment, etc.), by defining a "design", by establishing the conditions governing its protection and the scope of protection including the exclusive right to use the design[3]. The **Community Design** provides uniform protection throughout the Community for registered designs managed by the Office for Harmonisation in the Internal Market (Trademarks and Designs) in Alicante[4].

---

[1] Directive 89/104, OJ L 40, 11.02.1989 and Decision 92/10, OJ L 106, 11.01.1992.
[2] Regulation 40/94, OJ L 11, 14.01.1994 and Decision 2003/793 and Protocol, OJ L 296, 14.11.2003.
[3] Directive 98/71, OJ L 289, 28.10.1998.
[4] Regulation 6/2002, OJ L 3, 05.01.2002.

6.3. Public procurement

In a genuine single market, the public sector must also be open to intra-Community trade and competition. Indeed, **the requirements of the official authorities for works and supplies** of all sorts for the central civil service, regional and local authorities and for public undertakings (companies) and bodies accounts for 15% of the economic activity in the Community. At the end of the 1980s only 2% of the needs of the official authorities were covered by businesses from a Member State other than that of the official authorities concerned, notwithstanding the price, quality and service advantages that they could offer.

In some sectors, such as the aeronautical, energy, transport and telecommunications, procurement by public bodies constituted the largest, if not the sole, part of the market, virtually excluding it from the common market. Thus, the protected high technology industries, of particular interest to the public sector, were treated unfavourably in comparison to traditional industries, as the latter had benefited from the liberalisation of trade. These protected industries were **a paradise for inefficient suppliers of goods and services** who had connections with the civil administration, but public administrations were thus jeopardising their own efficiency. Moreover, the isolation of the markets of high technology industries held back their development, as those industries were the very ones most in need of a large market and the economies of scale that it could offer. It was evident that a common interest existed to open up public procurement to all Community businesses, but the vested interests in each Member State slowed down the adoption of the necessary common measures.

The principle of abolition of restrictions on freedom to provide services in respect of **public works contracts** and the award of public works contracts to contractors acting through agencies or branches was established in the early 1970s[1]. Nevertheless, the opening up of this sector to Community competition was achieved only in the 1990s through the coordination of procedures for the award of public works contracts in the Member States[2]. That coordination consists in the publication of notices of public works contracts in the Official Journal of the European Union so that all those interested in the Member States are informed at the same time. It also comprises common rules on the selection of candidates and on the award of contracts. The official authorities must refer to European standards and technical specifications agreed upon at European level [see section 6.2.3.], which must be met by the companies wishing to tender. The threshold as from which public contracts are subject to the Community arrangements is set at 5 million euro.

---

[1]   Directive 71/304, OJ L 185, 16.08.1971 and OJ L 1, 03.01.1994.
[2]   Directive 93/37, OJ L 199, 09.08.1993 and Commission communication, OJ C 121, 29.04.2000.

The **liberalisation of public supply contracts** was also completed in the 1990s[1]. Now, States, public bodies, etc., which propose to award a supply contract in excess of 200,000 euro have to publish a notice in the Official Journal of the EU in accordance with a uniform model. This is designed to provide firms concerned with all the information they need to be able to propose their candidacy, where restricted procedures are involved, or their tender, where an open procedure is involved. The contracting authorities are obliged to treat all firms on an equal footing and, to apply identical criteria for selecting a tender, published in advance. The products covered by the Community legislation include everyday supplies necessary for the functioning of services, such as hospital equipment, scientific research equipment and goods necessary for army maintenance, which are not specifically military.

The water, energy, transport and telecommunications, called **public utility sectors**, which were initially excluded from Community legislation on public procurement, are now covered as well[2]. The bodies in question and the activities concerned include the railway companies, port and airport authorities, gas and electricity distributors, undertakings which extract oil and gas, and suppliers of telecommunications, water and urban transport services. The contracting entities in these sectors, which, by virtue of the existence of exclusive government-regulated networks or concession rights, could formerly not resist political pressure to "buy national", are now obliged to call for tenders throughout the Community. Contracts must be awarded under proper commercial conditions and in accordance with the principle of non-discrimination by virtue of a flexible system including Community publication of invitations to tender, specification of the supplies and works adapted to encouraging tenders, and common rules applicable to all potential participants in the EU.

Public service contracts are subject to transparency and non discrimination requirements. Maximum transparency is sought in the sectors best suited to cross-border transactions and consequently considered priorities: maintenance and repair, computer technology, advertising, architecture, engineering and some financial services[3]. The "non-priority" services - the hotel business, education and training, social services and legal services - on the other hand, are subject to minimum transparency requirements.

6.4. Free movement of workers

One of the great achievements of European integration has been the transformation of economic migratory movements of the post-war period into free movement of workers. The freedom of movement of workers allows EU citizens to seek, within the Union, **better living and working**

---

[1] Directive 93/36, OJ L 199, 09.08.1993 and Directive 97/52, OJ L 328, 28.11.1997.
[2] Directive 93/38, OJ L 199, 09.08.1993 and Directive 98/4, OJ L 101, 01.04.1998.
[3] Directive 92/50, OJ L 209, 24.07.1992 and Directive 97/52, OJ L 328, 28.11.1997.

conditions than are available to them in their region of origin. It therefore boosts greatly the chances of improving the standards of living of the individual. At the same time, freedom of movement reduces social pressure in the poorest regions of the European Union and allows the living conditions of those remaining to improve. In the EU in general it facilitates the adjustment of the labour supply to the variations in the demand of undertakings and opens the way for more coherent and more effective economic policies at a European level. Thus, freedom of movement of workers contributes to the attainment of the objectives of the common market as well as to the flexibility and efficiency of the labour market.

Free movement is not restricted to workers. Article 18 of the EC Treaty, which has direct effect [see section 3.3.], gives every citizen of the Union the **right to move and reside freely** within the territory of the Member States. A citizen of the European Union who no longer enjoys a right of residence as a migrant worker in the host Member State can, as a citizen of the Union, enjoy there a right of residence by direct application of Article 18(1) EC[1]. The same right is enjoyed by his spouse, their descendants under the age of 21 and their dependent relatives in the ascending line. This right contributes to a concrete and practical expression of European citizenship [see section 9.1.]. Freedom of movement may contribute to the attainment of the objectives of the common market, while giving more flexibility and thus greater efficiency to the labour market. The challenge to the Union now is, however, to create a real European mobility area, in which freedom of movement becomes not only a legal entitlement but also a daily reality for people across Europe. This, calls for a complex interaction of common policies, some of which are explained below and some in the chapter on social progress [see sections 13.3, 13.4.2. and 13.5.].

6.4.1. The common labour market

The **EEC Treaty** had the objective, as regards workers, of creating a common labour market, which meant the free movement of labour within the Community and the abolition of any discrimination based on nationality between workers of the Member States as regards employment, remuneration and other conditions of work and employment. Under Article 39 of the EC Treaty (Art. 48 EEC), freedom of movement of workers entails the right, subject to limitations justified on grounds of public policy, public security or public health to accept offers of employment actually made, **to move freely** within the territory of Member States for this purpose, **to stay** in a Member State for the purpose of employment and **to remain** in the territory of that Member State after having been employed in it. The Community legislation that materialised those principles was completed in 1968

---

[1]   Judgment of 17 September 2002, Case C-413/99, Baumbast and R v Secretary of State for the Home Department, ECR 2002, p. I-07091.

and, thus, freedom of movement of workers was achieved, from the legal point of view, at the same time as customs union. This freedom was extended to all the workers in the European Economic Area in 1994[1] [see section 25.1.]. The worker can continue to reside, in the country in which he or she has settled after the termination of his or her employment. That takes specific form in the automatic renewal of the residence permit held by the person concerned as an employed person. The members of the family resident with him or her enjoy that right even after the worker's death. Nowadays, all persons residing legally in a Member State have equal rights of movement and residence in the other states of the Union [see sections 6.5.1 and 9.2.].

A directive implementing the **principle of equal treatment** between persons irrespective of racial or ethnic origin, provided in Article 13 of the EC Treaty, seeks to prohibit discrimination throughout the Community in different areas such as employment, education, social security, health care and access to goods and services[2]. It defines the concepts of direct and indirect discrimination, gives right of redress to victims of discrimination, imposes an obligation on the employer to prove that the principle of equal treatment has not been breached, and offers protection against harassment and victimisation in all the Member States.

The Community has set up a general framework for **combating discrimination** on grounds of religion or belief, disability, age or sexual orientation as regards employment and occupation[3]. A Community action programme to combat discrimination (2001-06) aims to promote measures to combat all forms of discrimination except that based on sex, which is the subject of specific Community action[4] [see section 13.5.5.]. The objective is to change practices and attitudes by mobilising the players involved and fostering the exchange of information and good practice. In particular, the programme seeks to set up databases and promote the networking of those involved.

6.4.2. Measures in favour of migrant workers

Adequate protection by European **provisions in the field of social security** is necessary for the effective use of the right of the citizens of one Member State to stay and work in another State of the Union. Without such protection, persons moving across borders to work or to look for a job, would risk losing all or part of their rights acquired or in the process of being acquired under national legislation (concerning, for example pensions, health insurance, unemployment benefits or family benefits). Article 42 of the EC Treaty (Art. 51 EEC) provides for the adoption of the measures

---

[1] Regulation 1612/68, OJ L 257, 19.10.1968 and Agreement on the EEA, OJ L 1, 03.01.1994, pp. 325, 572.

[2] Directive 2000/43, OJ L 180, 19.07.2000.

[3] Directive 2000/78, OJ L 303, 02.12.2000.

[4] Decision 2000/750, OJ L 303, 02.12.2000.

necessary for that purpose through arrangements to secure for migrant workers and their dependents: (a) aggregation, for the purpose of acquiring and retaining the right to benefit, of all periods taken into account under the laws of several countries, and (b) payment of benefits to persons resident in the territories of Member States. The system required by the Treaty was in fact adopted in 1958, but it has undergone many changes and improvements since then.

On the basis of Regulations 1408/71 and 574/72, **pensions of similar nature** acquired in the various Member States may be aggregated, but the person concerned may not obtain total benefits in excess of the highest pension he or she would have obtained if he or she had spent his or her whole insurance career under the legislation of any one of the States in which he or she had been employed[1]. This legislation covers also students moving within the Community, taking account of their specific situation and of the special features of the schemes under which they are insured. Civil servants and persons treated as such have equal treatment as regards general statutory pension rights and special schemes for civil servants prevailing in the Member States[2]. The supplementary pension rights of employed and self-employed persons moving within the European Union are equally guaranteed[3]. Rights and obligations comparable to those applying to EU citizens are granted to nationals of third countries who are legally resident in the Community and who satisfy the other conditions laid down in Regulations 1408/71 and 574/72[4].

The **unemployed person** who leaves for another Member State to seek employment receives, for a maximum period of three months from the date of departure, the benefits of the country in which he or she was last employed, to be paid for by that country. Repayments in respect of health care provided for members of the family resident in a Member State other than that in which the worker is employed and insured are made entirely to the institutions of the country of residence. Family allowances are granted under the legislation of, and at the rate laid down in, the country of employment. According to the Court of Justice, such allowances are not subject to requirements as to minimum period of residence[5].

Similar arrangements cover **self-employed persons** and their families[6] as well as employed persons or self-employed persons pursuing activities in the territories of two or more Member States[7]. Any insured person staying temporarily in a Member State other than the one in which he or she is insured, for tourist or employment purposes, may be admitted to hospital

---

[1] Regulation 1408/71, OJ L 149, 05.07.1971, Regulation 574/72, OJ L 74, 27.03.1972 and Regulation 631/2004, JO L 100, 06.04.2004.
[2] Regulation 1606/98, OJ L 209, 25.07.1998.
[3] Regulation 1223/98, OJ L 168, 13.06.1998.
[4] Regulation 859/2003, OJ L 124, 20.05.2003.
[5] Judgment given on 10 March 1993, Case C-111/91, Commission v Luxembourg, ECR 1993, I-840.
[6] Regulation 1390/81, OJ L 143, 29.05.1981.
[7] Regulation 3811/86, OJ L 355, 16.12.1986.

or receive refunds in respect of urgent medical care in the host State on presentation of the **European health insurance card** ("European card")[1]. This card replaced all paper forms needed for health treatment in another Member State provided for by Regulations 1408/71 and 574/72 giving entitlement to reimbursement of health care costs during a temporary stay in a Member State other than the competent State or the State of residence. The European card simplified access to care in the country visited, while providing a guarantee for the bodies financing the health system in that country that the patient is fully insured in his or her country of origin and that they can therefore rely on reimbursement by their counterparts.

For the effective functioning of a common labour market, it is also necessary that potential migrant workers have at their disposal adequate information regarding the number and nature of jobs available in the Community and the qualifications required. This is the task of the **European Employment Service (EURES)**, a network of some 400 "Euroadvisers" from the national employment services, employer organisations, trade unions, regional administrations and universities, specially trained to deal with the needs of transnational job-seekers and job-providers[2].

6.5. Freedom of establishment and recognition of diplomas

Freedom of establishment means the free movement of self-employed persons. For them, as for salaried workers, the basic principle is equality of treatment of all Community citizens, i.e. the abolition of discriminations based on nationality. **Freedom of establishment includes** the right to take up and pursue activities as self-employed persons and to set up and manage undertakings, in particular companies or firms within the meaning of the second paragraph of Article 48 (TEC), i.e., companies established under the conditions laid down for its own nationals by the law of the country where such establishment is effected. The freedom of establishment of companies extends to what is known as freedom of secondary establishment, i.e. the setting up of agencies, branches or subsidiaries (Art. 43 TEC).

6.5.1. Right of establishment

Whereas, freedom to provide services chiefly concerns the pursuit of an economic activity by a person in another Member State without having the principal or secondary place of business in that State, **right of establishment entails** permanent installation in a Member State in order to pursue an economic activity in that State. In fact, the situation of the person

---

[1] Decisions 2003/751, 2003/752 and 2003/753, OJ L 276, 27.10.2003.
[2] Decision2003/8, OJ L 5, 10.01.2003.

who establishes himself is characterised by the fact that he creates a permanent link with the country of establishment, unlike somebody who provides services in a country other then that of his permanent establishment.

The right for nationals of EU Member States to work or pursue activities as self-employed persons in the Member States means the **right to enter and to reside** in the member country in which they wish to work or pursue those activities. This right is extended to their spouses, children and other members of their families, including the registered partner if the legislation of the host Member State treats registered partnership as equivalent to marriage[1]. For periods of residence of longer than three months, Member States may only require Union citizens to register with the competent authorities in the place of residence. In fact, the self-employed person and his or her family members who have resided in a host Member State during a continuous period of five years have a right of permanent residence in that State. The members of the family enjoy the right of residence even after the self-employed person's death.

Under Article 46 (TEC), the principle of freedom of establishment does not concern national provisions providing for special treatment for foreign nationals on **grounds of public policy, public security or public health**. A Council Directive of 1964 contains an enumeration of the circumstances, which cannot be invoked as grounds for refusal of entry or deportation and a series of rules concerning the procedure, which must be followed where nationals of Member States may be refused entry or deported[2]. In order to take into account the concept of citizenship of the EU introduced by the Treaty of Amsterdam [see section 9.1.], as well as the case law of the Court of Justice, the Commission has laid down guidelines for correctly interpreting and applying the directive[3].

6.5.2. Recognition of diplomas

After removing obvious discriminatory practices, there could, however, remain other obstacles to the freedom of establishment, i.e. the numerous requirements of the Member States with regard to the training of employed and self-employed persons, and the detailed arrangements for pursuing industrial and commercial activities. Even though these requirements were not in themselves discriminatory, they could impede the free establishment, if they differed from country to country and obliged the interested person to **take a new examination** for the recognition of his or her professional competence. That is why Article 47 of the EC Treaty empowers the Council and the Parliament to issue directives for the mutual recognition of diplomas, certificates and other evidence of formal qualifications and for the coordination of national provisions concerning the taking up and pur-

---

[1]   Directive 2004/38, OJ L 158, 30.04.2004.

[2]   Directive 64/221, OJ 56, 04.04.1964 and OJ L 14, 20.01.1975.

[3]   COM (1999) 372, 19 July 1999.

suit of activities as self-employed persons. Such directives have in fact been adopted for certain professions, notably those of nurses, doctors, architects and lawyers.

However, the issuing of Directives aimed at the mutual recognition of diplomas, certificates and other evidence of formal qualification is not necessary any more, since the Community has adopted a **general system for the recognition of higher-education diplomas** awarded on completion of professional education and training of at least three years' duration[1]. The salient features of this system are the following: the principle of mutual trust amongst the Member States; the principle of the comparability of university studies between Member States; the mutual recognition of diplomas without prior harmonisation of the conditions for taking up and pursuing occupations, and lastly the principle that any divergence between Member States, in particular as regards training, should be offset by vocational experience. This system means, provided that the persons pursuing a profession fulfil certain minimum conditions as to qualifications, experience and professional education, that their qualifications will be recognised in all Member States and they will be authorised to pursue their activities without restriction.

A similar system relates to diplomas and certificates awarded on completion of **professional education and training of fewer than three years** of higher education or not covered by higher education. It covers two training levels: higher education or post-secondary diplomas where course duration is less than three years and secondary education diplomas. It also applies to certain non-graduates who have acquired professional experience[2]. There is provision for link-up between the two systems in order to cover professions that fall under the first system in one Member State and under the second in another.

A simple mechanism exists also for **recognising qualifications for professional activities** outside the scope of the general systems above, notably in the distributive trade and craft sectors. The directive that establishes it is based on the principle of the equivalence of qualifications[3]. A Member State may not, on the grounds of inadequate qualifications, refuse to permit a national of another Member State to take up or pursue any of the activities listed in the directive, without having first compared the knowledge and skills certified by the diplomas, certificates or other evidence of formal qualifications obtained by the beneficiary with those required under its own national rules. Where, the comparative examination shows a substantial difference, the host Member State must give the beneficiary the opportunity, either to demonstrate that he or she has acquired the knowledge and skills which were lacking or to undergo an adaptation period. According to the Court, all qualifications and experience must be

---

[1] Directive 89/48, OJ L 19, 24.01.1989 and Directive 2001/19, OJ L 206, 31.07.2001.
[2] Directive 92/51, OJ L 209, 24.07.1992 and Directive 2001/19, OJ L 206, 31.07.2001.
[3] Directive 1999/42, OJ L 201, 31.07.1999.

taken into account, that is to say, both those acquired in another Member State and those acquired in a non-member country[1].

6.6. *Freedom to provide services*

Article 49 (TEC) provides that restrictions on "freedom to provide services" within the Community shall be "abolished in respect of nationals of Member States who are established in a State of the Community other than that of the person for whom the services are intended". Any discrimination concerning the provision of services on the basis of nationality is prohibited directly by this Article (without the need of specific Community legislation). Under Article 50 (TEC), **services shall be considered as such** where they are normally provided for remuneration, in so far as they are not governed by the provisions relating to freedom of movement for goods, capital and persons. This Article specifies, however, that the provisions on the free movement of services **cover all activities of an industrial or commercial character** or of craftsmen and the activities of the professions.

The activity must be limited in time, must normally be pursued against payment and must involve some form of foreign aspect, unless the border is physically crossed. The person providing a service may, in order to do so, temporarily pursue his activity in the State where the service is provided, under the same conditions as are imposed by that State on its own nationals (third paragraph of Article 50 TEC). Services provided under a contract outside the country of establishment may be of a long duration. There is nothing, moreover, to preclude an activity for the provision of services from being of a magnitude such as to necessitate the acquisition of real estate in the country of provision of services. However, to constitute a provision of services rather than a permanent establishment, the person providing the service must remain established in his own country and his services must cross borders [see section 6.5.]. It appears that the freedom of establishment and the freedom to provide services cannot be clearly distinguished in all situations and that they often go together, since a person or company seeks establishment in another Member State in order to provide services in that state. This is why the two freedoms are usually considered as **one: the freedom of establishment and provision of services**.

Services represent almost 60% of the value added of the Community economy and cover a vast spread of economic activities, from banks and insurance to transport and tourism, not to mention data processing and management consultancy. They therefore play an increasingly large part in the economy and employment and are a linchpin for smooth operation of the EU's internal market. Their liberalisation is based on **the principle of mutual recognition**, according to which, if a service is lawfully authorised

---

[1]   Judgment of 14 September 2000, Case C-238/98, Hocsman, ECR 2000, p. I-6623.

in one Member State it must be open to users in the other Member States without having to comply with every detail of the legislation of the host country, except those concerning consumer protection. Control has to be exercised by the Government in the territory of which the company providing the services is established, with the authorities of the country in which the service is performed merely ensuring that certain basic rules relating to commercial conduct are observed. This system applies both to the traditional fields of transport, insurance and banking and to the new fields of services, such as information technology, marketing and audio-visual services.

Financial services - banks, insurance companies and stock exchanges - which are closely monitored by the official authorities, are particularly important, as they constitute a vast market and are indispensable activities for the proper functioning of the other economic sectors. Efficient and transparent financial markets foster growth and employment by better allocation of capital and reducing its cost. They therefore play an essential role in supporting entrepreneurial culture and promoting access to and use of new technologies. The freedoms of establishment and provision of services in the common market required that those services be liberalised from the protectionist measures applied by most Member States. This liberalisation, however, should reconcile two contradictory requirements, viz. the need to maintain very stringent criteria for control and financial security and the need to leave the branch concerned enough flexibility for it to be able to meet the new and ever-more complex requirements of its customers throughout the European market, particularly since the introduction of the euro. The Financial Services Committee helps define the medium- and long-term Community strategy for financial services issues examined below[1].

6.6.1. Banking

All restrictions on freedom of establishment and freedom to provide services in respect of self-employed activities of **banks and other financial institutions** have been abolished since the 1970s. The laws, regulations and administrative provisions of the Member States relating to the taking up and pursuit of the business of credit institutions have been coordinated within a single regulatory framework[2]. The right of access is based on the mutual recognition of supervision systems, i.e. application of the principle of supervision of a credit institution by the Member State in which it has its head office, and the issue of a "**single bank licence**" which is valid throughout the Community[3]. The single licence authorises a bank established in a Member State to open branches without any other formali-

---

[1] Decision 2003/165, OJ L 67, 12.03.2003.
[2] Directive 2000/12, OJ L 126, 26.05.2000 and Directive 2004/39, OJ L 145, 30.04.2004.
[3] Directive 89/646, OJ L 386, 30.12.1989 and Directive 92/30, OJ L 110, 28.04.1992.

ties or to propose its services in the partner countries. The principle of reciprocity governs the opening in the Community of subsidiaries of banks from non-member countries.

In the European internal market, the transparency, performance and stability of cross-border payment systems should match the properties of the best domestic payment systems. To this effect, a Parliament and Council Directive requires banks to execute **cross-border credit transfers** within reasonable time-limits (five banking business days for the originator's institution and one banking business day for the beneficiary's institution), makes double-charging illegal, requires the reimbursement of the full amount (up to a ceiling of EUR 12 500) in the event of non-execution of transfers and enhances transparency concerning the conditions applying to transfers[1]. A Commission notice supplementing this Directive provides a framework allowing banks to set in place cooperation arrangements aimed at making cross-border credit transfers more efficient without unduly restricting competition, particularly concerning market access and price competition[2].

A Directive on **deposit-guarantee schemes** is designed to protect depositors in the event of an authorised credit institution failing[3]. It stipulates that there must be a guarantee scheme in all Member States, financed by the banking sector and covering all deposits up to EUR 20 000 per depositor (EUR 15 000 in Spain, Portugal, Greece and Luxembourg). The scheme covers depositors not only in institutions in the Member State which authorise them, but also those in branches of such institutions set up in other Member States.

A clear regulatory framework for **electronic money** in the single market aims to enhance business and consumer confidence in this new form of payment, while ensuring that equal competitive conditions prevail for traditional credit institutions and other companies which issue electronic money[4]. Electronic money institutions are included within the general scope of the provisions of the banking coordination directives. Companies which issue electronic money but which do not wish to provide the whole range of banking services have nonetheless the opportunity to operate throughout the single market on the basis of a single licence issued by a single Member State, which places them on an equal footing with credit institutions [see also sections 14.2.1. and 17.3.5.].

6.6.2. Insurance

The laws, regulations and administrative provisions relating to the taking-up and pursuit of the business of **direct insurance other than life in-**

---

[1] Directive 97/5, OJ L 43, 14.02.1997.
[2] OJ C 251, 27.09.1995.
[3] Directive 94/19, OJ L 135, 31.05.1994.
[4] Directive 2000/46, OJ L 275, 27.10.2000.

surance have been coordinated[1] and the effective exercise of freedom to provide insurance services in the Community is a reality[2]. Community arrangements cover major industrial and commercial risks and provide adequate protection for minor consumers. Also coordinated are the legislations of the Member States concerning **credit insurance** and **suretyship insurance**, on the one hand,[3] and **legal expenses insurance**[4], on the other.

The coordination of the provisions of the Member States and the freedom to provide services **in the field of life assurance** offer policy-holders the choice between all the different types of contract available in the Community, while guaranteeing them adequate protection. The freedoms of establishment and provision of services are implemented through the mutual recognition of authorisations and prudential control systems, thereby making it possible to grant a single authorisation valid throughout the Community[5]. The coordination of the basic rules of prudential and financial supervision provides for single authorisation valid throughout the Community, along with the checking of all of a broker's activities by the Member State of origin.

A **single authorisation system** enables an insurance company with its registered office in a Community Member State to open branches and operate services in all the Member States without the need for authorisation procedures in each country[6]. This system is designed to ensure the free movement of insurance products within the Community and give European citizens the opportunity to take out insurance with any Community insurer, thus finding the coverage best suited to their needs at the lowest cost, while enjoying an adequate level of protection. An Insurance Committee helps the Commission exercise the implementation powers conferred on it by the Council in the field of direct insurance[7].

The approximation of the laws of the Member States relating to insurance against **civil liability in respect of the use of motor vehicles**, and to the enforcement of the obligation to insure against such liability affords adequate protection for the victims of road accidents, irrespective of the Member State in which the accident occurred[8]. The Community legislation imposes compulsory cover for all passengers of the vehicle, covering the entire territory of the Community, including cases where the passenger is the owner, the holder of the vehicle or the insured person himself[9]. Thanks to this legislations and to the Multilateral Guarantee Agreement between national insurers' bureaux signed in Madrid on March 1991, Member

---

[1] First Council Directive 73/239, OJ L 228, 16.08.1973 and Directive 2002/87, OJ L 35, 11.02.2002.
[2] Directive 88/357, OJ L 172, 04.07.1988 and Directive 92/49, OJ L 228, 11.08.1992.
[3] Directive 87/343, OJ L 185, 04.07.1987.
[4] Directive 87/344, OJ L 185, 04.07.1987.
[5] Directive 2002/83, OJ L 345, 19.12.2002 and directive 2004/66, OJ L 168, 01.05.2004.
[6] Directive 92/49, OJ L 228, 11.08.1992 and Directive 2002/87, OJ L 35, 11.02.2003.
[7] Directive 91/675, OJ L 374, 31.12.1991.
[8] Directive 2000/26, OJ L 181, 20.07.2000.
[9] Directive 90/232, OJ L 129, 19.05.1990.

States do not need to make any checks on insurance against civil liability in respect of vehicles which are normally based in a Member State or in certain third countries[1].

6.6.3. Stock exchanges and financial services

Community law on stock exchanges and other securities markets is directed towards widening the range of investments at Community level while protecting investors. The conditions for the admission of securities to official stock exchange listing are coordinated and the **single market in securities** is a reality[2]. Investment services in the securities field can be freely conducted, although monitored, throughout the EU financial area by the Directive on markets in financial instruments[3]. This directive establishes a comprehensive regulatory framework governing the organised execution of investor transactions by exchanges, other trading systems and investment firms and makes sure investors enjoy a high level of protection when employing investment firms, wherever they are located in the EU. An investment firm in any Member State can carry out its activities anywhere in the European Union on the basis of a single authorisation (called a "European passport) issued by the Member State of origin. The conditions governing authorisation and business activity have been harmonised for this purpose. Prudential supervision, based on uniform rules, is carried out by the authorities of the home Member State, but in cooperation with the authorities of the host Member State. Investment firms have right of access to all the regulated markets in the EU. Common standards pertain to the prudential supervision of financial conglomerates (credit institutions, insurance undertakings and investment firms) in order to create a level playing field and legal certainty for the financial establishments concerned.

The equity capital of investment firms and credit institutions must be adequate to safeguard market stability, guarantee an identical level of **protection against bankruptcy** to investors throughout the European Union and to ensure fair competition between banks, which are subject to specific prudential provisions, and investment societies on the securities market. In order to fulfil these objectives, a Directive lays down minimum initial capital requirements and sets the equity capital, which must permanently be held in order to cover position, settlement, exchange and interest rate risks[4]. All Member States must provide for minimum compensation for investors in the event of the failure of an investment firm, authorised to provide services throughout the Union[5]. In cases of insolvency, collateral security is provided[6]. The directive setting up common rules for collateral

---

[1] Commission Decision 91/323, OJ L 177, 05.07.1991.
[2] Directive 2001/34, OJ L 184, 06.07.2001 and Directive 2003/71, OJ L 345, 31.12.2003.
[3] Directive 2004/39, OJ L 145, 30.04.2004.
[4] Directive 93/6, OJ L 141, 11.06.1993 and Directive 2004/39, OJ L 145, 30.04.2004.
[5] Directive 97/9, OJ L 84, 26.03.1997.
[6] Directive 98/26, OJ L 166, 11.06.1998.

pledged to payment and securities settlement systems aims to limit credit risk and improve the functioning and stability of the European financial markets[1].

In order to combat fraudulent use of privileged stock exchange information, ensure the integrity of European financial markets and enhance investor confidence in those markets a directive prohibits **insider dealing and market manipulation (market abuse)**[2]. Member States must prohibit any person who possesses inside information (as defined in the directive) from using that information by acquiring or disposing of for his own account or for the account of a third party, either directly or indirectly, financial instruments to which that information relates. "Market manipulation" means notably transactions or dissemination of information, which give false or misleading signals as to the supply of, demand for or price of financial instruments or which employ fictitious devices or any other form of deception or contrivance.

6.6.4. Services of general interest

Services of general interest are "market" and "non-market" services which the public authorities class as being of general interest and subject to specific public service obligations. Article 86 of the EC Treaty specifies that undertakings entrusted with the operation of (market) services of general economic interest are subject to the rules contained in the Treaty, in particular to the rules on competition, in so far as the application of such rules does not obstruct the performance of the particular tasks assigned to them (postal, telecommunications, transport, electricity, broadcasting, etc.). However, advantages granted to operators of these services must not enable them to compete unfairly at the expense of other companies[3]. The evolutionary concept of "**universal service**", developed by the Community institutions, refers to a set of general interest requirements, which should be satisfied by the operators of such services to make sure that all citizens have access to certain essential services of high quality at prices they can afford[4]. It is sensitive to national diversity and takes into consideration the special features of the European model of society [see section 13.1.].

Article 16 of the EC Treaty specifies that, without prejudice to Articles 73, 86 and 87 (TEC), and given the place occupied by services of general economic interest in the **shared values of the Union**, the Community and the Member States must take care that such services operate on the basis of principles and conditions which enable them to fulfil their missions. A Protocol to the EC Treaty inserted at Amsterdam asserts that **public service broadcasting** is directly related to the democratic, social and cultural

---

[1] Directive 2002/47, OJ L 168, 27.06.2002.
[2] Directive 2003/6, OJ L 96, 12.04.2003.
[3] COM (2002) 636, 27 November 2002.
[4] COM (2000) 580 and COM (2001) 598, 17 October 2001.

needs of each society and to the need to preserve media pluralism. Therefore, the provisions of the Treaty are without prejudice to the competence
of Member States to provide for the funding of public service broadcasting,
provided that certain conditions are met, notably that such funding does not
affect trading conditions and competition in the Community [see section
10.2.].

6.7. Free movement of capital

Freedom of capital movement is another essential element for the
proper functioning of the large European internal market. The liberalisation
of payment transactions is a vital **complement to the free movement of
goods, persons and services**. Borrowers - individuals and companies notably SMEs - must be able to obtain capital where it is cheapest and best
tailored to their needs, while investors and suppliers of capital must be able
to offer their resources on the market where there is the greatest interest.
That is why it is important that the member states of a common market free
capital movements and allow payments to be made in the currency of the
member state in which the creditor or beneficiary is established. Obviously, all these conditions must pre-exist before the passage to the stage of
an economic and monetary union, involving the circulation of a single currency.

To this end, a 1988 Directive ensures the **full liberalisation of capital
movements**[1]. Under this Directive, all restrictions on capital movements
between persons (natural or legal) resident in Member States were removed in the beginning of the nineties. Monetary and quasi-monetary operations (financial loans and credits, operations in current and deposit accounts and operations in securities and other instruments normally dealt in
on the money market) in particular were liberalised.

However, the EC Treaty, which replaced the EEC Treaty in 1992, went
even further than the 1988 Directive in the liberalisation of capital movements. The principle of the free movement of capital and payments is now
expressly laid down in the Treaty. Article 56 (TEC) declares, in fact, that
all restrictions on the movement of capital between Member States and between Member States and third countries are prohibited. The main change
as compared to the previous situation is the extension in all but a few cases
of the **obligation to liberalise capital movements to and from third
countries**. Nevertheless, Article 59 authorises temporary safeguard measures to be taken where they are justified on serious political grounds or
where capital movements to and from third countries cause serious difficulties for the functioning of economic and monetary union. In addition,
Article 58 authorises Member States to take all requisite measures to prevent infringements of national law and regulations.

---

[1]   Directive 88/361, OJ L 178, 08.07.1988 and OJ L 1, 03.01.1994.

On the basis of these provisions and of those liberalising banking, stock-exchange and insurance services [see sections 6.6.1. to 6.6.3.], the Community **financial market has been completely liberalised** since January 1, 1993. European businesses and individuals have access to the full range of options available in the Member States as regards banking services, mortgage loans, securities and insurance. They can choose what is best suited to their specific needs or requirements for their daily lives and for their professional activities in the large market. The Member States must, however, dissuade the exploitation of the financial market for illegal purposes, notably laundering money generated by criminal activities[1].

6.8. Trans-European Networks

A common policy on infrastructure trans-European networks **(TENs)** is needed for the good functioning of the common market. Indeed, the integration of national markets through the completion of the internal market can only have full economic and social impact, if businesses and citizens enjoy trans-European **transport, telecommunications and energy networks**, which optimise the use of the various legal instruments governing the operation of this market. With a view to enabling citizens, economic operators and regional and local authorities to derive full benefit from the setting up of an area without internal frontiers, the Community strives to promote the interconnection and inter-operability of national networks and access to these networks. It takes account in particular of the need to link island, landlocked and peripheral regions with the central regions of the Community (Art. 154 TEC). To speed up the implementation of networks, and to encourage public-private partnerships, the complex national rules and procedures are streamlined in the case of TENs, by having one approval procedure instead of requiring a series of different approvals for each element of the project.

Article 155 (TEC) provides that, in order to foster the **completion of trans-European networks**, the Community:

- establishes a series of guidelines identifying projects of common interest and providing the objectives, the priorities, the general lines of Community action and coordination with national decisions. These guidelines are adopted in accordance with the procedure contained in Article 251 (co-decision Council-Parliament) and require the approval of the Member State in question:

- adopts measures designed to harmonise technical standards;

- supports the financial efforts made by the Member States for projects of common interest, by carrying out feasibility studies and granting loan guarantees or interest rate subsidies. These decisions are taken by the Council and the European Parliament pursuant to the procedure of Article 251 (TEC);

---

[1] Directive 91/308, OJ L 166, 28.06.1991 and Directive 2001/97, OJ L 344, 28.12.2001.

- contributes to the financing of specific projects in the area of transport infrastructure through the Cohesion Fund.

The **financial instruments**, which facilitate the realisation of these networks, are notably the Cohesion Fund, certain actions provided for under the Structural Funds Regulations, the loans of the European Investment Bank and the loan guarantees of the European Investment Fund [see section 12.3.]. A Council Regulation lays down the legal rules for the granting of Community financial assistance in the field of trans-European networks[1]. It defines the types of aid, the project selection criteria and the procedures for examining, assessing and monitoring applications for funding. It encourages public private partnerships and risk-capital participation. The Community support to TENs can take the form of contributions to feasibility studies, interest-rate subsidies, loan guarantees and, in duly justified cases, direct grants to investments.

6.9. Appraisal and outlook

It took nearly a quarter of a century after the removal of customs duties and quantitative restrictions between Member States to complete in tandem customs union and common market. However delayed, the **achievement of a single market** is a great step forward in the process of European integration. Free movement reduces the manufacturing and transport costs of goods, facilitates exports and the realisation of important economies. The reduction of administrative and financial costs of intra-Community trade and the realisation of economies of scale tend to liberate the dynamism and the creativity of European businesses and to give them a solid base from which to tackle international competitiveness. In a global economy characterised by fierce competition, particularly between multinational companies, the economies and the companies of small and medium European countries would certainly be much worse off than they are today, if it was not for the large internal market that is now their safe haven and springboard for external markets. This is why, business interest groups back the multinational integration process [see section 1.1.2]. On its part, the Community helps businesses and particularly SMEs striving to adapt to the conditions of the single market [see section 17.2.].

The common market has also boosted the welfare of the citizens of the Member States. European consumers, previously confined in their respective national markets, now enjoy a huge choice of high quality goods and services at prices dictated by free competition. The free movement of workers, freedom to provide services and freedom of establishment for self-employed persons constitute **fundamental rights**, guaranteeing the citizens of the Community the right to pursue an occupation in any Member State. The citizen of a Member State, be he or she worker, businessman

---

[1] Regulation 2236/95, OJ L 228, 23.09.1995 and Regulation 807/2004, OJ L 143, 30.04.2004.

or tourist, can no longer be regarded as an alien in another Member State, but as an EU citizen, and no discrimination against him or her is permitted [see section 9.1.].

The implementation of the fundamental freedoms of the common market allows the **production factors of work and capital to operate** without hindrance. Businesses can manufacture and sell their products in accordance with a system of free competition in the Member State in which conditions are most advantageous to them. They can set themselves up wherever they wish in the common market and can call on a multitude of services and sources of capital, which exist in all the Member States. The liberalisation of capital movements contributes to a better allocation of resources within the Union. Public procurement in all Member States is open to tenders from all Community companies. In banking and insurance sectors, where obstacles to cross-border trade were particularly pronounced, the increase in cross-border competition is reflected in a growing number of branches and outlets in other Member States of the Union. The common market has, thus, demonstrated the benefits of multinational integration both concerning economic efficiency and the welfare of the citizens of the Member States.

All this **does not mean that all is well in the best possible single market**. The priority is now to make it work efficiently. This implies, in particular, adequate implementation of the measures taken for the completion of the internal market in every Member State, effective opening-up of public contracts, further mutual recognition of standards, more transparent rules for the internal market and simplification of the taxation system. These requirements of the good functioning of the common market are not met uniformly and constantly in all Member States. Therefore, penalties for failure to comply with the obligations arising out of the Community law in the internal market field must be reinforced and enforced. Hence, the common market is not yet a completely integrated internal market and this fact handicaps European companies competing in the global market with companies, which have as a base a large internal market.

Moreover, although the common market provides a basis for common policies, it cannot by itself solve the structural problems weighing down on European economies. Strong common economic, industrial and research policies are needed to hasten the modernisation of European economies and enhance the competitiveness of European companies in the global market. These policies can and should also boost employment, while safeguarding the European social model. It is an illusion to think that European citizens may be satisfied with a common market that promotes the interests of businesses and not their own interests as workers and consumers. They rightly see the common market not as an end in itself but as a means to their own welfare. If it is not successful in this end, the common market is an incomplete tool and European leaders should perfect it.

Bibliography on the Common Market

1. BARNARD Catherine. "The substantive law of the EU: the four freedoms". Oxford: Oxford University Press, 2004.
2. DEUTSCHE BUNDESBANK. "Regulation of the European securities markets", *Deutsche Bank Monthly Report*, v. 56, n. 7, July 2004, p. 33-48.
3. ENGEL Charles, ROGERS John. "European product market integration after the euro", *Economic Policy*, n. 39, July 2004, p. 347-384.
4. EUROPEAN COMMISSION. *Internal Market Strategy priorities 2003-2006*. Luxembourg: EUR-OP*, 2004.
5. EUROPEAN COMMITTEE FOR STANDARDIZATION (CEN). *Trading with and within Europe: Directives and Related Standards*. Brussels: CEN, 2003.
6. OLIVER Peter, ROTH Wulf-Henning. "The internal market and the four freedoms", *Common Market Law Review*, v. 41, n. 2, April 2004, p. 407-441.
7. PITELL Lisa. "Non-transferability of software licences in the European Union", *European Intellectual Property Review*, v. 26, n. 9, September 2004, p. 390-401.
8. RANDZIO-PLATH Christa. "Europe prepares for a single financial market", *Intereconomics*, v. 39, n. 3, May/June 2004, p. 142-146.
9. TRUILHÉ-MARENGO Eve. "Towards a European law of contracts", *European Law Journal*, v. 10, n. 4, July 2004, p. 463-478.
10. WOODS Lorna. *Free movement of goods and services within the European Community*. Aldershot: Ashgate, 2004.

DISCUSSION TOPICS

1. Could the common market be built on a free trade area agreement or did it presuppose a customs union? Reflect on the evolution of the multinational integration process.
2. Why has the completion of the common market been retarded and how has it been brought about? Consider the role of the common institutions in the completion of the common market.
3. The EFTA countries participating in the EEA agreement apply the fundamental freedoms of a common market. Do they still form a free trade area or have they moved to the stage of the common market?
4. Why does the realisation of the fundamental freedoms of a common market necessitate common policies and harmonisation of the legislation of the member states?
5. What is the "acquis communautaire" of the common market and how does it affect other common policies?

Chapter 7

ECONOMIC AND MONETARY UNION

Diagram of the chapter

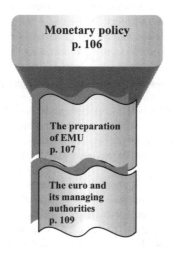

Monetary policy
p. 106

The preparation
of EMU
p. 107

The euro and
its managing
authorities
p. 109

Economic policy
p. 112

Economic
convergence
p. 113

Budgetary
discipline
p. 114

Financial
solidarity
p. 116

Economic and monetary union (EMU) is **an advanced stage of multinational integration** involving a common monetary policy and closely coordinated economic policies of the member states. EMU has to be based on a common market in goods and services, but is itself necessary for the proper functioning of the common market, as exchange rate variations between Member States' currencies hinder trade and investments.

In the early 1970s, the original six members of the European Economic Community tried already to establish an EMU and failed. The reasons were both external - the collapse of the international monetary system - and internal - the non-completion of the stage of the common market. This failure served, however, as a learning experience. The Member States of the European Community understood that they could not rush the multinational integration process, that they should complete the common market stage, adopt many accompanying common policies and commit themselves by treaty to the goal of EMU. The economic and monetary union initiated by the Maastricht Treaty [see section 2.2.] and completed for most Member States with the circulation of the euro is an evidence of the continuity of the multinational integration process [see section 1.1.2.].

7.1. The need for EMU

During the stage of the customs union, exchange rate variations are still possible and, to a certain extent, desirable, because the member states conserve the autonomy of their economic policies and can, by means of those variations, adjust their economies to the new conditions of competition prevailing between themselves and with the rest of the world. During the stage of the common market, however, the **exchange rate variations become more and more inconvenient** for the partners. While equal conditions of competition should prevail in a common market, the devaluation of the currency of a Member State could provide a competitive advantage to its industries, whereas the revaluation of the currency of another Member State could handicap its exports. In fact, **the devaluation** of the currency of a country, which is a member of a common market, could have an equivalent effect to imposing customs tariffs on all imported products and subsidising that country's exports. Conversely, **the revaluation** of a member country's currency would mean restricting its exports and encouraging its imports, factors which could get in the way of business expansion in countries with strong currencies.

A single market without a single currency is exposed to monetary and economic problems. On the **monetary level**, because of the possibility of upward or downward change in the value of certain currencies of the member states, there is an exchange risk in the event of credit sales to a business in a partner country, and this greatly restricts credit exports in member states. Indeed, an exchange rate adjustment, even a moderate one, may substantially alter the contractual obligations of firms operating in the different member states and at the same time affect the relative wealth of citizens and the purchasing power of consumers.

Currency fluctuations can penalise both investors who have financed their **foreign investments** by exporting capital from their countries and those who have had recourse to the resources of the host country. In the first case, devaluation of the currency of the country in which the investment took place or revaluation of the currency of the investor's country erodes the repatriated capital and profits. In the second case, devaluation in the investor's country or revaluation in the host country means higher amortisation and therefore a greater investment cost than expected. These risks could hinder businesses from investing in partner countries or from borrowing in them capital needed for their investments. Exchange risks, thus, would limit interpenetration of financial markets and therefore economic growth in a single market without a single currency.

From the **economic point of view**, if the common market were divided into autonomous markets as a result of divergent economic policies followed by the member states, the advantages expected of it, in particular economic growth and economic stability, would be greatly reduced. In reality, the interdependence of the economies of members of a common market accelerates the **transmission of cyclical fluctuations** and of the effects of measures intended to deal with them. Attainment of the economic objectives of a member state depends to a large extent on economic conditions in the other member states. An unfavourable economic situation in one member state leads to a reduction in its imports from the other members of the common market, which are affected in turn. On the other hand, a favourable economic situation in one member country has positive effects on the economies of the others and feedback effects on the former. If there were no coordination of economic policies, the differences in economic development - which would take the form of high interest rates in some member states and low rates in others and, conversely, of low exchange rates in the former and high exchange rates in the latter - could result in undesirable capital movements, that is to say from the poorest to the richest countries.

Negative effects can also ensue from **divergences in national short-term economic policies**. If, for example, a member state wished to pursue a deflationary policy by raising interest rates, whilst another member state followed an expansionist policy with low interest rates, capital would emigrate, for short-term investments, from the second country to the first and prevent the attainment of the objectives of both. Even if they pursued the same objectives, but by different means, two member states of a common market without a single currency could bring about undesirable movements of capital. If, for example, in order to pursue a deflationary policy, a state imposed quantitative restrictions on credit, whilst another raised interest rates, capital from the first might go to short-term investment in the second, causing balance of payments problems in the first and inflationary pressures in the second.

The semi-integration, or imperfect integration, which characterises a common market, generates situations that are unstable, and in the long term intolerable, for member states' economic policies. Those policies are no longer sufficient for regulating short-term economic situations because, firstly, some of their causes lie abroad and, secondly, some economic policy instruments are already beyond the control of the national authorities, including customs duties, import restrictions and export incentives [see sections 5.2. and 23.1.].It can be seen that the increasing interpenetration of the economies in a common market leads to a **dwindling of the independence of national short-term economic policies.** This means that the economies of the member states of a common market cannot be managed effectively by national authorities, i.e. the appropriate ministries and the central banks of those states. It becomes manifest that the loss of autonomy of the national economic and monetary policies of the member states of a common market needs to be counterbalanced by the establishment of a common economic and a single monetary policy. Hence, the member states of a common market that want to complete it need to pass to the next stage of multinational integration, which is that of economic and monetary union.

If economic conditions in the common market are to resemble those in an internal market, it is first and foremost necessary to eliminate exchange rate adjustments, which disrupt trade and investment by affecting in an unpredictable way their profitability. To this end, the member states of a common market must agree the full and **irreversible conversion of their currencies** at fixed parities or, better, **adopt a single currency**. In either case, they would thus establish a monetary union within which transaction costs (the costs of foreign-exchange transactions or the costs of exchange rate cover), would disappear altogether. The second possibility, however, which was rightly preferred by the EU, has some additional advantages. The single currency will permit a genuine comparison of prices of goods and services within the single market, it will become one of the main exchange and reserve currencies in the world and it will allow Europeans to pay for their imports from third countries in their own currency.

In other words, the single currency is a necessary attribute of a genuine single market. This is the reason why, in view of the completion of the single market, the Member States of the Community decided, in December 1991, in Maastricht to engage themselves in the track of economic and monetary union. By greatly facilitating the functioning of the single market, the single currency should provide a stable macroeconomic environment, which would be of considerable benefit to businesses. Under ceteris paribus conditions, this environment should normally foster trade, improve the allocation of resources, encourage savings, enhance growth and in the end create more employment.

7.2. The single monetary policy

The Treaty of Rome did not provide for the monetary organisation of the Community, because that Treaty aimed at the realisation of the first two stages of European integration, the customs union and the common. Moreover, at the time of drafting of the EEC Treaty an international monetary organisation existed, namely the Bretton Woods system, which ensured the convertibility of all the currencies of the Western World at fixed parities. This system warranted monetary stability, which is indispensable in a common market.

It was just at the time when the Bretton Woods system collapsed, **in early 1971**, that the Member States of the Community **began their effort to organise their monetary affairs** in an economic and monetary union. Acting on a proposal from the Commission based on the "Werner Report", the Council and the Representatives of the Governments of the Member States expressed their political will to establish economic and monetary union in accordance with a plan by stages beginning retroactively on 1 January 1971[1]. At the conclusion of that process the Community should have

---

[1]   OJ C 28, 27.03.1971, p. 1-4.

constituted a single currency area within the international system, possessing such powers and responsibilities in economic and monetary matters as would enable its institutions to administer the union.

With hindsight, that initial effort looks like a headlong rush without sound foundations, as it was not based on a real common market. However, that initial effort enabled the Members States to acquire precious experience and devise instruments and mechanisms that were, in 1979, transferred to the European Monetary System (which tried with variable success to stabilise the exchange rates of the common market countries), have been improved over time and were used for the second effort at establishing an economic and monetary union in the 1990s. This second effort had a better foothold than the first. The common market stage had been completed, the Member States had developed closer links through common policies and had engaged themselves in the Maastricht Treaty to advance in the stage of the economic and monetary union [see section 2.2.].

7.2.1. The preparation of EMU

The Treaty on European Union, signed at Maastricht in 1991 [see section 2.2.], provided for the introduction of a single monetary policy based upon **a single currency managed by a single and independent central bank**. According to the Treaty, the primary objective of the single monetary policy and exchange rate policy should be to maintain price stability and, without prejudice to this objective, to support the general economic policies in the Community, in accordance with the principle of an open market economy with free competition. These activities of the Member States and the Community should entail compliance with the following guiding principles: stable prices, sound public finances and monetary conditions and a sustainable balance of payments (Art. 4 TEC).

The 1971 experience served the EU to well prepare the changeover to the single currency. Although economic and monetary union was envisaged as a single process, there were, in fact, **three stages involved**. The **first stage**, marking the beginning of the whole process, came with the entry into force of the Directive on the complete liberalisation of capital movements in July 1990 [see section 6.7.]. The central objectives of this stage were greater convergence of economic policies and closer cooperation between central banks, incorporating greater consistency between monetary practices in the framework of the European Monetary System[1].

As provided for in Article 118 of the EC Treaty, the **composition of the basket of the ecu** was "frozen" on 1 November 1993, the date of the entry into force of the Maastricht Treaty, on the basis of the composition of the basket (in amounts of each national currency) defined on 21st September 1989 at the occasion of the entry into the basket of the peseta and the escudo. The European Council, meeting in Madrid on 15 and 16 December

---

[1] Decision 90/142, OJ L 78, 24.03.1990.

1995, decided that, as of the start of stage three, **the name given to the European currency should be the euro**, a name that symbolises Europe and should be the same in all the official languages of the European Union, taking into account the existence of different alphabets, i.e. the Latin and the Greek.

The **second stage** of economic and monetary union began on 1st January 1994 and ended on 31 December 1998. During that stage, the Treaty on European Union compelled each Member State to endeavour to avoid excessive public deficits and initiate steps leading to independence of its central bank, so that the future monetary union encompassed only countries which were well managed economically. A Council Regulation laid down detailed rules and definitions for the application of the excessive deficit procedure (EDP), including the definition of public debt, as well as rules for the reporting of data by the Member States to the Commission, which fulfils the role of statistical authority in the context of the EDP[1]. In the process leading to the **independence of central banks**, the Treaty prohibited them from granting governments overdraft facilities or any other type of credit facility and from purchasing public sector debt instruments directly from them (Art. 101 TEC). A Council Regulation clarified certain implications of this prohibition[2].

Together with the prohibition on the direct monetary financing of public deficits and in order to submit public borrowings to market discipline, the Treaty provided that public authorities should not have privileged access to financial institutions, unless this was based on prudential considerations (Article 102 TEC). The Treaty sought, thus, to institutionalise a sort of **market-induced budgetary control**. To this effect, a Council Regulation defined the terms "privileged access", "financial institutions", "prudential considerations" and "public undertakings"[3].

In **preparation for the move to the third stage**, the Treaty required a high degree of convergence assessed by reference to **four specific criteria** [see also section 7.3.1.]: (a) a rate of inflation which is close to that of the three best performing Member States in terms of price stability; (b) a government budgetary position without a deficit that is excessive, meaning a government deficit not exceeding 3% of GNP and total government debt not greater than 60% of GNP (subject to an appraisement by the Council deciding by qualified majority); (c) the durability of convergence achieved by the Member State being reflected in the long-term interest rate levels; and (d) the observance of the normal fluctuation margins provided for by the Exchange Rate Mechanism of the European Monetary System, for at least two years (Art. 121 TEC and Protocol on the excessive deficit procedure).

Following the procedure and the timetable set out in the EC Treaty, the Council, , meeting at the level of Heads of State or Government on 3 May

---

[1]   Regulation 3605/93, OJ L 332, 31.12.1993 and Regulation 475/2000, OJ L 58, 03.03.2000.

[2]   Regulation 3603/93, OJ L 332, 31.12.1993.

[3]   Regulation 3604/93, OJ L 332, 31.12.1993.

1998 decided that the 11 Member States **satisfied the necessary conditions for the adoption of the single currency** on 1 January 1999: Belgium, Germany, Spain, France, Ireland, Italy, Luxembourg, the Netherlands, Austria, Portugal and Finland. In July 2000, the Council agreed that Greece also fulfilled the convergence criteria and could therefore adopt the single currency. The Council had previously stated that Sweden did not at that stage fulfil the necessary conditions for the adoption of the single currency, because it did not participate in the mechanism of the European Monetary System. It did not examine whether the United Kingdom and Denmark fulfilled the conditions, because, in accordance with the relevant Treaty provisions, the United Kingdom notified the Council that it did not intend to move to the third stage of EMU on 1 January 1999 and Denmark notified the Council that it would not participate in the third stage of EMU. Member States benefiting from an "opt-out" and those, which do not meet the criteria from the outset, participate nevertheless in all the procedures (multilateral surveillance, excessive deficit...) designed to facilitate their future participation. The Governors of their central banks are members of the ECB General Council.

7.2.2. The euro and its supervising authorities

Stage three of EMU began on 1 January 1999 with the irrevocable fixing of conversion rates between the currencies of the participating countries and against the euro[1]. The ecu was replaced by the euro, and this became a currency in its own right, the currency of those Member States which participate fully in the single monetary policy (Art. 123 TEC). Since that date, monetary policy and the foreign exchange rate policy are conducted in euros, the use of the euro is encouraged in foreign exchange markets and new tradeable public debt must be issued in euros by the participating Member States. The participating Member States have a single monetary policy and a single currency - the euro[2]. They are monitored by the **European Central Bank (ECB)**, which replaced the European monetary Institute (provisional institution of the second stage) and formed together with the central banks of the Member States, the **European System of Central Banks (ESCB)**. Neither the ECB nor national central banks shall seek or take instructions from governments or Community institutions (Art. 108 TEC). The president, the vice-president and the other members of the Executive Board of the ECB were appointed by decision taken by common accord of the governments of the Member States, which adopted the single currency, after their appointments were endorsed by the European Parliament[3].

---

[1] Regulation 2866/98, OJ L 359, 31.12.1998 and Regulation 1478/2000, OJ L 167, 07.07.2000.

[2] Regulation 974/98, OJ L 139, 11.05.1998 and Regulation 2596/2000, OJ L 300, 29.11.2000.

[3] Recommendation 98/318, OJ L 139, 11.05.1998 and Decision 98/345, OJ L 154, 28.05.1998.

All central banks, including those not participating in the single monetary policy, are members of the ESCB from the start of the third stage. The **primary objective of the ESCB** is to maintain price stability. In addition, the ESCB must support the general economic policies in the Community with a view to contributing to the achievement of the objectives of the common policies referred to in Article 2 (TEC). The **basic tasks to be carried out through the ESCB** are: to define and implement the monetary policy of the Community; to conduct foreign exchange operations consistent with the provisions of Article 111 (TEC); to hold and manage the official foreign reserves of the Member States; and to promote the smooth operation of payment systems (Art. 105 TEC). However, exchange policy with regard to the currencies of third countries (US dollar, Japanese yen, etc.) is determined by the Council after consultation of the ECB (Article 111 TEC).

The **ECB** can adopt regulations and take decisions necessary for carrying out the tasks entrusted to the ESCB (Art. 110 TEC). National authorities must consult the ECB regarding draft legislation within its field of competence[1]. The ECB has powers to: apply minimum reserves and specify the remuneration of such reserves; impose fines and periodic penalty payments on firms for infringing its regulations or decisions[2]; and collect statistical information in order to carry out its tasks[3]. The ECB has the **exclusive right to authorise the issue of euro bank notes** within the Community. The ECB and the national central banks may issue such notes[4]. Member States may issue euro coins subject to approval by the ECB of the volume of the issue (Art. 106 TEC). The ECB must be consulted on any proposed Community act and may submit opinions to Community institutions or to national authorities on matters within its field of competence (Art. 105 TEC). A Council decision defines the scope and conditions of consultation of the Bank by national authorities concerning draft legislation within its field of competence[5].

The Amsterdam European Council of 16 and 17 June 1997 adopted a Resolution laying down the firm commitments of the Member States, the Commission and the Council regarding the implementation of the **Stability and Growth Pact** [see also section 7.3.2.]. In this Pact Member States commit themselves: to respect the medium term budgetary objective of "close to balance or in surplus" set out in their stability or convergence programmes; to correct excessive deficits as quickly as possible after their emergence; to make public, on their own initiative, recommendations made in accordance with Article 104 (TEC); and not seek an exemption from the excessive deficit procedure unless they are in severe recession characterised by a fall in real GDP of at least 0,75%.

---

[1]   Decision 98/415, OJ L 189, 03.07.1998.
[2]   Regulation 2531/98, OJ L 318, 27.11.1998 and regulation 134/2002, OJ L 24, 26.01.2002.
[3]   Regulation 2533/98, OJ L 318, 27.11.1998.
[4]   Decision ECB/1998/6, OJ L 8, 14.01.1999.
[5]   Decision 98/415, OJ L 189, 03.07.1998.

The Amsterdam European Council also agreed two Regulations that form part of the Stability and Growth Pact for ensuring budgetary discipline in the third stage of EMU. These Regulations set out a framework for **effective multilateral surveillance** and give precision to the excessive deficit procedure. The first concerns the continuity of contracts, the replacement of references to the ecu in legal instruments by references to the euro at a rate of one for one, the conversion rates and rounding rules[1]. In addition to this Regulation, the Directive on consumer protection in the indication of prices of products offered to consumers [see section 11.3.] sets down requirements concerning conversion rates, rounding rules, and the clarity and legibility of price displays[2].

The second Regulation provided for the conditions in which the currencies of the participating Member States would be replaced by the euro from 1 January 1999[3]. It also provided that, **as from 1 January 2002**, the European Central Bank and the central banks of the participating Member States should put into circulation banknotes denominated in euros and that, from that date, the euro notes and coins should be legal tender. A Regulation on denominations and technical specifications of euro coins intended for circulation provided that the first series of euro currency would consist of eight coins (1 cent, 2 cent, 5 cent, 10 cent, 20 cent, 50 cent, 1 euro and 2 euro)[4]. In parallel with the introduction of the euro on 1 January 2002, bank charges for cross-border payments in euro were brought into line with those applying at national level for euro transactions[5]. A Council Framework Decision aims at increasing protection against counterfeiting in connection with the introduction of the euro[6], while two Regulations lay down the measures necessary to this effect[7]. The Pericles exchange, assistance and training programme concentrates on promoting convergence of national measures so as to guarantee equivalent levels of protection of the euro against counterfeiting, on the basis of consideration of best practice[8].

At the starting date of the third stage, on 1 January 1999, the **exchange rate mechanism (ERM)** has replaced the European Monetary System, in order to link currencies of Member States outside the euro area to the euro and help to ensure that they orient their policies to stability, foster convergence and thereby help them in their efforts to adopt the euro. However, the voting rights of these Member States in the Council are suspended for all questions relating to the single currency. A central rate against the euro is defined for the currency of each Member State outside the euro area participating in the exchange rate mechanism. Accordingly, central rates are set for the "pre-in" currencies with a standard fluctuation band against the

---

[1] Regulation 1103/97, OJ L 162, 19.06.1997 and Regulation 2595/2000, OJ L 300, 29.11.2000.
[2] Directive 98/6, OJ L 80, 18.03.1998.
[3] Regulation 974/98, OJ L 139, 11.05.1998 and Regulation 2596/2000, OJ L 300, 29.11.2000.
[4] Regulation 975/98, OJ L 139, 11.05.1998 and Regulation 423/1999, OJ L 52, 27.02.1999.
[5] Regulation 2560/2001, OJ L 344, 28.12.2001.
[6] Framework Decision 2000/383/JHA, OJ L 140, 14.06.2000.
[7] Regulations 1338/2001 and 1339/2001, OJ L 181, 04.07.2001.
[8] Decisions 2001/923 and 2001/924, OJ L 334, 21.12.2001.

euro of 15% in either direction. Intervention at the margins will in principle be automatic and unlimited, with very short-term financing available,
but the European Central Bank and the central banks of the other participants could suspend intervention if this were to conflict with their primary
objective. On the other hand, formally agreed fluctuation bands narrower
then the standard one and backed up in principle by automatic intervention
and financing may be set at the request of the non-euro area Member State
concerned[1].

At 00.00 on 1 January 2002, the national currencies of the twelve
Euro-zone States ceased to exist. National notes and coins could be used in
most countries for a further eight weeks at the most, but it was no longer
possible to make payments in the old national currency units by card,
cheque or transfer. After this short period of dual circulation, during which
the old notes and coins were exchanged for the new ones, old banknotes
can be exchanged for a period of ten years only at central banks. The European institutions and the governments of the participating Member States
had carefully planned and therefore succeeded the tremendous enterprise of
the changeover to the euro. What these authorities had not foreseen and
hence neglected was the bid of many providers of goods and services to
profit from the rounding possibilities offered them by the new currency.
This uncontrolled profiteering has increased inflationary pressures in
economies already depressed from the unstable international environment.
Particularly vulnerable were the consumers of countries with multidigit
currencies, like Italy and Greece, who did not immediately perceive the
price increases in euro. The authorities of these countries should now do
their best to keep prices down. In the long term, however, it is probable
that heightened competition will stabilise prices inside the single market.

7.3. The common economic policy

The Treaty of Rome had considered it desirable that the Member
States **regard their conjunctural policies as a matter of common con-
cern**. Article 103 stipulated that they should consult each other and the
Commission on the measures to be taken in the light of the prevailing cir-
cumstances. Pursuant to that provision of the Treaty, the Council set up an
Economic Policy Committee for Short-term Economic and Financial
Policies[2]. That Committee, which consists of one representative for each
Member State and a Commission representative, has the task of preparing
the meetings of the **Economic and Financial Affairs (ECOFIN) Council**.
It is also responsible for the exchange, on a reciprocal and continuing ba-
sis, of information on decisions or measures envisaged by the Member
States which could have a considerable effect on the economies of the
other Member States or on the internal or external equilibrium of the

[1] OJ C 236, 02.08.1997, p. 5-6.
[2] Decision 74/122, OJ L 63, 05.03.1974.

Member State concerned or which could give rise to a considerable gap between the development of the economy of a country and the jointly defined medium-term objectives.

7.3.1. Economic convergence in the European Union

In contrast to monetary policy, Member States **retain ultimate responsibility for economic policy** within the economic and monetary union. They are, however, required to act in such a way as to respect the principle of an open market economy where competition reigns, to regard their economic policies as a matter of common concern and to conduct them with a view to contributing to the achievement of the objectives of the Community (Art. 98 and 99 TEC). Thus, the common economic policy complements the single monetary policy.

Since the second stage of EMU, i.e. since the 1st January 1994, economic policies of the Member States are coordinated at Community level. A Council Decision of 1990 is directed towards the attainment of progressive convergence of economic performance of the Member States[1]. To this effect the **Economic and Financial Affairs Council (ECOFIN),** acting by a qualified majority on a recommendation from the Commission, formulates, each year in the spring, a draft for the **broad economic policy guidelines (BEPGs)** of the Member States and of the Community, and reports its findings to the European Council. This discusses a conclusion on the broad guidelines of the economic policies of the Member States and of the Community. On this basis, the Commission recommends and the Council, acting on a qualified majority endorses the BEPGs, which lay down the common objectives in terms of inflation, public finance, exchange rate stability and employment (Art. 99 TEC)[2]. The BEPGs are at the centre of economic policy coordination in the European Union. They must be concise, concentrate on the main challenges facing the Union, with particular focus on the euro area, where coordination is most needed, and help to ensure that measures adopted in all Community economic coordination processes are consistent.

The Council, on the basis of reports submitted by the Commission, monitors economic developments in each of the Member States and in the Community as well as the consistency of economic policies with the broad guidelines (Art 121 TEC)[3]. This **multilateral monitoring** is based on convergence programmes presented by each Member State which specifically aim at addressing the main sources of difficulty in terms of convergence (Art. 99,3 TEC). It also involves a review of budgetary policies, with particular reference to the size and financing of deficits, if possible prior to the drafting of national budgets [see section 7.3.2.]. Multilateral monitoring

---

[1] Decision 90/141, OJ L 78, 24.03.1990.
[2] See for example the Recommendation of the Commission for 2003, COM (2003) 170, 8 April 2003 and Council Recommendation OJ L 195, 01.08.2003.
[3] See e.g., COM (97) 169, 23 April 1997.

aims at obtaining from the Member States reciprocal engagements for an autonomous coordination of their policies.

Where it is established that the economic policies of a Member State are not consistent with these guidelines, the Council may, acting by a qualified majority, make the necessary recommendations to the Member State concerned. It may decide to make its recommendations public (Art. 99,4 TEC). The Council may, acting unanimously on a proposal from the Commission, decide upon the measures appropriate to the economic situation, in particular if severe difficulties arise in the supply of certain products. **Where a Member State is in difficulties** or is seriously threatened with severe difficulties caused by exceptional occurrences beyond its control, the Council may, acting unanimously on a proposal from the Commission, grant, under certain conditions, Community financial assistance to the Member State concerned (Art. 100 TEC).

The move to the third stage of economic and monetary union has linked the economies of the Member States adopting the euro more closely together. They share a single monetary policy and a single exchange rate. Economic policies and wage determination, however, remain a national responsibility, subject to the provisions of Article 104 (TEC) and of the Stability and Growth Pact. Since national economic developments have an impact on inflation prospects in the euro zone, they influence monetary conditions in that zone. It is for this reason that the introduction of the single currency requires closer Community surveillance and coordination of economic policies among euro zone Member States. Close coordination should, in addition, contribute to the achievement of the Community objectives set out in Article 2 of the EC Treaty. In order to ensure further convergence and the smooth functioning of the single market, non-participating Member States must be included in the coordination of economic policies. This is particularly true for those Member States which participate in the exchange rate mechanism (ERM 2) [see section 7.2.4.].

7.3.2. Budgetary discipline and the single currency

Budgetary policy is perhaps the area in which differences between Member States are still at their strongest. This stems from the fact that the budget is the most characteristic manifestation of national sovereignty in economic terms. The budget is in fact the main instrument of orientation of the economy in general and of individual government policies, such as regional, social, industrial policies, etc. Through its expenditure side the budget has a direct influence on public investment and an indirect influence, through aids of all sorts, on private investment. Through its revenue side the budget acts on savings and on the circulation of currency. A state's budgetary policy may pursue short-term economic objectives (avoidance of a recession or stemming of inflation) or structural improvement objectives pertaining to the national economy and implemented through productive investments. Clearly, although it is difficult, coordination of budgetary policies is extremely important for economic convergence sought by the Treaty on European Union and for participation of a Member State in the third stage of EMU.

The **Stability and Growth Pact**, mentioned above [see section 7.2.4.], asserts that Member States remain responsible for their national budgetary policies. It provides, however, both for prevention and deterrence through two Regulations. The Regulation on the strengthening of the surveillance of budgetary positions requires Member States to submit stability pro-grammes (or convergence programmes in the case of the countries not par-ticipating in the single currency) presenting the medium-term objective for a government budgetary position that is close to balance or surplus[1]. The purpose of the second Regulation is to speed up and clarify the implemen-tation of the excessive deficit procedure, in particular as regards the sanc-tions to be imposed on Member States which fail to take appropriate meas-ures to correct an excessive deficit, and it lays down the deadlines which must be observed for the different stages of the procedure[2]. The economic policy strategy based on growth and stability-oriented macroeconomic policies and continuous progress in economic reform, allows a flexible re-sponse to changing economic conditions in the short run whilst safeguard-ing and strengthening the productive capacity of the economy over the me-dium term. Member States are required to compile and transmit to the Commission data on their quarterly government debt[3].

From the third stage of EMU, which began on 1 January 1999, the budgetary policies of the Member States are constrained by three rules: overdraft facilities or any other type of credit facility from the ECB or na-tional central banks to public authorities (Community, national or regional) are prohibited (Art. 101 TEC); any privileged access of public authorities to the financial institutions are banned (Art. 102 TEC)[4]; neither the Com-munity nor any Member State is liable for the commitments of public au-thorities, bodies or undertakings of a Member State (Art. 103 TEC). Im-plementing the new arrangements for economic policy coordination, the Council looks closely into actual and prospective developments in Member States' budgetary policies.

The Commission should monitor the development of the budgetary situation and the level of government debt in the Member States with a view to identifying gross errors. In particular it should examine compliance with **budgetary discipline** on the basis of the following two criteria [see also section 7.2.1.]: a) whether the ratio of the planned or actual govern-ment deficit to Gross Domestic Product exceeds a reference value (3% of GDP), unless either the ratio has declined substantially and continuously and reached a level that comes close to the reference value or, alterna-tively, the excess over the reference value is exceptional and temporary

---

[1]   Regulation 1466/97, OJ L 209, 02.08.1997.
[2]   Regulation 1467/97, OJ L 209, 02.08.1997.
[3]   Regulation 1222/2004, OJ L 233, 02.07.2004.
[4]   Regulations 3603/93, 3604/93 and 3605/93, OJ L 332, 31.12.1993.

and the ratio remains close to the reference value; b) whether the ratio of government debt to gross domestic product exceeds a reference value (60% of GDP), unless the ratio is sufficiently diminishing and approaching the reference value at a satisfactory pace (Art. 104 TEC and Protocol on the excessive deficit procedure).

If a Member State does not fulfil the requirements under one or both of these criteria, the Commission shall prepare a report, taking into account all relevant factors, including the medium term economic and budgetary position of the Member State. The Council shall, acting by a qualified majority on a recommendation from the Commission, and having considered any observations which the Member State concerned may wish to make, decide after an overall assessment whether an **excessive deficit** exists. Where the existence of an excessive deficit is decided, the Council shall make recommendations to the Member State concerned with a view to bringing that situation to an end within a given period. If there is no effective action in response to its recommendations within the period laid down, the Council may, first, make its recommendations public and, then, decide by qualified majority certain measures to be taken by the recalcitrant Member State (Art. 104 TEC).

7.3.3. Financial solidarity

The main Community instrument of financial solidarity is the **European Investment Bank** (EIB). According to Article 267 (TEC) the task of the EIB is to contribute, by having recourse to the capital market and utilising its own resources, to the balanced and steady development of the Community and the implementation of its policies. Thanks to its high credit rating, the Bank borrows on the best terms on the capital markets world-wide and on-lends to the Member States and their financial institutions - which distribute these global loans to SMEs. Since the EIB is a bank, it does not grant interest-rate reductions, but the financial institutions in the Member States and notably those whose vocation is regional development can borrow from the Bank and on-lend at more favourable terms. Some of the loans do have interest-rate subsidies attached, funded by the Community budget [see section 3.4.].

The EIB is a major source of finance for new industrial activities and advanced technology in sectors such as the motor vehicle industry, chemicals, pharmaceuticals, aeronautical engineering and information technologies. It also contributes to the establishment of trans-European telecommunications, transport and energy networks [see section 6.8.], reinforcement of industrial competitiveness [see sections 17.1. and 17.2.3.], environmental protection and cooperation in the development of third countries [see section 23.1.]. However, the main priority of the EIB is to contribute to the development of the least favoured regions of the European Union [see sections 12.1.1. and 12.3.]. These contributions account for around 70% of its financings in the Community.

Established in 1994, the **European Investment Fund (EIF)** is the specialist venture capital arm of the EIB Group. The EIF's tripartite share ownership structure - European Investment Bank (60%), European Commission (30%) and members of the banking sector (28 financial institutions) - facilitates the development of synergies between Community organs and the financial community, enhancing the catalytic effects of the EIB Group's action in support of small and medium enterprises (SMEs). The EIF's main objective is the financing of innovative and jobs creating SMEs through venture capital, in the Union and in the 12 applicant countries [see section 17.2.3.]. Acting as a "fund of funds", it acquires stakes in public or private sector venture capital funds with a view of strengthening the ability of European financial institutions to inject equity capital into SMEs, especially those in the growth phase.

7.4. Appraisal and outlook

As happened with the first effort at establishing an economic and monetary union in Europe, in 1971, the launch of the euro coincided with a highly adverse economic and monetary international situation: the terrorist attacks in New York and Madrid, the very important devaluation of the dollar, wars in Afghanistan and Iraq at the doorstep of Europe and high energy prices, probably related to these wars. In this global situation, the economies of the eurozone have run into unexpected difficulties, largely due to outside factors: the strong competition in world markets from companies working with undervalued currencies; the equally strong competition from countries practicing social dumping, i.e. countries with no social protection and therefore extremely cheap labour force; high prices of imported oil; and last but not least, the precarious situation in the Middle East. In this adverse global situation, the euro has shielded the economies of the eurozone from competitive devaluations, galloping inflation and increase in the prices of imports, more than 60% of which come from other euro countries. It is highly probable that if European economies had not the shield of the euro, they would have been in a much worse situation than the one they have found themselves when the euro became the strongest currency in the world.

In any case, the second effort at creating a European economic and monetary union was an unquestionable success, particularly in view of the great challenge of the changeover to the single currency. Not only was the physical introduction of the euro a historic event, it also represented an unprecedented strategic, logistical and practical challenge. From one day to the next, automatic cash dispensers (ATMs), instead of national currency, had to supply euro banknotes. Several million coin-operated machines and several hundred thousand ATMs had to be recalibrated. Some 15 billion euro banknotes and 50 billion euro coins replaced, in the space of a few weeks, a broadly equivalent quantity of national notes and coins in twelve countries with a combined population of some three hundred million.

Citizens and businesses were certainly faced with formidable problems in adapting their habits to the new currency. For the former the problems were mainly psychological. They had to forsake their sentimental attachment to a national currency, in some cases very prestigious, as the Deutsche Mark and in some cases very old, as the Greek Drachma born more than 26 centuries ago. Consumers had to familiarise themselves with the euro and make the necessary effort to construct for themselves a new scale of values. Traders had to display prices and give change in euros. Businesses had to adapt their equipment, prepare to use a new currency and make the most of the increased competition within the single market resulting from greater price transparency. Despite these difficulties and the Cassandras' catastrophic prophesies, the euro was circulated successfully, thanks to an exemplary planning and cooperation of national and European authorities.

Moreover, in spite of the great advance of multinational integration brought about by the EMU, national sovereignties have not suffered unduly. The Member States, which have moved to the third stage of EMU, have undoubtedly **lost the autonomy of their monetary policy**, since they are no longer at liberty to use the two main levers of this policy, the exchange rate and the interest rate (a freedom which they had already lost to a large extent, due to the interdependence of the European economies). At the same time, however, they lost responsibility for the parity of their currency and the equilibrium of their balance of payments, while enjoying shared responsibility for the parity of the euro against the currencies of third countries and the equilibrium of the collective balance of payments of the euro-zone countries. However, balance of current payments constraints exist for the zone as a whole. Therein lies the importance of close coordination of economic policies.

Price stability, which is a vital prerequisite for EMU, is also favourable to growth and the efficient use of the pricing mechanism for the allocation of resources. National budgetary policies and consequently government finances are subject to certain constraints anchored in the stability and growth pact, notably respect of the medium-term budgetary objective of close to balance or in surplus by 2004. The most direct "static gain" of the EMU consists of the ending, within the unified market, of all transaction costs inherent in the use of several currencies, costs representing between 0.3 and 0.4% of the GDP of the Union. Travellers, who previously lost important amounts in the exchange of their currency for those of the countries they visited, should particularly welcome these gains. "Dynamic gains", which cannot be measured directly, could take two forms: those resulting from heightened productivity and those generated by the elimination of the uncertainties concerning the long-term evolution of exchange rates.

The euro strengthens the single market and contributes to the maintenance of healthy fundamental figures, fostering sustainable growth. Stability in the euro zone, which is the fruit of the policies and structural reforms put in place by the European Union in recent years, is enabling the Union to face up to the global slowdown of economic activity, notably after the terrorist attack on the USA on September 2001. At the same time, the efforts made to consolidate public finances have provided the necessary room for manoeuvre to enable automatic stabilisers to come into play. They have also enabled the European Central Bank to play a central role in facing up to the shock affecting European economies.

Supported by progress achieved by the Member States in economic convergence (sound public finances, very low inflation, exchange rate stability) and the mechanisms for closer coordination of economic policies put in place as part of the introduction of the euro, economic and monetary union has already made the European Union a pole of stability in a world tormented by constant financial crises. In addition, the euro allows a **better balance of the international monetary system**, dominated since half a century by the dollar, which serves as a reference currency for almost 60% of world trade, whereas American exports represent around 12% of world exports. Its economic and commercial weight (16% of world exports) entitles the Union to play an important role in the necessary review of the international monetary and financial system. This review should focus on methods of crisis prevention and management, improved governance of the international monetary and financial system, development assistance and debt relief for developing countries.

As a matter of fact, the economic and monetary union is still in a trial phase. It has not consolidated itself. It suffers, in particular, from a disequilibrium between its strong monetary wing and its feeble economic one. The euro area is a monetary union working under a single monetary policy and **coordinated but decentralised economic policies**. While monetary policy management is the exclusive responsibility of the European Central Bank, economic and budgetary policies are a national matter. However, in an integrated monetary and economic zone, overspending and deficient restraint of inflation rates in some countries inflict a collective cost borne by all the countries sharing the same currency. There is a need, therefore, to reinforce existing economic, in particular fiscal, policy coordination mechanisms within the euro area and improve monitoring and evaluation of euro-area economic trends, including inflation, wage developments, investments and euro exchange rates. A revised stability and growth pact should aim at creating the conditions to foster employment and investment, while adhering to the medium-term objective of a budgetary position close-to-balance or in surplus. The strategy should be built upon further reductions of public debt, increases in employment rates and reforms of pension systems. In general, the pace of reform at Member State level needs to be significantly stepped up if the 2010 targets set by the Lisbon European Council are to be achieved [see section 13.3.2.].

Bibliography on the EMU

- BROWN Brendan. *Euro on trial: to reform or split up?* Basingstoke: Palgrave Macmillan, 2004.
- CASARES Miguel. *On monetary policy rules for the euro area.* Madrid: Banco de España, Servicio de Estudios, 2004.
- GRAUWE Paul de, KOURETAS Georgios, McKINNON Ronald. "EMU: current state and future prospects", *Journal of Common Market Studies*, v. 42, n. 4, November 2004, p. 679-867.
- KETTELL Steven. *The political economy of exchange rate policy-making: from the Gold standard to the Euro.* Houndmills, Basingstoke, Hampshire, England: Palgrave Macmillan, 2004.
- LJUNGBERG Jonas (ed.). *The price of the Euro.* Basingstoke: Palgrave Macmillan, 2004.
- MARTIN Andrew, ROSS George (eds.). *Euros and Europeans: monetary integration and the European model of society.* Cambridge: Cambridge University Press, 2004.
- PADOA-SCHIOPPA Tommaso. *The euro and its central bank: getting united after the union.* Cambridge, MA: MIT Press, 2004.
- SZAPÁRY György, HAGEN Jürgen von. *Monetary strategies for joining the euro.* Cheltenham: Edward Elgar, 2004.
- VINHAS de SOUZA Lucio, AARLE Bas van (eds.). *The euroarea and the new EU member states.* Basingstoke: Palgrave Macmillan, 2004.
- VOLBERT Alexander, MÉLITZ Jacques, von FURSTENBERG George (eds.). *Monetary unions and hard pegs: effects on trade, financial development, and stability.* Oxford: Oxford University Press, 2004.

DISCUSSION TOPICS

1. Why does a common market need a single currency in order to become a genuine internal market?
2. Why did the first attempt of the Community to create an economic and monetary union fail?
3. How does the common economic policy interact with the single monetary policy in an EMU?
4. Why is budgetary discipline indispensable in an EMU and how is it secured?
5. How does economic policy coordination affect the national sovereignty of member states participating in an EMU?

Chapter 8

TOWARDS A POLITICAL UNION

Diagram of the chapter

Justice and Home Affairs
p. 122

Judicial cooperation in civil matters
p. 123

Police and judicial cooperation in criminal matters
p. 123

Treatment of nationals of third countries
p. 125

The fight against terrorism in the EU
p. 126

Common foreign and security policy
p. 127

Decision making in CFSP matters
p. 127

The institutional framework of CFSP
p. 129

European Security and Defence Policy
p. 130

Political union is the last stage of the multinational integration process. It involves **common home and judicial policies and a common foreign and security policy**. According to the definition given above [see section 1.1.2.], a common policy entails a set of decisions, measures, rules and codes of conduct adopted by the common institutions set up by a group of states and implemented by the common institutions and the member states. A common policy does not exclude national policies, which continue to exist in all areas not covered by the decisions and rules agreed by the common institutions. By contrast, a common policy implies the non existence of a unique policy, which is the attribute of a federation of states. The stage of political union may by its development lead to a federation, but it does not necessarily imply it. Its development, however, requires the implementation by all the participating states of the common home and foreign policies agreed by the common institutions and the monitoring of this implementation by the common institutions. As long as these requirements are not met in certain sectors, political union, even though provided in a Treaty, is deficient or inexistent. In its place there may only exist intergovernmental political cooperation, leaving practically all freedom of action to the participants.

It ensues that the stage of political union is **the most difficult part of the multinational integration process**, because it requires weighty transfers of national competences to the common institutions. The guidelines for the common policies in this area have to be clearly set out in a treaty signed and ratified by all participating member states and the common policies that will materialise those guidelines have to be agreed by the common institutions according to the rules prescribed in this treaty. Such agreement presupposes that all member states participating at this stage have a common interest in a common policy worked out by the common institutions. Such common interest is difficult to be found in an area where national geopolitical interests have been built over the centuries. Hence, political integration cannot be built overnight. Time is needed to foster common political interests among formerly antagonistic nations and, therefore, to build common policies to pursue them.

8.1. Justice and home affairs

The common values underlining the objective of **an area of freedom, security and justice** are long-standing principles of the modern democracies of the European Union. The declared objective of the Union is to provide citizens with a high level of safety within an area of freedom, security and justice by developing **common action** among the Member States in the fields of police and judicial cooperation in criminal matters and by preventing and combating racism and xenophobia. The means that disposes the Union to this effect are: closer cooperation between police forces, customs authorities and other competent authorities in the Member States; closer cooperation between judicial and other competent authorities of the Member States; and approximation, where necessary, of rules on criminal matters in the Member States (Art. 29 TEU).

The integration of the Schengen acquis into the framework of the European Community rewards the efforts of the Member States which embarked on this cooperation and gives the citizens of the Member States, who are crossing internal borders without police controls, the sentiment of belonging to a union[1] [see section 9.2.]. Only **police cooperation and judicial cooperation in criminal matters** are now governed by an **intergovernmental framework**, improved by the creation of the new instrument of "framework decisions" (Title VI TEU) [see section 8.1.2.].

The **Constitutional Treaty** proposed to go a step forward, by extending the community method to virtually all aspects of the field of justice and home affairs, thus eliminating the so-called third pillar of the Union [see

---

[1]   Decisions 1999/435 and 1999/436, OJ L 176, 10.07.1999.

section 3.1.]. All measures would be adopted in the form of laws or framework laws through the normal legislative procedure, thus abolishing the current panoply of acts such as common positions and framework decisions. The principle of mutual recognition of judicial and extrajudicial decisions would guide judicial cooperation in criminal as in civil matters. The Court of Justice would have competence in all JHA matters. Common policies would be developed in the fields of border controls, visas, asylum and immigration (Art III-265). A uniform status of asylum for nationals of third countries would be valid throughout the Union (Art. III-266).

8.1.1. Judicial cooperation in civil matters

Judicial cooperation in civil matters is important since in a genuine European area of justice, individuals and businesses should not be prevented or discouraged from exercising their rights by the incompatibility or complexity of legal and administrative systems in the Member States. The main objective in this area is legal certainty and equal access to justice for all EU citizens, implying easy identification of the competent jurisdiction, clear designation of the applicable law, availability of speedy and fair proceedings and effective enforcement procedures. Procedural rules should respond to broadly the same guarantees, ensuring that people will not be treated unevenly according to the jurisdiction dealing with their case. The rules may be different provided that they are equivalent. The European Council of Tampere (15 and 16 October 1999), therefore, endorsed the principle of **mutual recognition of judicial decisions and judgments**, which is the cornerstone of judicial cooperation in both civil and criminal matters. This principle is already implemented by several Community instruments, which replaced pre-existing Conventions.

A Regulation on **jurisdiction and the recognition and enforcement of judgments** in civil and commercial matters, which replaced the 1968 Brussels Convention, lays down provisions concerning general jurisdiction and special jurisdiction in matters relating to insurance, consumer contracts, individual contracts of employment and some exclusive jurisdictions[1]. It also contains rules on prorogation, examination, admissibility, enforcement of judgments, authentic instruments and court settlements. Another Regulation established a general framework for activities aiming to **facilitate the implementation of judicial cooperation** in civil matters[2]. It has the following objectives: encourage such cooperation; improve mutual knowledge of the Member States' legal and judicial systems in civil matters; facilitate the correct application of Community instruments in this area; and improve public information on access to justice, judicial cooperation and the legal systems of the Member States.

---

[1] Regulation 44/2001, OJ L 12, 16.01.2001 and Regulation 2201/2003, OJ L 338, 23.12.2003.
[2] Regulation 743/2002, OJ L 115, 01.05.2002.

8.1.2. Police and judicial cooperation in criminal matters

Police and judicial cooperation in criminal matters (PJCCM) means that criminal behaviours should be approached in the same way throughout the Union. In concrete terms, terrorism, corruption, traffic in human beings, organised crime, should be the subject of minimum common rules relating to the constituent elements of criminal acts, and should be pursued with the same vigour wherever they take place. Article 29 of the TEU declares that the Union's objective is to provide citizens with **a high level of safety** within an area of freedom, security and justice. The Union is set to achieve this objective by preventing and combating crime, organised or otherwise, in particular terrorism, trafficking in persons and offences against children, illicit drug or arms trafficking, corruption and fraud. In the areas of PJCCM, Member States must inform and consult one another within the Council with a view to coordinating their action. To that end, they must establish collaboration between the relevant departments of their administrations (Art. 34 TEU).

In police and judicial cooperation in criminal matters the Council may, acting unanimously on the initiative of any Member State or of the Commission: (a) adopt **common positions** defining the approach of the Union to a particular matter; (b) adopt **framework decisions** for the purpose of approximation of the laws and regulations of the Member States, which are binding on the latter as to the result to be achieved but leave to the national authorities the choice of form and methods; (c) adopt **decisions** for any other purpose, which are binding but do not entail direct effect and must be implemented by the necessary measures adopted by the Council acting by a qualified majority; and (d) establish **conventions**, which, once adopted by at least half of the Member States, enter into force for those Member States, and may be implemented by measures adopted within the Council by a majority of two-thirds of the Contracting Parties (Art. 34 TEU).

The Council must consult the **European Parliament** before adopting any of the above measures and must give it adequate time to deliver its opinion, but is free to take or not take account of this opinion (Art. 39 TEU). Hence, the Parliament has a consultation role, but no co-decision or cooperation role in the field of PJCCM [see section 4.3.]. Another departure from the Community decision-making process is that the initiative for any PJCCM action can be taken not only by the Commission but also by any Member State (Art. 34 TEU). The competence of the **Court of Justice** of the European Communities is limited in giving preliminary rulings on the validity and interpretation of framework decisions and decisions, as well as on the interpretation of conventions in the field of PJCCM and on the validity and interpretation of the measures implementing them.

Judicial cooperation in criminal matters includes: cooperation between the competent ministries and judicial authorities of the Member States in relation to proceedings and the enforcement of decisions; facilitation of the extradition between Member States; compatibility in rules applicable in the Member States; prevention of conflicts of jurisdiction between Member States; and the progressive establishment of common rules relating to the constituent elements of criminal acts and to penalties in the fields of organised crime, terrorism and illicit drug trafficking (Art. 31 TEU).

Police cooperation should be organised both directly and through the **European Police Office (Europol)**. The Council should notably: enable Europol to coordinate specific investigative actions by the competent authorities of the Member States and assist them in investigating cases of organised crime; promote liaison arrangements between prosecuting/investigating officials; and establish a research, documentation and statistical network on cross-border crime (Art 30 TEU). The **Europol Convention** was signed on 26 June 1995[1]. Europol's remit includes the fight against terrorism[2] as well as forgery of money and means of payment[3]. The tasks of Europol include also trade in human beings and the sexual exploitation of children[4] and a joint action aims to combat trafficking in human beings and sexual exploitation of children[5].

Member States which intend to **establish enhanced cooperation** between themselves in the field of PJCCM may be authorised to make use of the institutions, procedures and mechanisms laid down by the Treaties (including the Community decision-making process and Court competence) provided that the cooperation proposed respects the powers of the European Community and aims at developing more rapidly an area of freedom, security and justice (Art. 40 TEU).

8.1.3. Common treatment of nationals of third countries

The Member States of the EU are all subject to **migration pressures**. The abolition of internal border controls and the notion of a common external border reinforces the desirability for the Union to develop more common approaches and closer cooperation in the immigration policy area. These are new concerns for the Community which emerged with the completion of the single market and which are taken into account by the Treaty on European Union.

In fact, the **abolition of checks at internal borders** of the Community is effective both for the citizens of the Member States and for third country nationals, once they have crossed the external frontiers of a Member State. In other words, freedom of movement applies to all those within the territory of the Community. This is why the Member States must have common rules for the crossing of their borders by foreigners and for the treatment of foreigners within their territory. This common need has led to the adoption

---

[1] Council Act OJ C 316, 27.11.1995 and OJ C 362, 18.12.2001.
[2] Decision, OJ C 26, 30.01.1999, p. 22.
[3] Decision, OJ C 149, 28.05.1999, p. 16-17.
[4] Joint Action 96/748/JHA, OJ L 342, 31.12.1996.
[5] Joint Action 97/154/JHA, OJ L 63, 04.03.1997.

of common policies in the fields of visas, immigration, the right of asylum, the status of refugees and extradition. Thus, a Directive determines: (a) the terms for conferring and withdrawing long-term resident status granted by a Member State in relation to third-country nationals legally residing in its territory, and the rights pertaining thereto; and (b) the terms of residence in Member States other than the one which conferred long-term status on them for third-country nationals enjoying that status[1]. Another directive lays down rules for determining which applicants for international protection qualify for refugee status and for subsidiary protection status, offered to persons who do not qualify as refugees but who would face a real risk of suffering serious harm, if returned to their country of origin[2].

8.1.4. The fight against terrorism within the EU

The terrorist attacks of 11 September 2001 in the United States have brought into being **a specific common policy for the fight against terrorism**, which has two wings: one within the European Union and within the realm of justice and home affairs policy; and one outside the Union, attached to the European security and defence policy [see section 8.2.3.]. In fact, in May 2000, the Union had already adopted a common strategy and action plan for the prevention and **control of organised crime**. The strategy entails notably: pooling and upgrading databases and analyses; strengthening the legal framework for preventing organised crime; strengthening the investigation of organised crime; boosting the role of Europol; and cooperating closely with the applicant and third countries[3].

In the light of the attacks in the United States on 11 September the Council decided to set up within Europol a team of counter-terrorist specialists for which the Member States appoint liaison officers from police and intelligence services specialising in the fight against terrorism, whose remit includes the following tasks: to collect in a timely manner all relevant information and intelligence concerning the current threat; to analyse the collected information and undertake the necessary operational and strategic analysis; to draft a threat assessment document listing targets, damage, potential *modi operandi* and consequences for the security of the Member States.

A framework decision aims to approximate the **definition of terrorist offences** in all Member States, including those offences relating to terrorist groups, and to provide for penalties and sanctions for natural and legal persons who have committed or are responsible for such offences[4].

---

[1] Directive 2003/109, OJ L 16, 23.01.2004.
[2] Directive 2004/83, OJ L 304, 30.09.2004.
[3] OJ C 124, 03.05.2000.
[4] Decision 2002/475, OJ L 164, 22.06.2002.

8.2. Common foreign and security policy

According to the European Union Treaty, the **objectives of CFSP** are: to safeguard the common values, fundamental interests, independence and integrity of the Union; to strengthen the security of the Union in all ways; to preserve peace and strengthen international security, in accordance with the principles of the UN Charter, the Helsinki Final Act and the Paris Charter; to promote international cooperation; to develop and consolidate democracy and the rule of law, as well as respect for human rights and fundamental freedoms (Art. 11 TEU). In order to pursue these ambitious objectives, the TEU gives the common institutions some simple **intergovernmental cooperation means**: defining the principles of and general guidelines for the common foreign and security policy; deciding on common strategies; adopting joint actions; adopting common positions; and strengthening systematic cooperation between the Member States in the conduct of policy (Art. 12 TEU).

In the framework of their **systematic cooperation**, which is in actual fact a follow on from their previous political cooperation, the Member States must inform and consult one another within the Council on any matter of foreign and security policy of general interest in order to ensure that their combined influence is exerted as effectively as possible (Art. 16 TEU). The diplomatic and consular missions of the Member States and the Commission delegations in third countries and their representations in international organisations must step up cooperation by exchanging information, carrying out joint assessments and contributing to the implementation of the CFSP (Art. 20 TEU).

Member States must **coordinate their action in international organisations** and at international conferences. All the Member States or those participating in such fora must uphold the common positions and keep each other informed of any matter of common interest. Member States which are permanent or temporary members of the United Nations Security Council must keep the other Member States fully informed and ensure the defence of the positions and the interests of the Union (Art. 19 TEU).

According to the **Constitutional Treaty**, the Union would have competence in matters of common foreign and security policy and the Member States should actively and unreservedly support this common policy (Art. I-16). But since this policy would still be in its infancy, the Member States would still have a large scope to exercise their national policies in this area.

8.2.1. Decision-making in CFSP matters

There are several departures from the Community method [see section 4.3.] concerning decision-making in CFSP matters. Whereas in Community decision-making only the Commission has the right to propose and hence the responsibility to define the common interest and ensure the coherence of action, in CFSP all the Member States and the Commission have the power to propose. The risks are inconsistency of the proposed action with the other policies of the EC/EU and disregard of the interests of the Member States in the minority, which cannot block the proposal. There are also two independent executive organs of the policy, since the Commission entrusts one of its members with the responsibility of the external relations of the Community and the Council appoints its Secretary General as High Representative for CFSP. Here again there is a risk of incoherence in the management of policy instruments and resources. Finally and most importantly, instead of the classical forms of Community acts [see section 3.3.], CFSP decisions take special forms, are usually taken by the Council acting unanimously and are not subjected to the control of the Court of Justice.

It transpires that the CFSP method is an improved intergovernmental cooperation method, but not much more than that. Probably, the most useful improvement is the definition by the European Council of **common strategies** in areas where the Member States have important interests in common. Since the definition of common strategies depends on the identification of common interests by the majority of the Member States, common strategies are a useful framework to find strategic answers to international crises and to increase the Union's efficiency by permitting decisions to be taken **by majority voting** (subject to the remark above). Common strategies set out their objectives, duration and the means to be made available by the Union and the Member States. On the basis of the general guidelines defined by the European Council, the Council takes the decisions necessary for defining and implementing the CFSP, usually by unanimous voting. It recommends common strategies to the European Council and implements them (Art. 13 TEU).

Common positions adopted by the Council define the approach of the Union to a particular matter of a geographical or thematic nature. Member States must ensure that their national policies conform to the common positions (Art 15 TEU). Article 3 of the Union Treaty contains an obligation to ensure the consistency of the Union's activities. Therefore, a common position adopted on the basis of Article 12 (TEU), while respecting the division of responsibilities set out in the Treaty, has to be compatible with the guidelines governing the EU's economic relations with a third country and with the objectives and priorities of its external policies, although it is the European Community that is responsible for adopting practical measures [see introduction to Part VI].

Joint actions adopted by the Council address specific situations where operational action by the Union is deemed to be required. They lay down their objectives, scope, the means to be made available to the Union, if necessary their duration, and the conditions for their implementation. Joint actions commit the Member States to the positions they adopt and in the conduct of their activity. Whenever a Member State plans to adopt a national position or take national action pursuant to a joint action, it must provide information in time to allow, if necessary, for prior consultations within the Council. Member States may take the necessary measures as a matter of urgency having regard to the general objectives of the joint action, and inform the Council immediately of any such measures (Art. 14 TEU).

8.2.2. The institutional framework of CFSP

Subject to the requirement laid down in Article 3 of the EU Treaty for the Council and the Commission **to ensure consistency in external relations**, and in accordance with their respective responsibilities under the Treaties, the Presidency, the Secretary-General/High Representative and the Commissioner for external relations, must cooperate closely in order to ensure overall continuity and coherence of action by the Union in external relations [see introduction to Part VI].

The **High Representative for the CFSP**, who is the Secretary-General of the Council, assists the Council in the matters coming within the scope of the CFSP, in particular through contributing to the formulation, preparation and implementation of policy decisions and, at the request of the Presidency, through conducting political dialogue with third parties (Art. 26 TEU). More specifically, according to the Helsinki European Council (10-11 December 1999), the High Representative of the Union **has the following tasks**:

- assist the Presidency in coordinating work in the Council to ensure coherence on the various aspects of the Union's external relations;
- contribute to preparing policy decisions and formulating options for the Council on foreign and security policy matters, so that it constantly focuses on the major political issues requiring an operational decision or political guidance;
- contribute to the implementation of foreign and security policy decisions in close coordination with the Commission, Member States and other authorities responsible for effective application on the ground.

The Presidency represents the Union in all matters falling within the CFSP. It is responsible for the implementation of common measures and expresses the position of the Union in international organisations and conferences. The Commission is closely involved in those tasks of the Presidency. The latter is assisted by the High Representative for the CFSP and may be assisted by the next Member State to hold the Presidency (Art. 18 TEU). The Presidency must consult the European Parliament on the main aspects and the basic choices of the CFSP and must ensure that its views are duly taken into consideration (Art. 21 TEU).

The Constitution's principal amendment to the provisions of the Treaty on European Union was the institution of a **Union Minister for Foreign Affairs**, who would wear two hats, being both one of the Commission's Vice-Presidents and the President of the Foreign Affairs Council. This association of the Commission and the Council in the person of the Foreign

Affairs Minister could be beneficial for the common foreign and security policy. Exercising the right of initiative of the Commission, the Union Minister for Foreign Affairs would contribute to the development of the CFSP, which he or she would carry out as mandated by the Council. The same would apply to the common security and defence policy (Art I-28). He or she would have responsibilities incumbent on the Commission in external relations and for coordinating the CFSP with other aspects of the Union's external action. By presiding over the Foreign Affairs Council, the Foreign Affairs Minister would contribute by his or her proposals to the preparation of common foreign and security policy and ensure implementation of European decisions adopted by the European Council and the Council of Ministers. The Foreign Affairs Minister would represent the EU in matters concerning the common foreign and security policy, conduct political dialogue on the Union's behalf and express the Union's position in international organisations and at international conferences and forums (Article III-305).

8.2.3. European security and defence policy

Common foreign and security policy covers all questions related to the security of the European Union, including the **progressive framing of a European security and defence policy (ESDP)**, which might in time lead to a common defence, should the European Council so decide. It shall in that case recommend to the Member States the adoption of such a decision in accordance with their respective constitutional requirements. The progressive framing of a common defence policy will be supported, when considered appropriate, by cooperation between the Member States in the field of armaments (Art. 17 TEU). The language used here gives an indication of the Member States' extreme caution in venturing into the field of common defence involving, in the long term, the integration of their Armed Forces. However, the objectives of the security policy were clearly defined at the Brussels European Council in October 1993. This policy must be aimed in particular at reducing risks and uncertainties which could impair the territorial integrity and political independence of the Union and of its Member States, their democratic nature, their economic stability and the stability of the neighbouring regions.

To assume their responsibilities across the full range of conflict prevention and crisis management tasks defined in the EU Treaty, the so-called **Petersberg tasks**, the Member States, at the Helsinki European Council (10-11 December 1999), have decided to **develop more effective military capabilities** and establish new political and military structures for these tasks. In this connection, the objective is for the Union to have an autonomous capacity to take decisions and, where NATO as a whole is not engaged, to launch and then to conduct EU-led military operations in response to international crises. For this purpose, a "common European **headline goal**" was set: to deploy 60 000 men in less than 60 days and to sustain them for at least one year, for the purpose of EU-led conflict prevention and crisis management tasks (Petersberg tasks). Although the goal was attained in 2003, the capability development mechanism (CDM) presents several problems, such as command and control arrangements for operational headquarters, the principles and framework for capability requirements and coordination and synergy with NATO. The "2010 headline goal" is the capability to deploy forces on the ground no later than 10 days after the decision to launch the operation.

To pursue the headline goal of the European Security and Defense policy (ESDP), the following permanent **political and military bodies** have been established within the Council:

(a) a standing **Political and Security Committee (PSC)** in Brussels, composed of national representatives of senior/ambassadorial level, deals with all aspects of the CFSP, including the common European security and defence policy. In the case of a military crisis management operation, the PSC will exercise, under the authority of the Council, the political control and strategic direction of the operation[1];

(b) the **Military Committee (MC)**, composed of the chiefs of defence or their military delegates and a Chair appointed by the Council on the Committee's recommendation, gives military advice, makes recommendations to the PSC and provides military direction to the Military Staff[2];

(c) the **Military Staff (MS)**, composed of military personnel seconded from Member States to the General Secretariat of the Council, provides military expertise and support to the ESDP, including the conduct of early warning, situation assessment and strategic planning for Petersberg tasks including identification of European national and multinational forces[3].

According to the Helsinki European Council, all Member States (defence ministers) are entitled to participate fully and on an equal footing in all decisions and deliberations of the Council and Council bodies on EU-led operations, but the commitment of national assets by Member States to such operations will be **based on their sovereign decision**. Russia, Ukraine and other European States engaged in political dialogue with the Union and other interested States may be invited to take part in the EU-led operations. A "European capability action plan", agreed by the Council on 19 November 2001, should incorporate all the efforts and investments, developments and coordination measures executed or planned at both national and multinational level with a view to improving existing resources and gradually developing the capabilities necessary for the Union's activities. The Council established a mechanism, called "Athena" having the necessary legal capacity for the financing of EU operations with military or defence implications[4].

---

[1] Decision 2001/78, OJ L 27, 30.01.2001.
[2] Decision 2001/79, OJ L 27, 30.01.2001.
[3] Decision 2001/80, OJ L 27, 30.01.2001.
[4] Decision 2004/197, OJ L 63, 28.02.2004.

The **European Defence Agency (EDA)** was set up in 2004 in order to develop projects and programmes aimed at supporting the development of European security and defence policy[1]. Subject to the Council's authority and open to participation by all willing Member States, the Agency aims at developing defence capabilities in the field of crisis management, promoting and enhancing European armaments cooperation, strengthening the European defence industrial and technological base (DTIB), creating a competitive European defence equipment market and promoting research aimed at leadership in strategic technologies for future defence and security capabilities.

Article 17 of the EU Treaty does not rule out the development of **closer cooperation between two or more Member States** on a bilateral level, in the framework of the Western European Union (WEU) and the Atlantic Alliance, provided such cooperation does not run counter to or impede multilateral cooperation. Thus, on 5 November 1993, France, Germany and Belgium took the important initiative of placing under common command certain units of their armies. The **Eurocorps**, which is placed under the authority of a "Joint Committee" made up of the Heads of Staff and political directors of the three countries, could be used autonomously by these three countries, or else placed at the disposal of NATO and the WEU.

The same Article 17 (TEU) underlines that the policy of the Union does not prejudice the specific character of the security and defence policy of certain Member States, respects the obligations of certain Member States under the **North Atlantic Treaty Organisation (NATO)** and is compatible with the common security and defence policy established within that framework. For the Member States concerned, this means that the actions and decisions they undertake within the framework of EU military crisis management will respect at all times all their Treaty obligations as NATO allies. In the case of an EU-led operation using NATO assets and capabilities, non-EU European allies will, if they wish, participate in the operation, and will be involved in its planning and preparation in accordance with the procedures laid down within NATO.

The European Council met in extraordinary session on 21 September 2001 in order to analyse the international situation following the terrorist attacks in the United States and to impart the necessary impetus to the actions of the European Union. Stating that terrorism is a real challenge to the world and to Europe, the European Council has decided that **the fight against terrorism** will, more than ever, be a priority objective of the European Union.

In the light of the **terrorist attacks in Madrid** on 11 March 2004, the Brussels European Council (25-26 March 2004) decided to revise the EU's action plan to combat terrorism, setting the following objectives: deepen

---

[1] Joint action 2004/551/CFSP, OJ L 245, 17.07.2004 and Decision 2004/658/CFSP, OJ L 300, 25.09.2004.

the international consensus and enhance international efforts to combat terrorism; reduce the access of terrorists to financial and other economic resources; maximise capacity within EU bodies and Member States to detect, investigate and prosecute terrorists and prevent terrorist attacks; protect the security of international transport and ensure effective systems of border control; enhance the capability of the European Union and of Member States to deal with the consequences of a terrorist attack; address the factors which contribute to support for, and recruitment into, terrorism. Moreover, the European Council declared that in the spirit of the solidarity clause laid down in Article 42 of the draft Treaty establishing a Constitution for Europe, the Member States and the acceding States shall act jointly in a spirit of solidarity mobilise all the instruments at their disposal, including military resources, if one of them is the victim of a terrorist attack.

The Constitutional Treaty strengthened the ESDP. More missions have been added to the so-called Petersberg tasks, such as joint disarmament operations, military advice and assistance tasks, conflict prevention and post-conflict stabilisation. The Constitution also states that all these tasks may contribute to the fight against terrorism (Article III-309). A solidarity clause was introduced whereby the other Member States would provide assistance if a Member State was the victim of terrorist attack or natural or man-made disaster. In this case, the Union would mobilise all the instruments at its disposal, including the military resources made available by the Member States, in order to assist the Member State concerned (Article I-43). More important is the **mutual defence clause** of the Constitution asserting that, if a Member State was the victim of armed aggression on its territory, the other Member States would have towards it an obligation of aid and assistance by all the means in their power, in accordance with Article 51 of the United Nations Charter (Article I-41(7)).

8.3. Appraisal and outlook

The two wings of the last storey of the European edifice are built at uneven pace. The wing of internal affairs has much advanced, while the wing of external affairs is far behind. This is due to the different methods used for the construction of each one. The Member States have accepted in Amsterdam a large-scale transfer of powers to the Community concerning **justice and home affairs**, a field that they had reserved in Maastricht for cooperation among their governments. The "communitarisation" concerns policies on visas, asylum and immigration and on judicial cooperation in civil matters. It implies, for these matters, instead of inadequate conventions and joint actions, the adoption by the Council and the Parliament of Community Directives and Regulations, upon initiative of the Commission and under the control of the Court of Justice [see section 4.3.]. It also means new transfers of national sovereignty through the development of a common policy concerning judicial and home affairs.

As in all areas where common policies exist, much progress was made since the entry into force of the Treaty of Amsterdam and particularly since the programme set by the Tampere European Council for the creation of an area of freedom, security and justice. The achievements of the common policy include: reinforcement of the rights of citizens and their families to move and reside freely in the territory of the Union; foundations of a common immigration and asylum policy; consolidation of the integrated management of external borders; better access to justice, notably through application of the principle of mutual recognition in the civil and commercial spheres; introduction of a European arrest warrant and establishment of Eurojust; and cooperation through legislation to combat cross-border crime and terrorism.

Some progress has also been made concerning the **common foreign and security policy** (CFSP). It has been given in Amsterdam more coherent instruments and a more effective decision-making procedure. Common strategies and "constructive abstention" give the possibility to the European Council and the Council to act by qualified majority, even if some Member States do not agree with a common policy. Through the recent development of the European security and defence policy (ESDP) and the strengthening of its capabilities, both civil and military, the Union has established crisis-management structures and procedures which enable it to analyse and plan, to take decisions and, where NATO as such is not involved, to launch and carry out military crisis-management operations. These are signs that the common foreign and security policy of the Union is slowly gaining momentum.

But the method of construction of the second pillar of the Union, that of the **common foreign and security policy** was not altered much by the Amsterdam and Nice Treaties on the European Union and, hence, this construction has progressed little if any at all. It is no wonder, therefore, that the Member States of the Union split radically on the first test of their supposedly common foreign and security policy, the March 2003 war and occupation of Iraq under American aegis, without the consent of the Security Council of the United Nations. The Constitutional Treaty would improve little the method of construction of the second pillar of the Union, which would thus resemble an imposing edifice sheltering internal economic and other common policies, an edifice having no gate to the exterior other than the small windows possibly opened by the foreign policies of the Member States, which, moreover, could contradict one another.

It should be stressed that **the economic unification of Europe has taken half a century** in order to attain the present adequately advanced stage of integration, with the economic and monetary union. Moreover, economic integration began with six surely europhilic nations. The stage of political union now concerns four times as many Member States, many of which are not europhilic, as they prefer slowing down rather than speeding up the progress of the integration process. Moreover, the political interests of the Member States, on which should be built common policies, are, at least for the time being, even more different than their economic interests. In view of these facts, the political union of Europe could be even more time-consuming than its economic union, without excluding however surprises coming from the developments of the world situation and the dissatisfaction of some nations of the Union with such developments.

To assume its responsibilities as a global power, the EU should rule out the use of unanimity and hence of the veto in the common foreign and security policy. This policy should be given the necessary resources (budget, efficient procedures, network of external delegations, etc.). The actual functions of the High Representative for the CFSP and of the Commissioner for External Relations should be merged into the tasks of the Minister for Foreign Affairs (envisaged by the Constitutional Treaty), ensuring coherent single representation of collective EU external interests, a leading role in crisis management and consistency with other common policies such as trade and aid to development. The Commissioner/High Representative for External Relations should be proposed by the European Council and named by the European Parliament [see section 4.4.]. Finally, the two wings of the foreign and security policy should back each other and make a coherent whole, because a foreign policy that cannot be enforced cannot be respected.

The European Union does not have to wait until it has built up its feeble military forces in order to have an independent international policy and world influence capable to rival those of the United States. The world today is not one in which military forces are automatically the most effective means of power. NATO is a relic of the Cold War. It no longer serves to protect Europe from any threat. On the other hand, for the United States, NATO has to exist because it provides the indispensable material and strategic infrastructure for American military and strategic deployments throughout Europe, Eurasia, the Middle East and Africa. NATO procures, indeed, to the United States a military presence, usually with extraterritorial privileges in most EU countries. If NATO is, as it claims, an alliance of independent and politically equal countries, the EU countries, which have an overwhelming majority in it, should have the democratic right to direct its political decisions towards their own national interests, which may but do not necessarily coincide with those of the USA.

Bibliography on JHA and CFSP

- DAVID Eltis (et al.). "The challenges of immigration", *European Review: Interdisciplinary Journal of the Academia Europaea*, v. 12, n. 3, July 2004, p. 313-398.
- EUROPEAN COMMISSION. *Green paper: Defence procurement*. Luxembourg: EUR-OP*, 2004.
- GUILD Elspeth (et al.). "An area of freedom security and justice : five years after its creation", *European Law Journal*, v. 10, n. 2, March 2004, p. 147-253.
- HIGGINS Imelda, HAIBRONNER Kay (eds.). *Migration and asylum law and policy in the European Union: FIDE 2004 national reports*. Cambridge: Cambridge University Press, 2004.

- KUIJPER Pieter Jan. "The evolution of the third pillar from Maastricht to the European constitution: institutional aspects", *Common Market Law Review,* v. 41, n. 2, April 2004, p. 609-626.
- LATAWSKI Paul, SMITH Martin. *Kosovo and the evolution of post-Cold War European security.* Manchester: Manchester University Press, 2003.
- MAWDSLEY Jocelyn, MARTINELLI Marta, REMACLE Eric. *Europe and the global arms agenda : security, trade and accountability.* Baden-Baden: Nomos, 2004.
- MOORE Anthony, CHIAVARIO Mario (eds.). *Police and judicial cooperation in the European Union: FIDE 2004 national reports.* Cambridge: Cambridge University Press, 2004.
- MÖRTH Ulrika, BRITZ Malena. "European integration as organizing: the case of armaments", *Journal of Common Market Studies,* v. 42, n. 5, December 2004, p. 957-973.
- SOLANA Javier (et al.). "Europe: élargissement, défense et sécurité". Défense nationale, année 60, n. 5, mai 2004, p. 5-144.

The publications of the Office for Official Publications of the European Communities (EUR-OP) exist generally in all official languages of the EU.

DISCUSSION TOPICS

1. Discuss the treatment of the common justice and home affairs policy in the Treaties of Maastricht and Amsterdam.

2. Should nationals of third countries be treated in the same way by all member states of a common market?

3. Comment on the development of the common foreign and security policy through the stages of the customs union, the common market and the economic and monetary union.

4. Compare the Community decision-making process, explained in section 4.2., to decision-making concerning the common foreign and security policy.

5. Do you perceive a spillover of economic into political integration in the case of the EC/EU or do you consider that the two processes develop independently from each other?

Part III: Policies concerning the citizens

Chapter 9.   Citizens' rights and participation
Chapter 10.   Information, audiovisual policy and culture
Chapter 11.   Consumer protection policy

European citizens are present at and are taking part both wittingly or unwittingly in, an experience that will leave its mark on the history of the planet for a long time: the gradual and free unification of nations, which until very recently were hostile to each other. The **keyword of the multinational integration experience is freedom**: freedom of movement of persons, of goods, of services and of capital [see chapter 6]; freedom based on human rights, democratic institutions and the rule of law [see section 8.1.], but, also and above all freedom of States and their people to belong or not to the Union. Economic and political freedom is the water of the mortar for the construction of the European edifice. The citizens who love these freedoms should normally be conscious or unconscious supporters of European integration, if only they realised the effects of this integration on their professional and everyday lives. As we will see in the next chapter, however, most citizens of the Union are unaware of the benefits of European integration.

The fact is that **all Europeans take part** in one way or another in the construction of Europe: the housewife filling her basket with products from the four corners of the European Union; the motorist choosing the car which suits him without regard to its origin; the worker employed by a Community firm in his country or the firm's country; the businessman rushing across borders to conclude deals with foreign partners; the student studying in a partner country; the young person participating in an exchange programme; the pensioner from a northern country who takes his vacations or his residence in a country of Southern Europe; the citizen of one of those countries who aspires to come into contact with the lifestyle and culture of his neighbours. They all participate in the construction of the large European edifice without realising it. Why? Because all these activities, which were difficult or unthinkable at the time of economic protectionism and which now appear so natural, bring the citizens of the Member States close to each other and to the process of European integration.

Each time the citizens choose a product or service from a partner country, they unknowingly contribute their grain of sand to the mortar necessary to cement the European edifice [see section 3.1.]. The citizens are not aware of the importance of these acts because they find them as natural as the air they breathe. In fact, they have become as essential to their daily lives as that air. They should, however, realise that their lives would be very different if they did not enjoy the freedom of choice made possible by European integration.

The title of this part of the book is misleading, since it limits the policies concerning the citizens to only three fields. In reality, measures of great importance to the individual in areas such as employment, social protection, the fight against poverty and health care are part of social policy and are dealt with in the Chapter on social progress. That Chapter also tackles the major issues of education and training, security at work and public health. Other measures of concern for the citizens are covered by the common policies on justice and home affairs, environment protection, etc. Thus, the following pages look at measures of interest to the individual not touched upon in other parts of this book, notably the rights of citizens, information, audiovisual and cultural activities and protection of consumers' interests.

Chapter 9

CITIZENS' RIGHTS AND PARTICIPATION

Diagram of the chapter

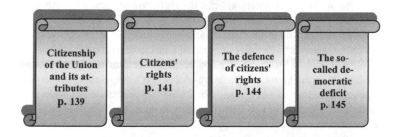

| Citizenship of the Union and its attributes p. 139 | Citizens' rights p. 141 | The defence of citizens' rights p. 144 | The so-called democratic deficit p. 145 |

In their great majority citizens ignore the many rights that they have acquired thanks to European integration, some of which are founded directly on the EC and EU Treaties, but most are based on the policies and the legislation derived from them. This ignorance is due to a deficient information of the general public, which the European institutions are trying unsuccessfully to develop, but which should be boosted by correct information from government sources and, of course, the media [see chapter 10]. A good cooperation between Community and national information sources is also necessary for an efficient protection of the health, safety and economic interests of European consumers [see chapter 11].

9.1. Citizenship of the Union and its attributes

The Treaty of Nice (following the Treaty of Amsterdam) establishes the **citizenship of the Union**, which is complementary to national citizenship. Every person holding the nationality of a Member State is a citizen of the Union. Citizens of the Union, thus defined, enjoy the rights conferred by the Treaty and are subject to the duties imposed thereby (Art. 17 TEC). Every citizen of the Union is, in the territory of a third country in which the Member State of which he or she is a national is not represented, entitled to protection by the diplomatic or consular authorities of any Member State, on the same conditions as the nationals of that State (Art. 20 TEC). Two Decisions specify the **right to diplomatic protection**[1]. This right is not

---

[1] Decision 95/553/EC, OJ L 314, 28.12.1995.

negligible, as there are many cases where one Member State is not represented in a third country. It includes assistance in the event of death, illness or serious accident, arrest, detention or assault as well as help and repatriation in the event of difficulty. In practical terms, EU nationals whose passport or travel document is lost, stolen or temporarily unavailable in a country where their own Member State has no representation, may obtain an **emergency travel document**, from the diplomatic or consular representation of another Member State[1].

In addition, every citizen of the Union residing in a Member State of which he or she is not a national has the **right to vote and to stand as a candidate** at European and municipal elections in the Member State in which he resides, under the same conditions as nationals of that State (Art. 19 TEC). Community directives lay down arrangements for the exercise of the right to vote and to stand as a candidate **in elections to the European Parliament** in the Member State of residence[2]. While including provisions to ensure freedom of choice and to prevent individuals from voting or standing for election in two constituencies at once, the Directive is based on the principles of equality and non-discrimination and is designed to facilitate the exercise by the citizens of the Union of their right to vote and to stand for election in the Member State where they reside.

The Directive laying down detailed arrangements for the exercise of the right to vote and stand as candidates in **municipal elections** ensures the same rights to Union citizens in elections by direct universal suffrage at local government level[3]. Member States may, however, reserve for their own nationals the posts of mayor and deputy mayor, which involve participation in an official authority or in the election of a parliamentary assembly.

Article 6 of the TEU states that the Union is founded on the principles of liberty, democracy, respect for **human rights and fundamental freedoms**, and the rule of law. While respecting the national identities of its Member States, the Union must respect fundamental rights, as they result from the constitutional traditions common to the Member States, as general principle of Community law. The EC Treaty explicitly acknowledges that human rights include economic and social rights, and lays down the principle of equal rights for citizens without discrimination based on sex, racial or ethnic origin, religion or belief, disability, age or sexual orientation (Art. 13 TEC). Upon a proposal from one-third of the Member States, the Parliament or the Commission, the Council, acting by a four-fifths majority of its members and with the assent of Parliament, can declare that a clear danger exists of a Member State committing a serious breach of fundamental rights and address to that Member State appropriate recommendations.

---

[1] Decision 96/409/CFSP, OJ L 168, 06.07.1996.
[2] Directive 93/109, OJ L 329, 30.12.1993.
[3] Directive 94/80, OJ L 368, 31.12.1994 and Directive 96/30, OJ L 122, 22.05.1996.

9.2. Citizens' rights

Protection of fundamental rights is a founding principle of the Union and an indispensable prerequisite for its legitimacy. The Cologne European Council (3 and 4 June 1999) concluded that there was a need to establish a **charter of fundamental rights** in order to make their overriding importance and relevance more visible to the Union's citizens. The charter, which was officially proclaimed at the Nice European Council (7-9 December 2000) by the European Parliament, the Council and the Commission, is divided into chapters dealing with the universal values of human dignity, freedom, equality, solidarity, citizenship and justice[1]. It is designed to make more visible and explicit to the European Union's citizens the fundamental rights, which are already derived from a variety of international and Community sources, such as the European Convention on Human Rights, the Community Treaties and the case-law of the Court of Justice. Alongside the standard civil and political rights and the rights of citizens deriving from the Community Treaties, the charter incorporates fundamental social and economic rights, such as the rights of workers to collective bargaining, to take strike action and to be informed and consulted. The charter is likely to become mandatory through the Court of Justice's interpretation of it as belonging to the general principles of Community law[2].

With the emergence of information systems spanning the entire internal market, the European Union has increasingly to concentrate on the **protection of the personal data** of its citizens [see also sections 17.3.5. and 17.3.6.]. Thus a Directive aims at the development of the information society and the service sector in the EU, while guaranteeing individuals a high level of protection with regard to the processing of personal data (safe harbour privacy principles)[3]. Accordingly, it imposes obligations on data controllers such as public authorities, companies and associations, and establishes rights for data subjects, such as the right to be informed of processing carried out, the right of access to data and the right to ask for data to be corrected. In any event, the Directive prohibits the processing of sensitive data, such as data revealing racial or ethnic origin, political opinions, religious or philosophical beliefs, or state of health, except in certain circumstances that are exhaustively listed, in particular when the data subject has given his explicit consent or where a substantial public interest requires such processing (e.g. medical or scientific research). Community legal acts on the protection of individuals with regard to the processing of personal data and the free movement of such data apply to

---

[1]   Solemn proclamation, OJ C 364, 18.12.2000.
[2]   COM(2000) 644, 11 October 2000.
[3]   Directive 95/46, OJ L 281, 23.11.1995.

Community institutions and bodies[1]. An independent supervisory body, the European Data Protection Supervisor, monitors the application of the relevant rules[2].

In addition to the fundamental rights, as defined in the Charter of the Union and in the European Convention for the Protection of Human Rights and Fundamental Freedoms signed in Rome on 4 November 1950, the citizens of the European Union have many rights, some of which they are not even aware of because they appear obvious. Their self-evident nature is a consequence of the existence of the Union and the membership of their State of origin to it. The Court of Justice has established that Community law, independent from the legislation of the Member States, can create obligations and rights for individuals[3]. These rights are so numerous that it would be tedious to list them all here. Almost all **the provisions of Community law examined in this book create rights** and obligations for the citizens of the EU's Member States, particularly as regards professional activities. The weight of this law is growing as European integration marches forward. It is superimposed on national law and in many cases simply replaces it [see section 3.3.]. It therefore has growing influence over the professional and day-to-day lives of European citizens.

Some examples may illustrate the importance of Community law **for the professional activities** of citizens. Traders have the right to consider the entire European Union as a potential market and therefore to purchase in any of the Member States and sell anywhere in the Union without any import duties or quantitative restrictions [see sections 5.1. and 6.2.]. Workers have the right to seek employment anywhere they wish in the Union, set up home with their family in the country where they are working and remain there even after they have lost their job [see section 6.4.1.]; they have the right to exactly the same social benefits as the citizens of the Member State in which they are residing [see section 6.4.2.]. Industrialists have the right to set up subsidiaries or branches anywhere in the EU where they feel that favourable growth conditions for their company exist and to transfer capital to and from these subsidiaries without restriction [see section 6.7.]. They have the right to borrow investment capital from a financial institution established in another country of the Union under the conditions prevalent in that country [see section 6.6.1.]. Businessmen have the right to be treated without discrimination by the public authorities of all Member States concerning all their professional activities, including the procedures for the award of public supply or works contracts [see section 6.3.]. Farmers have the right to guaranteed prices for their produce and therefore to a certain guarantee of income [see sections 21.4.2. and 21.4.3.]; sea fishermen also enjoy this right [see section 22.3.]. Members of the professions - lawyers, architects, doctors and so on - have the right to

---

[1] Regulation 45/2001, OJ L 8, 12.01.2001.

[2] Decision 1247/2002, OJ L 183, 12.07.2002.

[3] Judgment of 5 February 1963, case 26/62, van Gend en Loos, ECR 1963, p. 1.

set up a practice and to work in any Member State [see section 6.5.]. Women have the right for equal treatment with men in their professional life [see section 13.5.5.].

Some Community policies influence not only the professional life, but also the **everyday life of citizens**. Thus, important measures for the citizens in the fields of employment, vocational training, security at work and public health have their origin in the Community social policy. Furthermore, obligations imposed on industrialists by the Community policies of environment and consumers' protection have important effects on the quality of life of citizens. The citizens have the right to purchase goods - such as cars, electric and electronic appliances or clothes - in any one country of the Union at the conditions prevailing in that country and to take them to their country of origin without paying customs duties or any tax supplements [see section 5.1.2.]. They have the right to use any banking, insurance, telecommunications and audiovisual service offered in the large European market. They have the right to be treated by the administrative or judicial authorities of a country of the Union in the same way as the nationals of that country, i.e. without any discrimination on grounds of nationality (Art 12 TEC). This right covers a wide range of situations and human relations such as financial, contractual, family or student, which fall within the scope of Community law[1].

The Nice Treaty confers on every citizen of the Union a primary and individual **right to move and reside freely** within the territory of the Member States, subject to the limitations and conditions laid down in the Treaty and to the measures adopted to give it effect (Art. 2 TEU and Art. 18 TEC). Therefore, Directive 2004/38 replaced various instruments of Community law concerning freedom of movement and residence with a single text, aimed at reinforcing this fundamental entitlement of EU citizens by means of more flexible conditions and formalities and better protection against expulsion[2]. By virtue of this Directive, EU citizens enjoy right of residence provided that they satisfy certain conditions, notably if they themselves and the members of their families have sickness insurance covering all the risks in the host Member State. The directive facilitates considerably the freedom of movement and right of residence of family members of EU citizens, including the registered partner if the legislation of the host Member State treats registered partnership as equivalent to marriage. In addition, family members enjoy enhanced legal protection, notably in the event of the death of the EU citizen on whom they depend or the dissolution of the marriage, subject to certain conditions.

Many EU countries signed, on June 19, 1990, the **Schengen Convention** for the abolition of border checks at the frontiers between them, the

---

[1] Judgment of 12 May 1998, Case C-85/96, ECR 1998 I-2691.
[2] Directive 2004/38, OJ L 158, 30.04.2004.

reinforcement of controls at external borders and the cooperation among their administrations. To this end, they developed various cooperation tools, notably the Schengen Information System (SIS), a computerised data bank containing all search warrants issued by the Member States in the system and all supplementary information necessary in connection with the entry of alerts[1]. A Protocol annexed to the Treaty of Amsterdam integrates the Schengen "acquis" - i.e., the existing legislation - into the framework of the European Union[2] and allows the signatories to the Schengen Convention (the Member States of the Union minus the United Kingdom and Ireland plus Norway and Iceland[3]) to initiate between them, within the legal and institutional framework of the Union, cooperation in the areas covered by the Convention.

9.3. The defence of citizens' rights

Citizens should be conscious of their rights, some of which were mentioned above, to be able to defend them when they think that a Member State is not respecting them. They should also know that they are entitled to **defend their rights** acquired through Community law. They can do so by taking their case to the national courts, which can either issue a ruling or turn to the Court of Justice for a preliminary ruling[4], or by simply and inexpensively lodging a complaint with the Commission or a petition with the European Parliament (Art. 21 and 194 TEC). The Parliament has a Committee on Petitions which examines the complaints of citizens, mainly relating to social security, the recognition of professional qualifications or environment protection[5]. If the complaint concerns instances of mismanagement in the activities of the Community institutions or bodies, the citizen may address himself or herself to the **Ombudsman** appointed by the European Parliament (Art. 21 and 195 TEC)[6] [see section 4.1.3.].

Regardless of whether they are lodged with it or with the Parliament, the Commission is obliged to examine the **grievances of citizens**, which number around one thousand per year. Sometimes they are not justified and the Commission must explain to the citizen why this is the case. Not infrequently, however, they are justified and the Commission must address the Member State in question and ask it for explanations. If it does not get a good answer it must formally ask the Member State to correct its legislation or administrative practices which are causing injury to one or several

---

[1] Regulation 2424/2001 and Decision 2001/886, OJ L 328, 13.12.2001 and Regulation 871/2004, OJ L 162, 30.04.2004.

[2] Decisions 1999/435 and 1999/436, OJ L 176, 10.07.1999.

[3] Agreement, OJ L 149, 23.06.2000.

[4] Judgment of 25 July 2002, Case C-50/00 P, Unión de Pequeños Agricultores v Council, ECR 2002, p. I-6677.

[5] Resolution, OJ C 175, 16.07.1990, p. 214.

[6] Decision 94/114, OJ L 54, 25.02.1994, Decision 94/262, OJ L 113, 04.05.1994 and Decision 2002/262, OJ L 92, 09.04.2002.

citizens either of the State in question or of another Member State. If the Member State does not come into step with Community law as requested by the Commission, the latter must take the State to the Court of Justice, which will give a final ruling on the obligations of the Member State. According to the Court, the Member States are obliged to compensate for damage caused to individuals by violations of Community law attributable to them[1]. The citizens of the European Union therefore have powerful means at their disposal to obtain justice under Community law.

It goes without saying that if they are to defend these rights, they must be aware of them. The fact is that the vast majority of the citizens of the Member States are not **aware of their rights as citizens** of the European Union. The task of informing them therefore falls both to national and Community authorities, which are not very active in this area. The **information deficit**, examined in the following chapter [see section 10.1.], weakens the defence of citizens' rights.

9.4. The so-called democratic deficit

Numerous critics of European integration point out at the "democratic deficit" as cause of the indifference of the citizens of the Union, insinuating that the citizens do not participate in the Community decision-making process, which is therefore undemocratic and causes the estrangement of the citizens from European institutions. They overlook the fact that the alienation of citizens from politics is not peculiar to the EC/EU, but characterises practically all representative democracies, where a great proportion - in some countries the majority - of citizens abstain from national elections. They also neglect the fact that European **citizens already have almost the same influence** on the shaping of European law as they have on the shaping of national law. They indirectly influence it through the choice of the political parties, which make up the national governments and which therefore are involved in all European decisions adopted by the Council of Ministers. In addition, citizens have a direct say in the election of the members of the European Parliament, which has an important participation in the legislative process, thanks to improvements brought by successive European Treaties [see section 4.1.3].

It is true that the Parliament does not participate fully in all sectors of the European integration and that this situation should get better with a subsequent amendment of the Treaty, constitutional or not [see sections 2.5 and 4.4.]. But already the power and

---

[1] Judgment of November 19, 1991 in the joint cases C-6/90 and C-9/90, Francovich, ECR 1991, p. I-5357.

control of the European Parliament has greatly increased since the early days when it had a purely consultative role in the legislative process and when, as a consequence, the democratic deficit at European level was substantially greater than that at the national level. Now, most decisions are taken jointly by the Council, representing the democratically elected governments of the Union, and by the European Parliament, representing directly the citizens of the Union [see section 4.3.]. It follows that **the "democratic deficit" is another myth** propagated by eurosceptic circles. Paradoxically, these same circles are among the most vehement detractors of the Constitutional Treaty, which would practically eliminate the remnants of the democratic deficit, at least as far as the matters covered by the actual Community Treaty are concerned.

Furthermore, the viewpoints of European citizens concerning various common policies are also expressed by the **national parliaments**, which manifest a growing interest in European integration. Indeed, the Conference of European Affairs Committees (COSAC) of the national parliaments may examine any legislative proposal or initiative which might have a direct bearing on the rights and freedoms of individuals and may address to the European institutions any contributions which it deems appropriate on the legislative activities of the Union.

Article 191 of the EC Treaty states that **political parties at European level** are important as a factor for integration within the Union and that they contribute to forming a European awareness and to expressing the political will of the citizens of the Union. A regulation aims to establish a long-term framework for European political parties and their financing from the Community budget, while also laying down minimum standards of democratic conduct for such parties[1].

Far from being detached from the European integration process, national parliaments and the political parties, which dominate them, **are instrumental in** its launching, development and monitoring. The experience to date proves that practically all major parties in the great majority of the Member States are in favour of the general objectives of European integration. This is demonstrated by the fact that there is little or no change in a particular national policy towards European policies when there is a change of a parliamentary majority and, therefore, of a government in a Member State. Instead of showing public misgivings about the democratic legitimacy of European integration, the overall evidence brings out **an extraordinary political consensus** on the main elements of the common policies that determine it.

The **Constitutional Treaty** defines, for the first time, the democratic foundations of the Union, which are based on three principles: those of democratic equality, representative democracy and participatory democracy. The principle of **democratic equality** means that all citizens of the

---

[1]   Regulation 2004/2003, OJ L 297, 15.11.2003.

Union must receive equal attention from its institutions, bodies, offices and agencies (Art. I-45). The principle of **representative democracy** means that citizens are directly represented at Union level in the European Parliament, while Member States are represented in the European Council by their Heads of State or Government and in the Council by their governments, themselves democratically accountable either to their national Parliaments, or to their citizens (Art. I-46). The principle of **participatory democracy** means that the institutions must give citizens and representative associations the opportunity to make known and publicly exchange their views in all areas of Union action (Art I-47).

9.5. Appraisal and outlook

Given that the economic activities of the Member States are guided by European law, the **activities of individual citizens are influenced** and governed to a large extent by the common policies which dictate that law. Regulations on the right of entry and residence in the Member States, freedom of movement of workers, freedom of establishment of and provision of services by individuals and businesses, vocational training, protection of the environment and of the consumer, to mention but a few, are all the outcome of the various common policies. The **European social model** guarantees, not only fundamental human rights and the democratic and pluralistic principles, but also fundamental rights of workers: training adapted to the technical progress, fair pay allowing decent living conditions and social protection covering the hazards of life, illness, unemployment and old age [see section 13.5.]. This social model, which is defended by the majority of political parties in the Member States, places the European Union in the vanguard of social progress in the world.

Citizens are aware that the multinational integration process provides **a guarantee of peace and prosperity** in Western Europe and therefore support the idea of the Community in principle. But this Community - integrated since 1993 into the overall organisation of the European Union - is perceived as something distant, formless, cumbersome and incomprehensible. Citizens are largely unaware of the extent to which they are surrounded by the workings of the Union in their daily and professional lives. They hardly understand the rights that emanate from the citizenship of the Union and they ignore the rights that derive from European legislation.

Ignorance brings indifference and indifference is more dangerous for the European construction than the so-called democratic deficit, which is shrinking while indifference is expanding. The citizens need to know the rights that they are entitled to from European integration. Otherwise, the citizenship of the Union and the Union itself seem vague concepts, generating doubts, confusion or even rejection of the EU. The European institutions and the Member States should, therefore, permanently strive to ensure an easy access of the citizens to **simple and factual information**

about their rights and generally about the common policies that establish those rights. As we will see in the next chapter, European information is deficient or even non existent in many Member States, including those where it is needed most.

Bibliography on citizens' rights

- ARNULL Anthony. "From Charter to Constitution and beyond: fundamental rights in the new European Union", *Public Law*, Winter 2003, p. 774-793.
- DELEMOTTE Bernard (sous la dir. de). *Citoyens d'Europe*. Amiens: Licorne; Paris: L'Harmattan, 2004.
- DOUGLAS-SCOTT Sionaith. "The Charter of Fundamental Rights as a constitutional document", *European Human Rights Law Review*, n. 1, 2004, p. 37-50.
- DUTHEIL DE LA ROCHÈRE Jacqueline. "The EU and the individual: fundamental rights in the draft constitutional treaty", *Common Market Law Review*, v. 41, n. 2, April 2004, p. 345-354.
- EUROPEAN COMMISSION. *Citizens Signpost Service: activity report.* Luxembourg: EUR-OP*, 2004.
- HERVEY Tamara, KENNER Jeff (eds.). *Economic and social rights under the EU Charter of Fundamental Rights: a legal perspective*. Oxford: Hart, 2003.
- ILIOPOULOU Anastasia. "Le nouveau droit de séjour des citoyens de l'Union et des membres de leur famille: la directive 2004/38/CE", *Revue du droit de l'Union européenne*; n. 3, 2004, p. 523-557.
- IVALDI Gilles. *Droites populistes et extrêmes en Europe occidentale*. Paris: Documentation française, 2004.
- KECSMAR Krisztian. "Contractual solutions to the transfer of personal data from Europe to third countries without providing an adequate level of protection: inventory", *International Business Law Journal*, n. 3, 2003, p. 269-284.
- LEMMENS Koen. *La presse et la protection juridique de l'individu: Attention aux chiens de garde!* Bruxelles: Larcier, 2004.

DISCUSSION TOPICS

1. What are the advantages and disadvantages of European integration for the citizens of the Member States?
2. What rights and obligations do the common policies create for the citizens of the Member States?
3. What is the practical significance of the principles of liberty, democracy, respect for human rights and the rule of law, inscribed in the EU Treaty?
4. Can European citizens adequately defend their rights?
5. Discuss the existence and the importance of the so-called democratic deficit of the EU, comparing the structure and functions of European institutions to those of the Member States.

Chapter 10

INFORMATION, AUDIOVISUAL AND CULTURAL POLICIES

Diagram of the chapter

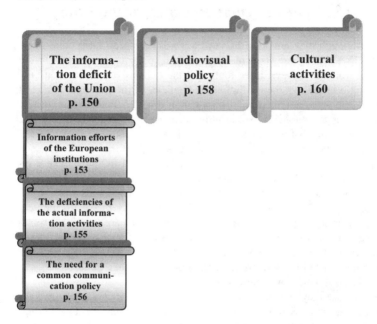

The information deficit of the Union
p. 150

Audiovisual policy
p. 158

Cultural activities
p. 160

Information efforts of the European institutions
p. 153

The deficiencies of the actual information activities
p. 155

The need for a common communication policy
p. 156

The point was made in the previous chapter that the citizens are silent, but indispensable, actors in the construction of Europe. The EC/EU could not have been built by the political elite, without the implicit consent of the citizens involved in the process. In fact, European citizens are generally in favour and consider as evident the fundamental principles and ideals the Union stands for, notably peace among their previously antagonistic nations, respect for human rights and the rule of law, economic development and social protection. The **public opinion survey known as "Eurobarometer"**, which is conducted each spring and autumn under the auspices of the Commission, shows that, in the spring of 2003, the EU (Fifteen) citizens were largely convinced that EU membership was a "good thing" rather than a "bad thing" (50% vs. 29%). They trusted the EU institutions more than their own government (44% vs. 37%). Nine out of ten Europeans support EU priority actions such as: maintaining peace and security in Europe, fighting poverty and social exclusion, fighting unemployment, fighting terrorism and organised crime and protecting the environment. The European public is even largely in favour of projects which are subject to controversy among the EU institutions and the governments of the Member States, such as a European constitution (63% vs. 10%), the EMU with a single currency (66% vs. 27% and 75% vs. 19% in EU 12), the common defence (74% vs. 15%) or the foreign policy (67% vs. 19%).

10.1. The information deficit of the Union

Although they are well disposed towards European integration, most citizens either ignore its achievements or take them for granted. In the Eurobarometer surveys, three fourths of the citizens say that they are not well informed about the institutions and policies of the European Union. It is interesting to note that good information greatly enhances the positive attitude of the public towards European integration. Indeed, 69% of the citizens saying that they are well informed have a positive image of the EU as against 34% of those who admit not being well informed. Also interesting are the findings that 74% of the citizens would like to be better informed on the EU and 83% support the notion that children should be taught in school about the way European Union institutions work. Civic education on EU institutions is even the first priority theme for the very large majority of Europeans. Apparently, the citizens are aware that something important is happening in Europe, in which they cannot participate for lack of general knowledge and day-to-day information and they call for better access to European affairs for themselves and their children.

The information deficit, acknowledged by the citizens themselves, means that they are ill informed about the reasons, the goals and the achievements of European policies, laws and measures. Ignorance brings disregard for the obscure phenomenon. At best, citizens take for granted or fail to see that the EC/EU is behind the many rights that they have acquired thanks to European integration, some of which we examined in the previous chapter [see section 9.2.], particularly the right to a peaceful, liberal and law secured existence. For uninformed Europeans, the peaceful coexistence and emulation of different European nations is self-evident and not to be attributed to unfamiliar Treaties, policies or common legislation. Uninterested citizens tend to forget the tariffs and other barriers hindering trade and therefore limiting their choice of goods and services from other European countries, in the pre-integration years. They do not recall the erstwhile controls at borders, the restrictions to movement, establishment and work in neighbouring countries, the limited amounts at their disposal when travelling abroad, the general restrictions to capital movements, the snags of dealing in several currencies, etc. Young Europeans tend even to disregard the bloody wars fought by their forefathers with nations that they themselves now consider friendly and allied to their own nation.

Many explanations have been advanced for the negative vote of the French and Dutch citizens at the referendums of 29 May and 1 June 2005 on the **ratification of the Constitutional Treaty**: national rather than European concerns, social protection versus free competition, fear of actual and future enlargements of the Union, etc. They all have their grain of truth; but to our mind, the main cause of the negative stance of two nations that were among the original builders of the European edifice is the ignorance of most citizens of the objectives and the achievements of European integration to date.

Instead of a democratic deficit, which as we explained in the previous chapter is largely overstated [see section 9.5.], we should rather speak about **an information deficit** in European affairs. The information deficit originates from the early days of the customs union and the common market, when the issues of European unification were too technical to really interest the public and the threat of the communist block was considered a sufficient justification of this unification. Now, however, that the communist threat has disappeared and the evolutionary integration process generates, every day, new common policies and laws affecting all sectors of the economy and society of the Member States, the citizens are bewildered about their impact on their lives. Furthermore, in order to judge the common enterprise on its true advantages and disadvantages, they need to have matter-of-fact information on the benefits and drawbacks already drawn and those expected from it, as well as on the real difficulties that it is facing in its management. Responsible for the information deficit are the institutions, which shy away from the development of a common information and communication policy, the governments of the Member States, which prefer to present the accomplishments of the Union as their own, and the media, which find more interesting to criticise the problems of the Union than present its achievements. Let us examine one by one these various factors of the information deficit of the Union.

The information deficit is partly due to the European institutions, notably the Commission, the Council and the Parliament, which do not join their forces to build a common communication policy. In their defence, it may be said that they are not encouraged - if they are not discouraged - by the governments of the Member States, which do not feel that they have a common interest in setting up a common information policy. In order to assume the political credit of modernisation, governments, when they propose innovating laws to national parliaments, transposing in effect Community directives, or when they change their administrative practices to comply with Community law, rarely take the trouble to explain to the general public that they are thus fulfilling their Community obligations.

Paradoxically, however, the providers of information themselves, the mass communication media, have their share of responsibility in the information deficit of the Union. In fact, the **media** can play an important role in the multinational integration process by shaping public opinion and by exerting pressure on the political decision makers for or against common policies. They may also ignore or report incorrectly important issues of the integration process and, thus, leave the public ignorant or lead it astray as to the advantages and disadvantages of particular common policies or the integration process in general. If the majority of the media adopt attitudes different from the majority of the political elite of a nation, concerning the issue of integration or particular aspects of it, this may lead to a different stance of the majority of the public from that of the majority of the political elite of the nation. We may thus have the following antidemocratic phenomenon: the popular media transforming the political consensus existing among the democratically elected leaders of a nation, concerning the major political issues discussed at European level [see section 9.5.], into a public opinion dissent on those issues, orchestrated by non-elected opinion leaders (media tycoons, trendy journalists, popular television speakers, etc.) and/or a vociferous minority (party, movement or union)[1].

In contrast to eurosceptic media, which systematically provide disinformation rather than information, unbiased mass media **rarely report the decisions of the EC/EU;** probably because they are too technical, too detailed and often quite difficult to understand by the general public and sometimes by the journalists themselves. Instead of bringing forward the need and/or the common interest of measures in discussion, the media (particularly the popular ones) tend to highlight the usual and comprehensible disagreements in the deliberations of the Council, stemming from different socioeconomic *structures, cultural traditions and vested* interests. Moreover, the media of a country tend to present as right the national points of view and as wrong those of the other Member States. When a compromise solution is found in the framework of the co-decision procedure of the Council and the Parliament (as happens with 95% of the technocratic proposals of the Commission, after thorough deliberation and many amendments introduced by the political bodies), and a Community measure (regulation, directive or decision) is adopted, the same media tend either to ignore it or to summarise its content in small print and in a language difficult to understand by the average citizen. Furthermore, as a compromise solution is halfway between the best possible solution and no solution at all, even an unprejudiced journalist can easily disregard or belittle the achievement that it represents and emphasize its shortcomings. The resulting information in such a case is half-right or half-wrong, according to one's standpoint. But, again, it should be said, in the journalists' discharge, that they need clear, simple and interesting press releases on which to work; and these can only be provided by the European institutions. We thus have a vicious circle: the governments do not mandate the European

---

[1]   The best example is the bitter opposition of the media tycoon Rupert Murdoch to the will of the Labour government of the UK to adopt the euro.

institutions to set up a common information and communication policy; hence the institutions do not provide interesting factual information to the media; and these, on their turn, do not report to the public the activities of the institutions worthy of note.

10.1.1. Information efforts of the European institutions

At present each of the three main European institutions has its own means and instruments to carry out its information policy. While preserving full autonomy, the Parliament and the Commission have established an Inter-Institutional Group on Information to coordinate their policies. They carry out jointly some priority information campaigns on subjects of topical interest, such as the euro (before its circulation), the new enlargement of the Union or the debate on the future of Europe. The Commission Representations and the European Parliament External Offices in the Member States are co-operating locally on an ad-hoc basis. Although it shares some means of communication with the Commission and the Parliament, such as the Europa server and the Europe by Satellite (EBS) - a television news instrument offering live coverage of the institutions' work and news summaries - the Council has a separate information and communication policy from the other institutions. As it has few budgetary resources for this purpose, it operates its own relations with the press and media. In general, except for a limited co-operation between the Commission and the Parliament, the three main European institutions have independent and heterogeneous information activities.

Although the Helsinki European Council in December 1999 called on the European Parliament, the Council and the Commission to pool their efforts to put out co-ordinated general information on the Union and to optimise the use of resources, the Commission did not seize the opportunity of this invitation to propose a common information policy. Instead, it published a communication on a new **framework for co-operation on information and communication**[1]. According to the Commission, this framework aspires to enlist support for objectives which include: developing a proper dialogue with the public; bridging the gap between the Union and the public; ensuring that people have access to the right information; keeping messages to the point; being proactive rather than reactive; creating a Europe that is close to people, familiar to them and means something to them.

All these could be good goals of a common policy of the institutions and the Member States. But, instead of proposing a common information and communication policy to attain them, the Commission proposed to continue developing and strengthening its own actions through journalists and the media, the networks, public and semi-public organisms, the private sector, the non governmen-

---

[1]   COM (2001) 354.

tal organisations and the civil society. It simply invited the other institutions and the Member States to join in this effort. Instead of building this partnership on Community instruments, e.g. a programme of common information and communication activities, it proposed that joint information activities be co-financed and co-managed through signed agreements (conventions) between the interested governmental and non-governmental organisations. Although work with the press should be the key to the immediate presentation of information on newly adopted common policies and measures, the press-related activities are not a priority or even a significant part of the framework for cooperation and communication proposed by the Commission. In this framework, each institution remains responsible for its press activities and for presentation, promotion and defence of its own policies and actions, as if these policies and actions were distinct from the Community policies that actually concern the citizens. The information and communication strategy for the European Union implemented by the Commission with the hypothetical voluntary synergy of the Member States, which should improve perception of the European Union and institutions and of their legitimacy[1], is clearly inadequate, as demonstrated by the indifference of citizens at the European elections of June 2004. Expressing its concern at the low voter turnout in those elections, the Brussels European Council (18-19 June 2004) recognised the need to strengthen a sense among the citizens of the importance of the work of the Union and its relevance to their daily lives. It would be up to the Commission to propose that the Union faces this need with a common communication policy.

As a matter of fact, **the Commission is the main provider of information on the EC/EU.** Major European affairs and problems, which occasionally attract television attention, are presented and commented in the press room of the Commission by its President, the competent Commissioner or a spokesperson. Rarely, is press attention attracted to the European Parliament and almost never to the Council of ministers. Although it practically monopolises Community information, the Commission is not a secretive organisation and it is even a good provider of information, as far as its activities are concerned. Its Representations in the capitals and other major cities of the Member States are open to the interested public. Its Office of Official Publications (EUR-OP) publishes hundreds of documents every year on all common policies. Its Europa server on the Internet gives free and user-friendly access to more than 60 databases, which each contains several hundred thousand documents in all Community languages. All the documents listed in the footnotes of this book are accessible at the

---

[1] COM (2002) 350, 2 July 2002.

Eur-lex database. The addresses of the general and of some of the most interesting free sites of Europa are the following:

- **(general for all sites)** http://europa.eu.int/index_en.htm
- **(general information)** http://europa.eu.int/geninfo/query_en.htm
- **(European legislation)** http://europa.eu.int/eur-lex/en/index.htm
- **(common policies)** http://europa.eu.int/scadplus/scad_en.htm
- **(official publications)**
  http://publications.eu.int/general/en/index_en.htm
- **(Bulletin of the EU)**
  http://europa.eu.int/abc/doc/off/bull/en/welcome.htm
- **(Who's Who in the institutions)**
  http://europa.eu.int/idea/en/index.htm
- **(calls for tenders)** http://ted.eur-op.eu.int/ojs/html/norecbrw.htm

Moreover, the Commission does not make any secret of its intentions concerning legislation in preparation. All its proposals are communicated directly to the press the day of their adoption and are published in the very informative monthly *Bulletin of the European Union*, available in paper and electronic form. In case of preparation of new policies or changes in existing policies, the Commission publishes **Green Papers** (reflection documents inviting a debate on the options of a policy before the preparation of proposals) and **White Papers** (general documents announcing a programme of actions)[1]. A White Paper usually presents the points of view of interested parties (organisations, associations, institutions...) at national and Community level on a Green Paper, along with the conclusions and intentions of the Commission. This step by step approach is meant to promote an exchange of views between the Commission and the interested parties on legislation in preparation.

10.1.2. The deficiencies of the actual information activities

A cursory view of the information activities of European institutions, gives the impression of a flood of documentation - coming mainly from the Commission - rather than of an information drought. But floods can be more harmful than droughts, if the soil is not prepared to receive the overflow; and in this case the soil is totally unprepared, because the citizens do not and never will make an effort to get the existing information, but rightly expect that they will be automatically informed, through their familiar media, about European affairs and decisions that are of interest to them. When they say in Eurobarometer surveys that they want to be informed about the institutions and policies of the EU, they mean that this information should come to them, not that they should go after it. Useful as they are to interested persons (researchers, interest groups and other spe-

---

[1] The index provides references to several Green and White Papers.

cialists), the Commission publications and Internet sites are ignored and are therefore useless for the large majority of citizens.

Indeed, information by the Commission suffers from two inherent defects. Firstly, it is addressed to a few initiated persons rather than to the average citizen, who does not read sophisticated publications or surf in the Europa server of the Commission. Secondly, information by the Commission reflects mainly its own proposals rather than the policies decided upon by the governments of the Member States and the Parliament of the peoples of the Union. Therefore, journalists and through them the public get the - partly right - impression that, through its information activities, the Commission defends its own policies rather than the common policies of the Member States.

The result of information deficiency, combined with disinformation on the part of eurosceptic media, is **the indifference or, worse, the dissatisfaction of citizens**, who quite sincerely believe that, instead of progressing in the field of European unification, the European Union is a theatre of infighting among European politicians; that it is totally unable to monitor global phenomena - such as globalisation, climate change and international conflicts - and that it is even responsible for some of their national problems, such as unemployment and the cost of living. It is this mismatch between high expectations and totally or partly false perceptions of the public that endangers European unification. The indifference and/or dissatisfaction of citizens, demonstrated in European elections, opinion polls and referendums, must be recognised as a major failure of the integration process and a grave danger for its future.

10.1.3. The need for a common communication policy

The signed but not ratified Constitutional Treaty of the Union provides for the information of workers and consumers, but not for that of the citizens. Whereas a Constitution should be based on the respect of its citizens, its authors have willingly or unwillingly disregarded the danger of disrespect brought about by the deficient information and civic education of the citizens of the Union. It is strange that, whereas the citizens themselves recognize their problem of understanding the European institutions and decisions, the political leaders ignore it or underrate it. If they ever examine seriously the Eurobarometers or other opinion surveys in their countries, they will understand that the citizens do not ask for a direct participation in the decision making process of the Union, but for a clear information as to how and why decisions are taken and as to what bearing they have on their lives. If this demand of the citizens was taken seriously into consideration, a common inf and communication policy, covering all other common policies, could easily be conceived and implemented.

By **common information and communication policy** we mean a policy with a common set of guidelines, decisions, rules, measures and codes of conduct adopted by the European institutions and implemented by the

European institutions and the governments of the Member States. If the constitutional Treaty did not explicitly call for such a policy, the Commission could, on the basis of the abovementioned Helsinki mandate of the European Council, take the initiative to propose it to the other institutions, as it usually does concerning all policies and measures. The Commission is the appropriate institution to consult, through a Green Book, national and professional experts, formulate and propose, in a White Book, a common communication policy with common goals, common means and multi-level implementation: European, national, regional and local. Thereafter, the Council and the European Parliament, with their own committees and experts, could work on the proposals of the Commission to make them acceptable to all parties concerned. The ensuing common information and communication policy should entail two basic elements: a common information and communication strategy of the European institutions and the governments of the Member States and a structure to carry it out, with at its head a European Press Agency.

The common strategy should encourage and give guidelines to the European institutions and the governments of the Member States to participate, together with regional and local authorities, in the common information tasks, in respect of the specific national and regional information needs. Coordination between the information services of the European institutions and the governments of the Member States should be assigned to a European Press Agency, i.e. an inter-institutional body, based in Brussels, depending from and representing all the European institutions: not only the three decision-making institutions of the Union, the Commission, the Council and the European Parliament, but also the European Ombudsman, the European Court of Justice, the Economic and Social Committee and the Committee of the Regions. Well publicised, the interventions of the European Ombudsman would guide citizens as to how better defend their rights. The important decisions of the Court of Justice merit more attention than what they actually get in legal publications. The opinions and reports of the two consultative Committees are hardly, if ever, given press coverage, even in specialised press organs. The European Press Agency should attract the attention of specific publics - i.e. professional and other non-governmental organisations and regional and local administrations - interested in the activities of the Ombudsman, the decisions of the Court of Justice and the opinions of the Committees.

But, of course, the attention of ordinary citizens should be attracted primarily to the activities and decisions of the main institutions, which have an effect on their professional and everyday lives. Press-conferences should present both the important proposals of the Commission and the major decisions of the Council and the Parliament. In the latter case, apart from the spokesmen of the institutions, it would be interesting to have the president of the Council and the chairman of the relevant parliamentary committee present a fresh decision to the press. Such a presentation should explain the problem addressed, the consequences of inaction, the reasons calling for common action in preference to individual action by the Member States, the main objectives aimed at by the decision and the most important means provided for attaining them. But, this common presentation should only be the basis of the information campaign on important decisions. On this basis should be built nationally oriented information by the ministers and the members of the competent parliamentary committee involved in a decision, addressed to the national media both in Brussels and at home.

It would, indeed, be quite reasonable that, upon adopting an important European law or measure, the responsible ministers give an accurate account to the journalists of their countries of the reasons of this law or measure, its goals and its effects on the professional or daily lives of the citizens of their states. Thus, each minister participating in the Council, which would have taken an important decision, would present in his or her own words and language the decision taken and/or circulate a press-release to national and regional media, based on the common press-release prepared by the European Press Agency. If he or she had voted against the measure taken, he or she should explain his or her disagreement, but also the reasoning having prevailed among his or her colleagues in the Council. The same information function should be performed by the members of the European Parliament, who should explain, through the media, why they have voted for or against a measure, along with the objectives and means agreed by the Assembly. Disapproval of a decision should not prevent the authorities and politicians of a Member State from participating in factual information about it. As a matter of fact, the concept of a common information and communication policy and respect for the democratic functioning of the institutions implementing it would call for the dissenting minority to join the majority in implementing a measure agreed by the latter.

Journalists, commentators and politicians of the opposition could, of course, criticise the measure taken and eventually blame the responsible minister for not having well defended national interests. In this way, citizens would have the double benefit of having a first-hand account of the reasons and objectives of a European measure, together with the arguments for and against it. They would thus be incited to think about the measure and take a stand on it, as they do about national measures and options. They would also come to know who and how represent them in Brussels. Eurosceptic media would, then, hopefully, avoid spreading false information about European decisions. In any case, they would not be able to claim that decisions are taken in secret by the "Eurocrats of Brussels", pointing at the Commission, when the citizens would be able to see for themselves that their own representatives, Ministers and European MPs, take part in the decision-making process in Brussels and can be appraised for their negotiating skills or called to account for any harm to national interests, actually or supposedly brought about by a common measure co-authored by them.

10.2. Audiovisual Policy

The audiovisual sector, which covers programme production and distribution ("software") and equipment manufacturing ("hardware"), has a great potential for growth and job creation in Europe. The European film and television programme industry, which plays a strategic role in the development of the audiovisual sector, is, in addition, **a prime vector of European culture** and a living testimony to the traditions and identity of each country. It must, therefore, illustrate the creative genius and the personality of the peoples of Europe; but, to do this, it must be competitive in an open, worldwide market[1].

In contrast to the information policy, the Member States of the Union have felt the need for a common audiovisual policy. A Protocol, annexed to the TEC in Amsterdam, asserts that **public broadcasting** in the Member States is directly related to the democratic, social and cultural needs of each society and to the need to preserve media pluralism [see also section 6.6.4.]. Member States may therefore provide for the funding of public service broadcasting in so far as such funding is granted to broadcasting organisations for the fulfilment of the public service remit as conferred, defined and organised by each Member State, and such funding does not affect trading conditions and competition in the Community.

The audiovisual sector in Europe took on a totally new face at the end of the 1980s, with the rapid growth in broadcasting by cable and telecommunications satellites and the emergence of the first European direct broadcasting satellites. However, **national markets in the Member States were too narrow** to be able to offer at competitive rates the equipment and programmes required by the new technologies and the proliferation of channels. This was a handicap for the European audiovisual sector, which was expected to be one of the principal service sectors in the 21st century.

Scattered and confined in their smallish national markets, European producers found themselves in conditions of uneven competition in the international arena as far as the costs were concerned. Europe should unify its audiovisual market to enable European producers to participate profitably in this technological revolution. Otherwise, it had to rely on powerful American and Japanese audiovisual industry, capable of covering cheaply international markets. American movies and serials and Japanese cartoons can defy world competition, because their cost is amortised on the large national market. European producers were doomed to disappear or be confined in their national markets.

At the same time a "technological revolution" was underway with the introduction of **high definition television (HDTV)** that gives to the image an almost perfect quality and makes it possible for the image to be accompanied by four sound channels, thus permitting, for example, a stereophonic sound and the simultaneous transmission of dialogues in two lan-

---

[1] COM (94) 96, 6 April 1994.

guages at the choice of the spectator. To prepare this revolution, the **Community's strategy on new technologies in the audiovisual sector** sought the cooperation between the Member States for the promotion of the European standard for HDTV, the aid for technological development and the aid to audiovisual operators for launching services using the new technology[1]. A single regulatory framework now covers the converging telecommunications, information technology and audiovisual sectors, including digital television[2] [see section 17.3.6.].

A particular regulatory framework was also necessary to permit the free provision of audiovisual services in the European space. To this end, a Directive concerning the exercise of television broadcasting activities (**"television without frontiers"**) aimed at the free movement of television programmes within the Community through the freedom to pick up and re-transmit programmes from another Member State. It consequently lays down the principle that compliance with the rules is to be enforced by the broadcasting State, without interference from the country of retransmission of the programme. The Directive introduced minimum harmonisation of advertising (breaks, duration, advertising for certain products, ethical rules), sponsorship, protection of minors and right of reply, while promoting the production and distribution of European audiovisual works. It stipulates that the Member States must ensure, "where practicable" and by appropriate means, that broadcasters reserve a majority proportion of their transmission time, excluding certain types of programme, for European works. The Directive also specifies that at least 10% of airtime or of the programming budgets should be earmarked for European works by independent producers. The 1989 Directive was amended in 1997 in order to clarify certain definitions of terms such as "television advertising" and "European works", to introduce rules on teleshopping and broadcasting for self-promotional purposes and to strengthen the protection of minors, in particular by making it compulsory for unencoded programmes likely to be unsuitable for minors to be preceded by a sound or visual warning[3].

10.3. Cultural activities

Culture was brought fully into the action scope of the Community through the Treaty of Maastricht [see section 2.2.]. The common cultural policy **does not aim at any harmonisation of the cultural identities** of the Member States, but, on the contrary, at the conservation of their diversity. Article 151 (TEC) states, in fact, that the Community should contribute to the flowering of the cultures of the Member States, while respecting their national and regional diversity and at the same time bringing the common cultural heritage to the fore. Its action aims at encouraging coop-

[1]   Decision 89/337, OJ L 142, 25.05.1989 and Decision 89/630, OJ L 363, 13.12.1989.
[2]   Directive 2002/21, OJ L 108, 24.04.2002.
[3]   Directive 89/552, OJ L 298, 17.10.1989 and Directive 97/36, OJ L 202, 30.07.1997.

eration between Member States and, if necessary, supporting and supplementing their action in the following areas: improvement of the knowledge and dissemination of the culture and history of the European peoples; conservation and safeguarding of cultural heritage of European significance; non-commercial cultural exchanges; artistic and literary creation, including in the audiovisual sector.

In order to achieve these objectives, **four means are employed**: cooperation between Member States; consideration for cultural aspects under other Community policies, including competition policy, concerning in particular aid to promote culture and heritage conservation (Art. 87 TEC); cooperation between the Community and its Member States with third countries and the competent international organisations; specific measures to support action taken by Member States which may take two forms: incentive measures, excluding any harmonisation of the laws and regulations of the Member States [see section 6.2.1.], adopted unanimously by the Council acting under the co-decision procedure after consultation of the Committee of the Regions; and recommendations unanimously adopted by the Council. The departure from the normal co-decision procedure [see section 4.3.] denotes that a Member State may not be forced by a qualified majority in the Council to take an action that it considers to be harmful to its cultural identity.

The European Union must strike a balance between the objectives arising from the completion of the internal market and those relating to the **protection of the national heritage**. In fact, a Council Regulation subjects the **export outside the Community of cultural goods** of artistic, historical or archaeological value to an export licence issued by the Member State on whose territory it is lawfully located[1]. In the same vein, a Directive provides for the return of cultural objects unlawfully removed from the territory of a Member State unlawfully removed from the on or after 1 January 1993[2]. It notably establishes a judicial procedure for the return of cultural objects and cooperation between the competent authorities of the Member States.

A rigorous, effective system for the **protection of copyright and related rights** is one of the main ways of ensuring that European cultural creativity and production receive the necessary resources and of safeguarding the independence and dignity of artistic creators and performers [see also sections 6.2.4 and 23.4.]. Therefore, **copyright** is protected at European Union level by a Directive that harmonises the term of copyright at 70 years after the death of the author in the case of literary, artistic, cinematographic or audiovisual works[3]. For the last two categories, calculation of the term of protection begins after the death of the last of the persons to survive from among the principal director, the author of the screenplay, the author of the dialogue and the composer of the music. The same Directive

---

[1]   Regulation 3911/92, OJ L 395, 31.12.1992 and Regulation 974/2001, OJ L 137, 19.05.2001.

[2]   Directive 93/7, OJ L 74, 27.03.1993 and Directive 2001/38, OJ L 187, 10.07.2001.

[3]   Directive 93/98, OJ L 290, 24.11.1993.

harmonises at 50 years the term of protection of the main **related rights** (those of performers, producers of phonograms or of films and broadcasting organisations). It also provides collective and obligatory management of the rights for cable retransmission through collective societies representing the various categories of rightholders.

10.4. Appraisal and outlook

Information is a key instrument of any policy making, let alone multinational policy-making. Citizens rightly distrust the common policies, which they do not understand for lack of proper information. The role of information has been underestimated and largely neglected in the EC/EU, with the result of a growing estrangement of the European public from European policies, which become ever more complicated as they advance and, hence, increasingly difficult to understand. As we saw above, three fourths of European citizens believe that they are ill informed about European affairs. This information deficit is endangering European unification. The more ignorant the citizens are about the institutions, the goals and the mechanisms of the integration process, the more easily **public opinion may be misled** about particular issues or the general thrust of the process.

The lack of generalised information combined with a sharp disinformation on the part of eurosceptic media is an explosive mixture placed under the foundations of European unification, because it separates citizens in two categories: the apathetics and the dogmatics. The vast silent majority is indifferent, because it finds living and working conditions generally acceptable in Europe, compared with other parts of the world, but does not credit the EC/EU with a significant role in shaping those conditions. On the other hand, a minority, which is systematically irritated against the deeds or supposed misdeeds of the European institutions (notably that of usurping national sovereignty), underestimates or even denies all the achievements of the Union in terms of peace, relative prosperity and unobstructed movement of goods, services, labour and capital. This situation is harmful, not only to the progress of European integration, but also to the good functioning of its democratic institutions [see section 4.3.] that are debased in the eyes of the citizens by some activists with dubious motives.

The states which participate in the integration process have, consequently, a common interest in developing **a common information and communication policy about this process.** This means using simple language, which can be used by the mass media, to put forward the reasons for European policies, the consequences of inertia and the benefits of common action in the interests of all participants. This would not be propaganda, but information necessary in a democratic community concerned with encouraging participation of all its members in communal life. This factual information is necessary in order to bring the citizens closer to the institutions of the Union and thus bridge the information and the democratic gaps. Priority should be given to information on issues close to the daily lives of citizens, such as price stability and employment as well as on issues of major political interest, such as the future of Europe and the place of the Union in the world. The Commission should take the initiative to propose a common communication policy with common goals, common means and multi-level implementation: European, national, regional and local.

Likewise, the European institutions - the Commission, the Council and the Parliament - should encourage the Member States to introduce the **teaching of the history, the institutions and the goals of European integration** in the high schools. This, again, would not be indoctrination dangerous for the democracy, but rather a civic education, necessary for the correct functioning of the democratic institutions at European level. The proper functioning of democratic institutions depends on well-informed and educated citizens. As revealed by public opinion surveys, practically all the citizens in all the Member States demand with insistence better information for themselves and better education for their children. They are right, because the two go together. The civic education of the young about the basic facts of European unification should, indeed, be the trunk on which would grow and be constantly developed, by the institutions and the Member States, the branches and leaves of the European information tree relating to all common policies and activities.

The cultural activities of the Union rightly emphasise the **cultural diversity of the nations that make it up** rather than trying to promote a common culture; but the national cultural identities should not overshadow the common cultural heritage of European peoples. Consciousness of a common cultural heritage is part of the process of an ever closer union among the peoples of Europe. The proper historical dimension, in particular, could contribute to a better mutual understanding of the cultures of European peoples. History lessons taught from the national angle, accentuate the divisions, the wars and the hatreds among European nations rather than their common cultural heritage. The Ministers of Education should one day agree on a textbook of European history and culture, which could make young Europeans understand that the national cultural particularities, which make up Europe's cultural wealth, are all parts of the same European civilisation of Greek-Roman origin.

In this respect, an effective **European audiovisual policy**, which is still in its inception phase, can enhance not only the common European cultural identity, but also the various national identities that enrich it. Certain Community measures could improve the industry's competitiveness, such as support systems for the distribution of non-domestic European works, the encouragement of private investment in European audiovisual production on foreign markets, the organisation of a pan-European prize-giving ceremony by the audiovisual profession and, last but not least, the launching of digital television in a competitive environment.

Bibliography on information, audiovisual and cultural policies

* BEICHELT Timm. "Euro-skepticism in the EU accession countries", *Comparative European Politics*, v. 2, n. 1, April 2004, p. 29-50.
* CRAUFURD SMITH Rachael (ed.). *Culture and European Union law*. Oxford: Oxford University Press, 2004.
* DULPHY Anne (et al.). *Les opinions publiques face à l'Europe communautaire: entre cultures nationales et horizon européen*. Bruxelles: PIE - P. Lang, 2004.
* EUROPEAN COMMISSION. *The management of copyright and related rights in the internal market*. Luxembourg: EUR-OP, 2004.
* EUROPEAN OPINION RESEARCH GROUP. *Eurobarometer 59: Public Opinion in the European Union, Spring 2003*. Brussels: European Commission, 2003.
* KOENIG Christian, HUSI Glori. "Public funding of digital broadcasting under EC state aid law", *European State Aid Law Quarterly*, v. 3, n. 4, October 2004, p. 605-612.
* MARCHETTI Dominique. *En quête d'Europe: Médias européens et médiatisation de l'Europe*. Rennes: Presses universitaires de Rennes, 2004.
* MOUSSIS Nicolas. "Pour rapprocher les citoyens de l'Union: une politique commune de la communication", *Revue du marché commun et de l'Union européenne*, n. 481, septembre 2004, p. 500-508.
* SABOURIN Paul (et al. eds.). *Langues et Union européenne: Colloque du 6 novembre 2003 à l'Assemblée nationale française*. Bruxelles: Bruylant, 2004.
* VREESE Claes de, SEMETKO Holli, "News matters: influences on the vote in the Danish 2000 euro referendum campaign", *European Journal of Political Research*, v. 43, n. 5, August 2004, p. 699-722.

DISCUSSION TOPICS

1. Consider the lack of a common information policy and its consequences on public awareness of the European integration process.
2. Discuss the relative importance of the democratic deficit and the information deficit of the European integration process.
3. Do the media that you are familiar with tend to give an objective and adequate view of the European integration process?
4. Is there a need for a common audiovisual policy of the EU?
5. Should the goal of a European cultural policy be a cultural uniformity or the defence of the particular cultures of the nations participating in the integration process?

Chapter 11

CONSUMER POLICY

Diagram of the chapter

Consumer information p. 166	Protection of health and physical safety p. 167	Protection of economic and legal interests p. 169

A common policy to protect consumers and users of products and services is essential for the functioning of the single market in the interest of the citizens. The aim of the common consumer policy is to ensure that the European Union's consumers draw maximum benefit from the existence of the internal market and play an active role in it. The single market must serve their maximum wellbeing and give them **a free choice of goods and services** of the best possible quality and at the best possible price, without consideration for their origin or for the nationality of their supplier [see section 6.1.]. Furthermore, within the single market consumers must enjoy a similar level of protection to that provided within a national market. For these reasons, the goods and services offered in the single market should be safe and the consumers should dispose of the necessary information so as to make the good choices.

Article 153 (TEC), gives the Community the task of contributing to the **protection of health, safety and economic interests** of consumers, as well to the promotion of their right to information, education and to organise themselves in order to safeguard their interests. The attainment of those objectives should be pursued through: (a) measures adopted pursuant to Article 95 (harmonisation of legislations) in the context of the completion of the internal market [see section 6.2.1.]; and (b) measures which support, supplement and monitor the policy pursued by the Member States. In order to help achieve the objectives of consumer protection, a Council Resolution demands that allowance be made for consumers' interests in **other Community policies**[1]. Obviously, the common consumer policy should in-

---

[1] OJ C 3, 07.01.1987, p. 1-2.

teract with other common policies, notably in the fields of agriculture, fisheries, environment protection and the harmonisation of legislations necessary for the internal market.

Following a public consultation, based on a Green Paper[1], the Commission set out its **consumer policy strategy** at European level for the years 2002 to 2006[2]. It defined three mid-term objectives: ensuring a high common level of consumer protection; guaranteeing effective enforcement of consumer protection rules; and guaranteeing the proper involvement of consumer organisations in EU policies. The Council called on the Commission to implement the strategy in line with the stated objectives, with particular emphasis on incorporating consumer protection into other Community policies and activities, and paying particular attention to specific areas such as services of general interest, the general safety of products and services[3].

11.1. Consumer information

Consumer information seeks to ensure that consumers are able to **compare the prices** for the same product within a country and are as well informed as possible on price differences between the Member States. The **indication of the prices** of the products represents an important means of information and protection of consumers. A Community Directive imposes the indication of the price per unit of measurement of all products sold in the shops, thereby giving the consumer a clear idea of the unit cost of the product in question and enabling him or her to compare different products and to make the best choice[4]. The selling price and the unit price must be unambiguous, easily identifiable and clearly legible. They must relate to the final price of the product and must refer to the quantity declared in accordance with national and Community provisions.

Labelling of products is also an important way of achieving better information and transparency for the consumer and ensuring the smooth operation of the internal market[5]. Two communications of the Commission are designed to encourage multilingual information and to improve cooperation between producers, distributors and consumers on the subject of labelling of products in the internal market[6]. The language requirements, the trade name, the stated quantity of the ingredients and other provisions are specified in the Directive on the labelling, presentation and advertising of foodstuffs[7].

---

[1]   COM (2001) 531, 2 October 2001.
[2]   COM (2002) 208, 7 May 2002.
[3]   Council Resolution, OJ C 11, 17.01.2003.
[4]   Directive 98/6, OJ L 80, 18.03.1998.
[5]   OJ C 186, 23.07.1992, p. 1-3 and OJ C 110, 20.04.1993, p. 1-2.
[6]   COM (93) 456 and OJ C 345, 23.12.1993.
[7]   Directive 2000/13, OJ L 109, 06.05.2000 and Directive 2003/89, OJ L 308, 25.11.2003.

11.2. Protection of health and physical safety

The effort to complete the internal market proved the effective trigger of a genuine policy to protect the health and physical safety of consumers. In the 1980s the Community placed the wellbeing of its citizens high on its list of priorities by adopting **general legislation guaranteeing the safety of individuals** in their capacity as users of products, regardless of the origin of the latter. This is the aim of a Directive on the approximation of the laws of the Member States concerning products which, appearing to be other than they are, endanger the health or safety of consumers[1]. This Directive prohibits the marketing, import and either manufacture or export of **dangerous imitations of foodstuffs**. Such products can be withdrawn from the market by a Member State and the Commission and the other Member States are informed of their existence.

A major Directive in the context of the single market was adopted in 1988 dealing with **toy safety**[2]. It sets the basic safety requirements that must be met by all toys manufactured in the Community or imported from third countries. The European standardisation committees then adopt harmonised standards and manufacturers respecting these are covered by a presumption that their toys meet the basic safety requirements defined in the Directive [see section 6.2.3.]. This Directive consequently promotes the free movement of goods while encouraging the manufacture of high-quality danger-free toys for the Union's children.

Since it is difficult to adopt Community legislation for every product, it is necessary to establish at Community level a general safety requirement. This general legal instrument is provided by a Directive on **general product safety**[3]. The purpose of this Directive is to ensure that products placed on the market, which are intended for consumers or likely, under reasonably foreseeable conditions, to be used by consumers even if not intended for them, are safe. Producers are obliged to place only safe products on the market, conforming to the specific rules of national law of the Member State in whose territory the product is marketed drawn up in conformity with the Treaty and in accordance with Directive 98/34 laying down a procedure for the provision of information in the field of technical standards and regulations [see section 6.2.2.]. Distributors are required to act with due care to help to ensure compliance with the applicable safety requirements, in particular by not supplying products which they know or should have presumed, on the basis of the information in their possession and as professionals, do not comply with those requirements. Member States must ensure that producers and distributors comply with their obligations, establish or nominate authorities competent to monitor the compliance of prod-

---

[1] Directive 87/357, OJ L 192, 11.07.1987.

[2] Directive 88/378, OJ L 187, 16.07.1988 and Directive 93/68, OJ L 220, 30.08.1993.

[3] Directive 2001/95, OJ L 11, 15.01.2002, repealing Directive 92/59, OJ L 228, 11.08.1992 from 15 January 2004.

ucts with the general safety requirements and lay down the rules on penalties applicable to infringements of the national provisions adopted. The Commission must promote and take part in the operation in a European network of the authorities of the Member States competent for product safety. This network must be coordinated with other Community procedures, in particular the **Community Rapid Information System (RAPEX)**, which is essentially aimed at a rapid exchange of information in the event of a serious risk.

Regulation 178/2002 lays down the general principles and procedures in matters of **food law and food safety** and establishes the European Food Safety Authority[1]. Whilst ensuring the effective functioning of the internal market, it aims at ensuring a high level of protection of human health and consumers' interest in relation to food, taking into account in particular the diversity in the supply of food including traditional products. It establishes common principles and responsibilities, the means to provide a strong science base, efficient organisational arrangements and procedures to underpin decision-making in matters of food and feed safety. The **European Food Safety Authority** must provide scientific advice, independent information and scientific and technical support for the Community's legislation and policies in all fields which have a direct or indirect impact on food and feed safety.

The Community legislation governing **food hygiene**[2], health issues related to the marketing of **products of animal origin**[3] and the organisation of **official controls** on such products[4] has been recast in 2004. Henceforth, a distinction is made between aspects of food hygiene and matters to do with animal health and official controls, thus providing scope for defining clearly the responsibilities of food business operators and the competent authorities in the Member States. A key point of the new legislation is that every operator involved in the food chain will bear primary responsibility for food safety, with a single, transparent hygiene policy being applicable to all foodstuffs and all operators (from the farm to the table), together with effective instruments to guarantee food safety and manage any future crisis in the sector. Administrative measures with criminal sanctions and financial penalties may be imposed on any Member State which fails to comply with Community feed and food law[5].

The food safety policy of the Community is based on the **precautionary principle**. This principle is an integral part of a structured approach to risk analysis based on assessment, management and communication of risk. In specific circumstances where, following an assessment of available information, the possibility of harmful effects on health is identified but scientific uncertainty persists, provisional risk management measures nec-

---

[1]   Regulation 178/2002, OJ L 31, 01.02.2002 and Regulation 1642/2003, OJ L 245, 29.09.2003.
[2]   Regulation 852/2004, OJ L 157, 30.04.2004.
[3]   Regulation 853/2004, OJ L 157, 30.04.2004.
[4]   Regulation 854/2004, OJ L 157, 30.04.2004 and Regulation 882/2004, OJ L 165, 30.04.2004.
[5]   Regulation 882/2004, OJ L 165, 30.04.2004.

essary to ensure the high level of health protection chosen in the Community may be adopted, pending further scientific information for a more comprehensive risk assessment. Indeed, according to the Court of Justice, when there is uncertainty regarding the risk to human health or safety, the Community institutions are empowered to take protective measures without having to wait until the reality and seriousness of those risks becomes fully apparent[1].

In accordance with the precautionary principle, a Directive aims at monitoring the deliberate release into the environment and on the placing on the market of **genetically modified organisms (GMOs)** as or in products[2]. Products containing GMOs must be clearly labelled and the public must be informed and consulted prior to the release and placing on the market of GMOs and products containing GMOs. Genetically modified micro-organisms may be used solely under conditions of contained use[3]. A Regulation provides a framework for the **traceability of products** consisting of or containing GMOs, and food and feed produced from GMOs, with the objectives of facilitating accurate labelling, monitoring the effects on the environment and, where appropriate, on health, and the implementation of the appropriate risk management measures including, if necessary, withdrawal of products[4]. Another Regulation lays down Community procedures for the authorisation and supervision of genetically modified food and feed and lays down provisions for the **labelling** of genetically modified food and feed[5].

11.3. Protection of economic and legal interests

With the opening up of the markets, the economic interests of the consumers had to be protected uniformly in the single market. Thus, the Directive on **liability for defective products** seeks to ensure a high level of consumer protection against damage caused to health or property by a defective product and at the same time to reduce the disparities between national liability laws which distort competition and restrict the free movement of goods. It establishes the principle of objective liability or liability without fault of the producer in cases of damage caused by a defective product. In the aftermath of the "mad cow" crisis, its scope was extended to primary agricultural products (such as meat, cereals, fruit and vegetables)

---

[1] Judgments of 5 May 1998, Cases C-180/96 and C-157/96, ECR 1998 I-2265.
[2] Directive 2001/18, OJ L 106, 17.04.2001 and Decisions 2002/811, 2002/812 and 2002/813, OJ L 280, 18.10.2002.
[3] Directive 90/219, OJ L 117, 08.05.1990, Directive 98/81, OJ L 330, 05.12.1998 and Decision 2001/204, OJ L 73, 15.03.2001.
[4] Regulation 1830/2003, OJ L 268, 18.10.2003.
[5] Regulation 1829/2003, OJ L 268, 18.10.2003.

and game products[1]. "Producer" is taken to mean: any participant in the production process; the importer of the defective product; any person supplying a product whose producer cannot be identified. The injured person does not need to prove the negligence or fault of the producer, but only the actual damage; the defect in the product; and the causal relationship between damage and defect. The producer's liability is not altered when the damage is caused both by a defect in the product and by the act or omission of a third party. However, when the injured person is at fault, the producer's liability may be reduced. "Damage" means: damage caused by death or by personal injuries; damage to an item of property intended for private use or consumption other than the defective product, with a lower threshold of 500 euros. The injured person has three years within which to seek compensation.

Going a step further, the Directive on certain aspects of the sale of consumer goods and associated guarantees introduced the **principle of the conformity of the product** with the contract[2]. The Directive is concerned both with commercial guarantees and with the legal guarantee, which includes all legal protection of the purchaser in respect of defects in the goods acquired, resulting directly from the law, as a collateral effect of the contract of sale. The seller is liable to the consumer for any lack of conformity which exists when the goods are delivered to the consumer and which becomes apparent within a period of two years unless, at the moment of conclusion of the contract of sale, the consumer knew or could not reasonably be unaware of the lack of conformity. When a lack of conformity is notified to the seller, the consumer is entitled to ask (in a logical sequence) for the goods to be repaired or replaced free of charge or for an appropriate reduction to be made to the price or to have the contract rescinded. On top of the legal guarantee, the commercial guarantee offered by a seller or producer should be legally binding under the conditions laid down in the guarantee document and the associated advertising.

A Directive seeks to protect consumers, traders and the public in general against **misleading advertising** and its unfair consequences[3]. It has the merit of defining a Community concept of "misleading advertising", namely advertising which in some way misleads the people to whom it is addressed, a concept which is very useful at a time when evolution in communications techniques, particularly television and Internet, means that advertising has become a transnational phenomenon. When a user considers that an advertising text or presentation has misled him or her, he or she can launch proceedings against the manufacturer. As amended in 1997, the Directive on misleading advertising introduced a uniform regulatory framework on **comparative advertising**, defined as the advertising that explicitly or by implication identifies a competitor or goods or services offered by a competitor. Such advertising is allowed under certain condi-

---

[1] Directive 85/374, OJ L 210, 07.08.1985 and Directive 1999/34, OJ L 141, 04.06.1999.
[2] Directive 1999/44, OJ L 171, 07.07.1999.
[3] Directive 84/450, OJ L 250, 19.09.1984 and Directive 97/55, OJ L 290, 23.10.1997.

tions, namely: it must not be misleading within the meaning of the Directive; it must objectively compare material, relevant, verifiable and representative features of goods and services, including prices; and it must neither create confusion in the market place between trade marks or trade names nor discredit or denigrate a competitor's marks, goods, services or activities.

A number of Directives concern **contractual relations**. The Community is concerned in particular with the protection of consumers in respect of contracts negotiated away from business premises (**door-to-door sales**). A Directive grants consumers seven days in which to reconsider and renounce any agreement on a door-to-door sale[1]. The trader must inform the consumer in writing of the right of renunciation at his or her disposal.

In the same spirit, a Directive lays down minimum consumer protection rules concerning **distance contracts** regardless of the technology used (e.g. mail-order, telephone, fax, computer, television, etc.) and regardless of the product or service marketed, with the exception of financial services[2]. The underlying purpose of the Directive is to provide consumers with information in advance and to ensure that transactions are transparent. When any offer of goods or services is made, and when a sales contract is drawn up, the identity of the supplier and the commercial nature of the proposal must be clearly stated (at the beginning of the call in the case of a telephone communication). Other details, which must be made clear, include the price of the proposed product or service, the technical characteristics, the arrangements for payment and the conditions governing withdrawal from the contract. The consumer's agreement must be obtained before any goods or services, for which payment is required, are supplied. The consumer is entitled to a period of seven working days in which to withdraw from the contract without penalty. A supplier who fails to fulfil his or her obligations must reimburse any sums paid.

A special directive concerning the **distance marketing of consumer financial services** provides for common rules for selling contracts by phone, fax or Internet. It is designed to offer consumers much-needed protection and rights and to increase their confidence in e-commerce, both within individual Member States and across borders[3]. Its main features are: the prohibition of abusive marketing practices seeking to oblige consumers to buy a service they have not solicited ("inertia selling"); rules to restrict other practices such as unsolicited phone calls and e-mails ("cold calling" and "spamming"); an obligation to provide consumers with comprehensive information before a contract is concluded; and a consumer right to withdraw from the contract during a cool-off period, except in cases where there is a risk of speculation.

---

[1]   Directive 85/577, OJ L 372, 31.12.1985 and OJ L 1, 03.01.1994.
[2]   Directive 97/7, OJ L 144, 04.06.1997 and Directive 2002/65, OJ L 271, 09.10.2002.
[3]   COM (1998) 468.

Another Directive concerns **unfair terms in contracts** concluded between a consumer and a professional[1]. It establishes, in particular, a distinction between contractual terms negotiated among the parties and terms which the consumer has not negotiated expressly. A non-negotiated clause is to be regarded as unfair where it creates a significant imbalance, to the detriment of the consumer, between the rights and obligations of the parties to the contract. The Directive establishes the principle that consumers are not bound by unfair terms in contracts, and makes Member States responsible for implementing appropriate and effective means of ensuring that professionals cease to use such terms.

Uniform protection in the European Union is provided to all consumers who use credit to finance their purchases. The Directive on **consumer credit** obliges the Member States to apply common rules to all forms of credit, thus avoiding the distortion of competition among suppliers and protecting consumers without regard to their nationality. This is done by certain prescribed guarantees, notably the calculation of the effective annual rate of interest and all the cost factors which the consumer must pay in order to obtain the credit. As amended in 1998, the Directive provides for the application of a single Community formula for calculating the annual percentage rate of charge for consumer credit[2].

A Council Directive on **package travel, including package holidays and package tours**, protects millions of tourists against possible corrupt practices by the organisers of these popular holidays[3]. Contract clauses must be recorded in writing and the consumer must receive a copy of them. The information supplied cannot be misleading: brochures placed at the disposal of the consumer must contain clear and precise information on prices, means of transport, type of accommodation, its situation, category and so on. In principle, prices cannot be revised, unless express provision is made for this in the contract. Even when surcharges are possible, they are subject to certain conditions. If the organiser cancels the package, the consumer has the right either to another package of equivalent or higher quality, or to reimbursement of all sums already paid, without prejudice to any compensation. The consumer also has the right to compensation if the organiser does not supply a large part of the service agreed upon. Finally, the organiser or the travel agency must give proof of sufficient guarantees to ensure repayment of the sums paid or the repatriation of the consumer in the event of insolvency or bankruptcy.

Still in the field of tourism and of cross-border vacations, a Directive protects purchasers of **timeshare rights** to one or more immovable properties[4]. The purchaser must be provided with a description relating, in particular, to the property itself, its situation, details of any communal services to which the purchaser will have access and the conditions governing such

---

[1] Directive 93/13, OJ L 95, 21.04.1993.
[2] Directive 87/102, OJ L 42, 12.02.1987 and Directive 98/7, OJ L 101, 01.04.1998.
[3] Directive 90/314, OJ L 158, 23.06.1990.
[4] Directive 94/47, OJ L 280, 29.10.1994.

access, the period of enjoyment, the price and an estimate of the charges payable. The contract and the document describing the property covered by the contract must be drawn up in the official Community language (or one of the languages) of the Member State in which the purchaser resides or, if he or she so wishes, in the language (or one of the languages) of the Member State of which he or she is a citizen. In addition, the vendor must provide the purchaser with a certified translation of the contract in the official Community language (or one of the languages) of the Member State in which the property is situated. In any case, the purchaser is entitled to withdraw within 10 days without giving any reason. Any advance payment by the purchaser before the end of that cooling-off period is prohibited.

11.4. Appraisal and outlook

The European Union shows a growing interest in the protection of the physical safety and of the economic interests of its citizens. This is a natural evolution since the single market has increased not only the choice of goods and services from the partners, but also the risks to consumers of all the Member States from defective products, notably foodstuffs, produced in one of them. Those risks were amply demonstrated during the mad cow crisis, which originated in the United Kingdom in 1996, and the scandal of dioxin-contaminated foodstuffs of Belgian origin, in 1999 [see section 5.1.3.]. While on these occasions, the Community consumer protection legislation proved its usefulness at preventing the spread of diseases and contaminations, it also revealed its limits, concerning its implementation by the Member States. With the increasing number of economic transactions between individuals and businesses from different Member States, there is also a growing need for their protection from dishonest business practices through uniform measures, supplementing the different national measures. Moreover, consumer representatives should be given the support they need to be effective in increasingly complex and technical debates, and the consumer's voice should be heard more systematically in the decision-making process.

Consumer protection is not only a necessary complement of other common policies, such as agriculture and fisheries, but also an important factor contributing to the affection or disaffection of European citizens towards the Union. Human nature tends, indeed, to disregard all the good attributes of a socio-political organisation, such as the European Union, when a serious, albeit temporary, problem shows the defects of this organisation. This is why, the European institutions should be very careful, not only to enact Community legislation, which safeguards the health and the economic interests of all European citizens, but also to impose on the Member States to strictly implement this legislation by adequate national measures.

Bibliography on consumer protection policy

- DAVIES Gareth. "Consumer protection as an obstacle to the free movement of goods", *ERA-Forum: Scripta Juris Europaei*. n. 3, 2003, p. 55-66.
- GUYOT Cedric. *Le droit du tourisme: régime actuel et développements en droits belge et européen*. Bruxelles: De Boeck, 2004.
- HERVEY Tamara, McHALE Jean. *Health law and the European Union*. Cambridge: Cambridge University Press, 2004.
- KARSTEN Jens, SINAI Ali. "The Action Plan on European Contract Law: perspectives for the future of European contract law and EC consumer law", *Journal of Consumer Policy*, v. 26, n. 2, June 2003, p. 159-195.
- MICKLITZ Hans, REICH Norbert, WEATHERILL Stephen. "EU treaty revision and consumer protection", *Journal of Consumer Policy*, v. 27, n. 4, December 2004, p. 367-399.
- REMY-CORLAY Pauline (et al.). "European contract law", *ERA-FORUM: Scripta Iuris Europaei*, n. 2, 2003, p. 39-145.
- SNYDER Francis (et al.). "Food safety in European Union law", *European Law Journal*, v. 10, n. 5, September 2004, p. 495-648.
- TOKE Dave. *The politics of GM food*. London: Routledge, 2004.
- WEATHERILL Stephen (ed.). "The protection of the weak party in a harmonized European contract law", *Journal of Consumer Policy*, v. 27, n. 3, September 2004, p. 243-356.
- ZANOLI Raffaele (et al.). *The European consumer and organic food*. Aberystwyth: University of Wales, School of Management and Business, 2004.

DISCUSSION TOPICS

1. Discuss the need for a consumer protection policy in the context of a common market.
2. Outline the respective responsibilities of national and Community authorities in tackling problems endangering public health.
3. What are the lessons to be drawn from the mad cow and dioxin crises?
4. Is there a need for a common legislation concerning contractual relations in a common market?
5. Compare the objectives of the Directives on general product safety and on liability for defective products.

Part IV: Horizontal policies

In **Part IV we examine the horizontal policies of the Union,** that is to say the objectives set, the means employed and the measures taken in common by the Member States of the Union in order to support and supplement their policies in five broad areas of their economic and socio-political activities: regional development, social progress, taxation, competition and environmental protection. All these common policies were launched during the stages of the customs union and the common market and are being continuously developed in order to further the higher goals set for the stages of economic and monetary union and political integration.

The **common regional policy** by means of the Structural Funds aims to help the poorer regions of the Community to face the increased trade and competition from the more developed regions imposed by the single market and the economic and monetary union. Such a union, implying abandonment of the use of exchange rate adjustment as a means of balance of the national economy, would be to the detriment of the poorer Member States without an efficient common regional policy revolving around sufficient capital transfers from the richer to the poorer regions of the EU. The common regional policy aims, therefore, at the economic and social cohesion of the Union.

The acceleration in the process of European integration since the middle of the 1980s has resulted in major progress in the **common social policy**, spanning fields such as vocational training, social protection and worker health and safety. This process is stepped up in the economic and monetary union, which takes out of governments' hands many economic and monetary instruments and hence their ability to tackle their social problems alone. Therefore, the Amsterdam Treaty identified the promotion of a high level of employment as a Community objective and introduced a coordinated strategy for employment.

The **common taxation policy** has gone beyond the Treaty requirements of fiscal neutrality. The Member States succeeded in replacing their various cumulative multi-stage turnover taxes with a uniform value added tax, the structures of which have been closely harmonised. The abolition of tax frontiers, made possible by the approximation of VAT rates and excise duties, made a vital contribution to the final completion of the single market. As economic and monetary union advances, approximation is also required for company and savings taxes.

The **common competition policy** plays the role of economic regulator in the common market. It prevents market compartmentalisation, abolished in the single market, from being restored by means of agreements between large companies. It also prevents multinational companies from exploiting their dominant position or monopolising a market by acquisition of independent firms. As regards State interventionism, the role of the common competition policy is to confine it to aid which fits in with the common objective of adjusting the structures of the European Union's production mechanism to internal and external changes.

The **common environment policy** is vital for the quality of life of the citizens of the Union. In a European economy, which faces strong international competition, the challenge of policy-makers is to take measures that make it possible to painlessly achieve the objective of growth, which is compatible with the essential requirements of the environment. The EU follows, indeed, a coherent programme for sustainable growth. However, the EU cannot work alone for the protection of the environment of the globe. Using its economic power, it should lead the way to a better international coordination in this area.

Chapter 12

REGIONAL DEVELOPMENT POLICY

Diagram of the chapter

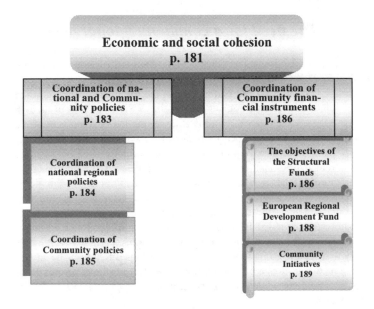

Economic and social cohesion
p. 181

Coordination of national and Community policies
p. 183

Coordination of Community financial instruments
p. 186

Coordination of national regional policies
p. 184

Coordination of Community policies
p. 185

The objectives of the Structural Funds
p. 186

European Regional Development Fund
p. 188

Community Initiatives
p. 189

The main objective of the common regional policy is the reduction of existing regional disparities and the prevention of further regional imbalances in the EU by transferring Community resources to problem regions using the financial instruments of the Community known as the Structural Funds. The common regional policy of the EU does not seek to supersede national regional policies. In accordance with the principle of subsidiarity [see section 3.2.], the Member States, through their own regional policies, are the first ones who must solve the problems in their regions by promoting infrastructures and financially supporting job-creation investments. However, the common regional policy coordinates national regional policies by formulating guidelines and establishing certain principles in order to **avoid competition for regional aid between Member States**. It coordinates also the various policies and financial instruments of the EU to give them a "regional dimension" and thus more impact on regions most in need of care.

The **Committee of the Regions** set up by the Treaty of Maastricht in order to enhance the role of regional authorities in the institutional system of the Union [see section 4.2.4.], plays an important role in the forecasting of regional tendencies and in the management of structural interventions of the EU. In the enlarged Union, where the unequal distribution of wealth among regions would be greatly increased, the democratic legitimacy and the role of the Committee of the Regions should also be increased [see section 4.4.].

12.1. The need for a common regional policy

By assisting the problem regions build up their infrastructure networks, the Member States and the Union can help them to both develop their markets for the benefit of all and better balance the European economy in the light of future changes. Of course, each Member State carries out its own regional policy, which generally aims at favouring the development of the national territory's less prosperous regions by means of **transferring resources from wealthier regions**. The means normally used by Member States to remedy regional problems are of two types: firstly, improving the infrastructure and the social and cultural development of backward regions, and secondly, various premiums, subsidies and tax incentives for attracting private investment in these regions. The general objective of these measures is to create or re-establish a better distribution of economic activities and population over the national territory. To do this, certain governments also try to discourage investments in highly developed regions. The advantages of such measures are twofold: favouring the transfer of resources towards poor regions while halting the disproportionate expansion of congested regions.

Certainly, it is primarily up to the national authorities to solve the problems of their regions, namely by promoting infrastructures or giving incentives to businesses to attract their investments in disadvantaged regions. The scale of the effort required to stimulate economic activity in the least advanced regions means that public funds must be used in conjunction with private investment. **Regional aid**, when judiciously applied, is a vital instrument to regional development and to continued and balanced expansion within the European Union. But given the possibility of competition inside a single market between the various regions in order to attract Community and foreign investments (including those from partner countries), the advantages granted can go beyond compensation for material difficulties faced by investors in the areas to be promoted. Thus, part of the aid granted would merely serve a reciprocal neutralisation. The national regional actions would simply be more expensive and grant unwarranted profits to benefiting undertakings [see also section 15.5.]. Therefore, the prime objective of EU regional policy is to **coordinate national regional**

policies by formulating guidelines and setting priorities at European level, which effectively help close the gap between regions.

In addition, the EU has a common interest in regional development through structural change. The very essence of economic integration is **the optimisation of the market mechanism** at a European scale. But a market policy based on some sort of spontaneous balance between the various economic parameters essentially benefits rich regions. Indeed, prior to the creation of the common market, economic activities had developed in a national context; certain activities usually grouped in certain regions were protected from international competition by customs barriers. With the opening of borders, European and foreign (American, Japanese...) companies wanting to set up business in the EU market are normally attracted in European regions where infrastructure is most developed, where labour is most qualified, and where the economic environment is most adapted to their activities. Economic concentration invites more concentration. The common regional policy strives to make up for this tendency in order to achieve **a better-balanced growth within the common market**. Its goals and mechanisms are coordinated and interact with those of other common policies, notably social, enterprise, environment, agricultural and fisheries policies.

12.1.1. Priority regions

All the Member States of the European Union are experiencing disparities in the levels of development and living standards from one region to another and the gaps are wider still when measured across the Union as a whole. At the beginning of the 1990s, some **52% of the total population of the Union (EU-12) lived in problem regions**. The per capita gross domestic product (GDP) in the ten poorest regions of the Union was only about one quarter of that in the ten richest regions. Unemployment in the ten regions worst hit was up to seven times greater than in the ten most fortunate regions. From one country to another the ratio of young people receiving vocational training was about 1 to 2, the ratio for basic infrastructure about 1 to 3 and the ratio for grants for research and technology about 1 to 7.

Since the beginning of the 21st century, the Community regional policy recognises **two main types of "priority" regions and areas**: regions whose development is lagging behind and areas facing structural difficulties. The identification of the priority regions and areas at Community level is based on the common system of classification of the regions, referred to as the "Nomenclature of Territorial Statistical Units (NUTS)", established by the Statistical Office of the European Communities in cooperation with the national institutes for statistics and ensuring that these non-administrative units correspond to comparable economic, social, geographical and environmental circumstances[1].

In 2001, per capita GDP, expressed in terms of purchasing power standards in the 211 "NUTS level II" regions of the EU, ranged from 53% of the EU-15 average in the Dytiki Ellada region of Greece to 263 % in Inner London in the United Kingdom. One region in 10 showed a GDP figure of more than 125% of the EU average, while roughly one in five was below 75%. The feature, which these regions have in common, is their excessive dependence on a limited range of traditional economic activities that can no longer provide sufficient productivity, employment and income. The consequences are common to all these regions, namely per capita GDP below the Community average, high and prolonged unemployment and a continuous outward population flow.

Regions whose development is lagging behind, termed "Objective 1 regions" in Community jargon are basically regions corresponding to level II of the Nomenclature of Territorial Statistical Units (NUTS level II) whose per capita gross domestic product (GDP) is less than 75% of the Community average. The outermost regions (the French overseas departments, the Azores, the Canary Islands and Madeira), which are all below the 75% threshold, and the areas **with very low population density** (less than 8 inhabitants per square kilometre), which are situated in the north and east of Finland and the northern half of Sweden[2]. The exact list of regions eligible under Objective 1 was drawn up by the Commission and is valid for seven years from 1 January 2000[3]. These regions are faced with a combination of handicaps: insufficient or rundown infrastructure - transport, energy or telecommunications; weak or outdated industrial structures whose production methods often fall short of the mark and whose products are ill-adapted to the marketplace; agriculture where archaic structures prevail; population exodus combined with urban decay; and high rates of unemployment particularly among young people and unqualified or poorly qualified workers. All of the regions whose development is lagging behind are situated at the periphery of the country to which they belong and/or of the European Union. A quarter of the population of these regions live on islands, some of which are very small (Greek islands[4]) or very far from the heart of the Union (Canaries, Azores, Madeira, Overseas Departments). This is an additional development handicap, for remoteness from the main centres of economic activity and the main centres of consumption renders their products less competitive and makes them less attractive to private investment. Therefore, the Commission envisages a stronger partnership for the outermost regions[5].

---

[1]   Regulation 1059/2003, OJ L 154, 21.06.2003.
[2]   Regulations 1447/2001, 1448/2001 and 1452/2001, OJ L 198, 21.07.2001.
[3]   Decision 502/99, OJ L 194, 27.07.1999.
[4]   Regulation 2019/93, OJ L 184, 27.07.1993 and Regulation 1782/2003, OJ L 270, 21.10.2003.
[5]   COM (2004) 343, 26 May 2004.

The **regions with structural problems** whose socio-economic conversion is supported under Objective 2 of the structural policy include in particular: areas undergoing socio-economic change in the industrial and service sectors; declining rural areas; urban areas in difficulty; and depressed areas dependent on fisheries. According to the Regulation laying down general provisions on the Structural Funds [see section 12.3.], these regions constitute about 10% of the population of the Community in the case of the industrial areas, 5% in the case of the rural areas, 2% in the case of the urban areas and 1% in the case of the fisheries areas. The total population of the Objective 2 regions must not exceed 18% of the total population of the Community. Accordingly, the Commission set a population ceiling for each Member State on the basis of certain criteria fixed by the Regulation laying down general provisions on the Structural Funds[1].

12.1.2. Economic and social cohesion of the Union

The wider European market reinforces the polarisation of pre-existing economic activities and thus **accelerates the agglomeration and concentration process**. If measures were not taken at national and European level, the completion of the internal market would tend further to widen existing inequalities in the distribution of economic activities throughout the territory of the EU. That is why, the objective of economic and social cohesion, implying the desire to reduce disparities between the various regions of the Community, was introduced by the Single European Act [see section 2.1.]. On top of the single market, **the achievement of economic and monetary union** promises enhanced prospects for the developed and the less favoured regions alike. The reduction of trans-frontier transaction costs and the elimination of exchange rate risk may promote regional specialisation and intra-Community trade in goods and services. The weaker regions can benefit from this specialisation by exploiting more fully their comparative advantages. Furthermore, increased capital mobility in EMU, supported by the single currency and the tendency towards quasi-uniform inflation rates, tends to equalise interest rates for any given level of risk, which should favour the less developed regions where capital is often relatively scarce and capital costs, therefore, relatively high.

At the same time, however, Member States participating in the euro-zone **lose certain fiscal and monetary policy options** as well as the ability to adjust the exchange rate. Exchange rate flexibility is important in that, in principle, it enables a country, through devaluation, to offset a loss in international competitiveness in a relatively painless manner. As such, it facilitates short-term adjustment to general, or country-specific economic shocks. The removal of the possibility of exchange rate adjustment, therefore, represents a more important loss to the least developed countries of the euro-zone, which are the ones that must carry out the most important

---

[1]   Decision 503, OJ L 194, 27.07.1999.

structural changes. Those countries must invest most, while spending least so as to conform to the Maastricht criteria and to the requirements of the Stability Pact [see section 7.2.1. and 7.3.2.].

In addition, those countries could **lose the advantage of lower labour costs.** As long as markets were protected by customs and other barriers, salaries in certain countries were much lower than in others, compensating for the lower productivity of a labour force that was not very qualified. But in a common market, and even more in an economic and monetary union, freedom of movement for workers, better information on respective situations, and trade union demands tend to align revenues towards the levels already attained in the more prosperous regions. This may be a positive outcome from a social point of view but it is one which engenders inflationist tendencies and creates difficulties for businesses in areas where productivity is low. If these businesses have to shut down, the workers lose their jobs and their revenue increase is merely an illusion.

From both an economic and social point of view, neither the weakest member countries nor the European Union can tolerate a substantial part of their patrimony being left to underdevelopment because of economic integration. The prosperity of certain areas of the union cannot be paid for by the decline or stagnation of other areas. Wide **disparities are intolerable in a community**, if the term is to have any meaning at all. Furthermore, disparities do not just imply a poorer quality of life for the disadvantaged regions, but indicate a failure to take advantage of economic opportunities that could benefit the Union as a whole.

For all these reasons, the Treaty on the European Union states in its Article 2 that the strengthening of **economic and social cohesion is a fundamental objective of the Union**. Article 158 (TEC) specifies that in order to promote its overall harmonious development, the Community shall develop and pursue its actions leading to the strengthening of its economic and social cohesion, aiming, in particular, at reducing disparities between the levels of development of the various regions and the backwardness of the least-favoured regions, including rural areas. Although all Community policies can contribute to reinforcing economic and social cohesion, as is stated in Article 159 (TEC), a major role is, certainly, played by the **Structural Funds** (Art. 161 TEC). In the Community terminology "Structural Funds" or simply "Funds" mean the European Regional Development Fund (ERDF), the European Social Fund (ESF), the European Agricultural Guidance and Guarantee Fund (EAGGF) - Guidance Section, and the Financial Instrument for Fisheries Guidance (FIFG).

The situation in which certain Member States find themselves necessitates special efforts to promote economic and social cohesion and thus enable them to comply with the convergence criteria required inside the EMU. Indeed, among these criteria is, in particular, the one on curbing public deficits [see section 7.3.2.]. In order to satisfy this condition, the **less wealthy countries must apply very strict budgetary disciplines**, whereas they need, at the same time, pursue and even increase public investments in order to close the prosperity gap with the other Member States.

In order to cope with these contradictory requirements, Article 161 (TEC) and a Protocol annexed to the Treaty of Maastricht [see section 2.2.] have provided for the creation of the **Cohesion Fund**. This must contribute financially to projects in the fields of the environment and transport infrastructure for trans-European networks [see section 6.8.] in Member States whose per capita GNP is less than 90% of the Community average (Greece, Spain, Portugal and Ireland) and which are implementing a programme aiming to fulfil the conditions of economic convergence announced in Article 104 of the EC Treaty[1]. In conjunction with the fulfilment of the conditions of economic convergence as set out in Article 104 of the Treaty and with the need for sound management of the government deficit, conditionality in the granting of the Fund's financial assistance takes account of the obligations of the beneficiary Member States with regard to excessive government deficits, the Resolution of the European Council on the Stability and Growth Pact [see sections 7.2.1. and 7.3.2.] and the stability of the euro.

The objective of economic and social cohesion means a great deal more than the mere redistribution of funds to the poorest Member States and regions. It requires coherent action through a coordination of national and common economic policies. Therefore, the common regional policy has two wings. Firstly, it seeks to **coordinate national regional policies** by formulating guidelines and establishing certain principles in order to avoid distortion of competition between Member States through their regional aid schemes. Secondly, it **coordinates the various policies and financial instruments of the EU** to give them a "regional dimension" and thus more impact on regions most in need of care. These two wings of the Community regional policy are examined in the rest of this chapter.

12.2. Coordination of national and Community policies

The first part of Community regional policy is the coordination and monitoring of the **regional policies of the Member States**. Article 87 (TEC) states that any aid which distorts or threatens to distort competition by favouring certain undertakings or the production of certain goods shall, in so far as it affects trade between Member States, be incompatible with the common market. But in the very same article 87, paragraphs 3(a) and (c) specify that the following may be considered to be compatible with the common market: "aid to promote the economic development of areas where the standard of living is abnormally low or where there is serious

---

[1] Regulation 1164/94, OJ L 130, 25.05.1994 and Regulations 1264/1999 and 1265/1999, OJ L 161, 26.06.1999.

underemployment" and, more generally, "aid to facilitate the development of certain economic activities or of certain economic areas, where such aid does not adversely affect trading conditions to an extent contrary to the common interest". In monitoring regional aid, the Commission should seek on the basis of economic criteria to determine which are the least-favoured regions of the EU and establish for each of them the level of aid intensity so that the aid be targeted at those areas of the Union which are really experiencing difficulties. The monitoring of State aid thus makes a considerable contribution to the economic and social cohesion of the Union.

12.2.1. Coordination of national regional policies

The European Commission determines the compatibility or incompatibility of a given regional aid with the common market. Article 88 (TEC) states that the Commission shall, in cooperation with the Member States, keep **under constant review all systems of aid** existing in those States. It must be informed, in sufficient time to enable it to submit its comments, of any plans to grant or alter aid. The Member States notify the Commission of proposed levels of regional aid and the latter either approves or amends them, often to lower levels. The Member State concerned must not put its proposed measures into effect until the procedure initiated by the Commission has resulted in a final decision. If the State concerned does not comply with this decision within the prescribed time, the Commission or any other interested State may refer the matter to the Court of Justice directly, which happens quite often.

The successive enlargements of the Community have boosted its regional diversity and accentuated the need for new instruments to control regional aid. This is why article 158 (TEC) gave fresh impetus to the aim of stronger economic and social cohesion and stipulated that the Community should attempt to close the gap between its regions and help the less-favoured regions to catch up. In response to these requirements, the Commission introduced new **regional aid guidelines** for the application of Article 87, paragraph 3 (a and c) of the EC Treaty[1]. The guidelines, which are applicable in the period 2000 to 2006, lay down the aid ceilings to be applied according to the severity of regional problems and are based on four fundamental principles: (a) aid should be concentrated on the poorest regions for maximum effectiveness; (b) the total amount of regional aid should be reduced and better distributed between the "cohesion regions" (Spain, Greece, Portugal, Ireland) and the more prosperous regions; (c) the real effect of aid on employment should be taken into account and, to that end, consideration given to the possibility of granting aid not only on the basis of investment but also in the light of the number of jobs created; and (d) there should be consistency between the regional aid maps and those

---

[1]   OJ C 212, 12.08.1988, p. 2-5.

used for the Structural Funds[1]. Regional **aid for large investment projects**, while covered by the regional aid guidelines, is also subject to specific rules, because it might be granted to large firms which are little affected by region-specific problems[2].

12.2.2. Coordination of Community policies

The general Regulation on the Structural Funds specifies that the Commission and the Member States must ensure that the operations of the Funds are consistent with other Community policies and operations[3]. Indeed, several **common policies favour by their nature the process of integration and cohesion**. Thus, the common social policy has an important impact on labour law, health and security at work, free movement of workers and equal opportunities for men and women in the poor regions of the Union. Community research programmes develop research capabilities in weaker Member States strengthening their scientific and technological base and accelerating innovation and economic development. The common agricultural policy has also a positive cohesion effect, with the cohesion countries receiving net transfers through it.

Since any economic activity is of necessity localised in one area, the majority of the Community's measures, be it in agriculture, industry, transport or research, have an impact at regional level. The Community's regional policy consequently attempts to ensure consistency between regional objectives and those of other common policies through the method of **regional impact assessment (AIR)**[4]. The purpose of assessing Community measures from a regional viewpoint is to correct any negative regional effects, which they may have, or to enhance any positive ones. A Community framework for cooperation supports awareness-raising on sustainable urban development and urban environment, through development and transfer of good practices and cooperation between actors involved in sustainable development[5].

The "**Community initiatives**", dealt with in the following part of this chapter, play also a role in coordinating the objectives of several common policies. Indeed, Community initiatives seek to: contribute to resolving serious problems directly related to the implementation of other Community policies; promote the application of Community policies at the level of the regions; or favour the solving of problems common to certain categories of regions. Thus, the INTERREG initiative favours the enlargement process towards Central and Eastern European countries, LEADER aims at rural development [see section 21.5.2.], while URBAN and EQUAL pursue the objectives of the common social policy [see section 13.5.6.].

---

[1] OJ C 74, 10.03.1998.
[2] Communication from the Commission OJ C 70, 19.03.2002.
[3] Ibid.
[4] OJ C 36, 09.02.1979, p. 10-11.
[5] Decision 1411/2001, OJ L 91, 13.07.2001 and Decision 786/2004, OJ L 138, 30.04.2004.

12.3. Coordination of Community financial instruments

According to Article 10 of the general Regulation on the Structural Funds[1], coordination between the various Funds must be carried out in particular through:

(a) the plans, the Community support frameworks, the operational programmes and the single programming documents [see section 12.3.1.];

(b) the monitoring and evaluation of assistance under an Objective [see section 12.3.1.]; and

(c) the indicative guidelines published by the Commission that help the competent national and regional authorities to draw up development plans and to carry out any revision of the assistance.

In order to maximise the stimulus provided by the budget resources deployed, making use of appropriate financial instruments, the Community assistance provided in the form of grants may be combined in an appropriate way with loans and guarantees of the **European Investment Bank (EIB)** [see section 7.3.3.]. The latter is the longest standing regional development instrument, for the Treaty of Rome called upon it to ensure a balanced and smooth development of the common market in the interests of the Community (Art. 267 TEC). Almost 75% of EIB financing in the Community contribute to regional development, although they pursue other objectives such as those of promoting SMEs and trans-European networks [see section 6.8.]. The EIB notably supplies long-term capital for the financing of infrastructure projects in the fields of transport, energy and telecommunications.

12.3.1. The objectives and methods of the Structural Funds

According to Article 159 (TEC), the "Structural Funds", i.e. the European Regional Development Fund (ERDF), the European Social Fund (ESF), the European Agricultural Guidance and Guarantee Fund (EAGGF) - Guidance Section, and the Financial Instrument for Fisheries Guidance (FIFG), should participate in a coordinated way to the attainment of the objective of economic and social cohesion in the Community. To this end, the Regulation laying down general provisions on the Structural Funds ascribes to the Funds the attainment of the following three **priority objectives** for the period 2000-2006[2]:

---

[1]   Regulation 1260/1999, OJ L 161, 26.06.1999 and Regulation 1105/2003, OJ L 158, 27.06.2003.

[2]   Ibid.

- **Objective 1** promotes the development and structural adjustment of regions whose development is lagging behind, i.e. whose average per capita GDP is below 75% of the European Union average, through funds coming from the ERDF, ESF and EAGGF-Guidance and FIFG [see section 12.1.1.]. Almost 70% of the total funding is reserved for the Objective 1 regions and almost 20% of the Union's total population should benefit from the measures taken under this Objective. This Objective also covers the most remote regions (the French overseas *départements*, the Azores, Madeira and the Canary Islands) as well as the areas eligible under the former Objective 6 created pursuant to the Act of Accession of Austria, Finland and Sweden;

- **Objective 2** supports, through all four Structural Funds, the economic and social conversion of areas facing structural difficulties and in particular areas undergoing socio-economic change in the industrial and service sectors, declining rural areas, urban areas in difficulty and depressed areas dependent on fisheries. 11,5% of the funding goes to these regions, which account for some 18% of the Union's population;

- **Objective 3** contributes to the adaptation and modernisation of policies and systems of education, training and employment outside the regions covered by Objective 1 and provides a policy frame of reference for all measures promoting human resource development. Objective 3 is, in fact, the reference framework for the measures taken under the Title on employment in the EC Treaty and under the European Employment Strategy [see section 13.3.]. The ESF alone is responsible for this Objective and disposes of a little over 12% of the Structural Funds.

In order to attain the objectives stated above, the work of the Structural Funds is based on four principles: the **concentration** of measures on those objectives; **programming**, which results in multiannual development programmes; additionality; and partnership. These specific principles of structural operations are compatible with the general principle of **subsidiarity** [see section 3.2.], according to which the implementation of assistance is the responsibility of the Member States without prejudice to the powers vested in the Commission, notably for managing the general budget of the European Communities [see section 3.4.].

Programming means the organising, decision-making and financing process carried out in a number of stages to implement on a multiannual basis the joint action of the Community and the Member States to attain the Objectives mentioned above. **Additionality** means that Community action is viewed as a complement to the corresponding national action or a contribution to it; it must not replace but rather bring added value to national initiatives.

The Commission evaluates the plans and action proposed by the Member States and draws up, with the agreement of the national authorities, the **Community Support Framework (CSF)** for Community structural operations in a certain region. This Framework includes:

(d) a statement of the strategy and priorities for joint Community and national action; their specific objectives; evaluation of the expected impact; the economic policies, the strategy for developing employment and the regional policies of the Member State concerned;

(e) an indication of the nature and the duration of the operational programmes not decided at the same time as the Community support framework, including their specific aims and the priorities selected;

(f) an indicative financing plan specifying, for each priority and each year, the financial allocation envisaged for the contribution of each Fund, where appropriate the EIB and the other financial instruments.

Instead of a CSF, the Commission may, at the request of the State concerned, adopt a **Single Programming Document (SPD)**, which is produced by a simplified procedure whereby the strategic priorities, programming procedures and aid granted are all included in a single document. Hence, an SPD contains the same information to be found in a Community support framework and operational programme, notably: (a) the strategy and priorities for joint Community and national action; (b) a summary description of the measures planned to implement the priorities; (c) an indicative financing plan; and (d) the provisions for implementing the SPD. SPDs are generally employed in respect of Objectives 2 and 3. They are exceptionally employed in respect of Objective 1, where the Community allocation does not exceed EUR 1000 million. Each CSF or SPD is supervised by a Monitoring Committee set up by the Member State.

12.3.2. European Regional Development Fund

The **European Regional Development Fund (ERDF)** has been reformed four times since its creation in 1975, demonstrating both the Community's growing commitment to regional development and its increased experience on this matter. The new ERDF Regulation is characterised by considerable flexibility at operational level. The Fund can make use of all forms of financial operation, such as co-financing of regional operational programmes, regional aid systems and major projects for infrastructures and productive investments, the granting of global subsidies to assist local development initiatives and support for technical assistance and for preparation and assessment measures[1].

The Regulation laying down general provisions on the Structural Funds provides that the main task of the ERDF is to contribute to the **attainment of Objectives 1 and 2** defined by that Regulation[2] [see sections 12.1.1 and 12.3.1.]. In addition, in the regions designated under Objective 1, the ERDF may contribute towards the financing of **investment in education and health** that is beneficial to the region's structural adjustment. It also

---

[1] Regulation 1783/1999, OJ L 213, 13.08.1999.
[2] Regulation 1260/1999, OJ L 161, 26.06.1999 and Regulation 1105/2003, OJ L 158, 27.06.2003.

contributes to the implementation of the **Community initiatives** for cross-border, transnational and inter-regional cooperation ("INTERREG") and for economic and social regeneration of cities and urban neighbourhoods in crisis ("URBAN") [see section 12.3.3.]. Finally, the ERDF contributes to the financing of **innovative measures**, notably studies, pilot projects and exchanges of experience.

12.3.3. Community Initiatives

Outside the CSFs and the SPDs [see section 12.3.1.], the Structural Funds operate individually or collectively to support **programmes of common interest called Community initiatives**. Whereas Community Support Frameworks are underpinned by national development plans, Community initiatives are transnational programmes whose objectives are the same for all of the eligible regions as they aim to resolve problems which have a particular relevance for the Community. However, by way of application of the principles of partnership and subsidiarity, national, regional or local authorities are deeply involved in drawing up and implementing Community initiatives, in particular through the operational programmes which they submit to the Commission.

Community initiatives are, in fact, **operations of Community interest** carried out at the initiative of the Commission to supplement those implemented under the priority objectives. These Community initiatives should concentrate on promoting cross-border, transnational and interregional cooperation, economic and social regeneration of cities and urban neighbourhoods in crisis, rural development and the development of human resources in the context of equal opportunities[1].

The four Community initiatives in operation for the period 2000 to 2006 are:

- **INTERREG**, financed by the ERDF, is concerned with transnational and interregional cooperation intended to encourage the harmonious, balanced and sustainable development of the whole of the Community area;
- **URBAN**, financed by the ERDF, is geared to the economic and social regeneration of cities and urban neighbourhoods in crisis, so as to promote sustainable urban development [see section 13.5.6.];
- **LEADER**, financed by the EAGGF-Guidance Section, is aimed at rural development [see section 21.5.2.];
- **EQUAL**, financed by the European Social Fund, is focusing on transnational cooperation for new means of combating all forms of discrimination and inequalities in relation to the labour market [see section 13.3.2.].

---

[1] Ibid.

12.4. Appraisal and outlook

The common regional policy has grown in importance since the Treaty made it an **essential instrument of economic and social cohesion**, itself necessary for the progress of economic and monetary union, implying the convergence of the Member States' economies. Indeed, the regional policy of the Union promotes the concept of European solidarity by completing and guiding the action of the Member States in view of a balanced European integration, profitable not only to the poor regions, but also to the rest of the Union.

In view of the new objective of economic and monetary union that it set, **the Treaty of Maastricht** provided both a frame of reference and support for the common regional policy, notably by establishing economic and social cohesion as a fundamental objective of the Union, creating the Cohesion Fund, setting up the Committee of the Regions and promoting trans-European infrastructure networks. By signing and ratifying this Treaty, the Member States acknowledged that the objectives of the EMU and of economic and social cohesion should be pursued in parallel. As seen in the Chapter on economic and monetary union, such union, implying the abandonment of the use of exchange rate adjustment as a means of rebalancing the national economy, would not be feasible without an efficient regional policy revolving around sufficient capital transfers from the richer to the poorer regions of the EU [see sections 7.2.1. and 7.4.]. The problem for the least-favoured regions is, in particular, to ensure that the effort to stabilise the budget does not choke off the investment in basic infrastructure, education and training which those regions require.

Helping the poorer Member States fulfil the requirements for participation in the EMU is in the interest of all. Indeed, the capital transfers carried out in the framework of an efficient regional policy are not just an offering to the less fortunate in the Union. They are also in the economic interest of the more prosperous States, since they develop markets for their products and help to stimulate growth in all the territory of the Union.

The efforts of the Union to develop its poorest regions are proving to be successful. The gross domestic product (GDP) per head of poorer regions is converging towards the Community average. Between 1986 and 1996, GDP per head in the 10 poorest regions increased from 41% of the EU average to 50%, and in the 25 poorest regions it rose from 52% to 59%. GDP per head in the four Cohesion countries went up from 65% of the EU average to 77% in 1999. The structural and cohesion policies have largely contributed to these results. But it is not only the poorest Member States which have benefited. Estimates show that almost 40% of all funding that flows into the poorest Member States returns to the richer ones in the form of purchase of know-how or capital equipment. The Cohesion Fund enabled the beneficiary countries (Spain, Greece, Ireland and Portugal) to sustain a substantial level of public investment in the areas of the environment and transport, while complying with the goals of reducing expected budget deficits through the convergence programmes drawn up in the context of economic and monetary union. In any case, substantial disparities remain, both in terms of GDP and unemployment, so that assistance must be reviewed periodically to ensure that it is concentrated in the regions that most need it.

Bibliography on regional policy

- CYPHER James, DIETZ James. *The process of economic development.* London; New York: Routledge, 2004.
- EUROPEAN COMMISSION. *Rural development: the impact of EU research (1998-2004).* Luxembourg: EUR-OP*, 2004.
- *The TRANSVISION blueprint: Bridging historically and culturally close neighbouring regions separated by national borders.* Luxembourg: EUR-OP*, 2004.
- *The AGRIBLUE blueprint: Sustainable territorial development of the rural areas of Europe.* Luxembourg: EUR-OP*, 2004.
- *The UPGRADE blueprint: Foresight strategy and actions to assist regions of traditional industry towards a more knowledge based community.* Luxembourg: EUR-OP*, 2004.
- MAGNIER Patrice, RERREAULT Jacques, BESNAINOU Denis. *Rapport de l'instance d'évaluation sur les fonds structurels européens et les politiques régionales.* Paris: Documentation française, 2004.
- MARTIN Carmela (et al.). "Catching up and EU accession: issues of real and nominal convergence", *Empirica*, v. 30, n. 3, 2003, p. 199-334.
- MORA Toni, VAYÁ Esther, SURIÑACH Jordi. "The enlargement of the European Union and the spatial distribution of economic activity", *Eastern European Economics*, v. 42, n. 5, September-October 2004, p. 6-35.
- PASQUIER Romain (et al.). *L'Europe au microscope du local.* Paris: L'Harmattan, 2004.
- TEMPLE LANG John. "Declarations, regional authorities, subsidiarity, regional policy measures, and the Constitutional Treaty", *European Law Review,* v. 29, n. 1, February 2004, p. 94-105.

The publications of the Office for Official Publications of the European Communities (EUR-OP) exist generally in all official languages of the EU.

DISCUSSION TOPICS

1. What is the need for a common regional policy in the stages of the common market and of the economic and monetary union?
2. What is the meaning of economic and social cohesion in the EU?
3. Which are the two wings of the common regional policy and how do they complement each other?
4. Outline the objectives and methods of the Structural Funds of the EU.
5. Discuss the role of the common regional policy within an enlarged Union containing a large number of poor regions.

Chapter 13

SOCIAL PROGRESS POLICIES

Diagram of the chapter

Social cohesion in the EU
p. 196

Employment policy
p. 197

Education, training and youth policies
p. 201

Living and working conditions
p. 206

The employment strategy of the Union
p. 198

Foundations of training and education policies
p. 202

Social dialogue p. 206

Worker information, p. 207

Social protection p. 209

The actions of the European Social Fund
p. 200

Education and training programmes
p. 203

Organisation of work, p. 211

Equal treatment for women.p 212

Fight of social exclusion, p. 215

Safety at work, p. 216

Free movement of workers see section 6.4.

Public health protection, p.217

Given the varied economic structures of the Community Member States, their social problems were from the outset - and still are to some extent - quite different. It would not have been possible at the start - and that still holds true - to entrust the common social policy with the task of solving all the Member States' social problems. Such a solution depends to a great extent upon economic policy, which is still to a large degree in the hands of the individual governments. But as European integration advances and the Member States delegate significant economic and monetary policy instruments to the European Union, the latter **commits itself increasingly to the advancement of social progress** for all the peoples who make it up.

As we will see below, the Treaty of Rome aimed mainly at the free movement of workers [see section 6.4.] and relied above all on the functioning of the common market to improve living and working conditions in all Member States [see section 6.1.]. In line with the reform of the Structural Funds, which constituted the financial side of economic and social cohesion, the European Council, despite the opposition of Mrs. Thatcher, who was then Prime Minister of the United Kingdom, agreed in December 1989 on the **Community Charter of the fundamental rights of workers**, which represented the legal side of social cohesion and stressed particularly the alignment of social standards in the Member States: social protection; freedom of association and of collective bargaining; equal treatment for men and women; information, consultation and participation of workers; the protection of health and safety at the workplace; and the protection of children and adolescents, the elderly and the disabled. The Commission, which had proposed the Charter, proposed immediately after its adoption by the majority of heads of State of Government, a series of Community laws in order to implement it. But due to the unanimity rule required and the negative position of the United Kingdom, very few social measures were adopted before the completion of the internal market, which they should in principle follow in step. In order to get out of the impasse, eleven (out of the then twelve Member States), on the one hand, and the United Kingdom, on the other, signed at Maastricht a Social Protocol allowing the former to adopt alone the social measures that they deemed useful.

However, the anomaly of a common policy where one Member State did not share the others' objectives was corrected at Amsterdam, in June 1997, when **the Labour British Government decided to accede** to the social provisions of the new Treaty and to accept the Directives that had already been agreed under the Social Agreement. Protocol N° 14 on social policy annexed to the TEC and the Agreement on social policy attached thereto were repealed. The new Chapter 4 on Social Policy of the TEC incorporates most of the provisions of the Maastricht Social Agreement, notably: the objectives of the Community Charter of the Fundamental Social Rights of Workers and the measures to achieve those objectives.

It should be noted that the Community Charter of the Fundamental Social Rights of Workers of 1989 was surpassed by the **Charter of Fundamental Rights of the European Union** solemnly proclaimed in Nice, on 7 December 2000, by the European Parliament, the Council and the Commission[1] [see section 9.2.]. The 2000 Charter exceeds the 1989 Charter, on the one hand, because it guarantees not only social rights but all rights and freedoms of the citizens of the Union and, on the other, because it is an official document agreed by all Member States whereas, as seen above, the Social Charter was not agreed by the United Kingdom.

---

[1]   Solemn Declaration, OJ C 364, 18.12.2000.

13.1. The need for a common social policy

The objectives of the common social policy are very close to those of the common regional policy. The latter is directed towards improving the lot of the least-favoured regions of the European Union, the social policy that of its poorest citizens. Both seek to **even out the economic and social imbalances** in the Union and to ensure that the advantages ensuing from the functioning of the common market are shared amongst all the countries and all the citizens. Several of their measures are complementary, and their financial instruments are closely coordinated in order to put them into effect.

A Community social policy, which was necessary for the social cohesion of the Community as early as the stage of the progressive implementation of the common market, was provided for in vague terms in the EEC Treaty. Although its signatories stated that they were resolved to ensure social progress by common action and affirmed as the essential objective the improvement of the living and working conditions of their peoples, they remained entirely independent in the field of social policies. They placed their faith above all in the automatic improvement of social conditions, relying on the **knock-on effect that economic integration would produce**. They were not wrong in that, but they were not completely right either.

It is certain that the progressive integration of the economies in itself promotes the convergence of the social conditions of the States of the Community. The most characteristic social features of the Community during the first forty years of its existence have been the moderate growth of the population, increased life expectancy and shorter working life, the widespread extension of compulsory education and the mass entry of women into economic activities. In addition to those general phenomena there have been structural changes within sectors and sectoral movements from agriculture to industry and from the latter to the service industries. Thus, it is not by chance that the problems of employment, social security and the vocational training of certain categories of workers (the young, the old and women) are priorities in every Member State. It is, therefore, true that the closer the economic conditions become in a multinational integration scheme, the more the **social problems of the member states become similar** and more similar, not to say common, solutions become necessary. Likewise, the free movement of workers and transnational trade union contacts have promoted a degree of **upward levelling** of wages, social benefits and social protection.

Increased prosperity brought about largely by European integration, did not, however, resolve all the Community's social problems. It even made some of them more acute or gave rise to new ones, viz. problems of disadvantaged regions and categories of persons who do not participate fully in the general progress; problems of structural unemployment; problems relating to the distribution of income and wealth; contradictions between economic and social values and, on occasion, dramatic changes in lifestyle with negative consequences for the behaviour of young people. Since the Treaty on the European Community actually calls for a social model based on the market economy, democracy and pluralism, respect of individual rights, free collective bargaining, equality of opportunity for all, social welfare and solidarity, it instructs the common institutions to strive to attain those objectives.

13.2. Social cohesion in the European Union

Economic and social cohesion is an objective of the Community (Art. 2 and 3 TEC). Whereas the common regional policy deals mainly with economic cohesion, the common social policy tries to strengthen social cohesion. Article 136 of the EC Treaty declares that the Community and the Member States, having in mind fundamental social rights such as those set out in the European Social Charter signed at Turin on 18 October 1961 and in the 1989 Community Charter of the Fundamental Social Rights of Workers, have as their objectives the promotion of employment, improved living and working conditions, so as to make possible their harmonisation while the improvement is being maintained, proper social protection, dialogue between management and labour and the development of human resources. This last goal entails effectual education and training policies. Article 136 states also that the objectives of social progress and cohesion that it sets should ensue not only from the functioning of the common market, which will favour the harmonisation of social systems, but also from the procedures provided for in the Treaty and from the approximation of provisions laid down by law, regulation or administrative action (particularly in the context of the single market). However, the measures taken by the Community and the Member States to attain the objectives of Article 136 must take account of the diverse forms of national practices, in particular in the field of contractual relations, and the need to maintain the competitiveness of the Community economy.

To attain social cohesion in the Union **minimum social standards are needed**, having regard to differing national systems and needs, and to the relative economic strengths of the Member States. The establishment of a framework of basic minimum standards guarantees acceptable social and physical security conditions to all the workers in the Union. At the same time, it provides a bulwark against reducing social standards to increase the competitiveness of the businesses of one Member State and, hence, against using low social standards as an instrument of unfair economic competition. These basic standards should not over-stretch the economically weaker Member States, but they should not prevent the more developed Member States from implementing higher standards.

The **effort to complete the single market** at the end of the 1980s was to mean a fresh start for the Community's social policy and its financial instrument, the European Social Fund (ESF). The Single European Act and, later on, the Maastricht Treaty stated that "in order to promote its overall harmonious development, the Community shall develop and pursue its actions leading to the strengthening of its economic and social cohesion" (Art. 158 TEC). The Structural Funds, and especially the **European Social Fund** (ESF), represent the main instruments for promoting social cohesion within the Union [see section 12.1.2.]. As we saw under the heading of co-ordination of financial instruments in the chapter on regional development, the ESF contributes to the attainment of the Objectives set out set out in the context of the Community structural policy, namely of Objective 3 [see section 12.3.1.].

The **social policy agenda,** proposed by the Commission and approved by the Nice European Council in December 2000, provides the roadmap for employment and social policy, in the period from 2000 to 2006, translating the policy objectives of the Lisbon strategy for economic and social renewal into concrete measures[1] [see section 13.3.]. A high level of social cohesion is central to the Lisbon agenda. Strategies which strive for gender equality, for the eradication of poverty and social exclusion and for the modernisation of social protection systems, in particular pension and healthcare systems, play a key role in this agenda. In short, the Union aims at social progress and cohesion through the specific policies for employment, education and professional training, as well as through the promotion and improvement of living and working conditions, including social protection and social inclusion. These are the subjects examined in the following parts of this chapter.

13.3. Common employment policy

Unemployment became a matter of serious concern for all the countries of the Community around the mid-1970s. Until then employment problems in the Community merely consisted of structural and regional imbalances in a general context of full employment. A series of very variable economic factors led to the **rapid deterioration of the employment situation** in the Community, viz.: the inflation and economic recession of the late 1970s and early 1980s, resulting from monetary and energy crises [see sections 7.1. and 19.1.], lively competition from recently industrialised countries in Asia with cheap labour, a degree of saturation of demand in Europe for industrial goods and the evolution of the economy and of European companies towards a post-industrial stage. Many jobs thus became superfluous and disappeared. Others were created, but required new qualifications which most of the unemployed did not possess. At the same time, women, most of who had previously stayed at home, joined the labour market in force [see section 13.5.5.].

---

[1] COM (2000) 379 and COM (2003) 312, 2 June 2003.

Averaging more than 10% of the active population of the Member
States (with important differences between them), in the beginning of the
21st century, the unemployment rate of the European Union is seen as **its
gravest social problem**. The economic and social costs of this unemployment are enormous. They include not only the direct expenditure on providing social security support for the unemployed, but also: the loss of tax
revenue which the unemployed would pay out of their income if they were
working; the increased burden on social services; rising poverty, crime and
ill-health. Special concern focuses on the lack of prospects for new entrants
to the labour market, especially young people and women and for people
excluded from regular work [see section 13.5.6.]. Under the pressure of
these problems was endorsed the employment strategy of the Union.

13.3.1. The employment strategy of the Union

The EU Treaty sets among the objectives of the Union, mentioned in
Article 2 (TEU), that of promoting economic and social progress and a
"high level of employment". The new **Title on Employment** of the EC
Treaty urges the Member States and the Community to work towards developing a coordinated strategy for employment and particularly for promoting a skilled, trained and adaptable workforce and labour markets re-
sponsive to economic change (Art. 125 TEC). To this end, Member States
must regard promoting employment as a matter of common concern and
must coordinate their action in this respect within the Council (Art. 126
TEC). The Community must encourage cooperation between the Member
States, support and, if necessary, complement their action (Art. 127 TEC).
The European Council should each year consider the employment situation
of the Community and adopt conclusions thereon, on the basis of which the
Council should draw up employment guidelines, consistent with the broad
guidelines of economic policies [see section 7.3.1.], which the Member
States should take into account in their employment policies (Art 128
TEC). The Council, under the co-decision procedure with the Parliament
[see section 4.3.], may adopt incentive measures designed to encourage
cooperation between Member States and to support their action in the field
of employment through initiatives aimed at developing exchanges of information and best practices (Art 129 TEC). Indeed, a Council decision
aims at: fostering cooperation in the field of employment as regards analysis, research and monitoring; identifying good practices and promoting exchanges and transfers of information and experience; and developing an
active information policy[1].

An extraordinary European Council on employment took place in Luxembourg on 20 and 21 November 1997. It enacted the definition, as from
1998, of **guidelines for employment** and placed emphasis on harnessing
systematically the common policies of the Community in support of em-

---

[1]   Decision 98/171, OJ L 63, 04.03.1998.

ployment. In adopting the 1999 employment guidelines, the Council set out the subsequent procedures for monitoring the application of the guidelines by the Member States[1]. These guidelines help the Member States to devise their own strategies, while preserving the four-pillar structure established in 1998[2]: improving employability, i.e. giving unemployed people and workers in general better opportunities to find work, with the emphasis on suitable training; developing entrepreneurship; encouraging adaptability; and strengthening equal opportunities policies for women and men. By mid-June, each Member State must submit to the Council and the Commission a report concerning the implementation of the previous national action plan and describing the adjustments made to this plan in the light of the changes introduced by the current employment guidelines. By the end of the year, the Council adopts guidelines for the Member States' employment policies for the next year and publishes a recommendation on the implementation of employment policies in the Member States[3]. The Commission monitors the employment strategy pursued by the Member States and publishes an annual report on employment rates considering how each Member State could help to achieve the goal of raising employment rates as an objective of economic policy. The Council has provided a legal basis for Commission activities forming part of the European employment strategy, concerning analysis, research, cooperation and action in the field of employment[4].

Going a step further in the coordination of employment policies, the Cologne European Council (3 and 4 June 1999) adopted a **European Employment Pact** aimed at a sustainable reduction of unemployment. The European Employment Pact embodies a comprehensive overall approach bringing together all the Union's employment policy measures, which support and mutually reinforce one another. In the broad economic policy guidelines (BEPGs), the Member States and the Community agree annually on the main elements of their economic policy [see section 7.3.1.]; in the employment guidelines the Member States and the Community agree annually on the main elements of the coordinated employment strategy; in the macroeconomic dialogue (within the framework of the ECOFIN Council), information and opinions of the relevant Community institutions and the social partners are exchanged in an appropriate manner concerning the question of how to design macroeconomic policy in order to increase and make full use of the potential for growth and employment.

The Lisbon European Council (23 and 24 March 2000) agreed to a **strategic goal** to be pursued over the first decade of the 21st century, with the aim of boosting employment, economic reform and social cohesion within the framework of a knowledge-based economy. The three key elements of this strategy are geared to: preparing the transition to a knowl-

---

[1]   Resolution, OJ C 69, 12.03.1999, p. 2-8.
[2]   Resolution, OJ C 30, 28.01.1998, p. 1-5.
[3]   See, e.g. Decision 2003/578 and Recommendation 2003/579, OJ L 197, 05.08.2003.
[4]   Decision 98/171, OJ L 63, 04.03.1998.

edge-based economy and society by means of policies tailored more to the needs of the information society and research and development, stepping up the process of structural reform to boost competitiveness and innovation, while completing the internal market; modernising the European social model, investing in people and combating social exclusion; and sustaining a healthy economic outlook and favourable growth prospects by applying an appropriate macroeconomic policy mix. Implementation of the Lisbon strategic goal involves: fixing guidelines for the Union combined with specific timetables for achieving the goals in the short, medium and long terms; translating these European guidelines into national and regional policies; and periodic monitoring, evaluation and peer review.

13.3.2. The actions of the European Social Fund

According to Article 146 (TEC) the **European Social Fund (ESF)** aims to: (a) render the employment of workers easier and to increase their geographical and occupational mobility within the Community; and (b) facilitate their adaptation to industrial changes and to changes in production systems, in particular through vocational training and retraining. The ESF is administered by the Commission, which is assisted in this task by a Committee composed of representatives of the governments, trade unions and employers' organisations (Art. 147 TEC).

The framework and **political priorities** of the ESF for the period 2000-2006 are defined in Regulation 1784/99 on the European Social Fund[1]. This Regulation falls within the overall framework set up under Council Regulation 1260/99 laying down general provisions on the Structural Funds[2] [see section 12.3.]. The latter contains specific provisions concerning the ESF inviting it to intervene on the whole territory of the EU in pursuit of Objectives 1, 2 and 3 fixed by the general regulation [see sections 12.1.1 and 12.3.1.]. According to its own Regulation No 1784/99, **the ESF's task** is to support measures which aim to prevent and combat unemployment, develop human resources and foster social integration in the labour market, so as to promote a high level of employment, equal opportunities for men and women, sustainable development and economic and social cohesion. In particular, it must assist the measures taken in line with the European strategy and guidelines on employment.

The **Objective 3 of the Structural Funds**, which is the exclusive responsibility of the ESF, contributes to the adaptation and modernisation of national policies and systems of education, training and employment outside the regions covered by Objective 1 and provides a policy frame of reference for all measures promoting human resource development. In addition, the ESF encompasses three horizontal issues: promotion of local em-

---

[1] Regulation 1784/99, OJ L 21, 13.08.1999
[2] Regulation 1260/1999, OJ L 161, 26.06.1999 and Regulation 1105/2003, OJ L 158, 27.06.2003.

ployment initiatives (including territorial pacts for employment); the social dimension and employment in the information society; equal opportunities for men and women.

In accordance with the provisions laid down in the General Regulation governing the Structural Funds [see section 12.3.], the ESF helps to implement the Community initiative to combat all forms of discrimination and inequality in the labour market **(EQUAL)**[1] [see section 12.3.3.]. The Equal Initiative aims to promote new ways of **combating all forms of exclusion, discrimination and inequalities** in the labour market, in the context of implementing the European employment strategy [see section 13.3.1.] and the National Action Plans.

13.4. Education, vocational training and youth policies

The problems of employment and vocational training are related, as very often the jobs offered require qualifications, which those seeking employment lack. That is why **employment and vocational training policies are also linked**. In fact, training is an instrument of active labour market policy. At the same time, measures promoting vocational training or retraining promote the employment or re-employment of workers in sectors where qualified labour is needed. Many workers cannot secure employment without becoming specialised, but they cannot acquire specialisation through experience until they have found a job. Breaking this vicious circle through vocational training is vital as workers should be able to change more frequently jobs throughout their working lives in the future.

Vocational training is not only a basic human right, enabling workers to realise their full potential, but also a **prerequisite for technological progress** and regional development. Indeed, a skilled, adaptable and mobile workforce is an essential component in the competitiveness, productivity and quality of companies, since it allows industries and regions to adapt rapidly to the requirements of technology and market trends and thus to become or remain competitive. Unemployment is in fact rife especially in the traditional industries in decline (steel, shipbuilding, textiles...), whilst the new industries (information technology, telecommunications, aerospace...) are badly in need of qualified labour. The new qualifications can help the European economy to effect the necessary structural changes in the information society and enable it better to face competition from the newly industrialised countries. The EU's education and training policies aim therefore to develop human resources throughout people's working lives, starting with basic education and working through initial training to continuing training.

---

[1] Ibid.

13.4.1. The foundations of training and education policies

Underlying the common education policy is the collection and dissemination of information on the programmes and projects of the various higher education establishments in the Member States. An **Education Information Network** in the European Community, under the name of EURYDICE, is available to users with responsibilities in the field of education, such as the Community institutions, national authorities and officials responsible for higher education in the Member States[1]. The Eurydice network is the chief instrument for providing information on national and Community structures, systems and developments in the field of education. It assists the drawing up of comparative analyses, reports and surveys on common priority topics determined inter alia in the Education Committee and in the Advisory Committee on Vocational Training[2]. A Community action programme supports bodies and their activities which seek to extend and deepen knowledge of the building of Europe, or to contribute to the achievement of the common policy objectives in the field of education and training[3]. Another Community action programme provides financial support to organisations active at European level in the field of youth[4].

An organ of the common policy on professional training is the **European Centre for the Development of Vocational Training (CEDEFOP)**, located in Thessaloniki[5]. Cedefop's programme of work focuses on two priority areas, namely qualifications and vocational training systems. The former is essentially concerned with the transparency of qualifications and new occupations at European level and the impact of new forms of work organisation and qualifications on training systems. The latter is concerned with strategies for the optimum combination of types and phases of training with a view to achieving a lifelong learning process and with improved teacher training.

The **European Training Foundation**, established in Turin, supports the reform of vocational education and training and management training in over 40 partner countries and territories, divided into four main geographical blocs (Mediterranean region, western Balkans, eastern Europe and central Asia, candidate/acceding countries), and provides technical assistance to the Commission for the Tempus programme[6] [see section 13.4.2.].

As agreed at the Lisbon European Council (23 and 24 March 2000) [see section 13.3.1.], the *e***Learning initiative** is designed to make good the shortcomings in Europe in the use of new information and communica-

---

[1]   Resolution, OJ C 329, 31.12.1990, p. 23-24 and Council Conclusions, OJ C 336, 19.12.1992, p. 7.

[2]   Decision 2004/223, OJ L 68, 06.03.2004.

[3]   Decision 791/2004, OJ L 138, 30.04.2004.

[4]   Decision 790/2004, OJ L 138, 30.04.2004.

[5]   Regulation 337/75, OJ L 39, 13.02.1975 and Regulation 251/95, OJ L 30, 09.02.1995.

[6]   Regulation 1360/90, OJ L 131, 23.05.1990 and Regulation 2666/2000, OJ L 306, 07.12.2000.

tions technologies, thereby accelerating the pace of change in education and training systems and helping Europe to move towards a knowledge-based society[1]. The key objectives are focused on: improving infrastructure, notably equipping all schools in the Union; training the population at all levels by making schools, training centres and other places of learning accessible to all; development of high-quality multimedia services and content; and networking of schools (European Schoolnet). The Commission mobilises Community programmes and instruments to achieve these objectives.

A Council decision on the promotion of European pathways for work-linked training including apprenticeship established a **"Europass" document** recording, at Community level, periods of work-linked training, including apprenticeship undergone by an individual in a Member State other than that in which his/her training is based[2]. A Council Resolution invited the Commission to promote the **involvement of young people** in the development, execution and evaluation of Community youth activities and programmes[3].

Sporting activities are covered in a declaration to the final act of the Amsterdam Treaty, which contains two essential principles: that sport has a role in forging identity, which amounts to saying that national identities in this field should be respected; and that sports associations should be listened to by the bodies of the European Union when important questions affecting sport are at issue, which gives them a consultative function in these matters. A Council Resolution invited the Commission to devise, in cooperation with the Member States, a coherent approach with a view to exploiting the non-formal educational potential of sporting activities[4].

13.4.2. Education and training programmes

The Maastricht Treaty [see section 2.2.] has consecrated Community action in the fields of education, vocational training and youth. Article 149 (TEC) specifies that the Community contributes to the development of **quality education** by encouraging cooperation between Member States and, if necessary, by supporting and supplementing their action in the fields of: developing the European dimension in education, particularly through the teaching and dissemination of languages; mobility of students and teachers; cooperation between educational establishments; exchanges of information and experience; exchanges of young people and socio-educational instructors; and the development of distance education. Incentive measures, excluding any harmonisation of the laws and regulations of the Member States, are adopted by the Council acting in accordance with the procedure referred to in Article 251 (co-decision with the European

---

[1]   COM (2000) 318, 24 May 2000.
[2]   Decision 1999/51, OJ L 17, 22.01.1999.
[3]   Resolution, OJ C 42, 17.02.1999, p. 1-2.
[4]   Resolution 2000/C 8/03, JO C8, 12.01.2000.

Parliament). Community action must, however, fully respect the responsibility of the Member States for the content of teaching, the organisation of education systems and vocational training and their cultural and linguistic diversity. It is evident that the EU not only **respects the cultural diversity** of its Member States but also encourages it [see section 10.3.].

According to Article 150 of the EC Treaty, the Community implements a **vocational training policy**, which supports and supplements the action of the Member States and which aims to: facilitate adaptation to industrial changes, in particular through vocational training and retraining; improve initial and continuing vocational training in order to facilitate vocational integration and reintegration into the labour market; facilitate access to vocational training and encourage mobility of instructors and trainees; stimulate cooperation between educational or training establishments and firms; and develop exchanges of information and experience on issues common to the training systems of the Member States. This Article is the foundation of the common training policy.

The Union's new generation of education and training programmes is designed to develop a European dimension of education from the primary school to the university and to establish a genuine European market in skills and training. Indeed, the three programmes are interlinked by means of a **common framework encompassing six broad elements**: physical mobility for people; different forms of virtual mobility (use of new information and communications technologies); development of cooperation networks; promotion of linguistic and cultural skills; development of innovation through pilot projects based on transnational partnerships; and ongoing improvement of Community references (databases, exchanges of good practice) for the systems and policies relating to education, training and youth in the Member States. In the period 2000-2004, the three programmes gave the opportunity to 2.5 million young Europeans to participate in an exchange programme, thus promoting multination integration.

The **SOCRATES programme in the field of education** pursues four primary objectives: to strengthen the European dimension in education at all levels; to promote improvement of knowledge of the languages of the Union; to promote mobility in the field of education and remove obstacles in this connection, in particular by improving the recognition of diplomas and periods of study; and to encourage innovation in the development of educational practices. It comprises measures and projects intended to promote transnational cooperation in the field of education, centred around three themes: cooperation in higher education through the promotion of student and teaching staff mobility, the establishment of university networks and the incorporation of the European dimension into all levels of study (Erasmus and Lingua strands); cooperation in secondary school education through the promotion of partnerships between schools in different Member States and networks of schools for the joint pursuit of educational projects, with special reference to languages, the new information technologies, cultural heritage and environmental protection (Comenius strand); and measures applicable to all levels of education, concerning the promotion of language skills, open and distance education, and exchange of information and experience[1]. The projects funded by Socrates include joint syllabus development, masters' programmes, European modules, an Internet-based European schools network, integrated language courses and the development of the European dimension in a given academic discipline.

The **LEONARDO da Vinci programme in the field of vocational training** (2000-2004), which is endowed with EUR 1 150 million, aims at boosting quality, innovation and the European dimension in vocational systems and practices, through transnational cooperation[2]. The three objectives pursued by the action programme are social and occupational integration of young people, development of access to high-quality continuing training, and helping those in difficult circumstances to integrate better on the labour market. The Community measures implemented under the programme fall into five categories: mobility projects; pilot projects; linguistic competence; transnational networks; and reference material.

The action **programme in the youth field** (2000-2004) incorporates the pre-existing "**Youth for Europe**" programme, which seeks to help young people in their education outside the formal school system and the new "European voluntary service for young people"[3]. Both strands of the programme for youth focus on four aspects: individual mobility within the framework of European voluntary service; group mobility entailing transnational exchanges; initiatives giving young people an opportunity to play an active role in society; and activities tying in with other areas of Community action. The programme aims to help young people acquire the knowledge and skills to help them in their future development. It seeks also to foster a spirit of initiative, enterprise and creativity, promote respect for human rights and combat racism and xenophobia.

The **Trans-European Mobility programme for University Studies** (**TEMPUS III**) (2000-2006) is designed to promote, in line with the general guidelines and objectives of the Phare and Tacis programmes [see sections 25.2. and 25.4.], the development of higher education systems in the eligible countries (independent States of the former Soviet Union, nonassociated countries of Central Europe, Mongolia and Mediterranean countries) through cooperation with partners in the EU Member States[4]. Joint European projects (JEPs), involving at least one Member State University, a partner in another Member State and a university in a beneficiary country, are the main instruments of the programme. In addition, Tempus III supports the provision of individual grants to teachers, trainers, university administrators, senior ministerial officials and other experts in the higher education field from the eligible countries or from the Community, with a

---

[1]   Decision 253/2000, OJ L 28, 03.02.2000 and Regulation 885/2004, OJ L 168, 01.05.2004.
[2]   Decision 1999/382, OJ L 146, 11.06.1999 and Regulation 885/2004, OJ L 168, 01.05.2004.
[3]   Decision 1031/2000, OJ L 117, 18.05.2000 and Regulation 885/2004, OJ L 168, 01.05.2004.
[4]   Decision 1999/311, OJ L 120, 08.05.1999 and Decision 2002/601, OJ L 195, 24.07.2002.

view to promoting, through courses, seminars and visits, the development
and restructuring of higher education systems in the eligible countries.

13.5. Common measures for the improvement of living and working conditions

The concern of the European Union for the living and working conditions of its citizens is not new, but its commitment in this respect has
grown apace with economic integration. In article 117 of the EEC Treaty
the States of the Community agreed on "the need to **promote improved
working conditions and an improved standard of living for workers**, so
as to make possible their harmonisation while the improvement is being
maintained". They expected such a development to ensue, in the first place,
from the functioning of the common market, which would favour the harmonisation of social systems and, to the extent necessary, from the approximation of provisions laid down by law, regulation or administrative
action.

In Article 136 of the EC Treaty the Member States declare having as
their objectives the promotion of employment, improved living and working conditions, proper social protection, dialogue between management
and labour, the development of human resources with a view to lasting
employment and the combating of social exclusion. Under Article 137 of
the EC Treaty, the Community **supports and complements the activities
of the Member States** tending to improve, in particular: the working environment so as to protect workers health and safety, the working conditions,
the information and consultation of workers, the integration of persons excluded from the labour market and the equality of opportunities between
men and women. The Council and the Parliament adopt, by means of Directives, minimal requirements for the gradual implementation of these objectives. These subjects are examined below.

13.5.1. The social dialogue in the EU

The social dialogue which was under way from the beginning of the
Community, was consecrated first by the Single European Act and then by
the Treaty on European Union, which commits the Commission to develop
the **dialogue between management and labour at European level** by
submitting to them its guidelines for proposals in the social field (Art. 138
TEC). Social dialogue at European level covers the negotiations between
European social partners themselves and between them and the organs of
the European Union. This dialogue contributes to the improvement of mutual understanding between the social partners and to the stimulation
and/or acceptance of economic and social policies implemented at European level.

At general European level the social partners are represented by the European Trade Union Confederation (ETUC), the Union of Industries of the European Community (UNICE) and the European Centre of Public Enterprises (CEEP). The **Tripartite Social Summit for Growth and Employment** is intended to ensure that there is continuous consultation between the Council, the Commission and the social partners on economic, social and employment matters[1]. The summit consists of representatives, at the highest level, of the Council Presidency, the two subsequent Presidencies, the Commission and the social partners.

At sectoral level, the social dialogue is promoted through the Sectoral Dialogue Committees, which are established in those sectors where the social partners make a joint request to take part in a dialogue at European level, and where the organisations representing both sides of industry fulfil certain criteria[2]. Since 1995, the Commission and the social partners have set up, in Florence, the European Centre for Industrial Relations (ECIR)[3].

The dialogue between social partners may lead to common opinions and/or, should the partners so desire, to **contractual relations, including agreements**. Such agreements may be implemented either in accordance with the procedures and practices specific to management and labour in each Member State or, in matters concerning working conditions, at the joint request of the signatory parties, by a Council decision on a proposal from the Commission (Art. 139 TEC). Thus, the social partners negotiated and signed, on 14 December 1995, a collective agreement, that entitles both male and female workers to unpaid **parental leave** of at least three months' duration and to time off work in the event of an unforeseen family emergency. At the request of the social partners, a 1996 Directive, which originally excluded the United Kingdom but in 1998 was extended to it, lays down minimum requirements concerning parental leave and absence by dint of "force majeure"[4].

13.5.2. Worker information, consultation and participation

In addition to the social dialogue, the 1989 Social Charter, now incorporated in the EC Treaty (Art. 136 and 137), stipulates that information, consultation and participation for workers must be **developed along appropriate lines**, taking account of the practices in the various Member States. Such information, consultation and participation must be implemented in due time, particularly in the following cases:

---

[1] Decision 2003/174, OJ L 70, 14.03.2003.
[2] Decision 98/500, OJ L 225, 12.08.1998, p. 27-28.
[3] COM (95) 445, 25 December 1995.
[4] Directive 96/34, OJ L 145, 19.06.1996 and Directive 97/75, OJ L 10, 16.01.1998.

- when technological changes which, from the point of view of working conditions and work organisation, have major implications for the work-force, are introduced into undertakings;
- in connection with restructuring operations in undertakings or in cases of mergers having an impact on the employment of workers;
- in cases of collective redundancy procedures; and
- when workers, especially transboundary ones, are affected by the employment policies of the company where they are employed.

A general framework for minimum requirements relating to the right of employees to be informed and consulted is applicable to undertakings and establishments operating **within a single Member State** and with at least 50 or 20 employees respectively[1]. The emphasis is on fostering social dialogue and ways of ensuring information for employees and effective consultation of their representatives at the earliest possible stage of the company decision-making process. Employers must inform employees about: the recent and foreseeable development of the company's activities and its economic and financial situation; the situation, structure and reasonably foreseeable developments of employment within the company; decisions which may lead to substantial changes in work organisation or in contractual relations (consultation between the employer and employees entails dialogue and exchange of views, including efforts to reach prior agreement on the decision in question).

The information and consultation of workers **in multinational companies** is pursued by Directive 94/45 - extended in 1998 to the United Kingdom - providing for the establishment of a **European Works Council** or a procedure for the purposes of informing and consulting employees in European-scale undertakings[2]. The companies or groups of companies concerned are those with more than 1000 employees in total in the Community and with at least two establishments in different Member States, each employing at least 150 people. The Directive also covers undertakings or groups of undertakings with headquarters outside the territory of the Member States, in so far as they meet the above criteria. The Directive provides for the establishment, at the initiative of the company or group management or at the written request of at least 100 employees or their representatives in at least two Member States, of a "special negotiating body" with the task of concluding an agreement between the management and the employees' representatives, on the scope, composition, powers and term of office of the European committee to be set up in the undertaking or group, or the practical arrangements for an alternative procedure for the information and consultation of employees.

In parallel with the regulation on the statute for a European company , with the Latin designation *Societas Europaea* (SE) [see section 17.2.1.], the Council adopted a directive supplementing this statute with regard to

---

[1]   Directive 2002/14, OJ L 80, 23.03.2002.
[2]   Directive 94/45, OJ L 254, 30.09.1994 and Directive 97/74, OJ L 10, 16.01.1998.

the involvement of employees[1]. The rules relating to **employee involvement in the SE** seek to ensure that the creation of an SE does not entail the disappearance or reduction of practices of employee involvement existing within the companies participating in the establishment of an SE. Therefore, when the management or administrative organs of the participating companies draw up a plan for the establishment of an SE, they must as soon as possible after publishing the draft terms of merger or creating a holding company or after agreeing a plan to form a subsidiary or to transform into an SE, take the necessary steps (including providing information about the identity of the participating companies, concerned subsidiaries or establishments, and the number of their employees) to start negotiations with the representatives of the companies' employees on arrangements for the involvement of employees in the SE. For this purpose, a **special negotiating body** representative of the employees of the participating companies and concerned subsidiaries or establishments must be created in accordance with the provisions laid down in the directive. The special negotiating body and the competent organs of the participating companies must determine, by written agreement, arrangements for the involvement of employees within the SE. Member States must lay down standard rules on employee involvement which must satisfy the provisions of the directive.

13.5.3. Social protection

Article 136 (TEC) names proper social protection and improved living and working conditions among the objectives of the Community and the Member States. **Social protection in the strict sense** usually means social security, while **social protection in a broad sense** includes social security among other social rights of the citizens. In fact, under the heading "solidarity", the Charter of Fundamental Rights of the European Union[2] [see section 9.2.] mentions several rights, such as: the workers' right to information and consultation within the undertaking; the protection in the event of unjustified dismissal; fair and just working conditions; protection of young people at work; and, of course, social security and social assistance.

Concerning this last subject, namely social protection in the strict sense, the Charter of Fundamental Rights declares that the Union recognises and respects the entitlement to social security benefits and social services providing protection in cases such as maternity, illness, industrial accidents, dependency or old age, and in the case of loss of employment, in accordance with the rules laid down by Community law and national laws and practices. The Charter acknowledges that everyone residing and moving legally within the European Union is entitled to social security benefits and social advantages in accordance with Community law and national

---

[1] Regulation 2157/2001 and directive 2001/86, OJ L 294, 10.11.2001 and Regulation 885/2004, OJ L 168, 01.05.2004.

[2] Solemn declaration, OJ C 364, 18.12.2000.

laws and practices. According to the subsidiarity principle, however, the Member States must apply Community law if and where it exists. Concerning social security, Community provisions concern only the implementation of the principle of equal treatment for certain categories of workers, i.e. immigrants [see section 6.4.2.] and women [see section 13.5.5.]. For the rest, social security is covered by the national law of each Member State.

In fact, the Member States have preferred coordination rather than harmonisation of social protection and particularly social security legislation. On these subjects the Council decides alone (without the Parliament) and by unanimity, which means that any Member State may veto the adoption of Community legislation (Art 137 TEC). It is true that as systems of social protection reflect the traditions and existing social benefits of each individual State, it is not easy to change them. However, in an internal market and even more in an economic and monetary union, differences between the various social security systems can constitute distortions of competition, hinder the free movement of labour and exacerbate regional imbalances. Therefore, a regulation aims to coordinate national social security systems so as to eliminate obstacles to freedom of movement, whether for purposes of study, leisure or work, without losing any social security rights or protection to which they are entitled[1].

The Community has already made headway when the term "social protection" is taken in its broadest sense to cover social security and the right to work. An important Community measure for the social protection of employees, particularly those of multinational companies, is the Directive on the approximation of the laws of the Member States relating to **collective redundancies**[2]. Employers who envisage such redundancies have to hold consultations with workers' representatives on the possibilities of avoiding or reducing such redundancies. Moreover, the employer has to notify any proposed collective redundancy to the competent official authority and may not implement it before the expiry of a period of 30 days which the authority uses to try to find solutions to the problems that have arisen and/or to lessen the impact of the redundancies. This Directive is particularly important for workers employed by multinational companies which operate in one or more EU countries, as it prevents such companies from taking advantage of differences between national laws.

In the same vein, a Directive on the approximation of the laws of the Member States aims at safeguarding employees' rights in the event of **transfers of undertakings**, businesses or parts of businesses[3]. Before any such amalgamation, the workers' representatives have to be informed of the reasons for it and of its consequences for the employees and of the measures envisaged in their favour. In principle, the workers' rights and obligations are transferred to the new employer for at least a year and agreement

---

[1]   Regulation 883/2004, OJ L 166, 30.04.2004.
[2]   Directive 98/59, OJ L 225, 12.08.1998.
[3]   Directive 2001/23, OJ L 82, 28.03.2001.

on the conditions of the take-over has to be reached in consultation with the work force. Failing agreement between the employer or employers and the workers, an arbitration body gives a final ruling on the steps to be taken in favour of the workers. A representation scheme not dependent on the employer's will is necessary for compliance with the Directive[1].

But the workers' interests also need to be protected **in the event of the insolvency** of their employer, especially where assets are not sufficient to cover outstanding claims resulting from contracts of employment or employment relationships, even where the latter are privileged. To prevent such situations, a Council Directive obliges Member States to set up guarantee institutions independent of the employers' operating capital so that their assets are inaccessible to proceedings for insolvency[2]. In such an eventuality, those institutions must settle the claims of employees arising prior to the insolvency of the employer, including contributions under social security schemes.

A Directive on the **protection of young people at work** prohibits work by children (less than 15 years of age or still subject to compulsory full-time schooling), with the exception of certain cultural, artistic or sporting activities. Children of at least 14 years of age may take up combined work/ training schemes, in-plant work-experience schemes and certain light work[3]. The Directive asks Member States to strictly regulate work done by adolescents of more than 18 years of age, by imposing specific rules in respect of working time, daily rest periods, weekly rest periods and night work, and laying down technical, health and safety standards.

13.5.4. The organisation of work

Social protection in the EU covers also **atypical work**, i.e. other forms of work than that for an indefinite period, such as work for a specific duration, interim work, temporary work and seasonal work. These different forms of work enable companies to organise their work and their production in such a way as to improve productivity and thus become more competitive. Similarly, they enable workers to adapt the hours they work to suit their personal and family circumstances. But in a single market, certain essential conditions must be determined both to avoid distortions of competition and to protect the workers who opt for or accept (for want of something better) these new forms of work. These two objectives are contained in the Directives on atypical work. Thus a Directive guarantees satisfactory health and safety conditions of workers with a fixed-duration employment relationship (whose duration is fixed by objective criteria) or a temporary employment relationship (between the employer - a temporary employ-

---

[1] Judgments given on 8 June 1994, Cases C-382/92 and C-383/92, Commission v United Kingdom, ECR 1994, p. I-2435.

[2] Directive 80/987, OJ L 283, 20.10.1980 and Directive 2002/74, OJ L 270, 08.10.2002.

[3] Directive 94/33, OJ L 216, 20.08.1994.

ment agency - and the employee)[1]. Another Directive, based on a frame-work agreement on fixed-term work concluded between the social partners, ensures compliance with the principle of non-discrimination *vis-à-vis* employment of indefinite duration[2].

Contract duration is but one of the areas where there have been changes in the organisation of work in Europe. Alongside traditional work practices of indefinite time, recent years have seen the growth of **new forms of work**: homeworking (out-workers), part-time work, job sharing, job splitting, being "on call", distance working, etc. These new work forms have arisen as a result of new technologies, to accommodate companies' needs for flexibility and to meet the personal and family demands of many workers. However, they can obscure the situation of these workers if there is no written proof of the essential points of the employment relationship. Therefore, a Directive provides for the drawing up of a written declaration **regarding an employment relationship**[3]. It stipulates that an employer shall notify an employee of the essential aspects of the contract or employment relationship by written declaration not later than two months after the commencement of employment. Essential aspects are considered to be: the place of work, the nature of the work and the category of employment, the duration of the employment relationship, the number of hours worked and paid holidays, pay and social rights.

A Directive concerning certain aspects of the **organisation of working time** lays down a basic set of minimum provisions covering more particularly: the maximum weekly working time (48 hours), the minimum daily rest period (11 uninterrupted hours), the minimum period of paid leave (4 weeks), conditions relating to night work and the maximum period of such work (8 hours), and breaks in the event of prolonged periods of work[4]. Although, in theory, most workers in the European Union enjoy better organisation of working time than is embodied in the European Directive, this is intended to exercise a pressure on the Governments of the Member States to better enforce the relative legislations. Another Directive aims to prevent part-time workers from being treated less favourably than full-time workers, concerning particularly employment conditions and continuing training[5].

13.5.5. Equal treatment for men and women

Article 141 of the EC Treaty (ex-Art. 119 EEC) stipulates that each Member State shall ensure the application of the principle that men and women should receive **equal pay for equal work**. This principle means: (a) that pay for the same work at piece rates shall be calculated on the basis

---

[1]   Directive 91/383, OJ L 206, 29.07.1991.
[2]   Directive 1999/70, OJ L 175, 10.07.1999.
[3]   Directive, 91/533, OJ L 288, 18.10.1991.
[4]   Directive 2003/88, OJ L 299, 18.11.2003.
[5]   Directive 97/81, OJ L 14, 20.01.1998 and Directive 98/23, OJ L 131, 05.05.1998.

of the same unit of measurement; and (b) that pay for work at time rates shall be the same for the same job. The original Community's concern for equality of the sexes - compared to its non-commitment in other important issues - stemmed from the fact that competition between Community countries could be distorted by the employment in some of them of women who were paid less than men for the same job. Moreover, unequal conditions of employment and remuneration between the sexes could be eliminated only through Community action, as no country could go it alone with a reform, which would be likely to alter conditions of competition to its detriment, in particular in industries employing large numbers of women. In any case, the EC Treaty places the achievement of equal treatment between men and women among the tasks of the Community (Art. 2 TEC).

The original Member States did not hasten to take the legislative and administrative measures necessary in order to implement the principle of non-discrimination based on the sex, as they were invited to do by Article 119 (EEC). However, the Court of Justice in three famous judgments bearing the name of Gabrielle Defrenne, air hostess of Sabena, established that, although Article 119 had a horizontal direct effect and could be evoked in national courts, it needed **interpretation by the Community legislative authority**, particularly concerning indirect or disguised discriminations and equal working conditions other than payment[1].

The opinion of the Court was followed by the Commission in its proposals and finally by the Council, which adopted a Directive on the approximation of the laws of the Member States relating to the **application of the principle of equal pay** for men and women[2]. The purpose of that Directive was to eliminate any discrimination on grounds of sex as regards all aspects and conditions of pay. It called on the Member States to "cleanse" their legal provisions of all discriminatory aspects and to repeal all collective or contractual provisions that were at variance with the principle of equal pay. Thus, for instance, the Court of Justice has established that the employers' contributions in favour of a pension scheme should be considered as part of gross payment and that, in this context, the burden of proof of non-discrimination based on sex should be borne by the employer[3]. A Commission code of practice on the implementation of equal pay for work of equal value for women and men, drawn up in close collaboration with the social partners, aims to provide concrete advice for employers and collective bargaining partners at business level to ensure that the principle of equality is applied to all aspects of pay[4].

---

[1] Judgments of: 25 May 1971, ECR 1971, p. 445; 8 April 1976, ECR 1976, p. 455; and 15 June 1978, ECR 1978, p. 1365.
[2] Directive 75/117, OJ L 45, 19.02.1975 and Agreement on the European Economic Area, OJ L 1, 03.01.1994.
[3] Judgment of 11 March 1981, Worringham, ECR 1981, p. 767 and judgment of 17 October 1989, ECR 1989, p. 3199.
[4] COM (96) 336, 17 July 1996.

Equal pay was only one battle won in the war against discrimination against women, which was based on historical and cultural causes and was reinforced in practice by the education system, inadequate vocational guidance and the demanding role imposed on women as wives and mothers. Therefore, the Council adopted, in 1976, a Directive on the implementation of the principle of equal treatment for men and women as regards **access to employment, vocational training and promotion**, and working conditions[1]. That Directive prohibits any indirect discrimination, i.e. the ways in which women are disadvantaged in relation to men in spite of apparently equal treatment, viz.: individual or collective contracts concerning employment and working conditions. For example, according to the ECJ, a discriminatory recruitment system is contrary to Directive 76/207[2], as is a general exclusion of women from military posts involving the use of arms[3]. A specific Directive provides for the equal treatment between men and women engaged in an activity, including agriculture, in a self-employed capacity, and on the protection of self-employed women during pregnancy and motherhood[4].

The principle of equal opportunity means, among other things, that there should be no discrimination based on sex especially as regards: the scope and the conditions governing the right to any work regime; the calculation of contributions; the calculation of benefits and the conditions governing the duration and preservation of pension rights. Two Directives concern, indeed, the implementation of the principle of equal treatment for men and women in matters of social security[5] and in occupational social security schemes[6]. According to the ECJ, the provisions concerning social security do not apply to women who have never been employed, those who do not look for a job and those who have voluntarily stopped working[7].

On the contrary, again according to the Court, the principle of non-discrimination applies indifferently to both men and women. Indeed, in its "Barber" judgment the Court of Justice held that any sex discrimination in the granting or calculation of an occupational pension, notably the differentiation of the age of pension according to the sex, is prohibited by Article 119 (EEC)[8]. As the Barber judgment had important financial implications for the professional schemes of social security, the Council amended the 1986 Directive in order to bring it into line with Article 119 of the EEC Treaty as interpreted by the Court in this judgment[9]. According to the Court, however, different treatment of **stable relationships between two**

---

[1] Directive 76/207, OJ L 39, 14.02.1976 and Directive 2002/73, OJ L 269, 05.10.2002.

[2] Judgment of 30 June 1988, ECR 1988, p. 3559.

[3] Judgment of 11 January 2000, Case C-295/98 Kreil v Germany, OJ C 63, 04.03.2000.

[4] Directive 86/613, OJ L 359, 19.12.1986.

[5] Directive 79/7, OJ L 6, 10.01.1979.

[6] Directive 86/378, OJ L 225, OJ L 225, 12.08.1986 and Directive 96/97, OJ L 46, 17.02.1997.

[7] Judgment of 27 June 1989, ECR 1989, p. 1963.

[8] Judgment given on 17 May 1990, Case C-262/89, Barber v Guardian Royal Exchange, ECR 1990, p.1889.

[9] Commission proposal, OJ C 379, 14.12.1996.

persons of the same sex and marriages or stable relationships outside marriage between persons of opposite sex in matters of social security, does not constitute discrimination directly based on sex[1].

Measures must be taken in all Member States to improve the **health and safety protection of women workers** who are pregnant, have just given birth or are breast-feeding[2] [see also section 13.5.7.]. These measures on the one hand prohibit the dismissing of the women workers in question and their exposure to specific agents or working conditions which could endanger their health and safety, and on the other ensure the preservation of the rights derived from the employment contract and of maternity leave of at least fourteen consecutive weeks. In addition, according to the ECJ, the non-recruitment of pregnant women or the laying off of women who have a bad health condition after having given birth are discriminatory and cannot be tolerated[3]. The dismissal would be illegal even if the worker was recruited for a fixed period and because of her pregnancy was unable to work during a substantial part of the term of the contract[4]. A Declaration to the Final Act of the Amsterdam European Council of June 1997 urges the Member States, when adopting measures referred to in Article 141 (TEC) to aim at improving the situation of women in working life.

13.5.6. Action to combat social exclusion

Social exclusion represents one of the major challenges facing the European Union. The challenge cannot be addressed merely by offering better assistance to those who are excluded or at risk of exclusion from work, but also requires active measures to tackle the obstacles to social inclusion. Article 137 (TEC) gives the Community a specific role in **supporting and complementing the activities of the Member States** as regards the integration of persons excluded from the labour market. In compliance with the principle of subsidiarity however, initiatives to combat poverty and social exclusion are primarily the preserve of the Member States' local, regional and national authorities. The European Union can only complete and stimulate the work of the Member States in these fields by promoting the exchange of information, the comparison of experiences, the transfer of know-how and the demonstration of the validity of the projects based on partnerships. Thus, the Community action against social exclusion is mainly centred on vocational training [see section 13.4.2.].

A Community action programme, covering the period from 1 January 2002 to 31 December 2006, encourages cooperation between Member States to combat poverty and social exclusion[5]. The objectives of the **social**

---

[1] Judgment of 17 February 1998, Case C-249/96, ECR 1998 I-621.
[2] Directive 92/85, OJ L 348, 28.11.1992.
[3] Judgments of 8 November 1990, ECR 1990, I-3941 and I-3979.
[4] Judgment of 4 October 2001, Case C-109/2000, ECR 2001, p. I-06993.
[5] Decision 50/2002, OJ L 10, 12.01.2002 and Decision 786/2004, OJ L 138, 30.04.2004.

exclusion action programme are, in particular, to improve understanding of social exclusion and poverty, to organise discussions on policies pursued and mutual lessons, and to develop the capacity of actors to address social exclusion and poverty effectively, by promoting innovative approaches and supporting networks of all those involved at EU, national and regional levels. The URBAN initiative, on its part, can help in a number of inner-city neighbourhoods where an accumulation of exclusion factors exists [see section 12.3.3.].

13.5.7. Safety and health at work

Despite the limited competences that assigned the EEC Treaty to the European Community, Directives were adopted concerning the protection of workers, notably from the major accident hazards of certain industrial activities[1] [see section 16.3.5.] and exposure to asbestos[2]. After the 1987 Single Act [see section 2.1.] had increased the Community's authority as regards the health and safety of the work force, the Commission set up a mutual information system for legislative and administrative acts of the Member States concerning health and security of workers at the place of work[3]. At the instigation of the Commission, the Council adopted, in 1989, a **Framework Directive** on the introduction of measures to encourage improvements in the safety and health of workers at the workplace[4]. This Directive lays down three main principles: the employer's general obligation to guarantee the workers' health and safety in all work-related aspects, in particular by preventing professional risks, by keeping the work force informed and by training; the obligation of every worker to contribute to his own health and safety and that of others by using the work facilities correctly and respecting the safety instructions; the absence or limited liability for employers for things caused by abnormal unforeseen circumstances or exceptional events. By laying down the main principles concerning health and safety at work in the Community, the framework Directive is the foundation on which all other directives aiming at the improvement of the working environment to protect workers' health and safety (Art. 137 TEC) are superimposed.

This is particularly the case as regards the specific Directives laying down **minimum requirements notably on**:

- workplaces[5];
- work equipment and machinery[6];
- personal protective equipment[7];

---

[1]   Directive 96/82, OJ L 10, 14.1.1997 and Directive 2003/105, OJ L 345, 31.12.2003.
[2]   Directive 83/477, OJ L 263, 24.09.1983 and Directive 2003/18, OJ L 97, 15.04.2003.
[3]   Decision 88/383, OJ L 183, 14.07.1988.
[4]   Directive 89/391, OJ L 183, 29.06.1989.
[5]   Directive 89/654, OJ L 393, 30.12.1989.
[6]   Directive 89/655, OJ L 393, 30.12.1989 and Directive 95/63, OJ L 335, 30.12.1995.
[7]   Directive 89/656, OJ L 393, 30.12.1989.

- work using display screens[1];
- exposure at work to carcinogenic agents[2];
- safety and/or health signs in the workplace[3];
- exposure to the risks arising from physical agents (noise)[4].

These Directives guarantee the right to safety at work for the workers in all Member States, including those which previously had not high safety standards. Workers having an interim or specific duration work relation must enjoy the same health and safety conditions as the other workers of an undertaking[5]. As seen above, a directive aims at improving the health and safety of pregnant workers and workers who have recently given birth or are breastfeeding[6] [see section 13.5.5.]. The Council recommends that the Member States recognise, in the context of their policy on preventing occupational hazards and accidents, the right of self-employed workers to health and safety protection, and their duties in this area[7].

The **new Community strategy on health and safety at work** aims at a global approach to well-being at work, taking account of changes in the world of work and the emergence of new risks, especially of a psycho-social nature. According to the Commission, the strategy should be based on: consolidating a culture of risk prevention, including psychological and social risks such as stress, harassment, depression and alcoholism; combining a variety of political instruments, such as social dialogue and corporate social responsibility; and building partnerships between all players in the field of health and safety[8].

13.5.8. Public health protection

Public health was brought fully into the action scope of the European Union by a special title of the EC Treaty, which, as amended at Amsterdam to heed the "mad cow" and dioxin lessons [see sections 5.1.3. and 11.2.], states that a **high level of human health protection** shall be ensured in the definition and implementation of all Community policies and activities. Article 152 (TEC) invites the Community to contribute towards ensuring a high level of human health protection by encouraging cooperation between the Member States and by fostering cooperation with third countries and the competent international organisations.

The **programme of Community action** in the field of public health (2003-2008) complements national policies aiming to protect human health

---

[1] Directive 90/270, OJ L 156, 21.06.1990.
[2] Directive 90/394, OJ L 196, 26.07.1990 and OJ L 138, 01.06.1999.
[3] Directive 92/58, OJ L 245, 26.08.1992.
[4] Directive 2003/10, OJ L 42, 15.02.2003.
[5] Directive 91/383, OJ L 206, 29.07.1991.
[6] Directive 92/85, OJ L 348, 28.11.1992.
[7] Recommendation 2003/134, OJ L 53, 28.02.2003.
[8] Commission communication, COM (2002) 118, 11 March 2002.

and improve public health[1]. The general objectives of the programme are: (a) to improve information and knowledge for the development of public health; (b) to enhance the capability of responding rapidly and in a coordinated fashion to threats to health; (c) to promote health and prevent disease through addressing health determinants across all policies and activities. The programme should thereby contribute to: ensuring a high level of human health protection in the definition and implementation of all Community policies and activities; tackling inequalities in health; and encouraging cooperation between Member States.

The measures under the programme underpin the **health strategy of the Community** and should yield Community added value by responding to needs arising out of conditions and structures established through Community action in other fields, by addressing new developments, new threats and new problems for which the Community would be in a better position to act to protect its people, by bringing together activities undertaken in relative isolation and with limited impact at national level and by complementing them in order to achieve positive results for the people of the Community. The programme can provide a significant added value to health promotion by facilitating the exchange of experience and best practices and by providing a basis for a common analysis of the factors affecting public health. Also, the programme may have added value in the event of threats to public health of a cross-border nature, such as infectious diseases, environmental pollution or food contamination.

A Community **health-monitoring system** aims to facilitate the planning, monitoring and evaluation of Community programmes, provide the Member States with appropriate health information to make comparisons and to support their national health policies. It entails action aimed at establishing Community health indicators, developing a Community-wide network for sharing health data and facilitating analyses and reporting in the health sphere. Actually, the Community leads actions against AIDS, cancer, particularly by combating smoking, and drug dependence.

13.6. Appraisal and outlook

The common social policy makes an important contribution to European integration, notably in helping achieve the **social cohesion** necessary among the Member States. It is interesting to note in the following paragraphs that each of the four wings of this policy makes a different contribution to the integration process. They, nevertheless, reinforce each other and interact with other common policies, notably the economic and monetary, industrial, research and development ones, in fostering the social cohesion necessary in an economic and monetary union.

---

[1]   Decision 1786/2002, OJ L 271, 09.10.2002 and Decision 786/2004, OJ L 138, 30.04.2004.

The **freedom of movement of workers** was essential for the completion of the common market and, therefore, was examined under that heading [see section 6.4.]. By virtue of the Community regulations adopted in their favour, migrant workers and self-employed persons from any Member State enjoy fair conditions compared with nationals of the host country with regard to access to employment, social security, the education and vocational training of their children, living and working conditions and the right to exercise union rights. The common labour market is handicapped, however, by the existence of different languages, customs and working methods and, although the EU is taking measures to overcome these hurdles to the free movement of workers, it will certainly need much time before it encompasses a really homogeneous labour market.

The **common employment policy** is striving to ensure that the national employment policies and the common policies of the EU, notably in the economic and monetary field, work together in a consistent manner so as to boost economic reforms and employment while maintaining price stability. The coordinated employment strategy aims to harness structural reforms and modernisation to improve the efficiency of the labour market, while maintaining a non-inflationary growth dynamic. The Lisbon agenda has shifted the focus of the European employment strategy from the fight against unemployment towards the wider priority of more and better jobs in an inclusive society and has helped employment creation in the EU [see section 13.3.1.].

The **common education and training policies** complement the common employment policy by encouraging the adaptation of the work force to the new conditions of the industrial and service sectors in Europe and in the rest of the world. The cooperation and exchange of experiences through the Community programmes helps the Member States develop the European dimension in education, the teaching of languages, the vocational training and retraining needed in the information society and in the global economy. At the same time, these programmes build networks of teachers, instructors and young people who participate actively in the European integration process.

The **common policy for the improvement of living and working conditions** is aimed at the convergence of social protection systems and through it at the social cohesion of the Union. Community directives fixing common minimum standards guarantee the rights, the physical safety and health of workers, particularly the women and the young, in all Member States. The establishment of a framework of basic minimum standards provides a bulwark against using low social standards as an instrument of unfair economic competition. The social bedrock, which is thus being built, is indispensable for the good functioning of economic and monetary union where the competition between the various regions of the Union is enhanced. However, economic and social developments in European countries make it necessary to modernise social protection systems in order to attain four main objectives: creating more incentives to work and provide a secure income; safeguarding pensions with sustainable pension schemes; promoting social inclusion; and ensuring the high quality and sustainability of health protection.

Bibliography on social policy

- BARNARD Catherine (et al.). *The future of labour law: liber amicorum Bob Hepple QC*. Oxford: Hart, 2004.
- CLASQUIN Bernadette (et al. eds.). *Wage and welfare: new perspectives on employment and social rights in Europe*. Bruxelles: PIE - P. Lang, 2004.
- DEBARGE Olivier (et al.). *Quel avenir pour l'Union européenne?: La stratégie de Lisbonne définie par le Conseil européen en 2000*. Bruxelles: Bruylant, 2004.
- DORSEMMONT Filip (et al.). "Corporate social responsibility: a threat or an opportunity for the trade union movement in Europe?", *Transfer*, v. 10, n. 3, Autumn 2004, p. 351-479.
- JOERGES Christian, RÖDL Florian. *Social market economy as Europe's social model?* Florence: European University Institute, 2004.
- LIND Jens, KNUDSEN Herman, JØRGENSEN Henning. *Labour and employment regulation in Europe*. Frankfurt am Main: P. Lang, 2004.
- MALTBY Tony (et. al.). *Ageing and the transition to retirement: a comparative analysis of European welfare states*. Aldershot: Ashgate, 2004.
- SHAW Ian, KAUPPINEN Kaisa. *Constructions of health and illness: European perspectives*. Aldershot: Ashgate, 2004.
- TAYLOR-GOOBY Peter. *Making a European welfare state?: convergences and conflicts over European social policy*. Oxford; Malden, MA: Blackwell, 2004.
- UEBELMESSER Silke. *Unfunded pension systems: ageing and migration*. Amsterdam: Elsevier, 2004.

DISCUSSION TOPICS

1. Discuss the development of the common social policy through the stages of customs union, common market, economic and monetary union, as outlined in the Treaties of Rome, Maastricht and Amsterdam.
2. What are the lessons to be drawn concerning the development of common policies from the momentary conflict between the common social policy and the national social policy of the UK?
3. How does the EU go about its social cohesion?
4. Consider the education, training and youth programmes of the EU in relation with employment qualifications, cultural identities and the building of human networks.
5. What is the significance of social protection in the EU context?

Chapter 14

TAXATION POLICY

Diagram of the chapter

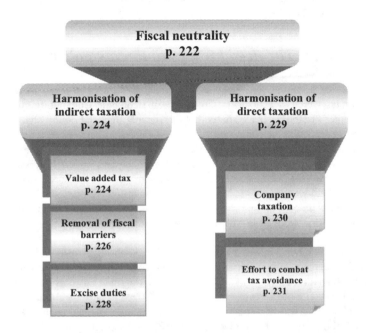

The EEC Treaty was very cautious as regards tax harmonisation. What it wanted above all was the introduction and observance of **the rule of fiscal neutrality in Community trade**, i.e. equal tax treatment for domestic production and imports from other member countries. Beyond that, the Treaty merely invited the Commission to examine how turnover taxes could be harmonised. The Treaty did not call for any harmonisation or other Community action with regard to direct taxes.

The fiscal objectives of the Treaty were attained rapidly. Cumulative multi-stage taxes, which did not guarantee fiscal neutrality, were replaced by **a new turnover tax, the value added tax**, and the structures of that tax were harmonised in all Community Member States, old and new. The principle of fiscal neutrality was thus guaranteed, but at the price of maintaining tax barriers, which were necessary for the collection of VAT and excise duties in the country of destination of goods.

However, in the single market goods must be able to move completely freely, and to achieve this, tax has to be imposed on them either in the country of origin or in that of destination. This led, at the end of the 1980s, to the **alignment of VAT and excise duties**. At the same time the harmonisation of direct taxes has begun, especially concerning those on companies and savings, in order to make the growth of companies and capital movement independent of tax considerations. Inside the economic and monetary union, tax harmonisation should progress at the same pace as economic integration.

14.1. The need for a common tax policy

Having economic and social structures which differed in many ways, the States which were to form the European Economic Community also had rather **dissimilar tax systems**, both as regards financial policy, that is to say in particular the composition of the tax burden as between direct and indirect taxes, and the technical organisation of taxation. In the short term there was no question of making a single fiscal territory of the European Community. But pending such unification, some urgent measures in the taxation field were needed for the common market to work properly. These measures were centred on achieving fiscal neutrality and equal conditions of competition among the Member States, the two subjects discussed below.

If the member states of a common market had absolute freedom in the fiscal field, they could very quickly **replace the customs barriers to trade by tax barriers**. They could in fact, while lowering their customs duties in accordance with the timetable laid down by the Treaty, raise their domestic taxes in such a way that the total burden on imports remained unchanged. It was therefore necessary that indirect taxes, in particular turnover tax, have no influence on intra-Community trade flows. In other words, **fiscal neutrality** between domestic production and imports from the partner countries was needed. To secure fiscal neutrality in a common market the turnover tax of the country of origin or of the country of destination would have to be imposed on all goods.

If the rule of **the tax of the country of origin** were adopted, there would be a danger of creating trade flows based artificially on the difference in the taxes rather than on the difference in comparative costs, but there would be pressure on the Member States to approximate the rates of their taxes, and fiscal frontiers could be removed, as imported goods would already have paid taxes at the rate of the country of origin. If, on the other hand, the system of the **tax of the country of destination** were applied, production could be concentrated where the comparative economic advantages were greatest rather than where taxation would be lower, as all products in competition on a market, whether of domestic origin or imported, would be uniformly subject to the tax on consumption in force on that market. However, under that system the tax barriers would have to be maintained in order to levy the taxes of the country of destination on imported goods and the Member States would not be encouraged to approximate the rates of their taxes. This was the price, which the founding Member States, in light of the low level of integration of their economies, paid in opting for the system of taxation in the country of destination.

Just behind the harmonisation of the structures of all indirect taxes came, of course, the harmonisation of their rates. It is obvious that in order to create completely impartial conditions of competition in the common market **a common system of taxes on consumption is needed**, comprising not only the same structures, but also very approximate rates or, indeed, the same rates wherever possible. In effect, the different rates of taxes could have a different influence on the consumption of various products in the common market and could distort the conditions of competition between the undertakings of the Member States. Where the tax burden on a product is lower in one country than in another, if the other conditions of competition are equal in both countries, the undertakings which manufacture the product in the first country are in a much more **favourable competitive position** than their counterparts in the second country, as they can have increased demand and high profits in their principal market.

Moreover, there are grounds for questioning whether, in spite of the harmonisation of tax structures and the alignment of indirect taxation, fiscal neutrality exists, when some states have much more recourse than others to **direct taxation**. It is true that such states tax the products of their partners less than do those which have more recourse to indirect taxes, but the terms of trade and productivity offset to a large extent the fiscal disparities of member states' companies. Moreover, states clearly apply certain categories of tax on the basis of historic habit, sociological structure and economic conditions. Some mainly apply indirect taxes, which are easily collected, whilst others have greater recourse to direct taxation, which is fairer from the social viewpoint. The member states of a common market need to have sufficient autonomy in the tax field so as to have enough room for manoeuvre to act in the light of their economic situations. Harmonisation of direct taxes can therefore only be a long-term objective of European tax policy.

In fact, the requirements for tax harmonisation increase together with progress in economic integration. Whilst fiscal neutrality in a customs union is ensured by the harmonisation of the structures of turnover tax and excise duties, in a common market and even more so **in an economic and monetary union** gradual harmonisation of the levels of those taxes and even of direct taxation are also necessary, to ensure fair competition throughout the single market. The long-term goal is to reach a taxation framework conducive to enterprise, job creation and environment protection in the Union[1]. While further development of the common taxation pol-

---

[1]   COM (96) 546, 22 October 1996.

icy depends on the progress of the common economic and monetary policies, further tax harmonisation may have spillover effects [see section 1.1.1.] on the development of the common enterprise, employment and environment policies.

14.2. Harmonisation of indirect taxation

Indirect taxes are **those on turnover, production or consumption of goods and services** - regarded as components of cost prices and selling prices - which are collected without regard to the realisation of profits, or indeed income, but which are deductible when determining profits. Customs duties are a form of indirect taxation. That is why, following the removal of customs barriers in a common market, Member States could be tempted to replace them with fiscal barriers, i.e. with internal taxes. That danger was foreseen in the EEC Treaty, Articles 95 to 98 of which contained provisions to obviate it, together with Article 99, which called upon the Commission to consider how the legislation of the various Member States concerning turnover taxes, excise duties and other forms of indirect taxation could be harmonised in the interest of the common market. Indeed, the Commission, assisted by two committees of experts, examined the harmonisation of indirect taxation and proposed the adoption by all Member States of a system of turnover taxes which did not distort conditions of competition either within a country or between Member States. Such a system was the tax on value added.

14.2.1. Value added tax

When it was **adopted for the first time, in France in 1954, value added tax (VAT)** was regarded as merely another tax on turnover or on consumption and did not attract the attention of other countries. It was only since 1962, with the publication of two reports ordered by the Commission recommending its adoption by all Member States, that its interest for the Community was understood. Acting on the basis of Commission proposals, the Council adopted on 11 April 1967 two Directives on the harmonisation of the legislation of Member States concerning turnover taxes[1]. Those two Directives laid the groundwork for the common value added tax system and a third one, adopted in 1969, introduced it in the tax systems of the Member States[2].

According to Article 2 of the first Directive of 1967, **VAT is a general tax on consumption**, i.e. a tax on all expenditure on goods and services. The tax is levied at each stage of an economic activity on the value added at that stage. It is paid by all those involved in the production and distribu-

---

[1]   Directive 67/227, OJ 71, 14.04.1967 and Directive 77/388, OJ L 145, 13.06.1977.
[2]   Directive 69/463, OJ L 320, 20.12.1969.

tion of a product or service, but it is not an element in the costs of those intermediaries and does not appear as an item of expenditure in their accounts, as it is not they who bear the tax, but the end consumer.

The tax is proportional to the price of the products and services irrespective of the number of transactions, which have taken place at the stages preceding that to which it is applied. At the time of each transaction, the amount of VAT, calculated on the price of the good or service, is reduced by the amount of the taxes previously paid on the cost of the various components of the cost price. The total sum which changes hands at each stage in the production or distribution includes the VAT paid up to that point, but the amount of the tax is recovered at each sale, except for the final sale to the **final consumer**, who purchases the product or service for his private use. The tax is paid to the State by the vendor in each transaction. However, the latter does not bear the burden of the VAT, as his purchaser has advanced the full amount of the VAT to him. Tax paid at previous stages, on deliveries made or services rendered to the taxable person, and the tax paid on imports, is deductible from the turnover tax of that taxable person. Given this **deductibility of taxes already paid**, VAT is neutral from the point of view of domestic competition, i.e. it does not favour vertically integrated undertakings, as did the cumulative multi-stage taxes. But VAT is also neutral from the point of view of international competition, since it cannot favour domestic products. Calculation of the tax paid is easy, as it appears on all invoices and documents accompanying the product.

The **sixth directive** on the harmonisation of turnover taxes established a package of common rules making it possible to define the scope of the tax and the method of determining tax liability, i.e. the territorial application of the tax, the taxable persons, the taxable transactions, the place of applicability of such transactions, the chargeable event, the taxable amount, the detailed procedures for applying rates of taxation, the exemptions and the special schemes[1]. These rules are known as "**the uniform basis of assessment of VAT**", and that basis is particularly important in that VAT is a basic source of revenue for the Community [see section 3.4.]. Moreover, the sixth Directive harmonised the laws on turnover tax structures of the Member States in the fields of the **provision of services**, agricultural production, small undertakings and exempt activities and operations linked with importation, exportation and international trade in goods. Subject to Council approval, a Member State may introduce into its legislation special measures for derogation from the common system of value-added tax, either in order to simplify the procedure for charging the tax or to prevent certain types of tax evasion or avoidance, or in the form of an agreement with a non-member country or an international organisation.

A directive amending the sixth directive put in place uniform **taxation rules for digital electronic commerce**, making it as easy and straightforward as possible to comply with these rules, particularly in the fields of

---

[1] Directive 77/388, OJ L 145, 13.06.1977 and Directive 2004/66, OJ L 168, 01.05.2004.

supply, electronic networks, services linked to software and computers in general, and of information, cultural, arts, sports, science, education and leisure services[1]. These rules allow Member States to subject to VAT services provided electronically and radio and television broadcasting services supplied on subscription or pay-per-view basis in the European Union and to exempt these services from VAT if they are provided for consumption outside the Union [see also sections 6.6.1. and 17.3.5.]. Another directive amended the rules for the application of VAT and harmonised the rules on the place of **taxation of natural gas and electricity**[2]. Supplies to dealers are taxable at the place of their business or fixed establishment for which the goods are supplied, whereas supplies to end consumers are taxable at the place of consumption of gas and electricity.

14.2.2. Removal of fiscal barriers

One of the main challenges to the **completion of the single market** was in the tax field [see section 6.1.]. Prior to 1992, goods and services moving within a Member State were taxed differently from those that were exported. On exportation, the product benefited from full tax remission and was in return subject to the VAT of the country of import at the crossing of borders. The tax was paid to the country in which the goods arrived at the final consumption stage. The protection, which that system afforded against tax evasion, depended on **controls at borders**. Without a check at the border to ensure that the goods which were the subject of an application for the reimbursement of tax had actually been exported, it would be all too easy for dishonest operators to invoice goods at the zero rate for exportation and subsequently resell them on the internal market, either free of tax, thus placing their competitors in a disadvantageous position with regard to price, or by including the tax component in the price, but keeping its amount for themselves. That would not only have constituted a loss of tax revenue for the exporting State, but also a source of serious trade distortion. For the authorities of the importing State, on the other hand, frontier controls were used to tax imported goods at the rates prevalent in the country in question, so as to collect the revenue due to them and, at the same time, make sure that these products did not unduly compete with national products.

However, the export refunds and import taxes, which accompanied intra-Community trade, and the resultant controls, constituted the so-called **"fiscal frontiers"**. To remove those barriers to trade, it was vital that cross-border trade be treated in the same way as purchases and sales within a State. The Commission actually proposed that all sales of goods and services should be taxed at the rate of the country of origin[3]. But the Council

---

[1]   Directive 77/388, OJ L 145, 13.06.1977 and Directive 2002/38, OJ L 128, 15.05.2002.
[2]   Directive 77/388, OJ L 145, 13.06.1977 and Directive 2003/92, OJ L 260, 11.10.2003.
[3]   Commission proposal, OJ C 250, 19.09.1987, p. 2.

did not follow the Commission's lead. In conclusions of 9 October 1989, adopted unanimously (necessary condition in order to counter the proposal of the Commission) [see section 4.3.], it considered that conditions could not be fulfilled for a system of taxation in the country of origin and that it was therefore necessary to continue, for a limited period, to levy VAT and excise duty in the State of consumption.

The Directive on the **approximation of VAT rates** completed the common VAT system. It stipulates that the Member States shall apply **a standard VAT rate of at least 15%**[1]. In fact, the standard VAT rate varies between 15 and 25% in the Member States. Thus, in 2002, it was 25% in Sweden and Denmark, 22% in Finland, 21% in Belgium and Ireland, 20% in Italy and Austria, 19.6% in France, 19% in the Netherlands, 18% in Greece, 17.5% in the United Kingdom, 17% in Portugal, 16% in Germany and Spain and 15% in Luxembourg. All the higher VAT rates have been abolished, leading to a significant fall in consumer prices in some sectors, such as automobiles.

The Member States enjoy the option of applying, alongside the normal rate, one (or two) **reduced rates**, equal to or higher than 5%, applicable only to certain goods and services of a social or cultural nature. Examples include foodstuffs, pharmaceuticals, passenger transport services, books, newspapers and periodicals, entrance to shows, museums and the like, publications and copyright, hotel accommodation and medical care in hospitals. The preservation of the zero and extra-low rates (below 5%) is authorised on a transitional basis, along with reduced rates on housing other than subsidised housing, catering and children's clothes and shoes.

The common system of VAT dispensed with customs procedures[2]. Intra-Community trade in goods between taxable bodies is subject to taxation in the country of destination. In the case of sales between companies subject to VAT, i.e. the vast majority, the vendor exempts the deliveries made to clients in other Member States. In his VAT return, he indicates, in a separate box, the total of his exempted intra-Community sales. In another return (usually quarterly), he lists the VAT number of his customers in the other Member States and the total amount of his sales to each of them during the period in question. The purchaser applies VAT to his purchase in another Member State, termed an "acquisition". He must declare the total amount of these acquisitions in a separate box in his normal VAT return and can request the deductibility of this VAT in the same return.

Individuals travelling from one Member State to another pay VAT there where they purchase the goods and are no longer subject to any VAT-related taxation or any border formality when they cross from one Member State to another. In return, the system of travellers' allowances (tax free sales in ports, airports, etc.) was abolished in intra-Community travelling[3].

---

[1] Directive 92/77, OJ L 316, 31.10.1992.
[2] Directive 91/680, OJ L 376, 31.12.1991 and OJ L 384, 30.12.1992.
[3] Directive 94/4, OJ L 60, 03.03.1994 and Directive 98/94, OJ L 358, 31.12.1998.

14.2.3. Excise duties

In a fiscally integrated Community a number of major **special taxes on consumption** (**excise duties**), i.e. taxes on the consumption of certain products, yielding substantial revenue to the States, must be maintained alongside VAT. Excise duties make it possible to impose a much larger tax burden on a small number of products than that borne by the vast majority of goods that are only subject to VAT, which has very few, and fairly low, rates. If the various excise duties in the Community States were abolished, the resultant losses of revenue would have to be offset by increasing VAT rates, which would be certain to have an inflationary effect on their economies. Thus, for example, manufactured tobacco products and mineral oils bear, without major drawbacks, very high taxes, which on average yield more than 10% of the tax revenue of the EU States. Moreover, within the overall context of a tax scheme, excise duties constitute **flexible components**, which can easily be manoeuvred if further tax revenue is needed. As they are separate taxes, excise duties can easily be adapted to the various economic, social and structural requirements. Lastly, they can be levied specifically in order to reduce consumption of certain products, such as tobacco products and alcoholic drinks, for public health reasons, and petroleum products for reasons of environment linked energy savings and reduction of energy dependence.

But if some excise duties had to be maintained in the Community two conditions had to be met so as **not to disturb the common market**: their structures had to be harmonised, so as to remove taxation indirectly protecting national production; and their rates had to be harmonised so as to eliminate, in trade between Member States, taxation and tax refunds as well as frontier controls, which disturbed the free movement of goods within the common market.

Taking account of these conditions, a Directive defines the **general arrangements** for the holding and movement of products subject to excise duty[1]. In contrast to the harmonised VAT system, the general arrangements for excise duties are definitive. The taxable event takes place at the stage of manufacture in the Community or of import into the Community from a third country. The tax is payable when the product is put up for consumption and must be acquitted in the country of actual consumption. The Member States have the option of introducing or maintaining taxation on other products and services, provided however that this taxation does not give rise to border crossing formalities in trade between the Member States.

Excise duties are paid by the consignee in the country of destination and the appropriate provisions are taken to this effect. For commercial operations, the Community system is similar to that applied within a state. The movement of products subject to suspended excise duty is run through

---

[1] Directive 92/12, OJ L 76, 23.03.1992 and Directive 96/99, OJ L 8, 11.01.1997.

interconnected bonded warehouses and is covered by an accompanying document, which has been harmonised at Community level. The payment of the excise due in the Member State of destination can be assumed by a fiscal representative established in this State and designated by the consignor. The appropriate provisions are taken to enable the exchange of information between all the Member States concerned by the movement of goods subject to excise with a view to ensuring effective fraud control[1]. Individuals can purchase the products of their choice in other Member States, inclusive of tax, for their personal use. Denmark, Finland and Sweden are, however, authorised by the Council to continue restricting the quantities of certain alcoholic drinks and tobacco products which individuals purchase in other Member States and import for their own consumption. Following these general guidelines, seven specific directives harmonise the structures and minimum excise duty rates on manufactured tobaccos, mineral oils, spirits and alcoholic beverages.

14.3. Harmonisation of direct taxation

Taxes on the revenue of undertakings (firms, companies, businesses) and private individuals, which are not incorporated in cost prices or selling prices and the rate of which is often progressive, may be regarded as direct taxes. The two important categories of direct taxes are **income tax and capital gains tax**. Article 92 of the EC Treaty prohibits, as regards such taxes, countervailing charges at frontiers, i.e. the application of remissions and repayments in respect of exports to other Member States. Derogations may not be granted unless the measures contemplated have been previously approved for a limited period by the Council. Apart from that provision, the EC Treaty does not deal with direct taxes and does not call for them to be harmonised.

Whilst the harmonisation of indirect taxes was necessary from the outset to avoid obstacles to trade and to free competition and later to make the removal of fiscal frontiers possible, the harmonisation of direct taxes was not considered indispensable at the common market stage. It gradually became clear, however, that the free movement of capital and the rational distribution of production factors in the Community required a **minimum degree of harmonisation of direct taxes**. In effect, the convergence of Member States' economic policies [see section 7.3.1.] necessitates a coordination of the fiscal instruments used by them. Likewise, the global competitiveness of European businesses requires that the taxation of companies operating in several Member States does not place them at a disadvantage in relation to their competitors restricting their activities to the purely national level. The Commission had tabled proposals to this end in 1969, right after the realisation of the customs union. The Council needed 21

---

[1] Decision 1152/2003, OJ L 162, 01.07.2003.

years of debate (!) before it could approve these proposals, vital for trans-national cooperation and company mergers in the single market.

14.3.1. Company taxation

The first Directive concerning business taxation, adopted by the Council in July 1990 relates to the taxation system applicable to the **capital gains generated upon the merger**, division, transfer of assets, contribution of assets or exchange of shares between two companies operating in different Member States[1]. National regulations consider this type of operation as a total or partial liquidation of the company making the contribution and subject it to capital gains tax. This is usually set in an artificial manner, since it compares the market value of the good in question (the company itself, a building, land or a share package) to the value entered in the balance sheet, traditionally underestimated. Such a calculation is unjust, insofar as no liquidation is taking place in effect, but two companies from different Member States are forming closer links. The Community solution consists of not taxing the capital gain at the time when the merger or contribution of assets takes place but rather when it is collected. This solution encourages the formation of "European companies", which usually result from the merger of companies originally established in different Member States.

The second Council Directive of July 1990 relates to the common fiscal system applicable to **parent companies and subsidiaries** situated in different Member States[2]. There can be little doubt that the decision by a company to set up a subsidiary in another Member State of the Community would be adversely affected by the fact that the dividends of the latter would be subject, on the one hand, to corporation tax in the country where it had its domicile and, on the other, to a non-recoverable withholding tax, in the Member State where the subsidiary would be domiciled. The Directive abolishes withholding taxes on dividends distributed by a subsidiary to its parent company established in another Member State.

A **code of conduct on business taxation** engages the Member States not to bring in any tax rules which constitute harmful tax competition and to phase out existing rules including withholding taxes on interest and royalty payments between companies forming part of a group[3]. A group within the framework of the Council has the task to assess the tax measures that may fall within the scope of the code and to oversee the provision by the Member States of information on those measures[4]. A Commission notice clarifies the application of the State aid rules to measures relating to direct business taxation[5].

---

[1]   Directive 90/434, OJ L 225, 20.08.1990.
[2]   Directive 90/435, OJ L 225, 20.08.1990.
[3]   Resolution, OJ C 2, 06.01.1998, p. 2-5.
[4]   Council conclusions, OJ C 99, 01.04.1998, p. 1-2.
[5]   Commission notice, OJ C 384, 10.12.1998.

A common system of taxation is applicable to interest and royalty payments made between **associated companies in different Member States**[1]. Therefore, interest or royalty payments arising in a Member State are exempted from any taxes imposed on those payments in that State, whether by deduction at source or by assessment. For budgetary reasons, Greece, Spain and Portugal may apply transitional measures in introducing the new system.

14.3.2. Effort to combat tax avoidance

The most important and urgent problems for the Community in the area of direct taxation were posed by **international tax avoidance**. In addition to the substantial budgetary losses for States and the fiscal injustice, international tax avoidance generates abnormal capital movements and distortions of conditions of competition. Therefore, a 1977 Directive instituted a **mutual assistance by the competent authorities** of the Member States in the field of direct taxation (income tax, company tax and capital gains tax) and certain excise duties and taxation of insurance premiums[2]. That Directive introduced a procedure for the systematic exchange of information directed towards enabling them to effect a correct assessment of direct taxes in the Community. It permits the Member States to coordinate their investigative action against cross-border tax fraud and to carry out more procedures on behalf of each other.

However, the liberalisation of capital movements as from 1 July 1990 [see section 6.7.], has **increased the risk of tax evasion**. In fact, Community residents can nowadays freely transfer their savings to bank accounts in any Member State without the corresponding income necessarily being declared to the tax authorities of the State of residence. Since, in several Member States, there is no "withholding tax" on bank interest paid to non-residents, investments would flow towards those States, thus avoiding any taxation. Such capital movements, motivated purely by tax considerations, would be contrary to the optimum allocation of resources, which is the objective of establishing a common financial area [see section 6.6.].

In order to lessen the risk of tax distortion, evasion and avoidance, it was necessary to intensify the exchange of information between tax authorities and to remove the encouragement to invest in a Member State, which applies a more favourable tax scheme than the Member State of the investor, by introducing in all the Member States a relatively low withholding tax. These objectives are aimed at by the Directive ensuring a minimum of effective **taxation of savings income** in the form of interest payments within the Community[3]. Under the terms of the Directive, each

---

[1] Directive 2003/49, OJ L 157, 26.06.2003 and directive 2004/66, OJ L 168, 01.05.2004.

[2] Directive 77/799, OJ L 336, 27.12.1977, Directive 2003/93, OJ L 264, 15.10.2003 and Directive 2004/56, OJ L 127, 29.04.2004.

[3] Directive 2003/48, OJ L 157, 26.06.2003 and directive 2004/66, OJ L 168, 01.05.2004.

Member State should automatically provide the other Member States with information on savings income of their residents. However, Belgium, Luxembourg and Austria may, for a transitional period (until the end of 2009), instead apply a non-final withholding tax to the interest on savings of non-residents. This should be applied at a rate of 15% for the first three years, after which it should rise to 20%, and the percentage of revenue transferred to the Member State of residence of the saver by the Member State of the paying agent should be 75%. In order to preserve the competitiveness of European financial markets, the European institutions entered into discussions with key third countries, such as the USA, Switzerland, Liechtenstein, Monaco, Andorra and San Marino, to promote the adoption of equivalent measures in those countries, notably effective exchange of information. Agreement in principle has been reached with the European countries.

14.4. Appraisal and outlook

The aim of creating a unified fiscal area in the European Union is ambitious, even if unification means the harmonisation of national tax laws rather than the creation of a federal tax system. Fiscal unification could only be achieved progressively, in line with the convergence of the national economies. It was, however, urgent for the common market to harmonise turnover tax structures and consequently to **achieve fiscal neutrality**, i.e. equal tax treatment of domestic products and products imported from the Member States. That was to a large extent achieved with the adoption of the VAT system by all the original Member States at the beginning of the 1970s and by the new Member States after their accession. Such a close harmonisation of turnover taxes as that resulting from the adoption by all Member States of the value added tax with a uniform basis of assessment was not called for by the Treaty of Rome. The Member States therefore went beyond what was required of them by the Treaty.

Twenty years later, under pressure from the completion of the single market which required the abolition of fiscal frontiers, the Member States also agreed to harmonise their excise duties, thus proving that when the political will exists, the technical problems of multinational integration can always be overcome. Indeed, the harmonisation of VAT rates and of excise-duty structures and rates, achieved in 1992, meant a great deal of **upheaval in the tax revenue of the Member States** that rely heavily on revenue from indirect taxation. However, despite the reservations and the predictions of impending disaster among some fiscal experts, they have been able to carry out this harmonisation without major upset. This fact tends to demonstrate that the multinational integration process brings about dynamic effects that are sometimes overlooked by conservative considerations [see section 1.1.2.].

The harmonisation of indirect taxation is very important, not just for the smooth operation of the internal market but also for the **convergence of economic conditions in the Member States** [see section 7.3.1.]. The VAT and excise duties arrangements enable companies to sell, purchase and invest in all the Member States without being subject to controls or formalities arising from the crossing of borders. Individuals can purchase goods in all the Community countries and, without restriction, bring them back for their personal consumption without any checks or taxation on border crossing.

Some very important areas of direct taxation, such as personal income tax, are not directly targeted by the harmonisation process, and the propensity to align the rates and the progressivity effect is markedly less. **As EMU advances**, however, a procedure for the coordination of national fiscal policies will have to be introduced to enable these policies to converge progressively in parallel with the convergence of economic policies. Such coordination should not necessarily aim at uniform tax rates, but should strive to reduce the continuing distortions in the single market, to get tax structures to develop in more employment and environment-friendly way and to prevent losses of tax revenue. Indeed, all Member States have common problems, notably that of capital evasion to fiscal paradises and even that of competition among themselves in order to attract capital while penalising their work forces. If they put together part of their sovereignty in the fiscal field so as to take common measures, Member States could better face international competition and avoid seeing the money market forces obstruct their common goals.

Bibliography on taxation policy

* BLAISE Yves (sous la dir. de). *Les impôts en Europe = Taxes in Europe: 2004*. Paris: Delmas, 2004.
* DEROUIN Philippe, MARTIN Philippe. *Droit communautaire et fiscalité: sélection d'arrêts et de décisions*. Paris: Litec, 2004.
* LACKÓ Mária. "Tax rates and corruption: labour-market and fiscal effects. Empirical cross-country comparisons on OECD and transition countries". *Research Reports = Forschungsberichte*, n. 309, September 2004.
* LYONS Timothy. "Direct taxation and the Court of Justice: the virtues of consistency". *ERA-Forum: scripta juris europaei*, n. 2, 2004, p. 174-184.
* MARTINEZ Jean-Claude (sous la dir. de). *Une constitution fiscale pour l'Europe*. Paris: Lettres du monde, 2004.
* MORE Patricia, STRAUB Olivier, Thomas Stéphanie. *Guide de la TVA intracommunautaire: formalités pratiques DEB/Intrastat*. Paris: Delmas, 2004.
* NEWEY Robert. "Cross-border enforcement of tax liabilities: recent European legislation from a UK perspective", *European Taxation*, v. 44, n. 12, December 2004, p. 528-534.
* ORGANISATION FOR ECONOMIC COOPERATION AND DEVELOPMENT. *Recent tax policy: trends and reforms in OECD countries*. Paris: OECD, 2004.

- RUDERMAN Julien. "Anti-avoidance provisions and primacy of European law over double tax treaties", *International Business Law Journal*, n. 3, 2004, p. 411-419.
- SCHÖN Wolfgang, "International accounting standards: a "starting point" for a common European tax base?", *European Taxation*, v. 44, n. 10, October 2004, p. 426-440.

DISCUSSION TOPICS

1. What is the significance of fiscal neutrality in a common market?
2. What was the interest for multinational integration of the adoption by all Member States of the value added tax?
3. How were "fiscal frontiers" removed inside the common market?
4. Outline the harmonisation of indirect taxation in the EU.
5. Discuss the need for harmonisation of direct taxation at the stages of the common market and of the economic and monetary union.

Chapter 15

COMPETITION POLICY

Diagram of the chapter

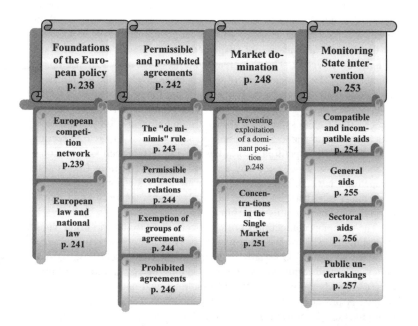

Foundations of the European policy p. 238	Permissible and prohibited agreements p. 242	Market domination p. 248	Monitoring State intervention p. 253
European competition network p.239	The "de minimis" rule p. 243	Preventing exploitation of a dominant position p.248	Compatible and incompatible aids p. 254
European law and national law p. 241	Permissible contractual relations p. 244	Concentrations in the Single Market p. 251	General aids p. 255
	Exemption of groups of agreements p. 244		Sectoral aids p. 256
	Prohibited agreements p. 246		Public undertakings p. 257

The essence of the single market is the possibility of undertakings to compete on equal terms on the markets of all the Member States. Therefore, the common competition policy is **essential to the achievement and maintenance of the single market** [see section 6.1.]. It ensures the competitive conduct of undertakings (firms, companies, businesses) and protects the interests of consumers by enabling them to procure goods and services on the best terms. It promotes economic efficiency by creating a climate favourable to innovation and technical progress [see section 17.1.]. It prevents anti-competitive practices on the part of companies, which might choke off the competitive dynamics generated by the completion of the single market.

While preventing market compartmentalisation from being restored by means of international agreements between multinational companies and while preventing market enlargement from securing windfall profits for dominant undertakings, the competition policy of the EU has to **establish**

for European industry the legal framework and economic conditions
which induce it to develop and modernise to cope with international competition. That is why, whilst action is taken without respite against im-
proper agreements or conduct on the part of (usually large) undertakings
which try to corner a share of the common market and the corresponding
profits, agreements and practices which enable SMEs to cooperate with
one another and to form strategic alliances without damaging the interests
of consumers or trade between Member States are concurrently permitted.

Common competition rules, necessary for preserving a level playing
field for all undertakings in the internal market, may go against national interests and have to be complied with by all governments, which accounts
for the **need for a neutral and respected referee placed above the clash
of national interests**. The EC Treaty allocates that role to the European
Commission. This is indeed one of the few areas in which the Commission
has autonomous, supranational power and it has the responsibility of taking
primary decisions [see section 4.1.2.]. Under the control of the Court of
Justice, the Commission establishes Community law on competition,
which provides a framework for and orientates national laws [see section
3.3.]. National competition authorities put into effect their own national
competition law which, in many respects, takes its cue from Community
competition law. This means that in many areas the implementation of
Community rules can be assigned to Member States' authorities and courts,
thus relieving the Commission from routine work.

The common competition policy affects virtually all the **other common policies**, which must comply with its rules. This is true in particular
of industrial policy, as regards structural and sectoral measures, regional
policy, as regards State aid for the poor regions, energy and transport policies, as regards the major public and multinational undertakings in those
sectors. A proactive competition policy facilitates business activity, wide
dissemination of knowledge, a better deal for consumers and efficient economic restructuring throughout the internal market[1]. Since competition
policy is impacting upon the economic performance of Europe, it is a key
element of a coherent and integrated policy to foster the competitiveness of
Europe's industries and to attain the goals of the Lisbon strategy.

15.1. The need for a common competition policy

Before the opening up of borders to intra-Community trade and competition, prices in some sectors in most countries were artificially maintained
at a level that allowed marginal undertakings to survive. **The consumer
bore the cost of protecting non-profitable businesses**. In other sectors,
unprofitable businesses were supported by aids of all kinds, and it was
therefore the taxpayer that kept them alive. Hence, both consumers and

---

[1]   COM (2004) 293, 20 April 2004.

taxpayers had a great interest in seeing the unprofitable undertakings disappear from the market thanks to the fair play of competition. This common interest of the citizens of the Member States is a major driving force of the multinational integration process [see section 1.1.2.].

National rules alone cannot ensure competition in a common market. They must be completed by Community rules to cover the cases, which affect trade between the Member States and where, therefore, there is Community competence. In contrast to national competition policies, the common competition policy has **a market integration objective**. It must ensure the unity of the common market by preventing undertakings from dividing it up amongst themselves by means of protective agreements. It must obviate the monopolisation of certain markets by preventing major companies from abusing their dominant position to impose their conditions or to buy out their competitors. Lastly, it must prevent governments from distorting the rules of the game by means of aids to private sector undertakings or discrimination in favour of public undertakings.

The very essence of the large market of the European Union is the liveliness of competition. The large market actually enables undertakings to produce on a large scale, to put in hand modern methods of production and to reduce their costs, to the **benefit of consumers**. Thanks to the common market, consumers have a choice between domestic products and products from partner countries, imported free of quantitative restrictions and customs duties [see section 5.1.]. Their choice naturally turns towards better-quality products, taking into account their price, irrespective of their origin. Consumers are therefore the judges of the performance of businesses in the large market. The least viable firms are obliged to modernise or shut down.

The increase of competition as a result of the creation of the common market involves the upheaval of supply conditions, the **renunciation of traditional habits and behaviour** and, in some instances, the loss of monopoly profits. Such developments cannot leave businessmen indifferent. Their attitude may be positive or negative. In most cases, they will endeavour to preserve or even increase their share of the market by reducing their cost prices through restructuring, investment outlay and rationalising production and distribution methods [see section 17.1.]. Such an approach is in the interest both of consumers, who benefit from plentiful supply on the best possible conditions, and of the businessmen themselves, as they learn to live with the common market and to cope better with international competition. Vertical agreements between producers and local distributors can be used pro-competitively to promote market integration.

In order to ensure that undertakings operating in the internal market enjoy the same conditions of competition everywhere, efforts have to be made to combat not only unfair practices on the part of undertakings, but also **discriminatory measures on the part of States**. Economic integration and the increasing liberalisation of international trade greatly weaken the classical methods of commercial protection, viz. high customs duties and quantitative restrictions on imports as well as technical barriers to trade. For that reason, States have more frequent recourse to **aids as an in-strument of economic policy**, especially given that increased competition and more rapid technological change reveal structural weaknesses in several sectors and regions. Some aids are doubtless justified on the grounds of social policy or regional policy, while others are necessary to direct businesses towards the requisite adjustments at an acceptable social cost. But the Member States' aid policies are often aimed at artificially ensuring the survival of sectors undergoing structural difficulties. Such aid measures run counter to the changes to the production structures inherent in technological progress and their social cost is often greater than the sums allocated to them, as they block production factors which could be better employed elsewhere. In addition, such uncoordinated measures at European level lead to spiralling aid, as each country finds itself obliged to follow in its neighbour's footsteps whenever the latter supports an economic activity. All these reasons necessitate European control of national aids.

One of the most intricate problems in the field of competition is posed by **public undertakings** and undertakings controlled by the public authorities. Member States use them as instruments for attaining various economic, political and social objectives such as directing investment towards certain sectors or regions, administering certain unprofitable public services, handling certain economic activities regarded as strategic, acting as the nation's standard bearer in the arena of international competition and employ persons who do not find jobs in the private sector. In return for the manifold services they render to governments, the latter tend to discriminate in favour of public undertakings. The various privileges, which are granted to them, can distort conditions of competition vis-à-vis undertakings in the private sector of their own nationality and those of their partners in the common market. It is this latter aspect of relations between Member States and their public undertakings that is of particular concern for the European institutions.

15.2. Foundations of the European policy

Protectionist agreements, concentrations, national aids and discrimination in favour of public undertakings are incompatible with the common market. They **must be controlled by the European institutions** on the basis of European criteria, because the Member States' competition policies, even when they are stringent, are not efficacious at European level. Therefore, Article 3 of the EEC Treaty, given over to the principles of the Community, provided for the institution "of a system ensuring that competition in the internal market is not distorted", and the whole chapter on competition allocated to the Community the task of organising intra-Community trade, free from tariff barriers, on the basis of the law of supply and demand.

The competition rules of the Treaty are interpreted and applied through Council regulations and Commission regulations as well as through general communications and individual decisions of the Commission. Regulation N° 17 of 1972, first Regulation implementing Articles 85 and 86 of the EEC Treaty[1], was replaced by Regulation 1/2003 on the implementation of the rules on competition laid down in Articles 81 and 82 of the EC Treaty (which have the same content as Articles 85 and 86 EEC)[2]. Whereas Regulation 17/62 was based on prior notification and centralised Commission authorisation of agreements, Regulation 1/2003 is based on ex post control and on a **decentralised application of the competition rules** of Articles 81(1), 81(3) and 82 by the national authorities and courts, thus relieving the Commission of the examination of trivial cases and the industry of the costs connected with notification. On the basis of this regulation, agreements, decisions and concerted practices caught by Article 81(1) of the Treaty, which do not satisfy the conditions of Article 81(3), are prohibited, no prior decision to that effect being required. This is also the case concerning an abuse of a dominant position referred to in Article 82 of the Treaty. On the contrary, agreements, decisions and concerted practices, which satisfy the conditions of Article 81(3) of the Treaty [see section 15.3.2.], are not prohibited, no prior decision to that effect being required.

15.2.1. European competition network

Council Regulation No 17 of 1962 laid down a system of supervision requiring restrictive practices affecting trade between Member States to be notified to the Commission in order for them to qualify for an exemption[3]. The Commission thus had the exclusive power to authorise restrictive practices meeting the conditions of Article 81 (3) (formerly Article 85(3)) of the EC Treaty. This system of centralised authorisation was necessary and proved very effective in establishing a **"competition culture" in Europe** at a time when the interpretation of Article 81 (restrictive practices) and Article 82 (abuse of a dominant position) was still uncertain and when the Commission was making an effort to integrate national markets which were still very heterogeneous. During the forty years of the existence of Regulation 17/62, however, a great number of individual decisions were made by the Commission applying the exemption criteria of Article 81(3) of the Treaty. National competition authorities and national courts are therefore nowadays well aware of the conditions under which the benefit of Article 81.3 can be granted. Individual exemption decisions taken by the Commission are thus no longer indispensable to ensure a uniform application of Article 81(3) of the Treaty. Moreover, a system of notifications, en-

---

[1] Regulation 17, OJ 13, 21.02.1962 and Regulation 3385/94, OJ L 377, 31.12.1994.
[2] Regulation 1/2003, OJ L 1, 04.01.2003 and Regulation 411/2004, OJ L 68, 06.03.2004.
[3] Regulation 17/62, OJ 13, 21.02.1962 and Regulation 1/2003, OJ L 1, 04.01.2003.

tailing a great scrutiny workload for the Commission, is no longer worka-
ble in a Union of 25 Member States.

Therefore, at the proposal of the Commission, Regulation 1/2003 replaced its absolute powers in the field of competition by a network of
competition authorities, called the **European Competition Network
(ECN)**, which is a key plank of the new enforcement system. Formed by
the Commission and the competition authorities of the Member States, this
network of public authorities applies the Community competition rules in
close cooperation, providing for an allocation of cases according to the
principle of the best-placed authority, the objective being that each case
should be handled by a single authority. In addition, the Commission consults an Advisory Committee on Restrictive Practices and Dominant Positions, composed of representatives of the competition authorities of the
Member States.

The Commission may continue to adopt so called "block" exemption
regulations by which it declares Article 81(1) of the Treaty inapplicable to
categories of agreements, decisions and concerted practices. It may still
adopt individual decisions prohibiting serious cartels affecting trade between the Member States and having the effect of restricting competition.
Where the Commission, acting on a complaint or on its own initiative,
finds that there is an infringement of Article 81 or of Article 82 of the
Treaty, it may by decision require the undertakings and associations of undertakings concerned to bring such infringement to an end. For this purpose, it may impose on them any behavioural or structural remedies which
are proportionate to the infringement committed and necessary to bring the
infringement effectively to an end.

On their side, **national competition authorities and courts** are empowered to apply Community law. They have the power to apply not only
Article 81(1) and Article 82 of the Treaty, which have direct applicability
by virtue of the case-law of the Court of Justice, but also Article 81(3) of
the Treaty. This means that national competition authorities are empowered to withdraw the benefit of a Community block exemption regulation
[see section 15.3.3.]. National competition authorities may take the following decisions: requiring that an infringement be brought to an end, ordering
interim measures, accepting commitments, imposing fines, periodic penalty payments or any other penalty provided for in their national law. National courts may apply Community competition rules in lawsuits between
private parties, acting as public enforcers or as review courts. They can apply Article 81 of the EC Treaty in three types of proceedings: contractual
liability proceedings (disputes between parties to an agreement); non-
contractual liability proceedings (disputes between a third party and one or
more parties to the agreement); and applications for injunctions. In any
case, national courts may ask the Commission for information or for its
opinion on points concerning the application of Community competition
law.

Compliance with Articles 81 and 82 of the Treaty and the fulfilment of the obligations imposed on undertakings and associations of undertakings under Regulation 1/2003 is enforceable by means of fines and periodic penalty payments. The rules on periods of limitation for the imposition of fines and periodic penalty payments were laid down in Regulation 2988/74[1], which also concerns penalties in the field of transport. The imposition or non-imposition of a fine, and the amount thereof, depend in particular on the gravity of the infringement, its duration and the size of the undertakings involved. An intentional infringement usually leads to a heavier fine than when undertakings are simply guilty of negligence. Practices that have already in the past been frequently punished by the Commission also carry heavier fines, as the earlier decisions of the Commission and of the Court of Justice should have alerted undertakings to the unlawful nature of such behaviour. The Commission may also impose on undertakings and associations of undertakings fines where, intentionally or negligently, they supply incorrect or misleading information, do not supply information within the required time-limit or refuse to submit to inspections.

Commission action in the area of competition is controlled, from the legal standpoint, by the **Court of Justice**, which can rescind or amend any formal Commission decision, i.e. negative clearances, decisions granting or refusing an exemption, orders to put an end to infringements, etc. [see section 4.1.5.]. The Court may also confirm, reduce, repeal or increase the fines and penalty payments imposed by the Commission. Any natural or legal person in respect of whom a decision has been taken may institute proceedings before the Court, as may any other person directly and individually concerned by a decision of which he is not the addressee. The Commission's competition policy is controlled, from the political standpoint, by the **European Parliament** [see section 4.1.3.], which adopts positions on its guidelines and scrutinises its annual report on competition.

15.2.2. European law and national law

In the field of competition, national competence and Community competence are autonomous and parallel, the latter being defined by the criterion of the effect of trade among Member States. In a concrete case there may be juxtaposition of the validity of European law and national law. In any case, **European law takes precedence over national law** [see section 3.3.]. National authorities may take action against an agreement, pursuant to national law, even where the position of that agreement with regard to Community rules is pending before the Commission. They can also apply the Community competition law. However, the decision resulting from **a national procedure may not run counter to the Commission's decision**. Where the latter precedes the national decision, the competent authorities of the Member State are obliged to observe its effects. Where, on the other

---

[1]   Regulation 2988/74, OJ L 319, 29.11.1974.

hand, the Commission's decision post-dates the national decision and is at variance with its effects, it is for the national authorities to take appropriate measures in conformity with it.

The **Member States cannot oppose Commission decisions**, whereas the Commission can request the competent authorities of the States concerned to proceed with any verification it deems necessary or to collect fines or penalty payments it has imposed. National courts can apply the Community law or refer matters of Community law to the Court of Justice of the European Communities for a preliminary ruling. Appeal courts are obliged to request a preliminary ruling where a decision on the point at issue is necessary to enable them to deliver their judgment.

15.3. Permissible cooperations and prohibited agreements

Article 81 of the EC Treaty declares that all agreements between undertakings, decisions by associations of undertakings and concerted practices which may affect trade between Member States and which have as their object or effect the prevention, restriction or distortion of competition within the common market shall be **prohibited as incompatible with the common market**. In particular, this article prohibits agreements which: (a) directly or indirectly fix purchase or selling prices or any other trading conditions; (b) limit or control production, markets, technical development, or investment; (c) share markets or sources of supply; (d) apply dissimilar conditions to equivalent transactions with other trading parties, thereby placing them at a competitive disadvantage; (e) make the conclusion of contracts subject to acceptance by the other parties of supplementary obligations which, by their nature or according to commercial usage, have no connection with the subject of such contracts. Prohibited agreements shall be automatically void.

However, under **paragraph 3 of Article 81,** the Commission may declare the provisions of paragraph 1 of that Article inapplicable in the case of any agreement or category of agreements between undertakings, any decisions by associations of undertakings and any concerted practice or category of concerted practices, on the following conditions: that they contribute to improving the production or distribution of goods or to promoting technical or economic progress, while allowing consumers a fair share of the resulting benefit, and that they do not afford such undertakings the possibility of eliminating competition in respect of a substantial part of the products in question. On the basis of Regulation 1/2003, agreements, decisions and concerted practices, caught by Article 81(1) of the Treaty, which satisfy the conditions of Article 81(3) of the Treaty, are not prohibited, no [2]prior decision to that effect being required. These conditions can, however, be controlled at any time by the European competition network [see section 15.2.1.].

It ensues that not all agreements between Community undertakings are prohibited - far from it. Most are even desirable with a view to improving the structures of European industry, as we see in the relevant chapter [see section 17.2.4.]. In parallel with the elimination of situations incompatible with the system of competition and market unity, the Commission has in fact always pursued a policy of encouraging cooperation between undertakings where, in its opinion, such cooperation is compatible with the common market and can produce favourable economic effects.

Over the years, the Commission has endeavoured to specify, in a double series of measures, some of which were individual and some general or sectoral (e.g., air transport or telecommunications) [see sections 17.3.6. and 20.3.4.], those agreements **not covered by the prohibition** in Article 85 paragraph 1 (present Art. 81 TEC) [see section 15.3.2.] and those which, although covered by the prohibition, were **likely to be exempted from it** [see sections 15.3.1. and 15.3.3.]. Individual exemption decisions do not lend themselves to ill-considered generalisation, as the conditions for exemption can only be specific on a case-by-case basis. However, some types of clearly defined agreements are covered by group exemptions.

15.3.1. The "de minimis" rule

In a notice on **agreements of minor importance (de minimis)**, the Commission quantifies, with the help of market share thresholds, what is not an appreciable restriction of competition under Article 81 of the EC Treaty[1]. The Commission holds the view that an agreement between undertakings, even if it affects trade between Member States, does not appreciably restrict competition within the meaning of Article 81(1) of the EC Treaty if :(a) the aggregate market share held by the parties to the agreement does not exceed 10% on any of the relevant markets affected by the agreement, where the agreement is made between undertakings **which are actual or potential competitors** on any of these markets; or (b) the market share held by each of the parties to the agreement does not exceed 15% on any of the relevant markets affected by the agreement, where the agreement is made between undertakings which **are not actual or potential competitors** on any of these markets. In these cases the Commission will not institute proceedings either upon application or on its own initiative.

Agreements entered into by SMEs whose annual turnover and balance-sheet total do not exceed EUR 40 million and 27 million respectively and which have a maximum of 250 employees are rarely capable of appreciably affecting trade between Member States and are not, in principle, investigated by the Commission. However, there exists a "blacklist of hardcore restrictions" - such as price-fixing, market-sharing or territorial protection - which, because of their nature are regarded as typically incompatible with Article 81(1) of the EC Treaty and hence liable to be caught by the ban on

---

[1] Commission notice, OJ C 368, 22.12.2001, p. 13.

agreements, even if the parties' market shares are below the above-mentioned thresholds.

15.3.2. Permissible contractual relations

Agreements between undertakings are not regarded as restricting competition and, therefore, do not need to be notified to the Commission where their purpose is a **form of authorised cooperation,** such as: the joint carrying out of comparative studies, the joint preparation of statistics and models, the joint study of markets, cooperation on accounting, joint financial guarantees, the joint execution of research and development contracts, the joint use of means of production, storage and transport and, under certain conditions, the joint performance of orders, joint selling, joint after-sales and repair service and joint advertising[1].

In order to lift any doubts the Commission specified in two communications the characteristics of very common contractual relations concerning exclusive representation and subcontracting, which do not fall under the prohibition of Article 81, paragraph 1, provided that they do not establish absolute territorial protection. Thus, the Commission considers that an **exclusive representation** contract concluded between a "commercial agent", who does not accept any liability for the financial risks involved in the transactions and he in fact acts only as a simple middleman for a "principal", is not covered by Article 81 paragraph 1[2]. **Subcontracts** are also allowed according to the Commission[3] [see also section 17.2.4.]. Subcontracting usually involves, for a small undertaking, known as the "subcontractor", performance of an order for a large undertaking, known as the "principal", in accordance with the directives of the latter. The Commission considers that the obligation to supply only to the latter manufactured objects or work executed does not restrict competition within the meaning of Article 81 of the EC Treaty (former Article 85).

15.3.3. Exemption of categories of agreements

Whereas the contractual relations mentioned above are not prohibited by Article 81, paragraph 1, the contractual relations mentioned below are in principle prohibited but can be exempted from the prohibition. Indeed, under paragraph 3 of Article 81, the Commission may declare the **provisions of paragraph 1 inapplicable** in the case of certain agreements or categories of agreements which contribute to improving the production or distribution of goods or to promoting technical or economic progress, while allowing consumers a fair share of the resulting benefit. A Council Regulation empowers the Commission to apply Article 81(3) of the Treaty

---

[1] OJ C 75, 29.07.1968, p. 3-6.
[2] OJ 139, 24.12.1962.
[3] Communication of the Commission, OJ C 1, 03.01.1979, p. 2-3.

by regulation to certain categories of agreements, decisions and concerted practices falling within the scope of Article 81(1)[1]. Another Council Regulation lays down the conditions under which the Commission may declare by way of regulation that the provisions of Article 81(1) do not apply to certain categories of agreements and concerted practices[2].

The instrument of the **"block-exemption" regulation** is used by the Commission to discharge a class of similar agreements whose pro-competitive benefits outweigh their anti-competitive effects. These Commission Regulations identify clearly-defined categories of agreements which automatically benefit from the exemption provision of Article 81, paragraph 3, provided that they do not seal off markets by preventing access and parallel trade. These block exemption Regulations are particularly useful for SMEs and were in many respects specifically designed for their benefit.

Following a 1997 Green Paper[3] and a communication of the Commission on the application of the Community competition rules to vertical restraints[4], Regulation No 17/62 and Regulation 19/65 have been amended with the aim of creating a single block exemption covering all vertical agreements or restraints[5]. Indeed, the Regulation of the Commission on the application of Article 81(3) of the Treaty to **categories of vertical agreements and concerted practices** has replaced three regulations, one on exclusive distribution, one on exclusive purchasing and one on franchise agreements. Such agreements are concluded between firms operating at different (vertical) levels of the production or distribution chain - in practice all industrial distribution and supply agreements between firms whose market shares do not exceed 30% - and govern the conditions under which distribution firms may acquire from producers, sell or re-sell final or intermediate goods or services. Above the 30% threshold, agreements are not presumed to be unlawful but may require an individual examination. The Commission has issued guidelines intended, first, to clarify how the provisions of the block exemption should be interpreted and, second, to explain the general criteria applicable when examining agreements not covered by the block exemption or when withdrawing the benefit of the exemption regulation[6].

The Commission is favourable to **joint ventures of a cooperative character**, particularly when they can introduce more quickly into Europe a new technology, the development costs of which are very high. Under certain conditions cooperative joint ventures concerning specialisation

---

[1] Regulation 2821/71, OJ L 285, 29.12.1971.
[2] Regulation 19/65, OJ 36, 06.03.1965 and Regulation 1215/1999, OJ L 148, 15.06.1999.
[3] COM (96) 721, 22 January 1997.
[4] COM (1998) 546, 30 September 1998.
[5] Regulations1215/1999 and 1216/1999, OJ L 148, 15.06.1999.
[6] Commission notice, OJ C 291, 13.10.2000.

agreements, research and development agreements, patent licensing agreements and know-how licensing agreements enjoy a block exemption[1].

15.3.4. Prohibited agreements

We shall not attempt, here, to describe all the forms of horizontal agreements which are prohibited by the rules of competition of the Treaties. Each case differs depending on the product concerned, the market involved and the imagination of the executives of the participant undertakings. We shall confine ourselves to **a few characteristic cases** of agreements incompatible with the common market, as emerging from Commission decisions. The Commission judges the advantages and disadvantages of an agreement or category of agreements not on the basis of purely legal criteria, but also using the criterion of the general interest of the producers and consumers in a sector. In addition, it applies the "de minimis" rule, discussed above, to agreements that infringe the rules of competition but the economic impact of which is insignificant.

The sharing of markets is particularly restrictive of competition and at variance with the objectives of the common market, as agreements based on the principle of reciprocal respect of national markets for the benefit of the participants established there have the effect of obstructing intra-Community trade in the products concerned. Through the system of fixing supply quotas on the basis of the total sales of members of the agreement, those members waive the freedom to apply an independent sales policy, but have, on the other hand, the possibility of applying a prices policy shielded from the competition of their partners. The following are celebrated cases of penalised market-sharing agreements: the case of the Community quinine producers, who had decided amongst themselves, by gentleman's agreements, on price regulation and quotas covering all their sales on the internal market and abroad[2]; and the case of the major sugar undertakings, which controlled intra-Community trade in sugar for human consumption[3]. In November 1994, the Commission decided to impose the highest fines ever (ECU 248 million) on 9 associations of undertakings and 33 European cement producers, parties to a general market-sharing agreement aimed at protecting national or domestic markets and concluded under the aegis of Cembureau, the European Cement Federation[4]. In July 2001, the Commission decided to impose fines of EUR 39.375 million and EUR 13.125 million respectively on SAS and Maersk Air for implementing an agreement to share out routes to and from Denmark[5].

Agreements on the fixing of prices or of other conditions of transactions seriously limit competition, because they prevent purchasers from

---

[1]   Regulation 151/93, OJ L 21 of 29.01.1993 and OJ C 43, 16.02.1993.
[2]   Decision 69/240, OJ L 192, 05.08.1969.
[3]   Decision 73/109, OJ L 140, 26.05.1973.
[4]   Decision 94/815, OJ L 343, 30.12.1994.
[5]   Decision 2001/716, OJ L 265, 05.10.2001.

benefiting from the competitive behaviour that producers would have shown had the agreement not existed. As they are coupled with reciprocal respect for national markets, they are also likely to have an adverse effect on intra-Community trade. The Commission has therefore prohibited: concerted practices for the purpose of the application by the participating undertakings, on the same dates and in respect of the same categories of product (colorants), identical rates of price increases[1]; horizontal price fixing agreements and horizontal exclusive dealing agreements[2]; the publishing by trade associations of tariff schedules or recommended charges without regard to any differences in firms' cost structures[3]; and concerted methods for calculating a price supplement, as was the case of a price cartel in the stainless steel sector[4]. In July 2001, the Commission imposed fines totalling EUR 218.8 million on eight firms (two German, two American and four Japanese), which participated in a secret cartel between 1992 and 1998 through which they fixed the price and shared out the world market for graphite electrodes[5].

Restrictions on access to the market by new entrants are also prohibited. Access to the market can be impeded where a large number of retailers on this market are tied by an obligation to sell only the products of the manufacturer with whom they have a contract or vertical arrangements having a similar exclusionary effect on third parties. This is why, the Commission condemned the exclusivity conditions imposed by Unilever as part of its terms for supplying freezer cabinets to its Irish retailers[6]. In other cases, new competitors can be prevented from entering the market through a horizontal agreement or concerted practice, as in the aforementioned case of the Dutch crane-hire market[7].

The most complicated cases are those of **exclusive distribution agreements,** which are covered by a category exemption, but not where they provide for absolute territorial protection **which prevents parallel imports**. This is the case of agreements, which stand in the way of the distributor re-exporting the products in question to other Member States or of such products being imported from other Member States in the concessionaire's area and being distributed there by persons other than the concessionaire. Commission policy on the matter was clearly set out in its decision of 23 September 1964 in the "Grundig-Consten" case, essentially upheld by the Court of Justice in its judgment of 13 July 1966[8]. The Commission continues to fight against distribution systems which impede parallel trade, such as that of Volkswagen, which prohibited its Italian dealers from selling Volkswagen and Audi cars to foreign buyers, thereby restricting in-

---

[1] Decision 69/243, OJ L 195, 07.08.1969.
[2] Decision 95/551, OJ L 312, 23.12.1995.
[3] Decision 96/438, OJ L 181, 20.07.1996.
[4] Decision 98/247/ECSC, OJ L 100, 01.04.1998.
[5] Decision 2002/271, OJ L 100, 16.04.2002.
[6] Decision 98/531, OJ L 246, 04.09.1998.
[7] Decision 95/551, OJ L 312, 23.12.1995.
[8] OJ L 161, 20.10.1964 and ECR 1966, p. 299.

tra-Community trade[1] or DaimlerChrysler, which instructed the members of its German distribution network for Mercedes passenger cars not to sell cars outside their respective territories and to oblige foreign consumers to pay a deposit of 15% to DaimlerChrysler when ordering a car in Germany[2].

15.4. Market domination

We shall see in the relevant chapter that, from the point of view of the Community's industrial and enterprise policies, concentrations of small and medium-sized undertakings into larger units are in principle desirable and should be encouraged, as they lead to economies of scale, the rationalisation of the production and distribution of products in the common market and promote technical progress [see section 17.2.1.]. But **if the concentration exceeds certain limits**, which vary from sector to sector, it may result in the formation of monopolies or, more often, oligopolies and the consequent restrictions of competition and intra-Community trade. This occurs in particular where an undertaking, which dominates a sector by virtue of its size and economic strength, acquires the smaller undertakings in competition with it one by one.

15.4.1. Preventing the exploitation of a dominant position

Article 82 of the EC Treaty (ex Art. 86 EEC) stipulates that "**any abuse by one or more undertakings of a dominant position** within the common market or in a substantial part of it shall be prohibited as incompatible with the common market in so far as it may affect trade between Member States". Apart from the fact that this Article does not prohibit the obtaining of a dominant position, but only abuse thereof, it leaves several issues obscure, although they are now clarified by various standard Commission decisions and judgments of the Court of Justice.

First, **domination of a given market** cannot be defined solely on the basis of the market share held by an undertaking or of other quantitative elements, but must also be looked at in the light of its ability to exercise an appreciable influence on the functioning of the market and on the behaviour of other firms. In its judgment of 14 February 1978 in the case of "United Brands Company v. Commission" the Court upheld and enlarged the definition of the dominant position adopted by the Commission as early as its decision of 9 December 1971 in the "Continental Can Company" case[3]. It thus stated that the dominant position referred to in Article 86 (EEC)"relates to a position of economic strength enjoyed by an undertak-

---

[1]   Decision 98/273, OJ L 124, 25.04.1998.
[2]   Decision of 10 October 2001.
[3]   Decision 72/21, OJ L 7, 08.01.1972.

ing which enables it to prevent effective competition being maintained on the relevant market by giving it the power to behave to an appreciable extent independently of its competitors, customers and ultimately of its consumers".

The definition of **the relevant market** or of the market in question is also of great importance, as the more strictly that market is defined in time and space, the greater the likelihood that a dominant position can be identified in the common market. In its judgment of 13 February 1979 in the "Hoffman-La Roche v. Commission" case, the Court of Justice felt, in common with the Commission[1], that each group of vitamins constitutes a separate market and that one product can belong to two separate markets if it can be used for several purposes[2]. The Court held that actual competition must be able to exist between products that belong to the relevant market, which presupposes an adequate degree of interchangeability or substitutability between such products. For the Commission, the assessment of demand substitution entails a determination of the range of products, which are viewed as substitutes by the consumer and their competition can thus affect the pricing of the parties' products. The Commission's notice on the relevant market is an analytical tool which makes it possible to calculate firm's market shares[3].

As regards the concept of the **distortion of trade between Member States,** which is the same for Articles 81 and 82 (TEC), the Commission and the Court of Justice agree that a concentration in which an undertaking occupies a dominant position in the common market or in a substantial part of it will always be of importance for trade between Member States. In its judgment of 13 July 1966 in the "Grundig-Consten" case the Court opined that the concept of damage to trade between Member States should be seen as a question of "whether the agreement is capable of constituting a threat... to freedom of trade between Member States in a manner which might harm the attainment of the objectives of a single market between States"[4]. It goes without saying that abuse of a dominant position is judged all the more harshly because it tends to compartmentalise the relevant market and make economic interpenetration more difficult. That was the case with British Leyland, which refused to issue type-approval certificates for left-hand-drive "Metro" vehicles in order to prevent the re-importation of such vehicles from other Member States[5].

Lastly, as regards the concept of **abuse of a dominant position,** Article 82 is more explicit, as it stipulates that "abuse may in particular, consist in: (a) ... imposing unfair purchase or selling prices or other unfair trading conditions; (b) limiting production, markets or technical development ...;

---

[1] Decision 76/642, OJ L 223, 16.08.1976.
[2] Judgment of 13 February 1979, case 85/76, ECR 1979, p. 461.
[3] OJ C 372, 09.12.1997, p. 5-13.
[4] Joined Cases 56 and 58/64, Consten-Grundig v Commission, ECR 1966, p. 299.
[5] OJ L 207, 02.08.1984 and case 226/84, British Leyland PLC v Commission, ECR 1986, p. 3263.

(c) applying dissimilar conditions to equivalent transactions with other trading parties ..." and "(d) making the conclusion of contracts subject to acceptance by the other parties of supplementary obligations" which have no connection with such contracts. We note that the concept of abuse of a dominant position is similar to the concept of restriction or distortion of competition given by article 81 TEC [see section 15.3.].

Generally speaking, an undertaking in a dominant position **may abuse its power on the market in one of the following ways**:

- by setting the prices on the dominated market;
- by imposing discriminatory commercial fees on service providers (as in the case of the Aéroports de Paris concerning groundhandling, catering, cleaning and freight handling services[1];
- by "tying" the products or services of the dominated market to other products or services (for example, the railway traction services in Germany offered by the Deutsche Bahn to specialised operators in the combined transport of goods operating in the port of Rotterdam[2]);
- by imposing on its customers agreements for the exclusive purchase of products (such as the vitamins in the Hoffmann-La Roche case) or services (as in the case of the company operating Frankfurt airport[3]);
- by restricting competition from imports (as in the case of Irish Sugar plc[4]); or
- by attempting to eliminate competition by "predatory pricing", i.e. by selling below cost for a short period of time until the competitors are driven out of the market (as in the case of Deutsche Post AG concerning the market for business parcel services[5]) and in the case of Wanadoo Interactive, a subsidiary of France Télécom, concerning access to the Internet by the general public[6].

It is certain that the Commission and the Court regard it as an abuse where an undertaking in a dominant position strengthens that position by means of a concentration or of **the elimination of competitors**, with the result that competition, which continued in spite of the existence of the dominant position, is virtually eliminated as regards the products concerned in a substantial part of the common market. The Commission accordingly imposed heavy fines on: AKZO Chemie, which is the chemical division of the Dutch multinational group AKZO, for having abused its dominant position on the organic peroxides market by trying to eliminate a small competitor from the market by applying prolonged, selective price-cuts designed to damage its business[7]; and British Sugar plc for imple-

---

[1] Decision 98/538, OJ L 252, 12.09.1998.
[2] Decision 94/210, OJ L 104, 23.04.1994.
[3] Decision 98/190, OJ L 72, 11.03.1998.
[4] Decision 97/624, OJ L 258, 22.09.1997..
[5] Decision 2001/354, OJ L 125, 05.05.2001.
[6] Commission decision of 16 July 2003.
[7] Decision OJ L 374, 31.12.1985 and judgment of 3 July 1991, case C-62/86, Akzo Chemie v Commission, ECR 1986, p. 1503.

menting a series of abuses designed to eliminate a smaller competitor from the retail sugar market[1].

15.4.2. Concentrations in the Single Market

Concentrations are arrangements whereby one or more companies acquire control of other companies and thus change the structure of the companies involved and of the market they operate in. The most **important forms of concentrations** of undertakings are the holding of a company in the authorised capital of another company or of other companies, the total or partial acquisitions by a company of the assets of other companies and, lastly, the merger of two or more companies which are legally independent into a new company. Concentrations allow economies of scale to be obtained, production and distribution costs to be reduced, profitability to be improved and technical progress to be speeded up. All of that facilitates the international competitiveness of Community undertakings and may provide consumers with part of the benefits of economic integration. It is, however, obvious that where the concentration in an industry exceeds certain limits it can lead to monopoly or oligopoly structures, which restrict competition and jeopardise consumers' interests.

As mentioned above, Article 86 of the EEC Treaty **prohibited abuse of a dominant position, but not its existence or creation**. This means that the EEC Treaty did not request authorisation by the Commission for a concentration operation, which could lead to a dominant position. The EC Treaty has not altered this situation. However, the Commission undertook to **fill the legislative vacuum in the EEC Treaty** on the basis of Article 3 (f) thereof. In the Commission's view, since that Treaty had the objective of ensuring the functioning of an undistorted system of competition, the exploitation of a dominant position should be regarded as abusive if it in practice prevented the functioning of undistorted competition. A concentration of undertakings that results in the **monopolisation of a market** should therefore be dealt with as abuse of a dominant position within the meaning of Article 86 of the EEC Treaty. For the first time in 1971 the Commission translated that interpretation into fact by adopting a Decision applying Article 86 (EEC) in the case of the concentration of an undertaking occupying a dominant position, namely Continental Can Cy, with a competing undertaking[2]. The Commission considered that Continental Can Cy had abused its dominant position by **taking control of one of its potential main competitors**, thus strengthening the said dominant position in such a way that competition in a substantial part of the common market was virtually eliminated with regard to the products concerned. The judgment delivered by the Court of Justice on 21 February 1973 confirmed the correctness of the Commission's approach to the application of Article 86

---

[1] 88/518, OJ L 284, 19.10.1988.
[2] Decision 72/21, OJ L 7, 08.01.1972.

(Art. 82 TEC) to abuse of the dominant position by the concentration[1]. More recently, the Court has ruled that any merger, which created or strengthened a **collective dominant position** enjoyed by the parties concerned, was likely to prove incompatible with the system of undistorted competition envisaged in the Treaty[2].

Thus, with the support of the Court of Justice, the Commission could exercise an *a posteriori* **control of concentrations** of undertakings, one of which had already achieved a dominant position. However, knowing that "prevention is better than cure", the Commission wanted a preventive policy in the field of concentrations. Already in 1973, it had submitted to the Council a proposal for a regulation on the control of mergers. It took sixteen years of discussions in the Council for the **Regulation on the control of concentrations between undertakings** finally to be adopted in December 1989. Still, this Regulation provided a high threshold for obligatory notification of concentrations and the Commission, after some new discussions, succeeded, in June 1997, to persuade the Council to reduce it[3].

After the 1997 and 2004 amendments of the Regulation, compulsory notification covers mergers involving undertakings whose aggregate world-wide **turnover** exceeds 2.5 billion euro (general threshold), and the turnover in each of at least three Member States exceeds 100 million euro. The system whereby a merger is referred to the national authorities by the Commission or vice versa is simplified, with the aim of ensuring both that the authority best placed to examine the situation is given charge of the file, in accordance with the subsidiarity principle [see section 3.2.], and that multiple notifications are avoided. Thus, the Commission only takes action on mergers if they have a Community dimension and on restrictive practices only if they affect trade between Member States. In these cases its position, its experience and its powers of inquiry place it at the best level to assess the factors involved. Moreover, the Commission can authorise a national anti-cartel office to investigate a concentration, which may have significant effects on a local market. The Commission has to base its decision principally on criteria of competition, but may also **take into consideration other factors**, such as economic and technical progress.

To ensure the effective application of the principle of compulsory notification, the Commission has adopted a Regulation covering, among other points, time limits and hearings, the form, content and other **provisions relating to notifications**[4]. According to this Regulation, notifications relating to Regulation 139/2004 on the control of concentrations between undertakings and to Article 57 of the EEA Agreement must be submitted in the manner prescribed by "Form CO" or, under certain conditions in "Short Form", while reasoned submissions for a pre-notification referral must take the "form RS". The forms are set out in the Annexes of the Regulation.

---

[1] Case 6/72, Europemballage Corporation v Commission, ECR 1973, p. 215.

[2] Judgment of 31 March 1998, Joined Cases C-68/94 and C-30/95, ECR 1998 I-1375.

[3] Regulation 4064/89, OJ L 395, 30.12.1989 and Regulation 1310/97, OJ L 180, 09.07.1997.

[4] Regulation 802/2004, OJ L 133, 30.04.2004.

The procedures established for dealing with notifications enable the Commission to make effective use of its powers in this area. The Commission grants authorisation, within the space of a month, to the vast majority of operations which do not create or reinforce a dominant position in the common market or a substantial part of it[1]. In a large number of cases the authorisation of the Commission is granted subject to compliance with conditions and obligations[2]. Only when serious doubts exist as to the operations' compatibility with the common market does it decide to open a detailed investigation as provided for in the second part of the procedure.

15.5. *Monitoring State intervention*

Competition in the common market can be distorted not only by the behaviour of undertakings, but also by State intervention. The **arguments adduced by governments for intervening** in economic activities are numerous, but they all have a socio-political ring: to prevent the closure of undertakings which might give rise to collective redundancies, which are unacceptable in social and regional terms. At national level, undertakings experiencing difficulties make public opinion and the official authorities aware of their predicament, especially when they are big companies, regarded as "flagship undertakings" and/or they occupy a large number of workers whose jobs are endangered.

The social and regional consequences of structural changes should indeed be attenuated, but the changes themselves should **not be opposed by artificially ensuring the survival** of obsolete industries or sectors in decline. The question should be asked, on a case-by-case basis, whether aid is really needed, rather than a radical change in production structures and methods, and whether aid for an industry in difficulty in one Member State of the EU might not harm the interests of the same industries established in the other Member States. It is, indeed, obvious that State intervention may involve a conflict of interests between the economic operators benefiting from such intervention and their competitors in the other Member States, which will be placed in a less favourable position and will press their governments to redress the situation. Unilaterally conceived State initiatives cannot, therefore, but trigger reciprocation from partner countries and lead to costly operations for everyone. In order to avoid retaliation from partner countries and squandered resources, therefore, a "code of good conduct" is needed for the Member States in this area.

In fact, as other forms of protectionism recede, the importance of State aids as an anti-competitive mechanism tends to grow. Beyond their negative effect on competition, State aids can also have **serious implications for economic cohesion** within the EU [see section 12.1.2.]. Large and well

---

[1] See, for example, Commission Decision 95/404, OJ L 239, 07.10.1995, (Swissair/Sabena).

[2] See, for example, Commission Decision 97/816, OJ L 336, 08.12.1997 (Boeing/McDonnell Douglas).

developed Member States are able to outbid less developed Member States on the periphery of the Union in the aid race. Indeed, the four largest Member States account for 88% of all aid granted in the Union.

Aid of a regional character was examined in the chapter on regional development [see section 12.2.1.]. The following paragraphs look at other State operations: general aid, sectoral aid, national monopolies and public undertakings.

15.5.1. Compatible and incompatible aids

Article 87 of the EC Treaty (ex Art. 92 EEC) stipulates that "any aid granted... which distorts or threatens to distort competition by favouring certain undertakings or the production of certain goods shall, in so far as it affects trade between Member States, **be incompatible with the common market**". Given the high degree of integration of the Community's economy, most national subsidies are likely to be considered trade-distorting, even for products which are not exported to other Member States, if they compete on their home market with imports from other Member States. The Commission has devised a mechanism for fixing and revising the reference rates used to calculate the grant equivalent of aid[1]. The form of the aid is irrelevant: for example outright grants, soft loans, tax concessions, guarantees, the supply of goods or services at less than cost are all subject to Community State aid control. However, under the **"de minimis" rule**, aid of less than EUR 100 000 over three years is judged not to affect trade between Member States and thus need not be notified to the Commission[2].

Paragraph 2 of Article 87 considers that the following shall be **compatible with the common market**, provided that aid is granted without discrimination related to the origin of the products concerned: aid having a social character granted to individual consumers, aid to make good the damage caused by natural disasters or exceptional occurrences and aid granted to certain areas of Germany affected by the division of that country (before 1991).

Paragraph 3 of Article 87, for its part, stipulates that the following **may be considered to be compatible** with the common market: aid to promote the economic development of areas with economic or social problems; aid to promote the execution of an important project of common European interest or to remedy a serious disturbance in the economy of a Member State; aid to facilitate the development of certain economic activities or of certain economic areas, where such aid does not adversely affect trading conditions; aid to promote culture and heritage conservation[3]; and such other categories of aid as may be specified by decision of the Council.

---

[1]   OJ C 31, 03.02.1979.

[2]   Regulation 69/2001, OJ L 10, 13.01.2001.

[3]   Point inserted at Maastricht.

The Council has empowered the Commission to adopt block exemption regulations for certain **categories of horizontal aid** (in favour of SMEs, research and development, environment protection, employment and training) and for aid below a given threshold[1]. A Commission decision of 22 July 1998 clarifies the circumstances in which public funding for training may be caught by the competition rules on State aid and sets the criteria which it applies in ascertaining whether such aid is compatible with the common market. A Commission notice of 11 November 1998 sets out the criteria it applies when examining or reviewing Member States' arrangements relating to direct business taxation.

So that the Commission may adopt a position on the possible application of one of the above derogations from the incompatibility of aid, the Member States are obliged, under Article 88 paragraph 3 of the EC Treaty (ex Art. 93) to **inform it in sufficient time**, through a detailed questionnaire, of any plans to grant new aid or alter existing aid. Such aid may not be granted by Member States until the Commission has taken a final decision on it. In case the Member States fail to fulfil their obligation to notify proposals to grant aid, the Commission reserves the right to take a provisional decision requiring them to recover, with interest, any aid paid illegally pending a final decision by it on the compatibility of the aid with the common market[2]. In order to increase legal certainty and transparency in the Commission's decision-making process, a Council Regulation lays down detailed rules for the application of Article 88 of the EC Treaty[3].

15.5.2. General aids

Aid from which any undertaking whatsoever can benefit, without regard to its geographical location or to the sector to which it belongs, is regarded as general aid. Owing to this lack of a specific character, such aid cannot lay claim to an exemption provision provided for in the Treaty. The Commission has to be able to verify, prior to their being granted, that general aids are in **response to genuine economic or social needs**, that they lead to an improvement in the structures of beneficiary undertakings and that they do not give rise to problems at Community level. The Commission tries to prevent aid that does not pursue clearly defined objectives. For that reason, it requires Member States, when applying general aid arrangements, either to notify it in advance of the relevant regional or sectoral programmes or, if there are no such programmes, to inform it of significant individual cases. It also tries to obviate an excessively high intensity of aid (aggregation) for a single undertaking under various aid schemes[4].

---

[1]   Regulation 994/98, OJ L 142, 14.05.1998.
[2]   OJ C 156, 27.06.1995, p. 5.
[3]   Regulation 659/1999, OJ L 83, 27.03.1999.
[4]   COM (98) 73, 18 February 1998.

The Commission systematically prohibits **State export aid** within the Community and normally prohibits aid, which does not have a **counterpart in the Community interest**. Aid on which no time limit is placed and which is required to support current activities ("**operating aid**") is just as unacceptable as aid for intra-Community exports. According to the Court of Justice, State **participation in the capital of undertakings** is likely to be considered State aid coming within the scope of Article 92 *et seq.* of the EEC Treaty (Art. 87 *et seq.* TEC).

However, certain general aids are granted to achieve **legitimate objectives** and may be approved by the Commission under certain conditions, specified in its communications. In addition to regional development aids [see section 12.2.1.], this is generally the case for research and development aids[1], aids in favour of small and medium-sized enterprises[2], environmental protection aids[3], vocational training aids[4], aids for rescuing and restructuring firms in difficulty[5] and aids for employment[6].

15.5.3. Sectoral aids

In principle, **sectoral aids pose fewer problems than general aids**, in that their field of application and scope are more clearly delineated. The Commission's policy on sectoral aids involves examining whether the problems facing these industries may, depending on the case, justify the granting of State aid while ensuring that such aid does not unduly delay the necessary changes, does not distort competition to an extent counter to the common interest and is in line with the attainment of the Community's objectives, or at least will not hinder that goal.

The symbiosis of national economies in the common market is reflected by very similar economic developments in the Member States, even though their economic structures are not homogeneous. The difficulties justifying intervention by a Member State are often to be found in some or all of its partners. A "**Community framework**" encompassing national measures may therefore be elaborated when the conditions in a sector so dictate. Such a framework includes guidelines for the objectives to be attained at Community level and a description of how to achieve that. The framework for aids to sectors in crisis takes varying legal forms, but is generally based on the criterion of "overcapacity", for which the definition and implementing provisions have gradually been refined to take fuller account of the features of the specific market in question such as progress in production technologies and the degree of globalisation. Such frameworks

---

[1] OJ C 45, 17.02.1996, p. 5-14 and OJ C 78, 10.03.2001.
[2] Regulation 70/2001, OJ L 10, 13.01.2001.
[3] Commission decision, OJ C 37, 03.02.2001, p. 3-15.
[4] Regulation 68/2001, OJ L 10, 13.01.2001.
[5] OJ C 288, 09.10.1999.
[6] Regulation 2204/2002, OJ L 337, 13.12.2002.

exist for aids to shipbuilding[1], maritime transport[2], the steel industry[3], the synthetic fibres industry[4] and the motor vehicle industry[5].

On 13 February 2002, the Commission approved the recasting of the rules applicable to regional aid to **large investment projects**, including in steel, the motor vehicle and synthetic fibres sectors[6] [see section 12.2.1.]. The overhaul is aimed at setting up a quicker, simpler and more transparent system of controlling public authority support for major investment projects in the European Union. The reform enhances Member States' responsibility as regards implementation of the State aid rules and guarantees proper control of State aid levels in an enlarged and more heterogeneous Community.

15.5.4. Public undertakings

While remaining neutral with regard to the legal position on ownership in the Member States, the EC Treaty stipulates, in **Article 86**, that "in the case of public undertakings and undertakings to which Member States grant special or exclusive rights, Member States shall neither enact nor maintain in force any measures contrary to the rules contained in this Treaty ...". Such undertakings therefore **have the same obligations as private firms,** including those laid down in Article 12 (prohibition of discrimination on grounds of nationality) and 81 to 89 inclusive (rules of competition). Article 86, paragraph 3 (TEC) confers on the Commission the task of ensuring the application of these provisions and the power to address directives or decisions to Member States where necessary.

However, Article 86(2) allows exceptions to the rules of competition of the Treaty **in favour of public utility undertakings**, entrusted with the operation of services of general economic interest (water, energy, transport and telecommunications) or having the character of a revenue-producing monopoly, so as not to obstruct the performance, in law or in fact, of the particular tasks assigned to them. Nevertheless, the development of Community trade must not be affected by aid to these undertakings to such an extent as would be contrary to the interests of the Community.

Indeed, governments grant certain public enterprises **statutory monopoly protection**. Such exclusive monopoly rights are awarded for various public policy reasons, such as ensuring security of supply, providing a basic service to the whole population or avoiding the costs of duplicating an expensive distribution network. Such practices are common, notably for utilities (energy and water), postal services, telecommunications and to some extent in broadcasting, transport (air and maritime), banking and in-

[1] Regulation 1540/98, OJ L 202, 18.07.1998.
[2] COM (96) 81 and OJ C 205, 05.07.1997.
[3] Decision 2496/96, OJ L 338, 28.12.1996.
[4] OJ C 96, 30.03.1996, p. 11-14 and OJ C 368, 22.12.2001, p.10.
[5] OJ C 279, 15.09.1997, p. 1-8 and OJ C 368, 22.12.2001, p. 10.
[6] Communication from the Commission OJ C 70, 19.03.2002.

surance. These exclusive rights could prevent, however, the creation of a real internal market in the sectors in question, if Member States could protect from competition their monopolistic enterprises. Member States must, therefore, not take measures, which could lead their public enterprises enjoying monopoly rights to infringe Community rules on competition or the free movement of goods and services.

In any case, greater **transparency of the financial relations** between States and their public undertakings is needed, in order to enable the Commission to decide whether transfer of public funds to those undertakings are compatible with the rules laid down in the Treaty. That is precisely the aim of a Commission Directive, which obliges Member States to supply the Commission, at the latter's request, with information on public funds made available directly or indirectly to public undertakings, thus covering not only "active transfer" of public funds, such as the provision of capital and the covering of losses, but also "passive transfers", such as the forgoing by the State of income of profits or of a normal return on the funds used[1].

Commission directives have paved the way for liberalisation in the **satellite telecommunications** sector, thus helping the development of trans-European networks in this sector and facilitating the European information society. The Commission Directive on free competition on the Community markets in **telecommunications terminal equipment** (modems, telex and telefax terminals, private satellite stations, etc.) prohibits any exclusive rights to import, market, connect, bring into service and maintain such equipment[2] [see section 17.3.6.]. Similarly, the Commission Directive on competition in the markets for **electronic communications networks and services** aims at: the abolition of existing exclusive and special rights; the prohibition of the granting of new rights in the electronic communications sector; and the guarantee of the right of firms to benefit from freedom of establishment and freedom to supply services[3].

15.6. Appraisal and outlook

Competition policy has traditionally been seen as a prerogative of the nation-state. The EC/EU is the first group of states to practice a policy, which tries to deal with the impact that distortions of competition have on trade. The basic objective of the common competition policy is to prevent the unity of the common market from being called into question by measures that have the effect of giving preference to certain economic operators (businesses, companies) and of restoring the partitioning of domestic markets. In fact, whatever means are used to **correct the rigours of competi-**

---

[1] Directive 80/723, OJ L 195, 29.07.1980 and Directive 93/84, OJ L 254, 12.10.1993.
[2] Directive 88/301, OJ L 131, 27.05.1988 and Directive 94/46, OJ L 268, 19.10.1994.
[3] Directive 2002/77, OJ L 249, 17.09.2002.

tion, the usual effect consists in raising prices to restore business profitability, at the expense of the consumer or the taxpayer.

The administrative practice developed gradually by the Commission and confirmed by the case-law of the Court of Justice has made it possible to interpret and improve the rules of the Treaty in order to establish a range **of principles of fair behaviour** which, while not hindering free enterprise, indicates to economic operators the rules to be complied with to ensure that free trade and equal opportunity are guaranteed within the common market. The practices of businesses directed towards impeding imports or exports, fixing production or sales quotas and generally sharing the market are accordingly actively proceeded against. Agreements, which have the effect of concentrating demand on specific producers, and exclusive distribution agreements which prevent traders and consumers from purchasing products in any Member State, are also prohibited. Companies which practice the prohibited restrictions of competition, thus jeopardising the unity of the common market, have to expect to have heavy fines imposed on them.

Legal proceedings are also brought against undertakings which **abuse a dominant position** by refusing to supply a long-standing customer, by applying discriminatory prices, unlawful practices which cause or could cause damage to customers or consumers or, lastly, by absorbing one another thus eliminating competition in a market. It would be absurd to take legal action against horizontal agreements between undertakings whilst at the same time permit the monopolisation of certain markets through uncontrolled vertical integration of undertakings in a dominant position. That is why the Regulation on the control of major concentration transactions filled a legal vacuum which had been causing problems for a long time. The **control of concentrations** does not mean the prohibition of concentrations. Just as concentrations are dangerous when they strengthen the dominant position of major undertakings, so are they desirable when they strengthen the competitive position of small and medium-sized enterprises. Refraining from a strictly legal approach to problems of competition, the Commission conducts in fact two parallel policies: a policy for the elimination of abuse by major companies and a policy of encouragement of cooperation and concentration between SMEs [see sections 17.1.4 and 17.2.4.].

As regards State aids, the role of the Community competition policy is not only to prevent national initiatives that are harmful to intra-Community trade or to the economic activity of the other Member States, but also to limit state intervention to aid which fits in with the prospect of adjusting the structures of the Community's production mechanism to changes in demand and to the international division of labour. The Commission tries to ensure that aid to undertakings does not constitute the resurgence of protectionist measures in a new form. The common competition policy is thus not only pivotal to the good functioning of the single market, but also a complement to Community sectoral policies - in particular in the industrial, energy, agriculture and transport sectors - aimed at improving production structures. It influences the competitiveness of the

European economy and hence helps to orient the Union's macroeconomic framework towards better employment conditions.

Bibliography on competition policy

- BAEL Ivo van, BELLIS Jean-François. *Competition law of the European Community*. The Hague: Kluwer Law International, 2005.
- CAHILL Dermot, COOKE John, WILS Wouter (eds.). *The modernisation of EU competition law enforcement in the European Union: FIDE 2004 national reports*. Cambridge: Cambridge University Press, 2004.
- DAVEY Lesley, HOLMES Marjorie. *A practical guide to national competition rules across Europe*. The Hague: Kluwer Law International, 2004.
- EEKHOFF Johann (ed.). *Competition Policy in Europe*. Berlin; New York: Springer, 2004.
- GERADIN Damien. *Remedies in network industrie : EC competition law vs. sector-specific regulation*. Antwerp; Oxford: Intersentia, 2004.
- GIANNAKOPOULOS Themistoklis. *Safeguarding companies' rights in competition and anti-dumping - anti-subsidies proceedings*. The Hague: Kluwer Law International; Athens: Sakkoulas, 2004.
- KATE Adriaan ten, NIELS Gunnar (eds.). "Antitrust in the U.S. and the EU: converging and diverging paths?", *The Antitrust Bulletin*, Thematic issue, v. 49, n. 1-2, Spring-Summer 2004, p. 1-434.
- KORAH Valentine. *An introductory guide to EC competition law and practice*. Oxford; Portland, Or.: Hart, 2004.
- RITTER Lennart, BRAUN David. *European competition law: a practitioner's guide*. The Hague: Kluwer Law International, 2004.
- SUFRIN Brenda, JONES Alison. *EC competition law: texts, cases, and materials*. Oxford: Oxford University Press, 2004.

DISCUSSION TOPICS

1. What is the significance of a common competition policy in a multinational integration scheme?
2. Discuss the respective roles of the Commission and of national authorities in the common competition policy.
3. Give some examples of permissible business cooperations and of prohibited agreements in the EU.
4. How does the EU try to prevent the domination of its internal market by large companies?
5. Which State interventions are considered incompatible with the common market?

Chapter 16

ENVIRONMENT POLICY

Diagram of the chapter

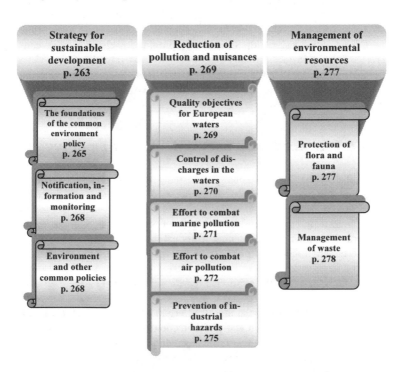

Up to the end of the 1960s no European country had a clearly defined environment policy. Student unrest in France and Germany
in May 1968, the United Nations Conference on the Human Environment,
held in Stockholm in June 1972, and the publication in the same period of
the report by the Club of Rome on "the limits of growth" alerted European
public opinion to the **ecological problems of economic development** and
questioned the hierarchy of the values extolled by the consumer society.

The Governments of the Community States were obliged hastily to design measures against pollution and nuisances so as to **open a safety valve
to an ecological movement** likely to swing the pendulum to the other extreme, to impose "zero growth", to block technological progress and with
it, perhaps, economic and social progress. But all the Member States had to
act together, as any country which took measures on its own against pollu-

tion or nuisances, or measures more stringent than its neighbours, would be likely to penalise its industry, which would have to bear the cost. Having done so, it would be forced to block the placing on its market of more pollutant, noisy or dangerous products from its more lax partners, which would bring the risk of technical barriers to trade [see section 6.2.].

The Summit Conference of Heads of State and Government held in Paris in 1972 opened the way to the implementation of a common policy on environmental protection. The Commission went to work and prepared wide-ranging action programmes for the reduction of pollution and nuisances and for the management of environmental resources. In record time by Community standards the Community provided itself with many concrete measures, a fact proving that, when there is pressure from public opinion, political will and the absence of deep-rooted national policies, the European institutions are capable of **legislative work comparable to that of an individual State**.

16.1. The need for a common environment policy

In the mosaic of States called Europe the **common market in terms of pollution** was established before the common market in goods. Polluted air and water moved freely across borders well before the idea emerged to open them to foreign goods. Each European State was thus immediately concerned by what was happening in its neighbouring countries with regard to the environment. It must not be forgotten that virtually every large lake and large watercourse in Europe is shared by two or more States, that the Mediterranean and the North Sea represent a common heritage for several European States and that those seas, lakes and rivers are used as common dumping grounds for the industrial waste of several countries. In the field of nature conservation and the protection of wildlife, too, a country that protected migratory birds or endangered species would be wasting its time if its neighbours killed them. If the mess was to be stopped, action therefore had to be taken together.

Not only neighbourliness, but also the comparable socio-economic development of the European countries, argued in favour of Community action to protect the environment. The **phenomena common to all European States** of the expansion of industrial activities, the increase in the urban population within megalopoles and the drift away from increasingly large tracts of territory originally used and maintained by agriculture required comparable measures and means to be utilised in the Member States to cope with them.

Common environmental problems **needed common solutions**. Short of seriously affecting the competitive capacity of its economy, no European State could hope to resolve its environmental problems by acting on its own. The fight against pollution in fact imposes certain expenditure on industrialists to adapt their products or their manufacturing processes. Such expenditure is all the greater, the more stringent are the standards laid down by the public authorities. If a State of the Union imposed stringent and **costly anti-pollution measures** on its industry, it might penalise it vis-à-vis its competitors from other States which were less attentive to the damage caused by pollution or which had different ideas as to how to apportion expenditure for the fight against pollution. Competition would therefore be distorted in the common market. It was therefore necessary for the same rules to be imposed on all European producers.

The free **movement of goods** within the common market would also be affected if each Member State laid down different standards for products put on sale on its market [see section 6.2.]. The country, which laid down more stringent standards than its neighbours, for example, on restrictions on the noise of certain engines or on the exhaust emissions of motor vehicles, would impede imports of related products from other countries. Protection against pollution and noise could thus quickly deteriorate into protection against foreign products. In other words, national environment policy could be used to thwart the internal market in a very subtle manner.

Lastly, it has to be said that the **European institutions are better placed than governments** to have a long-term view of environmental problems and requirements. Even when they are certain of remaining in office for fairly long time, national governments, being preoccupied with short-term problems, are rarely in a position to plan long-term strategies in this non-profit-making sector. Its relative detachment from the day-to-day problems peculiar to each Member State and its right of initiative with regard to the harmonisation of legislation make it possible for the European Commission to conceive a long-term programme against pollution [see section 4.1.2.]. Let us not forget, however, that in the case of the common environment policy, as in any other common policy, the "Eurocrats" of Brussels (the Commission), assisted by national technocrats (scientific and administrative committees), only propose the measures considered scientifically and technically necessary to protect the environment. It is the politicians in the European Parliament and the Council who take the final decisions [see section 4.3.], taking into consideration the industrial and political cost of precautionary measures proposed. These decisions, however, are taken collectively and concern all Member States.

16.2. Common strategy for sustainable development

The European Union's environment programme now aims at **sustainable development**, which takes into account the present economic and social needs without jeopardising, through resource misuse, the **development possibilities of future generations**[1]. To be sustainable, growth must be

---

[1] COM (2001) 31, 24 January 2001.

decoupled from negative environmental impacts and be based on sustainable consumption and production patterns. This means that short term economic gains at the expense of the environment should be replaced by a more sustainable model of economic and social development, which may constitute the basis for greater efficiency and competitiveness, both at a Union level and internationally.

The Göteborg European Council (15-16 June 2001) approved a **European Union strategy for sustainable development**, proposed by the Commission[1], based on:

1. **coordinated development of common policies** addressing the economic, environmental and social dimensions of sustainability and having sustainable development as their core objective;
2. **a set of headline objectives** to limit climate change and increase use of clean energy, address threats to public health, manage natural resources more responsibly and improve the transport system and land-use management;
3. **steps to implement the strategy** and review its progress at every spring meeting of the European Council (Cardiff process launched in 1998).

The **sixth Community environment action programme** sets out environmental objectives for the years 2001 to 2010 and outlines the action that needs to be taken to achieve them[2]. The programme focuses on four priority issues:

1. **tackling climate change** by reducing greenhouse gases according to the objectives of the Kyoto Protocol [see section 16.3.4.], i.e. achieving the Community's target of reducing emissions by 8% by 2008 to 2012 (compared to 1990 levels) and by 20 to 40% by 2020, through structural changes and stronger efforts on energy-saving, especially in the transport and energy sectors, the establishment of an EU-wide emissions trading scheme, further research and technological development;
2. **nature and biodiversity**, i.e. protecting and restoring the structure and functioning of natural systems and halting the loss of biodiversity notably through: the implementation of environmental legislation; protection, conservation and restoration of landscapes; completion of the Natura 2000 network to avert the threats to the survival of many species and their habitats in Europe; new initiatives for protecting the marine environment; and a thematic strategy for protecting soils[3];
3. **environment and health**, i.e. achieving a quality of the environment which does not endanger human health, necessitating *inter alia:* a fundamental overhaul of the Community's risk-management system for chemicals[4], a strategy for reducing risks from pesticides, protection of water quality in the Union, noise abatement and a thematic strategy for air quality;

---

[1]   COM (2001) 264, 15 May 2001.
[2]   Decision 1600/2002, OJ L 242, 10.09.2002.
[3]   COM(2001) 162, 27 March 2001.
[4]   See Commission White Paper, COM (2001) 88, 13 February 2001.

4. **sustainable management of natural resources** by decoupling resource use from economic growth, in particular through: improved resource efficiency; taxation of resource use; increased recycling and waste prevention with the aid of an integrated product policy.

16.2.1. The foundations of the common environment policy

The legal basis of environment policy was considerably enlarged by the Single Act of 1987 [see section 2.1.] and **firmly established by the Maastricht Treaty** [see section 2.2.]. As revised at Amsterdam, Article 2 of that the EU Treaty sets the achievement of balanced and sustainable development among the objectives of the Union. The common environment policy has now the **following objectives**: preserving, protecting and improving the quality of the environment; protecting human health; rationalising the utilisation of natural resources; promoting measures at international level to deal with regional or world-wide environmental problems (Art. 174 TEC).

According to Article 175 (TEC), the Council acting under the **co-decision procedure** with the European Parliament [see section 4.3.] and after consultation of the Economic and Social Committee and of the Committee of the Regions takes the measures necessary for the implementation of the objectives of Article 174. Still, **the unanimity of the Council** acting after consultation of the European Parliament and the ESC is needed for: provisions primarily of a fiscal nature; measures concerning town and country planning; and measures significantly affecting a Member State's energy supply.

The Member States finance and implement environment policy. However, without prejudice to the principle that the polluter pays, if a measure involves costs deemed disproportionate for the public authorities of a Member State, notably a cohesion State [see section 12.1.2.], the Council, in the act adopting that measure, lays down appropriate provisions in the form of temporary derogations and/or financial support from the Cohesion Fund (Art. 175 TEC).

Indeed, the activities, which the Community undertakes or wishes to undertake to protect the environment and conserve nature in Europe and in the rest of the world, are becoming increasingly costly and must be planned over the long term. Awareness of this provided the impetus for the creation of a **financial instrument for the environment, LIFE**, which seeks to promote the development and implementation of the Community's environment policy and legislation by financing priority projects in the Community, such as the "Natura 2000" network, and by providing technical assistance to the associated countries of Central and Eastern Europe as well as countries in the Mediterranean region or in Baltic coastal areas[1]. It

---

[1]   Regulation 1973/92, OJ L 206, 22.07.1992 and Regulation 1655/2000, OJ L 192, 28.07.2000.

provides financial assistance for preparatory measures, demonstration schemes, awareness campaigns, incentives, technical assistance and measures necessary for the maintenance or restoration of biotopes, natural habitats and species [see section 16.4.]. In addition to LIFE, Community support through the Structural Funds and the Cohesion Fund facilitates the realisation of joint environmental projects (Jeeps) in the poorest Member States. Furthermore, the Community grants financial support to nongovernmental organisations active in the field of environmental protection, in order to help them contribute, to the development and implementation of Community environmental policy and legislation in different regions of Europe[1].

The common environment policy is based on the **precautionary and preventive action** principles, on the principle that environmental damage should to the extent possible be **rectified at source** and on the principle that **the polluter should pay** (Art. 174 TEC).

Indeed, the European Union's work on the environment is marked more and more by an integrated, **preventive approach** taking account of human activities and their consequences for the environment as a whole. The proactive policy of voluntary prevention is manifested in the Directive on **the assessment of the effects of certain public and private projects** on the environment and on natural resources, which takes into account the commitments entered into under the international "Espoo" Convention on Environmental Impact Assessment in a Transboundary Context, particularly concerning the types of project for which impact assessment is compulsory[2]. According to this Directive, the promoter of the project, whether it be industrial, agricultural or relating to infrastructure, has to supply detailed information on its possible consequences for air, water, soil, noise, wild animals and their habitats, etc. Member States should ensure that members of the public concerned have access to a review procedure before a court of law or another independent and impartial body established by law to challenge the substantive or procedural legality of decisions, acts or omissions subject to the public participation provisions of the Directive[3]. Another Directive imposes an assessment, including the preparing of an environmental report, during the preparation of a plan or programme and before its adoption or submission to the legislative procedure[4]. The authorities and the public affected or likely to be affected by or having an interest in the decision-making process have the opportunity to express their opinion on the environmental effects of a draft plan or programme.

The **"polluter pays" principle**, which is mentioned in Article174, paragraph 2, of the EC Treaty, means that the cost incurred in combating pollution and nuisances in the first instance falls to the polluter, i.e. the polluting industry. Given, however, that the polluting industry can pass the

---

[1] Decision 466/2002, OJ L 75, 16.03.2002 and Decision 786/2004, OJ L 138, 30.04.2004.
[2] Directive 85/337, OJ L 175, 05.07.1985 and Directive 2003/35, OJ L 156, 25.06.2003.
[3] Directive 2003/35, OJ L 156, 25.06.2003.
[4] Directive 2001/42, OJ L 197, 21.07.2001.

cost of the prevention or elimination of pollution on to the consumer, the principle amounts to saying that **polluting production should bear**: **the expenditure** corresponding to the measures necessary to combat pollution (investment in apparatus and equipment for combating pollution, implementation of new processes, operating expenditure for anti-pollution plant, etc.); **and the charges** whose purpose is to encourage the polluter himself to take, as cheaply as possible, the measures necessary to reduce the pollution caused by him (incentive function) or to make him bear his share of the costs of collective purification measures (redistribution function).

Based on the "polluter pays" principle, an important directive establishes a framework of **environmental liability** with regard to the prevention and remedying of environmental damage, including transboundary damage, but excluding damage caused by *force majeure* or expressly authorised activities[1]. It aims at preventing environmental damage to water resources, soil, fauna, flora and natural habitats and at making the polluters pay whenever damage cannot be avoided. Member States are required to ensure that all environmental damage is restored, which entails assessing the gravity and extent of the damage and determining the most appropriate restoration measures to be taken. Member States are also required to promote the development of financial security products and encourage operators to take out financial security cover.

A Council Framework Decision aims at the **protection of the environment through criminal law**[2]. It requires each Member State to take all necessary measures to ensure that any environmental damage is punishable by effective, proportionate and dissuasive penalties including, in certain cases, imprisonment or extradition. These criminal penalties may also be accompanied by other measures, in particular disqualifying a person who has damaged the environment from engaging in an activity requiring official authorisation or from founding, managing or directing a company or foundation where there is a risk that the same kind of criminal activity may be pursued.

Another means for the prevention of pollutions is the "**ecolabel**", which guides the consumers towards "clean" products [see section 11.1.] and incites the industrialists to produce them, thus contributing to the efficient use of resources planned and to a high level of environmental protection[3]. The scheme functions on a voluntary basis and may be applied to a product belonging to product groups for which ecological criteria have been set by the Commission in accordance with the regulation.

---

[1]   Directive 2004/35, OJ L 143, 30.04.2004.

[2]   Decision 2003/80/JHA, OJ L 29, 05.02.2003.

[3]   Regulation 1980/2000, OJ L 237, 21.09.2000.

16.2.2. Notification, information and monitoring

The **European Environment Agency**, which is established near Copenhagen, provides the Commission and the national authorities with the technical, scientific and economic information necessary for the framing and implementation of measures and legislation relating to the environment[1]. Being a Community body open to third countries because of the multinational character of problems and work concerning the environment, the Agency acts as a European network for monitoring and obtaining information on the environment.

In any event, the Commission receives information on the legislative or administrative intentions of the Member States. It verifies the transposition by the Member States of Community legislation into national law and initiates proceedings against States which either fail to implement Community provisions on the environment in full or correctly or do not give notification of domestic measures on the environment. The Commission has an important ally in the matter, namely **the citizens in the Member States**, who are concerned at environmental damage and make a growing number of complaints to it each year [see section 9.3.]. When it receives a complaint from an individual citizen or association, the Commission carries out an inquiry to verify the facts, and if it considers that Community law has been infringed it initiates the procedure provided for in Article 226 of the EC Treaty [see section 4.1.2.]. A Directive, implementing the UN Aarhus Convention, guarantees freedom of access to and dissemination of information on the environment held by public authorities and sets the basic conditions under which information on the environment should be made available to the public[2]. The latter, through pressure that it can exercise on national authorities can contribute a great deal to improving the respect of Community legislation.

16.2.3. Environment and common policies

Article 6 of the EC Treaty, stipulates that environmental protection requirements must be integrated into the **definition and implementation of other Community policies**. This is meant to ensure environmental protection in all its forms by means of prior analysis of the potential problems in this sector and of the adoption of measures which integrate environmental requirements into the planning and performance of economic and social activities. In fact, many environmental issues such as climate change, acidification and waste management can only be tackled by an interplay between the main economic public and private actors, not only by legislative means, but also by an extended and integrated mix of other instruments, such as standards, certification systems, voluntary schemes or economic instru-

---

[1]   Regulation 1210/90, OJ L 120, 11.05.1990 and Regulation 933/1999, OJ L 117, 05.05.1999.
[2]   Directive 2003/4, OJ L 41, 14.02.2003.

ments. Therefore, the sustainable protection of the environment depends to a large extent on the common policies pursued in the fields of industry, energy, transport, agriculture and tourism, which are in turn dependent on the capacity of the environment to sustain them.

In a communication, drawn up in response to a request by the Cologne European Council in June 1999, the Commission set out a long-term Community strategy for the progressive **integration of environmental issues with economic policy**[1]. The essential elements of this strategy are as follows: a transparent approach to environmental integration, based on efficient target setting derived from a comprehensive analysis of the available scientific and technical data; consistency of the economic policy with the strategy for sustainable development; integration of the examination of the environmental impact of economic activity and regulation into the process of multilateral surveillance of structural reform and into the economic reform process; incorporation of the objectives of environmental integration into the broad economic policy guidelines (BEPGs) [see section 7.3.1.]; contribution of taxation policies to environmental integration; use of an appropriate mix of market-based instruments and regulations, including the removal of subsidies which are harmful to the environment.

16.3. Reduction of pollution and nuisances

The efforts of the Community environment policy to combat pollution and nuisances are more specifically directed towards: the fixing of quality objectives for European waters, the control of discharges into the aquatic environment of the European Union, efforts to combat sea and air pollution, the prevention of industrial accidents and efforts to combat noise pollution. These various groups of activity are examined in succession below.

16.3.1. Quality objectives for European waters

Water is an element indispensable not only to human life, but also to many of man's activities, from fishing to industry, by way of agriculture. **Water plays an essential role in the natural ecological balance** by procuring a substantial proportion of the oxygen necessary for life. In addition, seas, lakes and rivers are of great value for recreational activities and leisure, which are indispensable for town-dwellers. The Commission considers that appropriate water pricing has a key role to play in the development of sustainable water policies given that the sustainability of water resources is at stake in many river basins in Europe, from both a quantitative and a qualitative point of view[2].

---

[1] COM (2000) 576, 20 September 2000.
[2] COM (2000) 477, 26 July 2000.

The physical interdependence of the various surroundings that make up the aquatic ecosystem, such as surface fresh water, groundwater and seawater, **necessitates the coherent management of these resources**. The fact that watercourses often cross several countries and that lakeshores also extend across the territories of several countries dictates the common management of these resources. Comparable, and sometimes common, management of water is indispensable, *inter alia*, to prevent distortions of competition between major water-using undertakings. Therefore, Directive 2000/60 establishing a framework for Community action in the field of water policy lays down a basis for coordinating the Member States' policies and measures to protect inland surface waters, transitional waters, coastal waters and groundwater[1]. The **principal objectives of this policy** are to:

- prevent further deterioration and protect and enhance the state of aquatic ecosystems;
- promote sustainable use of water based on the long-term protection of available water resources;
- ensure the progressive reduction of pollution of groundwater and prevent further pollution thereof;
- provide a sufficient supply of good quality surface water and groundwater as needed for sustainable, balanced and equitable water use; and
- protect territorial and marine waters.

To achieve these objectives, the EU States lay down quality objectives or quality standards so as to manage water rationally and limit water pollution. Supplementing Directive 2000/60 on water policy, a decision establishes a list of 33 substances or groups of substances, some of which are identified as "priority hazardous substances", discharges of which must be halted, and others as "priority substances under review"[2]. Quality objectives, which vary according to the intended use of the water (drinking water, bathing water or water suitable for fish-breeding), lay down the **pollution or nuisance levels not to be exceeded** in a given surrounding or part thereof. European directives fix certain mandatory values, which must not be exceeded, and some guide values, which Member States endeavour to comply with.

16.3.2. Control of discharges into the aquatic environment

To attain and maintain the water-quality objectives described above, strict methods must be used to **reduce pollution caused by certain dangerous substances** discharged into the European aquatic environment, i.e. inland surface water, groundwater, internal coastal waters and territorial sea waters. Some toxic substances discharged into the water are, of course, chemically or biologically diluted and decomposed until their toxicity disappears, but others are persistent, i.e. they retain their chemical composi-

---

[1] Directive 2000/60, OJ L 327, 22.12.2000.
[2] Decision 2455/2001, OJ L 331, 15.12.2001.

tion, and therefore their danger to the environment and to man, for a lengthy period, which can, in some cases, be several years.

For this reason a Community Directive contains provisions on the collection, processing and discharge of **urban waste water** and biodegradable water from some industrial sectors, and on the disposal of sludges[1]. In particular, the Directive stipulates that as a general rule, waste water which enters into collection systems must, before disposal, be subjected to secondary treatment in accordance with a timetable adjusted to the size of the population covered and the type and situation of the collection water. Another Directive concerns the protection of waters against pollution caused by nitrates from agricultural sources[2].

A Directive on pollution caused by certain dangerous substances discharged into the aquatic environment of the Community is directed towards curbing the process of the deterioration of that environment by **prohibiting or restricting the discharge of toxic substances**[3]. The latter are divided into two lists: a "black list" grouping particularly toxic, persistent and bioaccumulable substances, and a "grey list" which mainly concerns substances whose harmful effects are limited to one locality and depend on the properties of the receiving waters. The "black list" is constantly amended in the light of the development of scientific and technical knowledge of the toxicity of the various substances[4]. Whether substances from the first list or the second list are involved, the Directive provides for authorisations granted for all discharges into Community waters, issued by the competent authority of the Member State concerned for a limited period.

16.3.3. Effort to combat marine pollution

Of all forms of pollution, sea pollution is one of the most dangerous because of its consequences for fundamental biological and ecological balances, the degree of degradation already reached, the diversity of sources of pollution and the difficulty of monitoring compliance with measures adopted. Apart from the accidental spillage of hydrocarbons in the sea, the **main sources of sea pollution are land-based ones**, i.e. the discharge of effluent from land and discharges of waste at sea. Therefore, the measures taken to control discharges into the aquatic environment, examined above, combat marine pollution.

The danger of serious pollution from **massive discharges of hydrocarbons** for the coasts of the EC States and for the seas surrounding them became a matter of common concern, in 1978, after the shipwreck of the giant oil tanker "Amoco-Cadiz" and the serious pollution of the coasts of

---

[1] Directive 91/271, OJ L 135, 30.05.1991 and Directive 98/15, OJ L 67, 07.03.1998.
[2] Directive 91/676, OJ L 375, 31.12.1991.
[3] Directive 76/464, OJ L 129, 18.05.1976 and Directive 91/692, OJ L 377, 31.12.1991.
[4] Directive 86/280, OJ L 181, 04.07.1986 and Directive 91/692, OJ L 377, 31.12.1991.

Brittany that ensued. In June 1978 the Council set up an action programme of the European Communities on the control and reduction of pollution caused by hydrocarbons discharged at sea[1]. In order to implement this action programme the Commission set up under its aegis an Advisory Committee on the Control and Reduction of Pollution Caused by Hydrocarbons Discharged at Sea[2]. The Council established a Community information system (a computerised network of data) for the control and reduction of pollution caused by the spillage of hydrocarbons and other harmful substances at sea[3].

It should be noted that the Community effort to combat marine pollution is based on voluntary measures and cooperation between the Member States. Thus, a **Community framework for cooperation** in the field of accidental marine pollution from harmful substances, whatever their origin, aims at the prevention of the risks and at efficient mutual assistance between Member States in this field, including compensation for damage in accordance with the polluter-pays principle[4] [see also section 20.3.4.].

16.3.4. Effort to combat air pollution

Industrial and household activities depend much on the **burning of fossil fuels**. Such burning causes the emission into the air of sulphur dioxide (SO_2), due to the presence of certain quantities of sulphur in the fuel and of very fine particles of partly burned carbon and hydrocarbons which are highly pollutant for the air and highly toxic for human health. Since several of the most industrialised regions of the European Union are situated in frontier areas, **sulphur dioxide and suspended particulate matter** are carried from one European region to another according to wind direction. The European States therefore have to act in unison to prevent air pollution and at the same time to prevent the effects on the functioning of the common market resulting from barriers to trade in fuels and on the conditions of competition between industries using such fuels.

The framework Directive 96/62 defines the basic principles of a **common strategy on air quality objectives for ambient air**[5]. These are: the establishment of air quality objectives based on limit values and alert thresholds for the principal harmful substances; the assessment of air quality in the Member States on the basis of common methods and criteria; the maintenance and improvement of air quality; and the measures to be taken where there is a risk of the limit values being exceeded. The most polluting substances that the EU endeavours to reduce are: ozone in ambient air (tropospheric ozone), sulphur dioxide, carbon dioxide, carbon monoxide, lead and its compounds.

---

[1] Resolution, OJ C 162, 08.07.1978, p. 1-4.
[2] Decision 80/686, OJ L 188, 22.07.1980 and Decision 87/144, OJ L 57, 27.02.1987.
[3] Decision 86/85, OJ L 77, 22.03.1986 and Decision 88/346, OJ L 158, 25.06.1988.
[4] Decision 2850/2000, OJ L 332, 28.12.2000 and decision 787/2004, OJ L 138, 30.04.2004.
[5] Directive 96/62, OJ L 296, 21.11.1996.

In order to attain and maintain air quality standards, a whole gamut of measures to limit the **emission of sulphur dioxide and other pollutants** is, of course, required. Therefore, a Directive set limit values not to be exceeded and guide values to be used as reference points for air quality with regard to sulphur dioxide and suspended particulates[1]. Community Directives limit the sulphur content of certain liquid fuels[2], the emissions of sulphur and other pollutants from industrial plants[3], from large combustion plants[4], from municipal waste incineration plants[5] and from internal combustion engines installed in non-road mobile machinery[6].

A major source of air pollution addressed by the Community is pollution by emissions from motor vehicles. **Carbon monoxide** resulting from the incomplete combustion of organic substances used in fuel was tackled first owing to its adverse consequences for human health and the environment. A 1970 Directive concerning the harmonisation of legislation on measures against air pollution by motor vehicle emissions obliged Member States to introduce three types of test to control gas emissions from positive-ignition engines of motor vehicles[7]. The technical controls of vehicles laid down by that Directive led to a significant reduction in emissions of carbon monoxide and unburned hydrocarbons by each vehicle. However, that effect was to a large extent neutralised by the increase in the number of vehicles in circulation in the Community States. For that reason the 1970 Directive was adapted to technical progress on several occasions in order to reduce the permissible levels of carbon monoxide emissions.

Another first-category air pollutant is **lead** and its compounds. A large proportion of the total quantity of this element in the air comes from emissions from petrol-engine vehicles. A 1982 Directive fixed a limit value for lead in the air[8]. Compliance with that limit required very costly measures for the Member States motor-vehicle industry. In order to prevent barriers to trade and the upheaval of conditions of competition, it was necessary to proceed in stages with the approximation of the laws of the Member States concerning the lead content of petrol, allowing the European motor vehicle industry and the petrol production and distribution industry time to adapt to the new conditions. That was done in a 1985 Directive and **lead-free petrol** won little by little and without problems the markets of the Member States. New Directives, repealing the former ones, concern the quality of petrol and diesel fuels[9] and limit values for sulphur dioxide, nitrogen dioxide and oxides of nitrogen, particulate matter and lead in ambient air[10].

---

[1] Directive 1999/30, OJ L 163, 29.06.1999.
[2] Directive 93/12, OJ L 74, 27.03.1993 and Directive 1999/32, OJ L 121, 11.05.1999.
[3] Directive 84/360, OJ L 188, 16.07.1984 and Directive 91/692, OJ L 377, 31.12.1991.
[4] Directive OJ L OJ C 2001/80, OJ L 309, 27.11.2001.
[5] Directive 89/369, OJ L 163, 14.06.1989, and OJ L 1, 03.01.1994.
[6] Directive 97/68, OJ L 59, 27.02.1998 and Directive 2004/26, OJ L 146, 30.04.2004.
[7] Directive 70/220, OJ L 76, 06.04.1970 and Directive 2001/100, OJ L 16, 18.01.2002.
[8] Directive 82/884, OJ L 378, 31.12.1982.
[9] Directive 98/70, OJ L 350, 28.12.1998 and Directive 2003/17, OJ L 76, 22.03.2003.
[10] Directive 1999/30, OJ L 163, 29.06.1999.

Whereas it is a pollutant in the lower atmosphere (troposphere), with adverse effects on vegetation, ecosystems and the environment as a whole, **ozone** is a natural element in the upper atmosphere (stratosphere), produced by photochemical reaction. The **stratospheric ozone layer** is vital to mankind, as it filters a large proportion of the sun's ultraviolet rays. A reduction in that layer could lead to a large increase in the number of skin cancers or considerable damage to agriculture on the planet. Emissions of **carbon dioxide** (CO_2) and of chemicals such as chlorofluorocarbons (CFCs) and halons contribute to the "**greenhouse effect**" and hence to global warming. Effective combating of this phenomenon requires concerted action at international level. Therefore, the European Union is signatory of the Framework **Convention on Climate Change of the United Nations**, the objective of which is to stabilise greenhouse gas concentrations in the air at a level avoiding dangerous climate change[1]. Particular reference should be made to the Protocol on Substances that Deplete the Ozone Layer and therefore on the control of greenhouse gas emissions, signed at Montreal in 1987 and amended several times[2]. An EC regulation is intended to implement the commitment agreed by the parties to the Montreal Protocol, and provides for measures are designed to help to speed up the process of regeneration of the ozone layer[3].

The Conference of the Parties to the UN Framework Convention on Climate Change, held in Marrakech (Morocco) from 7 to 9 November 2001, paved the way for **ratification of the Kyoto protocol**, thus imposing an obligation on 38 industrialised countries (excluding the USA, which rejected their previous engagement) to cut their total greenhouse gas emissions by 5.2% and 8% (compared with 1990 levels) between 2008 and 2012[4]. The EU played a leading role, particularly in finding a compromise solution among industrialised countries for "flexibility mechanisms", such as the exchange of emission allowances with less polluting countries. In the framework of Directive 96/62, a 2002 directive (replacing the 1992 one) aims to bring about a significant improvement in management of the ozone problem by establishing long-term objectives, target values for 2010, an alert threshold and an information threshold for **concentrations of ozone in ambient air** in the Community, designed to avoid, prevent or reduce harmful effects on human health and the environment as a whole[5]. A directive on national emission ceilings for certain atmospheric pollutants and relating to ozone in ambient air set the limit values to be met by each Member State by 2010 and provided for measures to reduce pollution due to acidification and ozone[6]. A parallel directive in the energy sector fixed

[1]   Vienna Convention and Montreal Protocol, OJ L 297, 31.10.1988.
[2]   Amendment to the Montreal Protocol and Decisions 94/68 and 94/69, OJ L 33, 07.02.1994 and Decision 2002/215, OJ L 72, 14.03.2002.
[3]   Regulation 2037/2000, OJ L 244, 29.09.2000 and Decision 2003/160, OJ L 65, 08.03.2003.
[4]   Decision 2002/358, OJ L 130, 15.05.2002.
[5]   Directive 2002/3, OJ L 67, 09.03.2002.
[6]   Directive 2001/81, OJ L 309, 27.11.2001.

the target for renewable and environment-friendly energy sources to cover 12% of gross energy consumption by 2010[1] [see section 19.3.5.]. These targets are assisted by Community research on "sustainable development, global change and ecosystems" [see section 18.4.1.].

The Community strategy is based upon regulatory, sectoral and voluntary measures, such as the Directive to limit carbon dioxide emissions by **improving energy efficiency**[2] [see section 19.3.1.] and a mechanism for monitoring CO_2 emissions and other greenhouse gas emissions, which provides for the Member States to compile inventories of CO_2 emissions and national abatement programmes evaluated by the Commission[3]. The Community approach is based on **emissions trading**, one of the flexible mechanisms recommended in the protocol to attain the reduction target. Under this system, companies are allocated greenhouse gas emission allowances, in line with their government's environmental objectives, and can then trade them with each other to achieve the best cost-effectiveness[4]. The "Clean air for Europe" (CAFE) programme aims to establish a coherent, long-term thematic strategy and integrated policy to combat air pollution through cost-effective measures[5].

16.3.5. Prevention of industrial and chemical hazards

National and Community rules against pollution cannot in themselves prevent serious industrial accidents which are catastrophic for the environment, like those in Seveso in Italy in 1981 and Bhopal in India in 1984. For that reason, rules should be taken concerning controls on land-use planning when new installations are authorized and when urban development takes place around existing installations. Therefore, Directive 96/82 aims at the **prevention of major accidents which involve dangerous substances** and the limitation of their consequences for man and the environment, with a view to ensuring high levels of protection throughout the Community in a consistent and effective manner[6]. It provides for: definition, by each establishment covered, of a major-accident prevention policy; submission, by each establishment where dangerous substances are present in large quantities, of safety reports demonstrating that the major accident hazards have been identified, that the design, construction, operation and maintenance of the installation are sufficiently safe and that the emergency plans have been drawn up; taking account, in land-use policies, of the objectives of preventing major accidents, limiting the consequences and improving the procedures for consulting and informing the public.

---

[1] Directive 2001/77, OJ L 283, 27.10.2001.
[2] Directive 93/76, OJ L 237, 22.09.1993.
[3] Decision 280/2004, OJ L 49, 19.02.2004.
[4] COM (2000) 87, 8 March 2000.
[5] COM (2001) 245 and Council conclusions adopted on 29 October 2001.
[6] Directive 96/82, OJ L 10, 14.01.1997 and Directive 2003/105, OJ L 345, 31.12.2003.

Independently of accident hazards control, the framework Directive 96/61 aims at an **integrated pollution prevention and control (IPPC)**[1]. Its across-the-board approach involves the various media (air, water, soil) by applying the principle of the best environmental option, in particular in order to avoid transferring pollution from one medium to another. It provides that the operators of certain polluting plants submit requests for operating permits to the competent authority in the Member States, with the issuing of a permit being conditional on compliance with basic obligations such as not to exceed emission limit values set by the Directive. The Community has established a scheme for greenhouse gas **emission allowance trading** within its territory ("Community scheme")[2]. The scheme aims both to achieve a pre-determined emission reduction and to decrease the resulting costs. It is based on granting authorised emissions allowances, purchasing emissions permits from companies which have not used up their full allowance and imposing fines in the event of misuse of this scheme.

A European **pollutant emission register (EPER)**, introduced in 2003, contains data concerning emissions of 50 pollutants from some 20 000 industrial facilities across the EU. Both the public and industry may use EPER data to compare the environmental performance of individual facilities or industrial sectors in different countries and to monitor the progress made in meeting environment targets set in national and international agreements and protocols[3].

Major pollution of water, air and soil is caused by **chemical products discharged in the form of by-products or industrial waste**. The problems here are identifying the dangerous substances and monitoring their utilisation and disposal. This is why, under the Directive on the approximation of the laws relating to the classification, packaging and **labelling of dangerous substances** each Member State undertook to act as a representative of its European Community partners when authorising the introduction of a new chemical product into the whole Community market[4]. For that purpose, the producer or importer has to provide the State into whose market the product is first introduced with a **"base set"**. That dossier is composed of a whole range of information on the physico-chemical properties of the new product concerned, its possible effects on health and the environment and a general evaluation of the dangers. That information is forwarded to the Commission, which sends it to each Member State and to the Scientific Advisory Committee, which examines the toxicity and ecotoxicity of chemical compounds[5]. Businesses are authorised to place on

---

[1] Directive 96/61, OJ L 257, 10.10.1996 and Directive 2003/35, OJ L 156, 25.06.2003.
[2] Directive 2003/87, OJ L275, 25.10.2003.
[3] Decision 2000/479, OJ L 192, 28.07.2000.
[4] Directive 67/548, OJ L 196, 16.08.1967 and Directive 1999/33, OJ L 199, 30.07.1999.
[5] Decision 97/579, OJ L 237, 28.08.1997.

the market only "EC" labelled and, accordingly controlled, dangerous sub-stances[1] [see section 6.2.3.].

16.4. Management of environmental resources

The Community environment programme is not confined to the effort to combat pollution and nuisances, but also seeks to make an active contribution to improving the environment and the quality of life through the rational management of space, the environment and natural resources. The measures provided for in that section of the Community environment programme can be grouped under the headings of the **protection of flora and fauna** in Europe and the **management of waste** in the Community. The financial instrument LIFE can finance projects in these areas, such as the conservation of biotopes of particular importance for the Community, projects for the conservation of endangered species and the location and restoration of areas contaminated by waste and/or dangerous substances[2]. LIFE III (2000-04) consists of "LIFE-Nature", "LIFE-Environment" and "LIFE-Third countries" and allows participation by the applicant countries [see section 16.2.1.].

16.4.1. Protection of flora and fauna

Species of wild flowers and the animal populations form **part of European heritage**. Apart from the fact that they represent non-renewable genetic assets, they participate in many natural functions which ensure overall ecological balances, such as the regulation of the development of undesirable organisms, the protection of the soil against erosion and the regulation of aquatic ecosystems. The genetic assets represented by all present-day animal and plant species constitute a resource of ecological, scientific and economic interest of inestimable value for the future of mankind. However, industrialisation, urbanisation and pollution are threatening a growing number of wild species and undermining the natural balances resulting from several million years of evolution.

A Community Directive aims to **protect natural and semi-natural habitats** and wild fauna and flora[3]. It provides for the establishment of a European ecological network of special conservation areas, "Natura 2000", made up of sites which are home to types of natural habitats of species of interest to the Community. The Member States must take appropriate steps to avoid their deterioration or any other disturbances affecting the species.

---

[1] Directive 96/56, OJ L 236, 18.09.1996.
[2] Regulation 1973/92, OJ L 206, 22.07.1992, Regulation 1655/2000, OJ L 192, 28.07.2000 and Regulation 788/2004, OJ L 138, 30.04.2004.
[3] Decision 92/43, OJ L 206, 22.07.1992 and Decision 97/62, OJ L 305, 08.11.1997.

A significant means of protecting wildlife threatened with extinction is to restrict and **control rigorously international trade in plants and animals** belonging to such species and products made from them. Therefore, the Community implements the Convention on International Trade in Endangered Species of Wild Fauna and Flora (CITES), which aims at protecting 2.000 species through the stringent control of international trade. However, the relevant Community Regulation covers a wider field than the Convention, dividing the species into four classes to be given protection, ranging from statistical monitoring of trade to a total trading ban, depending on the degree of the threat of extinction[1]. Special attention is given to re-exportation, control of commercial activities involving such specimens and definition of the infringements, which Member States are required to penalise.

16.4.2. Management of waste

As the penalty paid for economic development and urbanisation, the accumulation of **waste destroys the environment** and is at the same time proof of regrettable profligacy. Waste of all kinds, i.e. household waste, industrial waste, sewage sludge from waste water, agricultural waste and waste from the extractive industries, accounts for some 3 billion tons each year in the EU.

Included amongst "waste" are **toxic substances** and substances which are hazardous for man and the environment, as they can pollute the water table by percolation, contaminate micro-organisms and appear in the food chain through complex and little-known means. But "waste" also includes scrap metal, paper, plastics and waste oils, which can be recycled, which is important in a Europe becoming increasingly poor in raw materials.

In view of the close interdependence of waste management and many industrial and commercial activities, the lack of a Community design for waste management is likely to affect not only environmental protection, but also the completion of the internal market by creating distortions of competition and unjustified movements of investment, or even the partitioning of the market. The objectives of a **Community strategy on waste management** are: (a) prevention, by encouraging the use of products which create less waste; (b) increasing its value, through the optimisation of collection and sorting systems; (c) the laying down of stringent standards for final disposal, as contained in the Council Directives on new municipal waste-incineration plants[2] and on existing municipal waste-incineration plants[3]; and (d) rules governing the carriage of dangerous substances, so as to ensure safe and economic carriage and the restoration of contaminated areas, taking into account the civil liability of the polluter.

---

[1]   Regulation 338/97, OJ L 61, 03.03.1997 and Regulation 1476/1999, OJ L 171, 07.07.1999.

[2]   Directive 89/369, OJ L 163, 14.06.1989 and OJ L 1, 03.01.1994.

[3]   Directive 89/429, OJ L 203, 15.07.1989 and OJ L 1, 03.01.1994.

The principle of producer responsibility is a key component in future Community legislation on waste management[1].

The "framework Directive" for Community waste policy obliges the Member States to take measures to ensure that waste is eliminated without endangering human health and without damaging the environment, and in particular without giving rise to risk to water, air or soil, fauna or flora, without causing discomfort through noise or smell and without affecting areas or landscapes[2]. It also aims to set up an integrated and appropriate network of waste disposal plants, to encourage disposal as close as possible to the waste production site, thus reducing the dangers inherent in waste transport, and to promote clean technologies and products which can be recycled and reused.

A directive aims at preventing or reducing as far as possible the adverse **effects of landfills** on the environment, particularly pollution of surface water, groundwater, soil and air, and on the global environment, including the greenhouse effect, and the resulting risks to human health during the whole lifecycle of the landfill[3]. An accompanying decision on the acceptance of waste at landfills lays down the procedures for characterising waste, for checking that it complies with the acceptance criteria and for on-site verification that it is identical to the waste described in the accompanying documents[4].

16.5. Appraisal and outlook

Thanks to the Treaty of Maastricht environment protection has graduated to the status of a common policy and falls into the **priority objectives of the Union**. Environmental constraints must be integrated into the definition and implementation of other common policies. The uniform application in all Member States of environmental standards is, in fact, indispensable not only for the preservation of Europe's environment, but also for the good functioning of the internal market and for economic and social cohesion.

It is very difficult to evaluate the specific results of the European measures in this area, first because the quality of the environment is a highly subjective notion and therefore difficult to define, and secondly because the policy to combat pollution is a **Sisyphean task**. The quality objectives that it lays down are incessantly thrust aside by economic development and urbanisation. It is true that the annual reports of the Commission to the Parliament and the Council on the implementation of the European Community's environment programme show that significant progress has been achieved on phasing out ozone-depleting substances, reducing

---

[1] COM (96) 399, 30 July 1996 and resolution, OJ C 76, 11.03.1997, p. 1-4.
[2] Directive 75/442, OJ L 194, 25.07.1975 and Directive 91/156, OJ L 78, 26.03.1991.
[3] Directive 1999/31, OJ L 182, 16.07.1999.
[4] Decision 2003/33, OJ L 11, 16.01.2003.

emissions of certain pollutants into the atmosphere and surface waters, improving water quality and reducing acidification. But, the state of the environment overall remains a cause for concern, particularly in respect to growing consumption of natural resources, chemical risks, soil degradation, global warming and biodiversity losses.

Moreover, serious problems and excessive delays in the enforcement and implementation of the environment directives exist in many Member States, which also have a bad record on producing the necessary reports and information in general. To make the Union a highly eco-efficient economy, the environmental dimension of the Lisbon Process [see section 13.3.] should be strengthened, so as to give equal attention to economic, social and environmental considerations in policy-making and decision-taking processes. In any case, a permanent vigilance is required of citizens, who can lodge complaints with the Commission whenever they observe that European standards are not being complied with by an undertaking or by public or private works in their country or a neighbouring country. Likewise, mechanisms are needed for handling complaints and carrying out environmental investigations outside the courts [see section 9.3.].

However, the European Union cannot work in isolation in this field. Even if it were to succeed in significantly reducing and preventing pollution in its territory, it would still be open to water and air pollution from the other countries of Europe and the other regions of the world. For that reason the Union must play a leading role in international negotiations and take more visible action in the framework of **international organisations** such as the Council of Europe and the United Nations. Thus, the accession to the Union of **Central and Eastern European countries**, must go hand-in-hand with increased consideration of environmental constraints, which have been tragically neglected in the past. The European Environment Agency, which is open to the other countries of Europe, plays an important part in this area.

The environmental interdependence of all the countries in the world is particularly marked with regard to the **greenhouse effect** and its climatic consequences for the globe. The Union is on target to meet the objectives set for 2008-2012 concerning greenhouse gas emissions, but their attainment requires significant efforts from the Member States. Therefore, the EU should promote the use and competitiveness of renewable energy sources, the reduction of greenhouse gas emissions from motor vehicles with the aid of fuels with low pollutant content and energy efficiency in buildings, equipment and industrial processes. It may encourage the best available technologies and research and development and provide, within the framework of the guidelines on State aid, flexibility at national level to ensure the effectiveness of policies and measures to tackle climate change. Common action is needed to progressively reduce or remove fossil fuel and other subsidies, tax schemes and regulations which militate against efficient use of energy. Conversely, economic measures, such as tax incentives or reduced VAT rates, are needed to encourage good practice by consumers and promote clean and renewable energy sources.

However, the European Union cannot curb the greenhouse phenomenon alone. It should summon other industrialised countries and, particularly, the United States, as the biggest emitter of greenhouse gases, to comply with standards agreed in international fora. In November 2001 at Marrakech, the EU - taking along Russia, Australia, Canada and Japan - saved the Kyoto protocol from sinking under the pressure of the United States abandonment of its responsibilities. This example shows that, when the EU wants, it can take the lead effectively in environment-friendly actions. It should take the initiative to call for international **environmental governance**, based on coherent international, regional, sub-regional and national institutional environmental architecture topped by a World Environment Organisation, capable of responding to current challenges.

Bibliography on environment policy

- BEYER Peter (et al.). "The draft constitution for Europe and the environment: the impact of institutional changes, the reform of the instruments and the principle of subsidiarity", *European Environmental Law Review*, v. 13, n. 7, July 2004, p. 218-224.
- BROWNE John. "Beyond Kyoto", *Foreign Affairs*, v. 83, n. 4, July/August 2004, p. 20-32.
- BUREAU Dominique, MOUGEOT Michel. *Politiques environnementales et compétitivité*. Paris: Documentation française, 2004.
- COMPTE Françoise, KRÄMER Ludwig (eds.). *Environmental crime in Europe: rules of sanctions*. Groningen: Europa Law, 2004.
- CORFEE MORLOT Jan, AGRAWALA Shardul (eds.). *The benefits of climate change policies: analytical and framework issues*. Paris: OECD, 2004.
- ECKSTEIN Anne. *Protection de l'environnement: bilan de la législation de l'Union européenne au 1er janvier 2004*. Bruxelles: Europe Information Service, 2004.
- JORDAN Andrew, LIEFFERINK Duncan. *Environmental policy in Europe: the europeanization of national environmental policy*. London: Routledge, 2004.
- KAVALOV Boyan, PETEVES Stathis. *Impacts of the increasing automotive diesel consumption in the EU*. Luxembourg: EUR-OP*, 2004.
- ONIDA Marco (ed.). *Europe and the environment: legal essays in honour of Ludwig Krämer*. Groningen: Europa Law, 2004.
- SHARMA Sanjay, STARIK Mark (eds.). *Stakeholders, the environment and society*. Cheltenham; Northampton, MA: Edward Elgar, 2004.

DISCUSSION TOPICS

1. Compare the efficiency of various national environment protection policies with that of a common European policy.

2. How does the common environment protection policy interact with other common policies?

3. Discuss the "polluter pays" and "prevention" principles of the common environment policy.

4. Consider the significance of the efforts of the EU to restrain fresh water and marine pollution.

5. Assess the effectiveness of the measures taken by the EU States at curbing atmospheric pollution and global warming.

Part V. Sectoral Policies

In **Part V we consider the sectoral policies of the Union**, that is to say, the policies concerning big sectors of the economies of the Member States, industry, research, energy, transports and agriculture. We will see that in the last three sectors the Treaties required explicitly the development of common policies, whereas for industry they asked for no policy as such, but the whole multinational integration process was geared towards the restructuring and competitiveness of European industry. Common research and energy policies were partially defined in the sectoral Treaties, notably that on Euratom. The various legal foundations of the five main sectoral policies certainly account for their dissimilar development; but so do as well the different requirements that the Member States set for those policies during the stages of the customs union, the common market and more recently the economic and monetary union.

Whilst, the EEC Treaty made no call for a common or Community **industrial policy**, it chiefly regulated the common market in industrial products (free trade, rules of competition, approximation of laws, tax provisions...). It assumed that the abolition of protectionist measures and the opening-up of the markets, thanks to the common market would provide sufficient impetus for the restructuring of sectors and undertakings. We saw that this assumption was partly invalidated because of national protectionism, which persisted until the early 1990s by means of technical barriers to trade [see section 6.1.]. Now that the single market has become a reality, small and medium-sized enterprises (SMEs) must adjust to the new conditions of heightened competition. The new **enterprise policy** of the Community shores up their efforts. The common enterprise policy, however, aims to help SMEs in both the industrial and service sectors adjust to the new conditions of the large internal market. This is also the goal of common sub-sectoral policies, notably in declining or fast growing industrial sectors, which need to be freed from old protectionist practices so as to better face the new conditions of competition in Europe and the world.

A common **research policy** is also a vital rung on the ladder of the European Union's industrial development. It is essential for the definition of industrial strategy, for technical progress in high-technology sectors, for the mastery of the Community's energy problems and, finally, for the adaptation of businesses to the post-industrial information society.

Research is a key feature of the common **energy policy**, the aim of which is to reduce Europe's dependence on imported energy and raise the competitiveness of European industry through the development of cheap, safe and clean energies. Due to its foundation on the ECSC and Euratom sectoral Treaties [see section 2.1.], the common policy is well advanced in the sectors of coal and nuclear energy and very little in the oil and gas sectors.

Unlike most other Community policies, **transport policy** was specifically mentioned in the EEC Treaty, even with the specification that it should be a common policy. We will note that diverging national interests have impeded progress of the transport policy during the first thirty years of the Community's existence; but the completion of the single market, which has resulted in strong growth in demand for transport services for both goods and persons, went in step with a large-scale liberalisation in the areas of road haulage, sea and air transport.

By contrast, the **common agricultural policy** (CAP) covered a great deal of ground during the first years of the Community. However, of all the policies examined in this book, the CAP has been the most controversial and the most versatile, since it is reformed every five years or so to respond both to internal and external requirements. The CAP presents, indeed, a good example of the constant adaptation of a common policy to new societal needs and to the changing European and international competition and trade requirements.

The **fisheries policy**, initially a part of the common agricultural policy, gives a good illustration of how a common policy can develop. It starts out with a few isolated measures addressing a particular situation or shared problems in a sector and, little by little there is a realisation that if the common achievements are to be safeguarded, other measures are required leading to a full-grown common policy. Thanks to this policy and despite the growing depletion of fishing resources in the waters of the Union and worldwide, there is a single market for fisheries products.

Chapter 17

INDUSTRIAL AND ENTERPRISE POLICIES

Diagram of the chapter

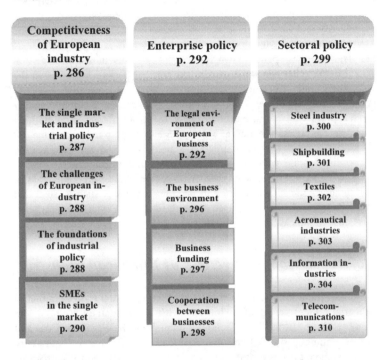

Competitiveness of European industry p. 286	Enterprise policy p. 292	Sectoral policy p. 299
The single market and industrial policy p. 287	The legal environment of European business p. 292	Steel industry p. 300
The challenges of European industry p. 288	The business environment p. 296	Shipbuilding p. 301
The foundations of industrial policy p. 288	Business funding p. 297	Textiles p. 302
SMEs in the single market p. 290	Cooperation between businesses p. 298	Aeronautical industries p. 303
		Information industries p. 304
		Telecommunications p. 310

The Treaty establishing the European Economic Community organised the achievement of customs union in great detail with regard to the industrial products of the Member States, but **made no call for an industrial policy as such**. In fact the founding fathers of the EEC had hoped that the liberalisation of trade and increased competition inside the common market could, on their own, bring about the structural changes that Community industry needed. As was explained in the chapter on the common market, this hope was tardily realised because of the persistence of technical obstacles to trade and, therefore, the tardy completion of the single market [see section 6.1.].

It took several years' effort, especially by the Commission, for all Member States to agree that a common industrial policy was necessary, firstly for the completion of the common market in industrial products and, secondly, to **cope with common structural and sectoral problems**. The first major aspect of this policy, which is linked with harmonisation of legislations and standardisation, was dealt with in the chapter on the common market [see section 6.2.].

In the absence of a specific structural policy for the industrial sector, a large part of the present chapter is devoted to **enterprise policy**. In the run-up to the completion of the single market, in the early 1990s, the Community has, in fact, paid close attention to small and medium-sized enterprises (SMEs), which account for almost 99% of the industrial fabric of the Community and for 70% of total employment in the private sector of the Member States and which face problems of integration in the single market. The enterprise policy, however, covers not only industrial firms but also firms in other economic sectors, in particular craft, tourism and the distributive trade. Concerning the **tourism sector**, in particular, it should be noted that, despite the common interest in developing a common policy for the promotion of European tourism, the Council, has done nothing more, until now, than invite the Member States to help implement the co-operation approach between tourism stakeholders through the open method of coordination, i.e. without using Community legal instruments[1].

The last part of this chapter deals with sectoral industrial policy, that is, Community policy for industries in decline in Europe, such as steel and shipbuilding, and "infant" or fast growing industries, such as information and telecommunications technologies.

17.1. The competitiveness of European industry

Whilst the European Treaties did not make provision for a Community industrial policy, they **dealt primarily with the industrial sector** of the Member States. In fact, the Treaties establishing the European Coal and Steel Community (ECSC) and the European Atomic Energy Community (EAEC) constituted sectoral policies in the relevant industrial sectors, while the Treaty establishing the European Economic Community (EEC) chiefly regulated the common market in industrial products [see section 2.1.]. But the ECSC and EAEC (Euratom) Treaties were more precise than the EEC Treaty or even the EC Treaty. They included provisions both on the attainment of the common market and on the structural policy of the sectors to which they related, and they gave powers to the Community institutions to formulate such policies.

Certainly, the customs union enhanced the ability of European industry to compete both on its own market and globally. As from 1968, with the introduction of the **Common Customs Tariff** and by virtue of its uniform duties, the Community had available to it a valuable instrument for conducting an effective commercial policy and for pressing on towards the

---

[1]   COM (2001) 665 and Council resolution, OJ C 135, 06.06.2002.

liberalisation of international trade [see section 5.2.1.]. That instrument has been used successfully by the Commission, which has negotiated, on behalf of the Community, the reduction of the customs protection of the major commercial powers within the framework of the General Agreement on Tariffs and Trade (GATT) [see section 23.4.].

However, the easing of international protectionism did not suffice to redress the competitive situation of Community industry. To be able to measure up to the American and Japanese multinational companies, European industries had to combine the production factors of capital and labour so as to minimise their production unit cost. In other words, they had to find the **dimension most appropriate to the new conditions of competition** and improve their productivity by seeking new products and new production methods. Only the large European market could offer them those conditions of competitiveness.

17.1.1. The single market and industrial policy

The completion of the single European market, topped by the single currency, presents businesses with an opportunity to **benefit from economies of scale**, to cut their administrative and financial costs, to gain easier access to public procurement in other Member States and to cooperate more closely with each other across borders. The advantages from economies of scale for investments on the domestic market are not only relevant for mass production, but also for the development of specialised products. As important as the size of the home market is its quality. The single market itself represents an essential step for business to look, think and act strategically beyond national borders. Certainly, the tendency of multinational enterprises to acquire a dominant position in the single market under the guise of achieving a sufficient critical size must be monitored by the competition authorities, allowing however European companies to pursue business strategies, which may safeguard their competitiveness at world level [see section 15.4.2.].

Several objectives of the Community industrial policy were attained through the completion of the single market. Thus, since the beginning of the1990s, **European standardisation** provides manufacturers with technical specifications recognised as giving a presumption of conformity to the essential requirements of Community directives [see section 6.2.3.]. European standards are not only required for the purpose of removing technical barriers to trade; increasingly they are also becoming a key element for the promotion of industrial competitiveness by lowering costs for producers and enabling the emergence of new markets, particularly for developing new technologies. At the same time, greater standardisation of products places a premium on product innovation, manufacturing excellence, design and reliability rather than on the more traditional factors of competitiveness like proximity to markets, distribution systems and customer loyalty.

Very important for European industrial competitiveness is also **public procurement**, which is now opened up thanks to the legislation of the single market [see section 6.3.]. Its importance for industry is threefold. Firstly, the vast size of public procurement - 16% of GDP - means that access to the public markets is very important for all firms. Secondly, public procurement may enhance technological capability by increasing the marketable demand of high technology products. Thirdly, public procurement being concentrated on a relatively small group of industries, these industries need a competitive market for public procurement in order to develop the necessary products and skills to be successful internationally.

17.1.2. The challenges of European industry

Although European industry now benefits from the advantages of a single large market, it is faced with new challenges. **Globalisation of economies and markets**, which enables greater economies of scale to be reaped and better specialisation for distinctive market segments, entails the intensification of international competition. In the context of this globalisation, European businesses must be able to face international competition. Although it has not deteriorated, apparent labour productivity in Community manufacturing still lags a good way behind that of the US and Japanese industry. Economic operators and public authorities in Europe must therefore pay more attention to the factors influencing productivity: technological development, investment in R&D, the rate of capacity utilisation, the cost and skill of the labour force, management skills and the organisation of production.

Apart from globalisation of markets and competition, European industry must prepare to face the challenge of the **new industrial revolution**, the one resulting from the development of information and communications technologies. These reduce the traditional distinctions between electronics, information technology, telecommunications and the audiovisual sectors [see sections 17.3.5 and 17.3.6.]. This revolution has far-reaching effects on production structures and methods. It spells changes in the way companies are organised, in managerial responsibilities and relations with workers, particularly concerning the organisation of work. There is therefore a need for structural adjustment and the steady shifting of resources towards the most productive outlets. In general, business competitiveness depends increasingly on the **ability to innovate**, notably by the development of new products and services.

17.1.3. The foundations of industrial policy

With the entry into force, in November 1993, of the Treaty of Maastricht [see section 2.2.], industrial competitiveness became one of the stated objectives of European integration. Article 3 of the EC Treaty states, in fact, that the action of the Community includes, *inter alia*, the **strengthening of the competitiveness of Community industry**. The Title on Industry of the TEC announces that the Community and the Member States must ensure the existence of the conditions necessary for the competitiveness of the Community's industry. For this purpose, in accordance with a system of open and competitive markets, **their action aims at**: speeding up the adjustment of industry to structural changes; encouraging an environment favourable to initiative and to the development of undertakings throughout the Community, particularly small and medium-sized undertakings; encouraging an environment favourable to cooperation between undertakings; and fostering better exploitation of the industrial potential of innovation and research and technological development policies (Art. 157 TEC).

This article forms the legal basis for Community action in the fields of industry and business. It specifies however that it does not provide a basis for the introduction by the Community of any measures that could lead to a distortion of competition. The objectives set out above may be **pursued by the following means**: the mutual consultation of the Member States and, where necessary, the coordination of their action, in liaison with and upon initiative of the Commission; the coordination with other Community policies and activities; and specific measures in support of action taken in the Member States decided by the Council acting unanimously on a proposal from the Commission after consultation of the European Parliament and the Economic and Social Committee. The unanimity rule required for specific measures in the industrial sector denotes the reluctance of the Member States to weaken national policies in favour of a common industrial policy. Hence, most industrial policy is carried out not at EU level but under the competence of the Member States.

Yet, industrial competitiveness depends on policies such as competition, the internal market, research and development, education, trade and sustainable development. Therefore, the common industrial policy must ensure that other common policies contribute to the competitiveness of Europe's industry. It therefore covers a very wide field, while many of its instruments are the instruments of other policy fields[1]. The **common industrial strategy is based on three principles**: consistent recourse to all common policies with a bearing on industrial activity, in particular that of protection of the environment[2]; improved access of Community businesses to non-Community markets and to measures against unfair trading practices and in favour of international industrial cooperation[3] [see sections 23.2.2. and 23.4.]; and the positive adjustment to industrial changes through a consistent approach[4]. On these principles is based the **Community action programme to strengthen the competitiveness** of European

---

[1] COM (2002) 714, 11 December 2002.
[2] Resolution, OJ C 331, 16.12.1992, p. 5-7.
[3] Resolution, OJ C 178, 15.07.1992, p. 1-3.
[4] COM (92) 2000.

industry[1]. Its broad action lines are: promoting intangible investment, e.g. by exploiting the competitive advantages associated with better protection of the environment; developing industrial cooperation; ensuring fair competition; and modernising the role of the public authorities, thus relieving businesses of unnecessary bureaucratic burdens. They have also agreed on a common policy framework in the **business services sector**, as a factor for the competitiveness of European industry and for the creation of employment[2].

17.1.4. SMEs in the single market

As was seen above, Article 157 (TEC) states, among other things, that the Community and the Member States shall encourage "an environment favourable to initiative and to the development of undertakings throughout the Community, particularly small and medium-sized undertakings". This is the base of the common enterprise policy, a policy in favour of small businesses, known in Community jargon as **small and medium-sized enterprises (SMEs)**. But what are the SMEs?

Until the mid-1990s, different definitions of SMEs were used in Community policies (competition, Structural Funds, R&D, tendering for public procurement, etc.). This diversity could give rise to doubts among public authorities and even to confusion among the businessmen concerned. Therefore, the Commission adopted a recommendation concerning the **definition of micro, small and medium-sized enterprises** used in Community policies[3]. An enterprise is considered to be any entity engaged in an economic activity, irrespective of its legal form. The category of micro, small and medium-sized enterprises (SMEs) is made up of enterprises which employ fewer than 250 persons and which have an annual turnover not exceeding EUR 50 million, and/or an annual balance sheet total not exceeding EUR 43 million. Within the SME category, a small enterprise is defined as an enterprise which employs fewer than 50 persons and whose annual turnover and/or annual balance sheet total does not exceed EUR 10 million. A microenterprise is defined as an enterprise which employs fewer than 10 persons and whose annual turnover and/or annual balance sheet total does not exceed EUR 2 million. However, the Commission recommends to remove from the SMEs category non-autonomous enterprises, i.e. those which have holdings entailing a controlling position (partner enterprises) or those that are linked to other enterprises.

This definition serves as a reference for Community programmes, policy and legislation concerning SMEs and thus provides an overall framework, which can increase the coherence, effectiveness and visibility of all measures to assist these enterprises. It should be noted that with this

---

[1] Decision 96/413, OJ L 167, 06.07.1996.
[2] COM (1998) 534, 21 September 1998.
[3] Recommendation 2003/361, OJ L 124, 20.05.2003.

definition, the Union(fifteen) numbers some 17 million SMEs, providing over 75% of its employment, accounting for 50% of investment and representing 60% of its wealth.

In addition to quantitative and easily verifiable criteria, SMEs are often also identified by **qualitative criteria**, focusing chiefly on the ownership of their capital, their management and their methods of financing. A SME is often a family business, whose management and ownership are in the hands of the same person(s). Day-to-day running of a SME falls upon the company head, enabling flexibility and rapidity in the decision-making process and a personalised relationship with staff, suppliers and customers. Finally, a SME is heavily dependent on self-financing due to difficult access to the financial markets and it often suffers from limited availability of financial resources. These qualitative identification criteria merge with a small undertaking's main characteristics, characteristics which can occasionally prove a handicap, but which can also be to their advantage.

Of course, SMEs have **their weak points, which are notably**: (a) the difficulty to face the complicated administrative and legal environment created by the completion of the internal market and the globalisation of production; (b) lack in management training for many businessmen and/or lack of willingness to delegate part of the management to qualified associates; and (c) funding difficulties, despite the increase and the differentiation of sources of financing in the large market. It is clearly more difficult and relatively more costly for SMEs than for large firms to have access to world technological capital, to avail themselves of the most sophisticated management techniques and business services and to find their proper place in the global economy and even in the EU's single market.

Small and, above all, medium-sized businesses, must, first and foremost, **rely on their own efforts to achieve success** in the single market. In order to succeed they must make the effort to adapt to their new environment by abandoning some of their family-style management habits and/or their production and marketing methods and cooperate with each other in order to overcome some of the handicaps which are attributable to their size, in particular with regard to supply and the distribution of their products over a number of Member States. In so doing SMEs must, however, **be assisted** by their trade organisations, their governments and the European institutions. That is why a common enterprise policy is needed to provide a framework for and coordinate the efforts deployed by the Member States to assist their SMEs, without distorting competition by favouring certain undertakings or the production of certain goods within the meaning of Article 87 of the EC Treaty [see section 15.5.1.].

17.2. Enterprise policy

The **European Charter for Small Enterprises,** endorsed by the Feira European Council (19 and 20 June 2000), states that the situation of small business in the European Union can be improved by action to stimulate entrepreneurship, to evaluate existing measures, and when necessary, to make them small-business-friendly, and to ensure that policy-makers take due consideration of small business needs. In this Charter the Member States pledged themselves to: strengthen the spirit of innovation and entrepreneurship; achieve a regulatory, fiscal and administrative framework conducive to entrepreneurial activity; ensure access to markets on the basis of the least burdensome requirements that are consistent with overriding public policy objectives; facilitate access to the best research and technology; improve access to finance and performance continuously, so that the EU will offer the best environment for small business in the world; listen to the voice of small business; and promote top-class small business support. The Charter commits the Member States to work along ten lines of action in order to achieve these objectives. The Charter has political rather than legal value, since it cannot be called upon in courts, but small business organisations in the member countries may exercise pressures on their governments to honour their commitments.

The multiannual **programme for enterprise and entrepreneurship** (2001-2005) provides for an enterprise policy to be implemented via a new coordination procedure with the Member States (the BEST procedure) [see section 17.2.2.] and aims in particular at the needs of SMEs in more than 30 countries (European Union, EEA and applicant countries)[1]. The programme is intended to enhance the growth and competitiveness of business in a knowledge-driven globalised economy, to promote entrepreneurship, to simplify and improve the administrative and regulatory framework for business so that research, innovation and business creation in particular can flourish, to improve the financial environment for business (in the form of loan guarantees and support for risk capital provision) and to give business easier access to Community support services, programmes and networks. The Commission has put forward an action plan to provide a strategic framework for boosting entrepreneurship through the multiannual programme[2].

17.2.1. The legal environment of European business

The objectives pursued by the Community through its efforts at harmonisation in the area of **company law and accounting** are: the mobility of firms in order to allow them to benefit from the advantages of a unified market; the equality of the conditions of competition between firms estab-

---

[1] Decision 2000/819, OJ L 333, 29.12.2000.
[2] COM (2004) 70, 11 February 2004.

lished in different Member States; the promotion of commercial links between the Member States; the stimulation of cooperation between firms across borders and the facilitation of cross-border mergers and acquisitions. Appropriate Community measures are needed to provide for legal structures which facilitate cross-border establishment and investment, and to smooth discrepancies between national systems of company law which discourage or penalise these activities.

By virtue of the freedom of establishment laid down by the EC Treaty, undertakings formed in accordance with the law of one Member State do not encounter administrative problems in establishing themselves in the territory of another Member State [see section 6.5.1.]. The same cannot be said of **the real economic and legal problems of establishment**, which cannot disappear by the sole virtue of the provisions of the Treaty. Indeed, as the common market develops, companies see a constant increase in the transnational dimension of their relations with third parties, be they shareholders, employees, creditors or others. That development multiplies the danger of conflict between the various national measures, which guarantee the rights of those people. It is accordingly understandable that the Community's first effort of structural policy concerned **the coordination of the company law** of the Member States by means of Council Directives, based on Article 54.3.g. of the EEC Treaty (Art.44.2.g TEC), which provides for coordination of the safeguards which are required by Member States of Community companies for the protection of the interests of members and others. On the basis of this article, a number of directives harmonised several aspects of the company law of the Member States.

The first Directive lays down a **system of disclosure** applicable to all companies in order to coordinate safeguards for the protection of the interests of members and others and to facilitate public access to information on companies[1]. It obliges Member States to keep a register of companies, which anyone may examine, and to ensure that certain information is published in a national gazette. Also to protect the interests of members and others, the second Directive provides for the harmonisation of the standards and procedures relating to the **formation of public limited liability companies** and the maintenance and alteration of their capital. An amendment to this Directive aims to ensure that this type of company does not make use of a subsidiary for the acquisition of its own shares[2]. The third Directive introduces into the legal systems of all member countries the procedure for **the merger of public limited liability companies**, with the transfer of the assets and liabilities of the acquired company to the acquiring company[3]. The sixth Directive regulates **the hiving-off process**, i.e. the division of an existing company into several entities[4]. The eleventh Directive imposes measures in respect of disclosure in the Member State in

---

[1]   Directive 68/151, OJ L 65, 14.03.1968 and Directive 2003/58, OJ L 221, 04.09.2003.
[2]   Directive 77/91, OJ L 26, 30.01.1977 and Directive 92/101, OJ L 347, 28.11.1992.
[3]   Directive 78/855, OJ L 295, 20.10.1978 and OJ L 1, 03.01.1994.
[4]   Directive 82/891, OJ L 378, 31.12.1982 and OJ L 1, 03.01.1994.

which a branch is situated, in order to ensure the protection of persons who through **the intermediary of the branch** deal with a company who is governed by the law of another Member State[1]. The twelfth Directive deals with **single-member private companies** and allows, under certain conditions, the limitation of liability of the individual entrepreneur throughout the Community[2].

More than 31 years after the Commission proposal for the creation of the **European company** (a record in Community legislation), the Council finally adopted the two legislative instruments necessary for its creation, the regulation on the statute for a European company and a directive supplementing this statute with regard to the involvement of employees[3]. These legal provisions, which will enter into force together on 8 October 2004, will make it possible for a company to be set up within the territory of the Community in the form of a public limited-liability company, with the Latin name *Societas Europaea* **(SE)**. The SE will be entered in a register in the Member State where its registered office is situated. Every registered SE will be publicised in the Official Journal of the European Union. An SE must take the form of a company with share capital of at least EUR 120 000. The rules relating to **employee involvement in the SE** seek to ensure that the creation of an SE does not entail the disappearance or reduction of practices of employee involvement existing within the companies participating in the establishment of an SE [see section 13.5.2.].

The **Statute for the European company** provides enterprises with an optional new instrument, which makes cross-border enterprise management more flexible and less bureaucratic and may help improve the competitiveness of European enterprises. The SE makes it possible to operate Community-wide while being subject to Community legislation directly applicable in all Member States. Several options are available to enterprises from at least two Member States wishing to form an SE: a merger, a holding company, the creation of a subsidiary, or transformation into an SE. The statute allows a public limited-liability company, which has its registered office and head office within the Community, to transform itself into an SE without going into liquidation. An SE may itself set up one or more subsidiaries in the form of SEs. The registered office of an SE may be transferred to another Member State under certain conditions, but without winding up of the SE or creating a new legal person. Subject to the Regulation on the statute of SEs, an SE should be treated in every Member State as if it were a public limited-liability company formed in accordance with the law of the Member State in which it has its registered office.

The statute for a **European cooperative society (SCE)** is modelled on that of the European company, with the changes required by the specific

---

[1] Directive 89/666, OJ L 395, 30.12.1989 and OJ L 1, 03.01.1994.

[2] Directive 89/667, OJ L 395, 30.12.1989 and OJ L 1, 03.01.1994.

[3] Regulation 2157/2001 and directive 2001/86, OJ L 294, 10.11.2001 and Regulation 885/2004, OJ L 168, 01.05.2004.

characteristics of cooperative societies[1]. It allows the creation of a new legal entity for the organisation of economic operations in two or more Member States in the form of a cooperative society. It is supplemented by a Directive providing arrangements for the involvement of employees in a SCE[2].

The harmonisation of company law and the creation of European companies facilitate the interpenetration of markets and the concentration of companies at European level. But it is also necessary for Community undertakings to be able **to cooperate easily amongst themselves**, which is by no means straightforward. The various forms provided for by national laws for cooperation between domestic undertakings are not adapted to cooperation at common market level, owing specifically to their attachment to a national legal system, which means that cooperation between undertakings from several countries must be subject to the national law governing one of the participating undertakings. Economic operators, however, do not readily accept attachment to a foreign legal system, both for psychological reasons and owing to ignorance of foreign laws. Such legal barriers to international cooperation are particularly important where the parties involved are SMEs.

It was therefore necessary to introduce a legal instrument covered by Community law, which would make adequate cooperation between undertakings from different Member States possible. This is the purpose of the **"European Economic Interest Grouping" (EEIG)**, an instrument for cooperation on a contractual basis created by a Council Regulation in 1985[3]. The EEIG is not an economic entity separate from and independent of its members, behaving autonomously and trying to make profits for itself. It is a hybrid legal instrument offering the flexibility of a contract and some of the advantages of company status, including notably legal capacity. It serves as an economic staging post for the economic activity of its members. It enables them, by virtue of pooled functions, to develop their own activity and thus increase their own profits. Each member of the Grouping remains entirely autonomous both in economic and legal terms. That is a pre-condition for the existence of the European Economic Interest Grouping and distinguishes it from any other form or stage of merger. The Grouping ensures the equality of its members. None of them could give the others or the Grouping itself binding directives. Lastly, the Grouping may not seek profit for itself, may provide services only to its members and must invoice them at the cost price. These services can consist of marketing, the grouped purchase of raw materials or the representation of its members' interests.

---

[1]   Regulation 1435/2003, OJ L 207, 18.08.2003.
[2]   Directive 2003/72, OJ L 207, 18.08.2003.
[3]   Regulation 2137/85, OJ L 199, 31.07.1985 and OJ L 1, 03.01.1994.

17.2.2. The business environment

In the run-up to the completion of the single market the Community has endeavoured in particular to remove any obstacles to cross-border business activity, so as to help companies take advantage of new commercial opportunities on partner countries markets and, in general, to improve the environment in which Union business operates. Nevertheless, because of the complex nature of certain European provisions and **inadequate knowledge of the European legislation** concerned [see section 3.3.], businessmen often regard that legislation as an impediment to the entrepreneurial spirit. The European Union should therefore ensure that the impact of its legislation on enterprises, in particular SMEs, is not in conflict with the common objective of seeing enterprises reach their full development in the single market.

The European institutions try, indeed, to take into account the problems and conditions which are specific to SMEs when drawing up and implementing common policies (regional, social, research, environment, etc.). All proposals presented by the Commission to the Council and the Parliament are accompanied by an **impact assessment describing their likely effects on businesses**, in particular small and medium-sized enterprises, and on job creation. Through the "impact assessment method", the Commission analyses the direct and indirect implications of a proposed measure (e.g. concerning businesses, trade, employment, the environment and health). The results of each assessment are made public[1]. The impact assessment also gives details of the consultations that have taken place with the trade organisations concerned by the proposal[2]. The Community's legislative authorities are thus kept fully informed of the implications of a proposal on business and employment [see section 4.3.]. In order to facilitate the consultation of interested parties, the Commission's legislative programme is published in the Official Journal [see section 3.3.], indicating all the **proposals subject to "preconsultation"** and assessing their impact on enterprises.

It is advisable, however, to ensure that Member States do not complicate matters when transposing Community legislation into national law. Therefore, the Council recommended to the Member States to implement programmes of **administrative simplification** covering both new legislative proposals and existing legislation and to examine the impact of all proposed legislation or rules on the administrative burden on enterprises[3]. In a resolution on realising the full potential of SMEs, the Council called on the Member States and the Commission to examine how the business environment for SMEs could be improved by removing the structural impediments resulting from the legal, financial and administrative frame-

---

[1] COM (2002) 276, 5 June 2002.
[2] Resolution, OJ C 331, 16.12.1992, p 3-4.
[3] Recommendation, OJ L 141, 02.06.1990, p. 55-56 and resolution, OJ C 331, 16.12.1992, p. 3-4.

work[1]. At the invitation of the Amsterdam European Council, the Commission set up in July 1997 a **Business Environment Simplification Task Force (BEST)**, consisting of independent experts, which has the job of proposing concrete measures to improve the quality of legislation and reduce the constraints on SME development.

In order to improve the European business environment, a directive aims at combating **late payment in commercial transactions** in the public as well as the private sector[2]. This directive obliged the Member States to limit the deadline for payment at thirty days from the invoice date, unless otherwise specified in the contract and it harmonised the interest on late payments at seven percentage points above the European Central Bank rate. It also provided for retention of title by the seller until the time of payment of the purchase price and accelerated recovery procedures for undisputed debts with a maximum 90 days between the lodging of the creditor's action and the time when the writ of execution becomes enforceable.

It is also necessary to improve the quality and flow of information on the internal market and other fields of Community policy directed towards enterprises, in particular SMEs. The **Euro-Info-Centre (EIC) network** is designed to respond to SMEs' requests for information covering in particular the internal market (legal, technical and social aspects of Community trade) and the possibility of benefiting from Community funding. The EICs have three major objectives: to provide information about all single market issues and opportunities of interest to enterprises; to assist and advise businesses on participation in European activities; and to act as a channel of communication between enterprises and the Commission.

17.2.3. Business funding

Many European SMEs experience financing problems. They have less equity capital than their counterparts in the United States or Japan and they are more dependent than large firms on direct institutional finance (bank overdrafts, short and long-term loans), which is more expensive. The Commission noted that the situation could be improved easily by providing them with effective advice regarding both their management methods and their relations with their financial backers[3]. It also suggested improving coordination and communication between the various European, national, regional and local programmes aimed at strengthening the financial position of SMEs. The risk capital action plan (RCAP), adopted by the Cardiff European Council in June 1998, encourages venture capital investments by the structural funds and other capital markets, particularly in the seed and

---

[1] Resolution, OJ C 18, 17.01.1997, p. 1-5.
[2] Directive 2000/35, OJ L 200, 08.08.2000.
[3] COM (93) 528.

start-up phases, which have traditionally been the weakest links of the financing cycle in Europe[1].

The **European Investment Bank (EIB)** through its Global Loans and the **European Investment Fund (EIF)** are the financial institutions of the Community in support of SMEs [see section 7.3.3.]. The EIF's activity is centred upon two areas, venture capital and guarantees. EIF's venture capital instruments consist of equity investments in venture capital funds and business incubators that support SMEs, particularly those that are early stage and technology-oriented. EIF's guarantee instruments consist of providing guarantees to financial institutions that cover credits to SMEs. Both instruments implemented by the EIF for SMEs are complementary to the Global Loans provided by the European Investment Bank to financial intermediaries in support of SME financing. EIF's instruments are implemented in the context of the multiannual programme for enterprise and entrepreneurship (2001-05) [see section 17.2.].

SMEs are particularly interested in the possibility of Community funding under the common regional policy. The Regulation on the **European Regional Development Fund**[2] provides for a series of measures to support local development initiatives and the activities of SMEs in Objective 1 and 2 regions [see sections 12.3.1. and 12.3.2.]. More particularly, it provides for:

- aid for services for undertakings, notably in the fields of management, market study and research and common services for many undertakings;
- the financing of the transfer of technology, including the dissemination of information and the implementation of innovation in the businesses;
- the improvement of the access of undertakings to capital markets, notably through the provision of guarantees and participations;
- direct aid for investment, in the absence of an aid system; and
- the realisation of small dimension infrastructure.

The Business and Innovation Centres (BICs), set up by the Commission and public and private regional partners, mainly in Objective 1 regions of the Structural Funds, are designed to promote business creation and expansion by providing a comprehensive programme of services (training, finance, marketing, technology transfer, etc.) to SMEs which are developing innovative technology-based projects][3].

17.2.4. Cooperation between businesses

The opening up of markets as a result of economic integration in the Community is bringing with it faster structural change and greater com-

---

[1]   COM (2001) 605, 25 October 2001 and COM (2002) 563, 16 October 2002.
[2]   Regulation 1783/1999, OJ L 213, 13.08.1999.
[3]   Special report No 5/93, OJ C 13, 17.01.1994, p. 1-11.

petitive pressures on businesses. In many situations, cooperation or partnership between small businesses in different regions or countries of the Community can **help to meet the challenge of the wider market** and to compete with larger ones, especially if the arrangements concerned are based on complementarity resulting in mutual benefits. Moreover, cooperation can foster the modernisation and diversification of SMEs. There are different forms of cooperation, e.g. joint ventures, syndicates, agreements covering non-financial links (the granting/purchasing of licences, the transfer of know-how, marketing, etc.) or the acquisition of holdings. It may be formal, i.e. based on a contract, e.g. via a European economic interest grouping [see section 17.2.1.], or informal. Before taking part in any form of cooperation, firms must of course consider whether that cooperation is legal, since cooperation agreements sometimes give rise to problems in connection with the provisions of the Treaties concerning competition [see section 15.3.]. Such cases are, however, rare. As stated in the chapter on competition, the Commission is in favour of cooperation between SMEs and agreements of minor importance[1] [see section 15.3.1.].

While cooperation between Community firms is regarded as desirable and is generally authorised, it still has to overcome problems of a technical and psychological nature. SMEs investing in other Member States prefer to create subsidiaries rather than joint ventures, or to enter into looser cooperation agreements without the obligation to create a new legal entity. Therefore, the Commission is currently studying the creation of an overall **business-support network**, in charge of partner search and other activities concerning SMEs.

17.3. Sectoral policy

Sectoral industrial policy is largely linked with commercial policy. The **commercial policy measures** that have the greatest consequences for industrial sectors are manipulations of the customs tariff, anti-dumping measures, trade agreements and various export incentives. By virtue of customs union, most of those measures are already in the hands of the European institutions [see section 23.3.]. Other sectoral policy measures are the **incentives used by governments** to modernise and guide national industries, such as grants to certain research bodies, to documentation centres and centres for the dissemination of knowledge, to productivity centres and to vocational training centres. Some such measures are already centralised at European level. The others **require Community coordination**, inasmuch as they may disturb conditions of competition on the single market.

Also still in the hands of governments are the most direct and best-known sectoral measures, i.e. **aids of every kind**: grants, loans, interest

---

[1]   OJ C 231, 12.09.1986, p. 2-4.

rate subsidies, etc. Aids for the improvement of certain sectors and aids to "infant industries" are characteristic examples of sectoral measures. The main grounds for them are employment promotion, regional development or even national prestige where important undertakings, regarded as "flag-ship companies", are involved [see section 15.5.3.]. Since sectoral aids and the conditions under which they are granted vary greatly from one EU State to another, they may affect trade between Member States and distort or threaten to distort competition. Therefore, the objective of industrial policy should be to create the conditions that allow better control of such aids. Moreover, the effectiveness of the Community's policies to promote greater cohesion could be improved by a progressive reduction in aid intensities in the central and more prosperous regions.

It is for that reason that Articles 87 and 88 of the EC Treaty provide for Commission control of the aids which States grant directly or indirectly to certain undertakings or the production of certain goods. Such **aids must be notified to the Commission**, which has the power to authorise them or prohibit them in accordance with the criteria laid down in the Treaty or under secondary legislation [see section 15.5.]. Thus, although the most powerful instrument of sectoral industrial policy is still in the hands of the governments, the Commission may prevent such national aids from distorting conditions of competition or running counter to the objectives of the EU's industrial policy.

The best way to prevent individual sectoral measures by governments that are harmful to the common interest and at the same time to restructure European industry is the **common sectoral policy**. This has developed in the most vulnerable sectors at international level, either because the markets are saturated (steel, shipbuilding, textiles) or because they are not yet well developed at European level (aeronautics, information industries, telecommunications). We shall examine Community policy in those sectors below.

17.3.1. Steel industry

The **Community rules for State aid** to the steel industry provide a framework for reasonable intervention without distortion of the competition conditions in the common steel market[1]. Moreover, the **steel market is closely monitored**, on the one hand, by way of information that steel companies must communicate to the Commission concerning their investments[2] and, on the other, in the framework of six-monthly **forward programmes** covering market developments and future prospects[3]. The "external aspect of steel", entails a few tariff quotas and the prior statistical monitoring of imports from Central and Eastern European countries to en-

---

[1]   Decision 2496/96, OJ L 338, 28.12.1996.
[2]   Decision 3010/91, OJ L 286, 16.10.1991.
[3]   See for example, OJ C 27, 29.01.2000.

sure that they do not harm the Community steel industry. Since the ECSC Treaty expired in July 2002, the regulatory framework on steel products came into line with the European policy applied to the whole of manufacturing[1].

In a resolution adopted on 14 March 2002, the European Parliament deplored the **American protectionist decision** to impose extraordinary tariffs of up to 30% on steel imports in violation of World Trade Organisation (WTO) rules. The Parliament backed the Commission in its decision to take a case immediately to the WTO and take all necessary measures to safeguard the EU steel industry in line with WTO rules [see section 25.7.]. Following the conditions laid down by the WTO safeguard agreement, the Commission imposed indeed provisional safeguard measures against imports of seven American steel products[2]. The Council established additional customs duties on imports of certain products originating in the USA and applied concession suspensions not only to steel products but also to other products with a view to offsetting the effects of the safeguard measures taken by the United States in March 2002[3].

17.3.2. Shipbuilding

The multilateral negotiations launched in 1989 under the auspices of the OECD between the main producing countries (European Union, Japan, South Korea, Norway, United States), which together account for more than 70% of world shipyard output, led to an agreement in July 1994 on the elimination of all obstacles to normal conditions of competition in the sector as from 1 January 1998. Consequently, a Council Regulation on aid to shipbuilding implements the provisions of the **OECD Agreement on respecting normal competitive conditions** in the commercial shipbuilding and repair industry, although this agreement, pending its ratification by the USA, has still not entered into force[4]. Hence, problems continue. Community inquiries reveal that South Korea is distorting competition on the world market in shipbuilding through dumping practices. The Council has authorised the Commission to initiate WTO proceedings against South Korea in May 2001 and introduced a temporary defence mechanism for the Community shipbuilding industry to counter unfair trade practices by the Republic of Korea in world shipbuilding markets until the conclusion of dispute settlement proceedings at the WTO[5] [see section 23.4.]. In any case, the Community Regulation prohibits contract-related aid (operating aid) as from 31 December 2000[6] [see section 15.5.3.]. The Commission concentrates its efforts on defending European industry against unfair trade

---

[1]   COM (1999) 453, 5 October 1999.
[2]   Regulation 560/2002, OJ L 85, 28.03.2002 and Regulation 142/2003, OJ L 23, 28.01.2003.
[3]   Regulation 1031/2002, OJ L 157, 15.06.2002.
[4]   Regulation 3094/95, OJ L 332, 30.12.1995 and Regulation 2600/97, OJ L 351, 23.12.1997.
[5]   Regulation 1177/2002, OJ L 172, 02.07.2002.
[6]   Regulation 1540/98, OJ L 202, 18.07.1998.

practices by shipbuilders in third countries and on improving its competitiveness by encouraging research and supporting closer industrial cooperation[1].

In a communication on Europe's maritime future, the Commission stressed the vital role played by **maritime industries**, which alongside shipbuilding encompass a vast range of products and industries, such as ship fitting, port services and the marine-resource industry, including fisheries and energy[2]. In keeping with its communication, the Commission, in Community guidelines, aims at harmonising the national aid schemes for maritime transport in order to permit national fiscal support to the development of the sector while making the schemes themselves more transparent[3] [see section 15.5.3.].

17.3.3. Textiles and clothing industries

On the internal level, the Commission **monitors national aids** and applies a policy aiming at preventing such aids from giving rise to distortions of competition within the Community or having the effect of transferring labour problems and structural difficulties from one country to another. Several schemes for aid to the textiles and clothing industries were accordingly prohibited or adjusted, and programmes for the orderly reduction of production capacity were able to be agreed on. The system for monitoring aids to **synthetic fibres** producers, which was introduced in 1977 and is renewed on a year-to-year basis, favours aid which seeks to re-absorb overcapacity through restructuring or reconversion of the industry[4] [see section 15.5.3.].

The **external aspect** of the common textiles policy aims at organising international trade in textiles in order to provide breathing space for the Community industry without frustrating the industrialisation hopes of the developing countries. Such organisation was sought within the framework of the General Agreement on Tariffs and Trade (GATT) through the arrangement on international trade in textiles, commonly known as the **"Multifibre Arrangement"** (MFA). However, the textiles agreement, concluded within the framework of the Uruguay Round aims at the progressive liberalisation of textile and clothing products within the World Trade Organisation [see section 23.4.]. In this context, the Commission proposes to strengthen the protection of intellectual property rights and measures to tackle fraud and counterfeiting in the fields of the internal market and commercial policy [see section 23.2.2.], to promote the harmonisation of customs duties under the WTO's Doha Development

---

[1] COM (97) 470 and COM (1999) 474.
[2] COM (96) 84, 13 March 1996.
[3] OJ C 205, 07.07.1997.
[4] OJ C 96, 30.03.1996, p. 11-14 and OJ C 368, 22.12.2001, p. 10.

Agenda, and to remove non-tariff barriers to trade in order to boost access to markets[1].

17.3.4. Aeronautical and aerospace industries

In a communication entitled " Europe and space: Turning to a new chapter", which was adopted in agreement with the European Space Agency (ESA), the Commission defined the objectives of a Community strategy for space: strengthening the foundation for space activities so that Europe preserves independent and affordable access to space; enhancing scientific knowledge; and exploiting the benefits of space-based tools for markets and society[2]. This strategy aims to establish the right political and regulatory conditions for space activities, to catalyse joint R & D efforts and to bring together all the players around common political objectives in projects of Europe-wide interest.

The user-oriented and policy-driven approach to space is articulated concretely in two Community initiatives: the development of a civil satellite navigation and positioning system (Galileo) and an initiative to build a coherent capacity in Europe for global monitoring for environment and security (GMES)[3]. The success of these initiatives depends on effective cooperation between the Commission, the Member States and the ESA. The Council shared the Commission's analysis and called upon it to prepare, together with the ESA, a comprehensive document on a European strategy for space[4]. The Commission suggested that priority should be given to the establishment of a defence equipment market, to the launch of a preparatory action to increase Europe's industrial potential in the field of security research, and to the creation of a genuine European space policy[5].

For the implementation of the development phase of the **Galileo programme**, a Joint Undertaking (within the meaning of Article 171 of the EC Treaty), combining public and private sector funding, was set up in Brussels[6]. The development phase of this programme should make it possible to make considerable progress in the development of satellite navigation technologies. The development phase should be followed by the deployment phase consisting of the production of satellites and terrestrial components, satellite launching and the installation of terrestrial stations and equipment in order to enable the system to be operational in 2008. Galileo will be compatible and interoperable with the US Global Positioning System (GPS). Thanks to a US-EU agreement signed on 26 June 2004, all users of satellite radionavigation will be able to use simultaneously, with

---

[1] COM (2003) 649, 29 October 2003.
[2] COM(2000) 597, 27 September 2000.
[3] COM (2001) 609 Council resolution, OJ C 350, 11.12.2001.
[4] Council resolutions, OJ C 375, 24.12.1999 and OJ C 371, 23.12.2000.
[5] COM (2003) 600, 13 October 2003.
[6] Regulation 876/2002, OJ L 138, 28.05.2002.

only one receiver, one or other of the two systems, or both at the same time.

The second stage of **the GMES initiative** is aimed at developing a global independent European monitoring capacity to be operational by 2008, by coordinating European activities in the field of satellite observation and remote sensing so as to provide support for government policies (in particular concerning the environment, agriculture, regional development, fisheries, transport and common foreign and security policy).[1]

Pointing out that major industrial, strategic, military and political interests are at stake in relation to Europe's capacity to control positioning and navigation services for its own territory, and that the existing system operates exclusively through American and Russian satellite signals, the Commission advocates developing **global navigation satellite systems (GNSS)** at European level offering a service meeting the needs of civilian users[2]. To this end, an Agreement between the European Community, the European Space Agency and the European Organisation for the Safety of the Air Navigation aims at developing and validating the operational capability of a European contribution to the GNSS[3] [see also section 18.4.1.].

17.3.5. Information industries

The economic and social development of nations depends, increasingly, on the use of information and knowledge, with the aid of the enormous progress made in **information and communications technologies (ICTs)**. Harnessing the opportunities opened up by the digitalisation of information in all its forms, these technologies are transforming dramatically many aspects of economic and social life, such as working methods and relations, the organisation of businesses, the focus of education and training, and the way people communicate with each other. The **information society** is the dawning of a multimedia world (sound - text - image) representing a radical change comparable with the first industrial revolution. It goes hand in hand with the "non-physical" economy, based on the creation, circulation and exploitation of knowledge. The conditions of access to information, to the networks carrying it (broad band networks called "information highways") and to the services facilitating the use of the data (including high value-added services, databases, etc.) are vital components of the Union's future competitiveness.

European States are undergoing a fundamental transformation: **from an industrial society to the information society**. Information society technologies increasingly pervade all industrial and societal activities and are key factors for the competitiveness of European companies. ICTs are also the vehicle for a growing number of societal services such as health,

---

[1]   COM (2004) 65, 3 February 2004.
[2]   COM (1998) 29, 21 January 1998.
[3]   Decision 98/434, OJ L 194, 10.07.1998.

education, transport, entertainment and culture. Since they are amongst the highest growth activities, and they are also highly skilled activities, these technologies have a high potential for employment creation.

The problem is that, although there is a strong demand for information in Europe, the suppliers could be anywhere in the world since the delivery is instantaneous. Indeed, **the United States and Japan have a head-start** as suppliers of information, because they each have a single system of standards and a single national language. Europe, thus, has to overcome large handicaps in this field. It should be noted that under the Information Technology Agreement, concluded in March 1997 under the auspices of the World Trade Organisation, tariffs on information technology products of countries accounting for 92% of world trade will be phased out completely by 1 January 2000, a fact which will intensify further investment competition[1] [see section 23.4.].

A multiannual Community programme aims to stimulate the development and use of **European digital content (*e*Content programme)** on the global networks and to promote linguistic diversity in the information society[2]. It proposes action over a period of four years in three specific areas: public sector information, linguistic and cultural customisation, and measures to make the market more dynamic. This action is intended to create an environment favourable to business initiatives where European creativity, cultural diversity and technological strengths can be commercially exploited. The sixth Framework Research and Development programme seeks, inter alia, to boost hardware and software technologies and applications at the heart of the creation of the information society and to harness the knowledge-based society for the benefit of the citizens[3] [see section 18.4.1.].

By guaranteeing recognition of **electronic signatures** throughout the European Union, a Directive on a common framework for electronic signatures was the first step towards establishing a European framework for development of electronic commerce[4] [see also section 6.6.1.]. This framework is provided by the so-called **electronic commerce directive**[5]. This Directive harmonises certain legal aspects, such as determining the place of establishment of service providers, the transparency obligations for providers and for commercial communications, the validity of electronic contracts and the transparency of the contractual process, the responsibility of Internet intermediaries, on-line dispute settlements and the role of national governments. It clarifies the application of key internal market principles (freedom of establishment of service providers and free movement of services) to information society services, affirming the country-of-origin prin-

---

[1] Decision 97/359, OJ L 155, 12.06.1997 and Regulation 2216/97, OJ L 305, 08.11.1997.
[2] Decision 2001/48, OJ L 14, 18.01.2001.
[3] Decision 2002/834, OJ L 294, 29.10.2002.
[4] Directive 1999/93, OJ L 13, 19.01.2000.
[5] Directive 2000/31, OJ L 178, 17.07.2000.

ciple by which service providers must comply with the legislation of the Member State of origin.

The action plan "eEurope" of the Commission, which was endorsed by the Feira European Council (19-20 June 2000), seeks to remove the key barriers to the uptake of the Internet in Europe, aiming in particular at: providing a cheaper, faster and more secure Internet; investing in skills; giving the public access to the Internet and encouraging its use[1]. The action plan is a success, since the number of households connected to the Internet has more than doubled, almost all schools and businesses are on line and Europe now has the world's fastest backbone research network[2]. A multiannual programme (2003-2005) established a legal basis for the monitoring activities under the eEurope 2005 action plan, the dissemination of best practice at European level and the improvement of network and information security (MODINIS)[3].

In the framework of the "eEurope" action plan, a regulation lays down the conditions for designating the registry responsible for the organisation, administration and management of the **Internet ".eu" country code top-level domain (ccTLD)** and establishes the general policy framework within which the Registry functions[4]. Domain names and the related addresses are essential elements of the global interoperability of the World Wide Web (www), since they allow users to locate computers and websites on the Web. TLDs are also an integral part of every Internet e-mail address. The ".eu" TLD should promote the use of, and access to, the Internet networks and the virtual market (electronic commerce) place based on the Internet, by providing a complementary registration domain to existing country code TLDs and should in consequence increase choice and competition. The establishment of the ".eu" TLD registry, which is the entity charged with the organisation, administration and management of the ".eu" TLD, should contribute to the promotion of the European Union image on the global information networks and bring an added value to the Internet naming system in addition to the national ccTLDs.

17.3.6. Telecommunications

Digital technologies, developed by the information industry, allow the integrated transmission of sound, text and image in one communication system and project Europe into the information era, radically changing the

---

[1] COM (2000) 330, 24 May 2000.

[2] COM (2003) 66, 11 February 2003.

[3] Decision 2256/2003, OJ L 336, 23.12.2003 and Decision 787/2004, OJ L 138, 30.04.2004.

[4] Regulation 733/2002, OJ L 113, 30.04.2002.

modes of consumption, production and organisation of work. On the other hand, advanced **communications technologies and services** are a vital link between industry, the services sector and market as well as between peripheral areas and economic centres. These services are therefore crucial for consolidation of the internal market, for Europe's industrial competitiveness and for economic and social cohesion in Europe. They can also contribute to social progress and to cultural development. The common policy on telecommunications is developing since the 1990s around four axes: the creation of a single market of telecommunications equipment and services; the liberalisation of telecommunication services; the technological development of the sector with the assistance of Community research; and the balanced development of the regions of the Union by means of trans-European telecommunication networks.

The **regulatory framework for telecommunications terminal equipment** follows and affects the new approach to standardisation, testing and certification that we have examined in the chapter on the common market [see section 6.2.3.]. A Council Decision and a Resolution on standardisation in the field of information technology and telecommunications pursue the objective of creating a **European market in telecommunications equipment**[1]. Such standardisation of information technology and telecommunications prevents distortions of competition and ensures exchanges of information, the convergence of industrial strategies and, ultimately, the creation and exploitation of a vast European information technologies and telecommunications (IT&T) market. European standards are used in many Community policies, above all those connected with the single market, *e*Europe [see section 17.3.5.], general product safety and environment protection. A Directive establishes a single market for radio equipment and telecommunications terminal equipment and prescribes the mutual recognition of their conformity based on the principle of the manufacturer's declaration[2].

European institutions and standardisation bodies endeavour to ensure the coherence with the regulatory framework applicable to information equipment in order to meet the challenge of interoperability. The Commission collates requirements with regard to standardisation on the part of users and establishes the priorities of a work programme, which is entrusted to the CEN (European Committee for Standardisation) and the CENELEC (European Committee for Electrotechnical Standardisation), with the participation of the CEPT (European Conference of Postal and Telecommunications Administrations). In addition to the European Telecommunication Standards Institute (ETSI), private organisations representing industry and consumers are involved in the pre-standardisation process and in the effective application of harmonised standards in the Member States, including for public contracts.

---

[1] Decision 87/95, OJ L 36, 07.02.1987 and resolution, OJ C 117, 11.05.1989, p. 1.
[2] Directive 1999/5, OJ L 91, 07.04.1999.

The creation of a single market in telecommunications services necessitated the progressive **liberalisation of telecommunications markets**, which were traditionally State monopolies. Telecommunications services had to be liberated and conditions of free provision of services by the networks had to be defined. To pursue this objective, which represents the second axis of the Community policy in this sector, the Commission adopted a Directive based on Article 90 of the EEC Treaty (Art. 86 TEC), requiring Member States to introduce arrangements ensuring free competition on the Community market in telecommunications terminal equipment (modems, telex terminals, receive-only satellite stations, etc.)[1] [see section 15.5.4.]. This Directive gives users the possibility of connecting terminal equipment, which they are able to procure freely without being obliged to apply to a single national telecommunications authority. Through its successive amendments, the Directive entitles suppliers of telecommunications services to use capacity on cable television networks for all telecommunications services, primarily data communications, "closed" corporate networks and multimedia services[2]. It also requires Member States to abolish the exclusive and special rights remaining in telecommunications, the restrictions on the installations used for mobile networks and the obstacles to direct interconnection between such networks. Last but not least, the Commission Directive provided for the complete liberalisation of voice telephony and telecommunications infrastructures on 1 January 1998.

Liberalisation of telecommunications services cleared the way for the **creation of the single market** in this sector. This is the aim of the "telecoms package", adopted in 2002. The package constitutes a single regulatory framework covering the converging telecommunications, media and information technology sectors. It is made up of a framework Directive and four specific Directives concerning access, authorisation, universal service and protection of privacy. National regulatory authorities must contribute to the development of the internal market by cooperating with each other and with the Commission to ensure the consistent application, in all Member States, of the provisions of those Directives.

Directive 2002/21 established a harmonised **regulatory framework** for electronic communications networks and services across the EU[3]. This Directive covers all electronic communications networks and services within its scope, namely: transmission systems and, where applicable, switching or routing equipment and other resources which permit the conveyance of signals by wire, by radio, by optical or by other electromagnetic means, including satellite networks, fixed (including Internet) and mobile terrestrial networks, electricity cable systems, networks used for radio and television broadcasting, and cable television networks. It sets out a number of principles and objectives for regulators to follow, as well as a series of

---

[1] Directive 90/388, OJ L 192, 24.07.1990 and Directive 1999/64, OJ L 175, 10.07.1999.
[2] Directive 95/51, OJ L 256, 26.10.1995 and Directive 96/19, OJ L 74, 22.03.1996.
[3] Directive 2002/21, OJ L 108, 24.04.2002.

tasks in respect of management of scarce resources such as radio spectra and numbering.

The aim of **the "access directive"** is to lay down a framework of rules that are technologically neutral, but which may be applied to specific product or service markets in particular geographical areas, to address identified market problems between access and interconnection suppliers[1]. It covers, in particular, access to fixed and mobile networks, as well as access to digital broadcasting networks, including access to conditional systems and other associated facilities such as electronic programme guides and application programme interfaces. The directive provides legal certainty for market players by establishing clear criteria on their rights and obligations and for regulatory intervention. It indicates clearly what obligations concerning access and interconnection can be imposed in which circumstances, whilst at the same time allowing for sufficient flexibility to allow regulatory authorities to deal effectively with new market problems that hinder effective competition.

The aim of the **"authorisation directive"** is to implement an internal market in electronic communications networks and services through the harmonisation and simplification of authorisation rules and conditions in order to facilitate their provision throughout the Community[2]. According to the Directive, "general authorisation" means a legal framework established by the Member State ensuring rights for the provision of electronic communications networks or services and laying down sector specific obligations that may apply to all or to specific types of electronic communications networks and services. The general authorisation system should apply to all such services and networks regardless of their technological characteristics and should limit administrative barriers to entry into the market to a minimum.

The aim of the **"universal users"** directive is to ensure universal service provision for public telephony services in an environment of greater overall competitiveness, with provisions for financing the cost of providing a universal service in the most competitively neutral manner and for ensuring a maximum of information transparency[3]. It also establishes the rights of users and consumers of electronic communications services, with corresponding obligations on undertakings. It aims to ensure the interoperability of digital consumer television equipment and the provision of certain mandatory services, such as leased lines. Finally, it lays down harmonised rules for the imposition of "must carry" obligations by Member States on network operators.

The **protection of privacy** directive translates the principles set out in Directive 95/46 [see section 9.2.] into specific rules for the telecommunications sector[4]. In fact, publicly available electronic communications services

---

[1] Directive 2002/19, OJ L 108, 24.04.2002.
[2] Directive 2002/20, OJ L 108, 24.04.2002.
[3] Directive 2002/22, OJ L 108, 24.04.2002.
[4] Directive 2002/58, OJ L 201, 31.07.2002.

over the Internet open new possibilities for users but also new risks for their personal data and privacy, in particular with regard to the increasing capacity for automated storage and processing of data relating to subscribers and users. Therefore, the Directive on privacy and electronic communications harmonises the provisions of the Member States required to ensure an equivalent level of protection of fundamental rights and freedoms, and in particular the right to privacy, with respect to the processing of personal data in the electronic communication sector and to ensure the free movement of such data and of electronic communication equipment and services in the Community.

17.4. Appraisal and outlook

Generally speaking, the EU intervenes in the industrial sector only to create an environment conducive either to the expansion of undertakings throughout the internal market (enterprise policy) or to the activity of certain industrial branches which present common problems, to enable them to cope better with increased competition at European and world levels (sectoral policy).

Although disparities remain between Member States' industrial structures, we are nonetheless in the presence of a parallel development of the various parameters in the secondary sector. **The completion of the single market**, in 1992, provided a fillip to the restructuring of European industry. The removal of the physical, technical and fiscal barriers to intra-Community trade gave rise to strengthened trade and therefore bolstered competition within the Community. Thanks to the removal of border controls and technical trade barriers, businesses can now supply a single product for the whole of the single market. Manufacturers no longer have to produce for fifteen separate markets. This situation increases competition enormously in the internal market. Greater competition results in the alignment of national suppliers' prices on those of foreign suppliers, who penetrate markets that had previously been protected. In the short term that squeezes the profit margins of undertakings which had been protected and/or enjoyed monopoly situations. Some of them are even forced to leave the market.

The elimination of the least competitive producers enables, however, those firms which survive to **expand on the market**. They are thus able to: better exploit and maximise their production capabilities, or even increase them (economies of scale); strengthen their domestic efficiency by restructuring and concentrating their activities and by improving allocation of human, technical and financial resources; improve their organisation and the quality and variety of their products, and innovate both as regards the production process and the products offered. This competitive pressure has already caused the wind of change to sweep the Union's industrial fabric.

Generally speaking, the large multinational companies are best equipped to conquer new markets, restructure their production, rationalise their organisation; but they often do all this by using less labour and more natural resources. On the contrary, small undertakings are labour-intensive and more concerned with the preservation of the environment, because they are closer to the populations surrounding their plants. Therefore, the European Union has developed a **policy towards small and medium-sized enterprises (SMEs)** to ensure that they are better informed about European facts (regulations, directives, standards, invitations to tender, research projects) and about the opportunities offered by the large market (exportation, cooperation, concentration).

Entrepreneurship and a well-functioning internal market are vital to growth and job creation. The regulatory environment should encourage entrepreneurial activity and make it as simple as possible to set up new businesses. Creation of a favourable business environment implies the **elimination of superfluous and niggling regulation**. The internal market must be made as unbureaucratic as possible. Both the Union and the Member States must therefore facilitate market entry and exit for businesses of all sizes, improve access to finance and know-how, improve regulation and reduce administrative burdens. The regulatory framework should be clear and predictable, while regulation should be limited to what is strictly necessary for achieving clearly-defined objectives. The common enterprise policy aims at this end, but it is not certain that the national policies follow suit. Member States should transpose faster Community legislation on the internal market and related subjects into national legal and administrative practice. On the other hand, company law and corporate governance practices need to be modernised in the wake of corporate governance scandals and in view of the growing trend for European companies to operate cross-border in the internal market, the continued integration of European capital markets, the rapid development of new information and communication technology and the enlargement of the EU to new Member States, most of which have not a long-established business culture.

Bibliography on industrial policy

- BILDT Carl (et al.). *Europe in space*. London: Centre for European Reform, 2004.
- BOULOUKOS Marios. "The legal status of the European company (SE): towards a European company 'à la carte'?", *International Business Law Journal*, n. 4, 2004, p. 489-517.
- CHEN John-ren. *International institutions and multinational enterprises: global players, global markets*. Cheltenham: Edward Elgar, 2004.
- CRANE Andrew, MATTEN Dirk. *Business ethics: a European perspective: managing corporate citizenship and sustainability in the age of globalization*. Oxford: Oxford University Press, 2004.

- DORIS Martin. "Cross-border contracting in the EU: interoperability problems and the impact of a Community wide optional instrument", *Tilburg Foreign Law Review*, v. 12, n. 1, 2004, p. 36-50.
- EUROPEAN COMMISSION. *Action plan: The European agenda for Entrepreneurship*. Luxembourg: EUR-OP*, 2004.
- JOHNSON Peter. *Industries in Europe: competition, trends and policy issues*. Cheltenham: Edward Elgar, 2003.
- MULLER Alan Rene. *The rise of regionalism: core company strategies under the second wave of integration*. Rotterdam: Erasmus Research Institute of Management, Erasmus University Rotterdam, 2004.
- SYKES Michael (ed.). *Understanding economic growth: macro-level, industry-level, firm-level*. Paris: OECD; Basingstoke: New York: Palgrave, 2004 .
- VELO Dario. "The European model of society and the European model of enterprise: the cosmopolitical enterprise", *The European Union Review*, vol 9, n. 1, March 2004, p. 7-28.

The publications of the Office for Official Publications of the European Communities (EUR-OP) exist generally in all official languages of the EU.

DISCUSSION TOPICS

1. How does the common industrial policy interact with other common policies?
2. How can the common market affect the restructuring and competitiveness of European industry?
3. What are the advantages and disadvantages of SMEs in the large single market?
4. How does the EU support the advent of the information society?
5. Outline the common strategy in the telecommunications sector.

Chapter 18

RESEARCH AND TECHNOLOGY POLICY

Diagram of the chapter

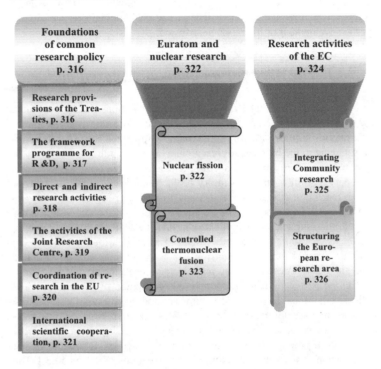

Economic and social progress and the competitiveness of European States at world level come about through efficacious scientific research and technological development. European research, however, is handicapped in the international arena as a result of the **fragmentation of research policies pursued in the Member States** of the Union and the resulting dispersion of efforts. The common research and development policy is therefore essential for European integration. The aim of that policy is to coordinate national research policies and to define and implement research programmes of European interest, i.e. programmes geared to the large market, of interest to all Member States and necessitating technical and human resources which Member States cannot put together individually. At world level, only the coordinated research of the Member States can allow the European Union to play a leading role in vast international programmes such as the one on global change.

Common research policy is closely **linked to the common industrial policy**, which we have just examined, and to the common energy policy, which we shall examine in the next chapter. Indeed, research is essential for the definition of industrial strategy, especially in high-technology sectors, by offering a common reference basis for technology forecasting and development. It is also necessary for the promotion of **reliable energy sources**, which reduce Europe's dependence on imported oil, particularly for the development of thermonuclear fusion.

18.1. The need for a common research policy

Although the challenges facing the European nations change over time, and with them the scientific and technical research priorities, certain immutable reasons militate in favour of a **common approach to research problems**. Owing to the high cost of research, a European policy is necessary in order to define the economic, social, political and even military objectives of research, to draw up an inventory of the resources available in terms of human resources, laboratories and funds, to set the priorities and to apportion the work. In this way it can be ensured that no important sector is neglected, that duplication is avoided and that the Union's human, material and financial resources are put to best use. Labour distribution can also ensure that Europe's smallest countries, which would otherwise be excluded owing to a lack of resources, can participate in research and development.

Europe is experiencing a massive transformation of its economy and society. Traditional industrial structures are undergoing rapid change. The problems that are observed in the structures of the traditional European industries, like textiles, shipbuilding and steel, are notably the results of the movement of production to countries with low wage levels induced by the globalisation of markets and economies [see sections 17.1. and 17.3.]. The transfer of European traditional industrial production to other countries can be offset only by new industries with a high level of technology.

Europe's industrial competitiveness, its jobs, its quality of life and the sustainability of growth depend on it being at the leading edge of the development and utilisation of **information society technologies**. Advances in information processing and communications are opening up exciting new possibilities [see sections 17.3.5. and 17.3.6.]. However, the increasing diversity and complexity of systems is also presenting new challenges for their development and use. Continuous efforts are required, in research, technological development and demonstration to tackle the universal issues such as access, ease of use, cost-effectiveness and interoperability and standardisation. They should also address the social changes brought about by the introduction and more widespread use of new information and communications technologies.

Innovation requires constant and organised interdependence between the upstream phases linked to technology, and the downstream phases linked to the market, such as the development of new business concepts, new means of distribution, marketing or design. This means that, in order to have **industrially efficient innovation**, the needs of the market should be taken into account, particularly by modernising the approaches and practices of marketing, and synergies in research and technological development (R & D) should be facilitated by trans-European cooperation. These considerations are particularly pertinent for SMEs, which are innovative by their nature, but which do not exploit efficiently their R & D potential because of their structural and financial handicaps [see section 17.1.4.].

Society is making increasing demands for better living conditions, better safety, and better use of scarce resources including secure and economic energy supplies and services. Availability of a sufficient and economic energy supply must be assured to promote industrial competitiveness and to maintain the quality of life for Europe's citizens [see section 19.1.]. At the same time, the environmental impact of energy production and use must be reduced. Indeed, rising population and per-capita use of resources, globalisation of economic markets and natural variability in earth systems are causing or exacerbating major environmental problems [see section 16.3.]. R & D in the fields of **energy, environment and sustainable development** is essential for the social well-being of Europe's citizens and the implementation of policies formulated at Community level or deriving from international environmental commitments - in particular, the implementation of the Kyoto Protocol [see section 16.3.4.].

The promotion of scientific and technological excellence is an essential prerequisite for Europe to succeed in the competitive environment of international research and scientific development. Access to **major research infrastructures**, in particular, is indispensable for researchers working at the forefront of science. The ability of European research teams to remain competitive with teams elsewhere in the world depends on their being supported by state-of-the-art infrastructures. As most of the major research infrastructures in Europe are operated by national authorities, principally for the benefit of their national researchers, access to these infrastructures is often restricted largely or even entirely to national research teams. The result is that researchers do not always have the opportunity to access the infrastructures most appropriate for their work. European R & D should therefore make available major research infrastructures in all Member States to competent multinational teams of researchers.

18.2. The foundations of the common research policy

Whilst we now see clearly the need for and objectives of Community research policy, that was probably not the case when the **EEC Treaty** was framed [see section 2.1.]. That is why the Treaty, apart from a rather vague reference to the coordination of research and the dissemination of agricultural knowledge in its Article 41 (Art. 35 TEC), did not give the Community Institutions any powers to finance or even coordinate Member States' research in the other sectors of the economy. This is now changed with the new provisions of the EC Treaty [see section 2.2.], the new concepts of the framework programme [see section 18.2.2.] and of direct and indirect actions [see section 18.2.3.] and, above all, the new missions of the Joint Research Centre [see section 18.2.4.]. These are the main subjects of this part of the chapter.

18.2.1. Research provisions of the Community Treaties

The Maastricht Treaty improved the position enjoyed by research in the process of European construction. Article 163 of the EC Treaty **consecrated research and technological development as a policy of the Community**, stating that the latter shall aim to strengthen the scientific and technological foundations of Community industry and boost its competitiveness at international level and shall promote the research activities deemed necessary by virtue of other Community policies. To this end, it adds, the Community shall in all the Member States encourage undertakings, including small and medium-sized enterprises, research centres and universities, in their research and technological development activities of high quality. Through its support for their cooperation efforts, the Community aims to enable undertakings to draw full benefit from the potential of the internal market, in particular through the opening up of national public contracts, the definition of common standards and the removal of legal and fiscal obstacles to cooperation.

The Community and the Member States coordinate their research and technological development activities (Art. 165 TEC). In pursuit of the objectives detailed in Article 163 (TEC), the Community conducts the following **priority activities**, complementing the R & D activities in the Member States (Art. 164 TEC):

(a) implementation of research, technological development and demonstration programmes, by promoting cooperation with and between undertakings, research centres and universities;

(b) promotion of cooperation in the field of Community research, technological development and demonstration with third countries and international organisations;

(c) dissemination and optimisation of the results of activities in Community research, technological development and demonstration; and

(d) stimulation of the training and mobility of researchers in the Community (Art. 164 TEC).

The **Euratom Treaty** gives an even more important place to the development of (nuclear) research, devoting its first Chapter to it [see section 2.1.]. Article 4 makes the Commission responsible for promoting and facilitating nuclear research in the Member States and for complementing it by carrying out a European Atomic Energy Community research and training programme. For purposes of coordinating and complementing research undertaken in Member States, the Commission calls upon Member States, persons or undertakings to communicate to it their programmes relating to the research which it specifies in the request. By its opinions the Commission should discourage unnecessary duplication and should direct research towards sectors which are insufficiently explored, of which it should publish at regular intervals a list. (Art. 5 EAEC).

18.2.2. The framework programme for R & D

A two-phased **decision-making process** exists for Community research programmes. Every five years, the Council acting under the codecision procedure with the European Parliament [see section 4.3.], after consulting the Economic and Social Committee, adopts a multiannual research and technological development **framework programme**. By laying down the objectives, the priorities and the overall funds for Community action and their apportionment in broad terms, the framework-programme constitutes a "guide" for decisions on specific programmes to be taken during the five years covered. In addition, the framework programme has the desired characteristic of making visible, for scientific establishments, undertakings or Member States, the medium-term research possibilities afforded by the Community. By providing clear indications of the specific measures that the Community intends to undertake, it allows the various European research operators better to programme their efforts and Community research to take its proper place in the concert of European cooperation actions.

The framework programmes are implemented through **specific programmes** [see sections 18.3. and 18.4.] adopted by the Council, acting by a qualified majority, after consultation of the European Parliament and the Economic and Social Committee (Art. 166 TEC). The **sixth framework programme** (2002-2006) takes account of the priority activities ascribed to Community R & D by the EC Treaty[1].With a budget of EUR 16.27 billion, this programme is intended to make a reality of the European research area by strengthening its foundations, by integrating research capacities in Europe more effectively, and by structuring and simplifying their imple-

---

[1] Decision 1513/2002, OJ L 232, 29.08.2002 and Decision 786/2004, OJ L 138, 30.04.2004.

mentation. This objective is based on two main principles: firstly, introducing instruments with integrating effects (networks of excellence, integrated projects, EU participation in jointly-implemented national programmes) and structuring effects (measures to promote closer links between research and innovation, human resources and mobility, development of infrastructures); secondly, greater concentration on certain priority areas where Community action can bring about the greatest value added (in particular genomics, information society technologies, food safety, sustainable development and the role of citizens and governance in the European knowledge-based society). In addition, the new framework programme fully integrates the accession candidate countries into all its activities and makes significant international cooperation possible, particularly as a result of the opportunity for third-country researchers and bodies to have access to a substantial part of the activities. The European Community framework programme is implemented through three specific programmes concerning the structuring, integration and strengthening of the European research area, as well as direct actions by the Joint Research Centre.

The parallel Euratom framework programme, with a budget of EUR 1.23 billion, covers all activities relating to research, technological development, international cooperation, dissemination and utilisation of results, as well as training in the following areas: waste treatment and storage, controlled thermonuclear fusion, the nuclear activities of the Joint Research Centre; as well as other activities relating to nuclear safety and safeguards (radiation protection, new processes for harnessing nuclear energy). The Euratom framework programme is implemented through two specific programmes concerning nuclear energy and direct actions by the Joint Research Centre.

18.2.3. Direct and indirect research activities

Community research policy does not necessarily mean the "communitarisation" of all programmes or the joint financing of all research and technological development (R & D) activities in the Member States. In application of the subsidiarity principle [see section 3.2.], a distinction has to be made between various forms of research. With regard to **fundamental research and basic research**, which necessitate very large investment and highly specialised researchers and whose results can be expected only in the fairly distant future, it is in the interest of the EU countries to pool their efforts in **direct actions** financed entirely by the European Union and bringing together researchers of several nationalities.

For the **development of leading-edge technology** (nuclear, information, aeronautical and aerospace technologies, etc), on the other hand, **indirect actions** promoting the coordination of research carried out in the Member States is better suited to ensure industrial success, the transnational restructuring of undertakings, the opening up of public contracts, and even the grouping of purchases by public electricity, telecommunications and transport services. European R & D are therefore distinguished into direct actions and indirect actions.

Direct actions are research activities proper pursued by the Commission in the research establishments of the **Joint Research Centre (JRC)** and paid for entirely from the Community budget [see sections 3.4. and 18.2.4.]. The European dimension of its research is one of the fundamental strengths of the JRC. Its activities are characterised by a multidisciplinary approach based on the broad span of its capabilities. This multidisciplinarity is reflected in the diversity of subjects covered by its institutes and helps it meet Europe's scientific challenges as they rise. The JRC, however, must carry out its activities in close cooperation with the scientific community and enterprises in Europe.

The second form taken by Community R & D, **indirect research**, which absorbs more than 80% of the financial resources of Community R & D, is conducted in research centres, universities or undertakings, with financial assistance from the Commission and on conditions laid down by the rules governing participation in the various programmes, notably the participation of at least two partners from different Member States. Community financial assistance covers, as a general rule, 50% of the total cost of research work.

The Commission, with the assistance of the Advisory Committees on Management and Coordination (ACMC)[1], prepares the research programmes on indirect action which are adopted by the Council. The Commission then publishes in the Official Journal of the European Union calls for tenders for researchers from the Member States, specifying the research objectives written into the European programme. The tenders are appraised by the Commission and the Committees on the basis of criteria determined in advance and aimed at ensuring the best possible results. There are no national quotas for research assistance. The main criteria for selecting projects are, firstly, their scientific and technical quality and, secondly, their effects on growth and competitiveness. The rules for the participation of undertakings (companies, firms), research centres and universities from Member States and from associated candidate countries in the implementation of the sixth EC and Euratom framework programmes aim at flexible operating conditions, at a large degree of autonomy in project implementation and at a broad dissemination of research results[2].

18.2.4. The activities of the Joint Research Centre

The JRC is an autonomous Directorate General of the Commission and acts as **a science and technology and reference centre** for the Union. It

---

[1] Decision 84/338, OJ L 177, 04.07.1984.
[2] Regulations 2321/2002 and 2322/2002, OJ L 355, 30.12.2002.

has at its disposal a unique combination of facilities and skills which transcend national borders. Close to the policy formulation process while remaining independent of vested commercial or national interests, it serves the common interest of the Member States. The largest establishments of the JRC are situated at Ispra (Italy), while specialised institutes are located at Geel (Belgium), Petten (Netherlands), Karlsruhe (Germany) and Seville (Spain)[1].

The mission of JRC is to provide customer-driven scientific and technical support for the conception, development, implementation and monitoring of Community policies. In implementing its mission, the JRC endeavours to coordinate R & D activities carried out in the Member States. Its work depends on intensive networking with public and private institutions in the Member States through, for example, research networks, joint projects or staff exchanges. This is important because the JRC's mission is complementary to the indirect action part of the framework programme. While the indirect actions are the main mechanism for developing and testing new ideas, the JRC's role is to help apply them in the service of the policy-maker. The two selection criteria for JRC activities are: relevance to Community policies and subsidiarity [see section 3.2.] implying that JRC research must be in an area where Community involvement is appropriate. The JRC provides notably support where it has special or even unique expertise and facilities in the Community or where it is entrusted with activities necessary for the framing and implementation of Community policies and tasks incumbent on the Commission pursuant to the Treaty which require impartiality, notably standardisation activities [see section 6.2.3.]. Thus, JRC operates in areas where its unique pan-European identity provides an added value to Community R & D. The JRC carries out two research programmes: one for the European Community and the other for the European Atomic Energy Community (Euratom).

18.2.5. Coordination of research in the European Union

Several scientific bodies assist the Commission in its tasks of conceiving and managing the Community policy of research and technological development. The **Scientific and Technical Research Committee (CREST)** is an advisory body which assists the Commission and the Council in the R & D field by identifying strategic priorities, establishing mutual consistency between national and Community policies, and helping to formulate Community strategy with regard to international cooperation[2]. The European Group on Ethics in Science and New Technologies (EGE) advises the Commission on ethical subjects related to research and new technologies,

---

[1]   Decision 96/282, OJ L 107, 30.04.1996.
[2]   Resolution, OJ C 264, 11.10.1995, p. 4-5.

such as the legal protection of biotechnological inventions or the cloning of human beings[1].

In fact, in order to implement Article 165 of the EC Treaty, which requires the Community and the Member States to coordinate their research and technological development activities, the coordination of national and Community policies is based as far as possible on **European scientific networks,** notably CREST. One of the main purposes of this coordination is to help determine the priorities for future Community R & D activities bringing Community added-value in compliance with subsidiarity, and help improve the use made of the resources available in the European Union. These scientific networks help knit the scientific fabric of the European Union.

18.2.6. International scientific and technical cooperation

International cooperation represents an important dimension of the *sixth* Framework Programme. Under the specific programme "integrating and strengthening the European Research Area"[2] [see section 18.4.1.], international activities are carried out in the **two forms** of:

- participation of researchers, teams and institutions from third countries in projects within the different thematic priority fields, related to issues arising at world level and being subjects of international efforts;
- specific international cooperation activities with some groups of countries, as a support to Community external relations and development aid policies.

European research is also **coordinated on a broader level than that of the Fifteen.** In fact, the specific research programmes of the Community are open to the participation of EFTA countries (Switzerland, Norway, Iceland, Liechtenstein) and of the countries of Central and Eastern Europe and the new independent States of the former Soviet Union [see sections 25.1, 25.2 and 25.4.]. **Scientific and technical cooperation (Cost)** covers the countries of the EFTA and of Central and Eastern Europe. It is managed by a Committee of Senior Officials and by specialised committees. It takes the form of memoranda of understanding by the Cost States on the execution of Cost activities in the most varied fields, such as medicine, transport or materials. The Council concludes coordination agreements between the Community and the Cost countries relating to concerted actions forming part of the Community research programme[3].

In 1988 the EAEC (Euratom) concluded a quadripartite Agreement (Community, Soviet Union, United States and Japan) for the execution of a conceptual design project for an **International Thermonuclear Experi-**

---

[1] Directive 98/44, OJ L 213, 30.07.1998.

[2] Decision 2002/834, OJ L 294, 29.10.2002.

[3] See e.g., Decision 88/615, OJ L 344, 13.12.1988 and Decision 92/181, OJ L 85, 31.03.1992.

mental Reactor (ITER), with the four parties providing equal contributions on an equal footing. In 1992, the four parties - Russia having replaced the Soviet Union - signed a Cooperation Agreement for the detailed study of ITER which it is hoped will demonstrate the scientific and technological feasibility of using fusion energy for peaceful purposes[1]. ITER should lead to a demonstration electricity generating power plant (DEMO). Euratom participation in the ITER initiative requires the implementation of an accompanying programme adapted to it, including the operation of the JET machine and the continuation of research into fusion physics and technology[2] [see section 18.3.2.].

18.3. Euratom and nuclear research

Nuclear energy has the potential to provide Europe with a secure and sustainable electricity supply at a competitive price. Efforts to develop the safety and security of nuclear energy systems can strengthen the Community's industrial competitiveness, through exploiting the European technological advance and enhance the public acceptance of nuclear energy. Minimising radiation exposure from all sources, including medical exposures and natural radiation, may improve the quality of life and may help in addressing health and environmental problems. The Commission has specific Treaty obligations in nuclear energy and it has always relied on the JRC to provide a technical support that can keep up with technological developments and face new challenges. However, both the focus of the Euratom Treaty and the missions of the JRC have undergone radical changes since the early days, the most important being that Euratom research is now mainly concerned with nuclear fission safety, on the one hand, and with thermonuclear fusion, on the other.

18.3.1. Nuclear fission

The sixth framework programme of the European Atomic Energy Community (Euratom) for nuclear research and training activities (2002 to 2006) comprises the following headings[3]:

- controlled thermonuclear fusion [see section 18.3.2.];
- management of radioactive waste;
- radiation protection;
- other activities in the field of nuclear technologies and safety;
- nuclear activities of the Joint Research Centre.

---

[1] Agreement and Decision 92/439, OJ L 244, 26.08.1992 and Decision 94/267, OJ L 114, 05.05.1994.

[2] Decision 2002/837, OJ L 294, 29.10.2002.

[3] Decision 2002/668, OJ L232, 29.08.2002 and Decision 2004/444, OJ L 127, 29.04.2004.

Nuclear fission energy supplies 35% of electricity in the Community. It constitutes an element in combating climate change and reducing Europe's dependence on imported energy. Some of the power plants of the current generation will continue to be operated for at least 20 years. For these reasons, the main objectives of the nuclear fission programme of Euratom are to help ensure the safety of Europe's nuclear installations, to improve the competitiveness of Europe's industry, to ensure the protection of workers and the public and the safe and effective management and final disposal of radioactive waste and to explore more innovative concepts that are sustainable and have potential longer-term economic, safety, health and environmental benefits. A further objective is to contribute, through education and training, towards maintaining within the Union a high level of expertise and competence in nuclear fission.

18.3.2. Controlled thermonuclear fusion

Euratom is also actively engaged in the development of controlled thermonuclear fusion, which is safe for the environment. **Thermonuclear fusion** is a process which occurs on the surface of the Sun, releasing prodigious energy. In the Sun's core at temperatures of 10 to 15 million degrees Celsius, hydrogen is converted to helium providing enough energy to sustain life on Earth. Man has conceived of reproducing on earth, in a controlled fashion, what happens on the Sun. In fact, by heating gases such as deuterium (abundant in all forms of water) and lithium (plentiful in the Earth's crust) or tritium (manufactured from lithium) to a temperature of 100 million degrees Celsius, their electrons are completely separated from the atomic nuclei, atoms fuse and a fantastic release of energy within that "plasma" ensues. However, one must first obtain that extraordinary temperature, which is feasible, and the plasma must thereafter be confined within a magnetic space known as a "torus", which is more difficult. The objective of Community research is to produce and contain plasma, which has the properties required for the reactors of the future, in a magnetic field known as "tokamak". For reasons bound up with the complexity of fundamental knowledge in physics and the technological problems to be resolved, the developments needed for the possible application of fusion for energy production take the form of a process in several steps, each of which has an impact on the next one.

Thermonuclear fusion research is pursued since 1978 at Culham (United Kingdom) in an establishment which does not form part of the Joint Research Centre, but which is administered by a **joint undertaking**, the Joint European Torus (JET), within the meaning of Article 45 of the Euratom Treaty[1] [see section 19.2.3.] and whose Board of Governors is made up of representatives of the participating States and of the Commis-

---

[1] Decisions 78/471 and 78/472, OJ L 151, 07.06.1978 and Decision 98/585, OJ L 282, 20.10.1998.

sion, with a budget 80% of which is financed by the Community[1]. The fusion physics and technology activities seek to develop the capacity, especially within an association of JET and the European industry, to construct and operate an experimental reactor. The Community research effort is currently geared towards the launching of the "Next Step" project and the construction of the demonstration machine (DEMO) in the context of the ITER international cooperation project[2] [see section 18.2.6.].

18.4. Research activities of the European Community

  The **sixth framework programme** is carried out to further the objective set out in Article 163(1) of the Treaty, "of strengthening the scientific and technological bases of Community industry and encouraging it to become more competitive at international level". In order to achieve this more effectively, and in order to contribute to the creation of the European Research Area and to innovation, this programme is structured around the following **three headings**, under which the four activities as set out in Article 164 of the Treaty [see section 18.2.1.] are undertaken:

- focusing and integrating Community research,
- structuring the European Research Area,
- strengthening the foundations of the European Research Area.

  The activities under these three headings should contribute to the integration of research efforts and activities on a European scale as well as to the structuring of the various dimensions of the European Research Area. We examine the activities under the first two headings in more detail below. Activities under the third heading aim to strengthen the coordination and support the coherent development of R & D policies in Europe by providing financial support for measures such as the opening up of national programmes.

  Networks of excellence aim to strengthen and develop Community scientific and technological excellence by means of the integration, at European level, of research capacities at national and regional level. A network of excellence is implemented by a joint programme of activities involving some or, where appropriate, all of the research capacities and activities of the participants in the relevant area to attain a critical mass of expertise and European added value. Each network aims at advancing knowledge in a particular area by fostering cooperation between capacities of excellence in universities, research centres, enterprises, including SMEs, and science and technology organisations.

---

[1] Decision 96/305, OJ L 117, 14.05.1996.
[2] Decision 2002/669, OJ L 232, 29.08.2002.

Integrated projects are designed to give increased impetus to the Community's competitiveness or to address major societal needs by mobilising a critical mass of research and technological development resources and competences. Each integrated project should be assigned clearly defined scientific and technological objectives and should be directed at obtaining specific results applicable in terms of, for instance, products, processes or services. Under these objectives integrated projects may include more long-term or "risky" research.

In order to help the **development of SMEs in the knowledge society**, SMEs, including small and micro enterprises, are encouraged to participate in all areas and all instruments of the sixth framework programme, in particular in the context of the activities carried out in the priority thematic areas. Specific targeted projects and coordination actions are used as a "stairway of excellence" to facilitate the access of smaller research actors of scientific excellence, including SMEs to the activities of the framework programme.

18.4.1. Integrating Community research

The activities carried out under the **specific programme** on "integrating and strengthening the European research area" (2002-2006)[1] represent the major part of the research efforts deployed under the sixth framework-programme. They are intended to contribute to the general objective of the Treaty of strengthening the scientific and technical bases of Community industry and encouraging it to be more competitive at international level, while promoting all the research activities deemed necessary by other Chapters of the Treaty. The Joint Research Centre (JRC) provides independent customer-driven support for the formulation and implementation of Community policies, including the monitoring of implementation of such policies, within its areas of specific competence.

In order to bring about European added value by assembling a critical mass of resources, the specific programme focuses on seven, clearly defined **thematic priority areas** where Community research efforts should be integrated by pulling them together and making them more coherent, on a European scale. The seven priority thematic areas identified by this programme are:

1. life sciences, genomics and biotechnology for health;
2. information society technologies;
3. nanotechnologies and nanosciences, knowledge-based multifunctional materials, and new production processes and devices;
4. aeronautics and space;
5. food quality and safety;
6. sustainable development, global change and ecosystems;
7. citizens and governance in a knowledge-based society.

---

[1]   Decision 2002/834, OJ L 294, 29.10.2002.

18.4.2. Structuring the European research area

The activities carried out within the specific programme entitled "structuring the European research area" are applicable to all fields of research and technology[1]. They have specific vocations, distinct from, and complementary to, the activities implemented within other parts of the framework programme, notably those within the "Integrating and strengthening the European Research Area" programme in the priority thematic areas. This programme has four main headings: research and innovation; human resources and mobility; research infrastructures; and science and society.

The activities carried out under the heading **research and innovation** are intended to stimulate technological innovation, utilisation of research results, transfer of knowledge and technologies and the setting up of technology businesses in the Community and in all its regions. To this end, the actions of this heading focus on improving the knowledge, understanding and capabilities of the actors involved - research workers, industrialists, investors, public authorities at European, national and regional levels, and others - by encouraging more intensive and fruitful interactions between them, and by providing strategic information and services, as well developing new methodologies and tools, to assist them in their particular endeavours.

The activities carried out under the heading "**human resources and mobility**" are intended to: support the development of abundant world-class human resources in all the regions of the Community by promoting transnational mobility for training purposes, the development of expertise or the transfer of knowledge, in particular between different sectors; support the development of excellence; and help to make Europe more attractive to third country researchers. Promoting transnational mobility creates opportunities for significantly improving the quality of the training of researchers, promotes the circulation and exploitation of knowledge, and helps to establish world-class centres of excellence that are attractive throughout Europe.

The development of a European approach with regard to **research infrastructures**, and the carrying out of activities in this area at Union level, aim at: ensuring wider access to the infrastructures existing in the different Member States; increasing the complementarity of the facilities in place; and multiplying optimum construction choices in European terms.

Science/society issues need to a large extent to be addressed at European level on account of their strong European dimension. This is bound up with the fact that very often they arise on a European scale (as the example of food safety problems shows). The activities carried out under this heading are intended to encourage the development of harmonious relations between science and society and an informed dialogue between researchers, industrialists, political decision-makers and citizens.

---

[1] Decision 2002/835, OJ L 294, 29.10.2002.

18.5. *Appraisal and outlook*

Competitiveness and sustainability are the keys to the long-term future of the Union's economy. They entail the capacity of citizens, enterprises, regions, nations and the Community to generate and use the knowledge, science and technology of tomorrow, in high-quality goods, processes and services, and in new and more efficient organisational forms. By strengthening the innovative capacity of the European industrial system and by fostering the creation of businesses and services built on emerging technologies and new market opportunities, European R & D helps EU countries face the major challenges of society, in particular employment. In parallel, research into sustainable mobility and environmentally and consumer friendly processes, products and services may contribute to improving quality of life and working conditions.

The promotion of sustainable development in Europe is not possible unless economic objectives relating to technological development, competitiveness and growth are reconciled with **societal goals** such as quality of life, employment, security, health and a high quality environment. Moreover, improving the quality of life of European citizens and disconnecting economic growth from environmental degradation contributes to European competitiveness and employment.

The individual and collective expertise of the Community's researchers is a considerable asset. However, scientific research takes place in **a strongly competitive worldwide environment** and compared with its main competitors, the Community has a relative shortage of researchers, a high fragmentation and duplication of research effort and a certain isolation of research teams, particularly in the peripheral and less-favoured regions of the Community.

The research and technological development powers vested in the Community, particularly since the 1990s, have provided a basis for raising the **competitiveness of European undertakings**, notably small and medium enterprises. The participation of SMEs in all R & D activities is stimulated and encouraged by the Community framework-programme. Their important potential to contribute to the innovation process is fully recognised. However, by comparison with performance elsewhere, the relative weakness of private-sector investment in R & D within the Union is striking. More effort is needed to strengthen the interactions between public research bodies and industry.

Europe has established **a leading R & D role in many areas**, notably nuclear safety, thermonuclear fusion, telecommunications' technologies and biochemistry. The Joint Research Centre, in particular, plays a principal role in various subjects such as climate change, bovine spongiform encephalopathy, genetically-modified organisms, safety of chemicals, nuclear forensics and cybersecurity. This role must be sustained and remain at the cutting-edge in order to prepare European industry for the challenges of the 21st century.

Bibliography on research policy

- BOGDANDY Armin von, WESTPHAL Dietrich. "The legal framework for an autonomous European Research Council", *European Law Review*, v. 29, n. 6, December 2004, p. 788-807.
- BOUCHER Stephen, HOBBS Benjamin (eds.). *Europe and its think tanks, a promise to be fulfilled: An analysis of think tanks specialised in European policy issues in the enlarged European Union*. Paris: Groupement d'études et de recherches "Notre Europe", 2004.
- CHRISTOFOL Hervé, RICHIR Simon, SAMIER Henry. *L'innovation à l'ère des réseaux*. Paris: Hermes, 2004.
- ENGWALL Lars (et al.). *CEMP: the creation of European management practice: final report*. Luxembourg: EUR-OP*, 2004.
- EUROPEAN COMMISSION. *Researchers in the European research area: one profession, multiple careers*. Luxembourg: EUR-OP*, 2003.

  - *Fusion research: An Energy Option for Europe's Future*. Luxembourg: EUR-OP*, 2004.

  - *Clean and competitive: EU research: environmental technologies*. Luxembourg: EUR-OP*, 2004.

  - *Scenarios for the future of European research and innovation policy*. Luxembourg: EUR-OP*, 2004.

- LAZONICK William, O'SULLIVAN Mary (eds.). *Corporate governance, innovation and economic performanc in the EU: CGEP: final report*. Luxembourg: EUR-OP*, 2004.
- SCHUBERT Uwe, SEDLACEK Sabine. *Towards an integration of environmental and environment-oriented technology policy: stimulus and response in environment-related innovation networks (ENVINNO): final report*. Luxembourg: EUR-OP*, 2004.

The publications of the Office for Official Publications of the European Communities (EUR-OP) exist generally in all official languages of the EU.

DISCUSSION TOPICS

1. Does the common research policy weaken or strengthen national research efforts?
2. What are the main types of Community RTD?
3. What is the role of the Common Research Centre?
4. Outline the activities of Euratom's nuclear research.
5. Outline the objectives of the specific research programmes of the European Community.

Chapter 19

ENERGY POLICY

Diagram of the chapter

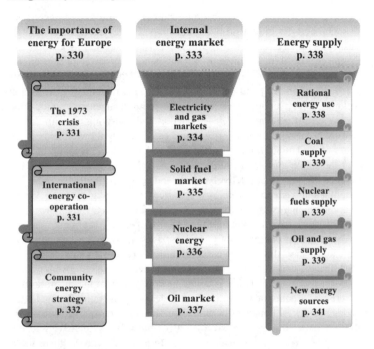

The importance of energy for Europe p. 330	Internal energy market p. 333	Energy supply p. 338
The 1973 crisis p. 331	Electricity and gas markets p. 334	Rational energy use p. 338
International energy co-operation p. 331	Solid fuel market p. 335	Coal supply p. 339
Community energy strategy p. 332	Nuclear energy p. 336	Nuclear fuels supply p. 339
	Oil market p. 337	Oil and gas supply p. 339
		New energy sources p. 341

Successive oil shocks, their impact on the economic and monetary system at international and EEC level and Community efforts to reduce its dependence on imported oil are the closely interrelated problems which topped the economic agenda in the1970s. The Community was ill prepared to cope with these problems, for when the founding Treaties were signed in the 1950s, it was almost self-sufficient in energy and hoped that a new source - atomic energy - would soon take over from coal, the traditional source. Time proved otherwise and it was oil which made a spectacular entry onto the Community market in the1960s.

In that **two Community Treaties dealt** uniquely with the energy of the past (coal - ECSC) and the perceived one of the future (nuclear - Euratom), the Commission did not have the legal instruments at its disposal to assume responsibilities in the energy sector (oil - EEC) which had since become the dominant player. The Community perceived the risks of its dependence from imported oil during the October 1973 energy crisis. From 1974 on-

wards, Community objectives began to be defined and steps taken to reduce dependence on imported crude oil and petroleum products. It was
from this point that a common energy policy began to take shape at a
snail's pace.

19.1. The importance of energy for Europe

Energy policy is important because **energy is at the core of economic
and social activity** in industrialised countries. Energy costs affect not only
industries with large energy consumption but also industry as a whole and
even the cost of living of citizens, notably because of the impact of energy
prices on transport cost and heating. While respecting the subsidiarity principle [see section 3.2.] and the environmental requirements for sustainable
development [see sections 16.2. and 16.3.4.], European energy policy aims,
therefore, at influencing energy production and consumption with the objective of securing economic growth and safeguarding the wellbeing of the
citizens of the Union. It must, on the one hand, ensure the smooth functioning of the single market in energy products and services and, on the other,
guarantee the supply of relatively cheap and secure (from the strategic and
environmental viewpoints) energy resources to the States of the Union.
The common energy policy thus revolves around two axes: the functioning
of the internal energy market and the security of energy supplies.

The common energy policy was not forgotten by the "founding fathers", since they **devoted two Community Treaties to this sector**: the
ECSC Treaty, which deals with coal and Euratom, which covers nuclear
energy [see section 2.1.]. They failed, however, to give the institutions of
the European Economic Community any clear responsibility for the hydrocarbons sector. Although with hindsight this may be questioned, in the
1950s coal was in abundant supply, was relatively inexpensive and met
65% of the energy requirements of the six founding countries. It was therefore seen as the energy, which would fuel the creation of the common market. Furthermore, impressed by the recent demonstration at Hiroshima of
the force of atomic energy, experts were predicting a bright future for its
peaceful use.

No clear need for a common or even for national oil policies was perceived in **the years when oil was cheap and supply certain**, which was
the case throughout the post-war years up to the early 1970s. This golden
era was anchored in major oil discoveries by Western oil companies in the
Middle East and Africa and in the legal system governing the exploitation
of oil reserves. The central principle of this system was the granting of a
prospecting and working monopoly over a given area by the producer
country to one or several foreign companies (licence). The activity spec-
trum of these companies covered all of the petroleum industry activities
(prospecting, production, transport, refining, storage and distribution) and
they enjoyed a strong position enabling them, in the vast majority of ex-

porting countries and in relation to most of the importing countries, to regulate petroleum output and marketing terms.

19.1.1. The 1973 crisis

The first occasion for a showdown between producer countries on the one hand and consumer countries and their oil companies on the other came with **the Kippur war between Israel and the Arab countries** from October 6 to 16, 1973. During this war and in the following months, the Arab countries successfully wielded the weapon represented by their oil resources. They notably placed an embargo, for several months, on exports to countries which were branded "enemies of the Arab cause" - including practically all the countries of Western Europe - while reducing their overall oil output level. They decided to overturn the principle of price setting for crude oil through agreements with the oil companies and hiked up prices on a unilateral basis. Finally, they stepped up their claims to holdings in the companies producing crude oil. Under the combined impact of these measures, oil prices quadrupled in just a few months and uncertainty clouded the quantity and price situation which the world's biggest importer, the European Community, would have to face. A common trade policy for oil could have considerably boosted the negotiating leverage of the EEC Member States, if only it had existed; but even after the bitter lesson of their weakness in the face of a united front of producing countries, the European States were **not ready to shed a bit of their sovereignty** in the oil sector in order to collectively negotiate the terms of their supply.

19.1.2. International energy cooperation

The **European Energy Charter** attempts to put some order in energy supply and demand conditions in Europe. It lays down the principles, the objectives and ways of achieving pan-European cooperation in the field of energy. Signed in the Hague on December 17, 1991 by almost all European countries as well as by the Community, Canada, the United States, and Japan, the Charter is in fact a code of good practice. Its interest is to give the first tangible demonstration of a consensus based upon solidarity and complementarity, in particular between the countries of Western Europe - with their know-how and advanced technologies - and those of Central and Eastern Europe, including the countries of the former Soviet Union, which have relatively abundant energy resources.

The **Charter pursues the following operational objectives**: expansion of trade, especially through free market operation, free access to resources and the development of infrastructure; cooperation and coordination of energy policies; and the optimal use of energy and protection of the environment. These objectives should be attained through the implementation of joint measures by the signatory countries in six specific priority fields: access to resources; use of resources; investment arrangements; liberalisation of trade; harmonisation of technical specifications and safety rules; research and technological development and innovation.

The implementation of the Charter is provided by the **European Energy Charter Treaty**, signed in Lisbon on 17 December 1994[1]. This Treaty is designed to develop new relations between the main European countries, most of the independent States of the former Soviet Union and Central and Eastern Europe, Canada, the United States and Japan concerning the transit of energy products between east and west, trade, investment and energy cooperation. The European Commission assists the Secretariat of the Conference, which is established in Brussels. The practical implication of the Energy Charter is the diversification of the supplies of European Union countries in oil and natural gas and, hence, their decreasing dependence from Middle Eastern sources.

19.1.3. Community energy strategy

Following the ideas of the Commission, a multiannual programme for actions in the field of energy, called "**Intelligent Energy - Europe**" (2003-2006), supports sustainable development in the energy context, making a balanced contribution to the achievement of the following general objectives: security of energy supply, competitiveness, and environmental protection[2]. Four specific areas are covered: rational use of energy and demand management, new and renewable energy sources, the energy aspects of transport, and international promotion in the field of renewable energy sources and energy efficiency. Six types of actions are proposed for each area: implementation of strategy, creation of financial and market structures and instruments, promotion of systems and equipment to facilitate the transition between demonstration and commercialisation, development of information and education structures, and the monitoring and evaluation of the impact of the actions.

The multiannual programme covers the following four specific areas:

(a) "**SAVE**", which concerns the improvement of energy efficiency and the rational use of energy, in particular in the building and industry sectors, including the preparation of legislative measures and their application;

(b) "**ALTENER**", which concerns the promotion of new and renewable energy sources for centralised and decentralised production of electricity and heat and their integration into the local environment and the energy systems, including the preparation of legislative measures and their application;

(c) "**STEER**", which concerns support for initiatives relating to all energy aspects of transport, the diversification of fuels, such as through new

---

[1] OJ L 380, 31.12.1994, OJ L Council Decision 98/537, OJ L 252, 12.09.1998 and Council Decision 2001/595, OJ L 209, 02.08.2001.

[2] Decision 1230/2003, OJ L 176, 15.07.2003 and Decision 787/2004, OJ L 138, 30.04.2004.

developing and renewable energy sources, and the promotion of renewable fuels and energy efficiency in transport, including the preparation of legislative measures and their application;

(d) **"COOPENER"**, which concerns support for initiatives relating to the promotion of renewable energy sources and energy efficiency in the developing countries, in particular in the framework of the Community cooperation with developing countries in Africa, Asia, Latin America and the Pacific.

19.2. Internal energy market

The **first wing of the common energy policy** aims to establish a genuine internal market for the products and services of the energy sector. Through the removal of barriers, whether of public or private origin, and the establishment of common rules, the opening up of energy markets should ensure the availability of energy on the most economic conditions for the end-user whether it be high energy consuming industries or just private individuals. The energy sector, a source of high value contracts, finds itself in the front-line of general public procurement policy and should benefit from the openness it provides [see section 6.3.]. Fiscal alignment by the convergence of the real rates of excise taxes, pursued by taxation policy, is crucially important for the completion of the internal market for oil products [see section 14.2.3.]. Last but not least, the introduction of competition in those sectors in which public monopolies persist could play a prime role in the integration of the markets and in the competitiveness of the EU economy [see section 15.5.4.].

The establishment of a real internal market for energy also depends on the development of **energy trans-European networks**, which should "irrigate" the whole territory of the European Union with cheap, diversified - from the supply point of view - and environment-friendly energy [see section 6.8.]. This development is particularly important for the less favoured regions, which previously had no access to the big interconnected networks for gas and electricity, this being a cause but also a consequence of their underdevelopment [see section 12.1.1.]. In the meantime, the Regulation on notifying the Commission of investment projects of interest to the Community in the petroleum, natural gas and electricity sectors aims at a certain coordination of trans-European energy investments[1].

In general, the full **application of Community internal market law** - and in particular of provisions relating to the free movement of goods and services, to monopolies, to undertakings (firms, businesses) and to State aids - is the main path to a better integrated energy market. The integration of this market is fundamental for the competitivity of the economy of the EU and for the wellbeing of its citizens. But the energy sector does not

---

[1] Regulation 1056/72, OJ L 120, 25.05.1972 and Regulation 736/96, OJ L 102, 25.04.1996.

fully benefit from this integration because the Member States still use the security of supply and the diversity of their energy situation as excuse for the preservation of their national monopolies and of their different regulatory frameworks.

19.2.1. Electricity and gas markets

The prime objective in the field of the internal energy market is to **liberalise and integrate the electricity and natural gas markets**. The most important challenge here is to apply the competition rules of the Treaty to the monopolies for transmission and distribution of gas and electricity, even though these are entrusted with the operation of services of general economic interest [see sections 6.6.4. and 15.5.4.]. Another issue is the reconciliation of the objectives of the prevention of trade barriers and of energy efficiency by way of the adoption of European standards established by the European Standardisation Bodies (CEN/CENELEC) [see section 6.2.3.]. A final problem is in the monitoring of the markets and the co-operation on interconnected systems between national regulatory authorities in both the gas and electricity sectors.

In the early 1990s, some concrete steps were taken in the direction of the integration of the electricity and gas markets. Thus, a Directive relating to the **transit of electricity** through the major European networks, aims at contributing to better integration of the internal market in electricity, through removing the obstacles to electricity trade between major networks[1]. Similarly, a Directive on the **transit of natural gas** through major networks aims at facilitating trade in natural gas[2]. Contracts on the transit of electricity and natural gas between major networks are negotiated between the entities with responsibility for these networks and the relevant bodies in the Member States. Transit conditions must be non-discriminatory and impartial as regards all the parties involved, must not contain unfair clauses or unjustified restrictions and must not place in danger either supply security or the quality of the service provided. Should a disagreement arise, parties concerned by transit contracts have the right to take their case to a conciliation body set up and presided by the Commission. A Directive, on the **transparency of gas and electricity prices** charged to industrial end-users, makes it compulsory for gas and electricity distribution concerns to communicate price data twice a year covering all the main categories of gas and electricity consumers[3].

Serious steps towards the **liberalisation of the electricity and gas sectors** were taken in the late 1990s. Community Directives, revised in 2003, set up common rules for the internal market in electricity[4] and gas[5]. They

---

[1] Directive 90/547, OJ L 313, 13.11.1990 and Directive 98/75, OJ L 276, 13.10.1998.
[2] Directive 91/296, OJ L 147, 12.06.1991 and Directive L233, 30.09.1995.
[3] Directive 90/237, OJ L 185, 17.07.1990 and Directive 93/87, OJ L 277, 10.11.1993.
[4] Directive 2003/54, OJ L 176, 15.07.2003.
[5] Directive 2003/55, OJ L 176, 15.07.2003.

are based on a balanced approach concerning access to the systems, public service obligations and competition rules and on the broad application of the subsidiarity principle [see section 3.2.], in order to take account of the different national electricity and gas systems, thus facilitating their incorporation into national law. The Directives lay down the rules relating to the organisation and functioning of the electricity and gas sectors, access to the market, the criteria and procedures applicable to calls for tenders and the granting of authorisations and the operation of systems. They also set up a European Regulators Group for Electricity and Gas, but they give the regulatory authorities in the Member States, an essential role in the smooth operation of the internal market.

A Regulation set up fair rules for **cross-border exchanges in electricity**, thus enhancing competition within the internal electricity market, taking into account the specificities of national and regional markets[1]. To this end, it established a compensation mechanism for cross border flows of electricity and set up harmonised principles on cross-border transmission charges and the allocation of available capacities of interconnections between national transmission systems.

19.2.2. Solid fuel market

The single market in the coal sector was **regulated, until July 2002, by the European Coal and Steel Community (ECSC) Treaty** [see section 2.1.]. Thanks to this Treaty, import and export taxes, taxes having equivalent effect, and quantitative restrictions on product movement were abolished. The Paris Treaty laid down rules for agreements, company concentrations and dominant positions, and prohibited unfair competitive practices and discriminatory practices, i.e. the application by a seller of dissimilar conditions to comparable transactions and especially on the grounds of the nationality of the buyer. It thus succeeded to ensure that users have equal access to sources of production and to promote the development of international trade. The "acquis communautaire" in the coal sector is now guaranteed by the EC Treaty.

The ECSC has enabled Europe to maintain a leading position in the field of mining technology and clean coal combustion. Considerable spin off effects have also been seen in other industries. Although the ECSC Treaty succeeded in creating a common coal market, it was **not able to prevent coal from being swept aside by oil**, which is a more flexible, easier to handle and a less expensive product. Preservation of coal's supremacy would have required measures much more drastic and expensive, in the form of a coal policy modelled on the Common Agricultural Policy [see sections 21.1 and 21.4.]. Europe of the1960's, awash with oil supply, was not prepared to pay the price of its energy independence. Thus, investment in the coal industry of the EU continued to fall during the 1990s in the face

---

[1] Regulation 1228/2003, OJ L 176, 15.07.2003.

of international competition and as a result of the gradual shift in Member States' domestic policies.

19.2.3. Nuclear energy market

The economic factors pertaining to the nuclear energy market have also not evolved in the manner predicted at the time of signature of the Euratom Treaty [see section 2.1.]. In the 1950's, it was thought that the arrival on the industrial scene of nuclear energy was just around the corner and the drop in energy prices, which caused this event to be postponed, could not have been foreseen. Nuclear energy in fact only attained economic competitiveness after the 1973 crisis and the momentous increase of oil prices. In the period prior to this, the **absence of a genuine nuclear energy market** forced each Member State to create an artificial one through vast government research programmes targeted more at the acquisition of basic knowledge than at the encouragement of industrial projects. This pushed the Member States off the straight and narrow path defined by the EAEC (Euratom) Treaty onto parallel technological roads, such as uranium enrichment systems, and sparked off a serious crisis in Euratom between 1965 and 1972.

Nevertheless, the Euratom Treaty provides for a well-functioning **common nuclear energy market**, characterised by: the abolition of customs duties, charges having equivalent effect and all quantitative restrictions on imports and exports of natural and enriched uranium and other nuclear materials (Art. 93 EAEC); the free movement and free establishment of individuals and companies in the common nuclear energy market (Art. 96 and 97 EAEC); the free movement of capital for the financing of nuclear activities (Art. 99 and 100 EAEC); the free determination of prices as a result of balancing supply and demand within the Supply Agency (Art. 67 EAEC) and the prohibition of discriminatory pricing practices designed to secure a privileged position for certain users (Art. 68 EAEC). Economic operators have to inform the Commission of major investment projects prior to their implementation (Art. 41 EAEC) and thus the Commission can inform governments and economic operators in the Member States of the aims and prospects for nuclear energy production in the Community (Art. 40 EAEC).

One interesting feature of the Euratom Treaty is that it offers special status and certain advantages to **joint undertakings**, which are of primordial importance to the development of the Community's nuclear industry (Art. 45 EAEC). The Council, acting unanimously on a Commission proposal, can grant each joint undertaking all or some of the advantages listed in Annex III to the Euratom Treaty, such as recognition that public interest status applies to the acquisition of immovable property required for the establishment of the joint undertakings or the exemption from all duties and charges when a venture is established (Art. 48 EAEC). In 1978, this status was granted to an undertaking of vital importance for the growth of the

Community nuclear industry, namely the joint venture which, as seen in the previous chapter, builds the **Joint European Torus (JET)**, a thermo-nuclear fusion prototype[1] [see section 18.3.2.].

Safety, a major feature of the common nuclear energy market, is perhaps the most important joint achievement in this field. This achievement is, however, of fundamental importance, because it determines the acceptance of the nuclear energy by the public. **Nuclear safety** is moreover approached from various different angles. Chapter VII of the Euratom Treaty provides for "safeguards". The Commission must be informed of the basic technical specifications of any nuclear plant. The Commission also has to approve procedures for the chemical processing of irradiated materials (Art. 78 EAEC). It must check that all ores, source materials and special fissile materials are not diverted from their intended uses as declared by the users (Art. 77 EAEC) and that the latter respect international safeguards and non-proliferation arrangements laid down by an Euratom Regulation[2]. The Commission can send inspectors to the Member States who must be given access at any time to all premises, all information and all individuals to the extent necessary to check the ores, source materials and special fissile materials used by the 750 or so nuclear installations, including some 130 reactors, in the Community (Art. 81 EAEC). The **Euratom Safeguards Office** has the task of ensuring that nuclear material is not diverted from its intended use within the European Union and that the Community's safeguards obligations under agreements with third countries or international organisations are complied with. In fact, during the early 1990's the Euratom Safeguards Office was called several times to take action in relation to cases of trafficking in nuclear materials from Eastern Europe, but in subsequent evaluations (in 1999 and 2000), the Safeguards Office did not find any indication that nuclear material had been diverted from its intended peaceful use[3].

19.2.4. Oil market

Although it is less developed than the nuclear market, a **single market in petroleum products exists** in many respects. On the basis of the EEC (now the EC) Treaty governing the oil market, all quantitative restrictions to trade between Member States and all measures having equivalent effect have been abolished. Tariff obstacles to trade in petroleum products were phased out in July 1968. On the external market, the Common Customs Tariff set a zero rate for oil and very low rates for refined products. The latter were further reduced in the framework of the General Agreement on Tariffs and Trade [see section 23.4.]. All the freedoms written into the

---

[1] Decision 78/471, OJ L 151, 07.06.1978 and Decision 91/677, OJ L 375, 31.12.1991.

[2] Regulation 3227/76, OJ L 363, 31.12.1976 and Regulation 2130/93, OJ L 191, 31.07.1993.

[3] COM (2001) 436.

Treaty of Rome, such as freedom of establishment and the freedom to provide services, are applicable in the oil sector [see chapter 6].

Even if the **common oil market is not yet perfect**, petroleum products can move freely from Member State to Member State. The big oil companies have been able to build refineries at certain nerve centres in the common market to supply refined products to networks covering neighbouring regions in two or more Member States. This means that refinery production and distribution activities can be rationalised to meet supply in surrounding regions without regard to national borders. Oil and gas pipelines consequently start their journey from the major ports of the Mediterranean and the North Sea, cut across one or several Member States and supply crude oil to the refineries of different oil companies situated in another Member State. Before the creation of the common market, it would have been unthinkable for a European state to entrust the supply of a product as vital as oil to the good will of one or several neighbouring countries. The European Community has rendered self-evident certain situations, which would have been inconceivable in the protectionist post-war period [see section 1.1.2.].

19.3. Energy supply

Security of energy supply, the second wing of the common energy policy, is defined as the ability to ensure the continued satisfaction of essential energy needs by means of, on the one hand, sufficient internal resources exploited under acceptable economic conditions and, on the other, of accessible, stable and diversified external sources. With this definition, most European countries had a more secure energy supply in the 1950s than they had in the 1970s or even in the 1990s, despite their efforts in those three decades. Indeed, at the beginning of the 1950s, the Community's energy economy revolved around indigenous resources, chiefly coal. In 1955, coal met 64% of gross internal energy consumption in the then Community of Six; but little by little, **demand switched from primary energy to processed energy**, chiefly electricity and petroleum products. Due to strong growth in demand for light petroleum products (chiefly petrol), heavy fuels became residual products, which refiners wanted to get rid of at any price, often below that of crude oil. Unfortunately for coal, its main competitors were these heavy, industrial use fuels. In that oil was almost exclusively imported from third countries, the consequences on the Community's energy independence were plain to see. Energy independence was sacrificed on the altar of rapid industrial growth, stimulated by low energy prices.

19.3.1. Energy objectives and rational energy use

Thanks in part to various measures taken by the Member States at the prompting of Community institutions and in part to the reduction of energy demand and the increase of internal production, notably in the North Sea, the EU, in 2000, imported about half of its total energy needs compared with two-thirds twenty five years earlier. However, despite these improvements, the problems have not gone away. The **European Union still has to cope with a massive oil bill**, vast amounts of investment, and the implications for environmental pollution and energy dependence that cannot be reduced in any significant manner in the medium term.

This is why, the Commission is proposing more drastic measures, notably **a tax based on the consumption of carbon dioxide**[1]. Such a tax would increase the price of energy, except for renewable sources, and help to save energy. It would thus set in motion dynamic changes, which would have beneficial consequences for the environment and a major impact on the Union's energy sector. This proposal is still under discussion within the Council, because it presents obvious difficulties, particularly due to its effects on the competitiveness of European industries compared to that of their competitors in the world. Other energy consuming countries should be persuaded to follow the Community's policies in this area, a particularly difficult task given the energy consumption habits of some countries.

19.3.2. Coal supply

Coal is the most abundant non-renewable energy source available and will continue to play a very important role as a regulator of the Union's energy market, particularly in the generation of energy. In any case, **the European Union does not face a problem in coal supply**, both as far as indigenous resources are concerned, which are abundant, and imports from several third countries, which are more competitive. After the expiration of the ECSC Treaty in July 2002, the common commercial policy of the EC covers the coal products [see chapter 23]. Any imported coal released for free movement in a Member State circulates freely in all the Community. However, there is Community surveillance of imports of hard coal originating in third countries[2]. The monitoring system entails the provision by the Member States of information concerning their imports of hard coal, including the prices charged and the breakdown of hard coal imports between electricity production and use in the Community steel industry.

19.3.3. Supply of nuclear fuels

Nuclear energy makes a significant contribution to the policy of diversifying energy supply and reducing overall emissions of CO_2. Supply of nuclear fuels is **a matter dealt with in some depth in the Euratom Treaty** [see section 2.1.]. Article 52 of this Treaty stipulates that supply of ores, source materials and special fissile materials is accomplished with re-

---

[1] COM (92)226, 27.05.1992.
[2] Regulation 405/2003, OJ L 62, 06.03.2003.

spect of the principle of equal access to resources and through a common supply policy. For this purpose, all practices that seek to provide certain users with a privileged position are forbidden. The Treaty set up a **Supply Agency,** the organisation of which is provided for in Articles 53 and 54 (EAEC). The Agency, which has legal status and is financially independent, is governed by Statutes adopted by the Council on the basis of a Commission proposal. The Euratom Supply Agency is under the control of the Commission, which issues it with policy guidelines, has a right of veto on its decisions and appoints its Director General[1]. In contrast with the coal and oil sectors, the nuclear sector is endowed with a strong common supply policy, exercised by the Agency, under the control of the Commission.

Article 52 (EAEC) grants the Agency two fundamental rights: (a) an option right on ores, source material and special fissile materials produced in the Member States and (b) the exclusive right to conclude contracts for the supply of ores, source materials and special fissile materials originating inside or outside the Community. The Agency's main role is to act as an **intermediary between producers and users.** Under Article 60 (EAEC), possible users periodically inform the Agency of their supply needs, specifying quantities, nature, places of origin, uses, price terms and so on, which would form the clauses of a contract which they would like to conclude. Producers inform the Agency of the supplies that they can put on the market, with all their specifications and notably the duration of the contracts. The Agency informs all potential users of supplies and of the demand volume brought to its attention, and invites them to order. Once it has all the orders, it makes known the terms at which they can be satisfied. In fact, the option right of the Agency, described in Article 57 (EAEC), gives it a *"de jure"* **monopoly** on the trade of ores, raw materials and special fissile materials intended for peaceful nuclear use in the Community.

19.3.4. Oil and natural gas supply

Contrary to the EAEC Treaty's concern for the supply of nuclear fuels, the **EEC Treaty did not show any particular interest** for the supply of oil and natural gas. The EEC Treaty did not even give the Community institutions the possibility of collecting and publishing information of vital importance for the common oil market, such as those covering investments, production or imports, as is done by the ECSC and Euratom Treaties for their respective areas. In light of the growing importance of oil in the1960s, this vacuum was partly filled by the Council.

The most important measure is the **strategic storage of petroleum products**. A Council Directive obliges the Member States to maintain a minimum stock level of 90 days' consumption for crude oil and/or petroleum products, as a buffer against the effects of accidental or deliberate interruption in supplies and against the economic and political leverage en-

---

[1]   OJ 32 11.05.1960, p. 777-779 and OJ L 193, 25.07.1975, p. 37-38.

joyed by suppliers[1]. Another measure is a Council Decision setting a Community target for the reduction of primary energy consumption in the event of supply difficulties of crude oil and petroleum products in order to ensure that these difficulties are spread fairly among all consumers[2]. A directive establishes measures to safeguard an adequate level of **security of gas supply**[3]. While contributing to the smooth functioning of the internal gas market, it provides for a common framework within which Member States should define security of supply policies compatible with the requirements of the competitive internal gas market.

In the context of the completion of the internal market, a Directive on the conditions for granting and using **authorisations for oil and gas prospecting, exploration and extraction** is designed to ensure non-discriminatory access to and pursuit of these activities by Community companies in non-member countries under conditions which encourage greater competition in this sector[4]. However, Member States have sovereign rights over oil and gas resources on their territories. They therefore retain the right to determine the areas within their territory to be made available for oil and gas prospecting, exploration and production.

19.3.5. New technologies and new energy sources

Fortunately for the Union, new energy technologies and new energy sources offer **an alternative route to supply security**. Moreover, **new and renewable energies** (solar, wind, hydroelectric, geothermal, biomass) can generate economic activity, thereby creating added value and employment in Europe. Furthermore, they both improve the quality of the environment and standards of living, and are particularly important for the less developed regions of the EU, which have considerable potential for the development of renewable energy resources. For these reasons, a directive commits the Member States to meeting national targets for their future consumption of **electricity from renewable energy sources** consistent with the indicative overall target of 12% of gross inland energy consumption in 2010[5]. In this context, a directive establishes a framework for the promotion and development of cogeneration, that is, the simultaneous generation in one process of heat and electrical and/mechanical power, as a means of improving security of energy supply[6].

The **ALTENER programme**, which is part of the multiannual programme for action in the field of energy (2003 - 2006)[7] [see section 19.1.3.], aims at the promotion of new and renewable energy sources for

---

[1] Directive 98/93, OJ L 358, 31.12.1998.
[2] Decision 77/706, OJ L 292, 16.11.1977.
[3] Directive 2004/67, OJ L 127, 29.04.2004.
[4] Directive 94/22, OJ L 164, 30.06.1994.
[5] Directive 2001/77, OJ L 283, 27.10.2001.
[6] Directive 2004/8, OJ L 52, 21.02.2004.
[7] Decision 1230/2003, OJ L 176, 15.07.2003.

centralised and decentralised production of electricity and heat and their integration into the local environment and the energy systems. It focuses among other things on legislation and standardisation to accelerate the maturity of the market for renewable energies such as hydroelectric power, biofuels (deriving from agricultural and forestry products, residues and waste) and biomass (from cereals, oil seeds, pulses and beets). The objectives of this programme, are to increase the share of environment-friendly renewable energies in the final demand and to achieve a significant reduction in carbon dioxide (CO_2) emissions. To this end, the programme aims at creating the right conditions, particularly in legal, socioeconomic and administrative terms, for the implementation of a Community action plan for renewable sources of energy, and to encourage private and public investment in the production and use of energy from renewable sources.

Under the thematic priority of "sustainable development, global change and ecosystems" [see section 18.4.1.], the **common research policy** tries to encourage the deployment of technologies and to help promote changes in energy demand patterns and consumption behaviour by improving energy efficiency and integrating renewable energy into the energy system[1]. The research effort is focused notably on: energy savings and energy efficiency, including those to be achieved through the use of renewable raw materials; the efficiency of combined production of electricity, heating and cooling services, by using new technologies; and alternative motor fuels, such biofuels, natural gas and hydrogen.

19.4. Appraisal and outlook

There is a general impression that a common energy policy is non-existent or, at best, ineffective. This impression arises chiefly from **confusion between energy policy and oil supply policy**. The latter is clearly of vital importance and is still lacking. But it is only a part of energy policy. It cannot be denied that the common coal, oil and nuclear energy markets have been largely achieved thanks to Community policy. But their existence tends to be taken for granted and similarly significant achievements are expected in the area of supply, notably oil supply. The fact that the EEC Treaty and now the EC Treaty did not provide for such a policy is often forgotten. The silence of the Treaty means, however, that the Member States do not want to commit themselves in a common policy for oil and gas supply.

Another fact often overlooked is that in the1960s, all the Member States chose to boost industrial growth through low energy prices rather than promoting indigenous energy production by high prices. This preference for the industrial rather than energy sector culminated, at Community level, in a system diametrically opposed to the one existing for agriculture

---

[1]   Decision 2002/834, OJ L 294, 29.10.2002.

[see section 21.2.]. It was a political decision, the advantages of which cannot be denied, even with hindsight of the post-1973 events. In any case, the Member States, due to their different energy situations and interests, have proven unable to conduct a common supply policy, which would have increased their negotiation power towards their main oil suppliers.

Thanks to the increase of internal production - notably in the North Sea - and to the diversification of fuels and suppliers, the Union is now in a much more comfortable situation than the one the Community has experienced in the mid-1970s. However, despite these improvements, the problems have not gone away. Since international political and economic developments are liable at any time to cause considerable increases in the price of oil and of products indexed to it, **the EU is always at risk** as regards competitiveness, employment and growth. This is why, a policy framework is needed in which Member States would be working towards agreed common objectives, notably balance and diversification in relation to the different sources of supply (by products and by geographical zones), the development of renewable sources and clean technologies, assisted by Community financial and fiscal measures and closely coordinated with other common policies, particularly the environment, transport and enterprise policies. Concerning hydrocarbon supply, in particular, the EU should ideally develop a common policy similar, as far as possible, to the one for the supply of nuclear fuels [see section 19.3.3.]. At least, it should promote greater coherence between national policies, more open relations with the producer countries, notably the OPEC countries, and enhanced cooperation with Central European countries and Russia.

Energy is certainly an important factor determining the economic performance of a country or of a group of countries such as the EU. The absence of a common oil and gas supply policy handicaps the common energy market and renders energy prices higher than they could be if the Union could use its economic weight to negotiate its overall supplies with producing countries as it does concerning its supplies of nuclear fuels. High energy prices mean a serious **competitive disadvantage for the businesses of the European Union** as compared with those of its main trading partners. Furthermore, economic performance is not measured only by industrial competitiveness, but also by the welfare of citizens in terms of the employment situation and the state of the environment. The reduction of greenhouse gas emissions requires common policies, such as a sustained commitment to energy efficiency and energy saving, a commitment to make more systematic use of energy sources with low or no CO_2 emissions and a reduction in the impact of the use of energy sources with high CO_2 emissions.

Bibliography on energy policy

- BOYLE Godfrey. *Renewable energy: power for a sustainable future.* Oxford; New York: Oxford University Press in association with the Open University, 2004.

- EUROPEAN COMMISSION. *European research spending for renewable energy sources.* Luxembourg: EUR-OP*, 2004.

    - *Trans-European energy network: TEN-E priority projects.* Luxembourg: EUR-OP*, 2004.

- INTERNATIONAL ENERGY AGENCY. *World energy outlook 2004.* Paris: OECD, 2004.

- JÄGER-WALDAU Arnulf (ed.). *Status report 2004: energy end-use efficiency and electricity from biomass, wind and photovoltaics in the European Union.* Luxembourg: EUR-OP*, 2004.

- JONES Christopher. *EU energy law: v. 1. The internal energy market.* Leuven: Claeys & Casteels, 2004.

- NOCERA Fabrizio. "Recent European Union legislation and the international nuclear third party liability regime: conflicts, problems and solutions", *Uniform Law Review*, v. 9, n. 1, 2004, p. 83-95.

- ORGANISATION FOR ECONOMIC COOPERATION AND DEVELOPMENT. *Renewable energy: market & policy trends in IEA countries.* Paris: OECD, 2004.

- ROGGENKAMP Martha, HAMMER Ulf (eds.). *European energy law report. 1.* Antwerp: Intersentia, 2004.

- YEOMANS Matthew. *Oil: anatomy of an industry.* New York; London: New Press, 2004.

The publications of the Office for Official Publications of the European Communities (EUR-OP) exist generally in all official languages of the EU.

DISCUSSION TOPICS

1. Discuss the energy objectives of the ECSC and Euratom Treaties.
2. How has the completion of the single market influenced the energy sector?
3. What measures has the EC/EU taken to promote its energy supply security?
4. Discuss the issue of security of oil supplies.
5. How can the common energy policy contribute to the attainment of the sustainable development objective of the common environment policy?

Chapter 20

TRANSPORT POLICY

Diagram of the chapter

The EEC Treaty sought **a common policy for inland transport**, namely roads, rail and inland waterways, but not for maritime and air transport (Art 84 EEC, Art. 80 TEC). The concept of a common transport market was consequently limited at the outset to inland transport and more specifically, in light of the highly specific situation of railway and inland waterway undertakings, to road transport. However road haulage services represent by far the bulk of goods carriage in the European Community. They, therefore, play a principal role in the good functioning of the single market by enabling the free movement of goods and persons. Thus, the common transport market had to be completed together with the single market for goods in 1992.

In addition to the integration of inland transport markets, Community policy in this sector seeks to **organise the various means of transport** in accordance with "Community rules", i.e. measures tending towards the ap-

proximation of the economic conditions and the structures of each mode of
transport in the Member States. For many years, the Community institutions concentrated upon harmonising road haulage rates, but achievements
are thin on the ground. The aim in the railway sector was to improve the
financial situation of railway companies, but the many provisions adopted
with this aim in mind have, thus far, had little impact. By way of contrast,
sea and air transport which only made their entrance onto the Community
stage in the middle of the 1970s, have seen spectacular progress recently,
not only in the completion of the internal market in these sectors, but also
of their Community organisation.

A communication of the Commission entitled "The common transport
policy - Sustainable mobility: perspectives for the future" provides an updated **framework for the future development of the transport policy**[1].
The Commission identifies three priority areas for action, for which it lists
the main measures designed to: improve the **efficiency and competitiveness** of Community transport by: liberalising market access, establishing
integrated transport systems and developing the trans-European network;
establishing **fair pricing** on the basis of the marginal social cost and improving working conditions; and improving **transport quality** through targeted action on safety, primarily on air, maritime and road transport, and
protection of the environment. Concerning in particular environment protection, the Commission believes that the introduction of a rational policy
for achieving a reduction in carbon dioxide emissions in the transport sector (accounting for 26% of total CO_2 emissions in the Union in 1995)
would make it possible to halve them by 2010[2] [see also section 16.3.4.].
To this end, the **"STEER"** programme, which is part of the multiannual
programme for actions in the field of energy (2003-2006)[3] [see section
19.1.3.], supports initiatives relating to all energy aspects of transport, the
diversification of fuels, such as through new developing and renewable energy sources, and the promotion of renewable fuels and energy efficiency
in transport, including the preparation of legislative measures and their application.

20.1. The special interest for the transport sector

Article 51 TEC (ex-Art. 61 EEC) makes the provision of services in
the transport sector dependent on the special clauses of the title relating to
transport. Article 71 TEC (ex-Art. 75 EEC) stipulates that the common
policy should take into account the **"distinctive features"** of (inland)
transport sector. At the outset, these distinctive features were based on the
facts: (a) that transport undertakings were dependent upon infrastructure
decided and built by the States; (b) that in general, competition took place

---

[1]   COM (1998) 716, 1 December 1998.
[2]   COM (1998) 204, 31 March 1998.
[3]   Decision 1230/2003, OJ L 176, 15.07.2003.

between large State controlled railway monopolies and a multitude of small road haulage and inland waterway transport operators; (c) that the State required certain undertakings, notably the railways, to fulfil public service obligations, which distort competition conditions; and (d) that supply and demand were extremely rigid in this sector.

The Treaty of Rome and its successor, the Treaty establishing the European Community, show **special interest in the transport sector for several reasons**. First of all, economic integration was expected to lead to growth in trade and consequently in transport flows. The EEC Treaty therefore saw the transport sector as one of the major motors of economic integration. On its side, the healthy operation of the transport sector depended to a large extent on healthy trade and business in the Community.

Secondly, transport costs, which put a serious strain on the cost price of certain goods, **could act as a barrier to trade** or a source of discrimination between European businesses of various nationalities. At the outset, the situation was most complex in the road transport sector, which represents 80% of goods carriage between the Member States. Depending on the routes, international road traffic was either restriction free or subject to prior authorisation or to the granting of authorisations in the framework of a quota. Authorisation issuing provisions (length of validity, possibility of return trip loaded, etc.) varied from one route to the next. The conditions governing Community transit differed from one State to the next and provisions relating to combined rail/road transport were practically non-existent. It is obvious that all this had to be changed in order to create a common market for transport.

Infrastructure choices for means of communication, their construction and use have considerable impact on regional development, the environment, town and country planning, traffic safety and energy consumption. Coordination of investment decisions can eliminate the risk of works whose socio-economic profitability is not sufficient and can open the way to the economies of scale offered by the wider internal market. The provisions of the TEC on trans-European networks and economic and social cohesion provide a new basis for the Community to devise a strategy for the development of transport infrastructure. This strategy should allow, amongst other things, the less favoured peripheral regions of the Union to take full advantage of the opportunities which stem from the completion of the internal market.

Nowadays, the priority in the transport sector is moving towards building modern infrastructures and, in particular, **trans-European networks**, which help complete the internal market by reinforcing the links between the Member States [see section 6.8.]. These networks also permit: better, safer travel at lower cost, thus improving both industrial competitiveness and quality of life; effective planning in Europe, thus avoiding a concentration of wealth and population; and bridge-building towards Central and Eastern European countries, which is essential in view of their integration into the Union. Building trans-European transport networks requires

Community action to coordinate the various national activities and so complete the internal market and facilitate interconnection and interoperability in the transport sector.

The continuing integration of the economies of the Member States necessarily entails increased transport movements across frontiers and places new challenges for the European transport policy. Thus, in addition to the consolidation of the internal market in transport, the Treaty of Amsterdam set two new objectives for the common transport policy: transport safety and environment protection. Article 71 of the EC Treaty declares that **transport safety** is one of the objectives to be attained by the transport policy. Safety requirements may fall within the area of the Community's exclusive powers, for example, because they affect the free circulation of vehicles or transport services. In other cases, in application of the subsidiarity principle [see section 3.2.], transport safety is a matter which should be addressed by the Community when it is in a position to act usefully.

20.2. The internal market for inland transport

Title V of the EC Treaty is devoted to transport policy. It states that common policy in the transport sector should be implemented via **common rules applicable to international transport**, through the admission of non-resident carriers to the national transport market and through all other appropriate provisions (Art 71 TEC). According to the Treaty, aids which respond to the need for the coordination of transport services or for the reimbursement for the discharge of certain obligations inherent in the concept of public service are compatible with the common market (Art. 73 TEC). Any discrimination, which takes the form of carriers charging different rates and imposing different conditions for the carriage of the same goods over the same transport links on grounds of the country of origin or destination of the country in question, must be abolished (Art. 75 TEC). The Member States may not impose rates and conditions involving any element of support or protection in the interest of one or more particular undertakings or industries, unless authorised by the Commission (Art. 76 TEC).

The first Community measures adopted in the inland transport sector sought **to integrate national transport markets** together with the creation of the general common market for goods and services. In this sector, it was necessary to create a genuine internal market in which transport operators from all the Member States would have access under the same conditions as those prevalent on their national markets. This implied freedom of establishment, the removal of barriers to freedom of movement and the harmonisation of competition conditions.

No special problems were encountered in the free movement of individuals and the right of establishment in the transport sector. The Regulation of 1968 on the **free movement of workers** within the Community was applied to the inland transport sector in the same way as to other economic sectors[1] [see section 6.4.]. The **right of establishment** formed part of the general programme to remove restrictions to the freedom of establishment adopted by the Council in December 1961 [see section 6.5.1.], but was also the subject of a specific Directive on mutual recognition of diplomas and certificates of road carriers[2]. It was the **free movement of services**, meaning free access of all operators in the transport market, that was the source of complex problems, due to restrictive national regulations in the Member States, particularly for road haulage services. This subject merits our particular attention.

20.2.1. Access to the common inland transport market

The **liberalisation of the internal goods carriage market** was at long last established by a Regulation on access to the market in the carriage of goods by road within the Community and departing from or en route to a Member State, or crossing the territory of one or several Member States[3]. This Regulation replaced the formerly existing quantitative restrictions and bilateral authorisations by qualitative conditions (fiscal, technical and safety) with which a carrier must conform in order to obtain the Community **road haulage operator licence** and which are specified in the directives on access to the transport profession, mentioned below. The licence is valid for six years, but the criteria for holding it have to be controlled every three years. Thanks to a uniform document, the **"driver attestation"**, the regularity of the employment status of a driver of a Community vehicle engaged in international carriage under cover of a Community authorisation can be effectively checked by inspecting officers of all Member States[4]. Should economic crisis hit the road haulage market, the Commission can take measures to prevent any further capacity increases on the market affected[5]. A Regulation laying down the conditions under which non-resident carriers may operate national **road haulage services within a Member State (cabotage)** is the culmination of many years of work towards the liberalisation of the road haulage sector[6]. These Regulations have completed the internal goods carriage market.

The **freedom to provide passenger transport services by road** for hire or reward or on one's own account is also guaranteed by a Council Regulation[7]. It notably provides for the liberalisation of shuttle services by coach and bus with sleeping accommodation, along with nearly all occasional services, and simplifies authorisation procedures by introducing a

---

[1] Regulation 1612/68, OJ L 257, 19.10.1968 and Directive 2004/38, OJ L 158, 30.04.2004.
[2] Directive 96/26, OJ L 124, 23.05.1996 and Directive 2004/66, OJ L 168, 01.05.2004.
[3] Regulation 881/92, OJ L 95, 09.04.1992 and Act of Accession OJ C 241, 29.08.1994.
[4] Regulation 484/2002, OJ L 76, 19.03.2002.
[5] Regulation 3916/90, OJ L 375, 31.12.1990.
[6] Regulation 3118/93, OJ L 279, 12.11.1993 and Regulation 3315/94, OJ L 350, 31.12.1994.
[7] Regulation 684/92, OJ L 74, 20.03.1992 and Regulation 11/98, OJ L 4, 08.01.1998.

Community licence based on a harmonised model. The detailed rules with regard to documentation covering the international carriage of passengers are laid out in a Commission Regulation[1]. Another Council Regulation lays down the conditions under which non-resident carriers may operate **national road passenger transport services (cabotage)** within a Member State[2]. It authorises cabotage, under certain conditions, for regular services performed during a regular international service, excluding purely internal urban and suburban services. Despite cabotage liberalisation, when a bus or coach company wants to gain a permanent foothold in another national market, the simplest way to do so remains to establish itself on that market. Thus, the impact of cabotage on the national markets of the Member States is marginal and insignificant, with cabotage operations carried out mainly in adjacent Member States.

The **admission to the occupation** of road haulage operator and road passenger transport operator and the mutual recognition of diplomas, certificates and other evidence of qualifications intended to facilitate for these operators the right to freedom of establishment in national and international transport operations are guaranteed by a Directive[3]. It stipulates that individuals or undertakings wishing to exercise the occupation of road haulier or road passenger transport operator must satisfy certain conditions relating to good repute (no insolvency), sufficient financial capacity for correct management of the undertaking and professional skills acquired through attendance of a training course or through practical experience.

20.2.2. Competition conditions in inland transport services

For there to be effective freedom to provide services, all transport operators in the Member States had to **be placed on an equal footing** from the viewpoint of competition conditions, a really difficult requirement. In effect, rail transport systems based on the exploitation of single networks constituted monopolies or oligopolies. Service obligations in the public interest tended to involve the granting of correlative special or exclusive rights. Rail transport operators frequently relied on public finance, including subsidies not compatible with the functioning of the common market.

After the achievement of customs union [see section 5.1.2.], a 1968 Regulation sanctioned the **application of competition rules** to the rail, road and inland waterway transport sectors[4]. This Regulation in principle forbids, for all three modes of transport, agreements between companies, decisions of association and concerted practices, along with abuse of a dominant position in the common market. Yet, an exemption is granted to

[1] Regulation 2121/98, OJ L 268, 03.10.1998.
[2] Regulation 2454/92, OJ L 251, 29.08.1992 and Regulation 12/98, OJ L 48, 04.01.1998.
[3] Directive 96/26, OJ L 124, 23.05.1996 and Directive 98/76, OJ L 277, 14.10.1998.
[4] Regulation 1017/68, OJ L 175, 23.07.1968 and Regulation 1/2003, OJ L 1, 04.01.2003.

agreements which contribute to productivity, along with certain types of agreements, decisions and concerted practices in the field of transport which have as sole object and impact the application of technical improvements or technical cooperation. A Commission Regulation of August 1969 facilitates the presentation of complaints, applications and notifications by natural or legal persons who claim a legitimate interest[1].

However, competition rules alone do not suffice to guarantee free competition in the transport sector. Competition conditions for different modes of transport and for the undertakings of different Member States running the same type of transport services must also be harmonised. The first step in this direction was taken by the Council Decision of May 13, 1965 on the harmonisation of **certain provisions affecting competition** in transport by rail, road and inland waterway[2]. Under this Decision, the Council agreed to take action in three fields: State intervention, taxation and social regimes in the transport sector. One of the most important measures in this sense was a Regulation providing for separate accounting of public service activities and commercial activities in transport undertakings, abolishing public service obligations and replacing them, when public interest justifies the preservation of transport services of no commercial viability for the operator, by **public service contracts** negotiated between governments and undertakings[3]. Many other measures harmonising the conditions of competition were taken in the fields of State aids, taxation and social legislation.

20.2.3. Transport infrastructure

Infrastructure plays a determinant role in the competition conditions enjoyed by the various modes of transport. Through its choice of means of communication, the State determines the expansion and link up possibilities of the various modes of transport. Transport undertakings are dependent upon the infrastructure, which they use, in as much as decisions on its construction and maintenance are taken by governments. However, transport users are usually **not obliged to pay the full cost of the infrastructures** that they use. This is particularly true of road infrastructures and has contributed to the phenomenal expansion of road transport. In other respects, transport networks having been designed largely from a national point of view, there were in post-war Europe many missing links, bottlenecks and obstacles to inter-operability between national networks.

At the instigation of the Commission, a **consultation procedure** and a Transport Infrastructure Committee were established in the late 1970s and improved over time[4]. This procedure enabled better planning at national

---

[1] Regulation 2843/98, OJ L 354, 30.12.1998.
[2] OJ 88, 24.05.1965.
[3] Regulation 1191/69, OJ L 156, 28.06.1969 and Regulation 1893/91, OJ L 169, 29.06.1991.
[4] Decision 1692/96, OJ L 228, 09.09.1996.

level both as regards time scale and geographical aspects. In addition, the European Investment Bank and the Structural Funds have much helped the financing of infrastructures. But the overall infrastructure deficit of the Community has increased with the accession of peripheral States. This is why, the development of transport infrastructures was provided for in the EC Treaty under the heading of trans-European networks.

Indeed, the new Article 155 of the EC Treaty calls for a series of guidelines covering the objectives, priorities and broad lines of measures envisaged in the sphere of **trans-European networks** [see section 6.8.]. These networks are not only necessary in order to complete the internal market, improve the links between the European regions, avoid traffic con gestions, reduce environment pollution and improve the competitiveness of European industries, but they can also enliven the European economy through the realisation of very big projects and thus contribute to its growth. Community financial assistance is granted under certain rules to projects of common interest[1]. Concerning trans-European transport networks (TEN-T) the goal is not so much the improvement of transport infrastructure in general but the integration of the Community's transport system through the completion and combination of its networks, taking particular account of its more geographically isolated regions.

A Commission White Paper entitled "**Fair payment for infrastructure use**" recommends the gradual harmonisation of infrastructure charging systems based on the "user pays" principle, according to which all users of transport infrastructure would have to pay for all the costs they generate, including environmental costs[2]. A first measure in this sense is the creation of a European **electronic road toll service**, which aims to secure the interoperability of toll systems in the internal market and to contribute to the elaboration of infrastructure charging policies at European level, making it possible to fund, in part, new infrastructure and to ensure a better traffic flow on the main routes of the trans-European network[3].

20.3. Sectoral organisation of the transport market

In addition to the proper functioning of the internal market for transport, the common transport policy also tackles the sector-by-sector **organisation of the various modes of transport**. This requires the approximation of the economic conditions and the structures of each mode of transport in the Member States. The Treaty of Rome did not call for specific action in this field, but nevertheless stated that there should be common rules applicable to international transport to or from the territory of a Member

---

[1]   Regulation 2236/95, OJ L 228, 23.09.1995 and Regulation 1655/1999, OJ L 197, 29.07.1999.
[2]   COM (1998) 466, 22 July 1998.
[3]   Directive 2004/52, OJ L 166, 30.04.2004.

State, or passing across the territory of one or more Member States (Article 75,1,a EEC). The European institutions slowly put in place common rules, first for road transport rates and for improving the financial situation of the railways and, then in reaction to the Court of Justice ruling of April 4, 1974 on the interpretation of Article 84 of the EEC Treaty[1], on the organisation of activities and the establishment of the internal market for the sea and air transport sectors. For concision's sake, all measures adopted in the last two sectors are examined in this part, since they often pursue simultaneously the two objectives of the common transport policy, namely the proper functioning of the internal market and the organisation of the sector.

20.3.1. Road transport

The part of road haulage in the total freight transport of the Community increased from around 50% in 1970 to almost 70% in 1990. This increase was partly due to the choice of the Member States **not to charge the prices of road transport with the cost of infrastructures**. The Member States have agreed a system providing a **free price setting** applicable to all carriage of goods by road between the Member States[2]. This tariff regime allows for the introduction of cost indexes, i.e. indicators of the various cost elements, which a haulier should take into account when drawing up a transport price to be negotiated with the client, but the real cost of infrastructures is not among those indicators.

The form and content of **registration certificates** for motor vehicles have been harmonised in order to facilitate road traffic within the Community, simplify procedures for the re-registration of vehicles in another Member State, and step up the fight against illegal vehicle trafficking[3]. Common rules command the recognition in intra-Community traffic of the distinguishing sign of the Member State in which motor vehicles and their trailers are registered[4].

The Community aims not only at the harmonisation of conditions of competition and the protection of the environment but also at **road safety**, which becomes an ever more important problem of the EU. The principal actions taken so far in the area of road safety have been concerned with the harmonisation of rules relating to vehicle construction and vehicle inspection, through the adoption of over 100 Directives, notably on: minimum tyre tread depth[5]; the periodic inspection of vehicles[6]; speed limiters for heavy vehicles[7]; the mandatory wearing of seat belts[8]; compulsory installa-

---

[1] Judgment of 4 April 1974, Case 167-73, Commission v French Republic, ECR 1974, p. 359.
[2] Regulation 4058/89, OJ L 390, 30.12.1989 and EEA Agreement, OJ L 1, 03.01.1994.
[3] Directive 1999/37, OJ L 138, 01.06.1999.
[4] Regulation 2411/98, OJ L 299, 10.11.1998.
[5] Directive 89/459, OJ L 226, 03.08.1989 and EEA Agreement, OJ L 1, 03.01.1994.
[6] Directive 96/96, OJ L 46, 17.02.1997 and Directive 1999/52, OJ L 142, 05.06.1999.
[7] Directive 92/94, OJ L 129, 14.05.1992.
[8] Directive 91/671, OJ L 373, 31.12.1991 and Directive 2003/20, OJ L 115, 09.05.2003.

tion of digital equipment to monitor the activities, notably the working hours, of lorry drivers (tachographs)[1]; and the general standards for the Community model driving licence in paper or "credit card" format, including harmonised codes for additional or restrictive information[2]. Minimum safety requirements for tunnels have become obligatory in the trans-European road network[3]. How many citizens realise that these life-saving measures are based on the - according to eurosceptic rhetoric - "niggling legislation of Brussels" [see section 10.1.]?

20.3.2. Railways

Railways, once the dominant means of transport, were **relegated by the car** in the 1960s. In the early 1990s, railway transport represented around 15% of freight transport in the Community, whereas twenty years before it represented practically the double. The bulky organisation of the railways has not given them sufficient flexibility to structure their service to new transport requirements, to the "European dimension" and to competition from other modes of transport. The Member States must shoulder part of the blame for the unfortunate situation in which their railways find themselves. They oblige the railways to bend to the requirements of public service and regional development, which is not required of their private competitors, the road hauliers, while not raising the capital endowment of railway undertakings in line with this obligation. This forces the railways into the red and hampers their modernisation.

Nowadays, however, there is some light at the end of the tunnel in the shape of the high speed trains, which have given a new lease of life to European railways. The new momentum has led to the "**railway package**" of measures designed to speed up market integration by removing major obstacles to cross-border services, ensure a high standard of operational safety on the railways and help to reduce costs and facilitate operations through greater harmonisation of technical standards in the railway industry.

Thus, a Directive on the **development of the Community's railways** purports to make relations between the railways and the public authorities more transparent and to ensure the financial, administrative, economic and accounting independence of the railway undertakings[4]. It entails the total opening of the rail freight markets. It also allows access to new railway operators into the combined transport market, in order to stimulate a higher quality of service from all concerned. Another Directive establishes the general framework for a uniform, non-discriminatory Community system regarding access to railway infrastructure, so that railway undertakings and

---

[1] Regulation 3821/85, OJ L 370, 31.12.1985 and Regulation 2135/98, OJ L 274, 09.10.1998.
[2] Directive 91/439, OJ L 237, 24.08.1991 and Directive 97/26, OJ L 150, 07.06.1997.
[3] Directive 2004/54, OJ L 167, 30.04.2004.
[4] Directive 91/440, OJ L 237, 24.08.1991 and Directive 2004/51, OJ L 164, 30.04.2004.

their customers can reap the full benefits of the internal market in this sector, while ensuring high standards of safety[1]. However, undertakings applying for a licence to the Community railway market must meet specified standards of financial fitness and professional competence[2]. The licences, granted by the Member State in which a railway undertaking is established, are valid throughout the territory of the Community. Harmonised technical specifications ensure the uninterrupted movement of high-speed trains throughout the European Union[3] as well the interoperability of the trans-European conventional rail system[4], while a uniform set of national safety rules purports to avoid distorting competition between modes for the transport of dangerous goods[5].

The **European Railway Agency** plays a key role in technically aligning the railway systems[6]. The Agency's areas of activity are, firstly, the development of common safety standards and the development and management of a system to monitor safety performance and, secondly, the long-term management of the system for establishing, registering and monitoring the technical specifications of interoperability.

Multimodal transport is encouraged by granting Community financial assistance to improve the environmental performance of the freight transport system (Marco Polo programme)[7]. This programme supports both the fight against congestion in the road freight sector and the objectives of improving the environmental performance of the transport system.

20.3.3. Maritime transport

Established in the early 1990s, the **internal maritime transport market** is functioning quite well. In 1986, the Council applied the principle of freedom to provide services, (Art. 49 and 50 TEC) to shipping services between the Member States and third countries[8]. In 1992, the freedom to provide services was extended to maritime transport within Member States **(maritime cabotage)** for Community shipowners who have their ships registered in and flying the flag of a Member State, provided that these ships comply with all the conditions for cabotage in that Member State[9]. For vessels carrying out mainland cabotage and for cruise liners, all matters relating to manning are the responsibility of the State in which the vessel is registered. However, for ships smaller than 650 Gt. and for vessels carrying out island cabotage, all matters relating to manning are the re-

---

[1] Directive 2001/14, OJ L 75, 15.03.2001 and Directive 2004/49, OJ L 164, 30.04.2004.

[2] Directive 95/18, OJ L 143, 27.06.1995 and Directive 2004/49, OJ L 164, 30.04.2004.

[3] Directive 96/48, OJ L 235, 17.09.1996 and Directive 2004/50, OJ L 164, 30.04.2004.

[4] Directive 2001/16, OJ L110, 20.04.2001 and Directive 2004/50, OJ L 164, 30.04.2004.

[5] Directive 96/49, OJ L 235, 17.09.1996 and Directive 2000/62, OJ L 279, 01.11.2000.

[6] Regulation 881/2004, OJ L 164, 30.04.2004.

[7] Regulation 1382/2003, OJ L 196, 02.08.2003 and Regulation 788/2004, OJ L 138, 30.04.2004.

[8] Regulation 4055/86, OJ L 378, 31.12.1986 and Regulation 3573/90, OJ L 353, 17.12.1990.

[9] Regulation 3577/92, OJ L 364, 12.12.1992.

sponsibility of the host State. The ability to transfer ships from one register to another within the Community may improve the operating conditions and competitiveness of the Community merchant fleet[1]. A Directive concerning the Agreement on the organisation of working time of seafarers, concluded by the European Community Shipowners' Association and the Federation of Transport Workers' Union in the European Union, is important for levelling both working conditions of sailors and competition conditions in this area[2].

Detailed rules were laid down for the application of Articles 81 and 82 of the EC Treaty (ex-Articles 85 and 86) to maritime transport in order to ensure that competition is not unduly distorted within the common market. Community guidelines for **State aid in the maritime transport sector** are intended to make public assistance transparent and to define what kinds of aid scheme can be introduced to support the Community's maritime interests[3]. Block exemptions [see section 15.3.3.] exist for certain concerted practices between liner shipping companies (**maritime conferences and consortia**), which generally contribute to ensure regular, sufficient and efficient maritime transport services[4], and for the carriage of cargo, to liner shipping consortia, which provide international liner shipping services from or to one or more Community ports[5]. Thanks to these exemptions from the general rules of Articles 81 and 82, shipowners may jointly organise services, thus rationalising their activities as maritime carriers and obtaining economies of scale and cost reductions, while at the same time providing users with a better-quality service. They allow notably the coordination and joint fixing of sailing timetables, the determination of ports of call, the exchange, sale or cross-chartering of space or "slots" on vessels, the pooling of vessels, port installations and operation offices.

International **safety standards for passenger vessels** are applied in the Community. Thus, the International Conventions for the Safety of Life at Sea (SOLAS) and for the prevention of pollution by ships (MARPOL) are applicable to the Member States - and therefore to ships flying their flags[6]. Clear and efficient safety procedures are applied to roll-on/roll-off (ro-ro) passenger ferries and high-speed passenger craft[7]. The Member States must subject such vessels to initial and annual surveys to check in particular compliance with the SOLAS Convention[8]. Passenger ships operating on domestic voyages, which are not covered by the SOLAS international Convention, are covered by a Community Directive, which is intended to guarantee maximum safety for passengers and, at the same time, to provide a level playing field based on convergent standards in Community ship-

---

[1] Regulation 789/2004, OJ L 138, 30.04.2004.
[2] Directive 1999/63, OJ L 167, 02.07.1999.
[3] OJ C 205, 05.07.1997.
[4] Regulation 4056/86, OJ L 378, 31.12.1986 and Regulation 1/2003, OJ L 1, 04.01.2003.
[5] Regulation 823/2000, OJ L 100, 20.04.2000 and Regulation 463/2004, OJ L 77, 13.03.2004.
[6] Regulation 2158/93, OJ L 194, 03.08.1993.
[7] Regulation 3051/95, OJ L 320, 30.12.1995 and Directive 2002/84, OJ L 324, 29.11.2002.
[8] Directive 1999/35, OJ L 138, 01.06.1999 and Directive 2002/84, OJ L 324, 29.11.2002.

ping[1]. In order to ensure that the maximum capacity of ships is not exceeded and to provide accurate information to the emergency services in the event of an accident, another Directive obliges shipping companies operating to or from Community ports to count and register the crew members and persons sailing on board passenger ships[2]. Ships using Community ports and sailing in the waters under the jurisdiction of the Member States must respect the international standards for ship safety, pollution prevention and shipboard living and working conditions (port State control)[3].

The independent **European Maritime Safety Agency** assists the Commission with drafting maritime legislation, monitoring application by the Member States and coordinating inquiries after accidents at sea or after accidental or illicit pollution caused by ships[4]. A Directive sets up common rules and standards for ship inspection and survey organisations in order to ensure a high level of competence and independence of these organisations[5]. To prevent marine pollution (such as that caused by the "Erika" and "Prestige" accidents off the coasts of France in December 2000 and Spain in December 2002), a Regulation established an accelerated phasing-in scheme for the application of the double-hull or equivalent design requirements of the MARPOL 73/78 Convention to single hull oil tankers[6].

20.3.4. Air transport

The liberalisation of air transport in the Community was achieved progressively, between 1987 and 1992, with three packages of Regulations. The third air transport package, adopted by the Council on 22 June 1992, constituted the final stage in the liberalisation of Community air transport. It has achieved the freedom to provide services within the Community, technical and economic harmonisation and free price setting.

The Regulation on the **licensing of air carriers** defines the technical and economic requirements which airlines must meet in order to obtain national licences authorising them to operate on Community territory without restrictions on the grounds of nationality[7]. The licences in question are: the air operator's certificate (AOC), which affirms the technical quality and competence of the airline concerned; and the operating licence, granted to undertakings which comply with certain conditions regarding nationality and which meet certain economic criteria and are covered by a suitable insurance scheme. This Regulation guarantees, then, that only airlines under

---

[1]   Council Directive 98/18, OJ L 144, 15.05.1998 and Directive 2003/24, OJ L 123, 17.05.2003.
[2]   Directive 98/41, OJ L 188, 02.07.1998 and Directive 2003/25, OJ L 123, 17.05.2003.
[3]   Directive 95/21, OJ L 157, 07.07.1995 and Directive 2002/84, OJ L 324, 29.11.2002.
[4]   Regulation 1406/2002, OJ L 208, 05.08.2002 and Regulation 724/2004, OJ L 129, 29.04.2004.
[5]   Directive 94/57, OJ L 319, 12.12.1994 and Directive 2002/84, OJ L 324, 29.11.2002.
[6]   Regulation 417/2002, OJ L 64, 07.03.2002 and Regulation 1726/2003, OJ L 249, 01.10.2003.
[7]   Regulation 2407/92, OJ L 240, 24.08.1992.

Community control, and with adequate technical and economic capacity, are able to take advantage of the opening up of the European market.

The Regulation on **access for air carriers** to intra-Community air routes opens up all airports on the territory of the Community to all those who are registered according to the above-mentioned Regulation[1]. It provides, in particular, for: the abolition of the previously existing sharing of passenger capacity between airlines; the unrestricted exercise of the **'fifth freedom'** (the right to pick up passengers in a Member State other than that in which the airline is registered and to disembark them in a third Member State); and the authorisation to undertake **cabotage operations** (to pick up passengers in a Member State other than that in which the airline is registered and to disembark them in that same Member State).

Finally, the Regulation on **fares and rates for air services** guarantees the unrestricted setting of new passenger fares and cargo rates for scheduled air services and charter flights under certain conditions safeguarding the interests of both the industry and of consumers[2]. It defines, in particular, the arrangements for the examination of new fares and rates by the Member States and the system of 'double disapproval' (whereby a new fare or rate may not be turned down unless both Member States concerned disapprove of it). If this is not the case, Community air carriers may freely fix passenger fares. Charter fares and air cargo rates are freely fixed by the parties to the air transport contract.

The EU encourages better information for air passengers, greater protection for passengers' rights, improved service and simplified handling of disputes[3]. A Regulation drawing up common rules for the **compensation of passengers refused the right to board** due to over-booking[4] is of particular importance to the ordinary citizen. It stipulates that should a passenger be refused the right to board, he has the right to choose between full reimbursement of the price of the ticket for the part of the journey, which he was unable to carry out, or rescheduling on a later date of his choice. Regardless of the choice made by the passenger, the air carrier must pay, immediately after the boarding refusal, compensation that varies in line with the distance of the flight and the rescheduling delay. The carrier must moreover offer passengers refused the right to board meals, hotel accommodation if necessary and the cost of a telephone call and/or telefax message to the place of destination.

As regards, more particularly, the operation of **air freight services,** a Council Regulation seeks to open up access to the market, liberalise fares and boost the operating flexibility of these services[5]. A Member State approves airfreight carriers whose licence has been issued by another Member State and which has been authorised by the State of registration to ex-

---

[1]   Regulation 2408/92, OJ L 240, 24.08.1992 and Act of Accession OJ C 241, 29.08.1994.
[2]   Regulation 2409/92, OJ L 240, 24.08.1992.
[3]   Council resolution, OJ C 293, 14.10.2000.
[4]   Regulation 295/91, OJ L 36, 08.02.1991.
[5]   Regulation 2408/92, OJ L 240 of 24.08.1992 and Act of Accession OJ C 241, 29.08.1994.

ercise third-, fourth- and fifth-freedom traffic rights. Fifth freedom traffic rights are exercised on a service, which is the extension of a service on departure from the State where the carrier is registered or a preliminary to a service whose end destination is this State. The prices applied by Community air carriers for freight transport are set freely by mutual agreement of the parties to the transport contract. Air carriers operating services within the Community must place all their standard freight rates at the disposal of the general public on request.

The establishment of **common rules in the field of civil aviation** aims at guaranteeing European citizens high safety and environmental protection standards and at facilitating activity in the aeronautics industry in Europe[1]. Aeronautical products are henceforth subject to certification to verify that they meet essential airworthiness and environmental protection requirements relating to civil aviation, notably to the design, production, maintenance and operation of aeronautical products, parts and appliances. Appropriate essential requirements cover operations of aircraft and flight crew licensing. They apply to third-country aircraft and other areas in the field of civil aviation safety. In order to respond to increasing concerns over the health and welfare of passengers during flights, the common rules aim, among other things, to develop aircraft designs which better protect the safety and health of passengers. An independent Community body, the **European Aviation Safety Agency** assists the Commission in the preparation of the necessary legislation and the Member States and the industry in its implementation. It is able to issue certification specifications and certificates as required. It is allowed to develop its expertise in all aspects of civil aviation safety and environmental protection.

A package of common rules on the use of airspace throughout the Community, called the "**single European sky**" package, aims at improving and reinforcing safety, and at restructuring airspace on the basis of traffic flow rather than according to national boundaries, at encouraging cross-border air navigation service provision and at establishing a framework for the modernisation of systems[2]. The specific regulatory framework is based on a system of authorisation for the supply of air navigation services that permit enforcement of the rules defined in Community law, conformity assessment mechanisms enabling Member States' authorities to check compliance, and provisions and procedures for payment of air navigation services. The measures concern an integrated, harmonised management of Community airspace, which implies the supply of services by flexible and efficient providers guided by demand from airspace users and therefore they entail a less rigid interpretation by States of national sovereignty over their airspace. Development of these measures requires, in addition to greater involvement of industry and the social partners, recourse to the technical expertise of the European Organisation for the Safety of Air

---

[1] Regulation 1592/2002, OJ L 240, 07.09.2002 and Regulation 1701/2003, OJ L 243, 27.09.2003.
[2] Regulations 549/2004 to 552/2004, OJ L 96, 31.03.2004.

Navigation (Eurocontrol) and the possible creation of a military cooperation framework.

Strong growth rates in air traffic inside and to and from Europe have
placed severe strain on some parts of the air transport infrastructure and
have worsened air traffic delays. In a 1995 Resolution, the Council invited
the Member States and the Commission to coordinate their actions in the
framework of the **European Organisation for the Safety of Air Navigation (Eurocontrol)**, the independent organisation responsible for coordinating the Member States' air traffic management systems, in order to
combat congestion and better manage crises situations in the European airspace[1]. As a matter of fact, the Directive, which is designed to achieve the
gradual harmonisation and integration of national air-traffic systems,
makes mandatory the technical specifications drawn up by Eurocontrol,
thus allowing the Commission to adopt Eurocontrol standards[2]. The accession by the European Community to Eurocontrol, aiming at ensuring consistency between the two institutions and improving the regulatory framework for air traffic management, forms part of the overall strategy to build
up a single sky over the single market[3]. Accession by the Community was
preceded, in 1997, by revision of the 1960 convention setting up Eurocontrol in order to extend Eurocontrol's powers to all aspects of air traffic
management and provide the organisation with more efficient decision-
making mechanisms, reinforcing discipline on the part of its Member
States[4].

20.4. Appraisal and outlook

Until the end of the 1980s, the Community achievements in the transport sector did not measure up to the clear need for a policy expressly mentioned in the Treaty of Rome as **a crucial cornerstone of the common
market**. In fact, during thirty years the Member States rejected measures
of liberalisation proposed by the Commission which, they maintained,
would upset competition conditions, both between the various modes of
transport and within each one of them. Council deliberations revolved
around the sophistic question of whether market liberalisation or harmonisation of competition conditions should come first.

The Council's failure to act, forcefully pointed out by the European
Parliament in its 1982 resolution, was chiefly due to an absence of **political commitment** to pushing economic integration in this field. As a consequence, national experts, who prepared the Council meetings, played a
very important role in examining the Commission's proposals. Since these
proposals, by their very nature, were likely to perturb vested interests and

---

[1]   OJ C 323, 04.12.1995.
[2]   Directive 93/65, OJ L 187, 29.07.1993.
[3]   Decision 2004/636, OJ L 304, 30.09.2004.
[4]   COM (2002) 292, 6 June 2002.

the economic policy concepts of the Member States, very often there was exaggerated defence of national interest and sectoral perception of the problems, which did not make sufficient allowance for the requirements of European integration. These requirements finally prevailed, however. Whether under pressure from the European Parliament and public opinion or the need to integrate transport into the post-1992 single market, **transport policy stepped on the accelerator** in the middle of the 1980s.

The greatest breakthrough for the common transport policy has undoubtedly been in the area of **liberalising international road haulage services** by a system of Community licences issued on the basis of qualitative criteria. The fact that the liberalisation introduced gradually since the early 1990s has not upset the road haulage market, shows that the fears of some national administrations of the common transport market upsetting their national markets were exaggerated.

In the area of **maritime transport**, which is the carrier for 85% of the EEC's external trade, the Member States undertook to apply the rules of free competition and the principle of free provision of services to this sector. They also agreed to fight unfair tariff practices and unsafe seafaring methods, while guaranteeing free access to ocean trades and even to cabotage. The market has not been adversely affected. Cargo volumes and the number of passengers transported have remained relatively stable.

As regards **air transport**, the liberalisation measures completed in 1992 have had a major impact on competition between air carriers. Additional routes were opened, new services were introduced, monopolies were put under pressure, inefficient national companies were forced to modernise or close down and new companies were created. Nevertheless, basic fares are still too high if compared to those in other regions of the world, especially the United States. The costs of air transport remain high, largely because of heavy infrastructure charges and airport fees. Access to the market is still too difficult, mainly due to bilateral agreements between the Member States and third countries.

In general, the European Union must find the answer to **several challenges in the field of transport**. In particular, it must face the problems caused by the saturation of existing networks, the uneven modal split and increasing pollution caused by most means of transport. At the same time, transport liberalisation involving the arrival of new entrants and greater competition between operators, engenders important structural changes, technical innovations and new investments; all, certainly, good developments, but which need to be coordinated at Community level. To answer these challenges the Community should adopt an overall approach aiming at: improving the infrastructure; rationalising the use of the means of transport; enhancing the safety of users; achieving more equitable working conditions; and protecting the environment.

Bibliography on transport policy

- ABEYRATNE Ruwantissa. "The decision in the 'Ryanair' case - the low cost carrier phenomenon", *European Transport Law: Journal of Laws and Economics*, v. 39, n. 5, 2004, p. 585-601.
- DEHOUSSE Franklin, THIRY Catherine, VAN DEN BRÛLE: "Vers le marché unique des transports ferroviaires: les avantages et les dangers de la stratégie européenne", *Studia diplomatica*, v. 57, n. 2, 2004, p. 1-131.
- EUROPEAN COMMISSION. *Road transport: Europe on the move*. Luxembourg: EUR-OP*, 2004.
  - *The single European sky: implementing political commitments*. Luxembourg: EUR-OP*, 2004.
- EUROPEAN CONFERENCE OF MINISTERS OF TRANSPORT. *Transport and spatial policies: the role of regulatory and fiscal incentives*. Paris: ECMT, 2004.
  - *Improving access to public transport*. Paris: ECMT, 2004.
- KAPLAN Daniel, LAFONT Hubert. *Mobilités.net: Villes, transports, technologies face aux nouvelles mobilités*. Paris: LGDJ, 2004.
- MARTINEZ Juan José, KERCKHOVE Marleen van. "EC state aid rules and the financing of inland transport infrastructure", *European Transport Law: Journal of Laws and Economics*, v. 39, n. 3, 2004, p. 357-362.
- SPERLING Daniel, CANNON James. *The hydrogen energy transition: moving toward the post petroleum age in transportation*. Luxembourg: EUR-OP*, 2004.
- STEHMANN Oliver, ZELLHOFER Georg. "Dominant rail undertakings under European competition policy", *European Law Journal*, v. 10, n. 3, May 2004, p. 327-353.

The publications of the Office for Official Publications of the European Communities (EUR-OP) exist generally in all official languages of the EU.

DISCUSSION TOPICS

1. Why was the common transport policy specifically provided for in the Treaty of Rome?
2. What are the relations between the single market for goods and the single market for transports?
3. Discuss the terms of competition between road and rail transport.
4. Can the common transport policy promote economic and social cohesion in the EU?
5. Has the upheaval of national policies and vested interests caused by the common transport policy been beneficial to EU citizens?

Chapter 21

AGRICULTURAL POLICY

Diagram of the chapter

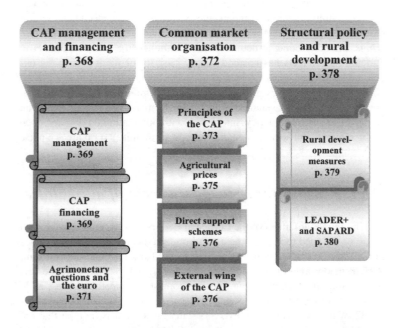

CAP management and financing p. 368	Common market organisation p. 372	Structural policy and rural development p. 378
CAP management p. 369	Principles of the CAP p. 373	Rural development measures p. 379
CAP financing p. 369	Agricultural prices p. 375	LEADER+ and SAPARD p. 380
Agrimonetary questions and the euro p. 371	Direct support schemes p. 376	
	External wing of the CAP p. 376	

The share of agriculture in the Union's gross domestic product (GDP) is just under 3%; but the sector accounts for some 5% of the employed civilian working population of the Fifteen and is the principal source of income in many rural communities. Moreover, food, beverages and tobacco account for about 20% of average European household consumer expenditure and form a substantial proportion of internal trade and exports of the Union. Finally and most importantly, the self-sufficiency of the EC/EU in basic agricultural products is vital, not only for the wellbeing of its citizens, but also for the political independence of its Member States. The economic, **social and political importance of agriculture** is, therefore, much greater than its share in the GDP of the Union.

Without a shadow of a doubt, agriculture is the economic sector where **the process of European integration is furthest advanced**. This achievement is all the more significant in that State interventionism and the conflicts of national interests complicated the task of creating a common policy in this sector. Indeed, prior to the common market, the Member States were actively interventionist in agriculture [see section 21.1.]. National interventionism had to be corrected to enable free trade and free play of competition in the agricultural sector. The creation of the **Common Agricultural Policy (CAP)** is therefore an exemplary achievement of the multinational integration process.

Nonetheless, the common agricultural policy is **extremely difficult to manage**, for it implies the use of common prices, common price management instruments, joint financing of support measures and common external protection. All these cumbersome but unavoidable mechanisms form part of the CAP's market organisation. The latter is one of **the CAP's two wings**, the other being structural policy. Although the common market in agricultural products has ensured supply security of foodstuffs at reasonable prices for consumers, it would not have been sufficient in itself to attain the other objectives of the Treaty, namely increased agricultural productivity and a higher standard of living for farmers. The latter required an active socio-structural policy, interacting with other common policies, such as the regional and social, to guarantee the Community's rural areas a place in the single market.

21.1. Reasons for special treatment of agriculture

The founding fathers of the European Economic Community were well aware of the need to include the agricultural markets of the Member States in the future common market. But they were also aware that the **common agricultural market could not simply be achieved** by abolishing the barriers to free movement and introducing common competition rules, as in the sectors of industry and the services [see section 6.2.]. This is why Article 32 of the EC Treaty (ex Art. 38) states in its first paragraph that the common market includes agriculture and trade in agricultural products, while specifying in paragraph 4 that the operation and growth of the common market in agricultural products must be accompanied by the introduction of a common agricultural policy.

There are several reasons why agriculture was afforded "special treatment". The most important is that due to the **very nature of agriculture**, which is at the mercy of weather conditions, crop and livestock diseases and many other factors which often elude human control and make it very difficult to ensure a perfect balance between agricultural output and the demand for foodstuffs. In addition, demand has very pronounced social and political characteristics. Governments are obliged to ensure that demand for basic commodities be satisfied at all times and at reasonable prices. The original Community was far from self-sufficient in foodstuffs and conditions on the world market provided no justification for the unilateral opening up of markets. Consequently, if food security was to be guaranteed at stable prices, the Community had to organise its own agriculture.

This was quite reasonable, since the agricultural output of the different Member States was complementary. Northern Europe could supply cereals, dairy products and meat, whereas Southern Europe could specialise in fruit and vegetables, citrus fruit and wines.

However, the diversity of the agricultural sector of the six founding Member States, which increased with each enlargement of the Community, generated difficulties for the unification of their agricultural markets, providing further justification for an **interventionist agricultural policy**. Different natural, structural, social and trade conditions, the prominence of agriculture in the national economy and different farming traditions led to the use in each European State of agricultural policy instruments which diverged considerably as to their application scope and magnitude. The common policy therefore had to not only align structurally different agricultural systems, but also to iron out tenaciously held privileges resulting from the interplay of national political institutions: State monopolies or similar regulations, price guarantees, farm income aid, export subsidies, direct or indirect import restrictions, customs protection and so on. A new agricultural policy stepping in the shoes of the national ones had to be defined. The complexity of the latter created the need for the blending of national policies into one common agricultural policy.

One could ask **why organise agricultural markets at all?** The answer is that the agricultural markets of the Member States were already organised in various ways at national level. Indeed, almost all states in the world intervene in one way or another to ensure the income of their farmers and stable supply for their consumers. The only difference is that the system of intervention varies from one to the other. They can however be divided into two main categories: direct income aid systems for farmers, which existed in the United Kingdom before its entry to the Community and was called deficiency payments; and the system of price support on the internal market combined with external protection, the system chosen for the bulk of the original EEC's agricultural production[1].

The system of support for agricultural prices was thought, at the time, to be better adapted to the interests of the original Community. In effect, under the alternative **direct income aid** system, agricultural products are imported at world prices, generally low when they are in ample supply, and the income of national farmers topped up by a subsidy from the budget. This system can be integrally applied in a few countries in the world, which are almost self-sufficient in agricultural products and/or where farmers are not very numerous. If the original EEC countries, which were not yet self-sufficient in agricultural products and had a large number of farmers, were to begin purchasing openly on the world market, initially lower world prices would drive out of work many European farmers and, then, as soon as demand would exceed supply, world prices would escalate

---

[1] OJ 11, 01.08.1958.

and cause important price increases and even penury of certain foodstuffs for low-income consumers.

Under the **system of price support**, on the other hand, in order to provide national farmers with sufficient income, internal prices which are higher than the world prices for agricultural products are practised and the difference is compensated by import levies or customs duties and by export refunds (subsidies)[1]. The higher prices stimulate agricultural output and productivity. They also tend to guarantee self-sufficiency in basic agricultural products and foodstuffs, which is another point in their favour. If they are set too high they can naturally lead to production surpluses, which is a negative point, but which results more from the manner in which the system is applied than from the system itself. Inasmuch, however, as agricultural prices determine farmer income, it is socio-politically very difficult for Agricultural Ministers within the Council to cut these prices, even if the Commission, in its pricing proposals, provides them with arguments in favour of reducing surplus production through prices [see section 4.3.]. These same Ministers are, however, conscious of their own failings, since they periodically accept to revise the system through a CAP reform [see section 21.2.].

As will be seen in the nest section, the CAP was reformed four times in forty years, blending gradually the systems of price and income support. Thus, after its major reforms, in 1992 and 1999, the **European model of agriculture** is based on competitive, multifunctional and sustainable farming. This means that European agriculture is broadening its horizons, since farmers also perform a range of additional tasks, notably in the fields of environment and countryside conservation. As a result of their high population density and geographical differentiation, European countries must produce these services in addition to actual farm produce itself. The EU cannot afford to confine nature and the environment to some reserves. Therefore, agriculture must also be maintained in less-favoured areas as well. Since it is not developed in a vacuum, however, the European model of agriculture has to prove its worth, both internally in addressing issues such as market development, rural development, satisfactory farm incomes and environmental protection, and externally, in facing the challenges of an enlarged Union and heightened competition inside the World Trade Organisation [see section 23.4.].

21.2. CAP foundations and reforms

The **objectives** of the common agricultural policy are specified in Article 33 of the EC Treaty (ex-Art. 39): higher agricultural productivity; guarantee of a fair standard of living to farmers; market stabilisation; supply security and reasonable prices for consumers. In order to attain these objec-

---

[1]   Regulation 800/1999, OJ L 102, 17.04,1999.

tives, Article 40 of the EEC Treaty (actual Art. 34 TEC) called for the **common organisation of agricultural markets** which, depending on the product, could take one of three forms: common coordination rules, compulsory coordination of the various national market organisations or European market organisation. It is interesting to note that it is always this last and most stringent concept that has been applied to the common organisation of agricultural markets.

Established in July 1966, the CAP was reformed a first time in April 1972, a second time in February 1988, a third time in May 1992 and a fourth time in March 1999. Four major reforms of a common policy in 33 years may indicate that the Member States that conceived it and those that joined them later on have never considered it as perfect; but may also show that they were willing to learn from their experience and able to **adapt their common policy** to the changing internal and external circumstances.

The political agreement of the Berlin European Council on the Commission's outlook paper called "Agenda 2000", resulted in the **fourth reform of the CAP**, in March 1999, taking account of the future enlargement of the EU. The reform package included a set of regulations that aimed to develop a more modern and sustainable European agricultural sector, thus ensuring that agriculture can be maintained over the long term at the heart of a living countryside[1]. This means that the CAP is henceforth targeted not just at agricultural producers but also at the wider rural population, consumers and society as a whole. Thus **the new CAP seeks to promote**:

- a clear connection between public support and the range of services which society as a whole receives from the farming community;
- a competitive agricultural sector which is capable of exploiting the opportunities existing on world markets without excessive subsidy, while at the same time ensuring a fair standard of living for the agricultural community;
- an agricultural sector that is sustainable in environmental terms, contributing to the preservation of natural resources and the natural and cultural heritage of the countryside;
- the maintenance of vibrant rural communities, capable of generating employment opportunities for the rural population;
- production methods which are safe and capable of supplying quality products that meet consumer demand and reflect the diversified and rich tradition of European food production.

The fifth CAP reform, carried out in September 2003, provides for a single farm payment for European Union farmers, independent from production and subject to compliance with environmental, food safety, animal and plant health and animal welfare standards, and requirements to keep all farmland in good agricultural and environmental condition ("cross-

---

[1] Notably, Council Regulations 1257/1999, 1258/1999 and 1259/1999, OJ L 160, 26.06.1999 and Regulation 583/2004, OJ L 91, 30.03.2004.

compliance")[1]. The reform is aimed at enabling the farmers of the twenty-five Member States to be more competitive and be more market-oriented whilst stabilising their income, and at channelling more resources into programmes on the environment, quality and animal welfare by reducing direct payments to large farms. It is expected also to strengthen the European Union's hand in the trade negotiations in the World Trade Organisation.

21.3. CAP management and financing

The unity of the European Union's agricultural market requires common prices, common support instruments for these prices, common external protection, joint financing and, in general, **joint management**, for which the European Commission has responsibility. The Commission, as for other areas of Community activity, is also invested with the power of initiative, i.e. the power to make proposals [see section 4.1.2.]. Hence, the genesis of any agricultural policy measure, adopted by politicians in the Parliament and the Council, is a Commission proposal, based on technocratic criteria.

Scientific committees, made up of experts from all Member States, give advice to the Commission on the very important matters of consumer health and food safety. Eight committees meet about ten times a year, and the Commission consults them whenever there is a legal requirement to do so, and whenever a matter of special relevance to one of them arises. A Scientific Steering Committee (SSC) has a multidisciplinary role. One of its tasks is to coordinate the work of the scientific committees to provide an overall view of consumer health matters, and to deliver scientific advice on matters not covered by the mandates of the other scientific committees, e.g. on transmissible spongiform encephalopathies. The operation of the scientific committees and, in particular, of the SSC, is based on the three principles of excellence, independence and transparency.

After all this preparatory work inside the services of the Commission, once a Commission proposal in the area of the common agricultural policy has been put before it, the Council entrusts the preparation of its proceedings to a committee of senior officials known as the **Special Committee on Agriculture** (SCA). In the area of agriculture, the SCA assumes the role normally fulfilled by the Committee of Permanent Representatives (Coreper)[2] [see section 4.1.4.].

---

[1] Regulations 1782/2003 to 1788/2003, OJ L 270, 21.10.2003 and Regulation 864/2004, OJ L 161, 30.04.2004.
[2] Decision 98/235, OJ L 88, 24.03.1998

21.3.1. CAP Management

After adoption of the basic regulations by the Council comes management of the common organisations. Management is either the joint responsibility of the Commission and Council or that of the Commission alone. For general policy decisions such as the annual setting of farm prices, undertaken in application of the basic regulations, the **full procedure** is used: the Commission after consulting professional organisations submits a proposal to the Council, which takes a decision after consultation with the European Parliament and very often the Economic and Social Committee as well as the Committee of the Regions [see section 4.3.]. For long-application management provisions, such as adjustments of market mechanisms or of basic criteria, a **medium-length procedure** is used: the Commission proposes measures to the Council, which takes a decision without consulting either the European Parliament or the Economic and Social Committee.

The implementation provisions for basic regulations and management measures in the strict sense of the term, which are applicable on average for a few weeks or a few months, are adopted by the Commission using a procedure known as the **"Management Committee" procedure**, whereby the Commission acts after having received the opinion of the relevant management committee[1]. Management committees comprise representatives of the Member States dealing with a specific sector. They give their opinion on the Commission's plans for the management of agricultural markets. There is a management committee for each category of product: cereals, milk products, beef and veal, wine, fruit and vegetables, etc. Very important management committees are notably: the Committee of the EAGGF, which deals exclusively with matters relating to the guarantee section of the European Agricultural Guidance and Guarantee Fund, such as regulations applicable to agricultural markets or price and income support policy; and the Committee on agricultural structures and rural development (STAR), which assists the Commission with the management of the EAGGF guidance section. **Regulatory committees**, also made up of representatives of all the Member States, play a role similar to that of the management committees for decisions about the regulations that apply in general areas such as food safety legislation, common veterinary or plant health standards, etc.

21.3.2. CAP financing

Article 34 of the EC Treaty (Art. 40 EEC) - devoted to the gradual development of the common agricultural policy - declared that one or several agricultural guidance and guarantee funds should be created to enable the common organisation of agricultural markets to fulfil its goals. On January

---

[1] Regulation 2602/69, OJ L 324, 27.12.1969.

14, 1962 during the first agricultural marathon, the Council opted for the creation of one single fund to finance all Community market and structural expenditure in the various agricultural sectors: the **European Agricultural Guidance and Guarantee Fund (EAGGF)**. The Fund was set up in 1962, but the arrangements on the financing of the common agricultural policy were finalised in 1970[1].

The Fund's **Guarantee Section** finances, in particular, expenditure on the agricultural market organisations, the rural development measures that accompany market support and rural measures in certain regions [see section 21.5.1.]. Indeed, the Regulation on the financing of the common agricultural policy provides for rural development measures to be financed by either the Guarantee Section or the Guidance Section of the EAGGF, according to the regional context[2]. Thus, the Guarantee Section provides for co-financing of rural policy in rural areas covered by Objective 2 and in rural areas outside Objectives 1 and 2 of the Structural Funds [see sections 12.1.1. and 12.3.1.]. The Guarantee Section finances also specific veterinary and plant-health measures, as well as the dissemination of information on the common agricultural policy. The EAGGF **Guidance Section** co-finances the Community initiative for rural development, known as LEADER+ [see sections 12.3.3. and 21.5.2.], and measures covered by Objective 1 programmes (excluding agri-environmental measures, early retirement, forestry-related measures and the aid scheme for agriculture in less-favoured areas, which fall under the EAGGF Guarantee Section).

EAGGF management falls to the Commission, which is assisted by the EAGGF Committee, made up of representatives of the Member States and chaired by the Commission. The Committee is consulted on either an obligatory or optional basis on all matters affecting the EAGGF in the framework of the "management committee" procedure, described above. Although the Commission has sole responsibility for EAGGF management, it nevertheless passes through the channel of state organisations or agencies in the Member States for the payment of intervention expenditure on the Community's agricultural markets[3].

Approximately half of the EU budget goes towards financing the CAP, or around 0.6% of Community GDP [see section 3.4.]. Given the size of the agricultural budget, it is essential for the credibility of the CAP that proper systems are in place to ensure that these funds are spent correctly and to prevent fraud. Indeed, European taxpayers have a right to expect that all public money is spent efficiently, whether this be under national or EU budgets. As seen above, **most of this expenditure is managed by the Member States**, who therefore have the main responsibility for administering payments and checks on payments.

---

[1] Regulation 729/70, OJ L 94, 28.04.1970 codified and repealed by Regulation 1258/1999, OJ L 160, 26.06.1999.

[2] Regulation 1258/1999, OJ L 160, 26.6.1999.

[3] Ibid.

However, it is clearly **the Commission's responsibility** - with the help of the EAGGF Committee mentioned above - to make sure that efficient systems and procedures are set up at national level, that the accounts presented by the Member States are correct and complete and that expenditure complies with specific rules and regulations. Commission auditors verify that Member States' payment and audit systems are reliable and that they meet Community standards. If the systems put into place by a Member State prove to be unsatisfactory, the Commission must, under the clearance of accounts procedure, refuse to finance all or part of the expenditure concerned. Recovery can be made for individual cases where irregularities have been found or where systematic failures are revealed. The financial consequences of irregularities are, however, borne by the Community, unless government departments of the Member States are responsible for the irregularities or incorrect payment of sums[1].

Fraud concerning agricultural expenditure often hits the headlines in the Member States and fuels the criticism of the CAP's opponents. A response to the problem has been given by a Council Regulation which requires the Member States to themselves scrutinise the transactions forming part of the system of financing by the Guarantee Section of the EAGGF[2]. Member States are thus responsible for prevention and suppression of frauds. However, the Community co-finances action programmes by the Member States designed to improve their structures for monitoring EAGGF Guarantee Section expenditure[3]. The 1992 reform of the CAP includes provisions for each Member State to set up an **integrated administration and control system (IACS)** for direct payments [see section 21.5.]. Under the IACS, Member States set up computerised databases to enable electronic crosschecks and on-the-spot checks of holdings.

21.3.3. Agrimonetary questions and the euro

The **introduction of the euro**, on 1 January 1999, ended the previously existing problems concerning the fixing of common prices and intervention measures. It led to a major reform and simplification of the agrimonetary system. Agricultural conversion rates have been discontinued. Agricultural prices and aid in the participating Member States is paid in euros. Community aid too is paid and collected in euros[4]. In the case of the Member States outside the eurozone, the euro exchange rate is used for the necessary conversions into their national currencies, unless they decide to make payments in euro. For those Member States the value of a payment is determined by the exchange rate on the date of the operative event (a price or an aid) and not on the date of actual payment. In the case of compensa-

---

[1] Regulation 1258/1999, OJ L 160, 26.06.1999.
[2] Regulation 4045/89, OJ L 388, 30.12.1989 and Regulation 2154/2002, OJ L 328, 05.12.2002.
[3] Regulation 723/97, OJ L 108, 25.04.1997 and Regulation 2136/2001, OJ L 288, 01.11.2001.
[4] Regulation 2800/98, OJ L 349, 24.12.1998.

tion for a drop in prices or other aid, the EAGGF must cover half of the compensation actually paid, matching the amount that the Member State actually contributes.

The use of **the euro benefits the CAP**, not only by simplifying its procedures and reducing its budget costs through the abolition of the green rates, but also through the simplification and transparency of aid schemes for farmers, price stability and increased competitiveness in Community agriculture. Like their American counterparts, who can use their national currency (the dollar) for export transactions, European enterprises now have the Euro and are able to invoice their products in the currency in which their costs are also denominated, thereby avoiding an exchange risk.

21.4. Common market organisations

The common agricultural market is underpinned by **common market organisations (CMOs)**, which remove obstacles to intra-Community trade and create common protection at the external borders. At present, almost all the Community's agricultural production is regulated by common organisations. Article 32 of the EC Treaty (ex-Art. 38) defines agricultural products as products of the soil, livestock products and fishery products, along with products of first-stage processing which are directly related to these products. Foodstuffs are considered as products of second-stage processing and are therefore not included in agricultural products. To make matters as clear as possible, products covered by the provisions under the heading "agriculture" are listed in Annex II of the Treaty. This is why, in Community terminology, agricultural arrangements are often stated as being applicable to "Annex II products".

The market organisation regulations, which came into force in 2000 as a result of **the fourth reform of the CAP** [see section 21.2.], concern the arable crops, beef, milk and wine sectors, the new rural development framework, the horizontal rules for direct support schemes and the financing of the CAP[1]. These regulations introduced gradual cuts in institutional prices - compensated by income support - with the objective of bringing Europe's agricultural prices into closer touch with world market prices, thus helping improve the competitiveness of agricultural products on domestic and world markets with positive impacts on both internal demand and export levels [see sections 21.4.2. and 21.4.4.].

The **fifth CAP reform** (September 2003) established common rules for direct support schemes under the common agricultural policy and support schemes for producers of certain crops (durum wheat, protein crops, rice, nuts, energy crops, starch potatoes, milk, seeds, arable crops, sheep

---

[1]   Regulations 1251/1999 to 1259/1999, OJ L 160, 26.06.1999 and Regulation 1782/2003, OJ L 270, 21.10.2003.

meat and goat meat, beef and veal and grain legumes)[1]. The reform takes account of increased consumer concerns over **food quality and safety and environmental protection**. Indeed, the full payment of direct aid is henceforth linked to compliance with rules relating to agricultural land, agricultural production and activity, which should serve to incorporate in the common market organisations basic standards for the environment, food safety, animal health and welfare and good agricultural and environmental condition. The reform includes a reduction in direct payments ("modulation") for bigger farms to finance the rural development policy and introduces a financial discipline mechanism to ensure that the farm budget fixed until 2013 is not exceeded. The reform of the support schemes for farmers concerns also the ten new Member States since May 2004[2].

The market organisation of each agricultural product uses different mechanisms defined by its basic regulation and adopted by the Council using the full-blown procedure [see section 21.3.1.], but all of them are underpinned by, on the one hand, internal market measures, more often than not relating to price setting and support, and, on the other, by a trade regime with third countries, which is in conformity with the Agreement on agriculture concluded in the context of the GATT Uruguay Round [see section 23.4.].

21.4.1. The principles of the CAP

Three basic principles defined in 1962 characterise the common agricultural market and consequently the common market organisations: market unity, Community preference and financial solidarity. Whereas, the introduction of the euro has consolidated market unity [see section 21.3.3.], the third and fourth reforms of the CAP [see section 21.2.] have had an important effect on Community preference and financial solidarity.

Market unity means that agricultural products move throughout the European Union under conditions similar to those in an internal market, thanks to the abolition of quantitative restrictions to trade (quotas, import monopolies,...) and the removal of duties, taxes and measures having equivalent effect. Market unity supposes common agricultural prices throughout the EU. The Council, acting on a proposal from the Commission, thus, early in each marketing year, sets common agricultural prices expressed formerly in ecu and, since 1999, in euro[3] [see section 21.3.3.]. In principle, the common agricultural prices should be attained through the free play of supply and demand so that the only variations in the prices paid to farmers in all regions of the Union result from natural production conditions and distance from main centres of consumption. But in reality,

---

[1] Regulations 1782/2003 to 1788/2003, OJ L 270, 21.10.2003 and Regulation 864/2004, OJ L 161, 30.04.2004.

[2] Regulation 583/2004, OJ L 91, 30.03.2004 and Decision 2004/281, OJ L 93, 30.3.2004.

[3] See, e.g., Council Regulations 1400/1999 to 1405/1999, OJ L 164, 30.06.1999 and Council Regulations 1671/1999 to 1680/1999, OJ L 199, 30.07.1999.

as will be seen below, the common market organisations incorporate intervention measures, the force of which varies according to product, in order to support the common prices should there be insufficient demand or external supply at lower prices.

Community preference, the second bulwark of the common agricultural market, signifies that products of Community origin are bought in preference to imported products, in order to protect the common market against low-price imports and fluctuations in world prices. This principle, spread throughout the world, is enacted through import and export measures. The European Union tries to bring the prices of imports into the EU at the prices practised on the common market. The price gap between the world market and the minimum guaranteed price in the EU was formerly covered by variable import levies, which after the GATT Uruguay Round have been progressively replaced by fixed customs duties [see section 21.4.4. and 23.4.]. To the extent that external prices taxed with import duties are at the same level as internal prices, it is not to the advantage of European traders to buy supplies from outside the EU and they therefore give preference to Community products. But whereas this was practically always the case with the import levies, it is much less certain with the customs duties.

The third basic principle of the common agricultural market is that of **financial solidarity**. It is implemented through the intermediary of the European Agricultural Guidance and Guarantee Fund (EAGGF) and signifies that the Member States are jointly liable as regards the financial consequences of the common agricultural markets policy. Since the European Union organises agricultural markets and defines and applies the intervention measures on them, it is logical that it is responsible for the financial consequences of these measures. The EAGGF Guarantee Section therefore covers all the expenditure rendered necessary by the common market organisations. The other side of the coin is that the customs duties, collected at the Union's frontiers on imports from third countries, do not go into the coffers of the Member States but are a source of revenue for the Community budget [see section 3.4.].

The 1992 CAP reform, which made possible the 1993 GATT Agreement [see section 23.4.], has affected the fundamental principles of the CAP, since it has supplemented the original price support with a direct income aid system. It has, in fact, introduced a **mixed system**: price support was reduced, but the farmers' revenue was maintained at its previous level by subsidies. In other words, the reduction of price support was compensated by the support of the revenue of the farmers. This system was amplified by the 1999 reform. The new policy for rural development seeks to establish a coherent and sustainable framework for the future of Europe's rural areas. It seeks to complement the reforms introduced into the market sectors by promoting a competitive, multi-functional agricultural sector in the context of a comprehensive, integrated strategy for rural development [see section 21.5.1.]. The guiding principles of the new policy are those of decentralisation of responsibilities - thus strengthening subsidiarity and partnership - and flexibility of programming based on a "menu" of actions to be targeted and implemented according to Member States' specific needs.

21.4.2. Agricultural prices and product quality

Prices are a central component of the common market policy and the terminology surrounding them is very complicated. This is due to the various different roles which agricultural prices play and to the need for them to be adapted to specific conditions on different markets. Generally speaking, prices play three roles in the common agricultural market: they guide production, trigger intervention mechanisms and secure common external protection.

The **guide price** (beef and veal, wine), which is also known as the **target price** (cereals, sugar) or the **norm price** (tobacco), is the price that the common market organisation seeks to guarantee to producers. It is set each year by the Council in accordance with evolution both of the cost of living and of supply and demand on each market[1]. It therefore guides the production of each of the agricultural sectors for which such a price exists.

The **intervention price** (cereals, sugar, butter, beef and veal, tobacco) or the **basic price** (pigmeat), which is a certain percentage lower than the guide price, is the price at which intervention organisations in each Member State must buy products of Community origin which farmers put in for storage. For fruit and vegetables, which cannot be stored, there are **withdrawal prices** below which producers' groups, in their role as intervention organisations, stop selling and send surplus quantities for distillation, to charities or for destruction until such time as more sluggish supply triggers a recovery of the market prices.

Connected with the question of agricultural prices is the question of the **quality of agricultural products** and foodstuffs. The quality and characteristics of these products are often linked to their geographical origin. Two Council Regulations are designed to raise consumer awareness of the producers' efforts to improve the quality of their products. The first establishes a Community system for the protection of **geographical indications and designations of origin** for agricultural products and foodstuffs[2], supplemented by lists of some 480 names of agricultural and food products drawn up by the Commission[3]. It spells out with what requirements a product or foodstuff should comply in order to qualify for a protected designation of origin (PDO) or for a protected geographical indication (PGI). The other Regulation introduces an instrument for registering the names of products,

---

[1] See, e.g., Council Regulation 1628/98 and Commission Regulation 1648/98, OJ L 210, 28.07.1998.

[2] Regulation 2081/92, OJ L 208, 24.07.1992 and Regulation 692/2003, OJ L 99, 17.04.2003.

[3] Regulation 1107/96, OJ L 148, 21.06.1996 and Regulation 2703/2000, OJ L 311, 12.12.2000.

thus enabling producers who so wish to obtain **certificates of the 'specific character'** of a traditional product (or foodstuff), the specific character being defined as the feature which distinguishes the product or foodstuff clearly from other similar products or foodstuffs belonging to the same category[1]. Another Regulation concerns **organic production** of agricultural products and indications referring thereto (labelling) on agricultural products and foodstuffs[2]. A European Union symbol (logo), based on the 12 stars symbol of the EU, identifies agricultural products and foodstuffs whose names are registered under the rules on the protection of geographical indications and designations of origin[3]. The Community finances generic, collective information and promotion campaigns (public relations, publicity and dissemination of scientific information) for agricultural products on the internal market[4]. It also finances measures promoting the conservation, characterisation, collection and utilisation of genetic resources in agriculture[5].

21.4.3. Direct support schemes for farmers

A number of common market organisations provide for support to be granted to farmers in the form of direct payments. In order to ensure that the Member States take account of environmental and employment issues when granting direct aid to farmers under market organisations, a Regulation lays down **horizontal rules, applicable to various market organisations**, notably: arable crops, cereals, olive oil, grain legumes, flax, hemp, bananas, tobacco, seeds, rice, beef and veal, milk and milk products, sheepmeat and goatmeat[6].

With a view to better integrating **environment protection** into the common market organisations, Member States must define appropriate environmental measures in respect of the situation of the agricultural land used or the production concerned, to be applied by farmers. However, Member States have three options at their disposal:

• Support in return for agri-environmental commitments;

• General mandatory environmental requirements; or

• Specific environmental requirements.

Member States may also decide on appropriate and proportionate penalties for environmental infringements involving, where appropriate, the reduction or even the cancellation of direct payments.

In order to **stabilise the employment situation** in agriculture and to take into account the overall prosperity of holdings, Member States may

---

[1] Regulation 644/98, OJ L 87, 21.03.1998.
[2] Regulation 2092/91, OJ L 198, 22.07.1991 and Regulation 1804/1999, OJ L 222, 24.08.1999.
[3] Regulation 2081/92, OJ L 208, 24.07.1992 and Regulation 1726/98, OJ L 224, 11.08.1998.
[4] Regulation 2826/2000, OJ L 328, 23.12.2000.
[5] Regulation 870/2004, OJ L 162, 30.04.2004.
[6] Regulation 1259/99, OJ L 160, 26.06.1999.

decide the criteria and the rate of reducing the amounts of payments to farmers in respect of the calendar year concerned in cases where:

- the labour force on their holdings falls short of limits, determined by Member States;
- the overall prosperity of their holdings rises above limits; or
- the total amount of payments granted exceed certain limits.

21.4.4. External wing of the CAP

The external wing of the common market organisations seeks to protect European agricultural prices against low price imports. In the same way as intervention on the internal market attempts to prevent the market prices falling too far below the intervention prices, intervention at the external borders tries to prevent low priced imports from upsetting the European market. The **threshold price** (cereals, sugar, dairy products, olive oil) or the **sluice-gate price** (pigmeat, eggs and poultry) is a minimum price above which imports from third countries enjoy free access. For products for which a target price or guide price exists, the threshold price is determined in such a manner that the sales price of the imported product, allowance made for transport costs, is on a par with this price. For products for which there is no guide price (fruit and vegetables, table wine), the **reference price** is the minimum price at which a third country product can be imported and a tax is collected if the reference price is not respected.

The gap between the world price and the threshold price was originally bridged by import levies. Following the GATT agreements of December 1993, this gap is now partially closed by **customs duties**. However, for certain product groups such as cereals, rice, wine and fruit and vegetables, certain supplementary mechanisms that do not involve the collection of fixed customs duties are introduced in the basic regulations of the CAP by a Regulation, which lays down the adaptations and transitional measures required in order to implement the agreements concluded in the GATT framework[1] [see section 23.4.].

The across-the-board **tariff concessions** which result from multilateral trade negotiations, such as those of the GATT and now the WTO, are only part of the commitments weighing upon the EU's agricultural relationships. There are in addition preferential bilateral agreements with the ACP countries [see section 24.2.] and the majority of Mediterranean countries [see section 25.5.], in the form of association agreements or cooperation agreements, which provide for concessions in the agricultural sector [see also section 5.2.2.]. In addition, tariff reductions are granted by the Community under the Generalised System of Preferences (GSP) to almost all the developing countries [see section 24.5.], notably in the framework of the United Nations Conference on Trade and Development (UNCTAD) and in the framework of the Europe Agreements with the countries of Central and

---

[1] Regulation 3290/94, OJ L 349, 31.12.1994 and Regulation 1340/98, OJ L 184, 27.06.1998.

Eastern Europe [see section 25.2.]. The Community supplies the Russian
Federation agricultural products free of charge from intervention stocks or
purchased on the EU market[1].

21.5. Structural policy and rural development

**"Agricultural structures" are taken as meaning all production and
work conditions** in the sphere of agriculture, i.e. the number or age spread
of people working in agriculture, the number and size of farms, the technical equipment on farms, the level of farmers' qualifications, producers'
groups, marketing and processing of agricultural products and so on.
Unlike market organisation and pricing policy, which requires uniform
provisions and centralised management, socio-structural policy **may remain more in the realm of the Member States** in that it has to be adjusted to the specificities of the different regions. But structural policy
blueprinting and supervision is brought under the wing of the Community
to promote economic and social cohesion and prevent uneven competition
conditions for Community producers [see sections 12.1.2. and 12.2.1.].
Thus, a Regulation has established an integrated administration and control
system (IACS) for Community aid schemes under the common agricultural
policy[2].

Measures designed to support the improvement of agricultural structures were introduced into the common agricultural policy as early as 1972.
For almost two decades, they have attempted and in some cases succeeded
to integrate agricultural structural policy into the wider economic and social context of rural areas. The 1992 policy reform stressed the environmental dimension of agriculture as the largest land user, but rural policy
was still carried out through a range of complex instruments. The 1999
CAP reform drove agriculture to adapt to new realities and further changes
in terms of market evolution, market policy and trade rules, consumer demand and preferences and the Community's next enlargement. The rural
development policy currently aims at **restoring and enhancing the competitiveness of rural areas**, thus contributing to the maintenance and creation of employment in those areas.

Financing from the EAGGF Guidance Section, like that from the other
Structural Funds, is granted under the Community support frameworks
(CSFs) and the single programming documents (SPDs) [see section
12.3.1.]. However, rural development and accompanying measures during
the period 2000-06 are financed by the EAGGF Guarantee Section or
Guidance Section, depending on their regional context.

Thus, Community support for early retirement, less-favoured areas and
areas with environmental restrictions, agri-environmental measures and af-

---

[1]   Regulation 2802/98, OJ L 349, 24.12.1998.
[2]   Regulation 3508/92, OJ L 355, 05.12.1992 and Regulation 1593/2000, OJ L 182, 21.07.2000.

forestation are **financed by the EAGGF Guarantee Section** throughout the Community. Community support for other rural development measures is financed by the **EAGGF Guidance Section** in areas covered by Objective 1 (integrated into the programmes) **and Guarantee Section** in areas outside Objective 1 [see sections 12.1.1. and 12.3.1.].

21.5.1. Rural development measures

According to **Article 33(2,a)** of the EC Treaty, in working out the common agricultural policy and the special methods for its application, account is to be taken of the particular nature of agricultural activity which results from the social structure of agriculture and from structural and natural disparities between the various agricultural regions. A common rural development policy should accompany and complement the other instruments of the common agricultural policy and thus contribute to the achievement of the policy's objectives as laid down in Article 33(1) of the Treaty. This policy should take into account the objectives set out in Articles 158 and 160 (TEC) for the common policy of economic and social cohesion and contribute to their achievement [see section 12.1.2.]. Rural development measures should, therefore, contribute to economic and social cohesion in regions whose development is lagging behind (Objective 1) and regions facing structural difficulties (Objective 2) as defined in the Regulation laying down general provisions on the Structural Funds [see section 12.3.].

The common rural development policy is based on Regulation 1257/99 on support for rural development from the European Agricultural Guidance and Guarantee Fund[1]. **The objectives of this single rural policy instrument** are to provide adequate support for the process of modernising agricultural production structures and to meet fully the requirements of the rural population, the complex economic and social microcosm of rural areas, and the needs of an environment which, while often fragile, is also rich in resources to be capitalised on. More specifically, rural development support measures are designed to:

1. **strengthen the agricultural and forestry sector**. The emphasis is on modernising agricultural holdings and on processing and marketing quality agricultural products. In addition, the viability of holdings should be reinforced through support measures for the establishment of young farmers and better conditions for early retirement. The forestry sector is recognised as a key element of rural development and there is support for the sector where it serves an ecological function;

2. **improve the competitiveness of rural areas**. Here, the main targets are to maintain the quality of life of the rural community and to promote diversification into new activities. The measures are designed to

---

[1] Regulation 1257/99, OJ L 160, 26.6.1999 and Regulation 583/2004, OJ L 91, 30.03.2004.

create alternative sources of income and employment for farmers and their families, and for the wider rural community;

3. **preserve the environment and Europe's unique rural heritage**. Agri-environmental measures are intended to promote environment-friendly agricultural methods. They are the only compulsory element in the new generation of rural development programmes, thereby taking a decisive step towards recognition of the multifunctional role of agriculture.

Regulation 1782/2003 (fifth CAP reform) [see section 21.2.] established: **common conditions for direct payments** under the various income support schemes in the framework of the CAP which are financed by the "Guarantee" Section of the European Agricultural Guidance and Guarantee Fund (EAGGF), except those provided for under Regulation 1257/1999; an income support for farmers ("single payment scheme"); and special support schemes for farmers producing certain crops[1]. In order to achieve a better balance between policy tools designed to promote sustainable agriculture and those designed to promote rural development, a system of progressive reduction of direct payments was introduced on a compulsory Community-wide basis for the years 2005 to 2012. All direct payments, beyond certain amounts, should be reduced by a certain percentage each year.

Community support may be granted under the conditions defined in Title II of Regulation (EC) 1257/99[2] for **the following rural development measures**:

- investments in agricultural holdings;
- setting up of young farmers;
- vocational training;
- early retirement;
- supporting less-favoured areas and areas subject to environmental constraints;
- improving processing and marketing of agricultural products;
- maintaining the agri-environment;
- afforestation.

21.5.2. LEADER+ and SAPARD

Since its launch in 1991, the LEADER Community initiative [see section 12.3.3.] has encouraged the active involvement of local rural communities in the development of their local economy. This participative approach to rural development has produced positive results. In particular, the experience gained from LEADER I and II has demonstrated that the territorial development strategy was the appropriate one to restore vitality

---

[1] Regulation 1782/2003, OJ L 270, 21.10.2003 and Regulation 864/2004, OJ L 161, 30.04.2004.
[2] Regulation 1257/99, OJ L 160, 26.6.1999 and Regulation 583/2004, OJ L 91, 30.03.2004.

to the rural territories, to stimulate the creation and maintenance of activities and hence to increase their attractiveness. The Community initiative, **LEADER+**, financed by the Guidance section of the EAGGF, goes a step further. Its objective is to encourage the implementation of high quality, original strategies for integrated sustainable development of rural areas. Leader+ is at the same time an instrument of assistance in the new rural development policy, accompanying and complementing the CAP, and an instrument of assistance in the economic and social cohesion policy aiming to ensure the viability of rural Europe[1] [see section 12.1.2.]. Its objective is to encourage, on the basis of local partnerships, the emergence and experimentation of rural territorial development strategies, integrated and in a pilot form.

LEADER+ is applicable in all rural areas of the Community, but the selected territories must have demonstrated their capacity to support the proposed development project in terms both of coherence and sufficient critical mass. The **development strategy** must demonstrate its foundation and coherence with the territory, its economic viability, its sustainable character (in environmental terms), its pilot character and more particularly its specificity and originality in relation to the operations of the mainstream programmes as well as the transferable character of the methods proposed.

The Special accession programme for agriculture and rural development **(SAPARD)** establishes the framework for Community support for sustainable agriculture and sustainable rural development for the pre-accession period for the following applicant countries: Bulgaria, the Czech Republic, Estonia, Hungary, Latvia, Lithuania, Poland, Romania, Slovakia and Slovenia[2]. Community pre-accession aid (of up to 75% of the total eligible public expenditure) is designed in particular to resolve priority problems in adapting the economies of the applicant countries in a sustainable manner and facilitating the implementation by them of the agricultural "acquis communautaire", focusing in particular on the common agricultural policy and in following the priorities of the reformed CAP. However, such aid should be applied to priority areas to be defined for each country, such as the improvement of structures for processing agricultural and fishery products, distribution, quality control of food as well as veterinary and plant-health controls and the setting-up of producer groups, integrated rural development projects and agri-environmental measures.

---

[1] Regulation 1260/1999, OJ L 161, 26.06.1999 and Regulation 1105/2003, OJ L 158, 27.06.2003.

[2] Regulation 1268/1999, OJ L 161, 26.06.1999 and Regulation 769/2004, OJ L 123, 27.04.2004.

21.6. Appraisal and outlook

The **common agricultural policy intrigues** those who take an interest in European integration, both because of its advance on other common policies and because of its complexity. The resources in its grasp represent nearly 50% of the Community budget [see section 3.4.]; the instruments that it applies are extremely varied and the terms that it uses to describe them would appear to be chosen precisely to prevent outsiders from understanding what they are. A close look, however, reveals that the complexity of the agricultural policy is due first and foremost to the variety of natural and economic situations which exist, the first relating to production and marketing conditions for different products, the second to the fact that the fifteen Member States have different structures and different climatic conditions.

Despite its complexity, the CAP has more than achieved its objectives. Customs duties, quantitative restrictions and measures having equivalent effect have been relegated to the dustbin of history and trade between the Member States has been fully liberalised. The **single agricultural market** signifies that a good originating in one Member State can be stored in another and marketed in a third. It can also be exported to third countries from any Member State. The merchandise of third countries gains entry to the common market by crossing just one of the Member States' borders. This liberalisation has led to considerable growth in the range of agricultural products and foodstuffs available to consumers.

In addition, the common market organisation has buffered the European agricultural market against major fluctuations on the world market. In normal times, it **has provided market stability** through a policy of staggering supply (storage, monthly increases), of surplus disposal (refunds, denaturing) or of diversifying supply (imports from third countries, export levies). In times of crisis, it has resorted to drastic measures ranging from import or export bans to the withdrawal from the market of part of production or even the reduction of production factors.

Market stabilisation is not an end in itself. It is a path to the other objectives of the common agricultural policy, notably that of food supply security. Thanks to the CAP, **the European Union has been spared any serious food shortages**, which would have jeopardised both the common agricultural policy and European integration itself. Comparison of the abundance of foodstuffs in Western Europe with the shortages in Eastern Europe, before and after the fall of communist regimes, is a sufficient gauge of the CAP's success. An additional and not less important one, is the independence of Western Europe in foodstuffs, which should be compared to its dependence on imported energy, namely oil [see section 19.1.1.]. The price of the Community's independence in foodstuffs has not been too high to pay. It goes without saying that the level of common prices corresponds to Europe's industrial and social development level.

These prices are naturally enough not below those of the world market, but they are not much above them either.

The so-called **"European model of agriculture"** aims at a sustainable development of rural areas through a diversified and multifunctional agriculture. The new CAP is based on two elements: lowering institutional prices for key products and offsetting the impact of these cuts on producer incomes by means of direct payments. While improving competitiveness of European agricultural products at world level, the 1999 reform has consolidated the foundations for a diversified and multifunctional agriculture contributing to sustainable development. The production of renewable raw materials and high quality food products, the protection of the environment and the maintenance of the vitality of rural regions and the countryside are considered services to the society, which have to be rewarded to ensure that they continue to be available in future.

In order to achieve the objectives of the overall agricultural and budgetary reform adopted by the Berlin European Council (Agenda 2000), **the Community effort should aim at**: stabilising the markets and improving the common market organisations (the first pillar of the CAP); introducing simpler and more sustainable direct support; achieving a better balance of support for sustainable agriculture and rural development; and consolidating and strengthening rural development (the second pillar). Supporting farming incomes is not the only issue, better results are also needed in terms of food quality, preserving the environment, animal welfare, landscapes and cultural heritage.

Bibliography on the common agricultural policy

- BULLER Henry, HOGGART Keith. *Women in the European countryside*. Aldershot: Ashgate, 2004.
- CAKMAK Erol. *Structural change and market opening in agriculture*. Brussels: Centre for European Policy Studies, 2004.
- CARDWELL Michael. *The European model of agriculture*. Oxford: Oxford University Press, 2004.
- CASTRO Paolo De, *Towards a new European agriculture: what agricultural policy in the enlarged EU?*. Roma: Agra Editrice, 2004.
- EUROPEAN COMMISSION. *Reform of the common agricultural policy: Medium-term prospects for agricultural markets and income in the European Union 2003-2010*. Luxembourg: EUR-OP*, 2004.
    - *New perspectives for EU rural development*. Luxembourg: EUR-OP*, 2004.
- JENTSCH Birgit, SHUCKSMITH Mark (eds.). *Young people in rural areas of Europe*. Aldershot; Burlington, VT: Ashgate, 2004.
- MOREDDU Catherine. *Analysis of the 2003 CAP Reform*. Paris: OCDE, 2004.
- O'CONNOR Bernard. *The law of geographical indications*. London: Cameron May, 2004.

- WICHERN Rainer. *Economics of the Common Agricultural Policy*. Brussels: European Commission, 2004.

The publications of the Office for Official Publications of the European Communities (EUR-OP) exist generally in all official languages of the EU.

DISCUSSION TOPICS

1. Why had the Treaty of Rome called specifically for a common agricultural policy?
2. Could the EU rely on world markets for the supply of agricultural products and foodstuffs as it does for the supply of energy products?
3. Discuss the management of the CAP.
4. Why does the CAP need a common financial instrument such as the EAGGF?
5. How does the CAP interact with regional, social and environment policies?

Chapter 22

COMMON FISHERIES POLICY

Diagram of the chapter

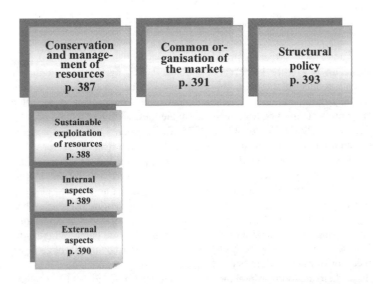

Fisheries policy, which the Treaty of Rome initially made part of the Common Agricultural Policy by placing fishery products, products of the soil and stock-farming products in the same basket, became a fully-fledged common policy in 1983. It no longer has much in common with the CAP, apart from the fact that it makes use of instruments of market organisation comparable to those of the CAP. Although the fishery sector does not carry the same weight in the Gross Domestic Product and does not employ as many people as agriculture, the establishment of a common policy required just as much effort as the Common Agricultural Policy.

The fishery resources policy, which embraces both internal and external policy, was the most troublesome to put into practice. It is the forum for such thorny questions as total allowable catch (TAC), the sharing out of TAC between the Member States (quotas) and access of the vessels from one Member State to the territorial waters of the others. Resources policy also has to cope with difficult negotiations with third countries to settle questions of access for Community vessels to their waters and vice versa. Although this kingpin of the common fisheries policy (CFP) is analysed first, it was the last arrival on the fisheries scene.

The origins of the two other pillars of the CFP date back to 1970. The common organisation of markets has clearly covered a great deal of ground since then and its reform, in 1981, opened the door to the final compromise on fisheries. Structural policy, for its part, has been torn by national differences on the question of resource conservation. For many years it was restricted to interim measures and was only firmly established with the agreement on resources, reached in January 1983.

22.1. Economic and legal framework

The market in fishery products is similar to that in agricultural products. This is why the EC Treaty stipulates that by agricultural products is meant products of the soil, stock-farming products and fishery products and that the operation and establishment of a common market for all of these products must be accompanied by the introduction of a Common Agricultural Policy (Articles 32 and 33). This is therefore the fundamental reason for and legal basis of a common policy in the fisheries sector.

The Treaty consequently placed fisheries policy and the Common Agricultural Policy in the same basket and the two were initially one and the same. More precisely, the organisation of the market and structural policy covering fisheries formed part of the Common Agricultural Policy. There is however a basic difference between products of the soil and stock-farming on the one hand and fisheries products on the other. Whereas the first two remain within the boundaries laid down by man, fish have no respect for frontiers! Migratory fish, such as herring and tuna, do not have to show their passports when they enter the economic zone of a Member State! There are therefore problems relating to fisheries resources, which simply do not exist for products of the soil and stock farming. This is the first reason why a specific common policy was required for fisheries products. This specificity is now acknowledged by the EC Treaty in Article 3, which speaks of a common policy in the fields of agriculture and fisheries.

The second justification for a common fisheries policy is specific to this sector. Between 1956 and 1965, world fish production rose by 50%. Investments over this period of economic growth, vessel modernisation and higher productivity pushed up catches to such a high level that stock replenishment was threatened and the commoner species, such as herring, began to be exhausted. In times of surplus, storage aid, export subsidies and import restrictions were required. In times of shortage, on the other hand, it was necessary to regulate and monitor fishing to ensure that the seas fished by the Member States did not become empty of fish. All of this had to be achieved at Community level, if the aim was a common fisheries market.

The implementation of the rule of the United Nations of a **200 mile fishery conservation zone** provided a striking illustration of the need for a common conservation policy for these new Community resources. The principle of free access to the fishing zones of Member States was incorporated into the Regulation establishing the fisheries structural policy, adopted as far back as 1970, the year in which accession negotiations were opened with four countries - the United Kingdom, Ireland, Denmark and Norway - all major fishing nations, the total catch of which amounted to double that of the six founding Member States.

The principle of equal access to fishing zones therefore formed part of the "acquis communautaire" (existing Community legislation) which applicants had to accept. Although they attempted to abolish the rule of equal access during accession negotiations, they only succeeded in postponing its full application. Articles 100 to 103 of the **Act of Accession** granted a temporary derogation to the 1970 Community Regulation, authorising the Member States to maintain until December 31, 1982 exclusive fishing rights for their vessels in waters up to six nautical miles from their coasts (stretched to twelve miles for certain regions of the acceding States and of France), provided that the historic fishing rights of vessels from other Member States were respected in these waters. Despite this temporary derogation, the principle of equal access to economic zones was one of the main causes for the negative votes of the Norwegian people on Community membership, in 1973 as in 1994 [see section 1.2.].

The Commission felt that **the total allowable catch** should be shared out in accordance with the golden rule of the common market, namely freedom from all form of discrimination [see sections 5.1 and 6.1.]. This amounted to equality of access for the vessels of the Member States to Community waters. However, the very uneven spread of fishery resources between the waters of the Member States and the fact that fishermen consider it their exclusive right to fish in the strip of coastal water under the jurisdiction of their State and to continue to fish in areas where they have traditionally fished, even if these areas are no longer covered by open access but fall into the economic zone of another Member State, give a measure of the difficulties faced by a Community policy of fishery resources management and conservation. To facilitate the management and development of the common fisheries policy, the Commission has established a permanent dialogue with professional and non-professional organisations (consumers, environment and development) inside the Advisory Committee on Fisheries and Aquaculture[1].

22.2. Conservation and management of resources

The need for a policy to conserve fishery resources became evident towards the middle of the sixties, when, after long years of overfishing, production began to stagnate and the Community's levels of self-supply began to fall for certain popular species, notably herring and tuna. Since a

---

[1] Decision 1999/478, OJ L 187, 20.07.1999.

similar situation prevailed in the rest of the world, the concept of a **total allowable catch (TAC)** was adopted by the United Nations Conference on the law of the sea, culminating in the extension of fishing zones to 200 miles[1]. Under the TAC rule, each coastal state uses scientific data to set a catch level which enables sufficient reproduction of fishery stocks, then it determines the amount which can be fished by its own vessels and that which can be granted to third countries in exchange for or through sale of catch rights. The central aim of the TAC is to conserve and enhance existing fishing zones in the interests of both the fishing industry and consumers.

In a Resolution of November 3, 1976 made public on May 7, 1981[2], the Council agreed that the Member States would extend, by concerted action, the limits of the fishing zones to 200 miles from January 1, 1977 for North Sea and North Atlantic coasts, without prejudice to action of a similar nature for other fishing zones under their jurisdiction, notably the Mediterranean. From January 1, 1977, the Community's exclusive economic zone therefore embraced numerous and potentially rich fishing grounds, the conservation and correct management of which was the responsibility of the Community.

While the extension of **the economic zones** to a distance of 200 miles off coasts - or to the median line when the distance between coasts did not permit a limit of 200 miles - extends the rights of coastal States in these zones, it also means greater obligations for them. The most significant of these obligations is that of conserving biological resources which, given the interdependence of fishery stocks, is a matter of some importance to fishermen and consumers both of the coastal state and of neighbouring states.

22.2.1. Sustainable exploitation of resources

The question of equal access conditions and that of the allocation of resources between Member States formed the crux of the design and implementation of the common fisheries policy. In this field as in many others, the diverging interests of the Member States proved to be a formidable obstacle. Many of them, pushed by the 200-mile rule out of the waters in which they had traditionally fished, had to fall back on the North Sea, where overfishing had already frittered away available resources. Since the three Member States, which had acceded to the Community in 1973 (United Kingdom, Ireland, Denmark), had much vaster and richer fishery zones than the founding members, the latter jealously coveted their resources. Founding members, to shore up their claims, called upon the Community principle of equal access to and working of fishing grounds in the sea waters under the sovereignty of the Member States by boats flying

---

[1] Decision 98/392, OJ C 155, 23.05.1997.
[2] OJ C 105, 07.05.1981.

the flag of one of the Member States. This principle, embodied in the 1970 Regulation establishing the policy of fishery structures, was fiercely fought by applicant States, who succeeded in winning a temporary derogation running to December 31, 1982. Hence, the Community conservation and management of resources policy was first adopted in 1983 and was completely reviewed in 2002[1] [see section 22.2.]. This policy covered both internal and external aspects that we examine successively.

22.2.2. Internal aspects

The Council framework regulation on the **conservation and sustainable exploitation of fisheries resources** lays down the basis for ensuring the long-term viability of the fisheries sector[2]. The approach is founded on scientific advice and the precautionary principle on the one hand, and on good governance and consistency with the other Community policies on the other. Among the measures which the Council may adopt are multiannual recovery plans for the most threatened stocks, including measures to reduce fishing effort where necessary, and multiannual management plans for other stocks. Where there is a serious threat to the conservation of resources or the marine ecosystem, the Commission and the Member States may take the necessary emergency measures lasting for six and three months respectively. The Member States may also adopt conservation and management measures applicable to fishing vessels inside their 12 nautical mile zone, provided that they are non-discriminatory and prior consultation between the Commission and the Member States has taken place, and that the Community has not adopted measures specifically for that area. Concerning access to waters and resources, the regulation lays down rules on allocating fishing opportunities and reviewing the access rules, and extends until 31 December 2012 the existing rules restricting access to resources inside the 12 nautical mile zones of the Member States.

To ensure the **effective implementation of the common fisheries policy** a series of measures are provided for: the establishment of a Community system of fishing licences, administered by the Member States and applicable to all Community fishing vessels, both in its waters as in those of third countries[3]; the issuing and management by the Member States of special fishing permits (authorisation of exploitation of specific fisheries)[4]; the setting of the objectives and detailed rules for restructuring the Community fisheries sector with a view to achieving a balance on a sustainable basis between resources and their exploitation[5] and of multi-annual guidance

---

[1] Regulation 2371/2002, OJ L 358, 31.12.2002 and Regulation 1242/2004, OJ L 236, 07.07.2004.
[2] Ibid.
[3] Regulation 3690/93, OJ L 341, 31.12.1993.
[4] Regulation 1627/94, OJ L 171, 06.07.1994.
[5] Decision 97/413, OJ L 175, 03.07.1997 and decision 2002/70, OJ L 31, 01.02.2002.

programmes (MAGPs) designed to implement these objectives and rules[1]; and the establishment of systems for the management of fishing effort and for control of the CFP.

When, for a particular species or related species, restriction of catch volume is necessary, the total allowable catch (TAC) for certain fish stocks and groups of fish stocks, the share available to the Community, the allocation of this share between Member States, total catch allocated to third countries and the specific conditions under which all this must take place are drawn up every year[2]. The same is true of the setting of guidance prices for fishery products[3]. The **annual allocation of catch quotas** between the Member States is a process almost as difficult as the annual setting of agricultural prices. In both cases, a delicate balance must be struck between the aspirations of the different Member States.

The annual setting of TACs and their allocation between the Member States are, naturally enough, based on certain criteria. **TAC setting** takes into account scientific opinions on the need to protect fishing grounds and fish stocks, balancing them against the interests of Community consumers and fishermen. It was mentioned above that quite often the latter interests weigh more than the scientific opinions. However, TAC setting also takes into consideration the agreements which the Community has with third countries, such as Norway and Canada. The allocation of the TACs between Member States (catch quotas) is also carried out in light of traditional fishing activities, possible loss of fishing potential in the waters of third countries and the specific needs of regions which are particularly dependent on fishing and its related industries. In order to improve the conditions for exploiting resources, **special fishing permits** may be issued to Community fishing vessels and to vessels flying third-country flags operating in the Community fishing area[4], or, inversely, to Community vessels operating in the waters of a third country in the context of a fisheries agreement[5].

A Community framework covers specific measures to conserve and manage **fishery resources in the Mediterranean**[6]. Projects which can be financed by the Community notably include the restructuring of traditional fisheries, the adaptation of specialised fisheries (sponges, coral, sea urchin), the monitoring of fishing activities, the development of a statistical network and the coordination of research and the use of scientific data. A Regulation lays down certain technical measures for the conservation of fishery resources in the Mediterranean[7]. Technical measures exist also for

---

[1] Commission decisions 98/119 to 98/131, OJ L 39, 12.02.1998 and decision 2002/652, OJ L 215, 10.08.2002.

[2] See, for example, Regulation 2287/2003, OJ L 344, 31.12.2003 and Regulation 867/2004, OJ L 161, 30.04.2004.

[3] See, for example, Regulation 2764/2000, OJ L 321, 19.12.2000.

[4] OJ L 171, 06.07.1994.

[5] Regulation 3317/94, OJ L 350, 31.12.1994.

[6] Regulation 3499/91, OJ L 331, 03.12.1991.

[7] Regulation 1626/94, OJ L 171, 06.07.1994 and Regulation 2550/2000, OJ L 292, 29.11.2000.

the conservation of fishery resources in the waters of the Baltic Sea, the Belts and the Sound[1].

22.2.3. External aspects

The external aspects of the resource policy are governed by the Council Resolution of November 3, 1976, known as **The Hague Agreements** and made public on May 7, 1981[2]. In this Resolution, the Council agreed that from January 1, 1977, fishing by third country vessels within the economic zone of the Community would be governed by agreements between the Community and the third countries in question. It also agreed that there was a need to ensure, through **Community agreements**, that the Community's fishing industry was granted or kept rights in the waters of third countries.

As a consequence, although the Community had not yet settled its internal fishery problems, by the end of 1976 it presented itself to the outside world as a single coastal State, obliging third countries which wished to fish in the fishing zones of the different Member States to conclude an agreement with the Community as such. The framework agreements negotiated by the Commission in the Community's name implied recognition of the Community's jurisdiction over the **Community 200 mile zone**, its right to set TACs within this zone and to give third countries access to the surplus part of TACs while obtaining access for the Member States to the surplus of co-signatory third countries.

Since this date, numerous fishery agreements have been concluded between the Community and countries with rich fishing grounds such as Madagascar, Angola, Mauritania, Morocco, Mozambique, the Seychelles and Senegal. These agreements and their renewal are negotiated by the Commission and concluded after a Council Decision, often in the form of an exchange of letters, defining the fishing rights of the Community and the financial compensation to be paid by it to the government of the country in question[3]. Fisheries agreements cover some 25% of supply of the Community market and are highly important to the sector, creating significant numbers of jobs in both the EU and partner countries[4].

22.3. Common organisation of the market

Contrasting sharply with the gestation of the policy for the management and conservation of fishery resources, the creation of a **common market for fishery products** did not come up against major difficulties.

---

[1] Regulation 88/98, OJ L 9, 15.01.1998 and Regulation 1250/98, OJ L 201, 17.07.1998.
[2] OJ C 105, 07.05.1981.
[3] See, for example, OJ L 349, 24.12.2002 and Decision 2003/384, OJ L 133, 29.05.2003.
[4] COM (96) 488, 30 October 1996.

Such a market organisation was moreover expressly provided for by the Treaty, with Articles 32 and 34 (ex-Art. 38 and 40 TEC) stipulating that the operation and development of the common market for agricultural products (including fishery products) should be accompanied by the establishment of a common (agricultural) policy and that the latter should incorporate common organisation of the market. Common organisation of the market in fishery and aquaculture products was born in October 1970 and amended several times at later stages. The most recent Regulation in this field aims at ensuring that the rules governing the organisation of the market in fishery products contribute positively to better management and utilisation of resources. It provides for consumers to be informed by means of labelling of fishery products when offered for retail sale, strengthens the role of producer organisations and overhauls the intervention mechanisms, the main purpose of which is to act as a safety net[1].

One of the measures necessary to implement the common organisation of markets is the application of **common standards for the marketing** of the products in question, to ensure that products which do not meet a sufficient quality level are not marketed and to stimulate trade on the basis of fair competition. A Regulation sets common marketing standards for certain fresh or chilled fish for human consumption[2]. In accordance with this Regulation, fish freshness plays a determinant role in assessment of its quality. The common marketing standards therefore take the form of a breaking down into freshness grading on the one hand and size grading on the other, the latter due to differences in consumers' buying habits. The application of these standards means that there must be inspection of the products subject to them. Member States must therefore submit products to a **conformity check**, which can take place at all the marketing stages and also during transport. The Member States must also take all appropriate steps to penalise infringements of marketing standards.

A **guide price** is set at the beginning of the fish marketing year for the main fresh or chilled products[3]. This price is based on the average of the prices recorded on wholesale markets or in representative ports during the three previous fish marketing years. It makes allowance for possible evolution in production and demand and for the need to ensure stable market prices and to contribute to supporting the income of producers, without forgetting consumers' interests. A **Community withdrawal price** is set in line with the freshness, size or weight and presentation of the product, which must be equal to at least 70% while not exceeding 90% of the guide price.

Within this range, producers' organisations can **set a withdrawal price** below which they no longer sell the products supplied by their members. Should this situation arise, the organisations must grant compensation to member producers in line with the quantities of the main fresh or chilled

---

[1] Regulation 104/2000, OJ L 17, 21.02.2000.
[2] Regulation 2406/96, OJ L 334, 23.12.1996 and Regulation 2578/2000, OJ L 298, 25.11.2000.
[3] See, for example, OJ L 351, 28.12.2002.

products withdrawn from the market. The organisations set up intervention funds formed by contributions based on the quantities put on sale or run a compensation system to finance these withdrawal measures. A **producers' organisation** is taken as being any recognised organisation or association of such organisations, set up on the initiative of producers in order to take measures ensuring that fishing is carried out in a rational manner, to improve sales conditions for their production and to stabilise prices.

22.4. Structural policy

The fishery sector is at least as vulnerable as agriculture. Production depends on several factors that cannot be controlled by producers: weather, water pollution, delimitation of fishing zones. The sea-fishing sector, which makes up the bulk of the fishing industry, has a highly specific social structure and arduous living and working conditions. Fishing is moreover often economically vital in certain coastal regions without other economic resources and it is a major breadwinner for the people living in these regions. This is why the common organisation of the fishery market must be accompanied by a common structural policy. This fact was recognised in 1970, which saw the combined adoption of the Regulation establishing a common structural policy and that of the Regulation creating a common organisation of the market for the fishery products sector.

Despite the structural measures that were thus implemented during the seventies and the eighties, the fisheries sector was confronted in the early nineties by a very serious structural crisis, characterised notably by: the widespread chronic overcapacity of the fleets; the over-capitalisation and high debt levels of the companies; the restrictions brought to certain fishing techniques in respect of the conservation of resources; the setting of Community standards with regard to hygiene, health, product quality as well as safety on board. Moreover, many coastal regions suffered from a fragile socio-economic fabric, in particular the areas dependent on fishing, for many of which - if one took account of the induced activities - fishing was the principal or even the only activity.

On account of the aggravation of the structural problems of the fisheries sector, when the Community revised the Regulations of the Structural Funds, in July 1993, it decided to establish a **Financial Instrument for Fisheries Guidance (FIFG)**. The tasks of FIFG are: (a) to contribute to achieving a sustainable balance between fishery resources and their exploitation; (b) to strengthen the competitiveness of structures and the development of economically viable enterprises in the sector; (c) to improve market supply and the value added to fishery and aquaculture products; and (d) to contribute to revitalising areas dependent on fisheries and aquaculture[1]. Community structural assistance in the fisheries sector is provided through

---

[1] Regulation 1263/1999, OJ L 161, 26.06.1999 and Regulation 179/2002, OJ L 31, 01.02.2002.

the FIFG under certain rules and arrangements aiming at preventing and eliminating illegal, unreported and unregulated fishing and at promoting the sustainable development of aquaculture[1]. To help Member States achieve additional reductions in capacity, an emergency measure (2003-2006) provides Community funds to part-finance their additional needs to scrap fishing vessels affected by recovery plans adopted by the Council[2].

22.5. Appraisal and outlook

The Treaty of Rome did not provide for a fully-fledged fisheries policy, for it included fishery products in the products to be covered by the Common Agricultural Policy. Little by little, however, the specific characteristics of the fisheries sector pushed for a separate common policy. Towards the end of the sixties, therefore, the Community began to turn its attention to the need to protect its resources in the Atlantic and the North Sea, under serious threat from overfishing. Its concern was heightened by the creation of exclusive economic zones, decided upon within the United Nations Conference on the law of the sea. A Community policy to conserve fishery resources was necessary to protect the most threatened species in Community waters. Its main manifestations have been the setting of total allowable catches (TACs), the allocation of catch quotas between the Member States and technical management and surveillance measures. Through an external fisheries policy, the Community has sought to guarantee its own fleet access to the waters of countries with surplus resources and to restrict access to Community waters for foreign vessels, notably Soviet, Polish and Japanese factory ships.

Six years of negotiations were required before, on January 25, 1983, the Community reached one of its "historic compromises". On this date, a Community system of resource conservation, endeavouring to protect the biological resources of the sea under severe threat from modern fishing methods, was added to the common fisheries policy. This system introduced measures to restrict fishing and set conditions under which it could take place, along with measures governing access to the waters of the Member States. Measures to conserve and manage fishery resources thus came to join the "common organisation of the market", which sets common marketing standards for fisheries and aquaculture products, dividing them up into a freshness grading and seeking to ensure that products which do not reach a satisfactory quality level are not marketed. It obliges the Member States to carry out conformity control checks on these products and to apply sanctions to any infringements. This policy therefore helps protect consumer interests. Producers' interests are not neglected either in the common fisheries policy. Structural policy, inaugurated in 1970, makes use

---

[1]   Regulation 2792/1999, OJ L 337, 30.12.1999 and Regulation 1421/2004, OJ L 260, 06.08.2004.
[2]   Regulation 2370/2002, OJ L 358, 31.12.2002.

of common measures to restructure, modernise and develop the fishery sector, to develop aquaculture, encourage experimental fishing and adapt Community fishing capacities to disposal possibilities.

This does not mean that the Community fisheries sector is riding on the crest of a wave. The CFP currently faces multiple challenges: a number of stocks are in a critical state, the Community fleet is suffering from over-capacity, the fisheries sector is beset by economic fragility and employment is on the decline. The depletion of resources, due notably to the over-fishing of juveniles combined with fleet over-capacity, make the entire European fisheries sector extremely vulnerable from the economic and social viewpoint. The results achieved in the areas of surveillance systems, inspection and surveillance activities, fleet controls and the application of penalties are not satisfactory, because there are many differences in how the Member States are implementing controls at national level and the co-operation and coordination arrangements established by them are not adequate. Some Member States do not fulfil their obligation to notify catches to the Commission and the multi-annual guidance programmes (MAGPs) have not ensured effective control of the real capacity of the fleets. In order to redress this situation, there must be reduction in both fishing and fishing capacity through more stringent regulation of access to resources and closer monitoring of vessel movements in order to respect the general interest. At international level, the EU should coordinate its development co-operation policy and the external aspects of the common fisheries policy, stressing the importance of environmental and socioeconomic factors for promoting sustainable and responsible fisheries.

Bibliography on the common fisheries policy

- CATARCI Camillo. *World markets and industry of selected commercially-exploited aquatic species with an international conservation profile.* Rome: FAO, 2004.
- CLOVER Charles. *The end of the line: how overfishing is changing the world and what we eat.* London: Ebury, 2004.
- CONCEIÇÃO-HELDT Eugenia de. *The Common Fisheries Policy in the European Union: a study in integrative and distributive bargaining.* London: Routledge, 2004.
- EUROPEAN COMMISSION. *Promoting more environmentally-friendly fishing methods: The role of technical conservation measures.* Luxembourg: EUR-OP*, 2004.
- *European code of sustainable and responsible fisheries practices.* Luxembourg: EUR-OP*, 2004.
- FOOD AND AGRICULTURE ORGANIZATION OF THE UNITED NATIONS. *Guide for identifying, assessing and reporting on subsidies in the fisheries sector.* Rome: FAO, 2004.
- HUSS H.H., GRAM L., ABABOUCH L. *Assessment and management of seafood safety and quality.* Rome: FAO, 2004.
- LEQUESNE Christian. *The politics of fisheries in the European Union.* Manchester: Manchester University Press, 2004.

- ØREBECH Peter. "The fisheries issues of the 2004 second European Union Accession Treaty : a comparison with the 1994 first Accession Treaty", *The International Journal of Marine and Coastal Law*, v. 19, n. 2, May 2004, p. 93-150.
- PALOMARES Maria Lourdes. *ACP-EU Fisheries Research Initiative: fish biodiversity: local studies as basis for global inferences*. Luxembourg: EUR-OP*, 2004.

The publications of the Office for Official Publications of the European Communities (EUR-OP) exist generally in all official languages of the EU.

DISCUSSION TOPICS

1. What is the need of a common policy for the conservation of fishery resources?
2. How is the fisheries sector organised at Community level?
3. What is the structural policy of the Community for the fisheries sector?
4. Discuss the similarities and differences of the common agricultural and fisheries policies.
5. How does the common fisheries policy relate with the common regional and environment policies?

Part VI: External policies

Chapter 23.   Commercial Policy
Chapter 24.   Development Aid Policy
Chapter 25.   External relations

The EU Treaty in its first pages (Article 2) declares that **the Union has the objective of asserting its identity on the international scene**, in particular through the implementation of a common foreign and security policy, including the progressive framing of a common defence policy, which might in time lead to a common defence. The **EC/EU is in fact present on the world stage in three roles**, played mainly under its European Community hat: common commercial policy, development aid policy and external relations. The first two are leading roles - as the EC/EU is the world's largest trading entity and the largest provider of funds for the developing countries - while the role of the external relations of the Community, which is for the time being secondary, is completed and often intermingled with the developing role of the Union in a common foreign and security policy (CFSP) [see chapter 8 and the European perspectives in the conclusions]. The three often overlap as development aid is tied in with commercial policy and commercial policy with the Community's external relations or the Union's CFSP. But, whereas the commercial and the development aid policies are managed with the successful Community method and have a global impact, the CFSP is run with the ineffective intergovernmental method and is common only in name. As the three policies should ideally support each other, the ineptness of the CFSP of the Union handicaps the performance of the policies of the Community.

The European Community/Union, through one or other of its international roles, has **diplomatic relations with 162 countries**, which for their part have representations in Brussels. The EC/EU has its own representations, set up by the Commission, in most of these countries and in **international organisations**. In organisations such as the General Agreement on Tariffs and Trade (GATT), the Community speaks in the name of and in place of the Member States, through the mouthpiece of the Commission [see section 4.1.2.]. It participates in the work of the Organisation for Economic Cooperation and Development (OECD) and has observer status in the United Nations and in some of its specialised organisations. It has relations with other international organisations, such as the Council of Europe. It is represented, by the President of the Commission, at the economic summits of the most industrialised countries, called "the G8", which bring together twice a year the Heads of State or Government of four of its

Member States - France, Germany, the United Kingdom and Italy - with those of the United States, Canada, Japan and Russia.

The European Community has signed and manages **association or co-operation agreements** with more than 120 countries and is also responsible for numerous multilateral agreements. When these agreements cover an area for which it has exclusive responsibility, such as international trade, agriculture or fisheries, the Community is the sole party to them on behalf of its Member States. In other cases (some agreements on the environment, transport and so on), the Community is a party in addition to its Member States.

If one adds the **international personalities** of the fifteen Member States - with their different and sometimes conflicting interests in the international arena - to the occasionally identical but at times distinct activities of the European Community and the European Union, one understands that the external relations of the former and the foreign policy of the later are bewildering subjects, not only for the partners of the Union, but also for the Member States themselves. Having examined the common foreign and security policy as a component of the future political integration of the Union, we now try to instil some systematic order in the study of the external relations of the Community.

Chapter 23

COMMERCIAL POLICY

Diagram of the chapter

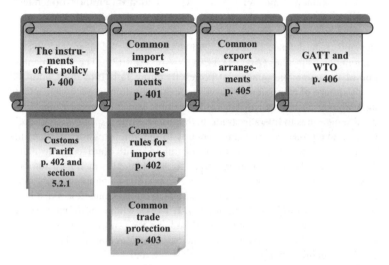

The creation of a **customs union** in the Community in 1968 was implemented internally through the abolition of customs duties, quantitative restrictions and measures having equivalent effect between Member States [see section 5.1.] and, on the external front, through the **introduction of a common customs tariff and a common commercial policy**. In fact, goods imported from third countries had to be treated in the same way by all Member States in order to circulate freely in the customs union [see section 5.2.]. But the customs union itself had to be integrated into the existing international economic order, regulated by the 1948 General Agreement on Tariffs and Trade (GATT).

This is why, in Article 110 of the EEC Treaty (Art. 131 TEC), the Member States declared that in creating a customs union, they intended to contribute, in accordance with the common interest, to the **harmonious development of world trade**, the gradual removal of restrictions to international trade and the lowering of customs barriers. They have kept their word. The creation of the customs union has led to strong growth in intra-Community trade, but the Community has not become introverted. Instead, it has developed into the world's biggest importer and exporter. In addition, the rules of the GATT [see section 23.4.], and the various international agreements drawn up under its aegis, formed the legal basis for the Community's own commercial policy instruments and action, notably in the field of tariffs, the application of safeguard measures, anti-dumping and anti-subsidies actions.

23.1. The instruments of the policy

The common commercial policy was founded on uniform principles, notably as regards tariff charges, the conclusion of tariff and commercial agreements and the harmonisation of liberalisation measures, export policies and trade defence measures, including those to be taken in cases of dumping and subsidies (Art. 133 TEC, ex-Art. 113 EEC). The implementation of the common commercial policy therefore falls **into the Community's sphere of competence**. The European institutions draw up and adapt the common customs tariff, conclude customs and trade agreements, harmonise measures to liberalise trade with third countries, specify export policy and take protective measures, notably to nip unfair trading practices in the bud. If agreements have to be negotiated with third countries, the Commission submits recommendations to the Council, which then authorises it to open negotiations. The Commission is the Community's negotiator and consults a special committee appointed by the Council to assist it in this task (known as "133 Committee"). It works within the framework of guidelines issued by the Council. In exercising the powers granted to it by Article 133 (TEC), including the conclusion of agreements, the Council acts by a qualified majority [see sections 4.1.4. and 4.3.].

In international agreements, **the Community as such, represented by the Commission** [see section 4.1.2.], is more often than not a party alongside the Member States, which means that it takes part in the negotiations, signs the agreements and if necessary participates in their management as a member of the organisation in question. In areas for which the Community has exclusive responsibility (agriculture, fisheries), the Member States are not at the forefront; the Commission negotiates and manages the agreements on the basis of a negotiating brief delivered by the Council (world commodity agreements, traditional trade agreements, preferential agreements, association agreements)[1]. According to Article 307 (TEC), rights and obligations arising from agreements concluded by the Member States before their accession to the Community [see section 1.2.] are not affected by the provisions of the EC Treaty [see sections 2.2. and 2.4.]; but to the extent that such agreements are not compatible with this Treaty, the Member States concerned must take all appropriate steps to eliminate the incompatibilities established[2].

Given the complexity of international relations and of external policy instruments in the broad sense of the term, the **Community powers occa-**

---

[1] See: judgment of 31 March 1971, case 22/70, AETR, ECR 1971, p.263; and opinion of 26 April 1977, ECR 1977, p. 741.

[2] See judgment of 14 October 1980, case 812/79, Burgoa, ECR 1980, p.2787.

sionally spill out of the framework defined in Article 133 (TEC). In such cases, the Community institutions cannot act alone [see section 4.3.]. They must draw in the Member States, a fact that considerably complicates the negotiating process and the conclusion of international agreements. However, the EC Treaty provides that the Council will be able, unanimously, to decide to extend the application of Article 133 (commercial policy) to international negotiations and agreements on services and intellectual property rights in addition to those already covered by this provision.

The **Common Customs Tariff (CCT)** is the key to the Community's commercial policy [see section 5.2.1.]. As seen in the Chapter on customs union and as will be seen later in this Chapter [see section 23.2.1.], the blueprinting and evolution of the CCT have taken place against the backdrop of the General Agreement on Tariffs and Trade (GATT). CCT tariffs were low at the outset, responding to the central objective of liberalisation of international trade. They have been cut even further in the framework of successive GATT negotiations [see section 23.4.]. It should be borne in mind that the Commission, acting on a negotiating brief issued by the Council, and not the Member States individually, is the Community's negotiator in the GATT/WTO arena.

Instead of becoming a **"Fortress Europe"** when the single market was completed in 1992 [see section 6.1.], as feared by some of its trade partners, the Community made important concessions in order to allow the conclusion of the GATT Uruguay Round in 1993. However, one of the central principles of GATT and WTO is that of balance of mutual advantages (global reciprocity). This means, for the European Union, that it can tie access for third country economic operators to the benefits of the single market with the existence of similar opportunities for European undertakings (businesses, companies) in the country in question, or at the least to the absence of any discrimination. This implies a case-by-case approach for third countries, but a common approach by the Member States. The single market obliges the latter to show a united face to third countries. At the same time, the globalisation of the economy is creating a state of interdependence and a growing realisation that trade problems need to be solved wherever possible in a multilateral framework.

23.2. Common import arrangements

The Customs Union is one of the linchpins of the common commercial policy. The other main elements are the **common import arrangements** and the **common protective measures**. Together they contribute to ensuring an even competition playing field for Community undertakings, giving them access to equal prices for imported raw materials and levelling the quantities and prices of competitor products.

23.2.1. Common rules for imports

The common rules for imports were established by Council Regulation of 22 December 1994[1]. **They apply to imports of products originating in third countries**, with the exception, on the one hand, of textiles subject to specific import arrangements, discussed under the heading of sectoral measures of the commercial policy, and, on the other, products originating from certain third countries, including Russia, North Korea and the People's Republic of China, mentioned below. Apart from those exceptions, imports into the Community are free and not subject to any quantitative restrictions. The Regulation strives to establish a balance between a Community market normally open to the world following the conclusion of the Uruguay Round and more rapid and simplified procedures in case of a risk of serious injury caused by imports of a product to Community producers.

The Regulation establishes a **Community information and consultation procedure**. The examination of the trend of imports, of the conditions under which they take place and of serious injury or threat of serious injury to Community producers resulting from such imports covers the following factors in practice: a) the volume of imports; b) the price of imports; and c) the consequent impact on the Community producers of similar or directly competitive products as indicated by trends in certain economic factors such as production, capacity utilisation, stocks, sales, market share, prices and so on.

Where the trend in imports of a product originating in a third country threatens to cause injury to Community producers, import of that product may be subject, as appropriate, to prior or retrospective **Community surveillance**. Products under prior Community surveillance may be put into free circulation only on production of an import document endorsed by the competent authority designated by Member States and valid throughout the EU, regardless of the Member State of issue. The surveillance may be confined to imports into one or more regions of the Community (regional surveillance).

Where a product is imported into the Community in such increased quantities and/or on such terms as to cause, or threaten to cause, serious injury to Community producers, the Commission may, acting at the request of a Member State or on its own initiative take **safeguard measures**, i.e.: limit the period of validity of import documents required in compliance with surveillance measures; alter the import rules for the product in question by making its release for free circulation conditional on production of an import authorisation granted under certain provisions and in certain limits laid down by the Commission. As regards Members of the World Trade Organisation (WTO), safeguard measures are taken only when the two conditions indicated above (quantities and terms of imports) are met. No safeguard measure may be applied to a product originating in a developing

---

[1]   Regulation 3285/94, OJ L 349, 31.12.1994 and Regulation2774/2000, OJ L 286, 11.11.2000.

country Member of the WTO as long as that country's share of Community imports of the product concerned does not exceed 3% and that the import share of all developing countries does not account for more than 9% of such imports.

23.2.2. Common trade protection

As seen above, the Community can introduce surveillance and safeguard measures in the framework of the common rules for imports when imports at prices viewed as normal are causing or risk causing serious injury to Community producers. In cases where the **export price is lower than the normal value of a like product (dumping)**, the Community can take trade protection measures, notably through the application of **anti-dumping duties**. Community rules being compatible with those of the World Trade Organisation, economic operators must comply with only one set of rules for imports into the EU [see sections 23.2.1. and 23.4.]. These rules apply automatically in the new States acceding to the EU, as of May 2004[1]. On the jurisdictional level, anti-dumping and anti-subsidy cases must be brought before the Court of First Instance[2].

According to the Regulation on **protection against dumped imports** from countries not members of the EC, anti-dumping duty may be applied to any dumped product whose release for free circulation in the Community causes injury[3]. A product is considered as having been dumped if its export price to the Community is less than a comparable price for the like product, in the ordinary course of trade, as established for the exporting country. The term like product means a product that is identical in all respects or has characteristics closely resembling those of the product under consideration. In order to determine the dumping, the normal price and the dumped price must be defined and these two values must then be compared. It should be noted that these definitions as well as the anti-dumping procedures are, after the Uruguay Round, similar in the EU and in other WTO countries.

Provisional measures may be taken by the Commission, after consultation with the Member States, no sooner than 60 days but not later than nine months from the initiation of the proceedings. The final conclusions of the investigation must be adopted within a further six months. The amount of the **provisional anti-dumping duty** must not exceed the margin of dumping as provisionally established. Investigation may be terminated without the imposition of provisional or definitive duties upon receipt of satisfactory voluntary undertakings from the exporter to revise his prices or to cease exports to the area in question at dumped prices.

---

[1] Commission notice, OJ C 91, 15.04.2004.
[2] Decision 94/149, OJ L 66, 10.03.1994.
[3] Regulation 384/96, OJ L 56, 06.03.1996 and Regulation 461/2004, OJ L 77, 13.03.2004.

Where a provisional duty has been applied and the facts established show that there is dumping and injury, the Council decides, irrespective of whether a definitive anti-dumping duty is to be imposed, what proportion of the provisional duty is to be definitively collected. If the **definitive anti-dumping** duty is higher than the provisional duty, the difference must not be collected. If the definitive duty is lower than the provisional duty, the duty must be recalculated. Provisional or definitive anti-dumping duties must be imposed by Regulation, and collected by Member States in the form, at the rate specified and according to the other criteria laid down in the Regulation imposing such duties.

The rules on **protection against subsidised imports** from countries not members of the European Community are also established by Regulation[1]. Here again the Community legislation is compatible with WTO rules and, therefore, business must comply with only one set of rules. A **countervailing duty** may be imposed for the purpose of offsetting any subsidy granted, directly or indirectly, for the manufacture, production, export or transport of any product whose release for free circulation in the Community causes injury. A subsidy is deemed to exist if: 1) there is a financial contribution by a government or by a private body entrusted by it (direct transfer of funds, loan guarantees, fiscal incentives, etc.); and 2) a benefit is thereby conferred.

Subsidies, which are not specific to an enterprise or industry or group of enterprises or industries, cannot be subjected to countervailing measures. Even when they are specific, subsidies cannot be subjected to countervailing duties, if they are given: for research activities; pursuant to a general framework of regional development; to promote adaptation of existing facilities to new environmental requirements. The amount of subsidies to be subjected to countervailing duties is calculated in terms of the benefit conferred to the recipient, which is found to exist during the investigation period. Where all conditions are met, a provisional or definitive **countervailing duty** is imposed following procedures similar to the ones described above concerning the imposition of anti-dumping duties.

In December 1994, the Council adopted a Regulation destined to improve Community **procedures on commercial defence** and to ensure the exercise of the Community's rights under international trade rules, in particular those established under the auspices of the World Trade Organisation (WTO)[2]. This Regulation allows the Community to respond to obstacles to trade, i.e. to any trade practice adopted or maintained by a third country in respect of which international trade rules establish a right of action. Thus, following the Community examination procedures and after consultation with the Member States, the Commission may take any commercial policy measures which are compatible with existing international obligations and procedures, notably: (a) suspension or withdrawal of any

---

[1]   Regulation 2026/97, OJ L 288, 21.01.1997 and Regulation 1973/2002, OJ L 311, 07.11.2002.
[2]   Regulation 3286/94, OJ L 349, 31.12.1994 and Regulation 356/95, OJ L 41, 23.02.1995.

concession resulting from commercial policy negotiations; (b) the raising of existing customs duties or the introduction of any other charge on imports; (c) the introduction of quantitative restrictions or any other measures modifying import or export conditions or otherwise affecting trade with the third country concerned. The Commission has thus initiated procedures concerning e.g.: the US Anti-dumping Act of 1916 and US practices with regard to cross-border music licensing[1].

An important trade defence instrument of the Community is related to customs action against goods suspected of **infringing certain intellectual property rights**, particularly counterfeit and pirated goods[2]. As these breaches have been escalating in recent years, notably as regards the methods used by fraud gangs and the internationalisation of traffic, and as other property rights such as geographical indications, designations of origin and new plant varieties are affected, the Community legislation has become more stringent [see sections 6.2.4 and 23.4.]. It gives customs administrations a legal arsenal enabling them, in collaboration with right holders, to better prevent and control intellectual property right infringements. Action by the customs authorities involves, for the period necessary to determine whether suspect goods are indeed counterfeit goods, pirated goods or goods infringing certain intellectual property rights, suspending release for free circulation in the Community, export and re-export. The measures applicable to goods which have been found to be counterfeit, pirated or generally to infringe certain intellectual property rights aim to deprive those responsible for trading in such goods of the economic benefits of the transaction and penalise them so as to constitute an effective deterrent to further transactions of the same kind.

23.3. *Common export arrangements*

Article 132 of the EC Treaty stipulates that the **aid arrangements applied to exports** by the Member States should be harmonised to ensure that there is a level competition playing field for the Community's exporting undertakings. As regards **export credits**, the Community applies the arrangement concluded in the framework of the Organisation for Economic Cooperation and Development (OECD) and providing guidelines for officially supported export credits ("consensus")[3]. These guidelines confine official support to the interest rates for export credits to certain countries. Concerning **export credit insurance** for transactions with medium- and long-term cover, a Directive aims to harmonise the various public systems for such insurance in order to prevent distortion of competition among EU firms[4]. It lays down the common principles which must be observed by ex-

---

[1]   OJ C 58, 25.02.1997 and OJ C 177, 11.06.1997.
[2]   Regulation 1383/2003, OJ L 196, 02.08.2003.
[3]   Decision 2001/76, OJ L 32, 02.02.2001 and Decision 2002/634, OJ L 206, 03.08.2002.
[4]   Directive 98/29, OJ L 148, 19.05.1998.

port credit insurers and which concern the constituents of cover (scope of cover, causes of loss and exclusions of liability and indemnification of claims), premiums, country cover policy and notification procedures.

The Commission contributes from the Community Budget [see section 3.4.] to **export promotion** and notably to closer cooperation at Community level and to research for joint action in favour of European exports (international exhibitions, trade forums, conferences, seminars) in coordination with Community programmes and with Member States' export promotion programmes. The cooperation with trade federations and with national export promotion organisations pursues two aims: first of all, to ensure that any activities on a particular market strengthen the Community dimension and secondly, to focus activities on a number of target countries, the list of which is topped by China, Japan, the countries of ASEAN (Association of South East Asian Nations) [see section 25.6.] and the countries of Central and Eastern Europe [see section 25.2.].

Community exports to third countries are free or, in other words, are not subject to quantitative restrictions, with the exception of a few products for certain Member States and of petroleum oil and gases for all the Member States[1]. However, when exceptional market trends, which cause scarcity of an essential product, justify protective measures in the opinion of a Member State, it can set in motion the **Community information and consultation procedure**. Consultations take place within an Advisory Committee and cover notably the conditions and terms of exports and, if necessary, the measures which should be adopted.

23.4. GATT and WTO

The **General Agreement on Tariffs and Trade (GATT)** came into being in 1947. Along with the International Monetary Fund and the World Bank it was one of the institutions set up in the post-war period to help regulate the international economy and prevent a recurrence of the disastrous protectionist policies undertaken between the two World Wars. GATT was charged with overseeing international trade in goods and, in particular, the liberalisation of this trade by means of a negotiated reduction in tariff barriers. The scope of the GATT was, therefore, somewhat limited initially, but the conclusion of the Uruguay Round negotiations enlarged its field of activities and placed them under the auspices of the **World Trade Organisation (WTO)**. The Member States of the EC were the contracting parties to the GATT, but, because of the common commercial policy, they participated as "the Community" in the work of GATT and now participate as such in the WTO. The Commission is the single negotiator and spokesman of the European Community in WTO [see section 4.1.2.]. The Community is signatory to a number of GATT agreements.

---

[1]   Regulation 2603/69, OJ L 324, 27.12.1969 and Regulation 3918/91, OJ L 372, 31.12.1991.

The EC Member States and other industrial countries made major tariff concessions - particularly in favour of the developing countries - during the successive GATT **negotiating rounds** between 1960 and 1979 under the aegis of the General Agreement on Tariffs and Trade [see section 5.2.1.]. Thanks to the Dillon (1960-1962) and Kennedy Rounds (1965-1967), the customs tariffs of the States participating in the General Agreement were slashed by nearly 50%[1]. Following the Tokyo Round (1973-1979), a fresh one-third reduction in customs tariffs was agreed upon, to be implemented in eight stages the last of which was timed for January 1, 1987[2]. The new cycle of multilateral trade negotiations got underway at the Punta del Este (Uruguay) Conference in September 1986.

The **Uruguay Round negotiations** encompassed the revision of GATT rules and disciplines, plus the adoption of disciplines for "new" areas: the trade-related aspects of intellectual property rights, trade-related investment measures and international trade in services. Also on the agenda were the sensitive issues of agriculture and textiles, areas in which trade was traditionally subject to special rules and for which the participants were to devise an agreement for their gradual incorporation into the GATT framework. The conclusion of the Uruguay Round, in December 1993, resulted in a strengthening of the rules and disciplines of international trade, thanks to the reform of the provisions on safeguards, subsidies, anti-dumping measures, the balance of payments, the "standards" and "public procurement" codes. All these GATT agreements have been incorporated into Community law [see sections 6.2.4 and 23.2.2.].

Market access for industrial products has been considerably improved by a reduction of one third or more in the customs duties imposed by the industrialised countries and many developing countries on the following sectors: building materials, agricultural machinery, medical equipment, steel, beer, spirits, pharmaceutical products, paper, toys and furniture [see section 5.2.]. The average level of tariffs for industrialised countries fell from 5% to about 3.5%, whereas it stood at 40% or more prior to the various rounds of GATT negotiations. In total, close to 40% of the EU's industrial imports are now duty free. On their part, developing countries apply substantial reductions of their customs duties on these products, whereas prior to the Uruguay Round they had taken very few such commitments. The EU played a major role in pushing through the conclusion, in March 1997, of the **Information Technology** Agreement under which tariffs on information technology products of countries accounting for 92% of world trade were phased out completely on 1 January 2000[3] [see also section 17.3.5.].

A first step was taken towards the liberalisation of world trade in services. It should be noted that trade is not limited to exchange of goods but also increasingly involves services, a sector which contributes nearly half

---

[1] Agreement and Decision 68/411, OJ L 305, 19.12.1968.
[2] Agreement and Decision 80/271, OJ L 71, 17.03.1980.
[3] Decision 97/359, OJ L 155, 12.06.1997 and Regulation 2216/97, OJ L 305, 08.11.1997.

of the EU's GDP. The **General Agreement on Trade in Services (GATS)** includes general rules for trade in this area, specific provisions for certain service sectors and national schedules showing the services and activities which each country agrees to open up to competition, with possible limitations[1].

The Uruguay Round negotiations included also the protection of **trade-related intellectual property (TRIPs)**[2]. Intellectual property concerns an ever-increasing part of world trade, be it related to pharmaceuticals, computer software, books or records. As trade has increased so too have cheating, counterfeiting and copying. A further problem has been the appropriation of brand names and, in the case of wines and foodstuffs, certain geographical appellations. The conclusions of the Uruguay Round have reinforced existing international conventions, for example the Bern and Paris Conventions for the protection of literary and artistic works, by bringing them within the ambit of the GATT dispute settlement procedures.

The Uruguay Round resulted also on an Agreement on **trade-related investment measures (TRIMs)**[3]. An illustrative list of non-permissible measures is included in the agreement, covering such things as local content rules, trade balancing and local sales requirements. Such measures must be phased out over a two- to seven-year period, depending upon whether the country is developed or developing. The TRIMs Agreement is particularly important for the EU, which is responsible for 36% of direct foreign investment in the world and receives 19% of such investments on its territory.

The **World Trade Organisation (WTO)**, established in 1995, has replaced the GATT, taking all the agreements concluded under its auspices, and settling trade disputes on a multilateral basis[4]. In fact, the WTO brings together under a single decision-making and administrative body the three agreements resulting from the Uruguay Round: the General Agreement on Tariffs and Trade (GATT), the General Agreement on Trade in Services (GATS) and the Agreement on trade-related aspects of intellectual property rights (TRIPs). The WTO operates on the basis of a ministerial conference, which must meet at least once every two years, and of a General Council made up of representatives of all the member countries. The European Community as well as all its Member States are members of WTO, a code of conduct defining the participation of the Community and its Member States in areas of shared power.

Thus, **the GATT continues to exist**, while frozen in its pre-Uruguay Round situation, for those countries that are not in a position to accept the entire package of its conclusions. On the contrary, the WTO is open to those who agree to abide by the entire Uruguay Round package of rules. This increases the certainty of the world exchange system, since all the

---

[1]   OJ L 336, 23.12.1994, p 191-212.
[2]   OJ L 336, 23.12.1994, p. 214-233.
[3]   OJ L 336, 23.12.1994, p. 100-102.
[4]   Decision 94/800, OJ L 336, 23.12.1994.

members of the WTO are perfectly aware of their own rights and obligations and of those of their partners. The national law of each contracting party must be in conformity with the rules of the WTO, thus precluding unilateral action.

23.5. Appraisal and outlook

A little known fact in Europe is that **the Member States of the European Union no longer have an independent foreign trade policy**. More than 60% of their trade is intra-Community and as such depends on the rules of the single market which prohibit any trade protection or trade promotion measures [see section 6.1.]. For the remaining 40% of their trade, the main instruments of commercial policy, the Common Customs Tariff, the common import arrangements and the common protective measures are in the hands of the organs of the EU, the Commission and the Council. Together they contribute to ensuring an even competition playing field for Community businesses, giving them access to equal prices for imported raw materials and other products they need. At the same time, the common commercial policy facilitates the work of Community importers who can use a uniform import licence, valid throughout the EU.

Being the world's leading commercial superpower, the Community is certainly respected and heeded in the context of the GATT and of the World Trade Organisation. One of the central principles of the latter is that of **balancing mutual advantages (global reciprocity)**. This means, for the European Union, that it can tie access for third country economic operators to the benefits of its single market with the existence of similar opportunities for European businesses in the country in question, or at the least to the absence of any discrimination. This implies a case-by-case approach for third countries, but a common approach by the Member States. The single market obliges the latter to show a united face to third countries.

However, whereas customs tariffs are diminishing thanks to the Uruguay Round and the rules of the World Trade Organisation impose in principle the freedom of international exchanges, **European companies are still faced with obstacles to trade and investment** in a large number of countries. Thus, an environment conducive to international exchanges and investments is still lacking in many Asian and South American countries and even the United States resorts to protectionist measures under pressure from its industries in difficulties, such as steel [see section 25.7.]. The European Community has the necessary power to redress these situations through a bilateral approach (action vis-à-vis the countries concerned) and a multilateral approach (actions within the World Trade Organisation); but the Member States must lend a supporting hand in combating trade barriers by joining forces with the European Commission. To face the problems arising from the **globalisation of trade**, the EC/EU should not try to block this irreversible phenomenon, as advocated by anti-globalisation groups, but to harness it by strict international rules and strong institutions [see European Perspectives in conclusions].

Bibliography on the common commercial policy

* AGGARWAL Vinod, FOGARTY Edward. *EU trade strategies : between regionalism and globalism*. Basingstoke: Palgrave Macmillan, 2004.

* CARDWELL M.N., RODGERS C. P., GROSSMAN M.R. *Agriculture and international trade: law, policy and the WTO*. London; New York: Oxford University Press, 2004.

* CHO Sungjoon. "A bridge too far: the fall of the Fifth WTO Ministerial Conference in Cancún and the future of trade constitution", *Journal of International Economic Law*, v. 7, n. 2, June 2004, p. 219 244.

* DAELE Karel. "Regulation 1383/2003: a new step in the fight against counterfeit and pirated goods at the borders of the European Union", *European Intellectual Property Review*, v. 26, n. 5, May 2004, p. 214-225.

* DREXL Josef. "International competition policy after Cancún: placing a Singapore issue on the WTO development agenda", *World Competition*, v. 27, n. 3, September 2004, p. 419-457.

* GRUBER Matthias. "Inside or outside?: The role of the WTO in the settlement of the transatlantic trade dispute on GMOs", *Intereconomics*, v. 39, n. 1, January-February 2004, p. 36-45.

* KINGSTON William. "Why harmonisation is a Trojan horse", *European Intellectual Property Law*, v. 26, n. 10, October 2004, p. 447-460.

* MATTOO Aaditya, WUNSCH-VINCENT Sacha. "Pre-empting protectionism in services: the GATS and outsourcing", *Journal of International Economic Law*, v. 7, n. 4, December 2004, p. 765-800.

* SNYDER Francis. "The gatekeepers: the European courts and WTO law", *Common Market Law Review*, v. 40, n. 2, April 2003, p. 313-367.

* YOUNG Alasdair. "The incidental fortress: the Single European Market and world trade", *Journal of Common Market Studies*, v. 42, n. 2, June 2004, p. 393-414.

DISCUSSION TOPICS

1. How does the customs union legislation interact with the common commercial policy?
2. Discuss the need and the scope of the common rules for imports.
3. Outline the common trade protection measures.
4. What are the functions of the World Trade Organisation?
5. Are the objectives of the common commercial policy compatible with the trade liberalisation objectives of the WTO?

Chapter 24

DEVELOPMENT AID POLICY

Diagram of the chapter

EC-ACP Association p. 413	**Overseas countries and territories** p. 415	**Aid for non associated countries** p. 415
Generalised system of preferences p. 416	**Cooperation at world level** p. 417	**Fight against hunger in the world** p. 417

Development aid reflects **both the search for solidarity** between the developed countries of the EU and the disadvantaged countries of the world **and the economic necessity for the Union** of guaranteeing its raw material supply and creating outlets for its products. Aware that advantages granted at world level, notably through the GATT negotiations mentioned in the previous chapter [see section 23.4.], diminished the attractiveness of regional preferences, the EC/EU has been caught up in a process of continually expanding its aid to developing countries. It now views every agreement with developing countries as an instrument in an all-embracing political, social and economic development strategy.

24.1. Objectives and instruments of the policy

Article 177 of the EC Treaty specifies that Community policy in the sphere of development cooperation is **complementary to the policies pursued by the Member States and must foster**: the sustainable economic and social development of the developing countries; the smooth and gradual integration of the developing countries in the world economy; and the campaign against poverty in the developing countries. Article 301 (TEC) allows the Community to apply politically motivated economic sanctions, thus making every cooperation agreement an instrument of a broad political, social and economic approach.

Indeed, the requirements for the implementation of operations in the framework of the Community cooperation policy contribute to the general **objective of developing and consolidating democracy** and the rule of law and to that of respecting human rights and fundamental freedoms in third countries[1]. The Community provides financial assistance and appropriate expertise aimed at promoting **gender equality** into all its development cooperation policies and interventions in developing countries[2]. Finally, the EU promotes the full integration of the **environmental dimension** in the development process[3] and, in particular, the conservation and sustainable management of tropical forests and other forests in developing countries[4].

The European Union currently has an impressive store of **development aid instruments**, spanning the Convention with the ACP countries, special relations with the Overseas Countries and Territories, aid for non-associated countries, the Generalised System of Tariff Preferences, participation in world commodity agreements and aid provided through non-government organisations fighting global problems such as hunger. The **decentralised cooperation approach** places local actors at the focal point of implementation and hence pursues the dual aims of gearing operations to needs and making them viable[5]. The EU participates fully in the International Monetary Fund and World Bank initiative for heavily indebted ACP countries by helping them reduce the net value of their obligations[6]. This variety of forms which development aid takes clearly demonstrates the EU's commitment to an outward-looking approach. In fact, in the 1990s, the EU and its Member States provided some 45% of official development assistance to developing countries in the world, whereas the United States provided less than 20%.

The European Union also has a wide range of **development policy resources**, from industrial and technological cooperation to trade promotion, food aid and financial aid. Financial aid also takes the form of European Investment Bank (EIB) loans and risk capital[7], EIB management of the Investment Facility[8], European Development Fund (EDF) subsidies; or grants under other Articles of the Community Budget, concerning in particular food aid. The EDF, is funded by a five-year specific contribution of the Member States but is an integral part of the Community Budget[9] [see section 3.4.].

---

[1]   Regulation 976/1999, OJ L 120, 08.05.1999.
[2]   Regulation 806/2004, OJ L 143, 30.04.2004.
[3]   Regulation 2493/2000, OJ L 288, 15.11.2000.
[4]   Regulation 2494/2000, OJ L 288, 15.11.2000.
[5]   Regulation 1659/98, OJ L 213, 30.07.1998 and Regulation 625/2004, OJ L 99, 03.04.2004.
[6]   Decision 98/453, OJ L 198, 15.07.1998 and Decision 2/2003, OJ L 152, 20.06.2003.
[7]   Decision 97/256, OJ L 102, 19.04.1997 and Regulation 2666/2000, OJ L 306, 07.12.2000.
[8]   Decision 2003/268, OJ L 99, 17.04.2003.
[9]   Financial Regulation, OJ L 83, 01.04.2003.

24.2. EC-ACP Association

In the first years following the entry into force of the EEC Treaty [see section 2.1.], the Community's development aid policy was more or less restricted to the association provided for in the fourth part of the Treaty and **covering the former colonies** of France, Italy, Belgium and the Netherlands. After most of these countries were granted independence, a first Convention was signed in Yaoundé (Cameroon) on July 20, 1963 between the EEC and an association of 17 African countries and Madagascar. The enlargement of the Community in 1973 substantially boosted the ranks of the associated countries, drawing in the former British colonies. This prompted an overhaul of the content of the agreement. The Convention signed in Lomé (Togo) on February 28, 1975 between the then nine Member States of the EEC and 46 States of **Africa, the Caribbean and the Pacific (ACP)** signalled a fresh start for the common development aid policy. The fourth EEC-ACP Convention, also signed in Lomé on December 15, 1989, firmly cemented cooperation between the EC Member States and 70 ACP States, including the whole of sub-Saharan Africa and, in certain aspects, South Africa.

The fourth Lomé Convention expired on 29 February 2000. Its successor, **the partnership agreement signed at Cotonou** (Benin) on 23 June 2000, although it is still based on the acquis of the four Lomé Conventions, heralds a fundamental change in relations between the ACP States and the Community and its Member States[1]. The term of the new agreement is 20 years. The addition of six Pacific Island States has raised to 77 the list of members of the ACP group of countries.

The partnership agreement combines substantial **political dialogue between the partners** with innovative forms of economic and commercial cooperation and new development cooperation mechanisms and strategies. Thus the agreement is supported by five interdependent pillars, namely the overall political dimension, encouragement of a participatory approach, a stronger bias towards the aim of reducing poverty, a new framework for economic and trade cooperation and reform of financial cooperation. The objective of good governance has been added to those of respect for human rights, democratic principles and the rule of law as one of the essential elements of the partnership. Under Article 11 of the Cotonou Partnership Agreement "the parties shall pursue an active, comprehensive and integrated policy of peace-building and conflict prevention and resolution within the framework of the partnership".

The Cotonou Agreement also includes provisions on cooperation in trade-related areas leading each participating country to negotiate a trade agreement with the Community. The purpose of these agreements is to help developing countries **integrate into the world economy**, step up production and stimulate trade and investment in compliance with World

---

[1]   Agreement and Council Decision 2000/483, OJ L 317, 15.12.2000 and OJ L 83, 01.04.2003.

Trade Organisation rules [see section 23.4.]. Where finances are concerned, the various instruments have been regrouped and rationalised so that all resources available under the European Development Fund (EDF) are disbursed via two instruments: a financial package from which subsidies is granted and another from which risk capital and loans is provided to the private sector. Operations must focus on a specific sector (health, transport, etc.) and combine many different aspects of cooperation (economic, environmental, social, etc.) in order to ensure that aid is better targeted.

The **joint institutions for cooperation** established by the former Lomé Conventions remain in force, namely:

- **the Council of Ministers**, consisting of members of the Council of the European Union, members of the European Commission and a member of the government of each ACP country, meets once a year to initiate political dialogue, adopt political guidelines and take decisions required for the implementation of the provisions of the Agreement;
- **the Committee of Ambassadors**, made up of the permanent representative of each Member State for the European Union, a Commission representative and a head of mission for each ACP state, assists the Council of Ministers;
- **the Joint Parliamentary Assembly**, made up of an equal number of representatives of Members of the European Parliament and representatives of the ACP States, may adopt resolutions and submit recommendations to the Council of Ministers.

The new system for programming the aid granted by the Community enhances the flexibility of the partnership and entrusts the ACP States with greater responsibility, particularly by establishing a system of **rolling programming** that eliminates the concept of non-programmable aid, i.e. aid programmed unilaterally by the Community. The ACP States now have greater responsibility for determining objectives, strategies and operations and for programme management and selection.

The programming process is centred on results. Financial assistance of a set amount is no longer an automatic right. Grants are allocated on the basis of an assessment of requirements and performances in accordance with criteria negotiated between the ACP countries and the Community. These criteria reflect the partnership's main objectives, such as progress in institutional reform, poverty reduction, etc.

The main instrument used for programming grants is the **country support strategy (CSS)**. An CSS is drawn up for each ACP country by the Commission and the country in question. The CSS sets out general guidelines for using the aid and is supplemented by an indicative operational programme containing specific operations and a timetable for their implementation.

In cases of fluctuation of export revenues, instead of the Stabex and Sysmin instruments of the previous Conventions, the new system of rolling and flexible programming (FLEX system) makes it possible to ensure additional support via the funds allocated within the framework of the CSS and the operational programmes (Annex II to the ACP-EC Partnership Agreement). Additional support in this area is needed because of the ACP States' vulnerability resulting from a high degree of dependence on export revenues in the agricultural or mining sectors in ACP States.

24.3. Overseas countries and territories

The regulations currently in force relating to the association of overseas countries and territories to the EC apply to twenty OCTs **dependent on France, the Netherlands, the United Kingdom and Denmark** (Greenland)[1]. While they come under the wing of Member States, and their nationals are recognised since 1996 as EU citizens, the OCTs do not form part of the Union, but they are associated with it and thus benefit from the EDF and the same types of development cooperation measures as ACP States. Community solidarity towards them is reflected chiefly by the near free access to the Community market for products originating in the OCTs, by the implementation of export stabilisation systems and by financial and technical cooperation drawing on the resources of the EDF and the European investment Bank.

The **fields covered by this financial and technical cooperation** are agricultural and rural development, fisheries, industrial development, the exploitation of mining and energy potential, transport and communications, the development of trade and services, regional cooperation and cultural and social cooperation. Depending on the development level and situation of the OCTs, an attempt is also made to establish firm cooperation between them and the ACP States. The partnership arrangements in favour of OCTs include many elements contained in the fourth Lomé Convention and establish a three-way Commission/Member State/OCT partnership. The mid-term review of the partnership arrangements aims to improve the rights of individuals and the status of OCT nationals in the European Union.

24.4. Aid for non-associated countries

The Community runs a programme of financial and technical aid for the developing countries of **Latin America and Asia**. The EU's relations with these countries are less structured than those with the ACP countries and take the form of cooperation agreements. These agreements are limited in scope. They do not provide for preferential access to EC markets for exports from Asian and Latin American countries, except under the Generalised System of Preferences, which is explained below. Aid is provided un-

[1] Decision 91/482, OJ L 263, 19.09.1991 and Decision 2001/161, OJ L 58, 28.02.2001.

der special inscriptions in the Community budget and, therefore, must be decided every year by the budgetary authorities.

The Community's cooperation with the countries of Asia and Latin America is now **focused on the poorest population groups** and on economic cooperation with high growth potential countries and regions [see also sections 25.6. and 25.8.]. It includes both financial and technical aid and new priorities such as the environment, the human dimension of development and the promotion of human rights[1]. Most of the funding is earmarked for the agricultural sector (agriculture in general, irrigation, fisheries) or for agriculture-related activities (agricultural and food research, rural credit). A certain proportion of the funding is set aside for rehabilitation and reconstruction operations in response to natural or manmade disasters[2]. A Community support programme provides aid to uprooted people (refugees, displaced persons etc.) in Asian and Latin American developing countries[3]. The Community has a development and cooperation agreement with the Republic of South Africa, which aims, among other things, to support South African efforts to consolidate the economic and social foundations of its transition process[4].

24.5. Generalised System of Preferences

The Community provided the initiative behind the **Generalised System of Preferences (GSP)**, the principle of which was taken on board by the other industrialised countries at the 2nd Session of the United Nations Conference on Trade and Development (UNCTAD) in 1968. Although it has traditionally come under Article 133 of the EC Treaty (ex Art. 113) and, therefore, in theory, under the common commercial policy, the GSP is in practice a tool of development. It offers some 130 developing countries tariff reductions or in some cases duty-free access for their manufactured exports and increasingly their agricultural exports as well. Being a tariff instrument, it operates purely at the level of tariffs which is already reduced thanks to GATT. Being an autonomous instrument, its preferences are granted (not negotiated) by the Community and are complementary to the multilateral liberalisation of trade within WTO [see section 23.4.].

After the conclusion of the Uruguay Round, the European Union updated the GSP by taking account of the **new international situation** and the stabilisation and association process in Europe. The GSP provides for a general scheme for tariff preferences for the period 1 January 2002 to 31 December 2004, a special scheme to help protect workers' rights, a special scheme to help protect the environment, a special scheme in favour of the

---

[1] Regulation 443/92, OJ L 52, 27.02.1992.
[2] Regulation 2258/96, OJ L 306, 28.11.1996.
[3] Regulation 443/97, OJ L 68, 08.03.1997.
[4] Regulation 1726/2000, OJ L 198, 04.08.2000 and Decision 2004/441, OJ L 127, 29.04.2004.

least developed countries and a special scheme to combat drug production and trafficking[1].

24.6. Cooperation at world level

Many developing countries are **heavily dependent on the export of just one or two commodities** and see their earnings rise and fall according to the fluctuations of the world prices of their products. As a consequence, international agreements concluded in the framework of the United Nations Conference on Trade and Development (UNCTAD) attempt to support or stabilise the production of certain commodities. These agreements generally cover three aspects: prices, quantities and mechanisms (production quotas, buffer stocks and so on). The producer countries see these agreements on commodities chiefly as a way of guaranteeing export earnings and ensuring a certain level of income for their producers, whereas importers view them as a way of guaranteeing supply of a given quantity of a product at a price set in advance. The agreements differ from one product to the next, some aiming at better marketing and heightened competitiveness, others involving attempts to intervene in the free play of market mechanisms at world level.

The United Nations **Common Fund for Commodities** supports the operation of agreements on certain commodities, which are regulated by organisations with specific responsibility for them. To this effect, the Fund has two "windows", one contributing to the financing of buffer stocks and national stocks coordinated at international level and managed by international organisations with specific responsibility for certain commodities; the other supporting measures other than storage (for example research and other measures seeking to improve productivity and marketing). The Community is a member of the Fund on the same footing as its Member States[2].

24.7. Fight against hunger and other afflictions

The European Community considers food aid, first and foremost, as a structural instrument of long-term development. The framework Regulation on **food aid policy and food aid management**, including special operations in support of food security, aims to promote not only the food security of the needy but also overall social and economic development in regions with a food deficit[3]. The measures covered concern support of food security (seed purchases, rural credit, storage facilities, marketing aids,

---

[1] Regulation 2501/2001, OJ L 346, 31.12.2001 and Regulations 814/2003 and 815/2003, OJ L 116, 13.05.2003.
[2] Agreement and Decision 1999/373, OJ L 182, 14.07.1990.
[3] Regulation 1292/96, OJ L 166, 05.07.1996 and Regulation 1726/2001, OJ L 234, 01.09.2001.

transport, distribution and processing of products, support for the private sector, training, research and development, and aid for women and producers associations) as well as schemes for early warning systems to identify famine risks.

In addition to normal food aid, the Community earmarks considerable quantities of agricultural products (cereals, sugar, vegetable oils) every year for **emergency food aid** to help the victims of disasters. It also grants considerable amounts for **emergency aid funding** to the ACP States and the OCTs on the one hand, through the European Development Fund, and to all other countries on the other, through the general Budget of the Community. Emergency aid is granted in response to difficulties created by political events or natural disasters such as cyclones, floods, droughts or epidemics. Emergency aid funding is used for foodstuffs, medical material, medical assistance, clothes, shelter, seeds and means of transport. Governments, specialised international and non-governmental organisations and the Commission take charge of the use of these credits.

Another Regulation lays down the objectives of **humanitarian aid** and the procedures governing aid and operations in this context[1]. More specifically, it sets out the types of situations eligible for Community financing, which include emergencies and their immediate aftermath as well as more drawn-out crises causing loss of life, physical suffering, trauma and significant material damage. By its humanitarian aid the Community tries to calm tensions and reduce sufferings so as to encourage the opening of negotiations and limit the scale of the disaster. The kinds of operation covered are specific projects or broader-based plans designed to bring in relief, help with short-term repair and rebuilding work, facilitate the arrival of aid, prevent crises from worsening and help with the repatriation and resettlement of refugees back home. Also included among the eligible operations are disaster-preparedness and activities to protect the victims of conflict.

The framework Regulation gives the **Commission overall control of all the aid mobilisation and delivery operations**. Commission control ends however when the aid is in the hands of the beneficiary country. Furthermore, the successful tenderer is responsible for the aid until its delivery to the location stipulated in the agreement concluded with the beneficiary countries. Finally, the Regulation stipulates that aid is to be monitored by professionals appointed by the Commission to ensure that the operation is correctly followed through. When, due to evolution in the crop or stock situation of a given country - for example should the harvest be exceptionally good - the supply of food aid would serve no purpose or would damage the local economy, it can be replaced by financial assistance[2]. The Community encourages the developing countries to strengthen their food security through the provision of financial support. Thus the Community

---

[1]   Regulation 1257/96, OJ L 163, 02.07.1996.
[2]   Regulation 1292/96, OJ L 166, 05.07.1996.

focuses its attention on **food strategies** where food security tops the list of priorities. The European Community participates actively in the Food Aid Convention[1].

The **European Community Office for Humanitarian Aid (ECHO)**, run by the Commission, has the role of enhancing the Community's presence on the ground, of grouping together all its emergency humanitarian actions and improving coordination with the Member States, other donors, NGOs and specialised international agencies. ECHO is wholly responsible for administering humanitarian and emergency food aid, and disaster preparedness. At present, the humanitarian aid of the EU exceeds 1 billion euros a year and its scope has been broadened to cover the violent ethnic conflicts in Africa, the consequences of the collapse of the Soviet Union and the aftermath of the fratricidal wars in former Yugoslavia. In fact, more than 95% of ECHO's activities cover man-made disasters.

24.8. Appraisal and outlook

The European Union and its member countries are **by far the largest providers of development funds in the world**. Whereas, in the beginning, it was limited only to Associated Countries and Territories, the common development policy now covers almost all the underdeveloped countries of the world. Moreover, the contribution of the EU to the development of countries in Africa, Asia and Latin America is not limited to grants, through the Community budget, and loans through the European Investment Bank. An important part of its development aid takes the form of trade concessions both to ACP and OCT countries, through duty free imports of their products, and to Asian and Latin American countries, through the generalised system of trade preferences [see section 24.5.]. In addition, the Community development aid policy strives - without much success up to now - to support democratic regimes, human rights, women's position and environmental protection in the recipient countries [see section 24.1.].

While much clearly remains to be done, given an international backdrop of economic crisis in the developing countries and the fratricidal conflicts and political instability in many of them, the association agreements of the EU with ACP and OCT countries and its cooperation agreements with Asian and Latin American countries are **a remarkable contribution to solidarity between the North and South** of the planet. Although aid cannot make up for a lack of sound domestic policies or trade outlets, it may be used as a lever for the implementation of economic and political reforms. What is therefore needed is an approach which encourages internal reforms in the developing countries, on the basis of the four main themes expounded in the Treaty on European Union: consolidation and development of democracy, sustainable economic and social development, integra-

---

[1] Convention and Decision 96/88, OJ L 21, 27.01.1996 and COM (1999) 308, 22 June 1999.

tion into the world economy and a battle against poverty. The adverse effects of climate change being particularly serious for the least advanced countries, the environmental dimension should be an integral part of the European Union's development policy, the principal objective being to create as many synergies as possible between action to combat poverty and that to tackle climate change.

By improving the arrangements for mobilising Community relief, the **European Community Office for Humanitarian Aid (ECHO)** is meant to provide both an efficient service to needy countries and a higher profile to European humanitarian interventions [see section 24.7.]. It should give, indeed, public opinion tangible evidence of the Community's role as an active contributor in the field of humanitarian aid. The visibility of the Community aid is necessary, because this aid comes out of the European taxpayers money [see section 3.4.]. EU citizens are entitled to know that they, through the Community budget, make a small contribution to the alleviation of the sufferings of the people of developing countries that the media relate every day.

In the future, the EU should ensure consistency between development cooperation, the common commercial policy and the common foreign and security policy [see section 8.2.], while establishing close relations with the partner countries. Greater coordination of development aid is needed both at the European Union level and worldwide. Internal coordination between the Commission and Member States would enhance the Union's overall effort and increase the effectiveness of this effort. A local EU action plan for coordination and harmonisation should exist in any partner country where two or more EU donors have a cooperation programme. Food security policy should go hand in hand with poverty reduction in the most vulnerable countries and its objectives and instruments should be fully integrated into the Community's overall development policy.

On the global scene, the enlarged Union is the world's biggest economy. Its ability to influence **global economic governance** is accordingly greater. As agreed at the Johannesburg World Summit on Sustainable Development in September 2002, the Union must defend a strategy for sustainable development based on the United Nations system and the international financial institutions and reject hegemony or unilateralism. To this end, it should promote the social dimension of globalisation, including bilateral and regional relations, development and external cooperation, trade policy, private initiatives and governance at global level. In view of the role they play in international development, the EU and its Member States should take the lead in revitalising the United Nations and its specialised organisations, the International Monetary Fund (IMF) and the World Bank in order to make them more effective in addressing the causes of hunger and poverty in the world, such as lack of peace, security and stability.

Bibliography on development aid policy

- ABASS Abou. "The Cotonou trade régime and WTO law", *European Law Review*, v. 10, n. 4, July 2004, p. 439-462.
- ADDISON Tony. *Development policy: an introduction for students.* Helsinki: United Nations University. World Institute for Development Economics Research, 2004.
- ARTS Karin. "ACP-EU relations in a new era: the Cotonou Agreement", *Common Market Law Review*, v. 40, n. 1, February 2003, p. 95-116.
- BUCKLAND Jerry. *Ploughing up the farm: neoliberalism, modern technology and the state of the world's farmers.* Winnipeg: Fernwood Publishing ; London: Zed Books, 2004.
- EUROPEAN COMMISSION. *Developing countries, international trade and sustainable development: the function of the Community's generalised system of preferences (GSP) for the ten-year period from 2006to 2015.* Luxembourg: EUR-OP*, 2004.
    - *External assistance reform: four years on (2000-2004)*, Luxembourg: EUR-OP*, 2004.
- HERDT Tom de, BESTIAENSEN Johan, D'EXELLE Ben. *Towards a local socio-institutional analysis of anti-poverty interventions: a critical review of methods and researchers.* Antwerp: University of Antwerp, Institute of Development Policy and Management, 2004.
- INGCO Merlinda, NASH John. *Agriculture and the WTO: creating a trading system for development.* Washington: World Bank, 2004.
- KAUFMANN Pascal, YVARS Bernard (sous la dir. de). *Intégration européenne et régionalisme dans les pays en développement.* Paris: L'Harmattan, 2004.
- PURVIS Martin, GRAINGER Alan (eds.). *Exploring sustainable development: geographical perspectives.* London: Earthscan, 2004.

The publications of the Office for Official Publications of the European Communities (EUR-OP) exist generally in all official languages of the EU.

DISCUSSION TOPICS

1. Do the EU countries have common interests in helping the development of the less fortunate countries of the world?
2. Which are the main axes of the common development aid policy?
3. Outline the development mechanisms used by the EC-ACP association.
4. How does the EU help other than ACP countries?
5. Could the common development aid policy be better linked to the common commercial policy and to the common foreign and security policy?

Chapter 25

EXTERNAL RELATIONS

Diagram of the chapter

European Free Trade Association and EEA p. 424	Candidates for accession p. 425	Balkan countries p. 429	Eastern European countries p. 430
Mediter- ranean countries p. 431	Asian countries p. 433	North Ameri- can countries p. 435	Latin Ameri- can countries p. 437

The **external relations of the European Community**, which date back to its first years of existence, should not be confused with the foreign policy of the European Union, introduced by the Treaty of Maastricht, but which comes more under intergovernmental cooperation than the Community procedure. As explained in chapter 8, the common foreign and security policy (CFSP) depends on a special decision-making process [see section 8.2.1.], whereas the external relations of the EC depend on the Community decision-making process [see section 4.3.]. However, the Community's external relations, tied in as they are with the common commercial policy and the Community's development aid policy, give a foretaste of a really common foreign policy and an indication of the scope which it will eventually assume.

The following pages will examine the relations which the European Community as a body has already established with many countries throughout the world. Although **these relations are of economic or commercial origin**, they have on more than one occasion stepped out of this setting into the purely political arena. This is notably the case of relations with other European countries. For the student of European integration it is interesting to distinguish the foreign affairs decisions taken under the common foreign and security policy procedure from those taken under the Community external relations procedure. In other words, it is interesting to see just where the European Community's external domain ends and that of

the European Union begins. The answer to this question is not straightforward.

25.1. European Free Trade Association and European Economic Area

As stated in chapter 1, the **European Free Trade Association (EFTA)**
was set up in 1959 on the initiative of the United Kingdom, which favoured trade liberalisation through intergovernmental cooperation rather
than through the multinational integration process aimed at by ECSC and
EEC [see sections 1.1.2. and 1.2.]. When the United Kingdom and Denmark switched allegiances from EFTA to the EEC in 1973, the scale of
their commercial relations with the other EFTA countries made it necessary to abolish customs barriers between the two groups of countries. As a
consequence, free trade agreements were signed in 1972 and 1973 between
the Community and the EFTA countries. These agreements abolished customs duties and restrictions on trade in industrial products. Furthermore,
the Community agreed to certain compromises on the Common Agricultural Policy, which were matched by reciprocal EFTA concessions in the
agricultural field. EEC-EFTA free trade has operated in a satisfactory
manner and has brought about sustained growth in trade between the two
groups of countries. This trade, by the end of the 1980s, represented 25%
of total Community trade and between 40% and 65% of that of the EFTA
countries.

In 1989, Jacques Delors, then President of the European Commission,
proposed and the European Council agreed to further strengthen the relations between the two European trade blocks. The negotiations were completed in October 1991 between the Community and EFTA as a body on
the basic, legal and institutional aspects of such a global agreement. The
Treaty on the European Economic Area (EEA) was signed in 1992 by
the governments of twelve EU countries and six EFTA countries. However, as a result of the negative Swiss referendum on the EEA Treaty, on 6
December 1992, and the accession to the European Union since 1 January
1995 of the former EFTA members Austria, Sweden and Finland, the EEA
Treaty associates to the EU **only Norway, Iceland and Liechtenstein**[1].
The new members of the EU have become contracting parties to the EEA
Agreement.

The institutional framework of the EEA comprises: the EEA Council, which is made up of members of the Council of the EU and the Commission plus one member for each signatory EFTA government, and which

---

[1] Decisions 93/734 to 93/741, OJ L 346, 31.12.1993, Agreement on the EEA, OJ L 1,
    03.01.1994, Decision of EEA Joint Committee 7/94, OJ L 160, 28.06.1994 and Accession of
    new Member States to the EU, OJ L 1, 01.01.1995.

provides political impetus for the implementation of the Agreement and lays down general guidelines; the EEA Joint Committee, comprising representatives of the contracting parties and responsible for the implementation of the Agreement; the EEA Joint Parliamentary Committee; and the EEA Consultative Committee, which provides a forum for representatives of the social partners. The EFTA countries, members of the EEA, participate in the decision-shaping process of the EU in the ambit of the Commission.

The aim of the EEA Treaty is to establish a dynamic and homogeneous integrated economic entity based on common rules and equal conditions of competition. The EFTA States, minus Switzerland, undertook to take on board existing Community legislation concerning the free movement of goods, persons, services and capital, subject to a few exceptions and transitional periods in certain sectors. Apart from the **implementation of the "four freedoms" of the common market** [see chapter 6], the EEA Agreement also provides for close relations between the Community and the EFTA countries to be reinforced and extended in areas which have an impact on business activity[1], notably social policy, consumer protection, environment, statistics and company law, research and development, information, education, the audiovisual sector, SMEs and tourism. In fact, the EFTA countries (including Switzerland in some respects) participate practically in the common market without participating in the decision making process that governs it, but by adapting its legislation to their circumstances.

25.2. Candidates for accession

Until the end of the 1980s, the part of Europe known as the **"Satellites of the Soviet Union"** was cut off from the rest of the continent by the "Iron Curtain" which closed off frontiers and by the planned economy system, which prevented normal economic relations with market economy countries. Quite apart from the political and ideological problems, trade with planned economy countries was hindered by the fact that their external trade was run by the State and trading relations therefore had to be established between States. When, at the end of 1989, the pace of history suddenly accelerated with the rapid and successive collapse of the Communist regimes in Central and Eastern Europe, the Community rushed to help the people of these countries, working to promote political reform and develop a private sector in their economies. Less than fifteen years after the fall of the Berlin wall, in May 2004, eight of these countries have become **members of the European Community/Union**, but some mechanisms that helped them achieve this status are still in force, in order to prepare the accession of other candidates mentioned in this and the following section.

---

[1] Regulation 2894/94, OJ L 305, 30.11.1994.

It is interesting to review these mechanisms, which have proved their effectiveness.

The first concrete manifestation of the Community's interest in its eastern neighbours was the 1989 action plan for the **operation PHARE** (Poland and Hungary: Aid for Economic Restructuring)[1]. This plan was designed as a framework for action by the Community and as an incentive for similar initiatives pursuing the same aims by other members of a group of 24 interested countries, including other European countries, the United States, Japan and Canada. The PHARE programme was extended, in 1990, to practically all the **Central and Eastern European countries (CEECs)**[2], in 1991, to the Baltic countries[3], in 1992, to Slovenia[4] and, in 2000 to Balkan countries [see section 25.3.][5].

Since that by the mid-1990s most CEECs had applied for membership in the EC/EU, new guidelines for PHARE on **pre-accession assistance** were proposed by the Commission and approved by the Council on 9 June 1997[6]. Aimed at gearing the programme to preparing the applicant countries for EU membership, the new guidelines are implemented by means of "accession partnerships" drawn up by the Commission. They provide the framework for the programming of PHARE funds focusing on two main priorities: institution building and financing investment. Institution building involves assistance to strengthen the applicant countries' democratic institutions and administrations with a view to facilitating adoption of the "*acquis communautaire*" (established Community law and practice) [see section 3.3.] and helping them meet the economic and political conditions for membership. Special attention under this priority is paid to justice and home affairs concerning notably fraud, illegal immigration and organised crime [see section 8.1.2.]. The second priority, the financing of investment, concerns areas where adoption of Community rules requires substantial resources (environment, transport, product quality, working conditions, etc.) and major infrastructure projects connected with the trans-European networks [see section 6.8.].

In parallel with PHARE and in relation with it three **specific but large-scale instruments** are designed for assistance to CEECs and are examined successively below: the European Bank for Reconstruction and Development, the European Training Foundation and the programme of trans-European mobility for university students.

On April 9, 1990 in Paris the text defining the operating provisions for the **European Bank for Reconstruction and Development (EBRD)** was

---

[1]   Regulation 3906/89, OJ L 375, 23.12.1989 and Regulations 1266/1999, 1267/1999, 1268/1999, OJ L 161, 26.06.1999 and Regulation 769/2004, OJ L 123, 27.04.2004.
[2]   Regulation 2698/90, OJ L 257, 21.09.1990.
[3]   Regulation 3800/91, OJ L 357, 28.12.1991.
[4]   Regulation 2334/92, OJ L 227, 11.08.1992.
[5]   Regulation 2666/2000 and Regulation 2667/2000, OJ L 306, 07.12.2000.
[6]   COM (97) 112, 19 March 1997.

signed[1]. It was inaugurated on April 14, 1991. The Bank's purpose is to support the transition to open market economies and promote private and individual enterprise in the countries of Central and Eastern Europe, which adopt and implement the principles of multi-party democracy, pluralism and market economics. The EBRD has two member institutions, the European Commission and the European Investment Bank (EIB) and forty member countries, including the EC and EFTA countries, the countries of Central and Eastern Europe, the independent States of the former USSR and the Baltic States. It has a capital of 20 billion euro, 51% of which is held by the EU Member States, reflecting the predominant role which the latter wish to play in the reconstruction of their Eastern neighbours[2].

This influence is even more marked in the area of the educational and training assistance offered to the countries of Central and Eastern Europe. The two instruments existing in this area were set up by the Community although they are open to operations by non-Community countries which are members of the Group of 24. The **European Training Foundation** is constituted in the form of an independent body which is cooperating closely with the European Centre for the Development of Vocational Training (**CEDEFOP**) [see section 13.4.1]. The Foundation is open to public or private sector participation by non-Community countries and focuses its action on vocational training, on-going training and training in certain specific sectors. Its role is to ensure efficient cooperation in the provision of aid to the countries in question, to help identify their training needs and to define a strategy which can help meet these needs. It acts as a kind of clearing house, matching up information on aid offers and requests and encouraging and helping multilateral assistance.

The **programme of trans-European mobility for university students (TEMPUS)** is cast in the same mould as existing Community exchange programmes, but is adapted to the specific needs of the countries in question[3] [see section 13.4.2.]. In addition to various complementary activities, it makes provision for joint training projects between universities and companies in Eastern European countries and their counterparts in at least two EU States. It also seeks to encourage the mobility of teachers, students and administrative officials. Its priority action fields are management, business administration and language learning.

Although Central and Eastern European countries, finding themselves since the early 1990s in a very difficult transition from centrally planned to free trade and competition economies, could have chosen membership of the EFTA and through it of the EEA [see section 25.1.], they all **applied for membership to the EU**, thus clearly indicating their preference for the multinational integration process rather than for intergovernmental cooperation [see section 1.1.2.]. On their side, the EU Member States responded

---

[1] Agreement and Decision 90/674, OJ L 372, 31.12.1990.
[2] Decision 97/135, OJ L 52, 22.02.1997.
[3] Decision 1999/311, OJ L 120, 08.05.1999 and Decision 2002/601, OJ L 195, 24.07.2002.

positively to this application, thus demonstrating that they did not view their successful enterprise as a club of rich countries.

The countries which request accession to the EU should, however, satisfy certain political and economic conditions. According to the **criteria established by the European Council in Copenhagen** in 1993, an applicant country should have: (a) stable institutions guaranteeing democracy, the rule of law, human rights and protection of minorities; (b) a functioning market economy and the capacity to cope with competitive pressure and market forces within the Union; and (c) the ability to take on the obligations of membership, including adherence to the aims of political, economic and monetary union. The EC/EU helps, however the candidate countries to comply with the criteria for their accession. In addition to their participation in various Community programmes and the assistance given through special programmes, notably PHARE, TEMPUS, ISPA and SAPARD [see section 21.5.2.], pre-accession assistance is granted to the countries trying to meet the criteria set at Copenhagen[1]. A Technical Assistance Information Exchange Office (**TAIEX**) allows the associated countries to call upon the experience of Commission and Member States officials in drafting, transposing and implementing legislation concerning the internal market.

The Copenhagen European Council (12-13 December 2002) confirmed that accession negotiations were concluded with **Cyprus, the Czech Republic, Estonia, Hungary, Latvia, Lithuania, Malta, Poland, Slovakia and Slovenia**, and welcomed these States as members from 1 May 2004. On the subject of Cyprus, the European Council confirmed that it would prefer a united Cyprus to accede to the European Union but pointed out that, in the absence of a settlement, the Republic of Cyprus would be admitted to the European Union, with the application of the *acquis communautaire* to the northern part of the island being suspended. Noting the important progress achieved by Bulgaria and Romania, the European Council confirmed its objective of welcoming these countries into the European Union in 2007 on the basis of the same principles that have guided the accession negotiations of the 10. With regard to Turkey, the European Council encouraged it to pursue energetically its reform process and announced that, if the European Council decided, in December 2004, on the basis of a report and a recommendation from the Commission, that Turkey fulfilled the Copenhagen political criteria, the European Union would open accession negotiations without delay. The Treaty of Accession of the ten new Member States was signed under the Acropolis of Athens on 16 April 2003. Partnership agreements, containing the principles, priorities, intermediate objectives and conditions of accession, were signed, in 2003, with **Bulgaria**[2], **Romania**[1] and **Turkey**[2].

---

[1] Regulation 622/98, OJ L 85, 20.03.1998 and Decisions 98/259 to 98/268, OJ L 121, 23.04.1998.

[2] Decision 2003/396, OJ L 145, 12.06.2003.

The financial and institutional consequences of the enlargement were spelled out by the Copenhagen European Council. The 10 acceding States will be able to participate in the 2004 European Parliament elections as members. The Accession Treaty stipulates that Commissioners from the new Member States will join the current Commission as from the day of accession on 1 May 2004. On the same date, the provisions contained in the Nice Treaty concerning the Commission and voting in the Council will enter into force [see section 2.4.].

25.3. Balkan countries

At the instigation of the Commission[3], the Council has adopted a common position concerning a **stability pact for south-eastern Europe**. The aim of the stability pact is to help ensure cooperation among the countries of this region in the adoption of comprehensive measures for the long-term stabilisation, security, democratisation, and economic reconstruction and development of the region, and for the establishment of sustainable good-neighbourly relations among these countries and between them and the international community. The European Union should play the leading role in the stability pact and should develop and implement it in close association with the Organisation for Security and Cooperation in Europe [see section 8.2.3.]. The Stability Pact is founded on the United Nations Charter, the principles and commitments of the OSCE, and the relevant treaties and conventions of the Council of Europe, in particular the European Convention on Human Rights[4].

Exceptional trade measures were introduced for western Balkan countries and territories (Albania, the Federal Republic of Yugoslavia, the Former Yugoslav Republic of Macedonia, Bosnia and Herzegovina, Croatia and the Kosovo) participating in or linked to the European Union's **stabilisation and association process (SAP)**[5]. The Thessaloniki agenda for the western Balkans, adopted by the Thessaloniki European Council (19-20 June 2003) enhanced the stabilisation and association process with elements from the enlargement process (twinning, allowing participation in selected Community programmes, European partnerships, strengthening of political dialogue and cooperation in the area of common foreign and security policy). In accordance, the Community pre-accession assistance programmes (Phare, ISPA and Sapard) were modified to allow the stabilisation and association process countries to participate in tenders, which were

---

[1]   Decision 2003/397, OJ L 145, 12.06.2003.
[2]   Decision 2003/398, OJ L 145, 12.06.2003.
[3]   COM (1999) 235, 26 May 1999.
[4]   Common Position 1999/3455/CFSP, OJ L 133, 28.5.1999.
[5]   Regulation 2007/2000, OJ L 240, 23.09.2000.

previously limited to the acceding or candidate countries, and therefore move towards EU integration[1].

After the change of regime in Serbia, the Union has stepped up its assistance to the Balkans by bringing under a single legal basis and a single programme the initiatives covered by the Phare and Obnova[2] programmes promoting close regional cooperation between recipient countries[3]. The aim of the assistance is the reconstruction and stabilisation of the region, support for democracy and the rule of law, promotion of human and minority rights, and economic development and market economy reforms. **European partnerships** cover Albania, Bosnia and Herzegovina, Croatia, the Former Yugoslav Republic of Macedonia and Serbia and Montenegro, including Kosovo[4]. The partnerships provide a framework covering the priorities resulting from the analysis of the partners' different situations, the preparations for further integration into the European Union and the progress made in implementing the stabilisation and association process. The Council decides by qualified majority the principles, priorities and conditions to be contained in the European partnerships

The EU has established a **monitoring mission** in the Balkans whose main purpose is to supervise political and security developments in the area of responsibility, give particular attention to border monitoring and help build confidence in the context of the Union's stabilisation policy for the region[5]. Advancement in the process of European integration in the region depends primarily on each country's own commitment and capability to carry out political and economic reform and adhere to the core values and principles of the Union.

25.4. Eastern European and Central Asian countries

The Community plays a decisive role in the provision of technical assistance and food aid to the new republics of the Commonwealth of Independent States (CIS). In 1990, it introduced a technical assistance programme in favour of economic reform and recovery in the former Union of Soviet Socialist Republics (TACIS programme). Such assistance generated significant impact on reform and led to partnership and cooperation agreements with 13 states in **Eastern Europe and Central Asia: Armenia, Azerbaijan, Belarus, Georgia, Kazakhstan, Kyrgyzstan, Moldova,**

---

[1] Regulation 769/2004, OJ L 123, 27.04.2004.
[2] Regulation 2454/1999, OJ L 299, 20.11.1999.
[3] Regulation 3906/89, OJ L 375, 23.12.1989, Decision 97/256, OJ L 102, 19.04.1997, Regulation 2666/2000 and Regulation 769/2004, OJ L 123, 27.04.2004.
[4] Regulation 533/2004, OJ L 86, 24.03.2004.
[5] Joint action 2000/811/CFSP, OJ L 328, 23.12.2000 and Joint Action 2002/921 and Decision 2002/922, OJ L 321, 26.11.2002.

Mongolia, Russian Federation, Tajikistan, Turkmenistan, Ukraine and Uzbekistan.

The **general programme of assistance** seeks to ease the 13 countries' transition towards a market economy, and to reinforce democracy and the rule of law[1]. It is founded on the principles and objectives set out in the **partnership and cooperation agreements (PCAs)** and commercial and economic cooperation agreements signed between the EU and each of those countries. The programme is focused on a limited number of significant initiatives, notably: support for institutional, legal and administrative reform, including the development of the rule of law; support to the private sector; and assistance for economic development. The Community assistance is applied in the framework of national and multi-country programmes, which comprise indicative and action programmes covering three to four year periods.

For the future, the Commission envisages a **European neighbourhood policy (ENP)** resulting, in the medium term, in a new contractual relationship of the EU with the most advanced of its eastern and southern neighbours in the form of European neighbourhood agreements. These should enhance EU relations in a number of areas such as political dialogue, trade and measures preparing the partners for progressive participation in the internal market[2]. On 14 June 2004, the Council approved the Commission proposals to pursue the ENP through action plans to be agreed jointly with the neighbouring countries concerned.

On 4 June 1999, the Cologne European Council decided on a **common strategy of the European Union on Russia**[3] [see section 8.2.1.]. The strategy seeks to make the Union and Russia work together in the many areas of common concern to bring peace, stability and prosperity to Europe on the basis of common values and shared objectives. The core of the EU-Russia relationship is the Partnership and Cooperation Agreement (PCA), with its aim of promoting Russia's integration into a wider area of cooperation in Europe and paving the way to a free-trade area between the European Community and Russia. Similar are the objectives of the **common strategy on Ukraine**[4].

25.5. *Mediterranean, Middle East*

The countries of the Mediterranean are of considerable economic significance for the European Union, constituting as a group one of its largest trading partners and having close historic and cultural ties with some of its

---

[1] Regulation 99/2000, OJ L 12, 18.01.2000.
[2] COM (2004) 373, 12 May 2004.
[3] Common strategy 1999/414/CFSP, OJ L 157, 24.06.1999 and common strategy 2003/471, OJ L 157, 26.06.2003.
[4] Common Strategy 1999/877/CFSP, OJ L 331, 23.12.1999.

Member States. A prosperous, democratic, stable and secure Mediterranean region, having close economic and political relations with Europe, is in the best interests of the EU. A new phase of close cooperation began in 1995.

An important Euro-Mediterranean ministerial conference took place on 27 and 28 November 1995 in Barcelona between the European Union and its twelve Mediterranean partners (Algeria, Cyprus, Egypt, Israel, Jordan, Lebanon, Malta, Morocco, Syria, Tunisia, Turkey and the Palestinian Authority). At the end of the proceedings, the ministers adopted a Declaration and a work programme instituting a regular political dialogue and enhanced cooperation fostering peace, security, stability and prosperity in the region. The three key components of the **Euro-Mediterranean partnership** based on the Barcelona Declaration are: to establish a common area of peace and stability through a political and security partnership; to create an area of shared prosperity through an economic and financial partnership; to establish a partnership in social, cultural and human affairs, thus developing human resources, promoting understanding between cultures and exchanges between civil societies.

The Feira European Council (19-20 June 2000), having regard to Article 13 of the TEU [see section 8.2.1.], has adopted a **common strategy of the European Union on the Mediterranean region**. The goals of the common strategy are:

- to make significant and measurable progress towards achieving the objectives of the Barcelona Declaration and its subsequent *acquis*;
- to promote the core values embraced by the EU and its Member States - including human rights, democracy, good governance, transparency and the rule of law;
- to encourage and assist Mediterranean partners with the process of achieving free trade with the EU and among themselves in the terms of the Barcelona Declaration, economic transition and attracting increased investment to the region;
- to strengthen cooperation in the field of justice and home affairs;
- to pursue, in order to fight intolerance, racism and xenophobia, the dialogue between cultures and civilisations.

The Commission proposes various measures to achieve these objectives. At trade level it recommends accelerating the association process with the countries of the region, i.e. concluding association agreements with Algeria, Syria and Lebanon[1] and the entry into force of the agreements already concluded with Jordan and Egypt with a view to establishing a free trade area by 2010. It also calls on all the partners to join the WTO by 2002, and to create a free trade area between their territories. In the context of the European initiative for democracy and human rights (EIDHR), the Commission has set out guidelines on how to make the most of the instruments available to the European Union and its Mediterranean partners

---

[1] OJ L 262, 30.09.2002.

for consolidating their common objective of promoting and defending universal human rights and fundamental freedoms[1].

A **Community budget heading called MEDA** constitutes the single financial instrument for the implementation of all cooperation activities with the countries concerned[2]. It provides for support measures in three areas: economic transition, economic and social development, and regional and cross-border cooperation.

25.6. Asian countries

The **Community Strategy for Asia** is founded on a development partnership and on political dialogue[3]. The priorities of this strategy include notably: backing cooperation schemes aimed at safeguarding peace and security; improving Europe's image in Asia and creating a climate conducive to the development of trade and investment; and improving coordination in the management of development aid so that the region's less prosperous countries experience economic growth and poverty is reduced [see section 24.4.].

The new agreement concluded with **India** is an advanced framework cooperation agreement emphasising economic cooperation and private sector investment, intellectual property rights, technology transfer and diversification of economic and trade relations[4]. Similar **non-preferential agreements, called "third generation"**, comprising three areas of cooperation, namely trade, economic and development cooperation, and making respect for human rights a key condition for the development of dialogue and partnership have been concluded with **Mongolia**[5], **Sri Lanka**[6], **Vietnam**[7] and **Nepal**[8].

Community aid has had a relatively positive impact in the countries belonging to the **Association of South-East Asian Nations (ASEAN)**, which comprises **Brunei, Indonesia, Malaysia, the Philippines, Singapore, Thailand and Vietnam**. The cooperation agreement between the Community and most of these countries dates back to 1980[9]. It is completed by

---

[1] COM (2003) 294, 21 May 2003.
[2] Regulation 1488/96, OJ L 189, 30.07.1996, Decision 96/706, OJ L 325, 14.12.1996 and Regulation 2698/2000, OJ L 311, 12.12.2000.
[3] COM (94) 314.
[4] Agreement and Decision 94/578, OJ L 223, 27.08.1994.
[5] Agreement and Decision 92/101, OJ L 41, 18.02.1993.
[6] Agreement and Decision 95/129, OJ L 85, 19.04.1995.
[7] Agreement and Decision 96/351, OJ L 136, 07.06. 1996.
[8] Agreement and Decision 96/354, OJ L 137, 08.06.1996.
[9] Regulation 1440/80, OJ L 144, 10.06.1980 and Decision 1999/295, OJ L 117, 05.05.1999.

trade agreements on manioc from Thailand and Indonesia[1] granting better access for their products to the Community market. As a follow-up to its communication on "Europe and Asia: a strategic framework for enhanced partnerships"[2], the Commission proposes revitalising the relations between the EU, ASEAN and the countries of South-East Asia, and identifies the strategic priorities, creating a framework for future bilateral agreements[3].

Relations between the Community and **China**, after the retrogression that followed the events of Tiananmen Square on June 4, 1989, are marking a steady improvement. A 1978 framework trade agreement evolved into the 1985 trade and economic cooperation agreement covering industrial and technical fields[4] and trade in textiles[5]. A 1998 Commission communication on "a comprehensive **partnership with China**"[6] opened the way for a new EU-China relationship embracing four main areas: upgrading the political dialogue; supporting China's transition to an open society based on the rule of law and respect for human rights; integrating China further into the world economy; and raising the profile of the EU in China. On behalf of the Community and its Member States, the Commission negotiated with China a whole series of commitments on the opening up of markets which are of particular importance to the European Union. These commitments were listed in the bilateral agreement signed by the People's Republic of China and the European Community on 19 May 2000, and are set out in the protocol of accession by China to the WTO[7] [see section 23.4.]. The EU's cooperation programme with China has expanded steadily and now focuses on supporting sustainable development to assist the overall reform process in China and the implementation of its WTO commitments[8].

Japan poses problems of a completely different nature for the European Union. Japan has a huge trade surplus with the Community, with its exports to the EU running at three times its imports from it. Japan is at an advantage compared with the other industrialised countries due to such specificities as a limited social security budget, low military expenditure and low aid level to the developing countries. But the success of Japanese policy is chiefly due to certain basic economic factors: strong competitiveness and productivity, rigid organisation of the domestic market, integrated industrial and trade strategy working towards precise and planned objectives. As regards more specifically trade relations with the EU, the determinant factors in the disequilibrium are: the concentration of Japanese ex-

---

[1] Decisions 82/495 and 82/496, OJ L 219, 28.07.1982 and Decision 90/637, OJ L 347, 12.12.1990.
[2] COM (2001) 469.
[3] COM (2003) 399.
[4] Agreement and Regulation 2616/85, OJ L 250, 19.09.1985.
[5] Agreement and Decision 95/155, OJ L 104, 06.05.1995.
[6] COM (1998) 181.
[7] COM (2001) 517 and 518, 19 September 2001.
[8] COM (2000) 552, 8 September 2000.

ports on a limited number of sectors, high quality, leading-edge products, marketed with highly effective marketing methods supported by a favourable financing system; and, on the other side of the equation, the closing of the Japanese market by various technical and administrative barriers as well as by prevalent Japanese national habits and attitudes. Nevertheless, the Community is becoming an increasingly important trading partner for Japan because of the size of the single European market and the efforts made to develop trade and cooperation.

Closer relations between the Community and Japan culminated in the adoption, on July 18, 1991, of a **joint declaration** similar to those defining the Community's relations with the United States and Canada. It sets out the general principles and objectives of cooperation between the two parties, notably stipulating that access to respective markets must be equitable and offer comparable opportunities through the removal of obstacles to trade and investments. It also stipulates the framework for dialogue, with annual summits and other meetings. As regards more especially trade in motor vehicles, the Community and Japan agreed on July 31, 1991 on a solution aiming at gradual liberalisation of the Community market as part of the completion of the single market, while avoiding market distortion caused by exports from Japan [see section 23.4.].

25.7. North American countries

The European Union is **the biggest trading partner of the United States** and is linked to this country by culture, tradition and cross-investments as well as by common economic and political interests embodied within international organisations such as the Organisation for Economic Cooperation and Development (OECD) and the North Atlantic Treaty Organisation (NATO). The United States were in 2000 the EU's leading investment partner: almost half of the extra-EU investments by Member States went to the United States (EUR 147 out of EUR 304 billion), and almost 80% of investments by non-member countries in the EU came from the United States (EUR 98 out of EUR 125 billion). From the political viewpoint, the United States has always supported European integration. This has not prevented strong economic antagonism between the two richest regions of the planet.

The fall of the Soviet Union and the emergence of the United States as the sole superpower led to the adoption on November 22, 1990 by the United States on the one hand and by the Community and its Member States on the other of a joint **transatlantic declaration**. Considering that their relationship is a vital factor for political stability in a changing world, the two parties confirmed their commitment to continuing and developing cooperation on an equal footing and, for this purpose, they agreed to consult one another on important subjects of common interest and to intensify their dialogue in a formal contact structure. The **transatlantic agenda**, signed in 1995, completed the Transatlantic Declaration and organised the cooperation between the two partners around four pillars: promoting peace, stability, democracy and development throughout the world, responding to global challenges, contributing to the expansion of world trade and closer economic relations, and establishing closer ties between the partners. In addition, an agreement between the Community and the United States established a cooperation programme in the field of higher education and vocational training[1].

After the **terrorist attacks** of 11 September 2001 against the United States, the European Council meeting in extraordinary session on 21 September 2001 declared its total support to the American people in the face of the deadly terrorist attacks and its willingness to cooperate with the United States in bringing to justice and punishing the perpetrators, sponsors and accomplices of such barbaric acts [see section 8.2.3.]. On 8 October 2001, the Council declared that the military action taken by the US in self-defence and in conformity with the UN Charter and the UNSCR 1368 was part of a wider multilateral strategy in which the European Union was committed to playing its part, including a comprehensive assault on the organisations and financing structures that underpin terrorism.

However, transatlantic relations are often a **controversial subject** for the EU, since the degree of solidarity with the United States differs considerably from one European country to another. It is, therefore, usually difficult to work out a common reaction to the initiatives of Washington. In general, the vision of the world and of international relations of the USA, which is largely based on national interest and the use of military force, is basically contrasting with the concept of international law that the European nations tend to place above national law. Even the best friends of the USA in Europe are sad to see the new American policy depart from the rules of international law, enacted with the active participation of the USA themselves, on issues such as: the ratification of the Kyoto protocol for the reduction of atmospheric pollution [see section 16.3.4.]; the exemption of American citizens from the jurisdiction of the International Criminal Court for war crimes [see section 8.1.2.]; the disrespect of the rules of the World Trade Organisation in general and particularly concerning the huge increase in American farm subsidies (70%) and the protection of American steel products; the invasion of Iraq without agreement of the UN Security Council; and, last but not least, the uneven interposition in the conflict between Israelis and Palestinians. On all these subjects the transatlantic declaration of 1990 has not served as a basis of dialogue and cooperation between equal partners. If this situation continues, the European Union will, sooner or later, adopt a foreign policy, which will increasingly diverge from that of the USA.

The Community's relations with **Canada** have originally been based on a cooperation agreement between Euratom and Canada on the peaceful use

---

[1]   Agreement and Decision 279/95, OJ L 279, 22.11.1995.

of atomic energy[1], on a cooperation agreement between the EEC and Canada on commercial and economic cooperation[2] and on a fisheries agreement[3]. The two parties adopted on November 22, 1990 a **joint declaration** based on the preferential relations introduced by the framework cooperation agreement which reinforces the institutional framework for consultations in order to give them a long-term horizon.

25.8. Latin American countries

As seen in the chapter devoted to development aid, the Community has been **granting aid to Latin America** as a group of non-associated countries for many years [see section 24.4.]. The Community is aware of its responsibility for development in these countries, home to some of the poorest people in the world. This awareness has been further accentuated since the entry of Spain and Portugal to the Community, two countries which share the same cultural heritage with Latin America. Thus, the Community develops ever closer relations with **regional groupings** in Latin America, i.e. the **Rio Group** (Argentina, Bolivia, Brazil, Chile, Colombia, Costa Rica, Dominican Republic, El Salvador, Ecuador, Guatemala, Honduras, Mexico, Nicaragua, Panama, Paraguay, Peru, Uruguay, Venezuela), the **Central American Integration**, the **Andean Pact** and **Mercosur**.

In 1986 the Community concluded a framework agreement for commercial and economic cooperation and development with the countries of the Central American Economic Integration or **San José Group (Costa Rica, El Salvador, Guatemala, Honduras, Nicaragua) and with Panama**[4]. The cooperation agreement between the Community and the countries of the **Andean Pact or Cartagena Agreement (Bolivia, Colombia, Ecuador, Peru and Venezuela)**, places particular emphasis on the consolidation of the regional integration systems and on the respect of democratic principles and human rights[5]. The main aims of the agreement are: to stimulate, diversify and improve trade; to encourage cooperation between industrialists; and to stimulate scientific and technical cooperation.

---

[1] OJ 60, 24.11.1959 and OJ C 215, 17.08.1991.
[2] Agreement and Decisions, OJ L 260, 24.09.1976.
[3] Decisions 81/1053 and 81/1054, OJ L 379, 31.12.1981 and Agreement and Regulation 3675/93, OJ L 340, 31.12.1993.
[4] Agreement and Regulation 2009/86, OJ L 172, 30.06.1986.
[5] Agreement and Decision 98/278, OJ L 127, 29.04.1998.

The European Union is also providing technical assistance to the common market between the **Mercosur** countries **(Argentina, Brazil, Paraguay and Uruguay)**. In the wake of the Solemn Joint Declaration between the European Union and Mercosur[1], an interregional commercial and economic cooperation framework Agreement between the EU and Mercosur was signed in Madrid on 15 December 1995[2]. Aimed at strengthening existing ties and preparing for eventual association, this Agreement provides: regular, institutionalised political dialogue; trade cooperation leading to trade liberalisation; economic cooperation geared to promoting reciprocal investment; cooperation on regional integration, intended to allow Mercosur to draw upon the experience of the European Union; and wider cooperation in fields of mutual interest, such as culture, information and communication, training on the multinational integration process and on the prevention of drug abuse.

The new opening provided by the Uruguay Round Agreements [see section 23.4.] and the developments in the various integration processes in Latin America are the two vital elements for **intensifying cooperation** between the EU and Latin American countries. In giving its support to the development efforts of the latter (at bilateral level) and to their integration efforts (at multilateral level) the European Union hopes to contribute to the political stability and economic and social development of a region of the world which, despite its current economic and social difficulties, is rich in raw materials and is a vast potential market.

25.9. Appraisal and outlook

Whereas at the outset the Community was viewed with indifference, scepticism or even hostility by the rest of the world, it is now **recognised as being a major economic, commercial and, potentially, political power**. In this and in the two preceding chapters we saw that the Community is dealing, negotiating and conversing with many countries large and small throughout the world, which see it as an important group of prosperous, democratic and peaceful countries. Curiously enough, those outside better perceive the common policies of EC/EU countries than those inside it [see sections 10.1. and 10.4.]. In fact, the Union's external policy is made up of a number of common policies, which support one another. It goes beyond the traditional diplomatic and military aspects, which are ostensibly in the ambit of the Union, and stretches to Community areas such as trade and customs affairs, development aid, justice and police matters, environment protection, external relations of agricultural and fisheries policies and external representation of the euro zone. Through its development

---

[1] OJ C 377, 31.12.1994.
[2] Agreement OJ L 69, 19.03.1996 and Council Decision 1999/279, OJ L 112, 29.04.1999.

aid policy, its common commercial policy and its external relations, the European Community has a **strong presence on the world stage**. It notably exerts a strong pressure, through its statements, representations and economic sanctions, on many countries practising serious violations of democratic principles and human rights [see section 24.1.]. It also advocates an effective multilaterism in the framework of an international society based on the rule of law.

However, the fragmentation of initiative, decision and action causes the **inadequacy of the Union's foreign policy**. The European Union cannot exert a political influence commensurate to its economic weight in the world affairs, as long as the external policies of the Community, examined in this part, are not well coordinated or better integrated in the common foreign and security policy of the Union [see section 8.2.]. As we will see in the "European outlook", it is up to its Member States to let the European Union become a world power by accepting to share their political sovereignty in the same way they share their economic and monetary sovereignty [see chapter 7].

The Union has the potential to **play a role as a world power**. To this end, it must propound its democratic values and its integration paradigm, stand up and be counted as the bearer of a shared and sustainable model of development. It must pursue an external policy open to dialogue between civilisations, cultures and religions, and based on cooperation with the countries at its borders and on the resolve to help the economic, political and social development of all the countries in the world. It is significant that after the fall of their communist regimes Central and Eastern European countries ignored the possibility of acceding to the European Economic Area and applied for membership to the EU in order to strengthen their feeble economies and stabilise their fragile democratic systems. By enhancing its power and image in the world arena, the EU could better help other countries in the world, torn by their economic and political differences, imitate its successful formula of multinational integration. In fact, Europe's experience with economic and political unification is being watched with close attention throughout the world and countries in other regions of the globe, notably in Latin America, are trying to imitate it. This could be a valuable contribution of the European Union to world peace and prosperity.

Bibliography on external relations

- CREMONA Marise. "The Union as a global actor: roles, models and identity", *Common Market Law Review*, v. 41, n. 2, April 2004, p. 553-573.
- EUROPEAN COMMISSION. *Central American integration: what's next?: the integration process in Central America and the role of the European Union*. Luxembourg: EUR-OP*, 2004.

- GOMES SARAIVA Miriam. *The European Union as an International Actor and the Mercosur Countries*. Florence: European University Institute, 2004.
- GOVAERE Inge, CAPIAU Jeroen, VERMEERSCH An. "In-between seats: the participation of the European Union in international organizations", *European Foreign Affairs Review*, v. 9, n. 2, Summer 2004, p. 155-187.
- INGLIS Kirstyn. "The Union's fifth accession treaty: new means to make enlargement possible", *Common Market Law Review*, v. 41, n. 4, August 2004, p. 937-973.
- KAUFFMANN Pascal, YVARS Bernard (sous la dir. de). *Intégration européenne et régionalisme dans les pays en développement*, Paris: L'Harmattan, 2004.
- KOUTRAKOU Vassiliki (ed.). *Contemporary issues and debates in EU policy: the European Union and international relations*. Manchester: Manchester University Press, 2004.
- NUGENT Neill (ed.). *European Union enlargement*. Basingstoke: Palgrave Macmillan, 2004.
- SCHUMACHER Tobias. *Survival of the Fittest: The First Five Years of Euro-Mediterranean Economic Relations*. Florence: European University Institute, 2004.
- SCHWABE Klaus (et al.). "The European Community and the dissolution of Yugoslavia", *Journal of European Integration History*, v. 10, n. 1, 2004, p. 5-202.

The publications of the Office for Official Publications of the European Communities (EUR-OP) exist generally in all official languages of the EU.

DISCUSSION TOPICS

1. What distinguishes the external relations of the EC from the common foreign and security policy of the EU?
2. Why have Central and Eastern European countries applied for membership to the EU rather than to the European Economic Area?
3. Could Russia and other Eastern European countries become one day members of the EU or else of the EEA?
4. Does competition in the world arena encourage or hamper the partnership between the EU and the USA?
5. How do the relations of the Community with Asian and Latin American countries interact with the common commercial policy and with the common aid to development policy?

Conclusions

EUROPEAN INTEGRATION
AND ITS PERSPECTIVES

Europe's history relates in the main the wars for the domination of some nations over the others and the battles of those others for their liberation from their oppressor or oppressors. After centuries of incessant wars, recurring aggressions, revolutions, massacres, human sacrifices, genocides, material destructions, economic disasters, Europe has arrived in the middle of the last century at the most devastating war of world history, the economic downfall of all European nations and the world supremacy of a non-European power. Fortunately, however, right after the Second World War, some inspired politicians, like Schuman, Adenauer, De Gasperi and Spaak, realised that the European nations, which had just ruined each other in a nonsensical war for the enlargement of their economic space, were in fact parts of **a single geographic, economic and political entity**, that could guarantee the prosperity of all in a single market.

Realists rather than idealists, those wise political leaders were fully aware of the difficulties of uniting Europe. The famous declaration of Robert Schuman of the 9th May 1950, inspired by Jean Monnet, was clear as to the step by step approach to be followed for European integration. The realisation of a customs union would fulfil the requirements for building a large common market and this would in turn establish the conditions and exert the pressures needed for the attainment of an economic and monetary union. This close economic integration would eventually necessitate a common foreign policy. Thus, political integration would follow the economic one.

Fifty years after the "invitation to union" of Robert Schuman we may say with confidence that the expectations of the fathers of European unification have been largely realised. The European Community/Union has built the three first floors of its edifice – the customs union, the common market and the economic and monetary union – and although work is still needed and done every day on them, it has started building the last floor, that of political union. Work at the one wing of this floor, that of home and judicial policy, is advancing satisfactorily. The big question is if and when work will get started on the wing of the foreign and security policy.

The work already accomplished qualifies the European model as a success story. Multinational integration has established peace in Western Europe, has turned the former enemies into good partners, has secured the equality of all participating nations under common laws, has ensured development opportunities and thus the relative prosperity of all. In short, the

European Community/Union has become an island of peace and prosperity in a world that is, unfortunately, still suffering from skilfully cultivated ethnic, racial, religious and other differences, battles for the glory of war-mongers, slaughters and displacements of populations for ethnic and/or economic reasons and, finally, the exploitation of the vast majority of mankind by an unscrupulous minority, equally distributed among various nations.

Unfortunately, despite the fantastic progress of science and technology during the previous century, civilisation has not much advanced in the world. Indeed, if "Civilisation" is taken to mean an advanced system of human values and social development guaranteeing peace, freedom of opinion and welfare for all persons, civilisation is not yet enjoyed by a huge part of mankind. In this sense of civilisation, multinational integration may be considered the **most important socio-political invention since the invention of democracy**, because it spreads and consolidates the values of the latter: the rule of law, the separation of the state from religion, freedom of initiative, equality of nations and individuals, well distributed welfare for all regions and social categories. These capital socio-political discoveries, which go hand in hand (since the concept of integration is inseparable from that of democracy) [see section 1.1.2.], were made on European soil. It is true that Europe invented also colonialism, fascism, anti-Semitism and bolshevism and other "isms", but these bad inventions ended in failures and are currently disavowed by the immense majority of Europeans. On the other hand, Europeans have a vital reason to promote the models of democracy, humanism and integration, that they have developed and are still improving, to the nations that are torn apart and starving, exploited by crooked demagogues and plutocrats of all kinds bearing all sorts of fancy banners. The reason is the protection of their own safety and wellbeing from all these false prophets.

In this book we have tried to throw light on all aspects of the phenomenon called multinational integration, which is complicated and difficult to understand even for those who are involved in it. The sad fact is that, because of the complex nature of the integration process and the lack of adequate edification, the citizens of the Member States do not realise that they take part in an experiment that may change for the better not only their own lives but also the course of history. If they did realise the potential of the multinational integration process, they would better accept the hurdles that it has to overcome and they would better appreciate its accomplishments. By presenting all the achievements of the integration process to date, our objective was not advertising **the success story of European integration** in order to embellish its institutions, which are far from perfect, but scrutinising the phenomenon in order to infer certain conclusions concerning its possible evolution and dissemination to other parts of the world. In what follows, we will try to assess the main findings of the study and propose some estimates concerning the advancement of the evolutionary process of multinational integration.

1. Main facts regarding European integration

The course of the multinational integration process in the European Community/Union is determined by *three* **currents that converge at certain points** and strengthen the main flow: (a) the increasing number of the participants; (b) the continuous raising of their goals through the passage from one integration stage to another; and (c) the constant increase of their activities by the development of common policies. It is worth recapitulating the main findings of our study on these major trends of European integration.

The membership has kept growing together with the tasks assumed by the team. The multinational integration process began in 1951 as a customs union concerning only the coal and steel sectors of six countries on the basis of the ECSC Treaty. In 1958, these same countries extended the operation of the customs union and of the common market to all the sectors of their economies, thanks to the EEC Treaty. In 1973, they were joined by three countries, which had originally preferred intergovernmental cooperation inside a free trade area. In 1992, the builders of the common market had become twelve, had completed the work on that stage of their integration on the basis of the Single European Act and had signed the Treaty of Maastricht leading them to the next stage of their integration [see sections 2.2. and 6.1.]. In 1995, the builders of the union were joined by three more states, which had originally believed in the benefits of the free trade area. At the dawn of the 21st century, the fifteen were finalising their economic and monetary union [see section 7.2.1.], were progressing in their political union thanks to the Treaty of Amsterdam [see section 8.2.] and were opening the door of their enterprise to ten more states [see section 25.2.].

Despite the successive enlargements, the multinational integration process in Europe has followed **a steady evolution in stages of ever closer economic convergence** - customs union, common market, economic and monetary union - and is proceeding towards the final stage of political union. The **customs union**, nowadays taken for granted and almost forgotten, formed the solid foundation of the entire European edifice. The problem-free removal of customs barriers to trade filled the apprentices of European construction with the enthusiasm necessary for climbing up the steep and unfamiliar road of integration [see section 5.1.1.]. The stage of the **common market**, completed in 1992, meant the freedom of movement within the single market of goods, persons, services and capital [see chapter 6]. These freedoms revolutionised trade and competition, the working methods and the economic conditions in the Member States of the Community. The reduction of administrative and financial costs of intra-Community trade and the realisation of economies of scale liberated the dynamism and the creativity of European businessmen and gave them a solid foothold from which to sustain international competitiveness [see section 6.2.].

In December 1991 in Maastricht, the Member States decided to initiate the next stage of their integration, viz. **economic and monetary union (EMU)**, implying a single monetary policy, necessary for the management of a single currency, and the convergence of national economic policies, with a view to achieving economic and social cohesion. EMU was based on the common market in goods and services, but itself served the proper functioning of the common market, by eliminating exchange rate variations between Member States' currencies, which hindered the interpenetration of capital markets, disturbed the common agricultural market and prevented the common industrial market from wholly resembling an internal market. This stage of the integration process was completed with the successful circulation of the euro, on 1st January 2002, just ten years after its conception.

At the same time that they designed their monetary integration, the Member States decided to coordinate their non-economic policies as well, i.e.: justice and home affairs policies, in order to achieve a common area of freedom, security and justice; and their foreign and security policies, so that the economic giant that they were creating through economic integration would have a voice commensurate with its size in the international arena [see section 2.3.and chapter 8]. They have, thus, reached the threshold of **political integration**; but although the new common policies in the political field were given a boost with the Treaty of Amsterdam, foreign and security policy is still detached from the prime objective of the EC/EU: an **"ever closer union among the peoples of Europe"**.

The preceding summary of events and trends demonstrates the **extraordinary success of the multinational integration process** as practised in Europe since the early 1950s. This success was due to the construction method taught by Monnet and Schuman, which is that of a step by step advance after careful evaluation of the previous experience. Brick upon brick, act after act, as taught by the old masters, the European edifice has been built up and is still expanding. Every new measure fits so well into the adjoining provisions that it fills a gap while consolidating the whole structure [see section 3.1.]. In fact, the successful formula of European integration is based on **common policies** built by **common institutions** following the **Community method** [see section 1.1.2.]. These three ingredients of the integration formula, amply brought out in the various chapters of this book, merit some concluding observations.

In the introduction of this book, we made the hypothesis that the fundamental elements of the multinational integration process are **common policies** pursuing common goals and **serving common interests** [see section 1.1.2.]. We supposed that the supreme interests of the citizens of the participating states are the assurance of peace with their neighbours and the increase of their wellbeing. On the basis of the findings brought out in the book, we may assert that the common policies of the European Community/Union serve well those interests. They have transformed the former enemies into partners. War between the members of the Union has become unthinkable and the wellbeing of their citizens has greatly increased through the constant development of their economies and through the abundance of good quality products and services inside the single market. In addition, the common policies attain a great number of secondary common goals. They monitor the free exchange of industrial and agricultural goods between the Member States. They stimulate and support the development of the poorer regions of the Union. They guarantee the rights of the citizens of the Member States to travel, to live and to work wherever they choose within its territory. They facilitate the access of all citizens to the universal banking, insurance, telecommunication and audiovisual services offered in the large European market. They bolster the competitiveness of European industries by imposing uniform rules of competition and by supporting their efforts in research and development. They prepare the future by laying the foundations of the information society and of transport, energy and telecommunications trans-European networks spanning the whole Continent. They try to protect in a uniform way the environment and the consumers of the member countries. Certainly, none of these policies is perfect, but all of them are under the constant scrutiny of the common institutions and they are amended very often, in order to be adapted to the new needs that emerge from internal or external causes.

The **common policies are closely knit together** and support each other. Two horizontal policies - regional and social - pursue the objective of economic and social cohesion [see section 12.1.2.], which is linked to the objective of economic and monetary union. Such a union, implying abandonment of the use of exchange rate adjustment as a means of balance of national economies, would be to the detriment of the poorer Member States, if there was not an efficient **common regional policy** operating capital transfers from the richer to the poorer regions of the EU [see section 12.1.]. In fact, thanks to the common regional policy the standard of living in the Union's poor regions was greatly increased and they have made good much of the disadvantage they were at. Likewise, inside an economic and monetary union, where governments gradually lose the ability to confront separately the social problems of their peoples, since monetary and many economic decisions are taken in common [see section 13.1.], the process of social integration is pursued through common employment, vocational training and social protection policies. The **common social policy** has already built a "European social model" which guarantees, not only fundamental human rights and the democratic and pluralistic principles, but also the fundamental rights of workers: training adapted to technical progress, fair pay allowing decent living conditions and social protection covering the hazards of life, illness, unemployment and old age [see chapter 13]. This model is the social bedrock of the European integration process.

Three other **horizontal common policies** - on taxation, competition and environment protection - ensure a level playing field for European businesses. The harmonisation of indirect taxes brought about by the common taxation policy is instrumental for levelling the competition conditions inside the single market of products and services. The common competition policy is not only a necessary instrument for the smooth functioning of the internal market, preventing new compartmentalisation by the agreements of large companies and protectionism by national administrations through national aids, but is also a complement to common sectoral policies - industrial, agricultural, energy, transport - aimed at improving production structures and achieving international competitiveness. The common environment policy is essential, both for even-handed competition between nations respecting both market laws and citizens' welfare and for the sustainable development of the European and world economy.

The large sectors of the European economy - industry, energy, transports and agriculture - are organised gradually at European level by the legislation of the single market and by specific legislation adopted in the context of **sectoral common policies** [see Part V]. In fact, the freedoms of the common market apply to the businesses of those sectors, either directly or through sector-specific adaptations. The sectoral common policies are therefore necessary for the smooth functioning of the customs union, the common market and the economic and monetary union. Both horizontal and sectoral policies, including research and development, strive to boost the international competitiveness of European businesses, while cementing the economic integration of the States of the Union.

The economies of the member states are greatly influenced by common policies. As these economies are gradually opened up to multinational trade and competition, **all economic parameters change**: trade increases enormously within the large internal market, both supply and demand conditions are modified dramatically, state intervention is curbed and new dynamics are set in motion, notably concerning trade and investment opportunities, mergers and joint ventures. The creation and/or extension of multinational companies and the cross investments between them tend to connect the national economies to one another. The common policies build, in fact, a new concept and context of political economy, which has to be reckoned with by politicians, economists and businessmen.

2. European perspectives

Common policies, as all other public policies, are there to answer societal needs which arise in a defined community of nations at a certain time. Therefore, not only the objectives that the member states set for each common policy, but also the means that they give to the common institutions to attain them and the measures that the latter adopt in order to implement them change in accordance with the economic, political and social needs that the states, which take part in the process, experience at a certain time. In the case of the EC/EU, the common policies are **in permanent evolution**, demonstrated, for all of them, by the constant amendment of the Community laws (regulations, directives, etc.) that form them, and, for some of them (e.g., agricultural, regional, social and research policies), by the amendment of the Treaty provisions that concern them. Moreover, a common policy tends to spill over into the area of other common policies, produce needs, cause reactions and nourish their development.

The constant evolution of all common policies, a fact brought out in each new edition of this book, causes the endless evolution of the multinational integration process. The development of common policies creates ever-stronger economic and political links between the peoples of Europe. Paradoxically, the constant progress of integration in all fields demonstrates both the soundness and the imperfection of the Community model. An organisation and a process that are in a state of permanent evolution can never be perfect. They may only be improved. The "**constant progress syndrome**" is the strong point and the permanent challenge of the European model of integration. It means that European integration will normally keep developing over time, trying to reach an integration ideal that will never be attained, since ideals, by definition, cannot be completely achieved.

Although, due to the constant progress syndrome, the common policies examined in this book are all expected to develop in range and improve in efficiency over time, two are practically inexistent: a common information policy and a common foreign and security policy. Both these failures are due to the reluctance of the Member States to entrust the common institutions with large scale tasks in these fields. They both cause the frustration of the citizens of the Union and endanger the very existence of the European integration model.

The absence of a common information policy results in the **information deficit** of the European Union, i.e. a deficiency of reliable information, readily available to the citizens, concerning European affairs and the integration process. Due to the information deficit, most citizens ignore or take for granted the positive and palpable effects of European integration, such as the customs free availability of goods from all over Europe, border free travel and, above all, peace and friendship among their erstwhile bellicose nations. They are unaware of the extent to which they are surrounded by the workings of the Union in their daily and professional lives [see sections 10.1. and 10.4.].

It is strange to see that the Member States, which have developed a great number of common policies in all fields examined in this book, have neglected to set up a common policy for presenting the goals and measures of those policies to their citizens. The neglect of information and/or communication is probably due to a bad habit carried over from the early days of European integration, when the common policies under development were too technical to really interest the citizens. Now, however, the citizens feel that the Union is influencing their lives and that they are left in the dark by the European institutions and their own political leaders as to its workings. They show their indignation about this state of affairs in European elections, referendums and opinion polls. The information deficit is, indeed, more responsible for the estrangement of the citizens from the

European integration process than the much decried democratic deficit [see sections 9.4. and 10.1.]. It is also worsening even as the integration process is deepening and spilling over an ever-growing number of economic, societal and political sectors.

The information deficit endangers the integration process. If citizens were led to believe that the disadvantages of integration were greater than its benefits, they might press their political leaders to disengage their country(ies) from the integration process or, worse, to block the progress of the integration process not only for themselves but also for their positively minded partners. If we consider the effects of the information deficit on some referenda, in the past (the Danish concerning the Treaty of Maastricht, the Irish concerning the Treaty of Nice and the French and Dutch concerning the Constitutional Treaty), this scenario is not as absurd as it seems at first glance. In a community of people, where a silent majority has no interest in the common affairs and goals, while a determined minority is strongly opposed to its objectives and institutions, there is a strong probability that the minority group would tend to grow over time and to become stronger and ever more convinced of its ideas and ideals. Unopposed by the silent majority, it might thus eventually succeed to reverse the working system that holds the community together.

Not only all governments but also all major political parties, which are generally pro-integration, should recognize that **the information deficit** combined with a systematic disinformation on the part of some europhobic media is undermining the common policies that they want to carry through, is debasing the democratic institutions set up and empowered by them to implement those common policies and is halting the progress of European integration. In other words, the political elite should acknowledge that a common information policy, which might have been a luxury as long as the integration process was confined to customs and technical matters, is a necessity now that the process is spreading ever more from the purely economic to the political field. Just as the Union is incorporating ten more Member States, whose citizens are even less informed about the goals, the means and the achievements of the integration process than the citizens of the erstwhile Fifteen, it is high time for the European institutions to forsake the old habits of discretion and neglect of the citizens' opinion. In chapter 10 we called for the inauguration of a common information and communication policy, covering all the activities of the European institutions and implemented by a European Press Agency in close cooperation with the governments of the Member States [see section 10.1.3.]. Such a common communication policy, combined with the civic education of young Europeans at school, would bring the citizens closer to the Union and would secure the achievements of all the other common policies.

A paradoxical effect of the information and civic deficit about European integration is that, while citizens seem to be indifferent to the European Union, they simultaneously expect ever more important results from it. This is notably the case concerning the **European presence in the world scene**, the second serious flaw of the European edifice. Eurobarometer surveys indicate constantly over a long period of years that two in three Europeans believe that the European Union should have an effective common foreign policy [see introduction to chapter 10]. Three in four citizens of the Twenty-five back a really common security and defence policy. These and many more specific findings of the opinion polls indicate that Europeans fail to understand how the economic giant that they have created, the most important power in international trade, now endowed with the strongest currency in the world, cannot make its voice heard in the world arena. They expect the Union to take the lead in monitoring regional conflicts, globalisation, environmental challenges and famines in the world. The tragic inability of the Union to prevent the Balkan wars at its doorstep or to enforce the rules of international law in the resolution of conflicts in the important for its oil supplies Middle East has greatly reduced the respect of Europeans for their common institutions. Public reasoning is quite simple: as long as the Union cannot act as a mature political giant, it cannot be respected. It is time for the infant giant to grow up.

The citizens' expectations for a powerful Union in the world include the dissemination and defence of the European ideals of peace, welfare, democracy, the rule of law and social justice on the world scene. Europe is open to the world and its citizens understand that they cannot live merrily in a prosperous island surrounded by the misery and envy of other nations. They understand that, for their own peace and security, the Union should contribute more to peace and sustainable development in the world. Europeans know as well that they cannot prevent the new technologies and free enterprise from shrinking the world to the virtual dimensions of a village; but they feel that this, as any village, should have a town hall and that they should have their representatives inside it. In other words, they expect the Union to play **an active role in the globalisation phenomenon** by enhancing the legitimacy and effectiveness of international institutions, notably the United Nations and its specialised agencies, so that these may impose the law in the fields of peace, durable development, social protection, commerce and competition. We have seen in part VI, that the EU is in the right track in some of these fields; but power sharing between the Community and the Union and between both of them and the Member States diminishes the potential of all in promoting their shared values to the rest of the world.

There is no doubt that the vast majority of European citizens want their integration to step up to the **stage of political union**, including a strong and independent foreign policy and an even stronger and more independent security and defence policy. Why do citizens understand that in an era of integration, globalisation and world predominance of a superpower, national sovereignty in matters of foreign policy and security has no real meaning, while their political leaders do not understand it? Because, for the later, national sovereignty is closely related to their own power, which they do not want to share with their partners, even though this power, in the present geopolitical environment, is waning all the time and only unity can bolster it.

One might suppose that the common foreign and security policy could develop as other common policies have developed in the past. There is, however, a fundamental difference between the common foreign and security policy and the common policies of the Community. Whereas the latter are governed by the Community method of decision-making [see section 4.3.], **the CFSP depends on intergovernmental cooperation**. This means that unanimity is required to make decisions in these fields, that the European Parliament does not participate in the decision-making process, that the Commission is not required to execute the decisions taken by the legislative organs and that the Court of Justice is not competent to settle disputes and enforce the implementation of the decisions taken. Thanks to the intergovernmental method of the CFSP, any Member State may block a common position or common action on an important matter, thus frustrating the will of all the others. Moreover, any Member State may eventually disengage itself from a decision taken, thus effectively bringing to an end a common action agreed upon. Obviously, the foreign and security policy cannot become "common" as long as it depends on intergovernmental cooperation.

The (now unlikely) coming into force of the **Constitutional Treaty** would improve a little the decision making procedure of the CFSP, but would not change fundamentally its intergovernmental character. It provides for a Union Minister for Foreign Affairs, who should be Vice-President of the Commission and who should contribute by his proposals to the development of the common foreign policy, which he should carry out as mandated by the Council of Ministers (Art. I-28). The European Union should conduct a common foreign and security policy, based on the development of mutual political solidarity among Member States, the identification of questions of general interest and the achievement of an ever-increasing degree of convergence of Member States' actions (Art. I-40, 1). Before undertaking any action on the international scene or any commitment which could affect the Union's interests, each Member State should consult the others within the European Council or the Council of Ministers. Member States should ensure, through the convergence of their actions, that the Union is able to assert its interests and values on the international scene (Art. I-40, 5). The common security and defence policy should include the progressive framing of a common Union defence policy. This should lead to a common defence, when the European Council, acting unanimously, so decides (Art. I-41,2). Until then, closer cooperation should be established, in the Union framework, as regards mutual defence. Under this cooperation, if one of the Member States participating in such cooperation is the victim of armed aggression on its territory, the other participating States should give it aid and assistance by all the means in their power, military or other, in accordance with Article 51 of the United Nations Charter (Art. I-41, 7).

All this is very good; but, **the unanimity rule prevails**. The Constitution excludes European laws and European framework laws in matters of the so-called common foreign and security policy, while they would be taken in matters concerning all other common policies of the Union. In fact, European decisions relating to CFSP should be adopted by the European Council and the Council of Ministers unanimously, except when they are implementing decisions of the European Council taken unanimously or if the European Council unanimously decides that the Council of Ministers should act by qualified majority (Art. I-40, 6,7).

Moreover, the unanimity rule prevails for the ratification of the Constitutional Treaty itself and for its eventual amendments. The Treaty signed in October 2004 provides in fact that it shall enter into force after being ratified by **all the High Contracting Parties** in accordance with their respective constitutional requirements (Art. IV-447). Worse, even the revision of the Constitutional Treaty - necessary for the continuous development of the Union [see section 2.5.] - would require ratification by all the Member States. This Treaty provides, in fact, that, if two years after the signature of the treaty amending it, four fifths of the Member States had ratified it and one or more Member States had encountered **difficulties in proceeding with ratification**, the matter should be referred to the European Council (Art. IV-443, 4). The same provision appears as a declaration of the Intergovernmental Conference annexed to the Constitutional Treaty in case of problems encountered in the ratification of this Treaty. But, what could the European Council do in this case? The probable answer is that the government, which would have encountered difficulties with ratification because of a negative vote of its parliament or of a negative outcome of a referendum, would not be disposed to persuasion inside the European Council, since it would be ensnared in a matter of constitutional order. Hence, both for the ratification of the Constitutional Treaty itself and for that of its future amendments, the problem of one or a few government(s), would become the problem of all, since they would not be able to put into force the Treaty that they would have signed.

This means that, even if and when the Constitutional Treaty were adopted, the CFSP would be run by intergovernmental procedure and that it could never become a really common policy through an amendment of this Treaty, if one or just a few countries did not want it. This stumbling block in the way of a real common foreign and security policy is put by the politicians negotiating the treaties against the will of their citizens. Whatever eurosceptic circles may say to the contrary, this is **democratic deficit par excellence**, i.e. disregard of the will of the people concerning the political maturity of their union. The democratic way would be for the peoples of the European Union to be given the possibility to pronounce themselves as to whether they want to have a real and effective common foreign and security policy or not. Of course, this way is not as easy as it sounds.

To become a really common policy, the CFSP should be integrated into the Community pillar governed by the Community decision-making process or, better, that the construction of the Union in pillars be abandoned and this be considered as a single structure. The European Commission should be involved in the CFSP both at the stage of the initiative for common action and at the stage of execution of the decisions taken by the decision-making authorities. The European Parliament should be involved in decision-making, both by agreeing on the common strategies initiated by the European Council and by laying down European laws and framework laws with the Council of Ministers. European strategies and European laws and framework laws should be taken by qualified majority, although this could be set at higher levels than those applying to other common policies, in order to make sure that a vast majority of the Member States, representing the great majority of the population of the Union agreed on a common strategy or a common action in the field of the CFSP.

However, it is practically certain that not all the Member States of the actual EU would be willing to hand over to the Union the competences necessary for building a genuine common foreign and security policy. The question then arises: would the Member States whose citizens aspire for a really common foreign and security policy be forever blocked by their partners who prefer to guard their national prerogatives rather than unite their forces in order to build a superpower capable of better serving their common interests? The probable answer is that sooner or later a number of states would, under the pressure of their citizens, want to gain their freedom to proceed to the integration stage of the political union and thus build a truly common foreign and security policy. It is probable that this would be the group of states, which would have a single currency on top of the single market. The interests of those states would become ever more common and it is natural that sooner rather than later they would feel the need to defend them in common through a genuine common foreign and security policy.

The subsidiary question to the one above is: how would the Member States of the EU, which would want to step up to the stage of political union, be able to do so, when the unanimity rule prevails for the amendment of the Treaty on the European Union and as long as some of the signatories of this Treaty do not want to make the concessions of national sovereignties necessary for taking this step? There are two possible answers to this question. The easier but limited way for building a common foreign and security policy would be through the enhanced cooperation of some Member States, provided for by the actual Treaty of Nice and reinforced by the Constitutional Treaty. The more difficult but sturdier way of proceeding to the political union of Europe would be through a Constitution democratically adopted and going beyond the Constitutional Treaty, signed in October 2004, which will probably never be brought into force. Let us consider these two possibilities.

Enhanced cooperation in the field of the common foreign and security policy is facilitated by the Treaty of Nice [see sections 4.3 and 8.1.2.] and even more so by the draft Constitution. The Constitutional Treaty provides that authorisation to proceed with enhanced cooperation should be granted by the Council of Ministers as a last resort, when it has been established within the Council of Ministers that the objectives of such cooperation could not be attained within a reasonable period by the Union as a whole, and provided that it would bring together at least one third of the Member States (Art. I-44, 2). Still, authorisation to proceed with enhanced cooperation should be granted by a European decision of the Council acting unanimously (Art. III-419). However, after the enhanced cooperation would be instituted, decisions could be taken by a qualified majority defined as at least 55% of the members of the Council representing the participating Member States, comprising at least 65% of the population of these States (Art. I-44, 3). Acts adopted in the framework of enhanced cooperation would bind only the participating Member States and would not be regarded as part of the acquis which would have to be accepted by candidate States for accession to the Union (Art. I-44, 4). In plain words, if at least one third of the Member States felt the need to build **a real common foreign and security policy** among themselves, they would still need the authorisation of the governments of the rest of their partners to do so. But, if they could succeed in obtaining this authorisation, they would surpass the ratification hurdle and would pioneer the way into political integration.

There is no question, however, that it would be much better, if all European states agreed to proceed to the political union of Europe; but such an agreement could only be sanctioned by a **new treaty or, better, by a European Constitution**, which would go beyond the actual Constitutional Treaty and would confer to the European institutions the necessary competences in the field of foreign and security policy. The experience of the Constitutional Treaty should lead the debate on a possible European Constitution. The faults committed in the drafting and in the handing over of this Treaty to the people should be avoided. The citizens of the Member States should be involved through their representatives in the drafting of the Constitution. This Constitution should satisfy the aspirations of European peoples to see their Union become a major actor in the international scene. It should reinforce the institutional framework of the Union so that this could function effectively in an increasingly complex internal and external environment. The Constitution should be put to ratification in a homogeneous way in all member countries, either by the national parliaments or by a referendum organised the same day in all Member States, after adequate explication of its contents. The Constitution should provide that only willing nations should adopt it and offer an alternative for those that would not want to do so.

All these requirements lead to the following suggestion. The European Council or the European Parliament should take the initiative to convoke a **constituent assembly** to draft a European Constitution. This assembly could be made up of the members of the European Parliament elected by the peoples of the Union with this specific mandate on top of their normal legislative mission. Prior to this election, a large public debate should take place in all Member States at the initiative of political parties. All options for the future of Europe should be aired. The candidates for the election to the assembly should expose their position on all the big issues of European politics. Consequently, the citizens of each State would have the option of sending to the assembly europhilic or eurosceptic representatives. The majority of the assembly would thus be constituted by europhilic or eurosceptic members regardless of their traditional political preferences. Of course, these preferences would also direct the debates in the assembly on many issues, such as human rights, social protection or free competition to be guaranteed by the Constitution.

If the majority of the assembly was constituted by eurosceptic members, it could turn down the drafting of a Constitution or restrain the integration process through it. If, on the contrary, the majority of the constituent assembly was made up of europhilic members, it could, through the draft Constitution, reinforce and speed up the integration process, particularly in the field of foreign and security policy. In any case, the outcome of the debates in the assembly would have a democratic legitimacy, since it would correspond to the will of the majority of the peoples of the Union. The draft Constitution should then be signed by the heads of State or government of the Union who agreed to its provisions. The ones who would not agree to these provisions should explain to their citizens the reasons of their disagreement and let them pronounce themselves, through referendum or general elections, if they agreed or not with their government.

The most important Article of the Constitution would be the one dealing with the ratification procedure. It would be up to the members of the constituent assembly to decide if the ratification should depend on the agreement of the parliaments of the Member States or of the citizens themselves through a referendum. But, in any case, the ratification procedure should be homogeneous and give each Member State the possibility to either ratify and, therefore, accept the bringing into force of the Constitution or reject ratification and, thus, be excluded from the integration process. Hence, the Constitution should come into force and be binding only for the nations that would have signed and ratified it.

The question would arise, of course, what would happen with the countries lagging behind concerning institutional arrangements and in particular decision-making provisions. This is a problem that may be dealt with transitional or temporary arrangements, consisting, for example, in **considering these Member States as abstaining in votes** until they ratify the Treaty. The problem of a standstill would thus not concern all the Member States but only the Member States left behind at their own will. In this case, these nations would be under pressure to catch up with the train of the integration process and the problem would probably be of small duration. Similar arrangements should be provided for the modification of the Treaty. With such arrangements the governments, parliaments and citizens of the Member States would know beforehand that if one Member State would go against the will of the majority for the deepening of the integration process, it would only succeed in placing itself in quarantine.

The CFSP could thus one day be closely united with the common commercial policy and with the aid to development policy, so that all three wings of the external action of the Union would work towards common goals by means of the so-called Community method. As is the case with other common policies, the common foreign policy would set the framework for the foreign policies of the Member States by fixing common goals, strategies, guidelines and actions that the Member States would be bound to follow. The qualified majority voting would also be applied to

European security and defence policy (ESDP) [see section 8.2.3.], thus making it really common and effectual. Europe can easily build up its power by bringing together the distinct and often overlapping military capabilities of the Member States. The existing military capabilities and military bodies of ESDP would only need to be strengthened and be completely self-sufficient inside NATO. The reinforcement and independence of ESDP would make third countries take Europe seriously as a world actor; but Europe would not need to emulate or duplicate the military power of the United States. The European Union is not threatened by any organised state and does not have any hegemonic or policing ambitions in the world. In order to become a world player it does not need to have great armed forces, bases and armaments deployed around the globe. It only needs to have the goodwill of governments and peoples of the rest of the world by fostering sustainable development, democracy, multinational integration and the overall respect of international law. These could be the common goals of the unified "common" foreign, commercial, development and defence policies. In an environment of global anarchic terror, this goodwill could be a stronger bulwark against terrorist attacks than any global defence system.

The group of states, which would have a single market and a single currency and which would have formulated a truly common foreign and security policy, **would not necessarily form a federation**. In fact, the very concept of the common policy excludes the concept of the single policy, which is an attribute of a federation of states. It means that a policy is built up and implemented in common by the common institutions and the governments of the Member States. A truly common foreign and security policy could be progressively developed among willing nations - through enhanced cooperation or a European Constitution - with the Community method restrained by the principles of conferral and subsidiarity [see section 3.2.]. These principles, which are applied since the beginning of the EC/EU, would imply that each member of the group participating in a real CFSP would keep intact its legal personality and sovereignty in all areas not placed under the common competence of the group. It could sign international agreements not conflicting with Community competence. It could keep its diplomatic representations in third countries and in international institutions. The representations of the members of the group would simply have instructions to follow the positions agreed in common, a fact that would enhance the position of the participating states in world affairs. In the field of defence as well, each member of the inner group would keep its own army, its armaments and its defence budget. The participating states would only place them under an integrated command, which would be responsible for their coordinated actions. This would not prevent separate actions, compatible with the CFSP, in case of non-agreement by the partners on a common action.

Of course, in order to play a leading role in the global scene, the European Union would need to **adapt and strengthen its institutions**. We have suggested a possible reform of the institutions in section 4.4. The members of the Commission should be proposed by the national parliaments, be elected directly by the citizens of each Member State and be nominated by the European Parliament. The President of the Commission and the Vice-president, responsible for foreign affairs, should be proposed by the simple majority of the heads of State or government (representing at least three fifths of the population of the Union) and nominated by the European Parliament. The European Parliament should invest, control and eventually dismiss a particular Commissioner or the Commission as a college. Its role in the decision-making process should be reinforced thanks not only to the extension of the co-decision procedure to all legislative matters, including the CFSP, but also to its task of coordinating and consolidating the opinions of the national parliaments, the Economic and Social Committee and the Committee of the Regions. These measures would contribute not only to the efficient functioning, but also to the democratic legitimacy of the European institutions. The citizens would feel much closer to a Commission that they would elect themselves directly and would control indirectly through their representatives in the European Parliament. Such governance would have many features of a federal character without being federal, since it would manage common policies and only that part of each common policy, which Member States would have agreed to confer to the competence of the Union.

We would thus have in Europe **a nucleus of States** pursuing their economic, monetary and political integration with the so-called Community method, which should in fact be called the "integration method", so as to be distinguished from the intergovernmental method, while not being identified with the Community alone. They would be the states, which would have signed and ratified the European Constitution or an enhanced cooperation agreement on the CFSP and would, thus, have marked their willingness to integrate their economic, monetary, security and foreign policies and thus create among themselves on top of the common market, an economic and monetary union and a political union. The States in the **second concentric circle** would remain at the stage of the common market as long as they wished and would be welcome to join the inner circle when they would be willing and ready to do so by ratifying the Constitution or an enhanced cooperation agreement concerning the CFSP. Of course, such **separation between the Community and the Union** would not be ideal for either, since it would entail institutional problems. However, institutional arrangements exist already concerning monetary affairs. They could be extended to foreign affairs. New legislation obtained with the abstention of Member States which would have not ratified the Constitution should not be binding on them until ratification, but should be implemented by them thereafter. Intergovernmental cooperation, in particular through the open coordination method, employing non-binding measures such as resolutions and recommendations could be used in a complementary way by both groups of states according to the principles of subsidiarity and proportionality [see section 3.2.].

In addition to the two circles of states pursuing their integration up to different points - all up to the point of the common market and some up to the point of the foreign and security policy - we would have the outer circle of **the European Economic Area** practising free trade through intergovernmental cooperation [see section 25.1.]. This circle - now limited to the EC/EU states, Norway, Iceland and Liechtenstein - could one day be widened to include Russia and other States of the former Soviet block having espoused an open market economy and wishing to have strong links with the European Community/Union. All these countries should, of course, belong to the large European family having the same values, similar democratic institutions and common ideals. With non-European countries in its periphery - i.e. Mediterranean countries in Asia and Africa, which have different cultures, traditions and regimes - the European Community/Union should build strong economic and political links through partnership and/or new neighbourhood agreements. A task of the common foreign and security policy of the Union would be to coordinate the commercial, development and foreign policies of the Member States of the Union to create a friendly and therefore secure area around Europe, notably in the Mediterranean and the Middle East.

A European Union, which would manifest its political as well as its economic integration, would greatly enhance its image in the rest of the world. The links, which this European Union would have with the European countries in the outer circle and with friendly countries in other regions of the world, would make it **a world player of prime importance**, basing the prestige and security of its members less on the force of arms and more on their assistance for the durable development of friendly countries. In a world which aspires for peace, social justice, economic progress and the rule of law, it is extremely important that a democratic and pluralistic Europe, with no expansionist ambitions, assumes the international role endowed upon it by its history, its culture and economic power. Its successful experiment of a peaceful and voluntary integration of nations, which only yesterday were fighting each other, is being watched closely by many nations throughout the world suffering from their ethnic, religious and other conflicts and could place the old continent at **the vanguard of the march of civilisation**, whose main objectives are world peace, political freedom, economic progress and social justice.

Bibliography on European perspectives

- ARNULL Anthony: "The Member States of the European Union and Giscard's blueprint for its future", *Fordham International Law Journal,* v. 27, n. 2, January 2004, p. 503-543.

- BADRÉ Denis. *L'attente d'Europe.* Paris: Albin Michel: Fondation Robert Schuman, 2004.

- BEAUD Olivier (sous la dir. de). "L'Europe en voie de Constitution: Pour un bilan critique des travaux de la Convention". Bruxelles: Bruylant, 2004.

- BOLKENSTEIN Frits, EPPINK Derk Jan. *The limits of Europe.* Tielt: Lannoo, 2004.

- CAMERON Fraser (ed.). *The future of Europe: integration and enlargement.* London: Routledge, 2004.

- DABROWSKI Marek, NENEMAN Jaroslaw, SLAY Ben. *Beyond transition: development perspectives and dilemmas.* Aldershot: Ashgate, 2004.

- DEARDORFF Alan (ed.). *The past, present, and future of the European Union.* Basingstoke: Palgrave Macmillan, in association with International Economic Association, 2004.

- HASELER Stephen. *Super-state: the new Europe and its challenge to America.* London; New York: I.B. Tauris, 2004.

- MOUSSIS Nicolas. "Communauté européenne ou Union européenne?: Proposition d'une séparation à l'amiable", *Revue du Marché commun et de l'Union européenne,* n. 468, mai 2003, p. 281-289.

- STEPHENSON Hugh (ed.). *Challenges for Europe.* Basingstoke: Palgrave Macmillan, 2004.

DISCUSSION TOPICS

1. On the basis of the data provided in this book, assess the role played by common policies in the European integration process.
2. What are the effects of common policies on the legal and political systems of the member states of a multinational integration process?
3. Is multinational integration a process with a definite or an open end?
4. Discuss the significance for European integration of the ratification and coming into force of the Constitutional Treaty and the possible developments in case of its non ratification by some Member States.
5. What is your opinion about the prospects of cooperation and/or integration of the European Union with other European nations?

INDEX AND GLOSSARY

Blood Debts

Celia de Fréine

Scotus
Press

Celia de Fréine was born in the North of Ireland and now divides her time between Dublin and Connemara. www.celiadefreine.com

Also by Celia de Fréine

POETRY
A lesson in Can't (Scotus Press, 2014)
cuir amach seo dom : riddle me this (Arlen House, 2014)
Aibítir Aoise : Alphabet of an Age (Arlen House, 2011)
imram : odyssey (Arlen House, 2010)
Scarecrows at Newtownards (Scotus Press, 2005)
Fiacha Fola (Cló Iar-Chonnachta, 2004)
Faoi Chabáistí is Ríonacha (Cló Iar-Chonnachta, 2001)

PLAYS
Desire : Meanmarc (Arlen House, 2012)
Plight : Cruachás (Arlen House, 2012)
Brian Merriman's The Midnight Court (Arlen House, 2012)
Mná Dána (Arlen House, 2009)

For the Women

First Published in Ireland by
Scotus Press
Dublin 6
www. scotuspress.com

© Celia de Fréine - Sep. 2014
ISBN: 978-0-9560 966-7-8

Production:

Cover & Design : Pat Pidgeon

Production & Setting: Colm McHugh

_____

Fonts: Goudy Old Style/Onyx

Cover Photograph: from a collection donated by
Pádraig Caomhánach to the National Library of Ireland

Contents

Foreword

Máire Mhac an tSaoi

A story is related in this collection of poems: a story about a woman on whom misfortune fell. There are additional indications that this woman lives in a world that is parallel to our own; Irish is spoken as an everyday language in this world. Thanks be to God for that — we wouldn't like it were the events recounted in this story to happen in any world in which we ourselves were living!

This particular woman had no idea of the penance that was in store for her. Even if she had, she honestly admits that she would not have denied life, cancelled the marriage feast, or shirked childbirth. At school she was full of music; as a young woman she welcomed love and marriage. When a son was born to her she received a blood injection. That was the beginning and the end for her. Symptoms surface one after the other: exhaustion, jaundice, an ugly rash. The doctors fail to make out what's wrong. Lupus – the wolf – is mentioned, defects in the immune system are mentioned; neither a remedy nor a satisfactory diagnosis is found. The woman continues to suffer and keeps an account in verse. In those verses we have an interpretation of the fullness of woman's existence: the normal illuminated through the abnormal – just as the experts recommend should be done – and, because this is a parallel world, we can enjoy the artistry of the poetry without our conscience being overly troubled by the subject.

Celia de Fréine feels she chose Irish as a medium because of the natural surrealism in that language. I fully understand her. I was persuaded of this strength of Irish a long time ago in Spain, when I saw how Garcia Lorca used the Andalucia dialect. This surrealism, associated with the vernacular, which has so far eluded the tyranny of the electronic, is a great boon. It is a strength I recognised immediately when I opened the first collection by this poet, *Of Cabbages and Queens*. Surrealism, the Gothic, folklore, she excels in them all. This present work, the biography of the woman on whom misfortune fell, goes deeper, to the core of the essence of life; the marvels of technique are underplayed, but those same marvels sustain a new pared-back storytelling throughout; a poetic style that is as bare as prose but as multifunctional as dialogue. For some time I had thought that poetry in modern Irish was as suited to every purpose as the English classical poetry of the Eighteenth Century. If I needed proof, it's in this book.

times when you'd press a knob on the oven
and conjure the six million
naked, shorn in the shower.

I think of the people of Omagh each time I heat the oven. This woman is a middle-class woman, like myself. She is knowledgeable about Europe and she expects us to recognise references to Jane Eyre and to Latin.

Let us rid ourselves, therefore, of the parallel conceit. In spite of the quality of her Irish, it's in today's Ireland, that the character in this adventure lives. In a miraculous way she weaves a cloak of dignity out of indignation, anger, deceit. It comes as no surprise that this is the Hepatitis C story, a story indescribable in how hard it is for the Irish citizen to come to terms with, or with the shame and guilt it awakens in us. The narrator does not flinch from the heartbreak that befell so many of our kinswomen as a result of the corruption and dishonesty in places where they expected and deserved to find succour and shelter.

A night on the town. A respite from Dáil debates
and the defensive tone of the Government Minister.
It isn't his fault a woman is dying

in a city hospital. But who is hastening
her to her grave? Who is asking her to sign
a form and accept a pittance?

Her twelve children are gathered round her
children whose feats she has cheered –
the first teeth, the first words.

She knows she'll never brush the fluff
from their graduation gowns
help them shop for trousseaux

smooth the silk in a grandchild's christening robe.
She would like her children to know
that none of this is her fault.

The twelve gathered round her know
they'll not hear her applaud
the day they graduate, realise

she'll not be there to embrace them
on their wedding day, see their likeness
etched on their children's faces.

You'd think that the poet, de Fréine, was trained from the very first to give voice to this hardship, that for this alone the feat of poetry was nourished in her. We have seen the shocking sparseness of the above narrative; here follows an example of the terrifying richness of colour and imagination:

It's no longer safe to enter that harbour –
toxins in the water might damage
the hull of any ship dropping anchor there:

when the moon is full jellyfish surge to the surface
tentacles at the ready, beside the reef
half-dead molluscs attack each other

and on the seabed barrels fester.
In years to come they may shatter
their contents explode.

Lover, keep your distance.

I don't think anything has yet been composed in modern Irish as powerful as those lines. That little poem is a faultless unit that rises to the height of perfection from the depths of terror. For me, the whole revival movement has been worth it so that its like could be provided. Forgive me, poor tormented woman, who set in motion the poetry of this book, I write this not to insult you - the opposite. I humbly thank you, whoever you are. Had I a magic wand, I'd release you from your misfortune. As it is...

It's there that the mystery of the aesthetic lives. De Fréine christens one of her poems 'another tale from Shahrazad'. That is enough for us to remember the close bond between pastime and death. These are stories for a Wake, the best of stories. Irish language poets are often accused of a shortness of breath. But this sequence of dramatic lyrics is remarkable because of the consistent standard of excellence throughout.

Máire Mhac an tSaoi
July, 2004

chalice of my blood

Had I known
when I played in the schoolyard

my blood was not the same
as that of other girls

my body was still
nourished by foreign blood

I could have prayed
this chalice be taken from me

I could have promised myself
before falling in love

to lure the man of my choice
through hospital maze

to find out whether we were suited
and if not

I could have begged Hymenaeus
not to lead me to the altar

I could have entreated him
to quench his torch

dismiss his minstrels
cancel the feast.

But even had I known
I'm sure I would have said

give me my children
give me my children whatever the cost.

miracle play

Strange how we went to a clutch
of plays on that first date
rotated in a quadrangle
watched as searchlights lit a caravan
of trailers and students projected tales
from the Bible onto the night air.

I remember what I was wearing –
a friend's cloak fashioned from rough tweed.

And when we had come full circle
and I had met his friends
and he mine
I sensed a plague
before us –
watched as the storytellers

sprouted carbuncles
smelt their bodies decay.
I wanted to tell them that fleas
in white linen were responsible
for the spread of the disease

beg them not to celebrate the resurrection
leave aside the seamless gown
but my lips were sealed
my legs dream-heavy
as the word of God
sounded a lament above us.

The next day I headed down the south circular road
and gave my friend back her cloak.

september – month of birthdays

My aunt used to visit
on my birthday

scrub the house from top to bottom
bake me a cake.

My son has no aunt
but I will keep the house clean

and organise parties for him –
whatever about cakes.

He stares wide-eyed from his crib
a child who didn't roar

when hauled arse-first
into the world.

I forgive them for whisking him off
for not laying him in my arms –

I trust them in this hospital
that's costing an arm and a leg.

I try to comply when a doctor says
I need an injection

of immunoglobulin
but my arm resists her needle.

She discharges her syringe
through a finer point.

The serum surges through me.

yellow humour

On every plate a fish eye watching
the stench of oil reminding me
of the school salmonella reunion

my husband and child waiting for their dinner
my son sobbing in his crib
the three of them a whirligig

television ads revolving
bowls of food flying at me
my oesophagus dragging up

all that's in my intestines
a strange yellow spreading
across my face and limbs

in the clinic my legs go from under me
as I describe my symptoms to the doctor.
He says I'm run down.

I dig my heels in
insisting
that I'm yellow

He brings me into his conservatory
to look at me in the clear light of day
insisting

there's nothing wrong with my skin
that its colour is normal.
My doctor is Indian.

blood is thick

My husband's family
are at pains to make out
who our kids resemble.

After much debate it's decided
our son has the eyes of a granduncle
and the nose of a great grandfather.

As our daughter takes after her mother
the origin of her features
is more difficult to determine.

Isn't it enough they have their father's name?
Isn't it enough his blood
is coursing through their veins?

pray continue

The obstetrician asks
how I'm feeling.

I tell him I'm sick and tired
and think

I have jaundice.
He says he's an obstetrician

who knows nothing
about jaundice and as far

as he's concerned
I'm fine and can resume

my conjugal duties
straight away.

pastor

Morning. In the fields around the city
and in the parts of the city that once
were fields men and women head to work
in the pasture that's theirs by tradition.
One, two, one, two, three – hirelings bustling.

Out here in the desert I imagine
these hirelings swallowed by archways
disappear through doors
sucked up in lifts.
One, two, one, two, three – hirelings bustling.

Afternoon. I see them bent over their lot:
write memos in their grey suits
sell newspapers in their pink pinnies
protect health in their white coats.
Four, five, four, five, six – hirelings striving.

I keep on changing nappies and sterilising bottles
and sometimes think I'd love
to be in there among them besides
being out here on my own rearing kids.
Four, five, four, five, six – hirelings striving.

Evening. Now that the day's pasture has been
grazed and decisions made on my behalf
I hear their voices raised in pubs.
I see them suckle tall glasses of beer.
Seven, eight, seven, eight, nine – hirelings having fun.

Out here in the desert I yield to chubby-hand
demands with no option but to accept
what the hirelings have decided on my behalf
in their grey suits, their pink pinnies, their white coats.
Seven, eight, seven, eight, nine – hirelings having fun.

sucker

When we came here first
we could scarcely

make it out
from the kitchen window –

a gnarled root
that sprouted a few shoots

among the irises
each autumn.

Over time its tentacles
have settled in the back wall.

Green at first, the leaves metamorphose
to the indeterminate hue of the colour blind.

petition

I confide in my friends
that I'm expecting an Easter Bunny.

He arrives on Spy Wednesday –
another little Judas.

I beg the ward sister
to test my liver function.

She reassures me – just because
I had jaundice after my last baby

doesn't mean it'll strike again.
She listens to my plea, even though

it's time for her to pray and wash
the feet of the Lord's disciples.

She advises me there's nothing to worry about
but that she can't test my liver function

when there's nothing wrong with my liver.

i wanna sleep forever

I could sleep for a week
if the pains in my legs
would let me.

I don two pairs
of leg warmers
which happen to be in vogue

because of the film *Fame*
and position a hot water bottle
behind my knees.

I could go to the doctor
but he'd say
these pains are normal –

the result of chasing
after three kids.
Their Daddy has come home.

He can chase after them
for the rest of the day
and cook the dinner while he's at it.

If that's a friend of mine
knocking on the door
wanting to come in for a chat

or inviting me out
tell her
I can't talk to her right now.

Tell her if I'm ever free again
all I wanna do
is sleep.

on her high wire again

When they tell her
not to brood
she pulls on
her battle leotard

and with her straightest arrow
shoots a rope towards
the mound of disbelief
that looms behind the clinic.

With only a spirit-level
as guide
and her soles as grip
she sets out.

Below her the medics
congregate
each face askance
in the noose of its stethoscope

She turns on her heel
mindful of other professions
she might have chosen
to play out life's drama

other venues – a big top – for example
where the audience would cheer
and she'd know
there was a net beneath her.

To the east she spies a lone boatman
row towards the quays.
He moors his currach
then soars to greet her

a rose snug in the ribbon of his fedora.

falling

It was on the day the picture
of my guardian angel fell

I was beset
by the first bout of despair.

It was a reproduction Italian job –
an angel wafting

behind two waifs
along a mountain pass.

Though the glass shattered
the picture itself

remained intact.
That night headlamps shafted

through the curtains
lighting the angel's face.

It was clear he could topple
again at any time.

love bite

Is it any wonder they're gaping at me
in the supermarket and me in this state again?

The way Mrs Kiss-my-Arse who spends
three hours a day cleaning her cooker

is gossiping at the counter with Mrs Excuse-Me
who reads the lesson on Sunday

you'd think I'd just spent the night
romancing a tall thin man from Romania.

Had such a man been courting me, I doubt
I'd be in a supermarket queue this morning.

As it is, I've no idea what came to me during
the night and left these marks on my neck.

Let that pair over there think what they like
while I lean on my trolley for support.

I've no wish to try to elaborate on the state
of my neck while I'm in this humour.

los angeles olympics

The neighbours are all inside
glued to their televisions.

Unbeknownst to them the white rabbit
from next door has escaped

into our garden followed by
the alsatian from round the corner.

My rash is spreading all the way
up my arms onto my neck.

If it reaches my face
I think I'll die. The oil

the doctor recommends oozes
onto my book *Journal du Voleur.*

When my child is born
I hope he or she does not

have oily skin or that he or she
does not become a thief.

Don't tell me if John Treacy
makes it to the stadium.

I don't want to see
the tricolour hoisted

or hear the strains
of *Amhrán na bhFiann.*

not of woman born

Rumour has it
the obstetrician doesn't like
to induce labour –

he prefers women to wait as long
as possible
before introducing oxytocin.

He's reluctant to investigate
when I tell him
matters are progressing

but discovers before long
my child's in distress.
What does he think I'm in

when the foetal heartbeat soars
and he's summoned back
to perform an emergency section?

I'm the last to meet my son.
The delivery man
gives a blow by blow account

of how one fist emerged
and then another
of how one small pugilist

took on the world
before the rescue team
could make out his sex.

comfort

My rash reminds me of a biblical epic
in which the good Lord visited a rash
of plagues upon the Egyptians.

The image foremost in my mind
is of a long green line that is fleshed out
to become an arm, a hand at its end

that reaches down from the heavens
and kills the first born in houses
not daubed with the blood of a lamb.

My rash is red.
The obstetrician promised it would clear
as soon as my child was born.

At first I had blamed it
on insects
but my GP disagreed.

More likely your washing powder
the district Nurse suggested.
Or maybe even your Comfort.

I've tried all the various powders
with and without Comfort
and it still hasn't cleared.

the indeterminate hue
of the colour blind

Last week our creeper reddened
the bricks on the back wall

causing them to quiver
during rain to form such a mass

as spread each time
Marnie saw red

before she knew
her mother was a whore

or that she herself
had murdered a sailor.

This morning a letter from the Corporation
pops through the letterbox

warning us that the tentacles
of our creeper have escaped

over the back wall
and are headed for the bus stop.

snowbound

I well remember that winter
when milk lorries couldn't
get through to the suburbs
and snow licked the tumour
on the cherry blossom.

I stayed inside stitching tulle on a tutu
while himself donned his rucksack
and headed for the shop
where he came upon a turkey
in the bottom of a freezer.

That night I saw his shadow framed
in the window, arms flailing,
while outside at the top of the crescent
a she-wolf and her cubs slunk
through the bollards into the next estate.

I felt shafts of cold air shoot
through the putty into the room,
searing my face as they made
for the *louvre* door where they settled,
peering out the way Mother would

from the top floor of that tenement.
And each time she'd see a gypsy approach
she'd scrape together the pennies
saved for my future
and make me

race down the stairs
and press them into the mendicant hand,
muttering from above
that to turn the indigent from the door
would be to invoke a curse.

in hot water

Dear Sam,

Don't hold it against me that I can't
celebrate your birthday with you.
Well I know it isn't every day
you reach the big Eight-0.

Indeed both of us have become used
to walking the selfsame road
turning on our heels at the same stile
scaling the same hill of crap.

Trying to escape that very hill
I pulled up to the fire this evening
More Pricks than Kicks
in my fist, but couldn't manage

to read past the first story
about the unfortunate lobster
and Belacqua who realises
at last the creature is about

to be dunked in boiling water
where he'll turn red, like my arm.
Don't hold it against me that I can't
celebrate your birthday with you.

My rash has come early this year.
I hate having to remind you –
it's only April,
April the thirteenth.

nip it in the bud

For the third day in a row
I can't turn my head
or get up without help.

A friend phones
and I tell her I've the flu.
There's a bad dose going, she says.

Christ, the pain has never
been this bad before –
attacking every bone in my body.

Earlier in the week
when I presented with my annual rash
the doctor prescribed

new pills, promising
they wouldn't make me groggy.
But they do.

As usual he discussed
all possible causes
underlining the one constant –

my rash occurs only when
I roll up my sleeves
and take out my trowel.

According to him such a chronic illness
could only be caused
by the primroses in my flowerbed.

the hour of the wolf

The specialist asks
if I've heard of lupus.

I tell him a friend
died from it. *No one*

dies from lupus
nowadays, he says.

I was at her funeral
where her sister mentioned

that their specialist had said
people with lupus

don't reach middle age.
He prescribes cortisone –

a steroid I've heard tell that
bloats the body. I see myself

in the guise of a *Michelin*
woman float up overhead

stare down on his pate
as he pummels my stomach.

getting on

My friend who hurt her back
and has been treated
with heat-packs and traction
can now move slowly and stiffly.

She invites me out for lunch.
The cortisone has begun to work –
I can now get dressed
and move slowly and stiffly.

With difficulty I ease myself
onto the passenger seat of her car.
The two of us barely manage to struggle out
and make our way to the restaurant.

We learnt Irish dancing together –
basketball and camogie.
Once during a crucial match
I slid the *sliotar* to her.

She rammed it into goal.
We lost the game – one : two.

enrolling

It's hard to believe I have
an auto-immune disease:
that inside me an
army of antibodies
is attacking my good cells.
I am self-destructing.

In an effort to find out why
I head into Hodges Figgis
and work my way through the index
at the back of every medical textbook.
I write to the Irish Lupus Society
peruse their pamphlets.

They used to show a film in school
about a priest called Fr Damien
who worked among lepers.
One day he put a foot into a basin
of boiling water and felt nothing
until he put in his other foot and was scalded.

if only

A friend sends me a card
hoping
I'm feeling better.

She's always sending cards
when I'm ill
and on rare occasions of celebration.

Her cards are well chosen –
pleasant and cheerful
as you'd expect from an American.

The latest is a reproduction
of a woman with hands spread
releasing a butterfly –

symbol of beauty and freedom
adopted by diagnosticians
to describe the rash that spreads

across the nose and cheekbones
of sufferers
from this chronic disease.

having fun

Yesterday the people
in this German hamlet
laughed at me
with my wide-brimmed hat
and long sleeves
while they rubbed oil
into their flesh
and sizzled
on the hillside.

Last night rain
spread from the east.

Today rather than spiral
down the corkscrew road
to the swimming pool
I decide to cut
through the wood.
The wet earth yields
beneath my feet
so I can slide
all the way.

It's cool and dull –
typical Dublin weather.

The locals have headed
off to work
the sun-worshippers
have gone sightseeing.
I undress
and dive
into the pool
down, deep down,
to its base turquoise.

morning ireland

The second day of the mid-term
break and I'm exhausted.

But I don't have to get up
or drag anyone out of bed.

I can lie back in the company
of the newscaster as he trawls

the four corners of the earth
in search of the latest scandal.

I'm dozing when I hear
the words *Anti-D*.

A doctor is interviewed but I can't
follow much of what is being said:

contaminated immunoglobulin
was pumped into thousands of women

clusters of whom contracted jaundice.

hearsay

According to radio reports
the hospitals have written
to all the women

who've been given the dodgy Anti-D.
We moved house –
my letter must have gone astray.

I phone the hospital.
Had I heard about it on the news?
they ask.

They'd heard about it on the news as well.
That was the first they'd heard about it.
Come in tomorrow, they say

and they'll give me a blood test.
Come in tomorrow and they might
have an idea of what's going on.

a wolf in sheep's clothing

The newspapers are full
of how the good-looking doctor
down in Cork

put two and two together
and made the Blood Board
go public.

Lines are open twenty four
hours a day. Ring anytime
and they'll allay your fears.

I spend the entire day
trying to get through. They couldn't
have pumped a poison serum

into thousands of women nursing their babies.
They never said it was a blood product.
And what about the wolf that's been ravaging me?

Contaminated blood + immune disease = AIDS.

There is no connection whatsoever
says the doctor on the other end of the line
when I get through the following day.

I don't believe him.
I don't believe anyone anymore.

the worst nightmare

There were days when you'd shove
your hand into a cupboard in search of a cabbage
and come upon the head of *Alfredo Garcia*

others when you'd thread a needle
and imagine you were darning a hole
out of which the evil of the world could escape

times when you'd press a knob on the oven
and conjure the six million
naked, shorn in the shower.

But at night the curtains drawn,
the door locked and bolted
you felt safe, yourself and your care.

No matter how many horror stories
swam into your mind
you never imagined this nightmare –

you lived in a democracy, yourself
and your care, under an elected government,
who cherished each citizen

far from the laboratories of jackbooted men.

where there's smoke

According to the Director of the Blood Board
blood samples have been flown

to Scotland for analysis.
The results take ten days.

It's seventeen days since
my sample was drawn from me.

I'll not spend another weekend
without an answer

is what I tell him
over the phone

adding that *I'll chain myself*
to the Board's railings, if necessary.

He wafts down the stairs
in a haze of smoke

saying he's referred me to a doctor
who's been drafted in

to deal with the crisis.
He mentions her name

but I don't hear it. The fumes
of nicotine have made me faint.

yes

The new recruit's first day
on the job and she's confronted
by a horde of sick women
who want to know why they're sick
and how sick are they.

She's only a messenger –
one who listens
when I describe my symptoms,
who doesn't think
I'm out of my mind.

But am I depressed?
What does *depressed* mean?

Does it mean
that I worry
when I get sick?
Do I feel
that I'm never going

to get better?
Do black thoughts
overwhelm me?
Do I feel at times
that I'm going to die?
If so, the answer is:
yes, I feel depressed. Yes.

lobby

They thought they'd
got away with it –

that we were going to sit back
and accept this mess.

They hadn't expected us
to summon meetings

have a specialist flown in
from a hospital in England

that had already
warned the Blood Board.

It is wonderful and awful.

I can no longer sit
in this hall of women

and listen to how
fifty per cent of us will develop this

and twenty per cent that.
I can no longer look

around me and transfer
these facts to the faces of my companions.

this is my body

This is my body
with the genes of my forebears
my mind with these thoughts.

This is my body that carried
bore and nursed children
with the genes of my forebears.

I see the life
that stretched ahead of me –
a long tunnel

like the one
revealed to those
at death's door

but instead of a man
in a white gown at its end
welcoming me

rows of small boxes
with labels
stretch all the way:

Roads A-Z
a choice of professions
the best of hobbies

but when I reach out
my hand towards them
they are swallowed by the tunnel.

This is my body
with the genes of my forebears
my mind with these thoughts.

This is the wound
that cannot be healed.

report

A magazine was what the nun recommended
we bring with us when going to a dance

not of course to read as we waited on one side
of the hall but for the journey home

should we be offered a lift and have to sit
on the knee of a boy in the back of a car.

Children of Mary. Temples of the Holy Ghost.

It was a good idea also to have a copy
of the *Messenger* to hand

to protect us each time we hopped on
to a bus or a train in case

we had to place our backsides on a seat
recently vacated by a man.

Models of Chastity.

At that time in Ireland there were troops of girls
on trains and buses that ran the length and breadth

of the country carrying in our satchels magazines
we never read. We might as well have boarded

ghost trains that hurtled through tunnels where ghouls
and werewolves were ready to swoop on us –

Children of Mary, Temples of the Holy Ghost

– rip the magazines from beneath us
paste their leaves to the windows

give cover while the *nosferatu* climbed
the buffers, stole in beneath the doors

pinning us to our seats, their contagion
permeating the pleats in our gymslips.

Models of Chastity.
Children of Mary. Temples of the Holy Ghost.

testing, testing

My favourite phlebotomist speaks with
a Northern accent. Her dress is white,

so too are her shoes – flakes of late
night whitewash spray the tiles. I stare

at her long thin laces when she says: *put
your hand on my knee*. She ties a blue band

round my biceps. I clench and unclench
my fist till my arm feels like it's going

to burst and my veins stand out like the maze
of Slobland streams I've seen when flying over

England. Her fingers are deft. Her vials
neatly ordered – lidded in green and red,

purple and blue, clearly labelled and placed
in plastic by her rubber-gloved hands.

pints

In the days when tights were worn
only by acrobats
a colleague regularly donated blood.

He'd lie back as it was siphoned from him
hoping to glimpse the dark
of a stocking top or glint of a suspender.

At regular intervals a fresh pelican pin
was added to the collection on his chest
proclaiming his continued suffering and lust.

In those days all I knew about the Blood Board
were the particulars of his lewd inclinations
and the fact that pints

of blood were exchanged
for those of Guinness.
I watch as my sons

are led away to be tested
the expectation of pints of stout
etched on their under-age faces.

dear children

If any of my tears brushed your cheeks
when I was upset, forgive me –
I was doing my best.

If when cooking the dinner
I cut my finger, forgive me –
I was trying to prepare a tasty meal.

If any drop of perspiration fell on you
as we belted up to music lessons, forgive me –
I was aiming to give you every chance.

Well you know how much money
I splashed out on bars of soap
and bottles of bleach –

if cleanliness is next to godliness
I should by now have carved out
a niche for myself among the archangels.

Had I known I could have stood
shoulder to shoulder with
the scrubbers who never boil

their tea-towels, wallowed in filth
alongside the million-germ-a-day
J Cloth brigade

or joined the ranks of those who –
and I've seen this in a country kitchen –
wash dishes with discarded knickers.

mentor

HIV AIDS Hep C
ELISA RIBA PCR
I could travel the four corners
of the earth giving lessons
on the above acronyms.

I listen as the registrar
answers a call
from a lecturer now retired
who wants to keep abreast
of the latest contagions.

I'd love to hear her say that Hep C
is an illness that came from China
that it was spread by fleas
that it escaped from Africa
and was spread by monkeys.
that it snuck in from Transylvania
disguised as a tall thin man.

But she tells him the truth:
it is a dangerous virus
rampant among drug-users
a plague waiting to erupt
as AIDS did during the eighties;
it is spread through blood transfusions,
Anti-D immunoglobulin, needles and sex.

At present not much is known
about it apart from the fact
that when someone dies
they are carried out
in a body bag, that one antidote
has been discovered which works
in twenty per cent of cases.

Later she asks me to sign a form
sanctioning the use
of my particulars for research.
I jot down my name as though
accepting an honorary degree.

without breaking a pane

Mesdames et Messieurs, meine Damen und Herren,
a dhaoine uaisle – bienvenue, wilkommen,
fáilte romhaibh to today's tour
of the best known theatre in this city.

It's our intention – as will become clear –
to achieve excellence in all matters.
Notice, for example, how anxious
this candidate is to gain admittance.

Listen to the way she responds
to that questionnaire – soon
she'll have all the answers off by heart
as she awaits the next stage in her trial.

Doesn't she deserve a round of applause –
remember she had to rise at an ungodly hour
bid farewell to her loved ones at her front door
summon the courage to endure this delay.

Notice the anxiety on her face as she's led
centre stage. Those men in masks are the
metteur-en-scène and his assistant trained,
I'm proud to say, by the Great Tantalus himself.

Notice how the lights are focused
over her head so that the excavation
can begin. It's no harm to remind you
at this stage that this is the theatre of cruelty

where only the most precise chiselling
will suffice and that the two engaged
in this work must be convinced
this woman is prepared to give herself

completely and utterly to the process.
Listen carefully: you will hear some problems
in her initial response. This is normal.
There – she has established a rhythm.

Notice how she is able to ascend
the scales in an even manner. Remember
she can get help – if she wants –
before she reaches the highest note.

No doubt, this is the hardest part in her trial:
We must depend on the two experts
to prevent her reaching those high decibels
and bringing the panes down about her.

lover

It's no longer safe to enter that harbour –
toxins in the water might damage
the hull of any ship dropping anchor there:

when the moon is full jellyfish surge to the surface
tentacles at the ready, beside the reef
half-dead molluscs attack each other

and on the seabed barrels fester.
In years to come they may shatter
their contents explode.

Lover, keep your distance.

inside

I saw a film once
about a nuclear power station
where safety procedures were lax.

Contaminated workers
regularly set off alarms
as they went to exit.

They had to be hosed down
like animals, scrubbed
until their skin burnished.

No one believed them
until a woman smuggled
plutonium out inside her body

and because it was inside no alarm sounded.

grace

Grace Paley has arrived in Dublin
and myself and a group of friends
have assembled in Trinity to hear her read.

A night on the town. A respite from Dáil debates
and the defensive tone of the Government Minister.
It isn't his fault a woman is dying

in a city hospital. But who is hastening
her to her grave? Who is asking her to sign
a form and accept a pittance?

Her twelve children are gathered round her
children whose feats she has cheered –
the first teeth, the first words.

She knows she'll never brush the fluff
from their graduation gowns
help them shop for trousseaux

smooth the silk in a grandchild's christening robe.
She would like her children to know
that none of this is her fault.

The twelve gathered round her know
they'll not hear her applaud
the day they graduate, realise

she'll not be there to embrace them
on their wedding day, see their likeness
etched on their children's faces.

I try to focus on Grace Paley's tone
one that reminds me of Sipowicz and Simone
as they coax confessions from their suspects.

But my thoughts of Sipowicz and Simone
tales of New York huckster shops
and Jewish neighbourhoods are not enough

to distract me from the lives of this woman's children
of how they will be, of how they should be.
I see her in her bed, I see her airbrushed

from the family photograph album.
The New York tone drones on:
one of the most interesting women writers

continues and all I can think of
is one of the most heroic women
who is dying in a city hospital
and of the Minister hastening her to her grave.

wise blood

I would like to reach out, take
this nurse by the shoulders and shake her.

I would like to kick back my chair, grab
those shelves of dusty files, fling them to the floor

and stamp on them. But I haven't the energy.
And the nurse is only doing her job –

I tell her *I did not have multiple partners.*
I did not inject drugs. Nor did I indulge

in body piercing or engage
a backstreet tattooist to carve

celtic whorls on my torso.
I rip off my shirt, show her a phenomenon

any tattooist would give his eye teeth for –
a design that can appear at any time

assume any shape or form
on any part of my anatomy.

daughter

Let's not argue.
You may no longer borrow
anything that's mine –
scissors, tweezers,
those innocent earrings.

Remember that fish restaurant
in Florence, the Japanese couple
on honeymoon at the next table
her lipstick untrammelled
no matter how many courses

she devoured, the way neither
of them noticed that the lobster
in the tank behind them
whose claws were tied
with yellow tape had run amok

and attacked the lobster
with green tape
and the one with pink?
That toothbrush in the far glass
is mine – yellow the colour

of the flag of the fever ship
anchored beyond the harbour.

luna

Luna / lunae
one of the first words

of Latin I learned
the word for moon

that governs the tide's
ebb and flow

woman's ebb and flow
for moon

that no longer governs
my body

*luna /lunae /*lunatic.

blood sacrifice

I gcoim na hoíche cloisim iad –
builders knocking down houses

in which citizens were born
raised and died
pubs with backrooms
attics that were safe during the Rising

the house where the hero lived
in which he planned the freedom
of the city where everyone would be equal.

I gcoim na hoíche dorcha
is cách ina gcodladh suain

An elderly woman falls on rough ground.
I cannot lend her a helping hand,
all I can do is watch as her blood
flows into the pool of progress.

An daoine iad nach sona dóibh
nó anamna i bponc?

another tale from Shahrazad

Let me relate to you another tale
to while away the hours of night:

once upon a time in Ireland
there was a great sickness:

innocent children died,
mothers spent their lives in mourning.

A cure was discovered – blood could be drawn
from the healthy and dispensed to the ill.

A Blood Board was established to manage
this system and ensure the vials used

remained uncontaminated.
By degrees the operatives

grew lax and broke the very rules
they themselves had laid down.

Germs made their way into the vials
and adopted the guise of genies.

The Board began to issue vials which,
when administered, caused illness.

This was apparent to some doctors
but when they explained to the Board

the operatives became confused:
they stopped issuing further batches

but didn't recall those already sent out.
These languished on shelves in presses –

rows of genies trapped in vials whose hearts
missed a beat each time the door opened

and a hand reached in, rows of genies
who couldn't wait to escape from their vials

and wreak havoc on the healthy.
Although this is a sweet and pleasant tale

it pales in comparison with the one
I'll tell tomorrow night if I survive.

because this is the truth

(i.m. Jonathan Wade 1942-73)

And some years ago the Lord
appeared to the artist and said:

your rulers mislead you,
they destroy the road you walk on –
all are greedy for profit and chase after bribes.
This city is fast becoming a harlot.

And the artist looked at what
he had painted: images of a city in decay –
mountains of twisted metal,
cliffs of rusted refuse.

He got out his palette, mixed his paints
and set to work, filling canvases
not with the images that surrounded him
but with those that were to come.

Today as I drove down the motorway
I saw what he'd painted before me –
gigantic pipes in light grey, charcoal,
grey-green, criss-crossing each other.

And I wept for the city
that had become a harlot.

diagnosis

For six months now samples of my blood have been
travelling back and forth across the Straits of Moyle.

I am referred to a new man. A professor.
He peruses the pink and white forms,

studies the test results in the buff folders
and announces I can forget all about

the insects, the primroses,
the Comfort, the washing powder.

It wasn't a wolf in sheep's clothing that caused
the rash, the jaundice, the pains, the exhaustion –

it was a cheetah in wolf's clothing –
I have never had an auto-immune disease.

After years of being told I was self-destructing,
that I was lacking in that most basic of instincts –

the will to survive – he is telling me
that I am not to blame for this disease.

I listen to what he has to say
watch as his lips form the words –

all my ailments have been caused by Hepatitis C.
His dictum reduces me to tears.

the book of evidence

As the date of the hearing approaches
the book of evidence expands into a volume
broad as the complete works of Shakespeare.

All privileged information, of course,
as the hearing is to be held *in camera*
but I'll let you in on its contents:

a sheaf of documents
that covers the high points of my life
my relationship with my husband, my children,

the work I can do
both inside and outside the home,
doctors' reports on how

my organs function,
specialists' statements on the pay
I'd be entitled to, had I worked fulltime

the pension I'd have, had I worked fulltime –
I'm not too sure how many years –

this is where I allow my mind to stray.
My solicitor counsels me not to worry –
my case is non-adversarial and non-litigious.

a price on my head

I am shown to a small pine-panelled seat
halfway between the judges' bench
and that of my legal team:

a seat I recognise from many a film
one from which I've heard the speech
of many a man sentenced to death.

The hearing is informal, as promised,
by my solicitor and both counsel.
The three sitting in judgment

aren't dressed in wigs or gowns –
they're wearing black and white
just like my own representatives.

From the dock I concur
with the statements of my team
answer questions posed by the judges

my head tennising between each trio.
All rise as the judges retire
to debate my case

and place a price on my head.

the cheque

When the cheque is ready
I ask my son to come with me to the solicitor's office
in case I collapse under its weight

and it drags me down through my torso,
thighs, shins into my feet,
out through my toes towards the canal

and soars above me into the clouds
the tiny flecks of figures
specks of rain falling over Ireland.

Who can place a price on my life?
Who can place a price on my mind?
Who can place a price on these words?
Who can place a price on my body?
Who can place a price on any body?

According to the news it was on this bank
that the latest victim was murdered –
a woman who came from a good home.

Gardaí prune buddleia, exposing beer cans,
congealing condoms, rats' tails
in their search for clues as to who killed her –

client or pimp – who drew her life from her
up through her feet, shins, thighs, torso,
pockmarked arms, up into the dark of night.

power corrupts

Throughout the city men and women
rise and eat breakfast.

Off they go, bouncing on their eggs,
sliding on their sausages, or swimming

through their cereal until they reach their jobs
in offices, shops, hospitals.

I see them swallowed by archways
disappear through doors

sucked up in lifts
and think I wouldn't like

to be out there in their company.
I understand now that it's the Good Shepherd

who gives his life for his sheep
that now and again the hireling who's not a shepherd

who doesn't own the sheep becomes confused.
I know now he can't be trusted

that he's reluctant to deal with problems
that he ignores memos

that his greed and arrogance spread
that he doesn't give a toss about the sheep

that when he sees the wolf coming
he flees and abandons the sheep

and the wolf captures them and kills them
that their blood fills the plain

seeping down into the earth.

headed for the bus stop?

A wind from the north-west wrenches
the leaves from the back wall

revealing again the tentacles.
The leaves, shrivelled and rusted,

cling to boots and shoes
make their way into the house

and up the stairs.
Out on the lake

the cries of those who drowned
echo off the blocks of flats.

in store

As you drew your hopscotch beds
you remembered it was said on the paper
that the world was to end that day
and the group who said it
had headed off, as had your friends.

When the rain came – a veil of drizzle –
you remembered Granda and his companions
waiting for the battle, the names of chessmen
on pieces of paper in their pockets in case
they were able to finish the game.

Off you went on one leg, your pickey
in front of you – one, two, three,
scissors, six, scissors, nine
until you reached ten
and could lay down both feet and rest.

How were you to know this was the game
that would decide what was in store, no matter
how many games of chess Granda won, no matter
how many pickeys you kicked into the right box?

sisters

(after Marina Tsvetaeva)

We have not escaped hell
though we had accepted our lot,
the chores apportioned to us

nor were we lured
from the cradles of our children
to bonfires lit by vagabonds.

As we leaned over those same cradles
innocent as the children in them
the vagabonds stole up to us.

Never fear, fine spinners,
good housekeepers,
it isn't we who are renowned

for slovenly needlework;
nor is there any point thinking
during those sleepless nights

what hand fate would have dealt us
had we not accepted our lot –
had we danced naked under the stars

would we have been punished just the same?
Our eyes are dry, our livers gnawed,
hair has fallen from our heads,

flesh has been clawed from our bones.
Definitely, dear sisters,
we have not escaped hell.

taken out and shot?

Late at night when I can't sleep
or can't read, and even
the drawl of Leonard Cohen
is not enough
to knock me out
I watch films.

I hear that the men
in white coats
are broken men
who can't sleep either.
I wonder what they do
late at night?

Do they spend time
in the company of Cohen
or do they watch
the same films as me
in their houses
seated on their settees?

I often see films
where men are dragged
from their beds
and shot for less
than what these did.
Would I like to see them

suffer the same fate?
Or would I prefer
them to live
in a limbo of ailments?
No.
I wouldn't wish that on anyone.

Afterword

Blood that Seeps Deep into the Earth
Luz Mar González-Arias

In the late 1970s about 1600 Irish citizens, most of them women, were infected with a contaminated blood product known as the "Anti-D" agent[1]. The product was revolutionary in the prevention of Rhesus disease but proved disastrous for the patients who received the batch manufactured in 1976 by the Blood Transfusion Service Board (BTSB) from a donor who had infective Hepatitis. A number of women were diagnosed with lupus, jaundice, fatigue, and a rash but the connection between their maladies and the toxic agent was not at first established. It was only in 1994 that the scandal was made public when evidence was provided that the BTSB had been alerted to the possibility of contamination, only to discount the alert[2].

This could work as a brief summary of the events. We could add more figures, and statistics, and even a longer list of ailments. But the official record would still be flooded with gaps and fissures. Flooded with questions: where are the private histories of the women infected? How did their communities react towards their maladies? What happened to their sexual lives? And how did it all affect their relationships with their own children? Celia de Fréine's *Blood Debts* provides answers. The collection is to date the only poetic articulation of

101

the Hepatitis C scandal in Ireland and it engages directly with the physical, emotional, sexual, and social dimensions of the illness developed by the poetic persona after giving birth in a Dublin hospital, where a contaminated blood product was pumped into her body.

Anyone familiar with de Fréine's work could argue that part of her enormous creative force is to be found in the rich terrain between languages, genres, geographies, and literary traditions: originally from County Down, she now divides her time between Dublin and Connemara; mainly known as a poet, she has also worked in playwriting, opera and filmmaking; her literary influences go from the English tradition to the Eastern European; much of her work has been published in Irish, but she herself has translated most of it into English and her recent collections have appeared in dual-language format. Her characteristic upsetting of boundaries is also the signature feature of *Blood Debts*, where the demarcation between the self and the outside world is made progressively more porous until it virtually disappears. All through the collection, this permeability facilitates the fluid transit of the poetic persona between within and without, private and public, sentient and non-sentient: 'inside', for instance, based on Stephen Poliakoff's television film *Stronger Than the Sun*, denounces the faulty safety procedures of a nuclear power station when a woman worker 'smuggled / plutonium out inside her body // and because it was inside no alarm sounded'. This porosity of bodily borders becomes an apt recourse to explore the ambiguous character of the products handled in our daily routines, as agents to aid us and also potentially harmful toxic material. And so, in 'comfort' the medical establishment is unable to diagnose the source of the rash the protagonist has developed. Instead of recognising it as a manifestation of the Hepatitis C virus, the GP and nurse suggest the source of this ailment is likely to be found in the chemicals she uses for her domestic chores: '*More likely your washing powder* / the district Nurse suggested. / *Or maybe even your Comfort*'. As the so-called risk theory has shown, the representation of the dangers a given society has to face is problematised by the intervention of the political, legal, and mass media machineries. The same rationale applies to this collection, where the 'authorities' blame the eponymous fabric softener above, the primroses in 'nip it in the bud', or the exhaustion of bringing up three children in 'i wanna sleep forever' for the woman's health problems, but a confrontation with the true source of the conflict does not take place.

One of the most interesting aspects of *Blood Debts* lies in its representation of ill embodiments. Medical terms like 'oxytocin', 'cortisone', 'phlebotomist' or 'immunoglobulin' are inscribed in the poetic text in what becomes one more skilful crossing of boundaries. While doctors and nurses are presented in much medical poetry as an ambiguous collective – professionals who participate in the cure of the patient but who also manipulate and dehumanise his/her body by treating it as a passive object of scientific research – de Fréine presents us with an even more poignant scenario: not only do the medics prove unable to provide an accurate diagnosis for the symptoms developed by the infected patient, but their constant silencing of the woman's pain contributes to her social and political segregation as well. In spite of her desire to resist – 'I need an injection // of immunoglobulin / but my arm resists [the] needle', says the protagonist of 'september – month of birthdays' – her powerlessness is made all the more evident when her body is manipulated by the doctor in charge in 'the hour of the wolf':

He prescribes cortisone –

a steroid I've heard tell that
bloats the body. I see myself

in the guise of a *Michelin*
woman float up overhead

stare down on his pate
as he pummels my stomach.

Blood Debts is also relevant in its depiction of Dublin city. In many of the poems de Fréine establishes an intelligent parallelism between the damage inflicted on women's bodies by the toxic agent and the degradation and contamination of their urban landscape under the rubric of progress. Dublin becomes both the emplacement and the embodiment of the action and interacts with the corporeal in ways that illustrate the poet's characteristic crossing over of boundaries. In this vein, in 'blood sacrifice', for instance, the focus is on the knocking down of emblematic buildings that are to be replaced by modern developments during the economic boom. The Dublin of the Rising is de-territorialised and re-territorialised again, this time according to the values of a globalised economy, here presented as a neo-colonial force that deprives the poetic persona of her own identity and the history of her people. However, the critique moves well beyond the dilapidation of historical Dublin. In the final lines of this poem a woman falls into a pothole left by a developer while the poetic persona can only look on: 'I cannot lend her a helping hand, / all I can do is watch as her blood / flows into the pool of progress'. The woman's blood soaking the soil of Dublin and the protagonist's inability to move because of the potential toxicity in her own blood poignantly emphasise the scapegoating of both figures by the structures of power.

Blood Debts is a necessary collection of poetry. Originally published in the Irish-language in 2004 as *Fiacha Fola*[3], the book was at the time the recipient of several literary awards that acknowledged its poetic strength[4]. De Fréine's English translations come out ten years after the original publication and twenty years after the Hepatitis C scandal entered the public domain. However, the freshness of the collection, its relevance and urgency remain untouched. In a literary tradition saturated with national muses of physical perfection, *Blood Debts* shifts the centre of representation to the non-normative corporeality of the poetic persona. De Fréine is not alone in this honourable pursuit. Particularly since the onset of the third millennium, Irish writers have turned ill embodiments into extraordinary literary material: Lia Mills, Dorothy Molloy, Joan Newmann, Paul Muldoon, Leanne O'Sullivan and Shirley McClure, to mention but a few, have written on the physical, social and psychological effects of eating disorders, cancer, disabilities, and disfigurement. *Blood Debts* focuses on the contaminated blood of the female protagonist. Toxicity running in someone else's body, since it is inside and not always obvious to the inattentive eye, would run the risk of passing unnoticed by the community, had it not been so skilfully turned into the subject-object of de Fréine's art. But the pertinence and validity of *Blood Debts* also lies in its representation of the Celtic Tiger phenomenon and the devastating impact it has left in the Irish landscape. In 2004 these poems were visionary in their depiction of the ruthless alterations of familiar geographies that, ten years on, are a visible reality.

Celia de Fréine is one of the great bards of her generation. And like the great bard she is, she masters the art of painting a detail, a nuance in colour, a small change of texture that may not be evident to the distracted observer. She shows us a path. And by doing so the picture is forever altered. Like the rash that spreads all over the body of the poetic persona in *Blood Debts*, her innocent blood 'seeping down into the earth' and leaving a shameful trace behind, her private history also spreads across the pages to become public and to remind us that some mistakes should never be forgotten. These poems may not cure the women to whom this book is dedicated. But there is no doubt they are part of the healing.

Luz Mar González-Arias,
University of Oviedo[5]
July, 2014

[1] The Anti-D agent is given to women with rhesus negative blood who have given birth to rhesus positive babies. This product prevents damage to the foetus in subsequent pregnancies.
[2] For a detailed study of the Hepatitis C scandal in Ireland, see Glenys Spray (1998): *Blood, Sweat and Tears: The Hepatitis C Scandal*. Dublin: Wolfhound.
[3] De Fréine, Celia (2004): *Fiacha Fola*. Conamara: Cló Iar-Chonnachta.
[4] *Fiacha Fola* was awarded Gradam Litríochta Chló Iar-Chonnachta in 2004 and a commission from *Bord na Leabhar Gaeilge* in 2002. Some of the individual poems were shortlisted in literary competitions like the Strokestown Poetry Competition, and the Seacat Irish National Poetry Competition. The Irish language original of 'chalice of my blood' ('cailís mo chuid fola') was awarded the inaugural Smurfit / Lá Award at Féile na Samhna in 2003.
[5] The author would like to acknowledge that her work on Blood Debts and the Hepatitis C scandal in Ireland has been funded by the Research Project FF2012-35872

Acknowledgements

*Thanks to Cló Iar-Chonnacht who published *Fiacha Fola*.

*Thanks also to Máire Mhac an tSaoi who gave permission for her Foreword to *Fiacha Fola* to be translated and included here.

*Thanks to Luz Mar González-Arias for her enthusiastic interest and encouragement.

*Thanks to Catherine Dunne, Phyl Herbert, Lia Mills, Fidelma Ní Ghallchobhair and Maggie O'Dwyer for their ongoing support.

* Thanks also to all at Scotus Press.

Fiacha Fola was awarded *Gradam Litríochta Chló Iar-Chonnachta* in 2004 in conjunction with *Údarás na Gaeltachta*.

*It was also awarded a commission from *Bord na Leabhar Gaeilge* in 2002.

*The Irish language original of 'chalice of my blood' was awarded the inaugural Smurfit / *Lá* Award at *Féile na Samhna* in 2003.

*The Irish language original of 'another tale from Sharazad' was shortlisted in the Irish language section of the Strokestown Poetry Competition in 2004.

*The Irish language original of 'grace' was shortlisted for the Seacat Irish National Poetry Competition in association with Poetry Ireland in 2002.

*Some of these poems, or earlier versions of them in either Irish or English, or both, were published in *Poetry Ireland Review*, *Comhar*, *An Guth 1*, *Breaking the Skin: twenty first century writing*, volume two, ed. by Nigel McLoughlin, Matthew Fluharty and Frank Sewell (Black Mountain Press) and *The New Irish Poets* ed. by Selina Guinness (Bloodaxe).

The Girl Who Saved
CHRISTMAS

Matt Haig

Also by Matt Haig

Father Christmas and Me
A Boy Called Christmas
Echo Boy
To Be a Cat
The Runaway Troll
Shadow Forest